P9-EDY-104

DATE DUE

PRINTED IN U.S.A.

EUROPEAN HISTORICAL DICTIONARIES
Edited by Jon Woronoff

Historical Dictionary
of
Modern Italy

Mark F. Gilbert and K. Robert Nilsson

European Historical Dictionaries, No. 34

The Scarecrow Press, Inc.
Lanham, Maryland, & London
1999

SCARECROW PRESS, INC.

Published in the United States of America
by Scarecrow Press, Inc.
4720 Boston Way
Lanham, Maryland 20706

4 Pleydell Gardens
Kent CT20 2DN, England

British Library Cataloguing in Publication Information Available

Library of Congress Cataloging-in-Publication Data

Gilbert, Mark.
    Historical dictionary of modern Italy / Mark F. Gilbert and K. Robert
Nilsson.
        p.   cm.   —   (European historical dictionaries ; no. 34)
    Includes bibliographical references.
    ISBN 0-8108-3584-3 (cloth : alk. paper)
    1. Italy—History—1870–1914—Dictionaries.   2. Italy—History—
20th century—Dictionaries.   I. Nilsson, K. Robert, 1927–.   II. Title.
III. Series.
DG555.G53   1998   98-41159
945'.08'03—dc21   CIP

⊖™ The paper used in this publication meets the minimum requirements of
American National Standard for Information Sciences—Permanence of
Paper for Printed Library Materials, ANSI Z39.48–1984.
Manufactured in the United States of America.

Contents

Editor's Foreword

Although Italy is one of the oldest countries in Europe, rooted as she is in Etruscan civilization, Magna Graecia, and the Roman Empire, she is also the newest of the European states, having been united under Piedmont in 1861. Since unification, Italy has been transformed socially, economically, and politically. Yet differences remain that separate the prosperous North and the far poorer South. In certain regions, vocal minorities clamor for autonomy; and class conflicts continue to exacerbate social and regional tensions. Italy's progress has, in fact, not been free of turmoil: the fascist regime, for example, was born out of World War I and laid to rest by World War II. Even a gentler, post-war regime has proven unable to deal with long-standing turbulence and uncertainty because it has been inefficient and often corrupt. Nonetheless, Italy remains one of Europe's most important countries and plays a significant role in European affairs. This Italy, its successes and failures, its advances and relapses, its unbounded promise incompletely realized, is examined in this *Historical Dictionary of Modern Italy.*

So much has happened in Italy since unification that there seems to be no end to what might be scrutinized. This volume has therefore focused on certain prominent individuals, basic institutions, crucial events, and fundamental features essential to understanding modern Italy. Entries are included not only on history and politics but also on economics, society, and culture. The objective is to provide readers with a broad overview concisely and precisely. The order in which the multitude of events occurred is traced in the chronology. Italy's geography, economy, and history are first presented in the Introduction and described more fully in the dictionary entries. The lists of abbreviations, kings, presidents, and prime ministers are useful references. The selective bibliography can lead readers to many other sources.

This historical dictionary was written by K. Robert Nilsson and Mark F. Gilbert. The former is Professor Emeritus at Dickinson College in Carlisle, Pennsylvania, where, since 1962, he taught European Political Systems, International Relations, and the Politics of Modernization and was director of the college's study program in Bologna, Italy, for ten of those years. For a time, he was chairman of the Italy Seminar at the Foreign Service Institute of the Department of State and was long editor of the newsletter of the Conference Group on Italian Politics and Society. Dr. Gilbert taught at Dickinson College's Center for European Studies in

Bologna, Italy, for two years and at Dickinson College in Carlisle for three before returning to residence in Trento. He has recently been appointed to the faculty at the University of Bath, England. Both have written on Italian politics in Europe and in the United States. Dr. Gilbert's most recent major work on Italy is *The Italian Revolution: The End of Politics Italian Style?* Between them, they have amply and authoritatively covered the field.

Jon Woronoff
Series Editor

Acknowledgments

When colleagues and friends undertake to write a book together, particularly when direct consultation is made difficult by distance (Carlisle to Trento must be close to 4,000 miles), some problems should be expected, despite the convenience of e-mail. We have accumulated many debts, some in common: to Vickie Kuhn and to Jon Woronoff. The rest are highly individual: it therefore seems best to recognize and acknowledge our debts separately. At Dickinson College, the secretary of the Political Science Department, Mrs. Victoria Kuhn, is friend and counselor to all its members, current and retired. She has manipulated diskettes and rearranged their contents to the exacting standards of our publisher despite the pressures on her energies exerted by an active department and a growing family. And she has done so, as always, cheerfully and helpfully. The editor of the publisher's series of which this book is part is Jon Woronoff who has been both patient and painstaking in his comments, flexible in his expectations, and thoughtful throughout the manuscript's preparation.

My work in Italian studies has been helped greatly by my coauthor, K. Robert Nilsson, who has been a good friend ever since I was a rookie Ph.D. in my first teaching job, and by the boundless enthusiasm and generosity of Professor Stephen Hellman of York University, Toronto.

I owe an immense debt to Dickinson College, and its political science department in particular. A liberal arts education is often considered an unjustifiable expense today: I can only say that Dickinson's gifted, open-minded, and friendly faculty are the best advertisement for such an education that one can imagine. It would be impossible to mention all the colleagues whose friendship and intellectual gifts made my stay at Dickinson so stimulating, but special thanks are due to Doug Stuart, Mark Ruhl, Russ Bova, Tim Lang, and Lisa Lieberman.

My wife, Luciana, is the real source of my interest in Italy: this book was finished a handful of days before our tenth wedding anniversary, which was probably the best present I could give her. My brother-in-law, Franco Gottardi, took a special interest in this project and allowed me to raid his bookshelves of several useful reference books. My mother-in-law, Leda, put up with my turning up at my "office" in her home at all hours—and never complained once.

My mother, father, and brother, Martyn, encouraged and supported me when I was many miles away for months on end. This book is dedicated to them.

Mark F. Gilbert
Bath, England
November 1998

My interest in Italy was originally stimulated by the late Professor C. Grove Haines, founder of the Bologna Center of the School of Advanced International Studies in Bologna. His support (by recommending a generous fellowship), encouragement, and example (his lectures remain models of coherence and thoroughness) made it possible for me to pursue that interest throughout my adult life. I have enjoyed it immensely.

My wife, Judy, indefatigable proofreader, and her late father, Aleardo Pelo, contributed immeasurably to my being at ease in Italy and in the Italian language. She has been most patient.

The college's computer center staff has converted Mac attachments to DOS rapidly and efficiently. The Dickinson College library staff and former Associate Dean Stephen MacDonald were generous with their time and support.

The book originated with Mark. I considered it the highest compliment to be invited by him to collaborate in its preparation. My series of post-retirement maladies, unfortunately, left him to shoulder the burden of making the final revisions required by the publisher.

For my part, the book is dedicated to Judy, to our children, and to their children.

K. Robert Nilsson
Robert Blaine Weaver Professor
Emeritus of Political Science
Dickinson College
Carlisle, Pennsylvania
November 1998

Acronyms
and
Abbreviations

ACI   Azione Cattolica Italiana
      Catholic Action

ACLI   Associazione Cristiana Lavoratori Italiani
      Christian Association of Italian Workers

AGCI Associazione Generale delle Cooperative Italiane
      General Association of Italian Cooperatives

AGIP Azienda Generale Italiana Petroli
      Italian General Petroleum Agency

AN   Alleanza Nazionale
      National Alliance

ANPI Associazione Nazionale dei Partigiani d'Italia
      National Association of Italian Partisans

BR   Brigate Rosse
      Red Brigades

CCD   Centro Cristiano Democratico
      Catholic Democratic Center

CDU   Cristiani Democratici Unificate
      United Christian Democrats

CGIL Confederazione Generale Italiana del Lavoro
      Italian General Confederation of Labor

CIPE Comitato Interministeriale per la Programmazione Economica
      Interministerial Committee for Economic Planning

CISL Confederazione Italiana Sindacati Lavoratori
      Italian Confederation of Workers' Unions

CISNAL
    Confederazione Italiana Sindacati Nazionali Lavoratori
    Italian Confederation of National Workers' Unions

CLN   Comitati di Liberazione Nazionale
    Committee for National Liberation

COBAS Comitati di Base
    Base [membership] Committees

COLDIRETTI
    Confederazione Nazionale dei Coltivatori Diretti
    National Confederation of Farmer-Owners

CONFCOOP
    Confederazione delle Cooperative
    Cooperatives' Confederation

COREL Comitato per la Riforma Elettorale
    Committee for Electoral Reform

DC   Democrazia Cristiana
    Christian Democracy Party

DN   Destra Nazionale
    National Right

ECSC   Comunità Europea per il Carbone e l'acciaio
    European Coal and Steel Community

EEC   Comunità Economica Europea
    European Economic Community

ENI   Ente Nazionale Idrocarburi
    National Hydrocarbons Agency

FGCI   Federazione Giovanile Comunista Italiana
    Italian Communist Youth Federation

FIAT   Fabbrica Italiana Automobili Torino
    Italian Automobile Factory: Turin

FIOM Federazione Italiana Operai Metallurgici
Italian Federation of Metal Workers

FUCI Federazione Universitaria Cattolici Italiana
Catholic University Graduates' Movement of Italy

FUCI-Laureati
Federazione Universitaria Cattolici Italiana-Laureati
Catholic University Graduates' Movement of Italy-Laureati

GAP Gruppi d'Azione Patriottica
Patriotic Action Group

GIL Gioventù Italiana del Littorio
Italian Youth of the [Fascist] Lictor

GUF Gioventù Universitaria Fascista
Fascist University Youth

IRI Istituto per la Ricostruzione Industriale
Institute for Industrial Reconstruction

ISTAT Istituto Centrale di Statistica
Italian Central Statistical Agency

LIT Lire Italiane
Italian Lira

LN Lega Nord
Northern League

LUISS Libera Università Internazionale per gli Studi Sociali
Free University for the Social Sciences

MSI / DN
Movimento Sociale Italiano / Destra Nazionale
Italian Social Movement / National Right

MUP Movimento d'Unità Proletaria
Movement of Proletarian Unity

MVSN   Milizia Volontario di Sicurezza Nazionale
       Voluntary Militia of National Security

ONB   Opera Nazionale Balilla
       National Balilla

OVRA   *No certain meaning for the fascist secret police. Perhaps*
       Opera Volontaria per la Repressione Antifascista
       Volunteer Organization for the Repression of Antifascism

PATT   Partito per l'Autonomia di Trentino-Tirolese
       Party for the Autonomy of Trentino-Tirolese

PCI   Partito Comunista Italiano
       Italian Communist Party

PdA   Partito d'Azione
       Action Party

PDS   Partito Democratico della Sinistra
       Democratic Party of the Left

PLI   Partito Liberale Italiano
       Italian Liberal Party

PLO   Organizzazione di Liberazione di Palestina
       Palestine Liberation Organization

PNF   Partito Nazionale Fascista
       National Fascist Party

PPI   Partito Popolare Italiano
       Italian People's Party

PR   Partito Radicale
       Radical Party

PRC   Partito di Rifondazione Comunista
       Communist Refoundation Party

PRI   Partito Repubblicana Italiano
       Italian Republican Party

PSDI   Partito Socialista Democratico Italiano
       Italian Socialist Democratic Party

PSI   Partito Socialista Italiano
       Italian Socialist Party

PSLI   Partito Socialista Lavoratori Italiano
       Italian Socialist Workers' Party

PSRI   Partito Socialista Riformista Italiano
       Italian Reformist Socialist Party

PSU   Partito Socialista Unificato
       Unified Socialist Party

RSI   Repubblica Sociale Italiana
       Italian Social Republic

SID   Servizio Informazioni Difesa
       Defense Information Service

SIFAR Servizio d'Informazione per le Forze Armate
       Armed Forces' Intelligence Services

SIM   Servizio Informazioni Militari
       Military Intelligence Service

SISMI Servizio per l'Informazione e la Sicurezza Militare
       Information and Military Security Service

SVP   Süd Tirol Volkspartei
       South Tyrolean People's Party

TAR   Tribunale Amministrativo Regionale
       Regional Administrative Tribunal

UdC   Unione di Centro
       Center Union

UDI   Unione delle Donne Italiane
       Union of Italian Women

UDN   Unione Democratica Nazionale
       National Democratic Union

UDS   Unione Democratica Socialista
       Democratic Socialist Union

UIL   Unione Italiana del Lavoro
       Italian Union of Labor

ITALY

showing regional
borders and capitals.

Reprinted by permission: Spotts & Wieser. 1986. *Italy: A Difficult Democracy.*
New York: Cambridge University Press.

Chronology

1797   Constitution of the Cisalpine Republic with the tricolor flag. Venetia is absorbed by Austria.

1802   Cisalpine Republic becomes the Italian Republic with Milan as its capital.

1804   Adoption of the Napoleonic *Code Civil* of 1803.

1805   Napoleon I crowns himself King of Italy in Milan.

1815   Congress of Vienna restores absolute rule in Italian peninsula.

1820   Middle class revolution in Naples and popular uprising in Palermo. Neapolitan troops invade Sicily. Five thousand die in street battles, September 1820.

1821   Austrian troops crush the revolt in Naples. Ferdinand I restored to the throne. Revolution in Turin; Charles Albert concedes a constitution, but then reneges.

1822   Congress of Verona.

1827   First edition of Manzoni's *The Betrothed*.

1831   Revolts in Central Italy against Papal rule. Austrian intervention. Mazzini founds *Giovine Italia*.

1833   Mazzinian conspiracy against the Kingdom of Piedmont-Sardinia discovered. Mazzini condemned to death in absentia. Mazzinian uprisings in Genoa and Savoy thwarted 1834.

1835   Cholera epidemic. More than 50,000 die over next two years.

1839   First railway between Naples and Portici.

1843   Publication of Gioberti's *On the Moral and Civil Primacy of the Italians.*

1846   Election of Pius IX: the "Liberal Pope."

1848   Revolutions in Palermo, Naples, and Turin. Constitutional monarchy introduced in Turin. Revolts against Austrian rule in Venice and Milan. War between Piedmont and Austria-Austrian victory at Custoza. Civil and political rights granted to Jews in Piedmont-Sardinia.

1849   Roman Republic proclaimed. War declared between Piedmont and Austria. Charles Albert abdicates after defeat at Novara. Victor Emmanuel II becomes king. Austria and France restore Papal authority.

1851   First performance of Verdi's *Rigoletto.*

1852   Cavour becomes premier in Piedmont.

1855   Piedmontese troops participate in the war in Crimea. New outbreak of cholera.

1858   An Italian nationalist, Felice Orsini, attempts to kill Napoleon III of France. Cavour signs the pact of Plombières with Napoleon and secures French aid against Austria.

1859   War between Franco-Piedmontese alliance and Austria leads to the peace of Villafranca (July). Cavour resigns. Bologna, Tuscany, Modena, and Parma reject Papal rule and appeal to be united with Piedmont.

1860   Cavour returns to power in Turin. Garibaldi's "Thousand" sail to the aid of a revolt in Palermo. Garibaldi establishes dictatorship in Sicily and invades the mainland. Cavour annexes central and southern Italy. October 26, 1860, Garibaldi yields his conquests to the Piedmontese throne.

1861   Victor Emmanuel II crowned *Re d'Italia* in March. Catholic Church boycotts elections. Cavour dies in June.

1862   An attempt by Garibaldi to invade the Papal state and liberate Rome is thwarted by the Italian army. Garibaldi himself is wounded.

1865   Florence becomes capital of Italy.

1866   Italy allies with Prussia and makes war on Austria. Italy defeated at Custoza and Lissa. After Prussian victory at Sadowa, Italy gains Venetia, but not the Trentino, despite Garibaldi's victories there.

1867   Garibaldi defeated at the battle of Mentana. Rome remains in Papal hands. Cholera epidemic kills thousands.

1868   Grist tax introduced by Quintino Sella.

1869   Death of Carlo Cattaneo, republican and democrat.

1870   Rome is occupied by Italian troops in September after the defeat of Napoleon III in the Franco-Prussian War. Only Vatican city left to the Pope.

1871   Law regulating relations between the Pope and the Italian state introduced. Verdi's *Aida* performed for the first time.

1872   Death of Giuseppe Mazzini.

1876   Agostino Depretis becomes prime minister, promises social and electoral reforms and the abolition of the grist tax–the "parliamentary revolution."

1878   Death of Victor Emmanuel II and Pius IX. Replaced by King Umberto I and Leo XIII. In November an anarchist attempts to kill Umberto who is saved by the bravery of his prime minister, Benedetto Cairoli.

1879   First telephones introduced in Italy.

1882   Death of Giuseppe Garibaldi. Italy joins the Triple Alliance. Depretis gives birth to *trasformismo* by persuading rightist deputies led by Marco Minghetti to join his government.

Electoral law extends the vote from 600,000 electors to over 2,000,000, but this is still less than 7 percent of the population.

1884   Cholera epidemic kills thousands, especially in Naples.

1885   Italian colonialism begins with the occupation of territories along the banks of the Red Sea.

1886   First child labor law.

1887   Five hundred Italian troops massacred at Dogali in Abyssinia. Depretis dies in July; in August Francesco Crispi becomes premier.

1889   Treaty of Uccialli with Menelik of Abyssinia. Italian colonial gains recognized.

1890   Death penalty abolished.

1891   Publication of the encyclical *Rerum Novarum*.

1892   The "Italian Workers' Party," forerunner of the Socialist party, founded in August.

1893   Banca Romana scandal brings down Giolitti.

1894   Sicilian peasants' uprising suppressed by Francesco Crispi.

1896   Renewed war between Italy and Abyssinia ends in the disaster of Adowa in March. Crispi's second government collapses. Showing of the first film, *The Arrival of the Train at Milan Station*.

1897   Conservative leader Giorgio Sidney Sonnino proposes increased executive power for the king and a reduction in the power of Parliament.

1898   Italian soccer championship begins. Year of bread riots throughout Italy. At least 80 and possibly as many as 300 workers are killed in Milan by government troops. Partito Socialista Italiano (PSI) leader Filippo Turati arrested.

1900　King Umberto assassinated at Monza by an Italian anarchist from Paterson, New Jersey. Victor Emmanuel III is crowned in July.

1901　Zanardelli cabinet formed in February: takes the side of labor in agricultural and industrial disputes. PSI deputies support the government in Parliament. Record year for strikes.

1903　Death of Pope Leo XIII and of Giuseppe Zanardelli, who is replaced by Giovanni Giolitti.

1904　PSI's revolutionary wing wins control of the party. First general strike in September. Year of violent labor discontent.

1906　First centralized trade union, the "General Confederation of Work," formed in Milan.

1908　A massive earthquake in December takes tens of thousands of lives in Sicily and Calabria. Messina and Reggio Calabria are devastated.

1909　Marinetti publishes the futurist manifesto in Paris. First *Giro d'Italia* bicycle race. Guglielmo Marconi wins the Nobel prize for physics.

1911　Italy declares war on Turkey and occupies Libya. Benito Mussolini leads violent strikes against the war; Italian atrocities against the civilian population cause an international outcry.

1912　Universal male suffrage introduced in May. Treaty of peace signed with Turkey in October after lengthy talks. The PSI expels its "ministerialist" wing and takes an increasingly revolutionary line.

1913　Record year for strikes and emigration–two million people emigrated between 1911 and 1913, mostly to the United States. "Gentiloni pact" signed between moderate Liberals and the "Catholic Electoral Union."

1914   Antonio Salandra becomes premier. One hundred thousand troops are needed to quell riots in northern Italy led by Mussolini. Italy remains neutral after the outbreak of war.

1915   Italy promises to enter the war on the side of Britain and France in April. War declared on Austria in May; on Turkey in August.

1916   Italy declares war on Germany in August after victory in the battle of Gorizia.

1917   Women lead strikes and protests against the war in the spring. Pope Benedict XV appeals for an end to the "useless slaughter." Disaster of Caporetto in October. Italian army suffers huge losses in men and material. Vittorio Emmanuel Orlando becomes premier.

1918   Italian victory in the battle of Piave restores the territory lost the previous year.

1919   Foundation of the Catholic Partito Popolare Italiano (PPI) and Mussolini's *Movimento dei fasci italiani*, soon to be known as the Partito Nazionale Fascista (PNF) and its members, Fascists. Electoral law introduces proportional representation. Italy is "robbed" of the territorial gains she expected by the Treaty of Saint-Germain. Gabriele D'Annunzio, with the tacit support of the Italian government, seizes Fiume on September 12.

1920   Strikes throughout the country; labor movement splits between communists, moderate trade unionists, and the PSI. Giolitti returns to power and in November signs Treaty of Rapallo, which resolves the border question with Yugoslavia. Italian troops expel D'Annunzio from Fiume in December.

1921   Formation of the Partito Comunista Italiano (PCI). Victory for the PSI and the PPI in national elections held in May. Thirty-five Fascists elected with Giolitti's backing. Ivanoe Bonomi forms new government. Major banking crisis.

1922   Death of Pope Benedict XV and Giovanni Verga, novelist. Bonomi and Facta governments collapse in the face of fascist lawlessness. Mussolini becomes premier after unopposed "March on Rome."

1923   Fascist power consolidated. Gentile reform of education; Acerbo electoral law introduced. Mussolini bombards and occupies Corfù.

1924   Fiume becomes Italian. Fascist victory in elections. Opposition parties, despite intimidation, obtain 35 percent of the vote. Giacomo Matteotti is murdered by a fascist squad, provoking the opposition parties to boycott parliament. First radio broadcasts.

1925   Mussolini takes personal responsibility for all the crimes committed by the fascists in 1924, including the murder of Matteotti. Manifesto of fascist intellectuals published; Croce publishes counter-manifesto. Anti-fascist newspaper *Non Mollare* founded in Florence.

1926   Three attempts on Mussolini's life lead to suspension of leading anti-fascist newspapers and passage of laws abolishing all opposition parties, establishing special tribunals for political cases and confiscating the possessions of anti-fascist exiles.

1927   Organization of the OVRA (secret police). "General Confederation of Work" is dissolved. Campaign to increase the birthrate begins. Grazia Deledda wins the Nobel prize for literature.

1928   New electoral law. Citizens are given the choice of voting for or against an approved slate of 400 fascist candidates. Introduction of an official textbook in schools.

1929   Signature of the Lateran pacts guaranteeing a degree of church autonomy from the regime. Plebiscite held under the new electoral laws produces a 98.4 percent majority for the fascist slate of candidates. "Justice and Liberty," anti-fascist organization, founded in Paris. "Italian Academy" founded in Rome; Benedetto Croce refuses to join.

1932   "Exhibition of the Ten Years of Fascist Revolution" in Rome. Italy wins the second-highest total of medals in the Los Angeles Olympics.

1933   Constitution of the "Institution for Industrial Reconstruction," to coordinate state investment in industry. In 1934 establishes dominant position in the banking sector.

1934   Law on corporations passed. Second plebiscite gives the fascist list a majority of 99.84 percent, in a poll characterized by lower absenteeism. The Italian soccer team wins the world cup (a feat they repeat four years later). After an attempted Nazi coup in Austria, Mussolini mobilizes troops in support of the Austrian government. Luigi Pirandello, a noted supporter of the regime, wins the Nobel prize for literature.

1935   France gives Italy a free hand in Abyssinia, and in October, Italian troops begin occupying the country. Italy is condemned by the League of Nations and limited sanctions are applied.

1936   Addis Ababa occupied by Italy in May. "Italian East Africa" is formed (comprising Somaliland, Ethiopia, and Eritrea), and King Victor Emmanuel III takes the title of emperor. In October, foreign minister Galeazzo Ciano signs a protocol committing Italy and Germany to conduct a joint campaign against Bolshevism and to sustain Franco in the Spanish Civil War. Large Italian expeditionary force is sent to Spain.

1937   Death of Communist leader Antonio Gramsci. Carlo and Nello Rosselli, the organizers of "Justice and Liberty," are murdered in France. All sexual relations are banned between Africans and Italians. Mussolini meets Hitler in Munich. In December, Italy leaves the League of Nations.

1938   Hitler makes official visit to Italy in May, shortly after occupying Austria with Italian support. Mussolini mediates between Britain, France, and Germany at Munich. So-called "third wave" of the fascist revolution begins: racial laws against Jews are introduced in November. Enrico Fermi wins the Nobel prize for physics. Fermi leaves for the United States rather than return to Italy.

1939   Parliament is abolished and replaced by a Chamber of Fascists and a Chamber of Corporations. "Pact of Steel" signed with Germany in May. Italy, however, refuses to enter the war in September, pleading military unpreparedness.

1940   Italy declares war on France and Britain in June. Angered by Hitler's refusal to allow Italy a place at the armistice talks with France, Mussolini invades Greece in October, but Italian forces are swiftly defeated. One hundred twenty thousand Italians are captured by the British in North Africa.

1941   The war in North Africa causes large casualties among Italian troops; Mussolini sends a contingent of over 60,000 troops to Russia to help the German war effort. War declared on the United States on December 11.

1942   German and Italian forces drive the British back in North Africa, but are decisively beaten at the battle of El Alamein. Eight Italian divisions are annihilated. Huge losses are also counted on the Russian front. The Action Party and Christian Democracy are formed.

1943   FIAT workers strike for "bread and peace" in March. Italo-German forces surrender in Tunisia. Sicily is invaded by Anglo-American troops in July. On July 25, the Fascist Grand Council deposes Mussolini. Marshal Badoglio becomes premier. Mussolini is arrested, but is later liberated by the Germans. On September 8, Italy surrenders to the Allies. German troops occupy Rome; 10,000 Italian soldiers are massacred by the Germans on the Greek island of Cephalonia. Mussolini establishes the Italian Social Republic at Salò on Lake Garda.

1944   Five former members of the Fascist Grand Council, including Ciano, are condemned to death by the Salò Republic at Verona in January. The Gestapo murders 335 political prisoners in Rome as a reprisal for a partisan attack. King Victor Emmanuel III is persuaded to make his son, Umberto, "Lieutenant-General of the Realm," clearing the way for the formation of a government that includes the PCI and the Democrazia Cristiana (DC) in June.

The PSI and the Action party, the other main resistance forces, remain uncommitted.

1945   The workers of northern Italy rise in rebellion in Genoa, Milan, and Turin. Mussolini is captured by partisans and shot on April 28. His body, and the corpses of other fascist officials, are exposed to public vilification in Milan's Piazza Loreto. Some 15,000 suspected fascists are executed during the spring. In June, partisan leader Ferruccio Parri is appointed prime minister of a leftist coalition. He is replaced by Alcide De Gasperi (DC) in December after a cabinet crisis.

1946   In May, Victor Emmanuel III abdicates on the eve of the referendum on the monarchy on June 2, and the election of a Constituent Assembly. By a narrow margin, Italy votes for a republic in its first ever free election by universal suffrage. The DC emerges as the largest party with 35 percent of the vote. Enrico De Nicola is appointed provisional head of state.

1947   May: De Gasperi forms a government without the participation of the PSI or the PCI. Italy loses its colonies and control over Trieste by the terms of the treaty of peace signed at Paris in February. The text of the new Constitution is approved by the assembly on December 22. After receiving the presidential signature, it comes into force on January 1, 1948. Victor Emmanuel III dies in exile in Egypt at the end of December.

1948   DC wins 48 percent of the vote in April 1948 elections. De Gasperi forms a cabinet that includes the small center parties. Luigi Einaudi of the Liberal Party (PLI) is elected first president of the republic. In July, an attempt is made to assassinate PCI leader Palmiro Togliatti. In response, riots break out in northern Italy. First showings of De Sica's *The Bicycle Thief*, Visconti's *The Earth Trembles*, and Rossellini's *Germany, Year Zero*.

1949   Italy joins NATO. Huge protests in southern Italy for land reform.

1950   Peasants occupy uncultivated land throughout southern Italy. A limited agricultural reform follows by the end of the year. Southern Development Fund created. The writer Cesare Pavese commits suicide.

1951   Nineteen forty-seven treaty of peace amended to allow Italian rearmament and to erase the preamble that described Italy as a "conquered enemy state."

1952   Italy joins the European Coal and Steel Community (ECSC). Bicycle racer Fausto Coppi wins the Tour de France. The following year he becomes world champion. Benedetto Croce dies in November.

1953   A "Swindle Law" is enacted, which changes electoral rules to give the winning coalition a "prize" in seats. In general elections held in June, the DC and its allies obtain less than 50 percent of the vote and the law is thus not applied.

1954   Alcide De Gasperi dies. Television broadcasts begin. Italy takes over administration of the former American and British zones of Trieste.

1955   Election of Giovanni Gronchi as president of the republic in April. The FIAT 600—the first popular Italian automobile—rolls off the assembly lines in Turin. Start of the "economic miracle." Italy admitted to membership in the United Nations.

1956   A narrowly proportional form of election law is adopted in March. Constitutional court instituted. The alliance between the PCI and the PSI weakens. Hundreds of intellectuals desert the PCI after the party backs Soviet oppression of the Hungarian revolution.

1957   Treaty of Rome establishing the European Economic Community (EEC) signed in March. Italy becomes one of the six founder members. Death of the anti-fascist historian and political thinker Gaetano Salvemini in September.

1958   DC wins uneventful 1958 elections. Amintore Fanfani becomes prime minister. Pope Pius XII dies and is replaced by the liberal Pope John XXIII.

1959   Publication of Di Lampedusa's *The Leopard* and first showing of Fellini's *La dolce vita*. Salvatore Quasimodo wins the Nobel prize for literature. Peak year for migration from the South to the booming cities of Lombardy and Piedmont.

1960 Fernando Tambroni forms a government with the support of the neo-fascist Movimento Sociale Italiano (MSI). Riots break out throughout Italy, and Tambroni is replaced by Fanfani. Rome hosts the Olympics: Italy is fourth in the medals table with thirteen golds.

1962 Fanfani forms a government that enjoys the parliamentary neutrality of the PSI. Antonio Segni becomes president of the republic.

1963 Defeat in the 1963 elections for the DC, which recedes to just 38 percent. The Partito Liberale Italiano (PLI) doubles its share of the vote, while the PCI obtains 25 percent for the first time. In October, almost 2,000 people die in Belluno and Udine after the collapse of a dam. In December, Aldo Moro forms a government that includes four PSI ministers.

1964 Moro government enters into a lengthy crisis, but eventually re-forms. During the crisis, General Giovanni De Lorenzo, head of the *Carabinieri* and former chief of the secret services, distributes to select police and army officials a plan for a coup d'état by the armed forces. Palmiro Togliatti dies in August. Failing health forces Segni to resign from the presidency. He is replaced by Giuseppe Saragat in December.

1966 Worst flooding of the century swamps Florence, Siena, and Venice. Volunteers from all over the world help save the cities' art treasures. The PSI and the Partito Socialista Democatico Italiano (PSDI) form a short-lived unified socialist party.

1967 Student sit-ins preface a long decade of tumult in the universities and factories. First pornographic movies and magazines appear.

1968 Student riots throughout Italy. In Sicily, an earthquake kills 300 people in January. Adultery is decriminalized. The PCI condemns the Soviet suppression of the Prague Spring.

1969 December: A bomb kills 17 and wounds nearly 90 in Milan's Piazza Fontana. Beginning of the so-called "strategy of tension" by mysterious neo-fascist groups.

1970   Enabling legislation passed instituting a regional tier of government and authorizing referendums. Divorce legalized in December. A group of ultra-rightists led by Prince Junio Valerio Borghese occupy the ministry of the interior briefly in December.

1971   Giovanni Leone becomes president of the republic in December on the twenty-third ballot.

1972   Giulio Andreotti forms the first of his seven governments in January. After elections in May, in which the MSI gains ground, Andreotti forms a second administration. Censorship laws are loosened: an explosion of hard-core pornography ensues.

1973   Neo-fascist lawlessness and speculation against the lira brings down the Andreotti government. The Pinochet coup in Chile prompts PCI leader Enrico Berlinguer to ponder a "historic compromise" with the DC in September.

1974   Italy votes by an unexpectedly large margin to retain the new divorce law in a May referendum. The *Italicus*, a train running between Rome and Munich, is blown up by terrorists. Twelve people are killed. Vittorio De Sica dies in November.

1975   Eugenio Montale wins the Nobel prize for literature. The writer and film director Pierpaolo Pasolini is murdered.

1976   High-ranking Italian politicians are accused of having received huge sums from the American aerospace company Lockheed. One thousand people are killed in an earthquake in Udine. A general election is held in June in a feverish climate prompted by the possibility that the PCI will "overtake" the DC and form a government. In the event, the DC remains at nearly 39 percent and the PCI gets just over 34 percent. The DC is left without a majority, but the PCI permits Andreotti to form an administration and to govern. A Communist, Pietro Ingrao, becomes Speaker of the Chamber of Deputies.

1977   The Red Brigades commit hundreds of terrorist acts and right-wing and ultra-left groups clash in Rome. Roberto Rossellini dies in June.

1978   Aldo Moro is kidnapped and, after 55 days imprisonment, murdered by the Red Brigades. Giovanni Leone is forced to resign from the presidency after the question of his involvement in the Lockheed affair and other financial scandals becomes publicly debated. He is replaced by Sandro Pertini. A moderate abortion law is passed. John Paul I dies only a month after assuming the Papacy; a Polish bishop, Karol Wojtyla, becomes the first non-Italian Pope since the sixteenth century.

1979   All cooperation ends between the DC and the PCI. In the ensuing elections, the PCI falls back to 30 percent of the vote. Italy enters the European Monetary System, and American nuclear missiles are installed in NATO bases in Italy. The Partito Repubblicana Italiano (PRI) leader Ugo La Malfa, one of post-war Italy's most respected politicians, dies.

1980   An Italian airliner crashes into the sea off the island of Ustica (Palermo) in June. Eighty people are killed. The Libyan air force and NATO are both suspected of shooting the plane down. In August a huge bomb devastates Bologna railway station, killing 85 people and wounding over 200. Neo-fascist terrorists are blamed. In October, southern Italy is shaken by an enormous earthquake that leaves 6,000 dead and hundreds of thousands homeless. Two of the PCI's historic leaders, Giorgio Amendola and Luigi Longo, die.

1981   John Paul II is seriously wounded by a would-be assassin in Rome. The P2 masonic lodge is discovered: 900 high-ranking Italian businessmen, army officers, journalists, and politicians are implicated in planning to transform Italian institutions by secretive means. In May, voters reject both a Catholic attempt to abolish the abortion law and a radical attempt to make the law more liberal in a national referendum. Giovanni Spadolini (PRI) becomes the first non-DC premier in the republic's history at the head of a five-party coalition that includes the PSI of Bettino Craxi.

1982   The DC elects Ciriaco De Mita as party leader. Spadolini's administration comes to an end in August after Craxi engineers a political crisis. Two prominent anti-mafia fighters, PCI deputy

Pio La Torre and general Carlo Alberto Dalla Chiesa, are killed by organized crime in Sicily. The Italian national soccer team wins the world cup for the third time.

1983   Thirty-two life sentences are given to the killers of Aldo Moro. In June, national elections result in a massive defeat for the DC, which sinks to less than 33 percent of the vote. Bettino Craxi becomes premier in August. Andreotti is accused of being the mastermind behind the Propaganda Due.

1984   During the campaign for the elections to the European Parliament, PCI leader Enrico Berlinguer dies of a stroke. Two million people attend the funeral and the PCI overtakes the DC in the Euro-poll, obtaining over 33 percent of the vote. Bettino Craxi and the church agree to revisions of the Lateran pacts, which end Catholicism's status as the official religion of the state.

1985   A referendum against a law passed by the Craxi government to end automatic cost-of-living increases is defeated. In June, Francesco Cossiga is elected president of the republic. Achille Lauro crisis roils Italian-American relations but boosts Craxi's standing with public opinion and the Arab world. Death of two of post-war Italy's most eminent novelists, Italo Calvino and Elsa Morante.

1986   The so-called "maxi-trial" against over 400 alleged mafiosi takes place in Palermo. After two years of hearings, life sentences are meted out to almost the entire leadership of *Cosa nostra*, including the boss of bosses, Michele "The Pope" Greco. Tensions between the DC and the PSI cause the downfall of Craxi's first government in June after nearly three years in power—a post-war record. Craxi forms a second cabinet in August on the understanding that he will give way to a DC premier in March 1987.

1987   Craxi reneges on his promise to resign, causing the most difficult and drawn-out government crisis of the 1980s. In June, elections are held to resolve the issue. The PSI does well, advancing to 14 percent, and the PCI's share drops again. Giovanni Goria (DC) becomes premier at the head of a hapless administration that is sabotaged mercilessly by the PSI. A referendum held in November abolishes Italy's nuclear power program. The writer Primo Levi commits suicide in April.

1988   Ciriaco De Mita replaces Goria, becoming premier in April. Italy is paralyzed by wildcat strikes called by unofficial trade unions in the transport sector. Death in May of Giorgio Almirante, historic leader of Italian neo-fascism.

1989   The DC removes De Mita from the party leadership, replacing him with Arnaldo Forlani. In July, De Mita is substituted as prime minister by Andreotti. The end of communism in eastern Europe provokes vast changes in the PCI. Its leader, Achille Occhetto, announces his intention to transform the party into a formation "new even in name." Death of the Sicilian novelist and political activist Leonardo Sciascia in November.

1990   Parliament whitewashes a report revealing that there was widespread electoral fraud in Naples in the 1987 elections. Sixty-seven percent of a special conference of the PCI back Occhetto's decision to create a new party. In October, Occhetto announces that the new party will be called the "Democratic Party of the Left" (PDS). Nineteen ninety regional elections reveal the local strength of the Lombard League. A secret network of underground anti-communist armed cells known as "Gladio" is discovered. Death in February of Sandro Pertini, Italy's most loved president and wartime hero. Italy plays host to the soccer world cup.

1991   Italian airmen and ships participate in the Gulf War. The PCI's Twentieth Party Congress votes in February to change the party's name. A faction leaves to form "Communist Refoundation" (PRC). Autonomist movements unite to form the Northern League. President Cossiga uses presidential powers to block investigation of his role in the creation of "Gladio" and attacks Italy's institutions in an endless series of public outbursts. A referendum on electoral reform passes by a huge majority in June against the wishes of the party hierarchies. Tens of thousands of Albanian boat people attempt to migrate to Italy.

1992   Treaty of Maastricht signed in February. General elections in April end in a historic defeat for the DC and a triumph for the

Northern League. President Cossiga resigns, provoking a major political crisis. After the mafia kills prosecutor Giovanni Falcone, Parliament elects Oscar Luigi Scalfaro (DC) to the presidency. The "Clean Hands" corruption investigation begins: hundreds of DC and PSI politicans, including Craxi, are implicated by the end of the year. In September, the lira collapses and the new government of Giuliano Amato (PSI) is forced to take emergency measures to save the country from bankruptcy.

1993   The Amato government collapses under the weight of the corruption investigations and public demands for change after a second referendum on electoral reform in April. The governor of the bank of Italy, Carlo Azeglio Ciampi, is appointed premier. The Northern League achieves a massive victory in local elections held in June. In December, political leaders of all parties publicly admit huge corruption in the trial of a Milanese businessman. Death, in November, of Federico Fellini.

1994   Victory, in elections held under new majoritarian rules, of the media entrepreneur Silvio Berlusconi. Together with the Northern League and the neo-fascists, Berlusconi forms a government in May. Berlusconi's government lasts until December, when the Northern League votes against the government in a vote of confidence. By December, Berlusconi, too, is under indictment. Antonio Di Pietro, the symbol of the "Clean Hands" investigation, mysteriously resigns.

1995   The most tormented and perilous government crisis of post-war Italian history is resolved by the appointment of Lamberto Dini, an economist and banker, at the head of a government of unelected technocrats. Dini is supported in Parliament by the Northern League, the Partito Democratico della Sinistra (PDS) and the remnants of the DC. The fierce polemics caused by this move cause the lira to plummet against the mark and lead to worries about Italy's political stability. Romano Prodi, a Bologna economics professor, forms a center-left coalition with the support of the PDS. The "Olive Tree Coalition," as it is known, rapidly wins public consent.

1996   Prodi wins national elections held in April, but his government is dependent upon the PRC for a majority in Parliament. The new government is forced to make harsh economic decisions in order to meet the deadlines laid down for monetary union by the Maastricht treaty. A bicameral commission on constitutional reform is announced.

1997   In March, Italy agreed to head a multinational United Nations force to assist in ensuring humanitarian aid to Albania. Over 16,000 refugees fled that country to land in nearby southern Italy. In April, administrative elections in many Italian cities saw Communist Refoundation gain while other major parties, both in the Olive Tree Coalition and in the opposition, fared poorly. In October, when the PRC protested deep budget cuts in pensions and health care by withdrawing its support of the government, Prodi resigned. In four days, the PRC reversed field in the face of domestic and international criticism for creating a crisis.

1998   Italy qualifies for membership of the Euro. However, both the bicameral commission on constitutional reform and the Olive Tree Coalition government collapse. In the autumn, Massimo D'Alema becomes prime minister.

Introduction

Geography and People

The long boot-shaped peninsula of Italy separates the Mediterranean basin into western and eastern halves. In addition, the largest islands in the Mediterranean sea, Sicily and Sardinia, are both part of Italian territory. Italy is just over 300,000 square kilometers in size (115,830 square miles), and some 1,500 kilometers (938 miles) in length. Its lengthy coastlines on both east and west have stood for centuries as invitation to freebooters, pirates, invasions, and—especially in the 1990s—clandestine immigration. The country's northernmost cities, Aosta and Bolzano, are in the heart of the Alps; Sicily, by contrast, is just a ferry ride away from North Africa. In all, there are 12 degrees of latitude between the southernmost tip of Sicily and the frontiers with France, Switzerland, and Austria. Almost all the country is mountainous. In Sicily, there are peaks exceeding 3,000 meters (9,847 feet), including Mount Etna, one of the world's largest active volcanoes. The Apenines run for 745 miles like the shinbone of the Italian boot through Umbria, the Marches, Abruzzi, Molise, and Campania. The highest peaks are Monte Rosa at over 4,600 meters (15,203 feet) and Monte Bianco at over 4,800 meters (15,755 feet). The only lowland areas are the fertile flood valley of the Po River, Italy's longest river, and the heel of the Italian boot, Apulia. Many of Italy's largest industrial cities (Turin, Milan, Bologna, Padua, Mestre-Venezia) are concentrated in the Po River valley, while Apulia boasts some of Italy's most important ports—Bari, Taranto, and Brindisi. Apulia's seashore is unusually gentle: for the most part, Italy's coastline is spectacular, rocky, and largely inaccessible.

The mountainous terrain ensures that population density is very high in the flatter, more accessible parts of the country and in the seaports. Big cities such as Milan, Genoa, Rome, and Naples all have densities of over 2,000 people per square kilometer; almost all of the country, including some of the most mountainous areas, has more than 200 inhabitants per square kilometer. Only the sun-scorched, barren uplands of Sardinia, southern Italy, and Sicily are sparsely inhabited. Even the Alps are dotted with villages and thriving small commercial centers.

1

Historical Development

A visitor to Italy today, observing the busy commercial success that pervades almost the entire peninsula, might be excused for thinking that the country had enjoyed a long history of Swiss-like political stability, economic development, social cohesion, and peace. In fact, Poland aside, no other European nation has been so constantly ravaged by war and invasion as Italy. The peninsula has been an enticing prize for the dominant European power of every epoch since the final collapse of Rome in A.D. 476. Beginning with the Lombards, who swept through all of northern and central Italy after A.D. 568 and gradually established (by the standards of the time) a well-administered, though loosely organized state that increasingly coveted the wealthy, but less politically cohesive South, Italy has absorbed waves of foreign invasion that have left their traces in the cultural and political DNA of the peninsula's inhabitants. At the risk of over-generalizing, it has been broadly true that the accidents of geography and history ensured that the North of the country has been influenced by northern Europe, and in particular the civilizations of France and Germany, while the South has been dominated by Mediterranean powers. The South, as a consequence, has known a more absolutist tradition of rule, while the cities of the North were freer to develop their own forms of rule. The Holy Roman Empire, to which northern Italy nominally belonged after A.D. 773 when the Lombards were defeated by the Charlemagne, was not able to exercise its authority in the peninsula after Charlemagne's death in A.D. 814, and political power in northern Italy was devolved to local noblemen and churchmen. The North's primary form of organization became the city-state: small, with a politically active aristocracy and a sometimes turbulent populace. These cities were hardly models of good government. They were riven with bloody factional strife and inter-family warfare, but they were economically dynamic and possessed—to use, anachronistically, the language of modern-day political science—a conscious political identity. This enabled them to unite against an outside aggressor: between 1152 and 1176, the efforts of Frederick Barbarossa to restore the Holy Roman Empire's authority in northern Italy were defeated by a league of northern Italian cities, the *Lega Lombarda*. In the South, by contrast, the Arabs, who occupied Sicily and much of southern Italy in A.D. 827, turned Palermo into one of the most prosperous and technologically advanced cities in the world in the ninth century. They were supplanted in the eleventh century by the Normans, who established a highly centralized form of government that brooked no opposition.

The last attempt to unify the peninsula until the nineteenth century took place at the beginning of the thirteenth century when Frederick Barbarossa's grandson, Frederick II, who had inherited the throne of Sicily from the Normans, endeavored to restore imperial authority over both the Papacy and the city-states. Italy was ravaged by a civil war between the supporters of the empire (the Ghibellines) and the Pope (Guelfs). After 30 years of constant fighting, the country was left prostrated but disunited upon Frederick's death in 1250. Frederick's successors continued the struggle, but the Papacy was aided by the French king of Anjou who made southern Italy part of the Angevin empire in 1266. By the beginning of the fourteenth century, Italy lacked any central authority whatever: neither the Papacy, the Angevins, nor the Holy Roman Empire were strong enough to impose order on the peninsula, which broke down into perpetual and internecine warfare. In 1316, the Papal curia was removed to Avignon in southern France, removing the one symbol of authority in central Italy, which soon degenerated into anarchy and baronial feuding.

Consolidation took place in the fourteenth century, which saw the rise of several native Italian principalities or republics to positions of power within the peninsula. Under the leadership of the Visconti family, Milan established itself as the dominant force in the North and Center of the country. Its main rivals were Venice, which enjoyed stable aristocratic government, a growing empire in Dalmatia, and domination over the northeast of the peninsula, and Florence, which overran nearly all of modern-day Tuscany. All three of these states eclipsed the Angevins, whose hold on southern Italy was somewhat tenuous, and who were replaced as rulers of southern Italy by the expansionary Kingdom of Aragon in the fifteenth century. The three great Italian states of northern and central Italy were the envy of Europe from 1300 onward. They were the most populous and wealthy cities of their day, with an advanced industrial base, sophisticated banking systems, and sublime levels of artistic achievement. The Renaissance, the revival of classical learning, was of course a European-wide phenomenon, but its home was in Italy, where the wealth of the noble families enabled artistic patronage on a grand scale. The fourteenth and fifteenth centuries are the age of Petrarch, Boccaccio, Michelangelo, Raphael, Benvenuto Cellini: before them had come the towering genius of Dante, the poet whose writings mark the transition of the ancient world to the modern.

Renaissance Italy, despite the creation in 1454 of an "Italian League" between Milan, Venice, Florence, the Papacy, and the Kingdom of Naples, was plagued by continual warfare. At the end of the fifteenth century it was invaded by Charles VIII of France, who was followed by the Spanish and the forces of the revived Holy Roman Empire. Italy became a battleground for the powers. This was the age of Niccolò Machiavelli, the Florentine diplomat whose willingness to accept the ruthless laws of realpolitik still shocks, but who saw clearly that the wealth and artistic glory of the Italian states counted for nothing in the absence of military preparedness, social discipline, and political unity. Machiavelli's classic, *Il Principe* (The Prince), was published in 1519, the same year that Charles of Ghent took the imperial title. By dynastic chance, Charles already possessed the crowns of Spain, Austria, and Burgundy, and thus controlled all of continental Europe from the Polish border to Spain—except Italy, which split the vast empire in half, and France, with whom he fought several bloody wars throughout his reign. France's hold on Lombardy was ended after the battle of Pavia in 1525, and in 1530 Charles conquered Florence. Charles annexed Milan for Spain; placed Florence in the hands of the Medici family; established the dukedoms of Savoy, Ferrara, Mantua, Urbino, Modena, and Parma; left Lucca, Venice, and Genoa as aristocratic republics; allowed Papal control over much of central Italy; and ruled Naples and the South through a viceroy. In the following decades, Venice, the one Italian state to retain some status as a European power, saw its empire in the eastern Mediterranean nibbled away by the rising power of the Ottoman Turks.

Italy thus entered a long period of domination by the Spanish crown (Charles had ceded control over Austria and Hungary to his brother Ferdinand), and the parts of the peninsula that were most directly ruled by Spain were drawn into the Spanish state's decline and eventual fall. Southern Italy, in particular, was bled dry by the need to subsidize the gargantuan edifice of the Spanish court, and was deeply influenced, politically, by the corruption and feudalism of Spanish rule. Italy became one of the chief prizes for the powers of Europe in the War of the Spanish Succession (1701-1713). The main beneficiary of the war, in Italian terms, was Austria, which annexed Lombardy in 1707 and added Mantua and the mainland South in 1714, with Sicily passing briefly under the control of the Dukedom of Savoy, which also expanded its influence in Piedmont. Savoy, a hereditary duchy enjoying great autonomy from the Holy Roman Empire, which had been governing a tract of territory on both sides of the Alps since the Middle Ages, exchanged Sicily for Sardinia in 1720, and the new Kingdom of Sardinia, and its capital, Turin, became an established power within the peninsula. The map of Italy was redrawn twice more before 1748. Austria's gains were reduced later in the same century after the short War of the Polish Succession (1733-1735), when Charles Bourbon of Spain became king of the Two Sicilies and reunited Naples with Sicily. In 1748, the peace of Aix-la-Chapelle, which brought to an end the War of the Austrian Succession, saw the Bourbons extend their influence, while Modena fell into Austrian hands. Between 1748 and 1796, the Italian peninsula was at peace: astonishingly, this was the longest period without major war since the fall of the Roman Empire.

In 1796, Napoleon invaded Italy at the head of the French revolutionary army, ending the Venetian Republic's long independent history and driving the Savoys from Turin; he returned again in 1800 to reestablish French dominion. Like the Lombards, Franks, Arabs, Normans, Angevins, Aragonese, French, Spanish, and Austrians before him, he drew and redrew the political map of the peninsula with scant regard for the wishes of its inhabitants. In so doing, however, he created the kingdom of Italy in 1805. Naples was added the following year, with only Sicily remaining outside French rule. Napoleon undertook an ambitious period of modernization: A unified civil code was introduced, the power of the clergy was reduced, internal customs duties were abolished. Many of these reforms were only partially implemented, but an important principle had at least been established. Italy, finally, was being treated as something more than a geographic expression: it had begun the process of becoming a state.

Modern Italy

The starting point in the story of modern Italy is the Congress of Vienna (1814-1815), where the great powers of Europe—notably Austria—put the lid of absolutist rule on the cauldron of Italian national and liberal sentiment brought to boil by the French Revolution and Napoleonic conquests in Italy. Four main powers dominated the peninsula after the treaty: Austria, which took sovereignty over Venice and Lombardy and exercised decisive influence over the nominally independent duchies of Tuscany, Modena, Parma, and Lucca; the Kingdom of Sardinia, comprising modern-day Sardinia, Liguria, Piedmont, Aosta, and Nice, which was restored to the House of Savoy; Naples, which was restored to Ferdinand IV of Bourbon and which swiftly annexed Sicily to create the Kingdom of the Two Sicilies; and the Papal states, consisting of modern-day Emilia-Romagna, Lazio, and the Marches, which was directly ruled by the Pope. The areas closest to the Austrian border (Trento and Friuli) were absorbed into Austria itself. All told, the Congress of Vienna left nearly five million Italians under direct Austrian rule.

The first half of the nineteenth century was marked by uprisings against absolute rule in Naples and Turin. Spurred on by the Carbonari, secret societies of progressive young noblemen, soldiers, professionals, and students, liberal revolutions broke out in Naples in 1820, Piedmont in 1821, and the Papal states in 1831. The goal of the revolutionaries—a constitution, similar to the one adopted in Spain in 1812, that compelled the crown to share executive power with a parliament elected by the wealthier classes—seems modest in retrospect, but it was bitterly resisted by the arch-conservative chief minister of the Austrian empire throughout this period, Metternich, who feared that the contagion of liberal ideas would spread to his own realm. Forceful Austrian intervention soon quelled all three uprisings, but the fact that the monarchies and duchies of Italy were reliant upon a foreign power for their continued existence inevitably led to the struggle against absolute rule transforming itself into a nationalist one. By 1848, the "year of revolutions," nationalist feeling was widespread among the Italian middle and upper classes. One of the leading nationalist theorists, the former priest Vincenzo Gioberti, who became prime minister of Sardinia after King Carlo Alberto, under popular pressure, granted constitutional rule; another, the republican Giuseppe Mazzini, became part of the committee of "dictators" that ruled Rome after a popular uprising had driven out the Pope. All of Italy from Venice to Palermo was incandescent with revolutionary activity in 1848-1849.

The Risorgimento

The revolutions of 1848 nevertheless met the same fate as their predecessors. Austrian troops crushed uprisings in Lombardy and Venetia; French soldiers restored the Pope's authority in Rome; the Sardinian army, which supported the rebels in Milan and Venice, proved woefully unable to match the Austrians on the battlefield and was crushed at the battles of Custoza and Novara. The rising star of Sardinian politics, Count Camillo Benso di Cavour, drew the conclusion that nationalist fervor was not by itself enough to ensure the expulsion of Austria from the peninsula: diplomacy and economic modernization were of greater importance. Cavour became premier of the Kingdom of Piedmont-Sardinia in 1852 and swiftly began building railways, opening protected markets to foreign competition, and strengthening the military. In foreign policy, he cultivated Britain and France, sending a contingent of Bersaglieri to the Crimean War in 1855, thereby winning a seat at the subsequent peace conference in Paris. In 1858, at Plombières, Cavour struck a cynical secret bargain with Emperor Napoleon III of France, under the terms of which he would surrender Nice and Savoy to France in exchange for guaranteed French assistance in a defensive war with Austria. At the same conference, it was foreseen that all of northern Italy would be annexed by Sardinia, that a French prince would rule over a central Italian state, and that Naples would be ruled by a figure acceptable to the French. The three kingdoms would be organized in a loose Italian federation, with the Pope as the nominal head. Cavour's conception of a united Italy, in short, recognized the necessity for a foreign and Papal role, and was principally directed at extending the Savoyard Kingdom of Piedmont-Sardinia's own power and ridding the peninsula of the Austrians.

In the event, all of Italy was unified by October 1860, and King Victor Emmanuel of Sardinia was crowned "Re d'Italia" in March 1861: Cavour, in other words, obtained more for the throne of Sardinia than he had originally intended. Historians have divided over how far his diplomatic, skills were responsible for this striking success. Cavour can take credit for forcing the Austrians' hand and tricking them into war in April 1859, and for having prepared the Sardinian army to the point where it was able to provide vital collaboration to its French allies in the summer of 1859. But both national feeling and sheer chance played an undeniably important role. Without such incidental factors as the incompetence of Austrian diplomacy, the vainglory of Napoleon III, and the military genius of the "hero of two worlds," Giuseppe Garibaldi, unification may have been postponed for several decades. National feeling led to the peoples of central Italy rising in support of Cavour after the outbreak of war with Austria, and to their eventual annexation by Piedmont-Sardinia in the Spring of 1860—although Cavour handled masterfully the diplomatic tensions caused by this move. Hostility to feudalism enabled Garibaldi to lead successful revolutions in Sicily and the rest of the South in the spring and summer of 1860 and might have led to Italian unification taking a more radical turn had Cavour not risked international displeasure by invading the Papal states and marching on Garibaldi's headquarters in Naples in October 1860. Garibaldi himself contributed immensely to Cavour's success by placing his nationalist principles ahead of his republican and socialist sympathies, and surrendering his conquests in southern Italy to Victor Emmanuel without bloodshed. Unification, in other words, was the outcome of a complex combination of human, diplomatic, and political factors. It remains true, however, that without Cavour's instinctive grasp of the principles of realpolitik, events might well have taken a vastly different turn. The Piedmontese statesman is the only Italian leader of the last two centuries who can stand comparison with such great figures in modern European history as Bismarck, Gladstone, Masaryk, Churchill, De Gaulle, and Adenauer.

Liberal Italy

The Italy that emerged in March 1861 was essentially Piedmont writ large. The capital of the new state was Turin, the constitution of 1848 was adopted in toto for the new kingdom, almost all of the dominant political figures were Piedmontese. The North of Italy was by far the richest part of the country and the only one that was industrialized. Many of Italy's subsequent problems can be traced to the lopsided balance of power within the new state. Southern Italy, in particular, was undeniably neglected by the northern power brokers in industry and politics, and was left to stagnate—with the complicity of its own ruling class of landlords and aristocrats—as a semi-feudal backwater.

In addition to immense economic difficulties, the new Italian state had to complete the process of unification. Venetia, Trento, and Trieste remained under Austrian control in 1861, and the Pope's authority in Rome was protected by a French expeditionary force that had no difficulty in crushing an attempt by Garibaldi and a small army of patriots to seize the city at the battle of Mentana in 1867. The questions of Venetia and Rome were resolved by astuteness. In 1866, Italy allied herself with Prussia against Austria and, despite a poor military performance, was rewarded with Venetia after the war. In 1870, the defeat of Napoleon III at the hands of Bismarck allowed Italy to march troops into Rome. The Papal state was reduced in size to the walls of the Vatican, and for the next 50 years, church-state relations were extremely tense. The church suspended all diplomatic relations with the Italian state, did its best to have Italy ostracized by Catholic nations such as France, and banned Catholics from taking part in Italian political life. Only in 1913, when the rise of socialism alarmed the Vatican hierarchy, was this ban relaxed.

Italian socialism arose in particularly intransigent form because the Italian state failed, in the 30 years following unification, to provide elementary social justice. Newly unified Italy was "liberal" in the sense that it could boast parliamentary institutions, but it was not in any way democratic. Unlike Britain, where the suffrage was extended to almost all the adult male population by 1884, and where trade unions were granted significant opportunities to organize manual workers, Italian governments were reluctant to concede basic political rights to the working class. From 1876 onward, after the "parliamentary revolution" brought Agostino

Depretis to power, Italy was governed by the so-called "parliamentary left," but Depretis, despite many promises, failed to widen the suffrage in any significant way. An electoral law extending the suffrage from 600,000 voters to just over 2,000,000 was passed against stiff parliamentary opposition in 1882, but this was still less than 7 percent of the adult population. Having passed this law, Depretis rid himself of his more radical parliamentary supporters by appealing to the conservative opposition to "transform themselves" into a force of government. Only in 1912, long after comparable European states, was universal male suffrage conceded, and the first election under these rules was held in 1913.

A similarly narrow-minded view prevailed in the political class's attitude toward socialism and trade unionism. Depretis's successors (he died in 1887)—even former radicals such as Garibaldi's onetime secretary, Francesco Crispi—took a harsh line with the nascent movements of the working class and peasants. Crispi used the regular army to crush a peasant revolt in Sicily in 1893-1894, and in 1898, a government that included prominent moderates suppressed bread riots in Milan with implacable zeal: hundreds of striking workers were killed by troops commanded by General Bava Beccaris. Repression made no difference to the growth of the workers' movements. Social conditions, including blatantly unjust systems of land tenure, made inevitable their appearance on the political scene. A greater show of tolerance, and a less ruthless defense of the propertied class's privileges, might have led the Partito Socialista Italiano (PSI) / Italian Socialist Party, which was founded in 1892, to develop into a moderate "labor" force on the British model. Its founder, Filippo Turati, was a pragmatic figure who warned against violent revolution, and other early Socialists, notably Leonida Bissolati and Ivanoe Bonomi, were willing to cooperate with relative progressives such as the several-times premier, Giovanni Giolitti, to win concrete social and political reforms. Instead, the PSI embraced both dogmatic Marxism and the violent syndicalism espoused by the French theorist Georges Sorel. By 1912, when Bissolati and Bonomi were expelled from the movement, the PSI had developed a counter-intransigence of its own. Its new voice was Benito Mussolini, who would soon quarrel with the PSI over the issue of intervention in the Great War, but who relished the turbulent mass politics offered by the labor movement.

Imperialism and War

Readiness to undertake the politics of violence was growing on the political right too. Italy's colonial adventures, which began with Depretis in the mid-1880s, and continued under Crispi in the 1890s, failed to leave Italy with an adequate place in the sun and, on two occasions—at Dogali in 1887 and Adowa in 1896—ended in military setbacks at the hands of Abyssinian tribesmen. By the first decade of the twentieth century, nationalist theorists (including some socialists) were claiming that Italy was a "proletarian" nation that had been robbed of its birthright by rapacious powers such as Britain and France. This resentful mood led directly to a short war with Turkey that ended with Italy occupying the Dodecanese Islands, including Rhodes, and most of modern-day Libya. These gains were confirmed by the Treaty of Lausanne in October 1912. Such a minor war (only 3,000 Italians were killed) was hardly sufficient for the more headstrong members of the nationalist intelligentsia, or for "futurist" thinkers such as Filippo Tommaso Marinetti, whose *Futurist Manifesto* (1909) described war as the world's only "true hygiene."

The desire for war at all costs was a decisive force in pushing Italy into war on the side of the Entente in May 1915, although a majority of the Italian people were opposed to intervention and Italy was bound by treaty to Austria and Germany. Italy had followed a pro-German foreign policy since 1882, when it joined the Triple Alliance. The Triple Alliance, which gave Italy an Austro-German military guarantee in the event of an aggressive French war over Italy's Mediterranean ambitions, made perfect sense in strategic terms, but it was unpopular with a vocal section of Italian public opinion, the so-called "irredentisti," who resented the fact that no effort was being made to recapture the "unredeemed" territories of Trento and Trieste. After the outbreak of war in August 1914, Italy's leaders saw the opportunity to bargain for a return of the Italian-speaking parts of the Austrian empire. Italy argued that she deserved compensation for entering the war, and a cynical auction took place between the two warring blocs of powers, with Austria eventually offering a generous territorial settlement in exchange for Italy's at least remaining neutral. Giolitti famously wrote that the Central Powers had offered "parecchio" (a large amount) and favored neutrality. The Entente offered more, however. The Treaty of London, secretly signed in April 1915, promised to satisfy all of Italy's "irredentist" ambitions, and many of her imperial dreams in the eastern Mediterranean too. Huge, intimidatory public demonstrations were held by the nationalists during what the poet Gabriele D'Annunzio called the "radiant May," and a climate of support for intervention was created. On May 24, 1915, Italian troops invaded Austrian-held territory near Trieste.

World War I was an unmitigated disaster for Italy. Italian troops took hundreds of thousands of casualties vainly trying to push the Austro-German forces back across the Isonzo River near Trieste and out of their impregnable strongholds in the Trentino and Venetian Mountains. No fewer than eleven Italian offensives took place on the Isonzo front before mounting losses and plummeting morale brought the Italians to an exhausted halt. In October 1917, an Austro-German counter-attack at Caporetto made short work of the demoralized Italians, who fell back to the Piave River, almost at Venice, suffering huge losses in men and materials. Here, fighting with immense bravery, the ordinary soldiers of the army narrowly succeeded in holding the line. When the Austrian empire collapsed in 1918, Italy reoccupied the territories lost in October 1917, but the defeat of Caporetto left an indelible scar on the national consciousness.

World War I brought Italy few compensations in terms of territory or prestige. Needing to placate Woodrow Wilson's desire to construct a new Europe on the principles of self-determination, Britain and France reneged on the Treaty of London, and Italy's dreams of establishing a colonial empire in the eastern Mediterranean were dashed. Italy's representative, Premier Vittorio Emanuele Orlando, briefly walked out of the peace conference at Versailles in 1919, but this show of petulance was to no avail. By the terms of the Treaty of Saint-Germain, Italy was grudgingly given a frontier with Austria at the Brenner Pass (thus absorbing German-speaking Bolzano), and Trieste came under Italian rule. Fiume (Rijeka), a city on the Dalmatian coast with a substantial Italian population, was given to the new Kingdom of Yugoslavia, a decision the nationalists regarded as an affront to Italy's dignity. With the tacit consent of the Italian government, Gabriele D'Annunzio, by now a war hero, led a column of bravos to Fiume and established his own petty dictatorship until a new Italian government, headed—for the last time—by Giovanni Giolitti, finally plucked up the courage in 1921 to drive D'Annunzio out and restore Fiume to its rightful owners.

Fascism

D'Annunzio's action at Fiume was symbolic of the violence and the contempt for the rule of law that was by now endemic in Italian politics. The years 1920-1922 are known in Italy as the "red biennial." They were years in which the PSI, which had been severely censured during the latter years of the war for its hostility to the conflict, celebrated its victory in the elections held in 1919 by taking to the streets and pressing the workers' economic demands. Street clashes between the PSI and the so-called

Fasci di combattimento, formed by Mussolini after the war became a commonplace, and the Italian state eventually degenerated into anarchy. Several figures, including the world-renowned philosopher Benedetto Croce, actually welcomed Mussolini's accession to power in October 1922 as a way of restoring the fundamental condition for a free society —law and order—to the political scene. But this judgment failed to recognize that the fascists were the principal organizers of the violence that was disfiguring Italian political life. Croce later argued in his *Storia d'Italia 1870-1915* that fascism had "nothing to do" with the course of Italian history since the Risorgimento. For him, fascism was simply a form of political gangsterism. A much younger contemporary (who died of a beating inflicted upon him by a fascist squad), Piero Gobetti, saw things differently. He said in his book *La rivoluzione liberale* (*The Liberal Revolution,* 1925) that: "Fascism is the autobiography of a nation." The point is still being debated among Italians.

Mussolini was the effective head of state from October 1922 to July 1943. King Victor Emmanuel III, whose refusal to sign an order to take emergency measures against Mussolini's illegality eased the fascist movement's path to power, acquiesced in every step in the creation in Italy of *lo stato totalitario*—the totalitarian state. In 1924, after a fascist squad kidnapped and killed an opposition deputy, Giacomo Matteotti, the king failed to side with the democratic forces who boycotted Parliament in protest. The king's silence, and the democrats' own reluctance to act unconstitutionally, probably saved Mussolini's career from an ignominious end. In 1925-1926, all opposition to fascism was outlawed, Mussolini became Duce, and by 1930 a new legal, electoral, and institutional structure—the so-called corporate state—had been erected to reflect the principles of fascist ideology. The state's presence in the daily life of the population was never as pervasive as in Nazi Germany or the Soviet bloc, nor were individual liberties ever entirely wiped out, but the intellectual rejection of liberal principles of constitutional government was as great as in Germany and Russia. The only non-fascist institution that exercised some limited degree of independence from the regime was the Catholic Church. The Lateran pacts, signed by Mussolini and Pope Pius XI in 1929, ended the long period of hostility between church and state and established Catholicism as the official state religion.

Mussolini was brought down by his decision to ally Italy with Germany in 1938. This move, which was accompanied by the introduction of the "racial laws" against Italy's Jewish community, constrained Mussolini to follow the German dictator on military adventures for which Italy was little prepared, and which eventually exposed the vaunted fascist state for the hollow shell it was. Despite Mussolini's defiance of the League of Nations during Italy's 1935 invasion of Abyssinia and Italy's involvement in the Spanish Civil War, Mussolini could have joined forces with Britain and France as late as 1940. Blinded by Germany's power, by his own anti-democratic ideology, or perhaps just by vainglory, the fascist dictator decided that Italy should sign the "Pact of Steel" with Hitler instead. Italy burned its bridges with the Allies by invading France in June 1940, and in 1941 invaded Greece, where its army was humiliated and had to be rescued by German troops. In North Africa, British and Commonwealth soldiers made short work of Italian forces whenever they were not stiffened by the presence of German troops, and Italy's colonial empire in Africa swiftly fell under British control.

By 1943, Italy's situation had become desperate. The Allies—including, since December 1941, the United States—invaded Sicily in June 1943, provoking the final crisis of the fascist state. During the night of July 24-25, 1943, the Fascist Grand Council, the cabinet of the fascist movement, passed a vote of no confidence in Mussolini's leadership. The king, shifting with the political wind, signed a warrant for the Duce's arrest and appointed Marshal Badoglio, the general who had led the war in Abyssinia, the country's new leader. Italy officially surrendered on September 8, 1943, whereupon Badoglio and the king fled to the Allied-occupied South, but surrender did not bring an end to conflict. For two years, Italy was once again a battlefield as the Allies inched their way up the peninsula against stiff German opposition. The North of Italy, meanwhile, was the setting for a brutal civil war between the mostly communist and socialist partisans and the squads of the newly constituted Italian Social Republic, which Mussolini, who had been spirited from jail by the Germans, presided over from Salò on the banks of Lake Garda. Thousands died in this internecine conflict: the Nazis also committed some of the worst atrocities of the war on Italian soil. Mussolini's own death, after the victory of the Allies in Europe, was itself an atrocity. Fleeing in disguise with his mistress and a handful of faithful followers, he was captured by partisans near the Swiss border. He and his followers were summarily executed and the bodies were strung up by the feet in Milan's Piazza Loreto, where they were vilified by the crowds. The leaders of post-war Italy had, above all else, to take into account the seething hatred that could endorse such a barbaric act. Thousands of acts of murder and violence were committed in the first months after liberation: Italy might very well have lapsed into a nationwide civil war had it not been blessed with political leadership of an exceptionally high caliber.

The First Republic

This leadership was provided by the men who headed the two most coherent and representative political formations to emerge during the wartime years: Alcide De Gasperi, the leader of the Democrazia Cristiana (DC) / Christian Democracy Party, and Palmiro Togliatti, of the Partito Comunista Italiano (PCI) / Italian Communist Party. Togliatti, who had spent the fascist years and the war as a leading functionary of the Comintern in Moscow, returned from exile in the autumn of 1943 and set the party's face against the revolutionary strategy that many Italian workers would have preferred. The PCI participated in the Allied-backed governments formed by Badoglio and Ivanoe Bonomi in wartime, and then cooperated fully with the post-war governments headed by Ferruccio Parri, a partisan hero of radical political sympathies, and De Gasperi, who became premier for the first time in December 1945. De Gasperi steered the country to the momentous elections of June 2, 1946, with great skill, and Italy voted to abolish the monarchy and elect a Constituent Assembly of delegates with remarkably little disorder. In the elections, De Gasperi's DC emerged as the largest party, with 35 percent of the vote, although the PSI and the PCI, the two next largest parties, jointly polled more votes than the DC. The assembly thus elected drew up a complex constitution that reflected socialist principles (Article 1 states that "Italy is a republic founded on work"), and established a parliamentary form of government that jealously guarded against the possibility of a powerful executive branch. Together with the proliferation of political parties caused by the adoption of a strongly proportional electoral system, this constitutional bias in favor of the legislative branch of government has been the chief reason for the notorious instability of Italian governments throughout the post-war period: Italy has had over 50 since the implementation of the Constitution on January 1, 1948.

While the Constitution was in preparation, De Gasperi—who had been one of the leaders of the Partito Popolare Italiano (PPI) / Italian People's Party, which had emerged in 1919 as the Catholic Church's organized political response to the PSI—purged his cabinet (allegedly at the behest of the United States leadership) of the PCI and the PSI. The April 1948 elections, held at the height of the post-war clash between the United States and the USSR, were marked by overt attempts by both superpowers to influence the political struggle in Italy. The DC took 48 percent of the vote and gained an actual majority of seats in Parliament, while the PCI replaced the PSI (from which the PCI had split in 1921; the PSI had thereafter always been the junior partner in this relationship) as the party of choice for the organized working class. De Gasperi, however, was astute enough to realize that the elections had not given the DC a free hand. He governed with the assistance of the "lay" (i.e., non-Catholic) center parties and introduced such important acts of social justice as the land reform of 1950. In foreign policy, he steered Italy back into the international community, brokering Italian membership in the North Atlantic Treaty Organization (NATO) and becoming one of the founding fathers of the movement for European unification. By the time of his death in 1954, the Italian economy was on the brink of the surge of sustained growth known as the "economic miracle" and a rising tide of unprecedented prosperity that eased many of the country's social tensions. De Gasperi's was an immense achievement, but one he could not have managed without the PCI's studied moderation. The immediate post-war period established the DC and the PCI as the two central forces in newly democratic Italy, a state of affairs that did not break down until the 1990s.

The "economic miracle" is the lasting achievement of Christian Democracy. Whatever the sins of the men who followed Alcide De Gasperi—and there were many—it is impossible to deny that under the DC, Italy became richer and more prosperous than at any other time in her history. Yet the DC did preside over social changes that accompanied the reduced dependence on the traditional agricultural economy, including the secularization of Italian society. Even changes of which the DC disapproved came irresistibly to pass: for example, divorce was introduced in 1970 and confirmed in a momentous popular referendum in 1974; obscenity restrictions were lifted; the universities were opened to the masses; a limited abortion act was passed in 1978 and defended, in its turn, by a popular vote in 1981; the Catholic Church's status as the official religion of the state was ended in 1984. The DC presided over this transformation in conventional mores and standards with some discomfort, occasional distress, and much flexibility of doctrine.

The same doctrinal flexibility enabled the DC to cooperate with the PSI during the 1960s (the so-called "opening to the left") and to survive a wave of industrial and social unrest in the early 1970s by forging a "historic compromise" with the far-sighted reformist leader of the PCI, Enrico Berlinguer. The so-called "government of national solidarity" (1976-1979) was an unnatural marriage of convenience, but it did at least defend Italian democracy from the attacks of the most merciless European terrorist movement of the 1970s: the "Brigate Rosse." Hundreds of judges, politicians, policemen, and civil servants were killed, wounded, kidnapped, or "kneecapped" by the terrorists in these years, the most famous victim being Aldo Moro, a five-times DC prime minister, and the architect both of the DC's strategies of "opening to the left" and of collaboration with the PCI.

Economy

The post-1945 prosperity of Italy is a crucial development in the country's history, and a source of great national pride. Resource-poor Italy industrialized later and less thoroughly than any other country in western Europe, and until the last two decades has always been regarded with some condescension by, notably, the British and the Germans. Although the period 1861-1914 saw high economic growth, investment in infrastructure (especially railways) and the emergence of a substantial but over-protected industrial sector, Italy still lagged behind other major countries in every index of well-being. Per capita income in 1914 was a quarter of the United States', a third of Great Britain's, and about half of Germany's. Fifty-five percent of the workforce still labored on the land (down from 75 percent in 1862): comparable figures for France, Germany, and Britain were 43, 35, and 12 percent. These agricultural workers, moreover, only rarely owned their own land. Nine-tenths of the land-owning population possessed less than a single hectare (a hectare is nearly 2.5 acres) of land, some three million hectares in all, while a smallish class of wealthy peasants and a few thousand wealthy landlords, the so-called *latifondisti*, owned most of the remaining 20 million or so hectares. These big landlords rented out strips of land to casual agricultural laborers in exchange for a tithe on the crops, and often left much of their land fallow. The grinding poverty bred by such a feudal form of agriculture was the main cause of the high migration rates of the pre-war years. Between 1911 and 1913 alone, nearly 2.2 million Italians left the country to look for a better life in northern Europe, the United States, and South America: the total for the whole period 1901-1914 is more than eight million.

An agricultural economy of this kind was not suited for the efforts required by modern war. The national debt increased sevenfold in the decade 1910-1920, as the Italian state struggled to meet the costs of a long, intensive war. In 1919-1920, the lira collapsed under the strain of the government's deficit spending, passing from Lit. 13 to the dollar to nearly Lit. 30 in a single year. Since Italy imported almost all its primary materials, and was even a large net importer of food, this devaluation unleashed inflationary pressures within the economy and squeezed the standard of living of the ordinary wage earners who had already been hard hit by increased taxation during the war. Adding to the difficulties of the economy, there was the problem of rapidly increasing unemployment, as the factories that had been churning out war materials were suddenly compelled to adjust to a peacetime economy in a near-bankrupt country. The Italian state's first experiment in public ownership of a manufacturing concern came in 1919 when the government intervened to save Ansaldo, a shipyard and armaments manufacturer based in Genoa.

One of Mussolini's initial attractions for Italy's most eminent financiers and economists was that he promised to discipline government spending and to follow classical laissez-faire doctrines to get the economy back on its feet. Fascism presided over the stabilization of the economy. Totalitarian ideology played a part in this process, but sheer necessity also forced the dictatorship's hand. The Italian economy was devastated by the Great Depression of 1929-1932 when unemployment levels reached 25 percent, and industrial output dropped by almost a third. Lack of demand brought hundreds of major industrial companies and banks to their knees, and Mussolini was compelled to create, in 1933, the public holding company that would eventually grow to be one of Europe's largest employers of labor—the Istituto per la Ricostruzione Industriale (IRI) / Institute for Industrial Reconstruction. IRI was originally intended to be a hospice for nursing depression-damaged enterprises back to market fitness, but it gradually evolved into a sprawling conglomerate that made everything from foodstuffs to oil tankers. For the next four decades, IRI dominated the Italian economy, and its leading executives were among the most powerful figures in the country.

It is a measure of Mussolini's vainglory and lack of judgment that he involved economically battered Italy in ambitious foreign policy adventures and the alliance with Germany. In 1938, Italy's industrial capacity had just about recovered its 1929 levels of production, which were themselves hardly higher than the levels reached prior to 1915. He repeated, in other words, the error of the Italian nationalists during World War I by waging modern war with a still unmodern economy. By the end of the conflict, war-blasted Italy's industrial production was only a quarter of pre-war levels. In 1946, Italy had the highest illiteracy rates, lowest rate of industrialization, worst infrastructure, lowest per capita income, and least efficient agriculture of any West European country except fascist Spain and Portugal. All these problems, moreover, were particularly acute in the South.

Nobody in 1945 observing the desperate socioeconomic backwardness of the Mezzogiorno and the smouldering rubble of the northern factories could have envisaged the dramatic "economic miracle" that was to transform Italian society over the following three decades. Even with the benefit of hindsight, it is easier to describe, rather than explain, the staggering surge in economic activity that transformed Italy into a world-class economy by the late 1960s. Led by the state-owned or state-protected giants (FIAT, the national gas company, ENI, Finsider steel), Italy began enjoying real economic growth rates of 6 percent or more per year from the mid-1950s onward. When, after 1958, tariff barriers were brought down among the EEC "six" (France, Italy, W. Germany, Belgium, Netherlands, Luxembourg), Italy's innovative consumer goods producers (motorcycles, household goods, electrical appliances, fashionable clothing) acquired markets all over Europe. The South was not left out. Post-war Italian governments pumped money into the Cassa per il Mezzogiorno—the Southern Italian Development Fund—to improve infrastructure, build an industrial base, and modernize communications. By the 1970s, southern Italians enjoyed approximately the same purchasing power (though not income per head) as northern Italians, although the Mezzogiorno's economy was unhealthily dependent on prestige projects by state-owned companies and hundreds of thousands of Southerners had headed to the booming factories of Lombardy and Piedmont in the 1960s. This move reinforced a long historical process. Lombardy's population grew by 141 percent in the century that elapsed between 1871 and 1971: the population of the nation as a whole grew by approximately 90 percent.

Thus the economic unity of North and South, a century after political unification, proved to be a flecting achievement. In textiles, optics, machine-tools, ceramics, furniture, agricultural products, Italy's northernmost regions have enjoyed a second economic miracle since the early 1980s. The main Turin to Venice highway across the Paduan plain is accompanied by an almost unbroken row of new factories, warehouses, and retail outlets. Rather like Britain in the early years of the Industrial Revolution, businesses in this region form "clusters" of producers who know one another well, place orders among themselves, and trust one another to deliver high quality goods on time. Add an obsession with design and traditional standards of craftsmanship, and the recipe for northern Italy's industrial success is not hard to decipher. The North of Italy is now richer in terms of per capita income than much of northern Europe (and, indeed, large parts of the United States). By all the indicators of personal wealth (car ownership per head, ownership of consumer goods, personal savings rates), Italy now ranks alongside wealthy countries like Germany, Holland, and Britain.

With this unprecedented affluence have come profound changes in personal behavior and in the composition of society. The birthrate, at just 1.3 children per adult woman, is the lowest figure in Europe, despite the fact that strongly Catholic Italy has the lowest divorce rate and number of births outside marriage of any industrialized country. This figure reflects both the fact that the modernization of the economy has led many working women to postpone both marriage and childbirth, and a widespread desire among Italians to maximize their potential for consumption by not having children. The lower birthrate and the booming economy have meant that for the first time in its history Italy has become an importer of people. Migrants from the countries of the North African shore, Albania, former Yugoslavia, and Eastern Europe have begun to arrive in large numbers. For Albanians, in particular, Italy is regarded as a promised land offering fabulous riches. These new migrants have not always been made welcome: a fact that shames the many Italians who remember the overt discrimination and ethnic stereotyping endured by Italian migrants to Switzerland and Germany in the 1950s. The best estimate is that there are today between 1.1 and 1.5 million people of foreign origin in Italy, by no means all of them refugees from poverty.

The Mezzogiorno, despite encouraging recent signs of growing entrepreneurship, has not shared in Italy's economic prosperity. Income per head in the poorest southern provinces (Agrigento and Caltanisetta in Sicily, Cosenza and Catanzaro in Calabria) is less than half the figure reached by the richest provinces (Trieste in Friuli, Bologna in Emilia-Romagna, Varese, Bergamo, and Milan in Lombardy). It is hardly an exaggeration to say that the Italian peninsula today harbors one economy that matches Germany in productivity and surpasses her in creativity and managerial flair; another that is barely more productive than Portugal, and a good deal less prepared than Portugal for the challenges globalization will inevitably bring in the coming decades. The most telling statistic is unemployment: levels of joblessness rose sharply in southern Italy in the late 1980s and 1990s, and today average well over 20 percent of the working population in such badly hit regions as Sardinia, Sicily, Calabria, and Campania. In the North, by contrast, unemployment has averaged 6 percent or less over the last decade, and there are some cities (Treviso, the home of the Benetton clothing group, being the classic example) where the vigor of local industry is such that it requires an influx of outside labor every year to keep the factories going.

The politicians had no answer to this regional disparity in economic performance or for the social pathologies—notably the revival of the mafia—that were generated as a consequence. Instead of dealing with the structural problems of the southern economy, which would have meant a painful period of retrenchment, the DC and PSI-dominated five-party coalition that controlled Italy between 1981 and 1991 preferred to throw money at the South's malaise, increasing wasteful subsidies, keeping open unproductive plants, doling out absurdly generous pensions and benefits, and giving local (often mafia-controlled) politicians unsupervised access to the public till. Such policies led to the Mezzogiorno's economy becoming assisted, that is, one that cannot stand on its own, and caused a surge in gang warfare as the criminal clans of southern Italy fought for a share of the influx of public money in state investment and for the relief of the effects of the 1980 earthquake.

The Crisis of the First Republic

The failure of Italy's politicians to take structural measures to render the Mezzogiorno more economically competitive reflected the nature of the DC's essentially distributive vision of politics. By the 1980s, the DC had been in uninterrupted power for over 40 years and had presided over the creation of one of the most dirigist economies in the non-communist world. Inevitably, the state-owned industries and banks were gradually absorbed into the patronage networks of the parties of government, which used them as a combination of employment agency and private bank, rather than as commercial undertakings. The results were predictable. IRI, which by now employed over 400,000 workers, owed some Lit. 40 trillion (at the time nearly $30 billion) by the mid-1980s and was losing more than Lit. two trillion every year. The state railways, the Post Office, and the publicly owned banks, were all characterized by inefficiency and the regular need for infusions from the national treasury. The possession of a party card, as opposed to managerial competence, was a sine qua non for a career in the state-run industries. Party-appointed placement dominated the national television service, turning its news programs into propaganda for the DC and its socialist allies. *Lottizzazione*, to give patronage its Italian name, was taken for granted in the universities, the health service, the highway authorities, the schools, the law, the civil service. In this way, as the Italian political scientist Sergio Fabbrini has argued, an oligarchy of "insiders" was created, who enjoyed privileges denied to the mass of "outsiders," especially the young. For example, certain categories of workers were rewarded with extremely generous pensions (until recently, it was possible for a state employee to retire on a minimum pension with just 14 years' service). Such an oligarchy could only endure so long as the parties of government did not exceed the limits of financial prudence. In the 1980s, as the DC and the PSI struggled for power within the five-party coalition, they failed to respect this elementary rule of systemic self-preservation. Public spending ballooned faster than a sharp increase in taxes; infrastructure was neglected, and those projects that were initiated were manifestly conditioned by corruption. In 1990, the national debt exceeded 100 percent of the Gross Domestic Product (GDP)—up from a relatively healthy 60 percent in 1980—imposing a crushing burden in interest repayments.

Italy, in other words, was increasingly being governed in a way that recalled Latin American countries like Colombia or Mexico at the same moment that its most prosperous regions were emulating Germany, Switzerland, and the rich economies of northern Europe. Such a contrast was bound to provoke a political reaction, and at the end of the 1980s the reaction duly came. The rapid rise of the Lega Nord, a populist mass movement preaching both free market remedies for Italy's state sector and the dismantling of the unified Italian state, was, in retrospect, a natural development, although it took both the political class and political observers by surprise. In the 1992 general elections, the Lega took 9 percent of the national vote and 17 percent of the votes in the North, inflicting a great defeat on the DC, which slipped under 30 percent for the first time in 50 years.

The rise of the Lega was only one of the major changes in the Italian political system at the beginning of the decade. Of equal importance were the transformation, between November 1989 and February 1991, of the PCI into the Partito Democratico della Sinistra (PDS) / Democratic Party of the Left and the growing popular movement for electoral reform, which led to changes in the electoral law that were bitterly opposed by the political elite in June 1991. Italy's politicians, particularly the prime minister, Giulio Andreotti, and the leader of the PSI, Bettino Craxi, seem to have underestimated the force of the reformist wind in Italian society. Indeed, the disappearance of the communists, and their replacement by a shaky new party that was insecure of its identity, seemingly convinced them that their hold on power was unassailable. They could not have made a greater error. After their shock defeat in the 1992 elections, the DC and the PSI were swept from power by the judiciary, popular fury, and the financial markets. The lira was devastated in the summer of 1992, collapsing against the deutsche mark and the French franc, and Italy came perilously close to a loss of international confidence. The most stringent austerity measures in post-war Italian history were introduced and, in short order, the political system erected by the DC crumbled ignominiously. Thousands of politicians, including almost all the most senior figures in the DC and the PSI, were indicted on corruption charges, or charges of association with the mafia, by prosecutors finally free of political interference. Italy was forced to face the fact that for the third time in her history as an independent state, she had fallen victim to a profound crisis of regime.

Ever since 1992-1993, Italians have been engaged in a debate over the new state that might replace the "First Republic." The debate has been fierce and inconclusive. Despite the rise of new political forces, such as Forza Italia, a party founded and marketed by the media entrepreneur Silvio Berlusconi, and the center-left "Olive Tree Coalition" headed by the current premier, the former academic and president of IRI, Romano Prodi, no new vision of Italy's future has caught the public imagination. One hundred and forty years after unification, Italy finds itself in a position analogous to the one inherited in 1861 by the new Kingdom of Italy. Then, as now, the nation's leaders had to repair devastated public finances. Then, as now, Italy faced the challenge of holding together two separate social and economic realities within the same country. Then, as now, Italy had to establish herself as a force that counted within the community of European nations. Contemporary Italy's politicians might do well to take a leaf from the book of solutions employed by the statesmen who led post-Risorgimento Italy. The virtues of public austerity, political courage, personal probity, and skillful diplomacy practiced by the so-called *destra storica* (historic right) during the governments of Luigi Federico Menabrea, Giovanni Lanza, and Marco Minghetti (1868-1876) have proved to be the exception rather than the rule in Italian history, but they remain valid guides for a country that has been all too prone to succumb to rhetoric, all-encompassing solutions, and cynical political horse-trading. This brief period is often passed over by historians giving a synoptic account of modern Italian history (a convention that we have followed ourselves in this introduction), but the achievements of Italy's governments in that period are unquestionable. At the cost of widespread peasant riots against the so-called "grist tax" on milled grain, the destra storica's austerity measures saved the nascent Italian state from bankruptcy and allowed Italy to take its place on the European stage. For a few brief years, Italy had what it has ever since struggled to find—a political class that subordinated its personal and class interests to the national interest.

THE DICTIONARY

ABYSSINIA. Some 20 years after unification in 1861, Italian governments embarked on a program of imperial expansion to answer the query, "Is Italy the least of the Great Powers or the greatest of the Lesser Powers?" After France had blocked Italian ambitions in Tunisia, Italy made inroads on the Red Sea, occupying several cities in what was to become Eritrea. Between 1887 and 1889, the Italian government aimed at establishing a protectorate over neighboring Ethiopia (Abyssinia) to which Britain agreed so long as Italy remain no less than 100 miles from the Nile and not interfere with the flow of its water. When Menelik, Ethiopian King of Kings, gave France a railway concession in exchange for munitions and other supplies and renounced the 1889 Treaty of Uccialli (which, in the Italian reading, had given Italy a protectorate over Abyssinia), Italy declared war. Menelik's 100,000-strong force roundly defeated the badly led 25,000 advancing Italians at Adowa on March 1, 1896. The immediate consequence in Italy was a wave of popular strikes and protests that forced the government of **Francesco Crispi** to withdraw the army and to resign. Crispi's successor, **Antonio Di Rudinì**, signed—in November 1896—a peace that left Italy with Eritrea but recognized the independence of Abyssinia.

Mussolini took Italy's revenge nearly four decades later. After creating border incidents in the unmarked area between Italian Somaliland and Abyssinia, the Duce provoked a brief but bloody war of conquest, opening hostilities on October 3, 1935. Foreign military observers were impressed by the speed of Italy's victory over a territory larger than metropolitan France, her ruthless use of aircraft against civilians, and her use of gas against the poorly equipped Abyssinian army. In May 1936, Addis Ababa fell and Emperor Haile Selassie fled the country, not to return until British forces recaptured Abyssinia in the course of World War II.

Mussolini's victory was also a diplomatic triumph. Playing on the imperial powers' fear of Germany, Mussolini was able to extract from the French a virtual blank check to do as he wished so long as no French colonies were threatened; from the British, a policy in the League of Nations of avoiding sanctions that might antagonize the Italian government. The league's threats regarding oil shipments and scrap iron sales did nothing to impede Italian acquisition of those war goods in trade with non-League members, including—conspicuously—the United States. Moreover, league threats enabled Mussolini to portray Italy to the Italian public as the struggling "proletarian" nation facing alone the hostility of the plutocratic European powers.

The conquest of Abyssinia, added to Eritrea (after the war, incorporated in newly independent Ethiopia) and Somaliland, created Italian East Africa, thereby enabling Mussolini to confer on King Victor Emmanuel the title of *imperatore* or emperor and to make of **Pietro Badoglio** viceroy of Abyssinia. For many, the conquest was proof of Mussolini's boast that **fascism** would show the world that Italy could be a nation of warriors. Subsequent failures in Greece and North Africa in 1940-1941 would prove that such hopes had no military basis. *See also* Fascism; Foreign Policy; Hoare-Laval Pact.

ACCADEMIA D'ITALIA (Italian Academy). The fascist regime's aspirations to renew Italy's status in literature and learning found expression in 1926 with the foundation of the Accademia D'Italia. The academy consisted of 60 eminent thinkers, divided into four distinct categories—the moral and historical sciences; literature; the physical, natural, and mathematical sciences; and the arts. The first 30 members were named in a royal decree, while the remainder were chosen by **Mussolini** himself from a list of names proposed by the academicians. From 1929 to 1944, the academy was housed in *La Farnesina*, the fifteenth-century palace in **Rome** that today houses Italy's foreign ministry. In 1939, the number of members was expanded to 80. These salaried academicians meant that Italy, no less than France, would have its guardians of the nation's intellectual and artistic life.

The academy's mission officially was to "coordinate the intellectual movement in Italy," but it had little success in this regard. From the historian's point of view, it is interesting to note just how many leading Italian intellectuals were willing to lend their names to an institution that had an obvious propaganda purpose. Its president between 1930 and 1937 was **Guglielmo Marconi,** the inventor of the wireless; **Gabriele D'Annunzio** succeeded him. Other intellectuals who either heard the siren call of **fascist ideology**, or were seduced by the extremely generous stipends offered by the institution, included the physicist **Enrico Fermi**, the dramatist **Luigi Pirandello**, the poet **Filippo Tommaso Marinetti,** the historian Gioacchino Volpe, and the philosopher **Giovanni Gentile**, who became president of the institution in 1944 and transferred its seat to Florence.

ACERBO, GIACOMO (1888-1969). First elected to Parliament in 1919 as a nationalist, Giacomo Acerbo soon switched to **Mussolini**'s **Partito Nazionale Fascista** (PNF) / National Fascist Party. In July 1921, he signed the so-called "pact of pacification" with the **Partito Socialista Italiano** (PSI) / Italian Socialist Party on behalf of the fascist movement. In November 1922, he entered Mussolini's first cabinet as undersecretary in the prime minister's office. In this role, he was responsible for the notorious Acerbo Law of 1923, which guaranteed electoral victory for the fascists and their allies in the elections of January 1924 by giving bonus seats to the party with a plurality.

Acerbo was one of the leading fascist officials tainted with the political responsibility for the murder of **Giacomo Matteotti** in 1924. He resigned his post, becoming deputy speaker of the Chamber of Deputies, although he returned to government office in the 1930s as minister for agriculture, and minister for finance in the last years of the regime. On July 25, 1943, he was one of the members of the Fascist Grand Council who voted to revoke Mussolini's dictatorial powers. Regarded by the fascist faithful as a traitor (he was condemned to death in the **Republic of Salò**), he was hardly looked upon with favor by Italian democrats. During the **Bonomi** government, he was arrested and sentenced to 30 years' imprisonment. After the war, however, he was soon amnestied. Acerbo, who by profession was an agricultural economist, returned to university teaching. He died in **Rome** in 1969. *See also* Electoral Laws.

ACHILLE LAURO. An Italian cruise ship, the Achille Lauro became famous in October 1985 when members of a splinter group from the Palestine Liberation Organization (PLO) took control of the vessel while it was en route to Port Said, Egypt, and terrorized its 500 passengers and crew. Sensitive to its relations with the Arab states, Italy tried to achieve a diplomatic solution to the crisis. With Egyptian cooperation, it was agreed that the terrorists would surrender in exchange for safe conduct to the Yugoslav capital of Belgrade. The only proviso was that no violent acts punishable by Italian law had been committed aboard the ship. When it became clear that an American tourist had, in fact, been killed, both the U.S. and the Italian governments wanted Egypt to allow extradition of the four perpetrators for trial. While en route to Yugoslavia, an Egyptian airliner carrying the Palestinians was forced to land at Sigonella in Sicily by two U.S. jets.

On landing, the Egyptian aircraft was immediately surrounded by both a detachment of *Carabinieri* and armed U.S. Navy Seals. Tensions subsided only when U.S. authorities instructed the Seals to recognize Italian territorial jurisdiction. This military standoff was only the beginning of the diplomatic crisis, however. When Prime Minister **Bettino Craxi** informed the Egyptian government of his intention to prosecute the Palestinians—one of whom was the notorious Abbu Abbas— the Egyptians insisted that they were guests of the Egyptian government and were in Italy against their will. President Ronald Reagan, however, continued to demand that the terrorists be extradited to the United States. Caught on the horns of a dilemma, Craxi chose to placate Arab opinion. It was decided that there was insufficient evidence to hold the terrorists and they were allowed to leave for Belgrade.

An internal political crisis followed. The pro-American **Partito Repubblicano Italiano** (PRI) / Italian Republican Party temporarily resigned from the government and the Craxi administration was forced to submit to a parliamentary vote of confidence. Craxi defended his actions vigorously. In a speech to the Chamber of Deputies, he criticized U.S. over-eagerness to apply military solutions to diplomatic problems and defended the Palestinian struggle for autonomy. The Achille Lauro incident was a watershed in Italian-American relations, since it illustrated that the geopolitical realities of Italy's position in the Mediterranean were potentially of equal or even greater importance for the country's foreign policy than the American alliance. *See also* Foreign Policy.

ACTION PARTY. *See* Partito d'Azione.

ALBANIA. During **World War I**, Italy offered hospitality to the provisional Albanian government in Durazzo (Durres), an Albanian port city over which Italy had established a protectorate de facto. Austria seized the city in February 1916. Control over Albania's inhospitable mountains was hotly contested by Austrian and Italian forces until war's end.

By 1926, the mutual assistance Treaty of Tirana ensured that Albania had become, in effect, an Italian protectorate: the banking system and much of the commercial life was already operating under

Italian auspices and financing. Within a year, the prime minister was crowned as Zog I. In 1931, large Italian loans under Italian supervision put most of Albania's economy under effective Italian control while purporting to modernize an abysmally poor and undeveloped country. The Italian response to a brief attempt by Zog to loosen Italy's hold was to send the Italian fleet to browbeat him into submitting to even greater Italian influence over Albania's army, schools, and economy. By the mid-1930s, most officers in the Albanian army were, in fact, Italian.

Germany's 1938 Anschluss with Austria and subsequent annexation of Czechoslovakia prompted **Mussolini** to consider redressing the Balkan balance by directly annexing Albania. Italy's sudden invasion forced Zog to leave for Greece, while a new Albanian Constituent Assembly asked for union with Italy, a request to which King Victor Emmanuel readily acceded.

In the next year, the virtual dismemberment of Rumania by the Soviet occupation of (formerly Russian) parts of Rumania and by cessions of other parts of Rumania to Hungary and Bulgaria led Mussolini to ask Greece for the right to use Greek bases in the event of hostilities. When he was refused, Italy invaded Greece from Albania on October 28, 1940.

Within a month, the Greeks had not only repelled the Italians but had occupied a quarter of Albania and taken nearly 30,000 Italian prisoners, obliging Germany to send 50,000 troops to Italy's assistance. Together with British defeats of Italian forces in Africa, Italian prestige plummeted and Mussolini's hopes of waging a **parallel war** in the Mediterranean independently of Germany were dashed. Hereafter, Italy was to be the subordinate partner in a relationship that was to continue costing Germany manpower and matériel.

When the post-war isolation of a rigidly Stalinist Albania came to an end in the late 1980s, thousands sought to leave. They naturally turned to the closest European nation. An overnight ferry ride was all that separated them from entry into the Common Market and to the wealth of Western opportunities. Italy suddenly found herself having to deal with boatloads of illegal, undocumented Albanian immigrants seeking refuge from deprivation. Police wearing surgical gloves herded the new arrivals into soccer stadiums, loaded them on busses to be shipped to northern cities and to **Rome** where, they were told, they would be provided with work permits and helped to find housing and employment. Stunned Albanians were then put on other busses and sent to airports for flights back to Tirana. Thereafter, they were reluctant to accept at face value any further Italian official assurances.

Beginning in early March of 1997, the disintegration of the Albanian state led Italy to begin evacuating Italian and European nationals. On April 14, 1997, Italy accepted the United Nations Security Council invitation to lead a coalition of forces from France, Greece, Hungary, Rumania, and Spain to protect humanitarian-aid deliveries. By mid-August 1997, all had ended the mission in Albania and been repatriated, although 600 Italian troops were to return to conclude training of local police and military forces. *See also* Foreign Policy; Immigration.

ALBERTINI, LUIGI (1871-1941). The founder of modern Italian journalism, Luigi Albertini was a native of the province of Ancona. After working in London on the *Times*, he began his career at the *Corriere della Sera* in 1896, and within four years he had become editor. A journalistic innovator, Albertini was a staunch critic of **Giovanni Giolitti** and a warm supporter of constitutional conservatives such as **Sidney Sonnino** and **Antonio Salandra**. The *Corriere* backed Italy's entrance into World War I in 1915; as the voice of Italian patriotism, the paper became one of the best-selling dailies in Europe, with sales of over a million copies every day.

Albertini's political influence waned after the rise of **Mussolini**. The *Corriere* opposed Mussolini's **March on Rome** in the name of constitutional legality, and following the murder of the Socialist leader **Giacomo Matteotti** in June 1924 openly supported the liberals and democrats who boycotted Parliament to protest Mussolini's conduct. Mussolini, as soon as he was able, returned the favor by depriving Albertini of his editorship in 1925. Albertini, who had been made a senator in 1914, conducted a dignified policy of parliamentary opposition to the fascist regime until his death in 1941. His three-volume *Origins of the War of 1914* is widely regarded as one of the greatest of all works of diplomatic history.

ALLEANZA NAZIONALE (AN) / National Alliance. The heir to the neo-fascist **Movimento Sociale Italiano** (MSI) / Italian Social Movement, the AN has established itself as the third-largest party in Italy. The AN was created by the party secretary of the MSI, **Gianfranco Fini**, in January 1994, when he persuaded a handful of former **Democrazia Cristiana** (DC) / Christian Democracy Party conservatives, plus a respected professor of politics, Domenico Fisichella, to add a gloss of relative moderation to the MSI. Fini then allied the neo-fascists with **Silvio Berlusconi** during the March 1994 electoral campaign. The MSI-AN obtained 13.5 percent of the vote—by far the best post-war performance of the Italian far right. In **Rome**, and other parts of southern Italy, the MSI-AN's share of the vote reached 25 percent. The MSI-AN subsequently took a prominent part in Berlusconi's government, a fact that drew intense criticism from European statesmen such as Jacques Delors and François Mitterrand.

In January 1995, following the collapse of Berlusconi's administration, the MSI officially renamed itself the AN. The party also abandoned—in theory, at any rate—its attachment to the corporatist economic principles traditionally espoused by fascism, and embraced the rhetoric of free market reforms and a smaller state. Fini additionally reassessed and criticized the MSI's historical legacy, in particular its long-standing defense of **Mussolini's Salò republic**. Stung by this rethinking (but *not* rejection) of the party's fascist past, a handful of extremists, led by **Giuseppe "Pino" Rauti**, left to form an openly fascist movement.

Since January 1995, the AN has been a sometimes frustrated junior partner in Berlusconi's right-wing "Liberty Pole" coalition, although Fini himself has emerged as one of the politicians most trusted by the Italian public. The AN maintained its share of the vote in the April 1996 elections but did not, as many expected, overtake Berlusconi's **Forza Italia** to become the largest right-wing party in Italy. Fini's unarguable skills as a political communicator cannot wholly disguise the party's somewhat unsavory origins. *See also* Giorgio Almirante; Gianfranco Fini; Movimento Sociale Italiano.

ALMIRANTE, GIORGIO (1914-1988). The historic leader of the **Movimento Sociale Italiano** (MSI) / Italian Social Movement, Almirante was an unapologetic defender of the **Republic of Salò** who nevertheless managed to bring the neo-fascist movement in Italy a degree of respectability. He was born in Salsamaggiore in the province of Parma in 1914. During the final years of the war he took part in the brutal civil war waged between the partisans and Mussolini's dying regime, as an officer in one of the republic's most notorious militia units, the *Decima mas*. After the war, he was elected one of the MSI's six deputies in the **Constituent Assembly**. Almirante was elected leader of the MSI in 1947, but in the 1950s and 1960s, the MSI's relatively moderate wing, headed by **Arturo Michelini**, won control. Almirante was not prepared to compromise with the DC, or to turn the MSI into a party that worked within the political system. As much as any communist, he rejected the institutions and economic system of capitalist democracy. As late as 1968, Almirante, despite his age, led neo-fascist hooligans in a street battle at the faculty of law at the University of Rome.

Despite such adventures, Almirante was reelected leader of the MSI in June 1969 upon the death of Michelini. He followed a more realistic policy of integrating the MSI into the political system and openly accepted democratic procedures, but successfully managed to retain the party's attachment to the principles of **fascist ideology**. He showed skill at exploiting the preoccupations of the "silent majority" alarmed by the anarchistic state of the nation's factories and universities, and linked the party with the monarchists to form the so-called "National Right" coalition in the elections of 1972, winning over 8 percent of the national vote. Almirante's strategy became known as "fascism in a double breasted suit," a phrase that captured his willingness to jettison the more obvious symbols of fascism, without rejecting its substance. At the same time, however, he was unable (or unwilling) to distance the MSI from the numerous far-right subversive organizations that spread terror in Italy in the early 1970s, and consequently never managed to complete fascism's transformation to respectablity. The MSI's vote declined steadily after 1972. Almirante shrewdly picked **Gianfranco Fini** as his heir apparent shortly before his death in **Rome** in 1988. Without Almirante's strategic vision, the wholesale modernization of Italian neo-fascism put into effect by Fini since the early 1990s would have been impossible, but his legacy is an ambiguous one. Unlike Fini, Almirante never dreamed of apologizing for the brutalities and excesses of the fascist dictatorship, or the death squads of Salò.

ALPS. The northern parts of Lombardy and Piedmont, and the whole of Trentino-Alto Adige and Valle d'Aosta, are home to some of the highest mountains in Europe, and to some of the most spectacular scenery. The highest peak in the western Alps is Monte Bianco (Mont Blanc) at 4,810 meters (15,788 feet), but several other mountains top 4,000 meters (12,800 feet). In the eastern Alps, the highest point is the Ortles group (3,899 meters or 12,798 feet), which is on the border between Lombardy and the Trentino. The eastern Alps are dominated by two mountain chains of breathtaking natural beauty, the Brenta and the Dolomites. Tourists come from all over the world to see the effect of the sunset on the pinkish Dolomite rocks of Val Gardena (Alto Adige) and Val di Fassa (Trentino). The Alpine regions are also famous for their lakes, and for the many elegant and expensive resorts that dot their shores. The three largest lakes are Lake Maggiore (Lombardy), Lake Como (Lombardy), and Lake Garda (Lombardy-Trentino-Venetia), but there are literally hundreds of smaller ones.

Culturally, the Alpine regions are sharply distinct from the rest of Italy. There are three main non-Italian ethnic groups: the French dialect-speaking Aostans (100,000-strong), the German speakers from Alto Adige (over 200,000), the *Ladino* speakers in the Trentino (approximately 30,000). But even the nominally Italian parts of Lombardy, Piedmont, and Trento speak **dialects** that are extremely difficult or even impossible for other Italians to understand. It is not an exaggeration to say that practically every valley speaks its own language.

These cultural and linguistic differences from the rest of Italy have been recognized politically. Trentino-Alto Adige and the Valle d'Aosta are special autonomous regions that enjoy—together with Sicily, Sardinia, and Friuli-Venezia Giulia—greater decisional power than most of the rest of Italy's regional governments. Three political forces represent the local minorities: the Union Valdotaine, the **Süd Tirol Volkspartei** (SVP) / South Tyrol People's Party, and the **Partito Autonomista Trentino Tirolese** (PATT) / Party for the Autonomy of Trentino Tirolese. To this list should be added the **Lega Nord** (LN) / Northern League, which began its meteoric flight in the valleys of northern Lombardy.

Tourism—mostly German—is the mainstay of the Alpine region's economy. The resorts of Courmayeur, Sestriere, Madonna di Campiglio, Val Gardena, and Cortina d'Ampezzo offer some of the best skiing in the world. Wine, fruit growing, dairy farming, forestry, and wood products, and the production of winter sports equipment are also major sources of income. *See also* Dialects in Italy; Minorities; Süd Tirol Volkspartei (SVP) / South Tyrolean People's Party.

AMATO, GIULIANO (1938-). The only leading member of the **Partito Socialista Italiano** (PSI) / Italian Socialist Party to emerge unscathed from the corruption scandals of 1992-1993, Giuliano Amato is an academic lawyer by profession: indeed, he is widely regarded as one of Italy's most able constitutionalists and intellectuals. His *Duello a sinistra* (*Duel on the Left*, 1980) suggested that the PSI had to overtake and replace the **Partito Comunista Italiano** (PCI) / Italian Communist Party as the main party of opposition in Italy, and was a decisive intellectual influence on the PSI's shift to the political center ground in the early 1980s.

Elected to Parliament in 1983, Amato passed to high ministerial office during the government of **Giovanni Goria**, becoming both vice premier and minister of the treasury. He continued as treasury minister under **Ciriaco De Mita**. In June 1992, Amato was chosen to head a government that would prove to be the most troubled administration of contemporary Italian history. Within weeks of taking office, the **lira** collapsed dramatically, the parties forming his majority had become targets for the judiciary, the **mafia** had murdered a famous prosecuting attorney, and Amato had to enact the largest act of budgetary belt-tightening since World War II—nearly Lit. 90 thousand billion ($60 billion) of new taxes and spending cuts. His government, which was rocked by regular ministerial resignations as the corruption investigations crept higher and higher up the political ladder, eventually fell apart in April 1993, after the referendums on political and electoral reforms. Amato, however, was personally untouched by the scandals.

In 1995, after being mentioned as a potential president of the European Commission, Amato became the head of the Italian anti-trust authority. In the current climate of deregulation and privatization, this post is a key one, but it seems unlikely that Amato will remain in this essentially technocratic job. Many believe that a new social democratic party could coalesce around him. He is certainly one of the few senior politicians in Italy with a clean past, substantial ministerial experience, high intellect, and international reputation. *See also* Lira.

AMENDOLA, GIORGIO (1907-1980). The son of **Giovanni Amendola**, he enrolled in the **Partito Comunista Italiano** (PCI) / Italian Communist Party in his native **Naples** in 1929. Two years later, he embarked secretly for Paris to participate in the organizational work of the PCI in the French capital. On one of his secret repatriations, he was arrested and tried by the Special Tribunal (for political crimes). His sentence was reduced—after an amnesty for the tenth anniversary of the advent of the regime—to five years of *confino*. He was given two more years for having organized protests among the other prisoners. In 1937, he accepted PCI orders to return to France to take charge of party publications.

When he reentered Italy in 1943, it was to assume responsibilities as the party's leading expert on the South and as one of the directors of party clandestine activities. After September 8, 1943, he represented the PCI on the Military Council of the **Comitati di Liberazione Nazionale** (CLN) / National Liberation Committees. In that capacity, he was one of the organizers of the Via Rasella partisan bombing of a German guards' vehicle, an event that led to the Fosse Ardeatine killings. From **Rome** he went to **Milan** where he narrowly escaped arrest, then on to **Turin** where he was one of the three directors leading what had become the insurrection.

In the **Parri** government, he was undersecretary to the Council Presidency, a post he retained in the first **De Gasperi** government until July 1946. He served in the **Constituent Assembly** and on the Central Committee of the PCI as well as in the newly elected Parliament to which he was regularly reelected. In 1976, he was also chosen for membership in the European Parliament.

By the time of the Eleventh Party Congress in 1966, Amendola had moved to the relative right within the Central Committee, closer to **Giorgio Napolitano, Enrico Berlinguer,** and **Luigi Longo.** Indeed, he had concluded that the **opening to the left**—while successfully driving a wedge between the **Partito Socialista Italiano** (PSI) / Italian Socialist Party and the PCI, causing the PSI to break the Unity of Action pact with the PCI—had failed to produce anticipated reforms. Therefore, he proposed reunification with the PSI. Such a union, if victorious, would permit the pursuance of policies of full employment and increased public spending on pensions, schools, hospitals, and housing. These classical reform goals reflected, in part, Amendola's generation. *See also* Monarchy; Rome.

AMENDOLA, GIOVANNI (1882-1926). Born in **Naples** on April 15, 1882, he was to become the leader of the **Aventine Secession.** This talented liberal deputy and one-time cabinet minister suffered beatings by fascist thugs on December 26, 1923, and again in 1925 (at Montecatini) at the hands of Carlo Scorza, a fascist who was to become secretary of the **Partito Nazionale Fascista** (PNF) / National Fascist Party in 1943 (when **Mussolini** replaced those who had begun to advocate Italian withdrawal from the war). While serving in the government of **Luigi Facta** as minister for colonial affairs,

Amendola had been one of the three who persuaded the prime minister to prepare for royal signature a decree of martial law to stop the fascist **March on Rome**. Facta's repeated failure to persuade the king and the latter's refusal to sign cleared the way for the call to **Rome** of **Mussolini** to form a government. Amendola's final parliamentary address, listing the wrongs committed in **fascism**'s name, was repeatedly interrupted by Mussolini and the blackshirts. In the violence-ridden elections of 1924, Amendola founded and led L'Unione Democratica Nazionale / the National Democratic Union (the constitutional opposition) only 14 of whose candidates were elected. After the **Matteotti** slaying, many deputies (from the **Partito Comunista Italiano** (PCI) / Italian Communist Party and the **Partito Popolare Italiano** (PPI) / Italian People's Party) withdrew from Parliament and retired to the Aventine Hill. Their leader, Amendola, was convinced that King **Victor Emmanuel III** would act against Mussolini, once the fascist leader was implicated in the kidnapping and murder of a parliamentary deputy. However, far from provoking the hoped-for public reaction, this move showed itself to be completely ineffective inasmuch as it removed the participants from positions of potential leadership in opposition and left the king able to say that he was constitutionally prohibited from acting without the support of Parliament. The king clearly disliked the prospect of having socialists in government more than he did the rule of fascism to which, after all, he was closely tied by virtue of his past support.

Amendola had been an editorialist for Bologna's daily, *Il Resto del Carlino* (1912-1914), and had supported the war in **Libya** as well as intervention in **World War I**. From the *Carlino*, he went to the more prestigious *Il Corriere della Sera* of **Milan**, where he served between 1914 and 1920, opposing the Balkan expansionism of Foreign Minister **Sidney Sonnino**. In 1922, he founded—and was editor of—*Il Mondo* of **Rome**. His impassioned anti-fascist editorials, especially after the Matteotti crime, were among the most telling and probably explain fascist motives in the several beatings administered to him. He had also signed **Benedetto Croce**'s *Manifesto degli Intellettuali*.

Amendola became one of those called *fuorusciti*, the anti-fascist voluntary expatriates. Their number grew and included—in addition to Amendola—**Francesco Nitti, Carlo Sforza**, Don **Sturzo, Gaetano Salvemini, Piero Gobetti, Claudio Treves, Pietro Nenni**, and **Filippo Turati**. From the aforementioned April 5, 1925, beating,

Amendola died a year later in Cannes, France, on April 7, 1926. In 1950, his ashes were removed to his native Naples.

ANDREOTTI, GIULIO (1919-). The personification of the Italian postwar political elite, Giulio Andreotti must be regarded as both a statesman of international reputation and as a deeply ambiguous political boss who may be implicated in terrible crimes. Born in Rome, Andreotti became a force in the nascent **Democrazia Cristiana** / Christian Democracy Party while president of **Federazione Universitaria Cattolici Italiana** (FUCI) / the Catholic University Graduates' Movement of Italy, during the war. A protégé of both **Alcide De Gasperi** (whose private secretary he became) and of Giovanni Battista Montini, the future Pope Paul VI, Andreotti founded the DC's daily newspaper, *Il Popolo* (The People), and was elected to the Constituent Assembly in 1946. His first major ministerial job came in 1954, when he was appointed minister of the interior by **Amintore Fanfani**, and for the next 40 years, he was an ever-present figure in Italy's shifting cabinets, usually holding posts of great sensitivity such as defense, the interior ministry, or foreign affairs. By the late 1960s, Andreotti was the leader of the right-wing faction within the DC and the chief point of reference for both the Americans and the Vatican.

Andreotti first became prime minister in 1972, at the head of a short-lived center-right coalition with the **Partito Liberale Italiano** (PLI) / Italian Liberal party. Unlike other key figures in the Italian defense establishment, he survived a bribery scandal in the mid-1970s when the American aerospace company Lockheed was accused of paying off leading DC politicians, and in 1976 was the logical choice as prime minister when the DC and the **Partito Comunista Italiano** (PCI) / Italian Communist Party chose to form the government of national solidarity after the inconclusive elections of that year. Like his mentor, De Gasperi, Andreotti offered the United States a guarantee that the growing communist presence in Italian political life would not deflect Italy's pro-western stance in foreign affairs. The government of national solidarity lasted until 1978, by which time Andreotti had skillfully succeeded in implicating the PCI in most of his government's most unpopular decisions. The kidnapping and murder of **Aldo Moro**, in March-May 1978, caused immense public criticism of Andreotti, who was accused of doing too little to save Moro's life: wildly, it was alleged that Andreotti and his American sponsors were happy to see the back of Moro, who was the architect of the policy of greater cooperation between the DC and the PCI.

Scandal continued to dog Andreotti in the early 1980s, when he was accused of being the mastermind behind the subversive **Propaganda Due** masonic lodge, and of being the political protector of a shady financier, Michele Sindona, who died in prison in 1987 after drinking poisoned coffee. Andreotti escaped unscathed from both scandals and served as foreign minister throughout most of the 1980s. In July 1989, after an internal power struggle within the DC, Andreotti became prime minister once more, at the head of an administration in which the DC effectively shared power with the **Partito Socialista Italiano** (PSI) / Italian Socialist Party of **Bettino Craxi**. He remained as prime minister until June 1992.

The famously witty Andreotti once said, in near-defiance of the dictum that "all power corrupts, but absolute power corrupts absolutely," that "power wears out those who do not have it." Many Italians believe that Andreotti has been corrupted by his half-century hold on the highest positions of the Italian state. In the spring of 1993, Andreotti was accused of being the Sicilian **mafia**'s political godfather by several former criminals who had decided to cooperate with the authorities. One *pentito* (state's witness) even claimed that he saw Andreotti exchange a kiss of greeting with Toto Riina, the mass murderer who emerged as boss of bosses in the mafia in the early 1980s. Even more sensationally, Andreotti was accused of having ordered the homicide of a well-known Roman journalist in 1979, in order to obstruct the publication of a major investigation into his financial dealings. Andreotti, who strenuously defends his innocence, has been on trial since 1995 for both crimes. If he were to be found guilty, it would be the most startling indictment imaginable of the post-war Italian political system. *See also* Compromesso Storico; Democrazia Cristiana; Mafia; Aldo Moro; Pentapartito; Propaganda Due.

ANTONIONI, MICHELANGELO (1912-). Post-war Italy's most intellectually challenging film director, Michelangelo Antonioni was born in Ferrara. His career in the cinema began in the 1940s, when he was an editor of *Cinema*, the film magazine directed by **Mussolini**'s son Vittorio. Antonioni was soon dismissed for political reasons. During the German occupation, Antonioni joined the **Partito d'Azione** and took an active role in the resistance.

Antonioni's early films were documentaries. His first feature film was *Cronaca di un amore* (*Chronicle of an Affair*, 1950), but his first real success was the internationally acclaimed *Le amiche* (*The Girlfriends*, 1955), which won the Silver Lion award at the Venice festival. Antonioni's masterpiece, however, is probably the 1960 film, *L'Avventura* (*The Adventure*), which won the Special Jury prize at the Cannes film festival. *L'Avventura* was followed in short order by two other classics, *La Notte* (*Night,* 1961) and *L'Eclisse* (*The Eclipse*, 1962). In these films, Antonioni's almost painfully austere direction reaches its peak. Alienation has seldom been portrayed this deftly by any artist, although Antonioni is careful, in all three films, to offer a counterpoint character, played in every case by the talented actress Monica Vitti, who retains normal human feelings of warmth, spontaneity, and friendship.

In the late 1960s, Antonioni directed two major English language films. *Blow Up* (1966) was a sardonic look at the "swinging sixties"; *Zabriskie Point* (1970) was a big-budget movie that somewhat didactically condemns the materialistic emptiness of modern Californian life. Antonioni has made few films since 1970, although *The Passenger* (1975) won critical acclaim. In 1994, Hollywood recognized the work of this most uncommercial of directors with an Oscar for lifetime achievement.

ARDITI. Sometimes drawn from the ranks of long-term prisoners whose sentences were reduced for undertaking hazardous wartime duty, infantry assault units (shock troops) of *arditi d'assalto* were highly effective on the Austrian front in **World War I**. Their distinctive uniform consisted of a black fez on which appeared a skull and crossbones carrying a dagger between its teeth, and a black shirt bearing the slogan "*Me ne frego!*" (I don't give a damn!), presumably after a wounded member who wrote this imprecation on his bandages. These commandos were used to infiltrate enemy lines at night and, using hand grenades and the silent dagger, wrought havoc with Austrian morale. They prided themselves on their contempt for human life, including their own.

The mythology inspired by their very irregularity appealed first to **Gabriele D'Annunzio**, then to fascists; both adopted not only the black shirt and the rest of the uniform that so many ex-*arditi* wore on punitive expeditions but much of their spirit as well: the dagger, the cudgel, and the song, "*Giovinezza*." *See also* Fascism.

AVENTINE SECESSION. Fascism might have been aborted but for the

Aventine secessionists whose boycott of **Parliament** left **Mussolini** with a solid majority of the **Partito Nazionale Fascista** (PNF) / National Fascist Party in the Parliament chosen in the violence-ridden 1924 general elections. The attempt by parliamentarians was probably the only one made to impede Mussolini's assumption of total power, but the Aventinians' preoccupation with constitutional and legal niceties proved no match for fascist **squadrismo**. When **Matteotti** gave his critical speech challenging the legality of seating fascist deputies, he was kidnapped, thus giving rise to accusations against the fascist leadership—the better to make the point that the Parliament in which the fascists were the dominant party was in league with murderers. The opposition almost to a man retired—the date was June 12, 1924—"to the Aventine," one of the seven hills of **Rome** to which members of the plebeian party had withdrawn (123 B.C.) in their struggle with the Roman aristocratic party. Mussolini's response was to expel them from Parliament in 1926. The Aventinians from the **Partito Comunista Italiano** (PCI) / Italian Communist Party returned to the Parliament in November 1924. In January 1926, the *Popolari* of the **Partito Popolare Italiano** (PPI) / Italian People's Party, on instructions from their party congress, also returned. But Mussolini insisted that they acknowledge that the fascist revolution was an accomplished fact. The Aventinians refused, and the Chamber, with a clear fascist majority, voted to expel all 123 Aventine deputies. This left a handful of liberals who had not joined the Aventine Secession in an otherwise totally fascist Chamber of Deputies. For the next several years, this Parliament passed laws that formalized the dictatorship of the Fascist Party and the state.

AXIS, ROME-BERLIN. *See* Foreign Policy.

AZIONE CATTOLICA ITALIANA (ACI) / Catholic Action. Founded in January 1908 to coordinate the new social organizations that had been established after the publication of the papal encyclical *Il fermo proposito* in 1905, Catholic Action is the evangelical arm of the Vatican in Italian society. Its major development came in the 1920s, during the pontificate of Pius XI. Anxious to avoid a clash with **Mussolini**, Pius abandoned the **Partito Popolare Italiano** (PPI) / Popular Party to its fate and relied almost entirely on the ACI to promote Christian values. It did so via four main institutions—the Federation of Italian Catholic Men, The Society of Catholic Youth, The Catholic University Federation, and the Catholic Women's

Union of Italy. For the most part, these organizations cooperated with the fascist state's initiatives, but the youth organizations, the Boy Scouts in particular, clashed with the totalitarian objectives of the state.

One of Pius's principal goals during the negotiations that led to the signing of the **Lateran pacts** in 1929 was the preservation of the Church's right to indoctrinate young people. Although Pius succeeded in this goal, the proliferation of ACI activities, in particular the publication of specialist publications for the family and women, and the use of church halls for meetings, film shows, and cultural activities, inevitably brought the ACI into conflict with the authorities. In June 1931, all Catholic youth associations were forbidden by law. Pius responded with the encyclical *Non abbiamo bisogno*, which criticized certain aspects of fascist ideology as being incompatible with Christianity. Despite this stand on principle, both Pius XI and his successor, Pius XII, were subsequently obliged to tighten ecclesiastical control over the movement.

With the return to democracy, there was a huge proliferation of specialist Catholic associations (for doctors, university and school teachers, jurists, chemists, even artists), and an impressive increase in the ACI's membership from the already imposing figure of 2.5 million in 1943 to over 3.3 million by 1959. In these years, the ACI—particularly under the leadership, 1952-1959, of Luigi Gedda—became one of the church's weapons in the ideological battle waged by Pius XII against the **Partito Comunista Italiano** (PCI) / Italian Communist Party. When Pope John XXIII ascended to the Holy See in 1958, the ACI's semi-political role became less accentuated. The theological innovations of the second Vatican Council (1962-1965) emphasized the essentially religious function of church-sponsored organizations. This reduction in what may reasonably be termed its propaganda role, and the increasing secularization of society, caused ACI membership to fall sharply in the 1970s and 1980s, but Catholic associations still penetrate into every sphere of Italian life and have a formative effect on the lives of many—perhaps most—Italians even today. *See also* Catholicism; Papacy.

-B-

BADOGLIO, PIETRO (1871-1956). Despite a lengthy military career, Pietro Badoglio is chiefly remembered today for negotiating Italy's surrender in September 1943. Badoglio's early battle honors were earned during Italy's colonial wars. During **World War I**, he was quickly promoted to the rank of general. He commanded an army corps at the battle of Caporetto, but even though the Austrian breakthrough occurred in his sector, he escaped blame, emerging as second in command to General Armando Diaz. After the war, he was appointed to the Senate in 1919, and served as ambassador to Brazil between 1923 and 1925 before becoming chief of the General Staff. Between 1929 and 1934, he was governor of Italy's colonies in **Libya**, where he suppressed the local nationalist movement with some brutality. The same willingness to use massive force was seen during the war in **Abyssinia** in 1935-1936. Badoglio, in command of the invading Italian forces, used poison gas and indiscriminate bombing to smash the underequipped troops of Emperor Haile Selassie. Badoglio's reward was to be made duke of Addis Ababa and viceroy of the new colony. In 1940, Badoglio was reappointed chief of the General Staff and also chaired the committee responsible for organizing Italy's efforts to achieve autarky. Badoglio, who was a reactionary and a monarchist rather than a convinced fascist, resigned when the Italian expeditionary force was humiliatingly defeated in Greece in 1941.

On July 25, 1943, King **Victor Emmanuel III** turned to Badoglio to replace **Mussolini** after the fascist leader's destitution of power by the Fascist Grand Council. In a radio address, Badoglio warned that Italy would remain in the war and that he would repress any attempts to disturb public order. In the next five days, troops fired upon anti-war protesters throughout Italy, killing and wounding several hundred people. On July 27, all political parties were outlawed and the Fascist Grand Council, Special Tribunal, and the Chamber of *Fasci* and Corporations were all eliminated, while the fascist militia was incorporated into the army. Italy's drastically worsening military and economic situation, however, constrained Badoglio to surrender to the Allies on September 3, 1943. News of the surrender was officially communicated on September 8, and the following day Badoglio, the king, and selected courtiers fled from **Rome** for the safety of Brindisi, already occupied by the Allies. There, they established a governmental seat.

Badoglio's first government endured until April 1944. It declared war on Germany in October 1943, but was unable to persuade even moderate opponents of **fascism** to join its ranks while it continued to be so closely associated with the king. When this problem was resolved by the appointment of Prince Umberto as "Lieutenant of the Realm," Badoglio was able to form a second cabinet that included liberals such as **Benedetto Croce** and **Count Carlo Sforza,** and the **Partito Comunista Italiano** (PCI) / Italian Communist Party leaders **Palmiro Togliatti** and Fausto Gullo. The administration, however, lasted little more than a month. Following the liberation of Rome, it was replaced on June 18, 1944, by a government led by **Ivanoe Bonomi** that was more representative of Italian democratic opinion. Badoglio retired into private life and spent the next ten years writing his memoirs and defending his military and political reputation. He died in his native Grazzano Monferrato (Piedmont) in 1956. *See also* Abyssinia; Fascism; Salò, Republic of.

BALBO, CESARE (1789-1853). One of the most prominent Piedmontese liberals, Balbo published in 1844 a hard-headed essay entitled *Delle speranze d'Italia* (*The Hopes of Italy*), which laid down a pragmatic policy for national unification that had immense influence on the political elite of Piedmont-Sardinia. Briefly, Balbo argued that all plans for the future of Italy were subordinate to ridding Italy of Austria, and that this desirable goal could only be achieved by the army of the Kingdom of Piedmont-Sardinia, not by popular insurrection. No democrat, Balbo's vision for Italy was a federation of constitutional monarchies guided by Piedmont. In 1847, together with **Camillo Bensi di Cavour,** Balbo founded the influential moderate newspaper, *Risorgimento.*

In March 1848, Balbo, who had played a prominent role in drawing up the so-called **Statuto Albertino,** became the first constitutional prime minister of Piedmont-Sardinia, an appointment that was confirmed by the first-ever free elections in Italy on April 27, 1848. His tenure as premier was brief. Following Piedmont's defeat at Custoza in July 1848, Balbo's government resigned. He died in his native Turin in 1853. *See also* Carlo Cattaneo.

BALBO, ITALO (1896-1940). Born in Quartesana, Ferrara (Emilia-Romagna), to a family of schoolteachers, he was—by the age of 14—one of the irredentists who volunteered to conquer the Albanian coast in order to make the Adriatic an Italian lake. At 17, he led a group of bicyclists on the road from Ferrara in the thick of the 1914 events of "red week" clad in his Garibaldine red shirt and ready to proclaim a socialist republic in Emilia-Romagna. His subsequent service in **World War I** (he became a lieutenant of Alpini), his nationalism, spirit of adventure, and natural combativeness equipped him well for his post-war activities as an organizer and leader of the action squads of the Po Valley. He found a natural home in the nascent fascism movement. Not only did he take the title *Ras* (an Ethiopian word for feudal leader), but his organizing talents led to the subordination of the entire Po Valley to the will of the action squads. His success led him to organize the *milizia*. He found time for a degree in public administration at Florence's Cesare Alfieri Institute. Prior to the **March on Rome**, some regarded him as a potential rival to **Mussolini** to head the **Partito Nazionale Fascista** (PNF) / National Fascist Party. He was put in charge of the militia after Mussolini came to power but had to resign after the murder of **Giacomo Matteotti** when it became known that he had authorized the militia to resume its violent ways. In 1926, he headed a movement to depose the king in favor of a fascist republic but was thwarted by **General Badoglio**. As minister of aviation between 1929 and 1933, he personally led a 24 Italian seaplane-group (he was an enthusiastic pilot) called, grandiloquently, an "armada" on trans-Atlantic formation flights to Chicago and to Brazil in 1933. Today's fascists enjoy pointing out that Balbo Boulevard is in Chicago, not in **Rome**. Mussolini was so irritated by Balbo's popularity that he made him Governor of Libya in order to remove him from the seat of power in Rome and from any temptation to challenge the Duce himself. By 1939, four Libyan provinces had been integrated with Italy as departments. Despite his vociferous dissent from the alliance with Germany, he was put in command of Italian forces in North Africa in 1940, when he was accidentally shot down by Italian anti-aircraft fire over Tobruk. He was probably the only fascist hierarch who was unintimidated by Mussolini. *See also* Quadrumvirate; Squadrismo.

BALKAN WARS. Italy's experiments in colonial expansion might be said to have begun with the temptation offered by Turkey's status as the "sick man of Europe." At the turn of the nineteenth century, classical diplomacy was still producing secret accords among the European chanceries as alliances were made and immediately counter-balanced by offsetting arrangements. The 1908 Austrian annexation of Bosnia and Herzegovina led to immediate talk of war in the Balkans involving Greece, Serbia, Montenegro, and Turkey at the head of an anti-Austrian coalition. Finally resolved diplomatically, the Austro-Turkish question carried in its wake the initial disintegration of Turkey and, as a consequence, Bulgaria's independence.

Beginning in 1887, Italy had made arrangements with Germany, Austria, England, France, and Russia securing the approval of each for eventual Italian initiatives in Tripoli (**Libya**), which was under Turkish suzerainty. When France and Germany resolved their differences over the German challenge to French primacy in Morocco, the Italian government insisted on a counter for French gains. In 1911, Italy landed troops and, within a month, proclaimed the annexation of Libya despite determined opposition by Turkey's Enver Bey.

In April and May 1912, Italian ships entered the Dardanelles and shelled, then occupied, the island of Rhodes in the Dodecanese. By the fall, Serbia, Bulgaria, and Greece had declared war on Turkey just as she was signing the Treaty of Lausanne with Italy. Under its terms, Italy was to end her occupation of the Dodecanese Islands in exchange for the Turks leaving Tripoli in Libya (although they were to retain religious primacy by appointing a *caliph*).

Early Bulgarian victories over Turkey might have widened the conflict. Similarly, Serbian occupation of parts of Albania challenged the fragile Balkan balance on which Austria, Germany, Russia, France, and Britain all relied. Faced with the prospect of having Serbia on the Adriatic, Italy drew closer to Austria in an anti-Serb policy that led to the final renewal of the **Triple Alliance** in July 1914.

BANCA ROMANA. The largest financial and political scandal of liberal Italy occurred in 1893-1894 as a consequence of the failure of the Banca Romana, which was one of six banks authorized to issue currency notes. A secret auditors' report in 1889 accused the bank of numerous breaches of the law and found the bank to be technically insolvent. The government, anxious not to cause panic in the market, did not act on the report. In December 1892, however, it was leaked to an opposition member of Parliament. The then prime minister, **Giovanni Giolitti**, was forced to form an impartial committee of inquiry that confirmed the calamitous state of the bank's books. The scandal widened in 1893 when it became clear that many politicians and newspapers had been bribed by the bank for silence and support. Giolitti introduced a banking reform law in August 1893 that reduced the number of banks authorized to print notes to just three and that intensified state controls over the emission of money. This action did not prevent a run on the banks at the end of the year and did not save Giolitti from being the most illustrious political victim of the scandal. In November 1893, a parliamentary inquiry found Giolitti guilty of negligence. The inquiry could find no proof that Giolitti had been bribed, but this suspicion obviously hung over the prime minister. Giolitti was forced to resign.

In 1894, the scandal spread further when documents provided by Giolitti proved that his political rival, **Francesco Crispi**, together with members of his family, had been beneficiaries of substantial undisclosed "loans" from the Banca Romana. When this fact was revealed by a five-man parliamentary committee of inquiry on December 15, 1894, Crispi responded by suspending a parliamentary sitting that intended to debate his involvement in the scandal. Fearing arrest, Giolitti left Italy for Berlin where he remained until February 1895. Crispi, meanwhile, kept Parliament closed until May 1895, when he called, and won, fresh national elections thanks to a large vote in his favor in **southern Italy**. In December 1895, Giolitti was finally absolved of any wrongdoing by the Chamber of Deputies. Crispi's large parliamentary majority, and growing public boredom, enabled the prime minister to cut his losses by burying the whole affair.

BANFI, ANTONIO (1886-1957). Less well known outside Italy than **Benedetto Croce** or **Antonio Gramsci**, Banfi has been one of the most influential thinkers of this century within the Italian academy. A philosopher of science who increasingly turned his attention to social theory, his thought departs from the central discovery of "modern" (i.e., post-Galileo) astronomy: that humanity is not the center of the universe or the reason for its existence. In his most famous book, *L'uomo copernicano* (*Copernican Man*, 1950), Banfi argues that this fact compels mankind to resolve the human dilemma by using our faculty of "critical reason" (instead of blind faith in man's metaphysical destiny) to create a free and progressive regime on earth. After 1945, Banfi increasingly identified "critical reason" with Marxism, which he seemingly regarded as a master science that superseded all other forms of social explanation. His essays on Marxism were published posthumously in 1960. Banfi was also the author of a number of works on the life and thought of Galileo Galilei and many works on pedagogy. Between 1940 and 1949, he edited the groundbreaking academic review *Studi filosofici*

(Philosophical Studies). In 1957, he died in his native **Milan** where he had taught throughout his career. His many students and followers have ensured that his ideas retain a central role in Italian intellectual life.

BANKING. An Italian institution that is both totally independent and widely respected in Italy and abroad is the Bank of Italy. The governor of the bank is a life appointee and is thus free from political pressures and has responsibilities analogous to those of the chairman of the Federal Reserve Board in the United States. Since **World War II,** more than 50 Italian governments have come and gone but there have been only six governors of the bank.

Relations between Italian banking and industry (especially **FIAT** and Ansaldo shipyards) have widened considerably in this century because of the Turco-Italian War over **Libya, World War I, World War II,** and the antecedent railway construction following unification.

Reduced activity on the Italian stock market meant that in 1931, it did not collapse but rather declined slowly. Italian lending banks, foreseeing serious losses, bought up shares in the hope that their action could sustain prices. Soon, banks held over one-third of Italy's large and medium firms. As these companies were unable to repay indebtedness, the banks—especially Banca Commerciale and Credito Italiano (still two of the three largest Italian banks)—sought government help, given in the form of the Istituto Mobiliare Italiano. It was created to lend money to the ailing companies. But worsening conditions led to the creation of the **Istituto per la Ricostruzione Industriale** (IRI). It was to have bought the banks' commercial holdings to liquidate them. In some cases, it not only acquired those companies but control of the banks themselves. Within a few years, IRI had evolved into a mammoth holding company under public control and able to reorganize industries in key sectors under the aegis of fascist **corporatism.** It was only in the 1980s that IRI, under **Romano Prodi**'s direction, began to divest itself of some of its less-profitable holdings, conspicuously the Alfa Romeo automobile company.

The Bank of Italy, once headed by **Luigi Einaudi**, helped bring monetary stability to Italy after World War II and aided in creating capital for investment by offering favorable lending rates. When, in 1962, the electrical industry was nationalized, it was the then governor of the Bank of Italy, **Guido Carli**, who won the struggle to keep the former electrical trusts as finance companies in order that their accumulated business acumen would ensure the wise investment of the compensatory payments. The opposite tack was taken by those who wanted the trusts abolished as symbols of the old way and as major opponents of the **opening to the left** and its program. Carli carried the day.

In the next year, Carli was able to forge, together with **Emilio Colombo**, a deflationary policy that curbed internal demand in order to deal with the balance of payments deficit and reduce inflation. The ensuing increase in business failures and unemployment made it necessary for the **Democrazia Cristiana** (DC) / Christian Democracy Party to postpone reforms. It also reduced labor's and the unions' bargaining power.

The banking system remains heavily regulated and is not well prepared for the integration envisaged for the **European Union.** Until recently, Italian banks were not free to lend for periods longer than 18 months. Credit controls are abundant and the number of bank branches, while increasing, is still significantly lower per 10,000 people than is true in Britain, France, or Germany. The effect has been to stifle competition and reward inefficiency. Especially because the administration of state-owned banks is headed by political appointees under the Italian spoils system called *lottizzazione* (**patronage**), the function of the bank seems as much that of protecting the jobs of appointees as making a profit. The number of employees per bank branch is double the European average, and each operation must be approved, checked, and signed by at least one supervisor. Cash is far more in use than non-cash payments (credit cards or checking accounts). The use of credit cards, for example, is at one-tenth the British or U.S. level.

A full 80 percent of Italian banks are state controlled, including the Banca Commerciale Italiana, Banca Nazionale del Lavoro, and the Banco di Roma. In preparation for the elimination of restrictions preventing foreign banks from competing on the Italian market, Italian banks in many cities have simply set out to acquire title to all urban spaces likely to be considered by foreign bankers as a site for a branch. The consequences are several: a further boost to already exorbitant real estate prices; the foreclosing of any available space for foreign occupancy; and the opening of many new branches of Italian banks.

BASSANI, GIORGIO (1916-). Along with **Primo Levi**, Giorgio

Bassani is probably the finest post-war writer produced by Italy's small (35,000) Jewish community. Born in **Bologna** in 1916, Bassani was raised in the Po Valley city of Ferrara, which provides the backdrop for his most important works. He was an active member of the resistance during the war and was jailed for his anti-fascist activities. He has written many books, but the most widely remembered are *Cinque storie ferraresi* (*Tales of Ferrara*, 1956), and *Il giardino dei Finzi-Contini* (*The Garden of the Finzi-Continis*, 1964), the poignant tale of a Jewish Italian family that was transformed into an Oscar-winning film by **Vittorio De Sica**. Together with **Di Lampedusa's** *Il Gattopardo* (*The Leopard*, 1959), which Bassani himself was instrumental in getting published, *Il giardino dei Finzi-Contini* broke the neo-realist monopoly in Italian arts and letters, and signaled a greater interest among Italian writers in introspection, fine writing, and traditional settings.

BASSO, LELIO (1903-1978). An uncompromising socialist, Lelio Basso was both one of the historic leaders of the **Partito Socialista Italiano** (PSI) / Italian Socialist Party and a stern critic of its policies in the 1960s. Born in the province of Savona (Liguria), Basso joined the PSI while a student and wrote for or edited several of the principal literary and ideological journals of the Italian left, including **Piero Gobetti's** famous *Rivoluzione liberale (Liberal Revolution)*. In 1928, he was arrested and confined on the isle of Ponza (Campania) for three years. Upon release, he was kept under strict surveillance—in March 1940 he served six months' intern- ment in a camp near Perugia.

In January 1943, Basso, who had always been one of the most outspoken voices of the PSI's "maximalist" wing, instituted a new party, the Movimento d'Unità Proletaria (MUP) / Proletarian Unity Movement. In August of the same year, the MUP merged with the by now almost moribund PSI, and the new party became the Partito Socialista Italiano d'Unità Proletaria (PSIUP) / Italian Socialist Party of Proletarian Unity. The party program contained many echoes of Basso's belief that the Italian socialist movement should struggle for a socialist revolution, not parliamentary democracy. He was soon criticizing the timidity of the party leadership, and between November 1943 and May 1944 he gave up his membership.

After returning to the fold, Basso became the PSIUP's chief organizer in northern Italy, successfully nurturing the party's clandestine networks in the factories of Lombardy and Piedmont. In

April 1945, he was one of the leaders of the Milanese insurrection against the Germans. His courageous clandestine work was rewarded in July 1945 when he became the vice secretary of the party. Basso was elected to the **Constituent Assembly** in June 1946 and was the author of several of the constitution's most important clauses. In the meantime, in January 1947 he had become party leader at the stormy **Rome** congress of the PSIUP, which saw the party's moderates, led by **Giuseppe Saragat**, leave the party. During Basso's tenure as leader, the newly renamed PSI identified itself closely with the **Partito Comunista Italiano** (PCI) / Italian Communist Party, even to the extent of condoning the February 1948 coup in Czechoslovakia, but the strategy proved electorally calamitous. Basso was replaced as party leader in July 1948 after the triumph at the polls of the **Democrazia Cristiana** (DC) / Christian Democracy Party.

Basso never yielded in his revolutionary beliefs. He opposed any arrangement with the DC, and in 1963, when **Aldo Moro** formed the first DC-PSI administration, Basso was one of 24 PSI deputies who broke ranks to found a new Marxist party that defiantly took the name of the PSIUP. In the late 1960s, Basso participated in the Russell War Crimes Tribunal on alleged American atrocities in Vietnam. He died in Rome in 1978. *See also* Partito Socialista Italiano.

BATTISTI, CESARE (1875-1916). Martyr, socialist, and soldier, Cesare Battisti was born in Trento (then still part of Austria) in 1875. He studied at universities in both Austria and Italy, where he came into contact with the liberal socialist ideas of **Gaetano Salvemini.** In 1895, Battisti founded *La Rivista popolare trentina* (*The Trento Popular Review*) to propagate socialist doctrines and the right of self-determination for Austria's Italian-speaking minority. In 1904, his activities earned him a prison term in Innsbruck jail. During **World War I**, Battisti abandoned his lifelong pacifism. The war seemed to him to be a golden opportunity both to liberate the Trentino and to bring about the collapse of the Austro-Hungarian empire, which he believed would be a prelude to the creation of a European federation of democratic socialist states. Battisti enrolled in the Italian army and served bravely as a junior officer. He was captured by the Austrians in July 1916, tried as a traitor, and hanged at Trento. **Filippo Turati** eulogized him as "a socialist in principle and in action" in a speech to the Chamber of Deputies in December 1916. In Trento, his memory is revered—several of the city's streets and squares are named after him and a monument consecrated to his name overlooks the city from a mountaintop.

BECCARIA, CESARE (1738-1794). Born in **Milan**, he studied jurisprudence at Pavia until 1758 and was drawn into an illuminist circle whose members published, between 1764 and 1766, the journal *Caffè*. In this setting, the young jurist wrote *Dei delitti e delle pene (Of Crimes and Punishment*, 1764). By arguing that prevention is more useful than repression or punishment, he launched the movement to make for individualized punishments in criminal law and to let the punishment fit the crime. For the first time, the possibility was considered that wrongdoers might be rehabilitated with humane treatment. After translation into virtually every European language (the French edition bore a commentary by Voltaire), these ideas spread to the entire Western world and—with the eventual adoption of the civil law in Africa, Asia, South America, and the Middle East—to the rest of the world as well. Frederick the Great of Prussia, Empress Catherine of Russia, and Pietro Leopoldo of Tuscany vied to incorporate Beccaria's ideas into programs of judicial reform. Speedy trials, elimination of torture and of the death penalty, equality of treatment and of punishment regardless of social class (the motto still appears in all Italian courts, *La Legge è Uguale per Tutti* / The Law is Equal for All) trace their origins to Beccaria. His book is probably the single most influential work on Western criminal (penal) procedure. The principles that only legislators (not judges) can make laws and that punishment can flow only from *illegal* acts (*nullum crimen sine lege*; *nullum poena sine lege*), or there is no crime in the absence of law, there can be no punishment in the absence of law—these dicta also stem from Beccaria. Having rejected offers of a post in St. Petersburg, he accepted a teaching appointment from the Austrian government. It took him to Brera in December 1768 where his course on David Hume became the basis for his *Elementi di economia pubblica* (*Elements of Political Economy*).

So impressed was the Hapsburg government that he was offered, and accepted, nomination to Austria's Supreme Economic Council (1771), simultaneously beginning his life as a bureaucrat and ending his extraordinary creativity. His daughter, Giulia (born in 1762), of his union with his first wife (who died in 1774) was to become the mother of **Alessandro Manzoni.**

BERIO, LUCIANO (1925-). One of the world's most important contemporary composers, Luciano Berio was born in the province of Imperia (Liguria). His father was an accomplished musician, and Berio's early training was at home. He completed his studies at **Milan** conservatory, where he graduated in composition and orchestral conducting in 1950, and in the United States. In the late 1950s, Berio emerged at the forefront of efforts to modernize the classical canon by integrating electronic sounds into his orchestral pieces. He edited an academic journal of avant-garde music, *Incontri musicali* (*Musical Encounters*), and collaborated with the noted writer **Italo Calvino** (*Allez-Hop*, 1959). In the 1960s and 1970s, Berio taught composition in some of the most prestigious conservatories in the world, including the Juilliard School in New York, as well as Harvard and Columbia Universities. He also met the soloist Cathy Berberian, who became the "voice" for some of his most complex and challenging works. In addition to electronic music, Berio is noted for having infused the classical form with themes from Japanese and Indian music, and for his interest in folk music and rock. His most famous works are probably *Folk Songs* (first version, 1964; second version, 1973) and *Coro* (*Choir*, 1976); more recent works include *Ofanim* (1988) and *Rendering* (1990).

BERLINGUER, ENRICO (1922-1984). Born in Sardinia, he joined the **Partito Comunista Italiano** (PCI) / Italian Communist Party at 21 and became active in the local youth section and in anti-fascist activity. At the end of 1944, he was called to **Rome** to serve on the national secretariat of the party's youth movement. He worked constantly within the party in various capacities. He was elected a deputy in 1968, was elected vice secretary to serve with **Luigi Longo** in the next year and, in 1972, became general secretary of the party, a position that he held for 12 years until his death. His rise was rapid.

Even his one-time adversaries admit that his rise was merited. Applying to party policy the strictures of both **Gramsci** and **Togliatti**, he advanced "polycentrism" and the notion of each country finding its own road to socialism. This doctrine came to be called **Eurocommunism**, and was wholly consonant with the **compromesso storico** (historic compromise), perhaps the most important single initiative in Italy since World War II. After the Khrushchev report (criticizing Stalin and Stalinism) at the XX Congress of the Soviet Communist Party and the Hungarian uprising of 1956, the PCI seemed destined to continue losing adherents. Nonetheless, party leaders such as Luigi Longo and, in his turn Berlinguer, displayed "a combative spirit and initiative" in criticizing the Soviet Union for its actions in Czechoslovakia, in promising to retain Italy's membership in the **North Atlantic Treaty Organization** (NATO), and in backing away from ideological dependence on the USSR. These perceived changes contributed to the electoral success of 1976 when the PCI came within a few percentage points of overtaking the **Democrazia Cristiana** (DC) / Christian Democracy Party. The fate of the **Partito Socialista Italiano** (PSI) / Italian Socialist Party in leading a reform movement within the **opening to the left** was, of course, well known to Berlinguer. Yet he saw the position of the PCI in 1976 as quite different from the PSI in 1963: the left was stronger in every way and a cautious alliance with the DC could be expected to lead to genuine structural change in Italian society and state. Together with Luciano Lama, then head of the Confederazione Generale Italiana del Lavoro (CGIL) / General Italian Labor Confederation, Berlinguer bent his efforts to persuading Italian workers to salvage capitalism by accepting a policy of relative austerity and wage restraint in exchange for greater investment in the south and among youth. The modesty of the results highlight Berlinguer's difficulties and seem to validate **Pietro Ingrao**'s warning that the PCI risked having to choose between confrontations with the state (which they could only lose) and being co-opted by the system (which would mean the end of the PCI as a revolutionary force).

The experiment of national solidarity between **Giulio Andreotti** and Berlinguer, despite its parallel with De Gasperi-Togliatti, failed to produce the reforms sought by the left. Berlinguer's burning of the bridges to the USSR antagonized the Soviet leadership and alienated many rank-and-file communists without alleviating the misgivings of Italy's middle class who were fearful lest the PCI's regularization on the national level might lead to higher taxes and property losses or worse. (**Silvio Berlusconi** was to allege that communists in government would mean either "exile or the gallows.")

Even before the XXV Soviet Party Congress, French and Spanish communist leaders had articulated in print and in speeches views concerning Eurocommunism that effectively mirrored Berlinguer's opinions. At international meetings in East Berlin, Warsaw, Belgrade, and Moscow, Eurocommunists talked of separate roads to socialism despite the efforts of Soviet translators to soften the impact. Berlinguer and others threatened to leave the conference altogether if further modifications were made to their addresses. In

1981, Poland's General Jaruzelski had suppressed Solidarnosč, claiming that he acted to preclude a Soviet invasion. These events provoked from Berlinguer the judgment that the "propulsive force" of Soviet direction had run its course. On his death in June 1984, even the Pope eulogized Berlinguer as an honorable man convinced of the rightness of his principles. *See also* Compromesso Storico; Partito Comunista Italiana; Trade Unions.

BERLUSCONI, SILVIO (1936-). A Milanese businessman who created Italy's first nationwide private television (TV) network, Silvio Berlusconi has led **Forza Italia** since its genesis in 1993.

Berlusconi made his first fortune in real estate dealings in the late 1960s and early 1970s. In 1977, he acquired his first media holding, a share in **Indro Montanelli**'s anti-communist newspaper, *Il Giornale Nuovo*, and at the end of the 1970s launched his first private TV company. By 1980, his flagship company, Canale 5, went on the air—it was the first private TV network to have a national audience. In the subsequent years, Berlusconi added two more private TV companies, Italia 1 and Rete 4, to his empire. This growing presence in the media sector was judged to be illegal by the courts in 1984; briefly, Berlusconi's TV channels were taken off the air. His close personal and political links with the then prime minister, **Bettino Craxi**, proved their worth, however. The Craxi government passed a decree law in October 1984, swiftly baptized the "Berlusconi Law," which retroactively legalized Berlusconi's activities.

In the mid- and late 1980s, Berlusconi added the **Milan** soccer team and the giant Mondadori publishing corporation to his holdings. He also established a near-monopoly over the production and sale of TV advertising, and started (less successful) TV companies in France and Spain. By 1990, he was the owner of one of the largest private companies in the world. In August 1990, the passage of a toothless law regulating media ownership appeared to have consolidated his dominance of the Italian private media for good. Berlusconi was forced to sell his stake in *Il Giornale* to his brother Paolo, but the right of a private entrepreneur to own three national television networks was protected by the new law.

The collapse of the Italian political system and Craxi's disgrace represented a threat to Berlusconi. He could be sure that a leftist government would attempt to break his monopoly on the media market. This appears to be one of the main reasons why, in December 1993, with a marketing blitz that recalled the launch of a new soap powder rather than a political party, Berlusconi founded Forza Italia and nominated himself as a potential prime minister. Skillfully allying himself with the **Lega Nord** (LN) / Northern League in northern Italy, and with the **Alleanza Nazionale** (AN) / National Alliance in the South, Berlusconi's right-wing coalition, the *Polo della libertà*, won an astonishing victory in elections to the Chamber of Deputies in March 1994. In terms of votes (though not parliamentary seats), Forza Italia became Italy's largest political party.

Berlusconi became prime minister in May 1994. His government was troubled by judicial inquiries into his business affairs, by the unruly behavior of the league's Senator **Umberto Bossi**, and Berlusconi's own reluctance to commit himself to a career as a politician. In November 1994, the judges of the Mani pulite or "Clean Hands" investigation in Milan declared Berlusconi to be under investigation on charges of corruption and irregularities in accounting. In December, the league joined with the opposition in voting no confidence and brought Berlusconi's administration down. Since then, Berlusconi has remained at the head of the right-wing coalition. The demagogic and at times threatening rhetoric he employed during the technocratic government of **Lamberto Dini** alarmed both the financial markets and many moderate voters, and has unquestionably tarnished his public image. *See also* Forza Italia; Mani Pulite; Radio Autodiffusione Italiana (RAI).

BERSAGLIERI. Organized in 1846 by General **Alfonso La Marmora Ferrero** as part of the army of the Kingdom of Piedmont-Sardinia, these assault infantry were praised by Anglo-French general officers for their performance in the Crimean War, contributing, in **Cavour**'s words, "much from the point of view of military prestige. This is something," he added, "which will be very useful to us."

Several particulars mark the Bersaglieri: their means of locomotion and their uniform. Light infantry, their march-step is a trot enabling them to cover great distances in short order and requiring that all be in excellent physical condition. Even their (brass) instruments play at a trot. In both twentieth-century general wars, they were issued sturdy, collapsible—hence, portable —bicycles that further enhanced their mobility. Second, their uniforms set them apart from the rest of the Italian army, an important factor in the morale of any armed force. La Marmora's original uniform was black with a high collar: that has given way to the standard-issue brown of other Italian troops. However, there remains of the original uniform the headgear: a flat-brimmed patent leather hat kept cocked at a jaunty angle over the right ear by a thick leather chin strap. To the low, round crown is affixed a cluster of shiny black and green feathers cascading over the right shoulder. In both **World War I** and **World War II**, as well as in United Nations missions in Lebanon, Somalia, Bosnia, and **Albania**, a smaller cluster of feathers adorned the steel helmets of these troops. Their non-dress uniform substitutes for the patent leather hat a soft red fez bearing a blue woolen tassel, which hangs midway down the back since the fez is worn on the back of the wearer's head.

BERTOLUCCI, BERNARDO (1940-). The son of a literary critic and poet, Bertolucci's own first book of poems won the prestigious Viareggio prize in 1962. In the same year, he directed his first feature film. Two years later, his first critically acclaimed movie, *Prima della rivoluzione* (*Before the Revolution*, 1964), which tells the story of a young aristocrat who flirts with revolutionary politics before settling down into a conventional marriage, won the Prix Max Ophuls at Cannes.

In 1968, Bertolucci joined the **Partito Comunista Italiano** (PCI) / Italian Communist Party, which was the prelude to an extraordinary burst of creativity at the beginning of the 1970s. *La strategia del ragno* (*The Spider's Stratagem*, 1970) and *Il conformista* (*The Conformist*, 1971) won Bertolucci international acclaim. The latter film, which describes a tormented young fascist intellectual coming to terms with his homosexuality, was a spectacular critical success. The film received an Oscar nomination and won the National Film Critics' award.

In 1972, Bertolucci's fame turned to notoriety after the production of *L'ultimo tango a Parigi* (*The Last Tango in Paris*, 1972). Its graphic sex scenes caused the film to be banned in Italy, and Bertolucci was deprived of his vote for five years. Critical opinion on the film's merits continues to be divided, with some regarding the film as a watershed for the cinematic art, others as embarrassingly overblown and pretentious. Bertolucci's real masterpiece is arguably the 1976 five-hour epic, *1900*, which was shot in his native Po River valley with an international cast that included Burt Lancaster, Robert De Niro, Gerard Depardieu, and

Donald Sutherland. A violent, squalid, heroic panorama of Italian life and politics from 1900 to 1945, the film contains some of the most moving—and most disturbing—images ever portrayed on film. In recent years Bertolucci has moved into the commercial mainstream. *The Last Emperor* (1987), shot on location in China, was an epic film of glorious beauty that told the tale of Pu Yi, the last emperor of China, who survived Japanese invasion and the cultural revolution to end his life as a gardener in Beijing. The film won several Academy Awards, including best picture.

BIANCHI, MICHELE (1883-1930). Born in Belmonte Calabro (Calabria), he came to be known as a firebrand syndicalist (and interventionist regarding **World War I**) in the heady days of organizing the field-workers in the Po Valley. When he tossed in his lot with **Mussolini** at the first 1919 meeting of the **Partito Nazionale Fascista** (PNF) National Fascist Party (at Piazza San Sepolcro in Milan), he retained the reputation for fanatical devotion to his syndicalist principles. He was chosen for membership on the first central committee of the newly formed PNF, of which he became the first secretary general. His relations with other fascist leaders were often strained, however. It was apparently Bianchi, as party secretary, who urged the **March on Rome** on an indecisive Mussolini. During the fascist coup in October 1922, Bianchi telephoned Rome pretending to be the prefect of Perugia reporting that only surrender to the fascists could avert serious bloodletting. Prime Minister **Luigi Facta** took this seriously and finally began the process of organizing resistance to fascism, publicizing a decree requesting emergency powers that resulted in the immediate dissolution of some fascist bands. The king refused to countersign the decree, however, thereby ensuring the victory of fascism. Before his sudden death in 1930 Bianchi became a PNF parliamentary deputy and, in 1929, minister for public works, a position he used to Calabria's advantage. *See also* Gran Consiglio del Fascismo; Quadrumvirate.

BISSOLATI, LEONIDA (1857-1920). A voice for moderate social democracy in early-twentieth-century Italy, Leonida Bissolati studied at Pavia and Bologna universities before becoming a lawyer and local politician in his native city of Cremona (Lombardy). Elected to Parliament as a Socialist in 1895, he became the editor of the daily newspaper of the **Partito Socialista Italiano** (PSI) / Italian Socialist Party, *L'Avanti!* His willingness to cooperate with relatively progressive liberals such as **Giovanni Giolitti** won him the reputation of being a "ministerialist" with the PSI's left wing. By 1910, Bissolati was diverging even from his fellow moderate **Filippo Turati**. Unlike Turati, who regarded reformism as a necessary tactical step on the road to the establishment of a socialist state, Bissolati became increasingly convinced that the introduction of such reforms as universal male suffrage should be themselves the objective of the socialist movement. Bissolati was consulted in 1911 on the occasion of the formation of Giolitti's new government, and although he refused any ministerial post, he had committed (in the eyes of PSI militants) the grave error of negotiating with the bourgeois state. Bissolati supported Giolitti's colonial war in **Libya** in 1912. This was the final straw for the party's "maximalist" wing, which expelled him from the party. Together with **Ivanoe Bonomi**, he formed a reform socialist party, but the new movement did not attract the mass membership he expected from the northern trade unions.

Bissolati had long been suspicious of Germany's hegemonic intentions in Europe, and had spoken out against Italy's involvement in the **Triple Alliance.** Accordingly, he was one of the warmest supporters on the Italian center-left of Italian intervention on the side of the Allies in 1915. Despite his relatively advanced age, Bissolati volunteered for the army and served at the front as a sergeant in the **Alpini**. He was wounded twice and received the Silver Medal for gallantry in combat. In June 1916, he became minister without portfolio and later, after the disaster at **Caporetto,** served as a minister under **Vittorio Emanuele Orlando.**

Although Bissolati was inclined to blame the anti-patriotic and pacifist activities of the PSI for the poor showing of the Italian troops, it would be wrong to regard his wartime ministerial experience as one in which he finally renounced his former ideals. In 1918-1919 he fought a stern political battle for the renunciation by Italy of its territorial gains in Dalmatia and the Tyrol. His argument that occupying these territories undermined the principle of national self-determination made no impression on the Italian nationalists who made Bissolati one of their favorite targets. Bissolati died in Rome in May 1920, despised and distrusted by both the nationalist right and the PSI.

BLACK ECONOMY. In the 1960s, those academics who studied the political and economic modernization of "developing" countries extolled the virtues of "cottage industries." This described productive work performed at home. A "jobber" might typically bring semi-finished products from household to household, paying each link in the chain for the items completed, embroidered, assembled, or stitched since the last visit. This not only augmented family incomes but allowed a mother to be with her small children while engaged in gainful employment.

Largely ignored was the price paid by the government, which is unable to levy taxes on the income so earned or to keep accurate production records. Yet the role of the black economy—or "submerged" or "underground" economy—as a social shock absorber in times of economic slowdown makes government tolerance understandable. As the fifth-ranking country in gross domestic product (GDP), Italy is not a third-world country, but already in 1979, the national statistical office began adding 9 percent to estimates of Italy's GDP and, in 1987, added another 15 percent. As much as one-quarter (and possibly more) of Italy's GDP is produced by the "black economy," unmeasured, unregulated, and untaxed. In areas of high unemployment, workers—whether skilled or unskilled—are easily persuaded to accept lower pay and to do without social protection in order to have an income, whether based on work that is part-time, full-time, or seasonal; in agriculture, small-scale manufacturing, or construction. For the employer, the savings are twofold: lower wages are paid and no contributions need be made for social security programs or retirement funds. Recent studies indicate that a full third of jobs in southern Italy are in the black economy. The national average is one in six. The number of self-employed is twice the average in the **European Union.**

In some cities of central Italy, modern computer technology has ensured that products such as sweaters and other knitwear (in Carpi) are designed and produced in constantly changed patterns so that no two are identical. Other instances of this "post-mass production" are found in Prato (near Florence) where most middle-class homes have a spare-room loom on which knitwear is prepared for the next stage in production, which might include embellishment by hand sewing. Precut leather glove parts by the caseload might be brought to a house in the *bassi* of **Naples** for stitching by machine. An entire family might be employed in this way.

Although Italy ranks among the richest of the industrial states, her economy continues to display several qualities more appropriate to developing countries: one is the incidence of retail outlets per unit of population; the other is the number of people engaged in "cottage industry," or the "black" economy, which employs 5 million workers, that is, over one-sixth of the entire work force, according to recent figures published by the Italian central statistical agency, ISTAT.

BLASETTI, ALESSANDRO (1900-). The most interesting film director of the fascist period, Alessandro Blasetti is widely regarded as a precursor of **neo-realism**. His first major movie, *1860*, which was made in 1934, is considered by many critics to be his masterpiece. A nationalistic portrayal of **Garibaldi**'s expedition to **Sicily**, it has a number of deftly handled battle scenes and, anticipating later directors such as **Roberto Rossellini** and **Luchino Visconti**, uses ordinary people rather than actors in several speaking roles. The final scene of the film, which the director cut after the war, was set in **Mussolini**'s **Rome**. The following year, Blasetti produced a more overtly fascist film, *La vecchia guardia* (*The Old Guard*, 1935), which celebrated the squadristi and the **March on Rome**. In 1941, he directed *La corona di ferro* (*The Iron Crown*), a mystical fairy tale with elaborate, costly sets and a more ambiguously pro-fascist message. In 1942, Blasetti abruptly shifted away from big-budget epics and made a simple drama about a traveling salesman who meets an unmarried pregnant girl and urges her family to show compassion for her. *Quattro passi fra le nuvole* (*A Stroll In The Clouds*, 1942), the film in question, is an important milestone in the Italian cinema's path to the classic neo-realist works of the late 1940s. Blasetti's post-1945 output was vast, but of generally lower quality, though an exception to this judgment might be made for his 1957 feature *Amore e chiacchiere* (*Love and Chatter*).

BLOCCO NAZIONALE. The general elections of November 1919 weakened the hold of Italy's traditional governing parties on power by rewarding the **Partito Socialista Italiano** (PSI) / Italian Socialist Party and the **Partito Popolare Italiano** (PPI) / Italian People's Party with a substantial share of the vote. Accordingly, in May 1921, **Giovanni Giolitti** tried to reestablish his parliamentary majority by forming a great coalition of liberals, conservatives, nationalists, reformist socialists, and **Mussolini**'s fascists to confront the two mass parties. As a political maneuver, the creation of this so-called "national bloc" was a success: the coalition obtained 275 seats in the Chamber of Deputies, compared to the 122 won by the PSI, the 107 won by the PPI, and the 16 of the newly constituted (in 1921) **Partito**

Comunista Italiano (PCI) / Italian Communist Party. The chief consequence of Giolitti's move, however, was to give legitimacy to Mussolini's fascists, who had been humiliated at the polls in 1919, but who now emerged with 35 seats. Giolitti's intention had been to "constitutionalize" the fascist movement, which many prominent Italian liberals regarded at this time as a strong form of liberalism that could restore order to the social and industrial anarchy unleashed by the end of **World War I**. Instead, the Italian bourgeoisie increasingly turned to **fascism** as their only salvation from the perceived perils of socialism.

BOBBIO, NORBERTO (1909-). Born and raised in **Turin**, Norberto Bobbio was professor of political and legal philosophy at the University of Turin from 1948 to 1979. A prolific scholar in these areas, Bobbio was made a life senator in 1985. Bobbio is not an unworldly academic, however. A member of the **Partito d'Azione** (PdA) / Action Party during the war, he has constantly tried to make his scholarship politically effective. His move away from what he saw as "sterile abstractions" in favor of political involvement began with the cold war. By the beginning of the 1970s, he had become a supporter of the **Partito Socialista Italiano** (PSI) / Italian Socialist Party, regarding it as a force that had moved away from the orthodox Marxist of the **Partito Comunista Italiano** (PCI) / Italian Communist Party and toward cooperation with the left of the **Democrazia Cristiana** (DC) / Christian Democracy Party in pursuit of a new progressivism. Yet he was never a PSI "loyalist." He was one of the few socialists who openly criticized **Bettino Craxi** in the 1980s.

Bobbio's books provide an intriguing portrait of Italy. For him, revolutionary rhetoric has abounded despite the fact that there has been neither a religious, political, nor social revolution in Italy. There have been many important revolutionary *movements,* but none has succeeded in transforming values and elite structure. Moreover, the intellectual has rarely succeeded in inspiring and guiding men of politics. Nowhere is this more emphatic than in Bobbio's assessment of the resistance. According to Bobbio, it was led by those who shared a desire to destroy **fascism** and to restore their separate pre-fascist political cultures—whether Catholic, liberal, or Marxist. The only newly born movement was the Action Party, but it was precisely this party's novelty that ensured that it found no space among the pre-fascist parties that came to dominate the Parliament after 1946.

Nevertheless, much of Bobbio's political activity has been directed toward promoting dialogue between Italy's political cultures. As a secular democrat and a liberal, tolerant and pluralistic himself while advocating tolerance and pluralism, he persisted in defining dialogue as a corrective to the limitless nature of human folly and exaggeration. In his view, dialogue is the only route to democracy. While in his late eighties, Bobbio remains a prominent figure in Italian life—his two most recent books both spent many weeks on the best-sellers list—and in the intellectual life of his native Turin. In recent years, this heir to the liberal-socialist tradition of **Piero Gobetti, Gaetano Salvemini,** and **Carlo Rosselli** has enjoyed growing international fame as a scholar and political thinker.

BOCCIONI, UMBERTO (1882-1916). The most important futurist painter and sculptor, and the most subtle theoretician of the futurist movement, Umberto Boccioni left his native Reggio Calabria before he was 20 years old to live in **Rome** and Paris, where he was greatly influenced by the work of Georges Saurat. Upon returning to Italy, he was one of the founders of the futurist movement: his *Tumult in the Gallery* (1909) was the first major work produced by a futurist artist. Boccioni's paintings, with their emphasis on urban, industrial themes, and their remarkable ability to capture movement, faithfully reflect the ideas of the "Manifesto of Futurist Painters," published in 1910, which Boccioni co-wrote with Carlo Carrà, Luigi Russolo, and Giacomo Balla. *The City Awakes*, painted in 1910 and currently housed in the Museum of Modern Art in New York, is arguably the finest example of his early work. Boccioni also published a "Manifesto of Futurist Sculptors" in 1912 and produced a number of powerful bronzes that attempt to portray the human form in the context of its environment.

Boccioni's style became increasingly abstract after 1911 and was greatly influenced by cubism. *The Dynamism of a Human Body* (1913), in which no obvious figure is visible, is a good example of his later work. He fought in **World War I** and died, tragically young, in 1916 in Verona after a heavy fall from a horse. *See also* Futurism.

BOLOGNA. Modern Bologna shows abundant signs of its Etruscan origins, its Roman past, and its wealth in the Middle Ages. Its long-lasting sense of civic engagement has been used to explain the remarkable "workability" and efficiency of this provincial and regional capital, with the highest per capita income in 1991 in all of

Italy. Papal for three centuries, part of Napoleon's Cisalpine Republic (1796-1814), followed by a period under Austrian rule, it is known chiefly for its university, the oldest in the West, having been founded in 1088. It is also known for its small-scale industry, its political energy, and its cuisine.

Since 1945 this city of nearly 400,000 has had both its mayor and a city council plurality drawn from the **Partito Comunista Italiano** (PCI) / Italian Communist Party. Innovative governance has made it a showcase city. For example, a housing plan, begun in 1970, expropriated (with compensation) and rebuilt war-damaged properties of the inner city. Preference in rentals was given to pensioners, students, and tenant **cooperatives**. Thus, while retaining a mix of citizens in the heart of the city, Bologna's center escaped being gentrified or converted to warehouses.

The imagination brought by the local PCI to metropolitan problems is further illustrated by the system of *quartieri* or neighborhoods. Each of these decentralized units has a meeting hall, a health center, and a records section. Identity cards, citizenship papers, wedding certificates and licenses, birth and death certificates, tax status, and residency records can all be procured from one's *quartiere*; in some, by computer. Eighteen were created in the original 1960 legislation; they have since been consolidated into nine of these mini-city halls. Each serves as a meeting place where *quartiere* residents meet to discuss measures under consideration by the city council. Thus, before any initiative is taken, all affected neighborhoods will have had an opportunity to judge its impact. Closing redundant schools or modifying traffic patterns are thoroughly debated before action is taken.

But all is not bliss in Bologna, the "fat and the learned" as it is called. Its political energies have sometimes been violent. During the German occupation, the Gothic Line which ran just south of the city was often at the center of partisan warfare. After protracted battles at several of the portals between partisans and the German garrison, the city was liberated on April 25, 1944, by the Polish Expeditionary Forces attached to the British Eighth Army. The local **Comitato di Liberazione Nazionale** (CLN) / National Liberation Committee had already established a de facto city administration.

The 1960s and 1970s were the years of maximum student activism, in Bologna as elsewhere. A meeting held (March 11, 1977) in the university's Anatomy Hall by a group of militant Catholics calling themselves *Comunione e Liberazione* (Communion and

Liberation) was set upon by student Maoists. Clashes between these groups raged in the university area and surrounding streets. Finally, the *Carabinieri* were called by the rector. Their teargas grenades drew the response of Molotov cocktails. Eventually, the forces of order employed firearms. One student, a known militant of **Lotta Continua,** was killed. The ensuing rioting brought tanks and armored personnel carriers into the university district while, in the city's main square, there seemed to be no alternative to letting student anger run its course while pressing the demonstrators constantly toward the periphery of the city. Student activists saw the PCI as part of the bourgeois establishment and condemned it as unfit to represent any hope of revolutionary change.

The invigorated student movement nourished the **Brigate Rosse** (BR) / Red Brigades producing a terrible response from the right. On August 2, 1980, hundreds were injured and 85 people killed when a bomb exploded in the second-class waiting room of Bologna's railroad station. Inconclusive trials point to a right-wing plot to destabilize the country, but as time passes this hypothesis is harder to prove. *See also* Police.

BOMBACCI, NICOLA (1879-1945). One of the leading figures of the fascist regime, Nicola Bombacci began his career as a political activist in the **Partito Socialista Italiano** (PSI) / Italian Socialist Party. He was one of the leaders of the party's "maximalist" wing, and won notoriety after the revolution in Russia in 1917 by appealing to Italians to follow the Bolshevik example. In 1918, he was arrested and condemned to over two years' imprisonment for anti-war activities, but was soon released and was elected to Parliament in 1919. In 1921, he was among the founders of the **Partito Comunista Italiano** (PCI) / Italian Communist Party, but was expelled in 1924 and drew ever closer to his former PSI comrade, **Benito Mussolini.** From 1927 onward, Bombacci was an open fascist, playing an important role as the regime's spokesman to the working class. He remained faithful to Mussolini even after the dictator's fall in July 1943, and became one of the most influential figures in the **Republic of Salò.** Together with Mussolini, Bombacci drew up the so-called "Manifesto of Verona," which outlined a confused program that incorporated socialist ideals such as the nationalization of public services with anti-semitic rhetoric. He was with Mussolini in the desperate flight to Dongo near the Swiss border in April 1945 and shared the dictator's gruesome end.

BONOMI, IVANOE (1873-1951). Born in Mantua (Lombardy), Ivanoe Bonomi was one of the most important early theorists of the nascent **Partito Socialista Italiano** (PSI) / Italian Socialist Party. He contributed to **Filippo Turati**'s influential magazine, *Critica sociale*, from 1895 onward, briefly edited the party newspaper *L'Avanti!*, and in 1907, published a controversial book, *Le vie nuove del socialismo* (*The New Roads of Socialism*), in which he argued that the workers' movement needed to reject Marxist dogma and concentrate on winning social reforms by adhering to British-style laborism—a position that found little support in the increasingly revolutionary PSI. Bonomi, who was elected to Parliament in 1909, was expelled from the PSI in 1912 along with others of the party's moderates. Together with **Leonida Bissolati**, Bonomi founded the Partito Socialista Riformista Italiano (PSRI) / Italian Reformist Socialist Party but it never obtained a mass following.

Bonomi supported the war and saw combat as a junior officer in a regiment of **Alpini**. His time at the front was relatively short. However, in 1916, he became minister for public works in the government of **Paolo Boselli** and later became minister of war under both **Francesco Saverio Nitti** and **Giovanni Giolitti**. Bonomi was himself prime minister between July 1921 and February 1922. His attitude toward the growing fascist threat was somewhat equivocal. During the elections of May 1921, he joined Giolitti as a candidate for the *blocco nazionale*. As prime minister, he did little or nothing to obstruct the outrages committed by the fascist squads.

During the **Mussolini** epoch, Bonomi eked out a precarious living as a writer of history books, the most important of which, *La politica italiana da Porta Pia a Vittorio Veneto* (*Italian Politics from Porto Pia to Vittorio Veneto*, 1943), later became a widely used school textbook. In June 1944, he returned to political activity, as the figurehead premier of the provisional government containing all the leading democratic forces in Allied-controlled Italy. His popularity with the British enabled him to survive a government crisis in November-December 1944, but after the end of the conflict in May 1945, the partisans of northern Italy would not accept his continuation in office. When he resigned, his place was taken by **Ferruccio Parri** of the **Partito d'Azione** (PdA) / Action Party who was to be succeeded by **Alcide De Gasperi**, thus ushering in nearly a half century of hegemony by the **Democrazia Cristiana** (DC) / Christian Democracy Party. Bonomi fought the June 1946 elections in the company of **Benedetto Croce**, **Vittorio Emanuele Orlando**, and **Francesco Nitti** as the leader of the Unione Democratica Nazionale (UDN) / National Democratic Union, but these remnants of pre-fascist Italy were humiliated at the polls, obtaining less than 7 percent of the vote. One last institutional burden awaited him: a member of the new Italian Senate by right, he was elected by his fellow Senators to be president of the first elected Senate in Italian history in May 1948 and remained in that position until his death in 1951. *See also* Salò, Republic of.

BONOMI, PAOLO (1910-1985). Long a militant in Catholic Action, he founded the farmers' lobby (Confederazione Nazionale dei Coltivatori Diretti: known by its acronym, COLDIRETTI). As a loyal member of the **Democrazia Cristiana** (DC) / Christian Democracy Party, he was rewarded by being put forward by his party as prime minister in the first post-fascist governments. Aside from lengthy service to his party in Parliament, he also organized the "Three-P Clubs" to be found in every Italian province. These, like the U.S. Four-H Clubs, aimed at encouraging future farmers to *Provare, Produrre, Progredire* or *Try* [new methods], *Produce, Progress*, a slogan bearing a striking resemblance to the earlier Believe, Obey, Fight (*Credere, Obbedire, Combattere*). *See also* Fascism; Fascist Ideology.

BORDIGA, AMADEO (1889-1970). Twentieth-century Italy's most prominent Trotskyite, Amadeo Bordiga was an engineer from **Naples** who played a prominent role in the "maximalist" wing of the **Partito Socialista Italiano** (PSI) / Italian Socialist Party. In 1919, Bordiga supported the party's entry into the Third International on Soviet terms, even though Lenin had insisted that the PSI could only become a member if it called itself a "communist" party and if it expelled such notorious moderates as **Filippo Turati**. When the PSI hesitated to bow to Lenin's demands at a special conference of the party in January 1921, Bordiga, together with **Antonio Gramsci**, left the PSI and founded the **Partito Comunista Italiano** (PCI) / Italian Communist Party. Bordiga's ideological position was clear. In the words of the motion adopted by the PCI's Second Congress in March 1922, the choice was "either communism or **fascism**." No alliance with the bourgeois parties (in practice, all other parties) was possible, only armed resistance to the fascists under the direction of the PCI (even if Bordiga must have been aware that the PCI lacked the military strength to assume this role).

After the "maximalist" wing of the PSI finally expelled Turati in October 1922, Bordiga's intransigence on this point caused the PCI itself to split. Some communists, at Soviet urging, rejoined the PSI, which was readmitted to the Third International, and others, led by Bordiga, refused. This fanatical adherence to party dogma demoralized the entire Italian left and unquestionably weakened the working class's response to fascism.

Bordiga was arrested and tried for "conspiracy against the state" in 1923, but remarkably managed to convince the magistrates of his innocence. Within the PCI, his position weakened as the Stalinist wing of the party gained strength. In 1926, at the PCI's Third Congress in Lyon, he lost the party leadership to Gramsci and was eventually expelled. After a period of internal exile, he was allowed to resume the engineering profession by the authorities in 1930. Bordiga dedicated himself to his work and took no further part in leftist politics, although in his old age he did write a two-volume history of Italian communism's left wing. At the time of his death in 1970, he had become a cult figure for the PCI's young critics in the student and workers' movements.

BOSELLI, PAOLO (1838-1932). Born in the Ligurian city of Savona, Paolo Boselli was elected to Parliament for the first time in 1870. An academic lawyer who specialized in industrial and maritime law, Boselli held a series of second-rank ministerial posts between 1888 and 1906.

In June 1916, Boselli, who had been a strong supporter of Italian intervention in **World War I**, was called upon to substitute **Antonio Salandra** as prime minister after initial Austrian successes had led to the fall of the city of Asiago. He formed a cabinet that contained representatives from all the political parties except the **Partito Socialista Italiano** (PSI) / Italian Socialist Party. Boselli, however, proved an inadequate choice as prime minister. His inexperience in military and foreign affairs, lack of a personal political base, and advanced age all hindered his ability to control either the authoritarian commander of the Italian forces, General Cadorna, or the unruly members of his majority. His government fell after the disaster of **Caporetto** in October 1917 emphasized the dramatic failings of the Italian war effort.

Boselli became a nationalist and a fascist after the war, although he held no further political office. He died in Rome in 1932.

BOSSI, UMBERTO (1943-). The charismatic leader of the **Lega Nord** (LN) / Northern League, Umberto Bossi was born into a working-class family in Varese (Lombardy). He has been a dance-band guitarist, odd-jobs handyman, hospital orderly, and part-time medical student before he found in political activity his true vocation. A chance meeting in 1979 with Bruno Salvadori, the leading ideologue of the autonomist Union Valdotaine (claiming to speak for the Aosta region of northwest Italy), gave Bossi the taste for the autonomist brand of politics. In 1982, Bossi founded the Lega Lombarda ("Lombard League") and shrewdly gave this new movement a populist program (recommending, for instance, a "Lombards first" policy in public administration). He soon revealed a genius for political propaganda. A string of electoral victories followed, and in February 1991, Bossi successfully united all the autonomist parties in northern Italy into a single party under his leadership—the LN. His goal in this period was to break the mold of Italian politics and compel what he disparagingly calls the "Roman parties" to transform Italy's highly centralized state into a federal republic based upon three "macroregions": the North, the Center, and the South.

When the political system seemed to collapse in 1992-1993, Bossi arguably overplayed his hand. Instead of projecting a moderate reassuring image to former **Democrazia Cristiana** (DC) / Christian Democracy Party voters in northern Italy, he used increasingly wild rhetoric (on one occasion warning that the North would "take up Kalashnikovs" if it were not granted greater autonomy from **Rome**). If so, it was one of the few tactical mistakes he has made. Bossi's political risk-taking is legendary in Italy, and he seems to have succeeded in establishing the LN as the party of choice for a substantial segment of the northern electorate (especially those who live in the Alpine regions of Lombardy, Venetia, Piedmont, and Friuli). In the 1996 elections, most experts expected the LN to be wiped out. Instead, the party increased its share of the vote and ensured that Bossi would have five more years in the parliamentary spotlight. Since then, he has launched his most recent scheme, the creation of the independent republic of "Padania" (the Po River valley) in northern Italy. In September 1996, showing his usual flair for publicity, he embarked on a symbolic voyage down the river Po to carry a flask of "sacred" water from the river's source to the sea at Venice. For all his antics, however, Bossi could not have made the LN a force to be reckoned with without years of misgovernment from Rome.

Bossi is the colorful and sometimes overly emphatic expression of a genuine mood of disquiet and frustration among the small-scale entrepreneurs of the Paduan Plain. *See also* European Union; Maastricht, Treaty of; Venice.

BOTTAI, GIUSEPPE (1895-1959). One of the leading fascist intellectuals, Giuseppe Bottai fought as a volunteer during **World War I**, rising to the rank of captain in the **Arditi**, the shock troops who took the heaviest casualties of all Italian units involved in combat. After the war, he was one of the original founders of the *fasci di combattimento*, organizing the fascist squads in his native Lazio. Nevertheless, he was widely regarded as one of the few genuine intellectuals among the hierarchs of the **Partito Nazionale Fascista** (PNF) / National Fascist Party. Editor of *Critica Fascista*, the moderation of his position on many issues and genuine openness to debate won him a relatively liberal reputation among the regime's opponents. It also caused him trouble with **Benito Mussolini**. His opposition to the PNF's increasing identification with the state almost caused his expulsion from party activity after Mussolini cracked down on internal dissent in October 1925.

Despite his aversion to the party state, Bottai held a number of important governmental posts in the 1920s and 1930s. Between 1926 and 1932, he was the most enthusiastic exponent of **corporatism** as an ideology and, as minister for the corporations, was entrusted with turning theory into practice. Subsequently, he became governor of **Rome** in 1936 and minister for education between 1936 and 1943. In this last post he enforced the **racial laws** and was also responsible for imposing on all schoolchildren compulsory membership in the regime's paramilitary youth organizations. On the other hand, his *Carta della scuola* (School Charter), because it opened public schools to workers, was widely praised among fascist dissidents on the left.

Between 1940 and 1943, Bottai published *Primato*, which seemingly sought to rescue Italian literature and culture from purely propagandistic uses. Its pages included essays by fascist left dissidents, distinguished anti-fascists, and regime-apologists.

When war broke out in 1939, Bottai—who had already expressed private doubts over the desirability of the alliance with Germany—was one of many prominent figures who opposed Italy's participation. Together with some of the old pre-war liberal politicians, he began to draw close to the crown in the hope of inspiring in **Victor Emmanuel III** some initiative that might withdraw Italy from the war. On July 25, 1943, Bottai was among the 19 members of the Fascist Grand Council who voted to deprive Mussolini of his powers. For this "crime," he was condemned to death *in absentia* by the **Republic of Salò.** In 1944, he fled Italy to North Africa where he joined the French Foreign Legion. In 1945, he was sentenced to life imprisonment by the High Court of Justice, but was amnestied in 1947 without having served a single day in prison. *See also* Fascism; Quadrumvirate.

BRIGATE ROSSE (BR) / Red Brigades. A terrorist movement whose leadership, especially in the early years, was drawn largely from profoundly Catholic elements of the sociology faculty at the University of Trento, the BR waged a ruthless war against the Italian state from 1971 onward. The Red Brigades set as their goal the embarrassment of the **Partito Comunista Italiano** (PCI) / Italian Communist Party by provoking the state into such repressive actions as to oblige all those who thought themselves revolutionaries to choose between acting on revolutionary rhetoric, on the one hand, or on the other, sustaining the dominance of an allegedly oppressive, bourgeois state. Their methods were violent: "kneecapping" (the wounding by gunfire aimed at the knee, which avoids a charge of attempted murder) and on occasion, kidnappings and assassinations. Their targets were, initially, those on the relative left end of the political spectrum who advocated or symbolized the collaboration between the reformist center parties or factions and parties of revolutionary tradition. Journalists, jurists, academics, and trade-unionists were all attacked, and the responsibility was always accepted—indeed, proclaimed—by the leadership of the Red Brigades. Despite the BR's violence, for many young Italians disgusted with what they perceived as the injustices of the political system, the *Brigatisti* was surrounded by the same aura of romanticism as was worn by Che Guevara and Fidel Castro.

The BR's boldest move was the kidnapping on March 16, 1978, of **Aldo Moro**. The meticulous planning of the daylight attack on the protective vehicles that preceded and followed Moro's automobile—his entire five-man police bodyguard was killed—enabled Moro's kidnappers to whisk him into hiding before a police response could be organized. In fact, as subsequent investigation eventually revealed, his hiding place was always in central **Rome** rendering police searches and road checks futile. After 55 days in captivity, and apparently following bitter quarrels as to his fate among the Brigades' leadership, Moro was murdered and his body left in the trunk of a small automobile parked—symbolically—midway between PCI national offices and the national headquarters of the **Democrazia Cristiana** (DC) / Christian Democracy Party in Rome. One line of behavior urged from some quarters was the enactment of measures expanding **police** powers and diminishing civil rights. This was not the method chosen by the Italian political leadership. Partly because the principal parties were divided between those ready to treat the BR as a legitimate interlocutor— the **Partito Socialista Italiano** (PSI) / Italian Socialist Party—and those who refused to contemplate such a course of action, no repressive measures were initiated. The inaction of the government and its avowed determination not to violate the constitutional rights denied the BR the provocation that they sought, and their own increasingly random violence gradually lost them most sympathy in public opinion. Clever police work—coordinated by Carlo Alberto Della Chiesa—also contributed to the BR's decline. In January 1983, Aldo Moro's killers—including the BR's chief strategist, Mario Moretti—were condemned to life sentences in Rome after a nine-month trial. Nevertheless, as late as April 1988, a BR cell was responsible for the murder of Professor Roberto Ruffilli, a close advisor to the then premier, **Ciriaco De Mita**, who was one of the leading advocates within the DC of Aldo Moro's philosophy of compromise with the PCI. Others who allegedly had inspired by their lectures the worst elements of the BR fled the country in order to avoid arrest. Professor Toni Negri of Padova, for example, remained in Paris until 1997 when he grandly announced his intention to return in order to put an end to the "years of lead."

When U.S. General James Lee Dozier was kidnapped and held prisoner by the Red Brigade (for 40 days between December 1981 and February 1982), his hiding place was uncovered by a combination of good police work and luck. Police and *Carabinieri* collaborated in a textbook raid on the apartment and freed the general unharmed, without a shot having been fired, taking several prisoners and uncovering incriminating documents that helped equip the Italian judiciary to incarcerate much of the top leadership of the BR.

The BR inspired several imitators, the most violent of which was a group called *Prima linea*—"Frontline." This group's most notorious member was Marco Donat Cattin, the son of a DC cabinet minister, who eventually gave evidence at the 1983 trial of his former comrades.

BROSIO, MANLIO (1897-1980). Born in Turin, he had a productive and lengthy career in the course of which Manlio Brosio established a reputation as an able diplomat and politician. He was a wartime partisan and, during the latter stages of the war, became leader of the **Partito Liberale Italiano** (PLI) / Italian Liberal Party, taking part in the second **Bonomi** administration as minister without portfolio and as vice-premier under **Ferruccio Parri** after the end of the conflict. The PLI bore substantial responsibility for the crisis that brought down Parri's short-lived administration in November 1945, but any hopes Brosio might have had of acceding to the premiership were dashed by the emergence of **Alcide De Gasperi**. Brosio was minister for war in the first post-war cabinet to be headed by this leader of the **Democrazia Cristiana** (DC) / Christian Democracy Party.

An anti-monarchist in a largely royalist party, Brosio joined the **Partito Repubblicano Italiano** (PRI) / Italian Republican Party in 1946, but gave up active politics for diplomacy in 1947. He was successively Italian ambassador to Moscow (whence he strongly urged a policy of neutrality on post-war Italian governments), London, Washington and Paris. In 1964, he became secretary general of the **North Atlantic Treaty Organization** (NATO), the only Italian to have held this post. In 1972, he returned to politics, being elected to the senate for the PLI. He died in his native Turin in 1980.

BUONARROTI, FILIPPO MICHELE (1761-1837). Conspirator, republican, agitator, Filippo Buonarroti was a disciple of Rousseau and an early communist. Born in Pisa, he became a French citizen during the revolution and was sent to Italy as a secret agent. After the fall of Robespierre, he took part in Babeuf's unsuccessful "conspiracy of equals" against the Directory and was forced to flee to Geneva. After the return of absolutism to Italy, he organized a secret society called the "Sublime Perfect Masters," a neo-masonic organization with elaborate rituals and hierarchy, whose task was to coordinate revolutionary activity in Italy. In fact, despite his tireless work for the cause, Buonarroti never obtained a serious following among the underground sects. The monarchism of the Carboneria was antithetical to him, although he exerted more influence than **Giuseppe Mazzini** among its sects. Buonarroti was a republican, like Mazzini, but his political philosophy was inspired by a Robespierrean vision of the need for a dictatorship of the enlightened that was at odds with Mazzini's more democratic goals. He broke with Mazzini in 1834. Buonarroti was the author of an important treatise on politics, *La conspiration pour l'égalité, dite de Babeuf* (*The Conspiracy for Equality, as told by Babeuf,* 1828), in which he reflected upon the impact of the French Revolution on European politics since 1789. He died in Paris in September 1837.

BUTTIGLIONE, ROCCO (1948-). Born in the Adriatic resort of Gallipoli (Apulia), Buttiglione initiated his career as a political philosopher under the conservative Catholic scholar Augusto De Noce. He is the author of numerous widely translated books and articles on Marxism and Catholic political thought and is personally and intellectually close to the Pope John Paul II, Karol Wojtyla.

In March 1994, Buttiglione entered politics and was elected to Parliament as a deputy for the reborn **Partito Popolare Italiano** (PPI) / Italian People's Party. Almost immediately, at the end of July 1994, he became party leader. Although a conservative, Buttiglione surprisingly sought to achieve good relations with the **Partito Democratico della Sinistra** (PDS) / Democratic Party of the Left and, in December 1994, joined with the PDS and the **Lega Nord** to defeat the government of **Silvio Berlusconi** in a parliamentary vote of no confidence. Buttiglione strongly supported President **Scalfaro**'s subsequent decision to establish a government of technocrats.

Impressed by the **Alleanza Nazionale** (AN) / National Alliance's renunciation of its fascist past at the beginning of February 1995, however, Buttiglione suddenly changed tack and proposed joining the right-wing alliance of **Forza Italia**, the Centro Cristiano Democratico (CCD) / Christian Democratic Center and the AN. The PPI's left wing, preferring the center-left **Olive Tree Coalition** launched by **Romano Prodi** strongly opposed this tactic and barely succeeded in passing a vote of no confidence in Buttiglione's leadership on March 8, 1995. Buttiglione took part in the April 1995 local elections in a common list with Forza Italia. In July 1995, the philosopher-politician launched a new centrist party, the Cristiani Democratici Unificati (CDU) / United Christian Democrats, which has won the legal right to make use of the shield and cross emblem of the old Democrazia Cristiana (DC) / Christian Democracy Party.

The CDU fought the general elections of April 1996 in the company of the CCD. Their joint list obtained a disappointing 5.8 percent of the vote. Since the elections, Buttiglione has shown signs of coolness toward the parties of the right, and is increasingly orienting his political strategy toward resuscitating a center party that would hold the balance of power between the PDS and Forza Italia-AN.

-C-

CADORNA, LUIGI (1850-1928). During **World War I**, General Cadorna was commander in chief of Italian forces on the Isonzo River from May 1915 to November 1917 when he was replaced by General Armando Diaz after **Caporetto**. At the Isonzo River, he had directed 11 battles on a 60-mile front which advanced Italian forces 10 miles toward Trieste. Britain's General Douglas Haig, about to attack in Flanders, demurred about sending British or French forces—as both Lloyd George and Foch wanted—to help Cadorna. Ludendorff, on the other hand, did not hesitate to send assistance to his Austrian ally. He despatched six German divisions in the hope that, together with the nine Austrian divisions already engaged, they might drive Italy from the war. When the battle opened, they very nearly succeeded when the Italian line broke at Caporetto. Allied reinforcements and a stiffened Italian resistance at the Piave averted disaster. Determined counter-attacks culminated in Austria suing for peace.

The Italian Commission of Inquiry on the Caporetto disaster assigned much of the responsibility to Cadorna for having used his position to undermine the prestige of rivals among other senior officers rather than in properly caring for his troops. Cadorna, on the other hand, attributed the losses to his men's "cowardice" making no mention of the remarkable containment at the Piave. *See also* Caporetto, Battle of.

CAIROLI, BENEDETTO (1825-1889). The eldest son of a family of patriots, Benedetto Cairoli's four brothers all died fighting for Italian unification. Benedetto himself was one of the "Thousand" who sailed with **Garibaldi** to **Sicily** in 1860. He was elected to Parliament in 1861, but returned to the battlefield to fight for the liberation of **Rome** in 1867. Romantic and quixotic, he could not match the political acumen of **Crispi** or **Depretis**. He nevertheless became prime minister three times between March 1878 and May 1881. Cairoli's governments were largely composed of politicians from northern Italy (he himself was from Pavia) and came to ignominious ends. His first government collapsed following an assassination attempt on King Umberto; the second as a result of the French occupation of Tunis. Cairoli was opposed to Depretis's style of government and allied with Crispi, **Zanardelli**, **Nicòtera**, and Alfredo Baccarini to form the so-called "Pentarchy," which led the parliamentary opposition to Depretis. Cairoli died in **Naples** at the villa of King Umberto in August 1889.

CALAMANDREI, PIERO (1889-1956). One of twentieth-century Italy's leading left-wing intellectuals, Piero Calamandrei was also a respected jurist, and a prominent opponent of **fascism**. Born in **Florence**, Calamandrei postponed his career as a professor of law to serve as a volunteer during **World War I**. He was an active anti-fascist from the very beginning of the regime. Together with Ernesto Rossi, **Gaetano Salvemini**, and **Carlo and Nello Rosselli**, he was one of the founders of an anti-fascist circle of intellectuals in Florence that the fascist squads brutally suppressed in December 1924; he signed **Benedetto Croce**'s 1925 manifesto of anti-fascist intellectuals; and in the 1930s honorably resigned his university chair rather than submit to taking a personal oath of loyalty to **Mussolini**, one of only eleven professors to choose this course.

In 1942, Calamandrei was one of the founders of the **Partito d'Azione** (PdA) / Action Party. He was elected to the **Constituent Assembly** in 1946, and became one of the principal authors of the Italian republican **Constitution.** In 1948, he was elected to Parliament as a member of the **Partito Socialista Democratico Italiano** (PSDI) / Italian Social Democratic Party, although he later strongly disagreed with his party's support for the **North Atlantic Treaty Organization** (NATO) alliance, and its increasing closeness to the **Democrazia Cristiana** (DC) / Christian Democracy Party. Unlike many in the PSDI, Calamandrei believed that democratic socialists could find intellectual common ground with the **Partito Comunista Italiano** (PCI) / Italian Communist Party both within Italy and without, and to this end he founded the intellectual review *Il Ponte* (*The Bridge*) in 1945. Ever since then, this magazine has been one of the most important forums for intellectual debate on the Italian left. Calamandrei died in Florence in 1956.

CALCIO. Catholicism is only the formal religion of Italy: *calcio* (association football or soccer) is the religion that inspires most fervor. It is impossible to have a full understanding of Italian social life in this century without knowing something about this hugely popular sport.

Soccer was imported from England in the late 1880s and took organized form in the early 1890s. The first soccer club was formed in 1893 in Genoa, and the first soccer championship, won by Genoa, took place in May 1898. The early championships were organized on a knockout basis, but after **World War I** the soccer clubs were placed into the system of leagues that is common for most professional sports in Europe. Today, the premier league, *Serie A*, consists of 18 leading clubs who play one another twice (once at home, once away) in a season that lasts from mid-September to the end of May. The championship winning club is the one that has amassed most points at the end of the season: clubs earn three points for a win (until recently just two) and one point for a tie. The four clubs that earn the fewest points in the season are relegated to *Serie B* and are replaced by the four clubs who do best in the junior championship. There is also a semi-professional *Serie C*, which is organized into northern and southern divisions, and a long array of amateur leagues at regional, provincial, and municipal levels. The biggest clubs in *Serie A*—Juventus (which plays in Turin), AC Milan, Internazionale of Milan, AC Roma—are among the wealthiest sporting businesses in the world. Games between the top teams are watched by as many as 80,000 people and by enormous TV audiences all over the globe. Many of the leading players from Germany, France, South America, and Africa play in Italy, and the top stars earn salaries that match those of basketball or baseball players in the United States.

Italy, along with Brazil, Argentina, and Germany, has been the most successful nation in international soccer competition. Its most famous clubs have won numerous trans-European and inter-continental club championships, and the *nazionale*, or national team, has won the World Cup on three occasions (1934, 1938, 1982) and been losing finalists twice (1970, 1994). In 1990, Italy hosted the World Cup, putting on a spectacular show in colossal state of the art stadiums especially built for the event. Italian soccer has historically been characterized by a heavy reliance on defensive, tactical play designed to frustrate opposition teams, but in recent years clubs have adopted a more adventurous, attacking style.

CALVINO, ITALO (1923-1985). The son of two expatriate Italian university botanists, Calvino was born in Havana, Cuba, although his parents returned to Italy in 1925. Calvino began his university studies in the same field as his parents in 1941, but the war intervened. Calvino was called up by the **Salò** republic but rather than serve, he went into hiding. In 1944, he joined the **Partito Comunista Italiano** (PCI) / Italian Communist Party and took part in some of the most intensive partisan fighting. As for so many Italians, this was an experience that shaped the rest of his life.

After the war, Calvino returned to the university, this time to study literature, and worked for the PCI and the publishing house Einaudi. His first political articles were published by the magazine *Il Politecnico,* and in 1946 he completed his first novel, *Il sentiero dei nidi di ragno* (*The Path to the Nest of Spiders*), a work in the neo-realist idiom that described the partisan struggle through the eyes of a child. It was the first novel in what would prove to be an extremely prolific career as a writer, critic, translator, and social theorist. Unlike his close friends **Cesare Pavese** and **Elio Vittorini,** Calvino evolved into a writer of *favole* (fables). *Fiabe italiane* (*Italian Fables*, 1956) and *Marcovaldo* (1963) are perhaps the high points of his literary output.

Calvino also showed notable political independence. In 1956, he broke with the PCI after the party condoned the Soviet Union's brutal suppression of the Hungarian workers' movement. While he never renounced his progressive sympathies, Calvino himself admitted that he became more detached from politics after 1956. This did not stop him, however, from joining in the intense debate over communism in the literary magazines of the Italian left, and being an outspoken opponent of the Vietnam War. By the 1970s, Calvino had become an internationally recognized writer, especially in France, which awarded him the *Légion d'honneur* in 1981, and in the United States, where he was invited to conferences and to give lectures. Calvino was preparing to give the Norton lectures on poetry at Harvard University when he died of a stroke in September 1985. He would have been the first Italian to perform this most prestigious of academic tasks.

CAPORETTO, BATTLE OF. A small town near what is today the Italian-Slovenian border, Caporetto was the scene of the greatest defeat in Italian military history. Following the failure of the Italian army's eleventh offensive on the Isonzo River in August 1917, the Austro-German high command launched a major counter-offensive. German assistance to Austria was not matched by the British and French until the situation became desperate.

On the first day (October 24, 1917), the Austro-German forces swiftly recovered the few miles that the Italians had taken (at a cost of 900,000 casualties) over the preceding two and a half years of fighting. The Italian line broke at Caporetto and was routed, stopping only at the Piave River—almost at Venice—where the new line held. Fortunately for Italy, not only did the Austro-German forces outrun their supplies but Britain and France sent reinforcements in early November. Losses at Caporetto were extremely high. More than 10,000 Italian troops had been killed, 30,000 wounded, and 293,000 captured. A measure of morale is provided by the desertion of some 300,000 soldiers.

CARABINIERI. *See* Police.

CARBONERIA. Secret societies of middle- and upper-class supporters of constitutional government and Italian unification, the *carboneria* (literally, coal-burners) sprang up in **Naples** and southern Italy during the Napoleonic occupation, but spread in the subsequent two decades to Spain and France, and to northern Italy. There, they came into contact with similar associations such as the *Federati* of Lombardy, and were infiltrated by the more radical followers of **Filippo Buonarroti.** Like the Freemasons, the *carboneria* were distinguished by a complex series of rituals, passwords, and emblems; were structured into a rigid hierarchy of grades of initiation; and were bound to absolute secrecy about their activities.

The *carboneria* were agents of revolution in the insurrections of Naples, Piedmont, and Lombardy in 1820-1821, and of hundreds of other revolutionary acts throughout the peninsula in the 1820s and 1830s. As such, they were the subject of bitter persecution from the authorities and from rival reactionary sects such as the *calderari* in the Kingdom of the Two Sicilies. The limits of the *carboneria* as a revolutionary organization were exposed by the failure of uprisings in central Italy in 1830-1831. Limited by their own secrecy and rituals to select categories of mostly wealthy students, soldiers, and professionals, the *carboneria* were able to establish provisional governments in Modena, Parma, and **Bologna**, but then lacked the numbers or coordination to fend off the Austrian troops that moved quickly to the aid of the Pope. The *carboneria* were thereafter eclipsed by Mazzini's *Giovine Italia*, which was much less elitist and ritualistic in its composition and behavior, and by the liberal reformers of the so-called neo-guelphist movement such as **Cesare**

Balbo and **Vincenzo Gioberti.**

CARDUCCI, GIOSUÈ (1835-1907). A poet who led Italian letters back
  to the classical tradition and away from the romanticism of **Giacomo
  Leopardi,** Carducci was born in Lucca (Tuscany) but spent almost
  all of his working life as a professor of rhetoric at **Bologna**
  University. In 1901 Carducci republished his life's work in a six-
  volume edition. The poems that have best withstood the test of time
  were published between 1861 and 1887; the most famous, perhaps,
  is *A Satana* (*Hymn to Satan*, 1862), in which he vaunted atheism and
  rationalism at the expense of all transcendental philosophies, German
  idealism, as much as traditional Catholicism. In 1876 he was elected
  to Parliament as a republican, but never took his seat. In his latter
  years, however, his views became less intransigent and radical, and
  became tinged with nationalism and a sense of Italian cultural
  superiority (he supported, for instance, Italy's colonial wars). By the
  1890s he was a popular national institution. Nominated to the Senate
  in 1900, in 1906 he became the first Italian to win the Nobel prize for
  literature. When he died in Bologna the following year, his funeral
  was attended by huge crowds.

CARLI, GUIDO (1914-1993). Born in Brescia (Lombardy), Carli
  worked for the International Monetary Fund between 1947 and 1950,
  before becoming a member of the controlling committee of the
  European Payments Union. In 1957-1958, he held the post of
  minister for foreign trade. In 1960, Carli was appointed governor of
  the Bank of Italy, a position he held until 1975. In 1976 he became
  president of Confindustria, the association of Italian manufacturers.
    Carli's political career began in 1983 when he was elected as an
  independent, but with the support of the **Democrazia Cristiana** (DC)
  / Christian Democracy Party, to the Senate. He was reelected in 1987.
  Carli served as minister of the treasury in Andreotti's sixth and
  seventh governments, 1989-1992. From this office, he did his best to
  protest against the growing national debt and to argue for the
  austerity that was anathema for the parties of government. Carli,
  however, was just one of three economics ministers and had no
  control over the departments of budget and finance. In effect, his
  reputation and international standing were being used as a fig leaf to
  cover the fiscal and monetary laxity of the parties of government. He
  died in Spoleto in 1993. *See also* Banking.

CARLO ALBERTO (1798-1849). Heir to the throne of Piedmont-Sardinia, Carlo Alberto vacillated between absolutism and liberal constitutionalism for most of his adulthood. He was born in Turin in October 1798 and was forced to take political responsibility at an early age when King Victor Emmanuel I appointed him Regent during the March 1821 insurrection in Piedmont. Carlo Alberto first tried to placate the insurgents by embracing the idea of a constitutional monarchy, but then reneged, joining the camp of his uncle, Carlo Felice, who crushed the insurrection and restored absolute rule. Carlo Alberto, in order to give proof of his faith in absolutism to the Congress of Verona (1822), served and fought as a common soldier in the French army that invaded and defeated the Spanish constitutionalists in 1823.

He became king of Piedmont-Sardinia in 1831. **Mazzini** greeted his accession to the throne by writing Carlo Alberto an open letter appealing to the new king to take the lead in the struggle for national independence. He responded by stamping out Mazzini's *Giovine Italia* movement, a policy that led to a farcical attempted coup by Mazzini's supporters in 1834. In other respects, however, Carlo Alberto was more liberal: he abandoned mercantilism, built railways, ended feudalism, and reorganized the army.

In the mid-1840s, responding to the liberalism of Pope Pius IX, who had instituted notable judicial, social, and political reforms in the Papal states, Carlo Alberto veered toward the creation of a constitutional monarchy. The **Statuto Albertino** adopted in March 1848 acted as the basic law of Italy until the ratification of the Republican constitution in 1948. Piedmont-Sardinia consequently escaped the upheaval of revolution in 1848, which, in Italy, led to popular insurrections against the Austrians in **Bologna** and **Milan**, as well as the creation of a republic in **Venice**.

In April 1848, Carlo Alberto declared war on Austria. The Piedmontese army was defeated at Custoza on July 25, and in August Carlo Alberto was constrained to make peace and allow the Austrians to retake Milan. The war, however, was not over. Incited by a nationalist Parliament and public opinion, Carlo Alberto attacked once more in March 1849. The Piedmontese were again defeated by the Austrians at Novara on March 23, and he abdicated the throne in favor of his son **Victor Emmanuel II**. He left for exile in Portugal, where he died just four months later. *See also* Statuto Albertino.

CARRISTI. The *carro armato* is the Italian description of a tank, whether metal-treaded or rubber-wheeled. In the argot of political journalism, the *carristi* are those who endorsed the use by the Soviet Union of armored vehicles to put down the Hungarian uprisings of October 1956, or who advocated a rigid pro-Soviet line toward Czechoslovak attempts at reform under Dubcek—in short, the most Stalinist elements of the former **Partito Comunista Italiano** (PCI) / Italian Communist Party. The term was also applied to "Kabulisti" (those who applauded Soviet intervention in Afghanistan). **Armando Cossutta,** now one of the leaders of the **Rifondazione Comunista** (PRC) / Communist Refoundation Party, was one of the foremost exponents of this position. Within the PCI, the *carristi* were in the majority in 1956, when the Eighth Congress of the PCI in December 1956 backed the Soviet Union's action despite fierce internal dissension and the walkout of many leading intellectuals, most notably the historian Furio Diaz and Antonio Giolitti, who became budget minister after the **opening to the left** as a member of the **Partito Socialista Italiano** (PSI) / Italian Socialist Party to which he had moved in 1957. In August 1968, by contrast, the PCI officially denounced the Soviet invasion of Prague, calling it "an unjust decision" that could not be "reconciled with the principle that each communist party and every socialist state has a right to autonomy and independence."

CASSA PER IL MEZZOGIORNO (Southern Development Fund). Southern problems of large-scale unemployment, inadequate transport, low rainfall, and poorly organized agricultural marketing have not always been ignored in the North. In fact, between 1947 and 1950, the Confederazione Generale Italiana del Lavoro (CGIL) / Italian General Confederation of Labor had advanced an ambitious plan to enhance employment by massive governmental investment aimed at resolving some of the South's most burdensome difficulties. Infrastructure projects are rarely tempting to private investors whose desire for short-term profits are little satisfied by long-term prospects. Thus land reclamation, rural electrification, and a national building program (housing, hospitals and schools) needed to be focused on the South, but should involve both North and South, trade union members and not, in dealing with long-standing problems. Industrial supporters of the **Democrazia Cristiana** (DC) / Christian Democracy Party saw no particular reason to act on a proposal favored by the left. That attitude changed when southern peasants began to occupy untilled land and forcefully to resist eviction. When the land reform was begun and the *Cassa per il Mezzogiorno* was created in 1950, it was said in **trade union** circles that both were offspring of their plan. Farmworkers in the South had been paid as little as Lit.150 daily (25 cents then) for as few as one hundred days of work available annually. Under the reform, idle farmlands were expropriated and distributed among farmworkers. In areas ridden by malaria for centuries, over two million acres were apportioned among 45,000 families in the first dozen years of the reform. The *Cassa* also paid up to 20 percent of the costs incurred by municipalities that built enterprise zones for small and medium industries in depressed areas of fewer than 200,000 inhabitants.

The *Cassa* was to be accountable to Parliament through a minister without portfolio (elevated to cabinet rank in 1965 as minister for the Mezzogiorno). Projects were to be approved by the Comitato Interministeriale per la Programmazione Economica (CIPE) / Interministerial Committee for Economic Planning giving rise to additional rivalries, tensions, and delays. Moreover, the local consortia, established to coordinate infrastructure investments and land allocations and to administer this largesse, became fiefdoms of local Demochristian faction leaders who were often accused of waste, favoritism, and inflated administrative overhead.

The early *Cassa* was guided by three coherent goals in dealing with the gap between North and South. The first objective was to address the land-tenure problem by a system of expropriation (paying the owners with 30-year interest-bearing bonds) and redistribution among those who actually worked the land. Most continued to reside in their home village.

The second phase was the building of the infrastructure needed not only for industrialization but to enhance the productivity of southern agriculture. This meant all-weather roadways, irrigation, flood control, electrification, modern port facilities, improved railways (most south of **Rome** were single track), quality control in storage and processing facilities, together with such essential social overhead expenditures as schools, clinics, and public housing.

The third stage meant luring the assignees from the mountain villages, which they had shown themselves reluctant to leave. The *Cassa* not only built houses on the assigned plots but made moving into them a condition of retaining assigned land. They also built community centers comprising a church, a meeting hall, a clinic and a pharmacy (not always staffed), and—in most cases—an elementary school. Yet people remained attached to their villages despite the relative absence of amenities of any sort. New, isolated, lowland houses, therefore, often were used as toolsheds by those who trudged daily between hilltop villages and newly acquired land. House occupancy involved signing a contract leaving ownership with the state until mortgage payments were completed over 30 years. Thus, the property could not be sold or transferred. Moreover, the contract created the obligation of forming and joining **cooperatives**.

Efforts were also made to encourage southern entrepreneurs and small industry. Industrial parks were set aside from expropriated lands and subdivision lots sold at subsidized prices with mortgage payments deferred. Local youth with no prospects beyond duplicating their fathers' lives were recruited into industrial training programs paid for by the *Cassa*, **FIAT**, and other private-sector firms, both domestic and foreign. Many theretofore unemployed individuals—both male and female (in a setting where women were still expected to stay at home with the children)—were introduced to factory discipline and to a totally new role for women outside the home. Of the many women who became the family's chief bread-winner, few were willing to continue playing the subordinate role to which tradition had accustomed them.

Locating a few large industries in the South—"cathedrals in the desert" as northern journalists dubbed them—produced cement factories (a necessary initial step for the building trades), oil refineries and petrochemical plants, vastly improved port facilities to ship both imported crude oil and the refined product, fertilizer plants, the Taranto steel mills of *Italsider*, asphalted highways, improved railways and airports, as well as the aforementioned infrastructure in elementary schools and modest housing.

Recent statistics, however, indicate exactly how unsuccessful these efforts have been in closing the North-South gap. Southern Italians enjoy today a far higher standard of living and level of consumption than was conceivable just one generation ago. However, it is equally true that life in the North and Center has improved even more rapidly, thus widening the separation of the country's regions. That conditions might have been worse without the efforts of the Southern Development Fund is not an easily testable proposition. What is clear is that many Southerners continue to feel that life has not been fair to them. In 1992, Italians in north-central Italy averaged $18,169 annual incomes while in the South, it was $10,133, barely over 55 percent of the northern average. Figures published in 1997 show that by 1994, per capita incomes in the 10 richest cities of north-central Italy averaged Lit. 27,200,000 while in the 10 poorest cities of the South the per capita average was Lit. 13,800,000. The former is 40 percent over the national average; the latter, 40 percent below that average. It is too soon to say whether the 1986 devolution of the *Cassa*'s functions to regional and local institutions will have the desired effect. *See also* Cooperatives; Land Reform; Latifondi; Lira; Southern Italy.

CATHOLIC ACTION. *See* Azione Cattolica.

CATHOLICISM. There can be few countries in which the influence of organized religion is as pervasive as Italy, and although Italians have adopted modern patterns of social behavior (the use of contraception, divorce, abortion) disapproved of by the Church, most Italians still describe themselves as practicing Catholics. Almost all children are baptized and confirmed, and the number of non-religious funerals is negligible. This is true even in the "Red," former Communist regions such as Tuscany and Emilia-Romagna. The Church follows "Roman" rites everywhere except **Milan**, where rites initiated by Saint Ambrose are followed, and two small dioceses in Apulia, where the Byzantine rites traditional for the area's Albanian minority are celebrated.

The Church is organized hierarchically, with the Pope, who is also bishop of **Rome**, as the spiritual and effective head of the Church in Italy, as well as of the Church worldwide. Beneath the Pope are nine cardinals (who have the right to vote in the Papal conclave), over 20 archbishops, approximately 250 bishops, and over 40,000 parish priests—approximately one for every 1,500 inhabitants. Nearly 4,000 young Italian men are studying for the priesthood—far fewer than in the early decades of this century, but still higher than in the 1970s and 1980s, when there was an authentic crisis of vocation. In addition, there are more than 125,000 nuns in the various orders. All told, there are about 200,000 "religious figures" in Italy.

The Catholic Church is an active promoter of social and youth associations through the various organizations coordinated by **Azione Cattolica** (ACI) / Catholic Action. More than four million people are members of one Catholic association or another. Seven percent of Italian schoolchildren go to the 1,600 Catholic schools; parish priests provide religious instruction in state schools; nuns are frequently employed in preschool care, nursing, old people's homes and charitable foundations for drug and alcohol addicts. Italians may give eight lire for every Lit. 1,000 that they pay in taxation to help the Church finance its charitable activities. Other religious faiths are growing in strength, however, not least because of immigration from North Africa. There are approximately 300,000 Italian Muslims, and some 35,000 Jews. Protestant churches of all denominations have about 200,000 members. In recent years, Buddhism has excited an increasing interest among young Italians. *See also* Azione Cattolica; Lateran Pacts; Lira; Papacy.

CATTANEO, CARLO (1801-1869). Milanese by birth, Carlo Cattaneo was both an independent-minded scholar and a political activist of great integrity. Between 1835 and 1844 he edited *Il Politecnico*, a review specializing in the scientific analysis of social questions, and achieved European-wide fame for his pioneering work in the social sciences. Although he had never participated in any of the secret revolutionary societies, he emerged as one of the leaders of the revolt against Austrian rule in **Milan** in 1848. When the Austrians defeated Piedmont-Sardinia at Custoza, he was obliged to flee to Paris. There, he wrote, in French, *L'insurrection de Milan en 1848* (*The Milan Insurrection of 1848*), a book that was sternly critical of King **Carlo Alberto**'s conduct of the war.

Cattaneo, in fact, was an unabashed republican, federalist, and democrat who was deeply suspicious of the unification of Italy as a constitutional monarchy. He was opposed to Piedmontese annexation of **Sicily** and **Naples** in 1861 (breaking with **Giuseppe Garibaldi** over this issue), and in 1867, on being elected to Parliament, he refused to swear an oath of loyalty to the crown and was thus unable to take part in the assembly's work. He spent most of his last years at Castagnola, near Lugano, as a somewhat disdainful critic of the new Italian state. For five years, 1859-1864, he brought out a second series of *Il Politecnico*. He died in Castagnola in 1869. In recent years, Cattaneo's life and work have enjoyed a revival: Italy's foremost institute of research in the social sciences is named after him, and the **Lega Nord** claims him as a distinguished pioneer of federalist doctrine in Italy.

CAVALLOTTI, FELICE (1842-1898). A picturesque figure much given to duels with his political rivals, Felice Cavallotti nevertheless played an important political role in liberal Italy. A radical, a democrat, and a republican, Cavallotti took part in **Giuseppe**

Garibaldi's expedition to **Sicily** in 1860 when he was barely an adolescent. After a career as a poet, playwright, and editor—in his native **Milan**— of the leading radical daily of the time, *Il Gazzettino rosa* (*The Pink Gazzette*), he entered Parliament in 1873 and soon became one of the leading critics of **Agostino Depretis**' reluctance to carry out social reforms. In 1879, he and Garibaldi founded the *Lega della democrazia* / League for Democracy. As leader of that body, he fought a fruitless battle for universal male suffrage, repression of the clergy, decentralization of the state administration, and improvements in public hygiene (he worked as a volunteer in **Naples** in 1884 when the city was stricken by cholera). He was a prominent figure in the **irredentist** movement and took an active role in the protests against Austrian rule in **Trieste** and, more generally, was strongly critical of the Italian government's link with Germany and Austria in the **Triple Alliance.** In 1886, he became leader of the radical party in Parliament. By then, he was Garibaldi's heir apparent in the public imagination, and campaigned against political corruption and took an active part in the parliamentary investigation into the **Banca Romana** scandal. In June 1895, in the wake of the scandal, he published an open letter addressed to "the honest people of all parties" that contained a richly documented account of the corruption of the then prime minister, **Francesco Crispi**. Rather than debate Cavallotti's accusations in the Chamber of Deputies, Crispi and his supporters voted to close Parliament for six months.

In the 1890s, Cavallotti and the Radicals united with the Republicans to press for social reforms of a more explicitly socialist character, but Cavallotti never quite arrived at an open endorsement of the nascent workers' movement. Cavallotti was killed in his 32nd duel in 1898 by a fellow parliamentary deputy, Ferruccio Macola.

CAVOUR, CAMILLO BENSO DI (1810-1861).The younger son of a noble family from **Turin**, Cavour entered politics by way of journalism. In 1847, he founded *Il Risorgimento*, a liberal journal that pressed for the establishment of a constitutional monarchy. Philosophically, Cavour was influenced by English utilitarianism, especially Bentham, and the classical economists (Adam Smith, David Riccardo, John Stuart Mill). But an even greater influence was the French philosopher and statesman Alexis de Tocqueville. Like de Tocqueville, Cavour was an aristocratic liberal, convinced of the need for wider political participation, but acutely aware of the dangers of the coming democratic age.

Cavour favored Piedmontese intervention in the Lombardy uprising against Austrian rule in 1848, and in 1849 was elected to the first constitutionally elected Parliament in Turin. His ministerial career began almost immediately; long interested in modern techniques of scientific farming, he became minister for agriculture in 1850. He was promoted to the finance ministry the following year. Cavour became prime minister in 1852. His sojourn in office was characterized by the far-reaching modernization of the Piedmontese economy and society. Faithful to his liberal principles, Cavour slashed tariffs and encouraged foreign investment, multiplying annual exports to the rest of Europe fourfold by the end of the 1850s, although the benefits of this increased economic activity went mostly to the propertied classes, and not to the urban poor. At the cost of perilously indebting the state, Cavour also initiated many public works to raise the standard of Piedmontese infrastructure to European levels, and modernized the organizational structure and military preparedness of the army.

Cavour's spell as prime minister was also characterized by an attack on the privileges of the church. In part to placate the anti-clerical left who were supporting him in Parliament, Cavour introduced, in 1855, a law abolishing the contemplative orders of monks (i.e., those who did not fulfill a teaching function or perform good works). The passage of the *legge sui frati* was one of the most strenuous challenges to Cavour's authority of his entire ministry, and thereafter he followed a more conciliatory policy toward the church, proclaiming his belief in a "free church in a free state."

Cavour's foreign policy initially aimed less at Italian unification than extending Piedmont-Sardinia's authority over the whole of northern Italy. The failure of the Piedmontese army to drive Austria out of the north in 1848-1849, however, had convinced Cavour that Piedmont-Sardinia would only be able to expand its territorial possessions in Italy with the help of Britain and France. To ingratiate Piedmont with the two liberal European powers, Cavour agreed to send a corps of Piedmontese soldiers to the Crimea in 1854, a move that secured him no concrete territorial advantage, but did enable him to raise the Italian question, in the teeth of fervent Austrian opposition, at the subsequent Paris peace conference in February-March 1856. Cavour's chosen ally was Napoleon III of France, against whom an assassination attempt was made by an Italian nationalist in January 1858. Cavour used the attack as a means of emphasizing the relative moderation of the Kingdom of

Piedmont-Sardinia, and in July 1858, he signed the pact of Plombières with Napoleon. By this agreement, Cavour ceded Nice and the Savoy to France and conceded that southern Italy and the central Italian states would be placed under the control of rulers favorable to France in exchange for a French guarantee of military assistance in the event of an Austrian war on Piedmont-Sardinia. Piedmont would add Lombardy and Venetia to its possessions after a victorious war.

This cynical deal was nullified by events once Austria had declared war on Piedmont in April 1859. Pro-Piedmontese insurrections broke out in Tuscany, Modena, and the Papal states (Cavour's agents had been at work), and Napoleon, seeing his own hopes of territorial gains in Italy evaporating, did his best to repair the damage by abandoning the war against Austria, and reneging on the pact of Plombières. The peace of Villafranca (July 1859) left Austria still in command of Venetia, and Cavour, who was no favorite of **King Victor Emmanuel II**, was forced to resign. Moody by nature, Cavour contemplated suicide after this disaster for his strategy.

He was out of office for a mere six months. The duchies of central Italy were determined to unify with Piedmont, and Cavour was called back to office to negotiate their annexation with Napoleon III. While Cavour was dexterously completing this task, radical nationalists, led by **Giuseppe Garibaldi**, were contemplating less diplomatic methods of completing Italian unification. Cavour was initially skeptical of Garibaldi's expedition to **Sicily** in the spring of 1860, but once the redshirts had seized power in **Palermo** and crossed into **southern Italy**, Cavour was quick both to take advantage of the collapse of the Kingdom of the Two Sicilies and to prevent the contagion of nationalist and democratic ideas from spreading. Piedmontese troops invaded the Papal states in September 1860, and at Teano on October 26, 1860, Garibaldi surrendered his conquests to the Piedmontese throne. Cavour's subtle realpolitik had been successful beyond his own intentions: Piedmont had effectively digested most of the rest of Italy, with the consent of the great European powers.

Cavour became the first prime minister of the Kingdom of Italy in March 1861. In June 1861, years of overeating and excessive drinking caught up with the Piedmontese statesman, and he died without warning at the still relatively young age of 51. Italy was left to face the challenge of completing its reunification without the services of the one nineteenth-century Italian statesman of comparable stature to Bismarck, Disraeli, or Metternich. *See also* Giuseppe Garibaldi; Monarchy; Risorgimento.

CENTRAL ITALY. The core of central Italy is Tuscany, with its spectacular scenery and the famous historical centers of Florence (the region's largest city), Pisa, Volterra (a major center of the pre-Roman Etrurians), and Siena. The other regions are Umbria (whose largest cities are the splendid cathedral hill towns of Assisi, Orvieto, Perugia, and Urbino—all damaged in the **earthquake** of 1997), the Marches (Pesaro, Ancona), the northernmost part of Lazio, and the Abruzzi, whose largest cities are Aquila and Pescara. The independent republic of San Marino is also to be found between Umbria and Romagna. In addition to tourism, the region boasts a flourishing wine industry (Chianti and Montepulciano) and substantial numbers of small enterprises specializing in high-quality craft products. The region does not have the same industrial dynamism that characterizes Venetia, Lombardy, or Emilia-Romagna, however, and incomes per head, while up to the European average, are less high than in northern Italy.

Politically, the area is mostly "Red." Tuscany and Umbria in particular are bastions of the **Partito Democratico della Sinistra** (PDS) / Democratic Party of the Left and were formerly strongholds of the **Partito Comunista Italiano** (PCI) / Italian Communist Party. The Abruzzi, by contrast, was a former fiefdom of the **Democrazia Cristiana** (DC) / Christian Democracy Party, and in 1992 the entire regional government was arrested and charged with looting development funds sent to the area by the **European Union.**

The region's terrain is dominated by the Apennines mountain chain, whose highest point is Gran Sasso (Abruzzi) at 2,914 meters (9,565 feet), site of the fortress in which **Mussolini** was briefly imprisoned in 1943. Both the Adriatic and the Tyrrhenian coastline attract tourists from all over the world.

CHRISTIAN DEMOCRACY. *See* Democrazia Cristiana.

CIAMPI, CARLO AZEGLIO (1920-). A lifelong public servant, the Tuscan Ciampi became governor of the Bank of Italy in 1979, an appointment that enabled him to warn publicly against the budgetary irresponsibility of the **Craxi** and **Andreotti** governments of the 1980s. In April 1993, following the collapse of the **Amato**

government, Ciampi was President **Oscar Luigi Scalfaro**'s choice to head an interim administration that would pass a new electoral law and restore calm and international confidence.

The first non-parliamentarian ever to be made premier, Ciampi formed a government that included several former communists in ministerial posts, as well as members of the **Democrazia Cristiana** (DC) / Christian Democracy Party and **Partito Socialista Italiano** (PSI) / Italian Socialist Party who had been untainted by the scandals that had brought the **Amato** administration down. This government fell apart even before its ministers had had the chance to take the oath of office when the refusal of the Chamber of Deputies to allow a judicial investigation into the private affairs of Bettino Craxi led to a walk-out by the **Partito Democratico della Sinistra** (PDS) / Democratic Party of the Left. Ciampi replaced the PDS's nominees with non-partisan technocrats and governed as ably as the circumstances permitted until the election of March 1994.

In 1995, he became president of the European Commission's advisory group on competitiveness, but he has since been recalled to politics by **Romano Prodi**. In May 1996, he was made the treasury and budget minister in the new center-left administration. He follows a tight money policy aimed at shrinking Italy's public deficit before the introduction of new European currency in the **European Union** in 1999. *See also* Maastricht, Treaty of.

CIANO, GALEAZZO (1903-1944). Son of one of **Mussolini**'s intimate advisors, Galeazzo Ciano married Edda, only daughter of the Duce and his favorite child. His fortunes in party and government circles quickly rose. By 1936, he was made a count as well as foreign secretary, a post that he retained until February 1943. In some interpretations, while the war in **Abyssinia** was meant to assuage the wounds remaining from Italy's 1896 humiliation at Adua, the "crusade" in Spain to assist Franco was desired by Count Ciano and his circle of younger fascists similarly to prove their mettle.

In the Grand Council meeting of July 25, 1943, Ciano was among those supporting the **Grandi** resolution to put the armed forces under royal control thereby ending Mussolini's role. Significantly, neither the police nor the militia intervened to prevent this *colpo di mano,* and fascism's founder was imprisoned at Gran Sassò. After Mussolini's liberation by German paratroopers and subsequent installation at **Salò,** the Duce had Ciano and a dozen others arrested, tried, and executed by a fascist firing squad prompting Winston Churchill's comment that his admiration for Mussolini had grown the moment that "he had his son-in-law shot." Perhaps Ciano's major contribution to posterity was the diary that he kept beginning with 1936. Parts had been secreted away by Edda who made them available to publishers after the war. Their account of Ciano's steadily growing doubts about Mussolini's mental stability repay scrutiny. *See also* Abyssinia; Fascism.

CINEMA. Few countries can boast a cinematic history as rich as Italy's. The first kinetographs appeared at the end of the nineteenth century, and techniques developed rapidly: by the eve of **World War I** director Giovanni Pastrone was producing such innovative epics as *Cabiria* (1914) and the *Gli ultimi giorni di Pompeii* (*The Last Days of Pompeii*, 1913), which won a worldwide public and are still regarded as masterpieces of the early cinema. In the 1920s and 1930s, the Italians struggled to match Hollywood as the big-budget movies made possible by the American film industry's superior financing made inroads into the Italian domestic market. The number of domestic films distributed in Italy dropped from over 200 in 1920 to less than a dozen a year by the end of the decade.

This decline had a political dimension: in **Mussolini**'s Italy, the domination of foreign films was seen both as a symptom of the failure of fascist policies of economic autarky and a relatively uncontrolled source of information about the rest of the world. Consequently, film production was centralized in 1935 in a single government-owned company, and the Italian government built "Hollywood on the Tiber"—the *Cinecittà* film complex near **Rome**. Influential film magazines such as *Nero e Bianco* (*Black and White*) and *Cinema* (the latter edited by Mussolini's son, Vittorio) were started. By 1942, nearly 100 films were being produced every year. While many of these films were propagandistic in tone, several were outstanding works of art. **Alessandro Blasetti**'s ambiguous fairytale *La corona di ferro* (*The Iron Crown*, 1941) and the romantic comedies of Mario Camerini were highly successful in technical, artistic and box office terms. Even some of the propaganda movies—Blasetti's *La vecchia guardia* (*The Old Guard*, 1935), Augusto Bianco's haunting *Lo squadrone bianco* (*The White Squadron*, 1936)—reached high artistic levels.

After the war, neo-realist and post-realist directors such as **Roberto Rossellini, Luchino Visconti, Vittorio De Sica,** and **Michelangelo Antonioni** made films hailed by critics everywhere.

Yet the average Italian did not watch their grimly beautiful depictions of working-class and peasant life. In the 1950s and 1960s Italians watched instead La Commedia all'Italiana and a whole new generation of actors, many of whom (Claudia Cardinale, Sophia Loren, Gina Lollobrigida, Vittorio Gassman, Marcello Mastroianni, Ugo Tognazzi) went on to achieve fame outside Italy. They also watched that unique Italian invention, the "spaghetti western" of **Sergio Leone** and, by the early 1970s, experimented with pornography in films.

The relentless competition provided by Hollywood has arguably been resisted more successfully in Italy than elsewhere in Europe except France, although American films do dominate the box office. Hit comedies still tend to star Italian actors and have Italian settings. Moreover, in the 1980s and 1990s a new wave of Italian directors has been making watchable, artistically successful films. Some of these films have even been successfully exported to the United States—Giuseppe Tornatore's *Cinema paradiso* (*Paradise Cinema*, 1991) and the Anglo-Italian coproduction *Il postino* (*The Postman*, 1995) being particularly good examples. The Italian cinema's resilience should not surprise anyone; there is a deep love for the cinema and its greatest artists in Italy. When the director **Federico Fellini** died in November 1993, there were several days of what amounted to unofficial national mourning. A similar emotional outpouring greeted the death, in December 1996, of Marcello Mastroianni.

COBAS. These *Comitati di Base* / Committees of the Base began as organizers of "wildcat" protests—particularly among highly skilled unionists (teachers, airline pilots, railway locomotive engineers) —against the leveling of wages achieved by trade-union negotiators. The *appiattimento* (flattening out) of incomes was the result of seeking to raise the earnings of those at the lowest levels and was therefore abhorrent to those whose skills were, in their view, inadequately rewarded and whose incentives for accepting greater supervisory responsibilities were undercut by the perceived meagerness of income increments.

Beginning in the 1980s, the COBAS initiated work stoppages to protest settlements reached by union federation negotiators. They insisted that the years of training and/or formal education needed for their work entitled them to a larger share of any increments. To trade unionists, the COBAS's position perfectly illustrates "corporativism," that is, the readiness of the members of a particular economic sector to use their numerical strength and/or strategic position to seek advantages for their own category without regard to the general interests of the working class or of the society as a whole. The roots of the COBAS, however, are also to be found in the Confederazione Generale Italiana del Lavoro (CGIL) / Italian General Labor Confederation of the late 1960s. Young workers not entirely acculturated to trade-union discipline sometimes regarded union moderation in negotiations as a betrayal. At the Pirelli tire plant in 1969, a compromise settlement resulted in the organization of a *Comitato Unitario di Base* (CUB) / United Base Committee. This workers' council attracted adherents from all skill levels by denouncing both the CGIL and the **Partito Comunista Italiano** (PCI) / Italian Communist Party as "soft on management." One of their demands was that wage differentials should be reduced. Thus began the *appiattimento* now under attack from the CUB's spiritual heirs.

Those who suffer inconvenience or deprivation from "wildcat" work stoppages are impatient with the COBAS. By breaking union discipline, COBAS members are anathema not only to other union members but also to management representatives who find a negotiated settlement rendered futile by these wholly autonomous groups. Their existence, moreover, shows union leaders the risks inherent in allowing too great a gap to form between themselves and rank-and-file members.

COLOMBO, EMILIO (1920-). Born in the deep south of Potenza in Basilicata, Colombo went from militance in **Azione Cattolica** to candidacy in the **Democrazia Cristiana** (DC) / Christian Democracy Party while still in his twenties. He was one of the youngest delegates to the **Constituent Assembly**. On election to the **Parliament** on the DC list, he served in the first governments of **De Gasperi** as undersecretary for agriculture. He served in the same role for **Pella**, **Fanfani** and **Scelba** in their cabinets. In the first **Segni** government, he was assigned the Ministry of Agriculture and Forests, a post that he retained in the **Zoli** government.

In Fanfani's first government, he was minister of foreign trade. He continued in that post in the governments of **Antonio Segni**, **Fernando Tambroni**, and Fanfani II and IV while becoming a member of the DC National Council. He became minister of the treasury in the **Leone** I, II governments and played the same part in

Moro I, II, and III and in **Rumor**'s first cabinet. He was to hold the treasury post longer than anyone in the history of the republic. For two years—1970-1972—he was president of the Council of Ministers. As minister for United Nations relations in **Andreotti** I, he continued serving in others' cabinets including those of Rumor IV and V, as well as Moro IV. In addition to constant reelection from Potenza-Matera, he was elected to the European Parliament in 1976, a body that he eventually served as president. He is the third Italian politician (after De Gasperi and Segni) to be given the Charlemagne award by the European Parliament for his contributions to European integration.

His service as foreign minister in the government of **Arnaldo Forlani** led to his appointment to the same post in **Spadolini** I and II and in Fanfani V. Then he was put in charge of the Budget Ministry in the government of the late **Giovanni Goria**. After Vincenzo Scotti's resignation as foreign minister in the **Amato** government, Colombo returned to that post.

His priestlike demeanor in no way contradicts his astute use of funds destined for the transformation of the South to the advantage of the local supporters of that DC faction of which he was *capocorrente* or "head." Municipal factional leaders who displayed the requisite loyalties could be assured that resources aplenty would come to them. When funds for southern development became inadequate to the South's needs, Colombo joined other southern DC leaders to persuade the cabinet, in 1957, to ordain that thereafter, 40 percent of total new state investment and 60 percent of its industrial plant would be earmarked for the South. Colombo's place in the *doroteo* faction of the national DC assured the needed support for these machinations. *See also* Cassa per il Mezzogiorno; Southern Italy.

COMITATI DI LIBERAZIONE NAZIONALE (CLN). National Liberation Committees. After the fall of **Mussolini** in 1943, the major political parties formed (in the city of Bari) Committees of National Liberation as agreed on by representatives of the **Partito d'Azione** (PdA) / Action Party, the **Democrazia Cristiana** (DC) / Christian Democrats, the **Partito Liberale Italiano** (PLI) / Italian Liberal Party, the followers of **Ivanoe Bonomi**, and the two Marxist parties, the **Partito Socialista Italiano** (PSI) / Italian Socialist Party and the **Partito Comunista Italiano** (PCI) / Italian Communist Party. King **Victor Emmanuel III** and Marshal **Badoglio** shared the view that all pre-war political parties should be excluded from post-war political life. The initial position of the various regional CLNs was that the king should abdicate and that they should be at the core of a new government. But to the surprise of all, when **Palmiro Togliatti** returned from the USSR (spring 1944), he insisted—in the svolta di Salerno (the Salerno turnabout)—on postponing the institutional question until after the war. In the meantime, his party was ready to cooperate with and even take part in a transitional government under **Badoglio**. Defeating the forces of Germany and their fascist allies was what mattered; political questions would be sorted out after the fighting had been brought to a satisfactory conclusion.

In June 1944, the king, without abdicating, turned over his powers to Crown Prince Umberto, styling him Lieutenant-General of the Realm. Badoglio resigned and **Ivanoe Bonomi** formed a cabinet of all six CLN parties. In the last year of the war, Allied forces continually moved northward against determined German resistance. Partisan units (especially the Comitato di Liberazione Nazionale-Alt Italia [CLN-AI] / CLN for Northern Italy), often led by former Italian army officers, took over whole towns in the Po Valley and the Lombard Plains, becoming the force behind the post-war talk of a "wind from the north," which was to produce a second **Risorgimento**, purifying the South which had been liberated by foreign armies while the North had liberated itself. (The wind blew somewhat erratically, largely because of tensions among partisan rivals. The *Fiamme Verdi* partisan division of Brescia was headed and manned by **Azione Cattolica** militants who were as hostile to the left partisans as to the Germans.) The partisans operated under the contradictory restraints imposed by Allied differences: for example, British policy favored the monarchy while U.S. policy seemed obsessive in its diffidence concerning the role of the organized left.

The CLN thus faced two enemies: the *Wehrmacht* on the one hand and the Allies on the other. In October 1944, in what ex-partisans continue to insist was a deliberate attempt to expose them to German wrath, they were first given coded radio instructions that the moment had come for them to mount an offensive openly. Those instructions were then countermanded and they were told to hold back until the spring. Since many units had thereby exposed themselves, German retribution was swift and devastating. The Allied command had apparently agreed that the CLN should not function as a co-belligerent Italian army but should act as saboteurs behind the lines and be prevented from laying the groundwork for too great a role or from becoming a genuinely revolutionary armed force.

Even after the German surrender in May 1945, the Allied decision to disarm the partisans was seen as confirmation of the suspicions held by many former *partigiani:* the Allies were to be the only armed force in Italy and the new Italian state was not to be of the National Liberation Committees. *See also* Monarchy.

COMITATO DI LIBERAZIONE NAZIONALE—ALTA ITALIA (CLNAI). *See* Comitati di Liberazione Nazionale.

COMMUNIST PARTY (PCI). *See* Partito Comunista Italiano.

COMMUNIST REFOUNDATION. *See* Partito di Rifondazione Comunista.

COMPROMESSO STORICO. The genesis of the *compromesso storico* (historic compromise) was three articles published by **Enrico Berlinguer** in *Rinascita* (*Rebirth*), weekly journal of political strategy and theory of the **Partito Comunista Italiano** (PCI) / Italian Communist Party in October 1973. Berlinguer argued that the PCI, which, at that moment, hoped to overtake the **Democrazia Cristiana** (DC) / Christian Democracy Party and become Italy's largest party, should avoid above all else the civil disorders and American intervention that the turmoil of the Allende experiment had provoked in Chile. He defined a program that would spur social change without antagonizing "vast strata of the middle-classes" or undercutting the efficiency of the economy. Berlinguer recommended that the party seek out "every possible convergence and understanding among popular forces" by working toward the transformation of Italian society in collaboration with the DC and the **Partito Socialista Italiano** (PSI) / Italian Socialist Party—a grand coalition of political forces that together would have the support of 75-80 percent of the electorate. The "left alternative" of a PCI-PSI coalition, Berlinguer argued, would have had the effect "of splitting the popular masses, liquidating *de facto* our encounter with Catholic [social] forces, moving the DC toward the right, thus isolating and defeating the left, and therefore, in the final analysis, bringing about the defeat of the cause of democracy and its development in our country."

There were four main implications of Berlinguer's argument. He was rejecting "proletarian internationalism"and the demand that national communist parties should accept subordination to the Soviet party. Each country had to find its own path to socialism. Second, his proposals were a rejection, in advanced industrial countries at any rate, of the doctrinal notion of a "dictatorship of the proletariat." Third, they embodied a perception of the class struggle as resolvable by a broadening of the consensus rather than by revolution. And finally, they implied acceptance of economic, ideological, and social pluralism as a prerequisite to building a socialist democracy based on an interclass consensus wide enough to overwhelm any opposition. By implication, this doctrinal change of course meant persuading non-Marxist Catholics and diffident, anti-communist socialists to accept a common program without, at the same time, alienating the communist mass membership.

Berlinguer's ideological innovations underpinned the PCI's decision to give its parliamentary support to the "government of national solidarity" formed by **Giulio Andreotti** after the 1976 general elections. They were also responsible for the February 1978 decision by the leaders of the principal **trade unions** to advocate an unpopular program of wage restraint, increased profitability, and increased returns on investments in order to attack unemployment, inflation, and the southern question. This decision may well have saved Italian big business from collapse. Eventually, however, the party's position opened such a gap between the PCI leadership and the union leaders on the one hand and the rank and file on the other that the PCI had to withdraw its benevolent support of the **Andreotti** government, leading to the elections of June 1979, in which the PCI's support fell back from its 1976 high.

The *compromesso storico* thus ended in political failure. Ideologically, however, Berlinguer had worked a change that outlasted his death in 1984. The PCI had determined that it intended to stabilize Italian capitalism, and render it more efficient and socially just, rather than fight it tooth and claw. This new-found emphasis on gradual change, of course, was resisted by many party members—particularly the older Stalinists—for they recognized that it meant a definitive abandonment of the party's traditional Leninist goals. *See also* Enrico Berlinguer; Armando Cossutta; Partito Comunista Italiano; Pietro Ingrao.

CONCORDAT. *See* Lateran Pacts.

CONFINO. This is one of several ways of dealing with those guilty of political or conspiratorial offenses. Introduced in the *Testo Unico di*

Pubblica Sicurezza (TUPS) in 1931, the Consolidated Text of the Public Security Law sets out that a person convicted of "conspiracy to commit a crime" (*associazione a delinquere*) or of acts compromising the security of the state may, as an alternative to incarceration, be ordered to leave his own city or town to take up residence in an assigned locality (*residenza obbligata)* where he would be free to move about, seek employment, and generally live a normal life so long as he reported in person to the local *Carabinieri* at specified intervals.

Carlo Levi described his experience of forced residence in *Cristo si è fermato a Eboli (Christ Stopped at Eboli).* The purpose was—and remains—to deprive the miscreant of the network of friends and allies who made him effective. The result has often been to see his efforts bent toward creating a new network in his new locale, thus spreading the influence of any organization of which he was a part. This practice is still in use today particularly for those accused of associating with known *mafiosi.* Especially under **fascism**, however, use was also made of "internal exile" or obligatory residence under **police** supervision in a place so remote and often so little populated as to be a virtual free-range prison. One was sent "to the border" or *al confine,* the very edge of the nation. Lipari and other islands acquired some fame because of the famous leaders of the left who escaped under most dramatic conditions—for example, Nenni, Rosselli, Turati.

A milder variant found in all prefectural states in dealing with particularly bothersome state employees and appointees is the assignment to duties, even with a promotion to sweeten the pill, to unpopular or hazardous sites. Aspiring to assignment in **Rome**, the civil servant, academic, railway worker, prefect, or magistrate might find exceptional zeal (e.g., in pursuit of the mafia) rewarded by transfer to Basilicata or **Sardinia.**

CONSOCIATIONALISM. At war's end, the **Democrazia Cristiana** (DC) / Christian Democracy Party leader **De Gasperi** and the secretary of the **Partito Comunista Italiano** (PCI) / Italian Communist Party, **Palmiro Togliatti,** used shared **patronage,** clientelism, and *lottizzazione*—or "parceling out" of government appointments—to prop up one another's maintenance of the system, illustrating what political scientists came to call "consociationalism."

This device allegedly helped to make a badly divided Italian polity manageable. In Italy's **Parliament**, it has meant the association of the minority (read, parties of the left, especially the former PCI) with governmental decisions and appointments. In a setting in which state holding companies administer banks, insurance firms, social security systems, subsidies, pension funds, communications, television and radio broadcasting, rail and other transport, as well as veterans' affairs and other public agencies, appointments are in the hands of the government, which ensures that responsibilities are distributed among parties and among factions within parties in such a way as to give all players a stake in perpetuating the status quo. The possibilities for corruption are apparent, but the stability engendered is important to the social order, much like its reviled antecedent, *trasformismo.*

Seating on legislative committees is also dealt with in this way as are the choice of presidents of the Chamber of Deputies and of the Senate, normally made from opposition parties' leadership. Before the political changes of 1992, the most recent speaker was **Nilde Iotti**. Her counterpart in the Senate was **Giorgio Napolitano**. Both were from the PCI.

When judicial investigations began to probe alleged corruption among those who shared power, everything associated with the governing DC and the **Partito Socialist Italiano** (PSI) / Italian Socialist Party was open to question, including consociationalism. Because it denied to opposition parties much of the incentive to censure the majority, the system was blamed for failing to hold the ruling coalition accountable. Beneficiaries of a system are rarely its most determined critics.

Electoral reforms and the elections of 1992, therefore, were seen as a victory over a device that had served to ward off some of the consequences of the realities of Italian political life. Some observers argue that the system functioned well for Italy and made it possible for industry to create wealth and survive "without governing." Others, Italian and foreign, have hailed the end of consociationalism as a deliverance. Clearly, as a phenomenon peculiar to Italy in extent, the system had outlived its welcome. *Stabilizing* it may have been, but it was simultaneously corrupting and left governments paralyzed in the face of the need for fiscal restraint and reform. It remains to be seen whether this characteristic of post-war practice will be continued. *See also* Patronage.

CONSTITUENT ASSEMBLY. When **World War II** ended, the form of government and the role of the **monarchy** itself were major issues to be decided by the Italian people. The resolution of these questions was left to the Constituent Assembly elected on June 2, 1946. Simultaneously, Italy's voting public—including, for the first time, women—was asked to choose the assembly's members and to decide on the question of whether or not to retain the monarchy. The delegates chosen included 207 (35.2 percent of the vote) for the **Democrazia Cristiana** (DC) / Christian Democracy Party; 115 seats (20.7 percent) for the left parties—Partito Socialista Italiano d'Unità Proletaria (PSIUP) / Italian Socialist Party of Proletarian Unity; and for the **Partito Comunista Italiano** (PCI) / Italian Communist Party—104 seats (19 percent); for the **Partito Liberale Italiano** (PLI) / Italian Liberal Party, 41 seats (6.8 percent). The newly formed Uomo Qualunque (UQ) / Common Man's Movement received 30 seats (5.3 percent); the **Partito Repubblicano Italiano** (PRI) / Italian Republican Party, 24 seats (4.4 percent); and the Partito Nazionale Monarchico (PNM) / National Monarchist Party, 16 seats (2.8 percent). Finally, the **Partito d'Azione** (PdA) / Action Party won 7 seats (1.5 percent).

The delegates representing these parties presented Italy with a parliamentary constitution with provisions for a Constitutional Court and for referenda (used most conspicuously for divorce, abortion, and electoral reform). It was to come into effect on January 1, 1948. The chief architects were, in fact, the DC and the PCI, each led by a person reluctant to see a strong executive branch that might, conceivably, fall into the hands of the other: hence the embrace of assemblyism and of **consociationalism**. Many of the delegates are found in this dictionary and are still active in Italian political life: **Giulio Andreotti, Emilio Colombo, Amintore Fanfani, Nilde Iotti,** and **Oscar Luigi Scalfaro**, president of the republic. Others who were part of the Constituent Assembly who are found in this dictionary but deceased are **Ivanoe Bonomi, Piero Calamandrei, Alcide De Gasperi, Guido Gonella, Giovani Gronchi, Luigi Longo, Alessandro Pertini,** and **Palmiro Togliatti.**

At the end of June 1946, the Constituent Assembly elected Enrico De Nicola provisional head of the Italian Republic. Alcide De Gasperi, who was the leader of the largest of the parties, was asked to form a government that included members of the DC, the PCI, and the PRI. *See also* Comitati di Liberazione Nazionale; Constitution of 1948; Monarchy.

CONSTITUTION OF 1948. At the end of **World War II**, deep divisions separated Italy's avowedly revolutionary left from a largely discredited right; her North, which had liberated itself, from a South that had been liberated by foreign armies. Moreover, partisan warfare in the North had left armed bands under, at most, the loose authority of political parties.

The first governments headed by **Ivanoe Bonomi,** then **Ferruccio Parri,** yielded to an almost uninterrupted succession of governments headed by the leaders of the **Democrazia Cristiana** (DC) / Christian Democracy Party—beginning with **Alcide De Gasperi.** DC governments were to continue for nearly 50 years.

The willingness of **Palmiro Togliatti,** secretary of the **Partito Comunista Italiano** (PCI) / Italian Communist Party, to accept the **Lateran Pacts** as part of the Constitution can be explained by examining those provisions that served the chief constituency of the PCI, that is, Italian workers. Articles 1 and 35 particularly recognize the role of the working class in Italy; the right to work (Arts. 4 and 36) and the corresponding *duty* to work. An egalitarian principle protective of workers (Art. 3) and the right to strike are defined and protected (Arts. 39, 40) as are the margins of industrial democracy (Art. 46). Concentrations of economic power are limited (Arts. 41, 42) while emphasis is put on the need for land reform (Art. 43). Finally, legal parameters of **cooperatives** are set out in Article 45.

Togliatti was convinced that the social transformation of Italy would be brought about incrementally through the electoral strength of the PCI and its allies. A workers' republic by parliamentary means did not seem entirely out of the question.

There are ways in which the Italian Constitution is exceptional: for example, as a matter of right, a defense counsel at every level of Italian justice (Art. 24) was ensured well in advance of the establishment of a similar right in the United States in the case of *Gideon* v. *Wainwright.*

Not only is **education** "obligatory and free," but even those who lack financial means "have a right to reach the highest possible level of studies" (Art. 34). Every worker is entitled to a pay reflective of the "quality and quantity" of his or her work but in any case, "adequate to ensure for himself and his family a free and dignified existence." He/she is also entitled to a day off per week, a right that may not be renounced (Art. 36). Female workers have "the same rights and, at the same job, the same pay as the male worker" (Art. 37). Moreover, working conditions must allow that the woman's "essential familial function be fulfilled and assure to the mother and child special and adequate protection."

Regarding the thorny question of extradition, the Italian Constitution states that an Italian citizen may be extradited only in conformity with international agreements and never in cases involving "political crimes" (Art. 26).

The deference to international norms is clear, too, in Article 11, which reads, in its entirety:

> Italy repudiates war as an instrument which offends the freedom of other peoples and as a means to resolve international controversies; it agrees, on a par with other states, to the limitations of sovereignty necessary to sustain a legal regime which will ensure peace and justice among nations; promotes and favors international organizations working toward that end.

Paramilitary groups and private armies of the sort that preceded **fascism** are expressly prohibited with exemplary clarity. "Secret associations are prohibited as are those which pursue . . . political ends by means of organizations of a military character" (Art. 18). The death penalty, too, is permitted only "in the cases covered by military justice in time of war" (Art. 27).

Unfortunately, many of these constitutional provisions have waited 50 years for **Parliament** to pass the necessary enabling legislation. *See also* Monarchy; Parliament.

COOPERATIVES. Italian cooperatives trace their origins to the Mutual Aid Societies formed by rural workers seeking unity of action to get the highest prices for the labor they sold and lower prices for what they bought. By 1886, the *Lega delle Cooperative* (League of Cooperatives) was formed. It proved the basis for the **Partito Socialista Italiano** (PSI) / Italian Socialist Party. Undermined by the fascist regime, cooperatives were restored by the **Comitati di Liberazione Nazionale** (CLN) / National Liberation Committees. In the negotiations that culminated in a new republican **Constitution of 1948**, they were given—in Article 45—specific standing.

A half-century later, over 100,000 cooperatives with nearly eight million members have an annual turnover in excess of Lit. 47 trillion ($31 billion). Until the demise of the **Democrazia Cristiana** (DC) / Christian Democracy Party and the PSI, the largest federations of cooperatives were closely affiliated with political parties: the *Lega* with the **Partito Comunista Italiano** (PCI) / Italian Communist Party and the PSI; the *Confcoop* (Cooperative Confederation) with the DC; and Associazione Generale delle Cooperative Italiane (AGCI) / General Association of Italian Cooperatives with the **Partito Repubblicano Italiano** (PRI) / Italian Republican Party, the **Partito Socialista Democratico Italiano** (PSDI) Italian Social Democratic Party, and the *Verdi* or Greens. In the 1880s, over three-fourths of the cooperatives were located in the northern regions, 14 percent in Italy's center, and half of one percent in the South. A century later, of nearly 16,000 coops in the *Lega*, 44 percent were in the North, 24 percent in the Center, and 32 percent in the South, traditionally diffident regarding cooperative efforts.

The *Lega* ranks fourth in annual turnover among Italian enterprises and includes the sixth-largest insurer in Italy (UNIPOL), as well as venture capital (*Fincooper*) and both merchant banking and commercial banking. Producers' cooperatives operate in areas as varied as agriculture, fishing, construction, metalworking, printing, and stone masonry. Service cooperatives range from office cleaning, waste disposal, and building maintenance to transport (trucking, taxis, commuter aircraft, and busses), while professional services can be sought from cooperatives of engineers, architects, doctors, caterers, tax consultants, labor consultants, accountancy, and marketing researchers. Consumers' cooperatives operate large supermarket chains (COOP Supermercati and Conad retailers).

Italian law allows ten persons to seek financing for a cooperative. If all the members are between 18 and 25 years of age, they are entitled to receive additional help from regional authorities. State subsidies are available for the first three years. Other benefits include an easing of the social security burden and preferential treatment in bidding for public contracts. *See also* Lira.

COPPI, FAUSTO (1919-1960). In the view of many experts, Fausto Coppi was the greatest cyclist of all time: nobody would deny that he was the most spectacular. His willingness to break from the main group in lengthy, solitary "fughe" of tens, even hundreds of kilometers, made him a byword for stamina and courage. His duels with another great Italian cyclist, Gino Bartali, are one of the greatest chapters in the history of the sport. In a career spanning 17 years (1939-1956), Coppi won 128 races, including the Tour de France twice, the Tour of Italy five times, and the World Road championship in 1953 by over six minutes from the second-placed finisher—a performance that many regard, even today, as the finest ever seen in a one-day race. He smashed the one-hour distance record in 1942. Had his career not been interrupted for four years (1943-1946) by the war, there seems no doubt that this imposing list of victories would be even longer. Coppi's life, however, is also important for non-sporting reasons. In September 1954, he caused a national scandal when the police, applying to the letter Italy's laws against adultery, arrested his married lover, Giulia Occhini. In 1955, Occhini was sentenced to three months' imprisonment for abandoning her husband's home and Coppi to two months. The sentences were conditional only, so neither actually spent time behind bars, but the affair highlighted the Italian state's readiness to interfere in the private lives of its citizens. The adultery laws were later repealed in 1969. Coppi died in his native Alessandria (Piedmont) in 1960.

CORFÙ. *See* Foreign Policy.

CORPORATISM. Corporatism was perhaps the most original idea to emerge from the fascist experience. Essentially, it was meant to include institutional devices for controlling all instruments of production—both management and labor—in the interests of an assertive national policy and of autarchy, that is, the organization of the economy so as to reduce or eliminate dependence on foreign sources of supply. Management and labor were to be organized—economic sector by economic sector—into guildlike units, membership in which was to be compulsory for the practitioners of a trade or the manufacturers of a given product. These "corporations" were recognized by the state and given a representational monopoly within their respective categories in exchange for observing certain state controls on the choice of leaders and the articulation of demands.

The Ministry of Corporations—headed by **Mussolini** himself—required that all members of unions be "of good moral character" (i.e., loyal to **fascism**) and that only those syndicates recognized by the Confederazione Italiana Sindacati Nazionali Lavoratori (CISNAL) / Italian Confederation of National Workers' Unions were to take part in corporatism's activities. Hence, Catholic and Socialist **trade unions** were effectively excluded: only contracts signed by fascist unions would have legal effect. Territorial organizations of employees in a particular sector or the employers (of

10 percent of the work force) formed federations of employers' associations or labor syndicates on provincial, regional, and national levels. Labor tribunals were organized as sections in each of the 16 Courts of Appeal to hear disputes left unresolved by conciliation. Their chief criterion was ostensibly the national welfare rather than either the interests of labor or capital. Strikes and lockouts were prohibited. At the national level, these territorial federations were to generate "corporations" that were to increase productivism within their sectors. This was to be syndicalism as administered by the omnipotent state through its National Council of Corporations made up entirely of Mussolini appointees and chaired by the secretary-general of the Fascist Party.

Although first implemented by the Italian fascists, corporatist doctrine was not entirely original. Its most important doctrinal antecedent was to be found in the Papal **encyclical** *Rerum Novarum* (1891), which was anti-liberal, anti-bourgeois, and defensive of the unorganized worker. Another was to be found in the work of a Rumanian writer, Mihail (sic.) Manoilescu, whose prediction that the 20th would be the century of fascism was taken as a portent by Mussolini who frequently used the idea of *Il secolo nostro* (our century) in his speeches.

State corporatism was introduced to the world almost simultaneously with the Great Depression. Its chief characteristic was that the leadership of each association was not selected by the members of each productive category, but by the **Partito Nazionale Fascista** (PNF) / National Fascist Party. Italy did not seriously apply corporatism during the two decades of fascist rule despite all claims of making the Italian state self-sufficient—autarchic. *See also* Fascism; Fascist Ideology.

CORRADINI, ENRICO (1865-1931). The founder and editor of the influential Florentine periodical *Il Regno* between 1903 and 1905, Enrico Corradini was one of the most widely read journalists and intellectuals in pre-fascist Italy. An ardent nationalist and implacably anti-socialist, Corradini was as responsible as any Italian for diffusing the philosophy of power worship, hyper-nationalism, and contempt for parliamentary procedure that proved a fertile breeding ground for **fascism**. Borrowing the language of his socialist adversaries, Corradini advanced the idea that Italy was a "proletarian nation," robbed of its rightful role and position in world affairs by plutocratic nations such as Britain and, above all, France. Through this lens, imperialism became a substitute for socialism, an alchemic experience that would forge Italy as a strong, unified state, and would solve the economic difficulties of the Mezzogiorno by providing a dignified outlet for emigration.

In 1910, Corradini was one of the founders of the Italian nationalist movement, and became editor of its newspaper, *L'Idea nazionale* (*The National Idea*). His was one of the loudest voices raised in support of intervention in May 1915, and he was one of **Giolitti**'s most contemptuous critics during and after the war. Corradini supported the fusion of the nationalist movement with the fascist party in 1923, and served as a minister under **Mussolini** in 1928. He died in **Rome** in 1931.

COSSIGA, FRANCESCO (1928-). Born in the Sardinian province of Sassari, Francesco Cossiga was active in the **Democrazia Cristiana** (DC) / Christian Democracy Party from his early teens, and in 1958, he was elected to the Chamber of Deputies. Cossiga's political career has been characterized by controversy. In 1964, he was the go-between during secret negotiations between his political patron, President **Antonio Segni,** and General Giovanni De Lorenzo, then head of the Italian Secret Service, who was later accused of plotting to overthrow the state. As a junior minister for defense in the late 1960s, Cossiga participated in the establishment of the so-called **Gladio** networks: secret groups of "patriots" who were supposed to organize and lead resistance to an eventual Soviet invasion of Italy. Many believe, however, that the real purpose of Gladio was to subvert a legitimately elected communist government in Italy; it has also been alleged that there was a link between Gladio and right-wing terrorism.

Cossiga was given the important task of combating the **Brigate Rosse** (BR) / Red Brigades in 1976. His tenure as minister of the interior was generally successful until the March 1978 kidnapping and May 1978 murder of **Aldo Moro. Police** incompetence during the Moro affair inspired conspiracy theorists to suggest that Italy's right-wing establishment, and its allies in the United States Central Intelligence Agency (CIA), were content to see Moro, the architect of the *compromesso storico* with the **Partito Comunista Italiano** (PCI) / Italian Communist Party, perish at the hands of his terrorist captors. In Cossiga's defense, it should be stressed that the BR's price for Moro's life—political recognition—was regarded as an unacceptable demand by all the principal political parties except the

Partito Socialista Italiano (PSI) / Italian Socialist Party. Cossiga resigned after Moro's death. In September 1979, President **Alessandro Pertini** asked him to form a government, which lasted for a year. In 1983, Cossiga moved from the Chamber of Deputies to the Senate and was immediately elected to the presidency of the upper chamber. In 1985, he became the eighth man to be elected as president of the republic. Just 57 years old, he was the youngest man ever to hold the office.

In the first five years of his presidency, Cossiga behaved with gray dignity; his deft handling of the 1987 government crisis was praised even by his political opponents. After the public disclosure of the **Gladio** networks in the fall of 1990, however, Cossiga took a more outspoken line: his "outbursts" became famous. He also provoked a constitutional crisis by availing himself of his formal power to chair the Consiglio Superiore della Magistratura (CSM) / High Council of the Magistracy, the governing body of the Italian legal profession, and then using that position to block judicial investigations into Gladio. Cossiga's antics were at least partly motivated by impatience at the inadequacies of the political system. He said in July 1991 that there was an "authentic and remarkable contradiction" between Italy's extraordinary post-war economic success and the miserable failure of its political institutions and parties. Disgusted by the behavior of the government parties, Cossiga resigned on April 25, 1992, with three months of his mandate still to run.

Since 1992, Cossiga, who is one of the few senior Italian politicians to have been untouched by the **Mani pulite** investigations into political corruption, or the concurrent investigations into collusion with the **mafia**, has been mentioned on several occasions as a potential premier. His political career is certainly not over. Cossiga has been the main force behind attempts to refound a centrist Catholic Party and to reunite the splintered fragments of the ex-Democrazia cristiana / Christian Democracy party. Since the political crisis in October 1998, when several of Cossiga's allies entered the government, he has emerged as a key figure once more. *See also* Gladio; Aldo Moro; Solo Plan.

COSSUTTA, ARMANDO (1926-). A card-carrying member of the **Partito Comunista Italiano** (PCI) / Italiana Communist Party and a partisan in the Garibaldi brigade when he was just 17 years old, Cossutta has never wavered in his communist faith. Imprisoned in the latter stages of the war, he rose in the hierarchy of the PCI by dint of becoming a contributor to both *L'Unità* and *Rinascita* (respectively, the daily newspaper and theoretical weekly of the PCI) and a tireless party worker in his native **Milan**. Then, in 1966, he was invited to join the national secretariat in **Rome**. Within ten years, he was put in charge of coordination with regional and other autonomous areas, a position that he held until 1983.

In these years, he was elected simultaneously to the Chamber of Deputies and to the Italian Senate on the PCI list in six elections beginning with 1972. In each case, he opted for accepting the Senate seat. Within the party, his was the voice of a shrinking minority of **carristi**. In the 1983 congress and in that of 1986, he was in the forefront of those who dissented from the party's seeming move away from its traditional acceptance of the Soviet model. Continuing in his losing battle in favor of Stalinist orthodoxy, Cossutta fought **Achille Occhetto**'s attempts to replace the PCI with a new progressive party every step of the way. The PCI's February 1991 decision to rename itself prompted Cossutta to depart and form a new movement, the **Partito di Rifondazione Comunista** (PRC) / Party of Communist Refoundation. Cossutta was elected its first secretary at its initial congress in January 1992 and has since become president of Rifondazione. The **Olive Tree Coalition**'s lack of a parliamentary majority since the elections in April 1996 has allowed Rifondazione and Cossutta to exercise a substantial degree of influence over government policy.

CRAXI, BETTINO (1934-). Born in Milan, Craxi's early political career was in local government. The protégé of Italian socialism's historic leader, **Pietro Nenni**, he was elected to the national executive committee of the **Partito Socialista Italiano** (PSI) / Italian Socialist Party in 1965, and three years later was elected to the Chamber of Deputies. In 1976, he took the place of Francesco De Martino as party leader after the PSI's poor performance in the elections of that year.

As party leader, he followed an opportunistic line trying to undercut the **Partito Comunista Italiano** (PCI) / Italian Communist Party's support among the organized working class by espousing far-left policies. He was the only politician to favor negotiating with the **Brigate Rosse** during the dramatic kidnapping of the **Democrazia Cristiana** (DC) / Christian Democracy Party leader, **Aldo Moro** in the spring of 1978. After the 1979 poll, President **Alessandro Pertini** gave Craxi the burden of trying to form a coalition government, but DC opposition blocked this move.

Despite the DC's hostility, Craxi realized that the 1979 elections had left the PSI as the fulcrum of the political system since the DC could not continue to govern without the PSI's parliamentary support. At the PSI's congress in April 1981, Craxi pragmatically transformed its platform along centrist, social democratic lines, and launched his own candidacy for the prime ministership with American-style attention to the publicization of his personality and image. Initially disappointed in his objectives (the first non-DC prime minister was **Giovanni Spadolini** of the **Partito Repubblicano Italiano** (PRI) / Italian Republican Party in June 1981), Craxi finally became premier in August 1983, at the head of a five-party coalition (DC-PSI-PRI-**Partito Socialista Democratico Italiano** [PSDI] / Italian Social Democratic Party and **Partito Liberale Italiano** [PLI] / Italian Liberal Party).

Craxi enjoyed the longest single spell in office of any post-war Italian prime minister. He governed until April 1987, winning a reputation for decisive leadership both in Italy and abroad. By standing up to the **trade unions** and the PCI when they tried to restore, via referendum, a law ensuring automatic cost-of-living pay increases, he weakened the power of organized labor. And although he was a strong supporter of the **North Atlantic Treaty Organization** and respected by the Reagan White House, Craxi did not hesitate to reject American demands for the surrender of the Arab terrorists who murdered an American citizen on the Italian cruise liner, the **Achille Lauro**, in 1985.

Despite these achievements, Craxi's premiership represented the beginning of the end for the Italian party system. Determined both to overtake the PCI and to rival the DC, the PSI plunged both hands into the pork barrel while in government. Italy's economic boom in the 1980s was largely due to the Italian state's generosity as the PSI and the DC competed to outspend one another with apparent disregard for Italy's public finances. By 1990, Italy's national debt stood at over 100 percent of GDP, and the country was risking bankruptcy.

For two years after the end of his premiership, Craxi engaged in a bitter struggle for power with the leader of the DC, **Ciriaco De Mita.** Craxi essentially won this political battle. The DC substituted De Mita with **Arnaldo Forlani** in February 1989, and the PSI was given a large number of important (and patronage-rich) ministries in the July 1989 government formed by **Giulio Andreotti.** Craxi,

Andreotti, and Forlani governed as a triumvirate until April 1992. These years saw the end of all moral restraint in Italian government.

Since December 1992, Craxi has become the target of dozens of corruption inquiries. He has been found guilty in four separate trials and has been condemned to long prison sentences. Since 1994, however, he has been residing—in defiance of a court order for his return to Italy—in his luxurious Tunisian villa. Reputable experts estimate that he has several hundred million dollars stashed away in bank accounts all over the globe. *See also* Mani Pulite; *Pentapartito*; Partito Socialista Italiano.

CRISPI, FRANCESCO (1819-1901). Almost alone of the major figures who created the Italian state, Francesco Crispi was a Southerner, from Agrigento in **Sicily**. He took an active role in the **Palermo** uprising in 1848 and was subject to political persecution both in Sicily and then in Piedmont (to which he had escaped in 1849) as a consequence of his republican ideals. A Mazzinian, Crispi was forced to live in exile until 1860 when he returned to Italy to organize the sailing of **Garibaldi**'s "Thousand" redshirts to Sicily. It was Crispi, on May 11, 1860, who proclaimed Garibaldi's dictatorship over Sicily.

Crispi became a parliamentary deputy in 1861. In 1864, he broke with the republicans by declaring himself willing to accept the **monarchy**. His anti-clericalism and pro-Garibaldi sentiments, however, ensured the continuation of his radical reputation, although his overweening ambition and violent temperament won him few friends. Following the victory of the constitutional left in 1876, Crispi became first speaker of the Chamber of Deputies, then minister of the interior. However, he was forced to resign from the latter post within three months after he was charged with bigamy. He was later acquitted on a technicality.

A scandal of this magnitude might have been expected to kill Crispi's career. Crispi, however, became the leading backbench critic of **Agostino Depretis**'s policy of *trasformismo*. Nevertheless, when, in 1887, Depretis offered him the post of minister of the interior, Crispi's lust for high office proved too strong. After Depretis's death in July 1887, Crispi finally reached the top of the greasy pole and became prime minister, a post that he held until February 1891, a tenure in office unmatched by any Italian politician until **Benito Mussolini**. Crispi occupied the posts of foreign minister as well as minister of the interior. As prime minister, he followed a policy of close collaboration with Germany (Crispi had first met Bismarck in the 1870s and was a warm admirer of the German statesman) and of overt hostility to the Catholic Church. Relations between the church and the Italian government became so bad during Crispi's premiership that Pope Leo XIII thought seriously of abandoning **Rome**. Crispi's second government (December 1893 and March 1896) was characterized by grandiose imperial ambitions, rising social tensions, and the violent repression of the Sicilian peasants' uprising in 1896. From December 1894 to May 1895, Crispi suspended Parliament rather than allow it to vote on a motion condemning his involvement in the **Banca Romana** scandal. Despite this undemocratic behavior, Crispi won a landslide victory in the eventual general elections. However, Crispi had been politically damaged as a consequence of having antagonized and alarmed every other important figure of the day. The calamitous defeat of the Italian expeditionary force in **Abyssinia** at Adua in 1896 brought his career to an ignominious end. He died in **Naples** in 1901. *See also* Banca Romana.

CROCE, BENEDETTO (1866-1952). One of the greatest philosophers in modern Italian history, and arguably one of the greatest philosophers of history of this century, Benedetto Croce became also a symbol of the intellectual resistance to **fascism**.

He was born in the province of Aquila (Abruzzi). When he was just 17, both parents and his sister died in an earthquake, and he was obliged to move to **Rome**, where he lived with his uncle, the economist and cabinet minister Silvio Spaventa. While in Rome, he began studying law, but soon became distracted by the lectures of the Marxist philosopher **Antonio Labriola**. Croce's first major book was an original critique of Marxism, *Materialismo storico ed economia marxista* (*Historical Materialism and Marxist Economics*), but Marxism soon came to seem a rudimentary and inadequate form of historical explanation for Croce. Of far greater interest were Hegel and Vico (whose current intellectual standing as one of the most important philosophers of the eighteenth century owes much to Croce's rediscovery of his work). Between 1902 and 1909, Croce, in the words of the title of his most famous book in this period, explained "what is alive and what is dead in the thought of Hegel."

In the same years, Croce founded and edited the intellectual review *La Critica*. Together with his collaborator, **Giovanni Gentile**,

Croce carried on an intellectual battle in the pages of his journal against both the growing irrationalism of the younger thinkers and against the waning influence of positivism and Marxism. Later, after Gentile himself had espoused **fascism**, Croce combated his former colleague's apologetics for **Mussolini** in *La Critica*. The review was published continually from 1903 to 1944—even **Mussolini** dared not totally silence Croce's voice.

Croce was a neutralist in 1915. During the war years, he became increasingly interested in the theory of historiography. After a brief spell as minister for education in 1920, Croce turned to actually writing political history. It was through the medium of narrative history that Croce made arguably his most effective protests against fascism. Croce's *Storia d'Italia, 1871-1915* (*History of Italy, 1871-1915*) and his *Storia d'Europa nel secolo decimonono* (*History of Europe in the Nineteenth Century*) snubbed the pretensions of fascism to be a new phase in Italian and European history. In elegant, erudite prose, Croce made the case for the liberal state and parliamentary institutions, and exalted the "religion of liberty." Croce was directly active in opposing the regime after the murder of **Giacomo Matteotti** in 1924. He countered Gentile's 1925 attempt to rally intellectual opinion to the fascist cause with a counter-manifesto signed by the cream of Italy's liberal intelligentsia, opposed the **Lateran pacts** in a famous Senate speech, and refused all intellectual collaboration with the regime. He was, for instance, almost the only prominent Italian intellectual who refused to contribute to Gentile's *Enciclopedia italiana*. Unsurprisingly, the fascists made life difficult for him. From the mid-1930s, Croce lived under virtual house arrest.

Croce lent his name and reputation to the **Partito Liberale Italiano** (PLI) / Italian Liberal Party after September 1943. He took part in the **Badoglio** and **Bonomi** cabinets, and was elected to the **Constituent Assembly** in June 1946. But direct political activity was never his forte. In 1947 he retired from politics to found the Institute for Italian Historical Studies. He died in 1952 in **Naples**, where he had lived almost continuously since 1886.

-D-

D'ALEMA, MASSIMO (1949-). The most impressive of the new generation of Italian politicians who have emerged from the collapse of the party system in 1992-1994, Massimo D'Alema has been the leader of the **Partito Democratico della Sinistra** (PDS) /

Democratic Party of the Left since the summer of 1994. D'Alema's entire career has been spent in the party organization of the former **Partito Comunista Italiano** (PCI) / Italian Communist party, first as head of the party's youth federation, then as a member of the party secretariat, then as a parliamentary deputy, and as managing director of *L'Unità*, the PCI's daily newspaper, between 1988 and 1990. As deputy leader of the PCI during the traumatic years of 1989-1991, when the PCI experienced a profound identity crisis following the collapse of communism in Eastern Europe, D'Alema played a crucial role in the party's transformation into the PDS.

When D'Alema took over as leader of the PDS from **Achille Occhetto**, many regarded him as an uninspired choice who would reflect the wishes of the party bureaucracy. It has instead become clear that D'Alema is one of the few contemporary Italian politicians with vision. As the title of a book of his speeches proclaimed, he envisages Italy becoming "a normal country." He interprets this as meaning that Italy must develop constitutional arrangements in which the government has the power to implement its policies without being held hostage by minority parties in Parliament; in which there is a genuine social market economy without the deformations of **patronage** politics; in which there is alternation in power between a center-left party and a center-right party. In a leading article in *L'Unità*, he announced that he wanted to build *uno stato snello* (A slimmed-down state) in Italy: an objective that is light years away from the statist dogma of the old PCI, and clearly distinct, too, from the issues-oriented radicalism preferred by Occhetto after the formation of the PDS.

Despite his own unquestionable political skills (which are offset by a cold, overly intellectual manner that wins him few friends when he appears on television), it cannot be said that he has made much headway in turning his vision for Italy's future into reality. His support was crucial for the formation of the **Olive Tree Coalition**, and the PDS dominates Italy's existing government, but D'Alema's attempts to broaden the PDS into a larger social democratic party have fallen foul of the factionalism of Italy's numerous leftist splinter parties who are reluctant to be swallowed by the PDS. In 1997, D'Alema chaired an important bicameral commission of Parliament that had the task of rewriting the **Constitution of 1948**. The bicameral commission failed after months of political wrangling. Despite this setback, D'Alema replaced **Romano Prodi** as prime minister in October 1998. *See also* Constitution of 1948; Partito

Democratico della Sinistra.

DALLA CHIESA, CARLO ALBERTO (1920-1982). A general in the
Carabinieri, Carlo Alberto Dalla Chiesa served the Italian state with
great bravery against two deadly internal enemies: the terrorists of
the **Brigate Rosse** (BR) / Red Brigades, and the Sicilian **mafia.**
Born in the province of Cuneo (Piedmont), Dalla Chiesa joined
the *Carabinieri* in 1942. Most of his career was spent combating
illegality in Campania and **Sicily**, although in 1968 he was placed in
charge of relief efforts after the tragic earthquake in **Palermo**. In the
early 1970s, he returned to Piedmont at a time of great political
activism and violence in the factories of **Turin**. His success in
combating terrorism in Piedmont led to his appointment as the
national coordinator of anti-terrorist activity following the tragic
kidnapping and death of **Aldo Moro**. Much of the Italian state's
success in tracking down and defeating the menace of the **Brigate
Rosse** (Red Brigades) can be attributed to Dalla Chiesa's persistence
and skill.

In December 1981, Dalla Chiesa became vice-commander of the
Carabinieri; a few months later, following the murder by the mafia
of Pio La Torre, a deputy of the **Partito Comunista Italiano** (PCI)
/ Italian Communist Party, he was sent to Palermo to direct the Italian
state's efforts to restore legality and order in Sicily. His tenure of the
job was short-lived; in September 1982, Dalla Chiesa and his young
second wife were ambushed and killed. Dalla Chiesa's death caused
a heated polemic in Italy. In two passionate and detailed books, Dalla
Chiesa's university professor son, Nando, has argued the thesis that
his father was assassinated by the crime bosses at the behest of senior
politicians within the **Democrazia Cristiana** (DC) / Christian
Democracy Party. *See also* Mafia; Police.

D'ANNUNZIO, GABRIELE (1863-1938). Poet, adventurer, novelist,
Gabriele D'Annunzio is one of the most flamboyant personalities in
modern Italian history. Born in Pescara in 1863, he published his first
collection of verse, *Primo vere* (1879), when he was just 16 years
old. In the 1880s, he became a celebrity thanks to a series of critically
acclaimed novels, of which *Il Piacere* (*Pleasure*, 1888) is perhaps the
most widely read today; collections of decadent, sensual verse (*Canto
Novo* in 1882 being the most significant); and a well-deserved
reputation for *don giovannismo*. An ardent nationalist, his verse
voiced the patriotic and imperialist sentiments of the **Crispi** era; in

1897 D'Annunzio was elected to Parliament as a representative of the extreme right. Within three years, however, D'Annunzio, inspired by the socialists' physical bravery in pursuit of their cause, had swung to the extreme left. Whether on the right or the left, certain themes are constant in his copious political writings: irrationalism, detestation of the masses, francophilia and anglophobia, contempt for the processes of bourgeois parliamentary democracy, and a fascination with war and violence.

D'Annunzio was naturally a partisan of Italian intervention in **World War I**, in which he fought with great bravery as a volunteer pilot in the Italian air force, even losing an eye in combat. It is claimed that he once flew a biplane over Vienna in order to drop from the sky pages of his poetry. When the war was over, he led an attempt by enraged Italian nationalists to defy the Treaty of Versailles (which had granted the city of Fiume [Rijeka] in present- day Croatia to the newly formed Yugoslavia, not to Italy). With the tacit support of many influential figures in Italian politics, D'Annunzio established his own little city-state in Fiume and ruled as *duce* for a year until the government of **Giovanni Giolitti**, at the end of 1920, compelled the poet and his "legionnaires" to abandon the city by arraying against them the army.

D'Annunzio plainly had much in common with **Mussolini**, but his relations with the fascist leader were marked by acute rivalry. For several months in 1922, D'Annunzio's splendid villa on the shores of Lake Garda became a meeting place for anti-fascists of all political persuasions who regarded the poet as a figure around whom national reconciliation might be possible. The **March on Rome**, however, put an end to D'Annunzio's hopes of emerging as a national leader. D'Annunzio did not add his voice to **Croce**'s dignified and courageous opposition to the fascist state. Like **Pirandello**, the poet made his peace with the new regime and even accepted, shortly before his death, the presidency of the **Accademia d'Italia.**

D'AZEGLIO, MASSIMO TAPARELLI (1798-1866). The fourth son of a prominent nobleman who was the legate of the Sardinian throne at the court of Pope Pius VII, Massimo D'Azeglio initially followed a literary and artistic career. He studied painting in **Florence** and **Milan**, where he met and married Giulia, the daughter of the novelist **Alessandro Manzoni**. D'Azeglio himself dabbled in literature: in 1833 he published *Ettore Fieramosca*, a novel of no lasting literary value, whose ardently nationalist and anti-Austrian content nevertheless make it an important historical document.

In 1845, with the encouragement of his cousin **Cesare Balbo,** D'Azeglio made a tour of the Papal states (Tuscany, Emilia-Romagna, the Marches). Upon his return, he wrote a celebrated exposé of the misgovernment prevailing in the regions under the church's control, *Degli ultimi casi di Romagna (Of the Most Recent Romagnole Cases,* 1846), which established him as a national political figure.

D'Azeglio was a moderate and a constitutionalist. After the disasters of the war of 1848-1849 (in which he fought and was wounded), he became prime minister of Piedmont-Sardinia and negotiated the peace agreement with the Austrians. D'Azeglio remained as prime minister until 1852, when he was substituted by **Cavour.** Thereafter, he held no office, but was a trusted counselor to King **Vittorio Emanuele II.** During the second war with Austria in 1859, he was an active publicist on behalf of the Italian cause. The extension of Piedmontese authority to southern Italy left him perplexed, however. He was convinced that no good could come of fusion with **Naples.** He died in **Turin** in 1866.

DE BONO, EMILIO (1866-1944). Born in the province of Milan (Lombardy), De Bono became a monarchist and conservative, acting as a conduit between Mussolini and the monarchy. In 1912, he had been chief of the General Staff in Libya. In **World War I,** he served in Albania and on the Austrian front. After the war, he joined the **Partito Nazionale Fascista** (PNF) / National Fascist Party, probably as a stepping-stone to higher office. Before the **March on Rome,** he had helped organize the militia. Once in power, Mussolini made him chief of police in **Rome,** but when the murder of **Giacomo Matteotti** by fascist thugs led to a public outcry, De Bono resigned from the post. In 1929, he became minister for colonial affairs and, in 1935, high commissioner for East Africa. In 1936, De Bono was put in command of ground forces in the war in **Abyssinia** despite his age (he was nearly 70). He was subsequently promoted to the rank of marshal in order to clear the way for **Pietro Badoglio,** who concluded operations in six months. De Bono was among those who voted to deprive Mussolini of his powers at the fateful meeting of the **Gran Consiglio del Fascismo** (Fascist Grand Council) on July 24-25, 1943, and was thus among those executed by firing squad on the Duce's orders in January 1944 at Verona. *See also* Dino Grandi; March on Rome; Benito Mussolini; Quadrumvirate.

DE CHIRICO, GIORGIO (1888-1978). Born in Greece, De Chirico is one of the most enigmatic painters of the twentieth century. After an early cubist period, he was influenced by the futurist painter Carlo Carrà. Together with Carrà, De Chirico gave birth to the so-called "metaphysical" school of art, which—by emphasizing stillness, emptiness, natural light, and the hyper-realistic depiction of objects—deliberately contradicted the frenzied celebration of motion that characterized futurist painting.

De Chirico's best work is unforgettable once seen: his figures are like a tailor's dummies—eyeless, mouthless, and disquieting. His street scenes are as different from the crowded thoroughfares and kinetically charged piazzas portrayed by **Umberto Boccioni** as can be imagined. De Chirico painted the porticoed squares of desolate villages baking under a blue Mediterranean sky, with large areas of murky shadow and houses whose large windows look out blankly on to the street. The few human figures are solitary individuals, engaged in aimless tasks, and usually draped in shadow. Both dadaism and surrealism, and much of the best fascist architecture, owed a great deal to De Chirico's work.

De Chirico's artistic production from the late 1920s onward is considered to have declined in originality and quality. He died in **Rome** in 1978.

DE GASPERI, ALCIDE (1881-1954). Born in Trento while that city was still Austrian, De Gasperi studied in Vienna and was elected to the Austrian Parliament as a representative of the Italian-speaking minority in 1911. Despite his irredentist views, he was allowed to travel to **Rome** in 1915 where he was introduced to **Sonnino**, then Italy's foreign minister. When, at the war's end, the "unredeemed territories" formerly under Austrian jurisdiction were annexed by Italy, he took part in the founding of the **Partito Popolare Italiano** (PPI) / Italian People's Party and became a member of its national council. He was elected to Italy's Parliament in 1921. In October 1922, in opposition to the PPI's leader, **Don Luigi Sturzo**, he recommended, successfully, that the PPI should take part in **Mussolini**'s government. He substituted Don Sturzo as leader of the PPI, but the increasingly dictatorial tendencies of Mussolini led him to oppose the regime. De Gasperi was one of the leaders of the **Aventine Secession** after the murder of **Giacomo Matteotti**. He was arrested and served a brief prison sentence in 1927-1928.

De Gasperi spent the remainder of the dictatorship in the Vatican library, mediating between new Catholic movements and the remnants of the old PPI. He was elected secretary of the **Democrazia Cristiana** (DC) / Christian Democracy in 1944 and authored the left-of-center party program published in occupied Rome by the DC's clandestine paper, *Il Popolo*. He served as foreign minister in the second government of **Ivanoe Bonomi** and in the government formed by **Ferruccio Parri** in June 1945. In December 1945, with the concurrence of the **Partito Comunista Italiano** (PCI) / Italian Communist Party, De Gasperi became prime minister himself. His ability to work with the PCI in the tense immediate post-war period testifies to his pragmatism. His leadership of the DC enabled the party to outdistance all others in the election of June 1946 whereupon De Gasperi formed a government in conjunction with the **Partito Socialista Italiano** (PSI) / Italian Socialist Party and the PCI.

On his first visit to Washington in February 1947, he was able to negotiate considerable economic aid for Italy on the apparent condition that he expel these Marxist parties from his government. Inasmuch as he needed their support for the treaty of peace and in the continuing preparation of the **1948 Constitution** and the inclusion therein of the **Lateran pacts**, he could not free himself of them until May 1947, when he formed a *quadripartito* in which the DC was supported by the small parties of the center-left and by the **Partito Liberale Italiano** (PLI) / Italian Liberal Party. This formula balanced parties of the right (PLI) and parties of the left (**Partito Repubblicano Italiano** [PRI] / Italian Republican Party and **Partito Socialista Democratico Italiano** [PSDI] / Italian Socialist Democratic Party) thereby enabling De Gasperi to prevent ecclesiastical dominance after the **monarchy**'s weight had been removed from the political scales. Even following the DC's huge victory in the April 1948 elections, he persisted with this strategy.

Despite the immobility of his party that this tidy balancing made inevitable, De Gasperi—in the eight governments that he headed between 1945 and 1954—led Italy to join the **North Atlantic Treaty Organization** (NATO), consolidated its new democracy, undertook a measure of **land reform**, and took an active role in the moves toward integrating Europe both economically and politically. In many ways, he had been the architect of his party and of its subsequent fundamental choices: Atlanticist, European, and—as **Aldo Moro** was to quote him as saying—"of the center moving toward the left." Both **consociationalism** and the **opening to the left** originate with De Gasperi. Outside Italy, he was regarded as one of the primary architects of the new Europe. *See also* Democrazia

Cristiana; European Union.

DELEDDA, GRAZIA (1871-1937). The only Italian woman writer to win the Nobel prize for literature (and one of the restricted group of women ever to win the world's most prestigious literary award), Grazia Deledda was born in Nuoro (Sardinia) in 1871, though from 1898 onward she lived in **Rome**. A self-taught writer, Deledda's many novels depict Sardinian characters in psychological and moral dramas of great intensity. During her lifetime, she was widely compared to Dostoyevsky, and although this comparison now seems overblown, there is no doubt that her best works—*Elias Portolu* (1903), *Cenere* (*Ashes*, 1904), *Canne al vento* (*Reeds in the Wind*, 1913)—are powerful works of art that deserve renewed critical attention. Deledda's last work was an autobiography, *Cosima*, that was published after her death in 1937.

DE LORENZO, GIOVANNI. *See* Solo Plan.

DE MITA, CIRIACO (1928-). Although he was born near **Naples** in Avellino (Campania), De Mita began his political activities while studying law at the Catholic University of Milan. In 1956, he was elected to the National Council of the **Democrazia Cristiana** (DC) / Christian Democracy Party and to the Chamber of Deputies in 1963. He first served in a government under **Mariano Rumor** as undersecretary of the interior. Between 1969 and 1973, he was vice secretary of the DC. In Rumor IV and V, he was minister for industry and commerce. With **Moro** IV and V, he was minister for foreign trade.

De Mita's southern influence was enhanced by his appointment to the ministry for the South in **Andreotti** III and IV. In 1982, he was elected secretary of the DC. Despite the extent of his local power base, De Mita led the DC in the direction of factional reform. Factions had always characterized the party inasmuch as they served the electoral needs of the local notables who were at their center. His detractors argue that he was mainly concerned with reforming others' factions, leaving his own still able to function effectively. The disappointing results of the 1983 elections showed that many Demochristians were alarmed. For many, he was too closely identified with the **opening to the left** and reformism generally.

Nonetheless, in 1988, De Mita was asked to form a government. In its short life, it led **Parliament** to approve modest reforms in the premier's office, in local governments, and in parliamentary voting procedures. But snipers—party members who, under cover of the secret ballot, vote against their party leaders' position are called *franchi tiratori*—from within the DC offered tenacious resistance to more deep-reaching reforms. After the party responded to **Andreotti**'s leadership by electing **Arnaldo Forlani** as its new secretary, De Mita was put in an impossible position and was forced to resign as president of the Council of Ministers to make room for Andreotti VI. In 1989, De Mita was made president of the DC, a post from which he resigned in October 1992.

By 1996, De Mita had spent 30 years in the Italian Parliament and had been his country's prime minister from April 1988 to July 1989. Despite the relative collapse of his party, De Mita brought an end to his self-imposed exile by once again agreeing to be a candidate in the April 1996 elections. Although widely suspected of complicity in the 1980 Irpinia earthquake-relief scandal, De Mita has never been indicted.

DEMOCRATIC PARTY OF THE LEFT (PDS). *See* Partito Democratico della Sinistra.

DEMOCRAZIA CRISTIANA (DC) / Christian Democracy Party. The DC was founded in September 1942. After the armistice on September 8, 1943, the DC took part in the governments that were formed in Allied-occupied Italy. Only in the summer of 1944, however, when the church threw its unambiguous backing behind the new movement, did the party emerge as a force of genuine weight. After the war, the leader of the DC, **Alcide De Gasperi,** became first foreign minister and then, from November 1945, prime minister. No party other than the DC would hold the premiership again until 1981, a cycle of institutional dominance unmatched by any other party anywhere else in democratic Europe. The DC's emergence at the core of the Italian political system was founded upon the broad appeal of its policies. In the immediate post-war period, the party defended the rules governing relations between church and state established by the **Lateran pacts,** evinced a strong commitment to European unification, was belligerently anti-communist, and proposed the wider diffusion of private property through land reform and measures to strengthen small owners of all kinds. These policies made the DC the natural party of the peasants, shopkeepers, small businessmen, clerical workers, and self-employed artisans who constituted a huge proportion of the electorate, but who were less well organized than the manual workers or the big industrialists. The votes cast by these middle-class electors established the DC as the largest party in the country in Italy's first free elections in 1946.

De Gasperi's resolute handling of the **Partito Comunista Italiano** (PCI) / Italiana Communist Party gave the DC an aura in American eyes. U.S. support for the DC (in the form of campaigns asking Italo-Americans to write to family and friends in Italy encouraging votes for the DC) was instrumental in the party's massive victory in the 1948 elections (48 percent of the vote and an absolute majority of seats), which laid the foundations for the party's subsequent political hegemony. De Gasperi dominated the party until shortly before his death in 1953. Once the De Gasperi era was over, the party's internal ideological divisions (the party encompassed all creeds from Christian socialists to extreme conservatives) burst out as De Gasperi's successor, **Amintore Fanfani,** tried to shift the party to the left.

By the end of the 1950s, the party was broadly divided into three main factional blocs, representing the party's left, center, and right, each of which was further subdivided into a vast array of sub-factions and individual cabals. Over the next 30 years, although these blocs regularly changed their names, and individuals habitually decamped from one faction to another, the basic structure remained approximately the same, and so did the form of politics that these internal divisions entailed. No one faction rode roughshod over the others; every faction (and sub-faction, and cabal) was consulted on policy questions, on questions of ministerial nominees, on state appointments, and got its share of all available **patronage**. The center group became the majority in 1958 and remained the party's center of gravity thereafter. In these circumstances, the party leader had to be above all a weaver of compromises. The DC was fortunate that for much of this period its dominant figure was **Aldo Moro**, an artful master of the black arts of coalition politics.

By the early 1970s, the DC had almost two million members and could count upon a solid 40 percent plurality of the electorate. But this state of affairs was less healthy than it looked. Increasingly out of touch with public opinion, the DC attempted to overturn the 1970 **divorce** law by referendum in 1974 and was humiliatingly defeated. The DC seemingly had no answer to the industrial and social strife that paralyzed Italy from 1968 onward. Worst of all, its long hold on power had had predictable effects on public ethics: major corruption scandals marred the two governments of **Mariano Rumor** in 1973-1974, and would continue to dog the DC until the collapse of the political system in 1993.

In the 1976 elections, the DC just managed to keep ahead of the PCI (39 percent to 34.5 percent), but could not muster a parliamentary majority. The solution was a government of national solidarity between the DC and the PCI in which the latter took no part but agreed not to vote against policies on which the PCI was consulted. This relationship lasted until the PCI leadership felt themselves excluded while, at the same time, facing the disenchantment of many in the rank and file.

In the 1980s, electoral arithmetic forced the DC to relinquish some of its hold on power. In 1981, **Giovanni Spadolini** became the first non-DC premier. In a bid to recapture its central role, the DC turned to its left and elected **Ciriaco De Mita** party secretary in May 1982. De Mita promised to end patronage politics and attempted to put fresh life into the DC's by now moribund stock of ideas, but the results were disastrous. The party received its lowest ever vote in the June 1983 elections (just under 33 percent) and was forced to allow the PSI's **Bettino Craxi** to assume the premiership. Craxi's ruthless exploitation of his party's position as the fulcrum of Italian politics eventually produced a tacit power-sharing agreement between the DC's leading oligarchs and Craxi.

The last two governments headed by a member of the DC, **Giulio Andreotti**'s sixth and seventh administrations (July 1989 to June 1992) illustrated in full the malaise of the DC. The party, once a movement of idealistic Catholic democrats, had become a conspiracy to defraud the state. Corruption was rampant at all levels of government, and in **southern Italy** links between important DC politicians and organized crime were commonplace. Such a party was incapable of resisting the challenges presented by the PCI's renunciation of communist doctrine, by new political movements such as the **Lega Nord,** and by public demands for political and electoral reform. In the April 1992 general elections, the DC's share of the vote fell below 30 percent, and the party entered into a crisis that proved to be terminal.

The subsequent **Mani pulite** and **mafia** investigations, which revealed the full, astounding extent of political wrongdoing, were the party's death knell. In January 1994, the party was officially wound up and replaced by a new formation with an old name, the **Partito Popolare Italiano.** *See also* Giulio Andreotti; Compromesso Storico; Alcide De Gasperi; Amintore Fanfani; Aldo Moro; Mani Pulite; Pentapartito.

DE NICOLA, ENRICO (1877-1959). President of Italy between 1946 and 1948, Enrico De Nicola was a figure of notable institutional standing in the final years of Italian liberalism. Politically close to **Giovanni Giolitti**, he was elected to **Parliament** for the first time in 1909. In June 1920, he became speaker of the Chamber of Deputies, a post he held until December 1923. Like many liberals, his attitude toward **fascism** was equivocal. In 1924, he was included in the list of approved fascist candidates by **Mussolini**, but shortly before the ballot he withdrew his nomination. Despite being nominated to the Senate in 1929, De Nicola played no political role during the fascist period.

De Nicola returned to active politics after the fall of Mussolini. In the spring of 1944, he resolved the crisis caused by the democratic parties' reluctance to take part in the administration of Allied-occupied Italy so long as **Victor Emmanuel III** retained the throne by suggesting that Prince Umberto should be made Lieutenant-General of the Realm. This scheme paved the way for the creation of the first government of **Ivanoe Bonomi** in June 1944. De Nicola was subsequently elected president of the republic by the **Constitutional Assembly** and oversaw the process of drawing up the **Constitution of 1948**. In that year, he was offered the opportunity to be post-war Italy's first constitutionally elected head of state, but he stepped aside in favor of **Luigi Einaudi**. He was made a life member of the Senate. In 1951-1952, he was briefly president of the Senate and, in 1955, he became president of the constitutional court—a post he held for two years. He died in his native **Naples** in 1959.

DEPRETIS, AGOSTINO (1812-1887) . The quintessential professional politician, Depretis was born in Pavia (Lombardy) in 1812 to a family of wealthy landowners. His political career started in his mid-thirties when he was elected to the Piedmontese parliament. Initially a Mazzinian, he remained in opposition until the war of 1859, but then entered into government service, acting as the intermediary in 1860 between the Piedmontese government and the *Garibaldini* in **Sicily**. This task ended in the harbinger of many future conflicts between Depretis and **Garibaldi**'s secretary, the young **Francesco Crispi**.

Depretis's first experience of ministerial office came in the 1860s, as minister for public works, but from 1867 onward Depretis was in opposition. After the death of **Urbano Rattazzi** in 1873, he became the most important figure on the moderate left and led the parliamentary opposition to the economic austerity of **Quintino Sella** and **Marco Minghetti**. In the 1874 elections, the left, ably exploiting public discontent with Sella's grist tax, won over 200 seats in the Chamber. In October 1875, Depretis made a famous speech in his hometown of Stradella in which he outlined the program the left would follow in government. The key points were faithfulness to the **monarchy**, and a series of major social reforms: including the abolition of the grist tax, the extension of the right to vote, and compulsory elementary education.

Depretis came to power in the so-called "parliamentary revolution" of March 1876 when rightist deputies from Tuscany and Lombardy switched their support to the left. Depretis formed a government that included numerous representatives from **southern Italy** and then called new elections in November 1876. The elections were an immense triumph for the left, which obtained over 400 seats, but were marred by unprecedented government interference with the press and the local electoral authorities.

The left's huge majority soon split into two main blocs: the "purists" headed by Crispi, and the "moderates" led by Depretis. Between 1876 and May 1881, Depretis headed two governments that introduced slowly and incompletely the main points of the 1875 program. Compulsory **education** between six and nine years of age was introduced in 1877, although it was imperfectly enforced; the grist tax was abolished, but little else was done to improve the lot of the poorest citizens. In 1882, Depretis's third government did finally introduce a reform to the suffrage: the vote was extended to more than 600,000 new electors—7 percent of the population could now cast a ballot. In foreign policy, Depretis was concerned to stay on good terms with Germany and Austria. In 1882, Italy adhered to the **Triple Alliance**, which would remain the focus of the nation's foreign policy until 1915, and began looking for its own "place in the sun" by colonizing territories along the banks of the Red Sea.

Prior to the elections in October 1882, Depretis sensed that he could liberate himself from the "purists" by opening to the right. Accordingly, he appealed to members of the opposition to "transform themselves" into moderate progressives. The maneuver was successful. Led by **Marco Minghetti**, over 70 former rightists gave their support to the government Depretis set up after the elections. The "purists" protested, but they, too, took part in the government at one time or another. Depretis's political career ended in February 1887 following the disastrous massacre of the Italian expeditionary force at Dogali in **Abyssinia**.

DE SANCTIS, FRANCESCO (1817-1883). As a young man, De

Sanctis took part in the 1848 uprising against absolutist rule in his native **Naples**. He was imprisoned for two years, and after his release, he was exiled first to **Turin** and then to Zurich, where he taught Italian literature at the university. He became a member of the Italian Parliament and the first minister for education of the new kingdom in 1861. He returned to Naples to teach at the university between 1871 and 1877; he became minister for education once more in 1878 and 1881, although it cannot be said that he introduced any great curricular or organizational innovations in this post. De Sanctis's importance, however, lies not in the list of public posts that he held, but in the quality of his work as a literary historian, which aroused educated Italians to a greater sense of their common literary and cultural heritage—an important step for a new nation. De Sanctis's *Storia della letteratura italiana* (*History of Italian Literature*, 1870-1872) is essentially a history of the culture and civilization of the Italian-speaking peoples from medieval times to the nineteenth century and is widely regarded as one of the finest pieces of scholarship of its age.

DE SICA, VITTORIO (1902-1974). A matinee idol in the 1930s, Vittorio De Sica transformed himself into one of the greatest film directors in cinema history. A native of the Ciociara, the region lying between **Rome** and **Naples**, De Sica began his film career early and by 1930 he had appeared in dozens of romantic comedies. He began his directing career in 1940, but it was not until his fifth film, *I bambini ci guardono* (*The Children Are Watching Us,* 1943), that De Sica showed signs of exceptional talent. In 1946, he produced the neo-realist classic *Sciuscià* (*Shoeshine*), a film that portrayed the moving story of two young vagrant shoeshine boys in the streets of war-torn Rome. De Sica used authentic street children to ensure that his characters behaved naturally, a technique he repeated in his next film, *Ladri di biciclette* (*The Bicycle Thief,* 1948). Ranked, in 1952, as one of the ten greatest films ever made, *Ladri di biciclette* tells the story of Ricci, a desperately poor Roman worker who gets a job as a bill poster provided, that is, that he have a bicycle, and his is stolen from him on his first day at work. Together with his son Bruno, Ricci scours the streets of Rome and eventually finds the thief but cannot prove his guilt. Frantic to keep his job, Ricci steals a bicycle that has been left outside an apartment building, but is caught by an angry crowd. The bicycle's owner does not press charges, and the film ends with Ricci and Bruno walking away into the crowd. They face an uncertain future, but the bond between them has been strengthened by their ordeal. Ricci was played by a factory worker called Lamberto Maggiorani with impressive dignity and restraint, but the movie is stolen by Enzo Staiola's Bruno, who is the quintessential street urchin.

De Sica approached the heights of *Ladri di biciclette* only once more in his career. In 1951 he made *Umberto D*, a grim story about the struggle of an aging clerical worker against destitution and despair. As usual, De Sica used an amateur actor, a professor from the University of **Florence**, as his protagonist. De Sica continued to make films for more than 20 years, but although he worked with some of the world's most talented actors, he never had more than modest critical success until 1970, when his adaptation of **Giorgio Bassani**'s novel *Il giardino dei Finzi-Contini* (*The Garden of the Finzi-Continis*) won the Oscar for best foreign picture. His own performance in the 1959 film *Il generale della Rovere* was probably the finest of his distinguished career. *See also* Neo-realism.

DE VECCHI, CESARE MARIA (1884-1959). A life-long conservative clerico-monarchist, he drew close to **fascism** (he joined in **Turin**) and to **Benito Mussolini** instrumentally, that is, because he was sure the movement and the Duce could be useful to the conservative cause. Physically distinctive because of his shaved head and extraordinary moustaches (on a British Indian Army colonel they would have been called pukka sahib), he was often the butt of cruel jokes by other leading fascists, even after he had been made count of Val Cismon because of his **World War I** heroism in the battles over that valley. While, in Milan, Mussolini awaited news of the fate of the **March on Rome** in October 1922, and **Antonio Salandra** was trying to form a cabinet, De Vecchi and **Dino Grandi** had gone to the capital where they tried to organize a coalition with nationalist leaders. De Vecchi acted as the go-between in negotiations between the king and the fascist leader during the final crisis of liberal Italy. His frequent gaffes as co-commander of the militia (together with **Italo Balbo** since August 1922) included publicly endorsing the violence of **squadrismo** in Turin. He was dismissed by Mussolini in May 1923 and sent off to Somalia as governor, whence he returned when war broke out.

After endorsing the Grandi motion against Mussolini in 1943, he was—as were all other like-minded members—condemned to death. He fled first to a monastery, then to South America, and returned to Italy ten years later to join the neo-fascist **Movimento Sociale Italiano** (MSI) / Italian Social Movement in which his monarchico-conservative position made him welcome to only some of the party's adherents. He died in **Rome** in 1959. *See also* Quadrumvirate.

DIALECTS IN ITALY. Dialects in Italy are not just regionally distinctive pronunciations of Italian. They are the popular speech of many for whom speaking the literary language as taught in school is a terrible struggle. Yet no inferiority should be imputed. Dialects have their own verb forms and vocabularies. Many have their own theatrical tradition, their own poets, and—most conspicuously—their own songs. Many Piedmontese leaders of newly united Italy, including the king, had to learn Italian as a foreign language.

As the Romans colonized the Italian peninsula, they met Etruscans, Ligurians, Oscans, Illyrians, Phoenicians, and Greeks. (Magna Grecia included Greek colonies in the river valleys of the Italian south, leaving a clear impact on local culture, including speech.) Not surprisingly, the pronunciation of the Latin learned by these people varied significantly. After the collapse of Roman unity, and the Germanic, Norman, and Arab invasions between the fifth and ninth centuries, the absence of a political center exacerbated the differences between North and South and further slowed the acceptance of a common speech.

By the Middle Ages, a gulf separated the use of Latin as a written language and neo-Latin vernaculars that, while initially only spoken, came to be written as well in the eleventh and thirteenth centuries.

Conceiving all dialects of the Romance languages as derived from Latin helps one see how in Italy (as in France, Portugal, and Spain), one powerful or wealthy region was able to ensure the widened use of their particular Latin dialect. Thus, Castilian became the dialect that the rest of centralized Spain had to accept as the standard, just as Parisian became the standard for unitary France and Tuscan the Italian literary language, for this was the language of Bocaccio, Dante, and Petrarch in the region whose wealth derived from having invented banking and being the major insurer of European trade with the Near and Far East.

In 1945, 50 percent of Italians spoke *only* a dialect. Before the advent of television, increased school attendance and the leveling effect on language of commercial films, most Italians found communication between people from differing regions as difficult as between people from separate countries. A Neapolitan and a Milanese can now converse in Italian; 50 years ago, unless they shared a knowledge of French, Latin, or another language, comprehension often suffered.

The vigor of dialects continues at the end of the twentieth century, especially in remote areas and among older generations. Spontaneity and intimacy are easiest in the dialect used in the home, among friends, and in the family, and it clearly distinguishes outsiders from those who "belong." Indeed, one's identity seems to depend on ties to territory in the form of ties "to the parish, the club, the neighborhood, the dialect." The global economy may require the loosening of such ties, but the price to be paid has yet to be calculated.

Dialectologists distinguish *Gallo-Italic* dialects (Piedmontese, Ligurian, Lombard, Emilian-Romagnol) from *Venetian* (Venetian, Trentin). In central Italy are the *Tuscan* and *Central* dialects (Umbrian, Marchigian, Roman) and *Southern* dialects (Campanian, Abruzzese, Molisan, Calabrese, Pulian, Lucanian, and Sicilian). To these must be added the Ladino dialect spoken in Friuli (called Friulano in Italian or—in dialect—*Fûrlans*). Sardinian is closely related to Catalan, the dialect that Francisco Franco tried for decades to stamp out in Spain.

DI LAMPEDUSA, PRINCE GIUSEPPE TOMASI (1896-1957). The scion of a noble Palermo family, Di Lampedusa is the author of *Il Gattopardo* (*The Leopard*, 1958), arguably the greatest twentieth-century Italian novel and one of the greatest historical novels ever written. The book tells the tale of the decline of the ancient Salina family after the **Risorgimento** and the rise of the middle class, represented in the novel by the figure of Don Calogero Sedàra, the mayor of a small village on one of the Salina family's estates, and his beautiful but unprincipled daughter Angelica. Prince Fabrizio Salina (the "leopard" is his family emblem) allows Angelica to marry Tancredi, his favorite nephew, convinced that the best way to preserve his power and position is to go along with the revolutionary spirit of the times. In a phrase that has become famous as a perfect definition of the perennial Italian vice of *trasformismo*, Tancredi tells his uncle that "If everything is to stay the same, everything has to change." The irony of the novel is that the social structure of liberal Italy does remain the same as before, but the Salinas are substituted by the upstart Sedàras and their ilk. At one point, Salina says that "after us will come the age of the hyenas and the jackals." This brief summary of the novel's plot, however, does not do justice to its thematic and philosophic complexity or its astoundingly vivid and sensuous descriptions. **Luchino Visconti** brilliantly captured the novel's sad beauty in his 1963 film version.

Despite the book's universal appeal and the author's manifest genius, *Il Gattopardo* was the center of a literary polemic when it first appeared. In many ways, conservative in personal philosophy and certainly profoundly pessimistic, the book was dismissed by the neo-realist establishment in the Italian literary world, and it was only thanks to the efforts of the writer **Giorgio Bassani** that the book saw the light of day in 1959—two years after the author's death.

DINI, LAMBERTO (1931-). Economist, banker, prime minister, Lamberto Dini was born in **Florence** in March 1931. An economist by profession, Dini worked for the International Monetary Fund from 1959 to 1975, rising to the position of executive director in 1976. In 1979, he returned to Italy as director-general of the Bank of Italy, a position he held until 1994 when he was persuaded to enter politics as minister of the treasury in **Silvio Berlusconi**'s short-lived administration. When Berlusconi's government collapsed in December 1994, Dini, who had been one of the government's handful of ministerial successes, became President **Oscar Luigi Scalfaro**'s choice to head an interim government of technocrats. Dini shepherded Italy through a difficult year, restoring international confidence in Italy's economic and political stability. His achievements as prime minister seem to have given the former bureaucrat a taste for politics. In February 1996, Dini founded a new centrist party called Rinnovamento Italiano (Italian Renewal) and campaigned in the April 1996 general elections as an ally of **Romano Prodi**'s **Olive Tree Coalition**. Following Prodi's victory, Dini, who was elected to the Chamber of Deputies as deputy for a Florence constituency, was made foreign minister. He showed signs of being uncomfortable as a member of Prodi's cabinet. The Olive Tree Coalition's reliance on **Rifondazione Comunista** / Communist Refoundation disquieted his conservative political instincts and made the job of reassuring Italy's European partners more difficult. Since the fall of the government in October 1998, Dini has continued as foreign minister. *See also* Banking.

DI PIETRO, ANTONIO (1950-). An intense, hardworking opponent of political corruption, Antonio Di Pietro was born in the Molise in 1950. He became first a policeman and then, in 1981, a public prosecutor. In 1985, he joined the district attorney's office in **Milan**, where he specialized in corruption investigations. In February 1992, he masterminded the arrest and prosecution of a Milanese businessman with close ties to the **Partito Socialista Italiano** (PSI) / Italian Socialist Party called Mario Chiesa, an event that initiated the **Mani pulite** (Clean Hands) inquiry that eventually led to the investigation and arrest of thousands of politicians and businessmen all over Italy. Di Pietro became a symbol of Italy's search for social and political regeneration, and was the subject of hundreds of flattering profiles in the foreign and domestic press. The high point of the "Clean Hands" inquiry was Di Pietro's ruthless but brilliant cross-examination of a dozen leading Italian politicians in December 1993 during the trial of a Milanese financier accused of having been the conduit for illegal donations to the political parties.

In 1994, the Mani pulite investigation, and Di Pietro personally, became the targets of violent political opposition as they dug into the financial affairs of the new premier, **Silvio Berlusconi**. Di Pietro resigned in protest at the atmosphere of intimidation surrounding the investigation in December 1994, but in 1995 had to survive an investigation into his own conduct as a prosecutor. Cleared of all charges against him, he became minister for public works in the **Prodi** government in May 1996. In the fall of 1996, he once more became embroiled in a web of accusations and inquiries, this time relating to charges that he had given lenient treatment to a Swiss-Italian banker involved in the "Clean Hands" scandal in exchange for cash. No hard evidence has so far appeared on his personal dishonesty, but Di Pietro believed that his position as a minister was incompatible with his being under investigation and resigned in November 1996 in order to clear his name. In November 1997, he was elected to the Senate, representing Mugello (Tuscany) where he won 68 percent of the vote. He had the support of the **Olive Tree Coalition**. Many observers believe that he will form a "party of the honest people" and run for president if a presidential reform is realized.

DI RUDINÌ, ANTONIO STARABBA (1839-1908). A Sicilian conservative, Rudinì came to national attention as mayor of **Palermo**. In 1869, he was briefly minister of the interior under **Luigi Menabrea**. The long sequence of governments of the "left" then kept him out of office until February 1891, when Rudinì—who had been the undisputed leader of the parliamentary right since 1886—became both prime minister and minister for foreign affairs. His first government was accompanied by several important events, notably the foundation of the **Partito Socialista Italiano** (PSI) / Italian

Socialist Party and the publication of the **encyclical** *Rerum Novarum*. His government was brought down in April 1892 by parliamentary opposition to his attempts to balance the budget coming from both the military right of **Girolamo Pelloux** and the parliamentary left of **Giovanni Giolitti.**

Rudinì returned to power in March 1896. His new administration was criticized by the noted economist **Vifredo Pareto** as a "government of gentlemen" who were too well bred to stamp out the corruption revealed during the **Banca Romana** scandal, but, in fairness, Rudinì could also boast some significant achievements. Military spending was capped; the war in **Abyssinia** was brought to an end in October 1896; civil government replaced military rule in Eritrea. These generally sensible policies were not rewarded at the polls. After the elections of March 1897, Rudinì had to rely upon the radicals to stay in office.

Rudinì's second spell as prime minister came to an end as a consequence of the 1898 bread riots, which his government suppressed with severity. At least 80 citizens were killed by troops commanded by General Bava Baccaris in **Milan.** Thousands of people, including several PSI deputies, were arbitrarily arrested and condemned to jail by military tribunals, and emergency laws limiting civil liberties were passed. In June 1898, Rudinì asked that these emergency provisions be made into permanent laws and, when parliament denied this request, appealed to the king to dissolve the Chamber of Deputies and institute a state of siege by royal decree. This near coup was too extreme even for a conservative court, and Rudinì was obliged to resign. He died in **Rome** in 1908.

DIVORCE. In strongly Catholic Italy, the right to divorce was one of the major social and political issues of the late 1960s and early 1970s. The right to legal separation was first proposed in October 1965 by the socialist deputy Loris Fortuna. Fortuna's bill met fierce resistance from the church. But, helped by a cross-party pressure group for reform—the "Italian League for the Institution of Divorce"—his ideas gradually won support. In November 1969, a parliamentary coalition of the "lay" parties that included the conservative **Partito Liberale Italiano** (PLI) / Italian Liberal Party, the Marxist Partito Socialista Italiano d'Unità Proletaria (PSIUP) / Italian Socialist Party of Proletarian Unity, and **Partito Comunista Italiano** (PCI) / Italian Communist Party defeated the opposition of the **Democrazia Cristiana** (DC) / Christian Democracy Party and the **Movimento Sociale Italiano** (MSI) / Italian Social Movement by 325 votes to

283 to pass a law that permitted the state, rather than the church alone, to authorize the dissolution of a marriage. The so-called *Legge Fortuna* became law in December 1970. Pope Paul expressed his "profound regret" for the decision, which the church held to be a violation of the **Lateran pacts.**

Within six months, more than a million Catholics had signed a petition for a referendum abrogating the new divorce law, and in January 1972, the Constitutional Court declared the proposed referendum legitimate. To avoid a divisive social clash over the issue, in February 1972 the political parties resorted to dissolving **Parliament**, and calling an early general election (which, by law, may not be held concurrently with a referendum) in order to postpone the referendum vote. In 1973, **Amintore Fanfani,** hoping to make political capital from the issue, turned it into a crusade (he famously warned that homosexual marriage would be legalized if Italians did not turn back the tide of sexual license of which the divorce law was a harbinger). Bowing to the inevitable, president **Giovanni Leone** called a referendum on the issue in March 1974.

The poll, which took place on May 12-13, 1974, illustrated the shift in Italian social mores that the previous two decades of economic growth and social transformation had worked. Some 87 percent of the electorate voted, and a resounding 59.3 percent voted against abrogating the divorce law. Huge numbers of Catholics, taking notice of Pope Paul's studied moderation during the electoral campaign, either abstained or voted in favor of the *Legge Fortuna*. The introduction of divorce has not shaken the foundations of the Italian family. While the number of divorces has increased from 10,000 in 1980 to 24,000-25,000 per year in the 1990s, this is still a very small percentage of all marriages contracted. Moreover, only 6-7 percent of Italian children are born out of wedlock, compared with figures of 30 percent or more for some industrial democracies. *See also* Catholicism; Referendums.

DOLCI, DANILO (1924-1997). An advocate of non-violent resistance and a civil rights activist on behalf of some of Italy's most deprived citizens, Danilo Dolci was born in **Trieste**, the son of a Sicilian father and a Slovenian mother. His entire adult life after 1952, however, was spent fighting on behalf of the peasant and fishing communities of western Sicily. His most famous tactic was the so-called "strikes in reverse," in which he led hundreds of villagers to repair roads for which funds had been allocated by Parliament but not actually allotted. Such non-violent methods led foreign journalists to call him "the Sicilian Gandhi," a likeness that Dolci always rejected. By embarrassing the Italian state as well as the local notables, he made powerful enemies. In addition, his struggle to gain water rights that were controlled by the local **mafia** added to the precariousness of his position. Yet he continued to organize cooperatives, to engage in hunger strikes, to agitate for irrigation projects and the dams that they entail. His popularity seemed to protect him from any reprisals by those whom he antagonized. In 1957, although not a communist, he was awarded the Lenin Peace prize worth $30,000. But in 1958, he was arrested and tried for the unauthorized work done on roads near Partinico and sentenced to eight months in prison. In 1965 and in 1982, he was nominated for the Nobel prize. In 1967, his allegations that leaders of the **Democrazia Cristiana** (DC) / Christian Democracy Party were guilty of collusion with organized crime led to his conviction for libel and to two additional years in prison.

Dolci was a prolific author of political pamphlets and published several volumes of poetry. Long suffering from diabetes, he contracted pneumonia and—in his last months—was confined to a wheelchair. He died in a Sicilian hospital on December 30, 1997.

DON STURZO. *See* Luigi Sturzo.

DOPOLAVORO, ISTITUTO NAZIONALE DEL (National Institute of Leisure Time Clubs). **Achille Starace** was the president of the Istituto Nazionale del Dopolavoro, a national agency that helped organize and that subsidized "after working hours" leisure-time clubs and organizations during the fascist period. Railway workers, tram operators, machinists, and others had their own distinct biking and hiking clubs, and singing groups, and were encouraged to participate in tennis and other sporting activities. Not only was the intent to heighten the solidarity of members but to contribute to their sense of indebtedness to the state while facilitating their physical conditioning.

This is one of the fascist institutions still employed in Italy with control now in the hands of the political parties who find support of such activities a useful ancillary way of encouraging solidarity among supporters. In some cases, facilities such as tennis courts are provided by the national agency. Other facilities such as meeting rooms are typically found in community centers, union offices, hiring halls, all of which are organized and subsidized by one or another political party. Their role is described in a study by an American sociologist as those "third places, neither home nor work."

DOSSETTI, GIUSEPPE (1913-1996). Born in Genoa, this passionately religious man—a professor of canonical law at the University of Modena—had fought in the resistance near Reggio-Emilia (Emilia) and had served the **Democrazia Cristiana** (DC) / Christian Democracy Party on its steering committee. Elected to the **Constitutent Assembly**, he subsequently was elected and reelected to the Chamber of Deputies between 1945 and 1952, a period in which he joined with **Fanfani** and other integralists to augment the role played in political and social life by Catholic social doctrine. In 1956, he ran unsuccessfully. Taking the vows of priesthood (he was ordained in 1959), he founded a small monastic order. He died in **Bologna** at age 83. *See also* Integralism.

DUCE, IL. *See* Mussolini, Benito.

-E-

EARTHQUAKES. In seismic terms, Italy is one of the nations most at risk in Europe. There have been three major earthquakes in twentieth-century Italy, as well as dozens of minor tremors. The worst quake occurred when Messina (Sicily) and its twin city Reggio Calabria were both destroyed on December 28, 1908, with the loss of nearly 100,000 lives—one of the worst natural disasters in European history. This tremor was measured at 7.5 on the Richter scale, one of the most powerful of all time.

There have been two major quakes more recently. In May 1976, more than 1,000 people were killed by an earthquake in Friuli-Venezia-Giulia, near the Yugoslav border. Volunteers came from all over Italy to clear away the wreckage and help the *friuliani* get back on their feet. In November 1980, meanwhile, a massive tremor (6.8 on the Richter scale) killed 6,000 people in Campania and Basilicata. This terrible natural calamity was compounded by the behavior of Italy's politicians, who turned the disaster into an opportunity to funnel huge sums of relief aid into the area and then to syphon it off to their client networks, to friendly businessmen, and organized crime (which carried great electoral weight in the **Naples** region). It has been calculated that over Lit. 50 thousand billion ($30 billion) were earmarked for earthquake relief, but most of this money was never spent on the reconstruction efforts, and even today, several thousand refugees continue to live in the prefabricated huts thrown up in the aftermath of the emergency. In September 1997, a series of earthquakes struck Umbria taking fewer lives but destroying priceless frescoes by Giotto in the church of Saint Francis in Assisi.

ECO, UMBERTO (1932-). One of the world's leading philosophers and a pioneer in the study of semiotics (the analysis of signs), Umberto Eco is that rarest of birds, a professor who is both internationally respected within the academy and widely read outside. Eco owes his popularity principally to his 1980 novel *Il nome della rosa* (*The Name of the Rose*), a philosophical "whodunit" set in a medieval Italian monastery that quickly sold more than four million copies in numerous languages, and became one of the publishing events of recent times. Since 1980, Eco has published two further novels, which have met lesser critical and public success, *Il pendolo di Foucault* (*Foucault's Pendulum*, 1988) and *L'isola del giorno prima* (*The Island of the Day Before*, 1994). Professor Eco's scholarly works have included monographs on the aesthetics of Saint Aquinas and medieval aesthetics more generally, the poetics of James Joyce, and, most famously of all, his several books on the theory of semiotics. He was the first Italian to give the Norton lectures on poetry at Harvard University in 1992. Eco is also a columnist for the weekly news magazine *L'Espresso* where he has a platform for his witty, acute, and occasionally whimsical views on popular culture, politics, and contemporary life in general. Eco lives in his native **Milan** and teaches at the University of **Bologna**.

ECONOMIC MIRACLE. By 1963, Italy had ceased to be a primarily agricultural country and became a modern industrial state. Between 1950 and 1970, income per head in Italy grew faster (on average over 6 percent per year) than any other major European country and had arrived at 80 percent of British levels by 1970. Between unification in 1861 and the end of the 1930s, real per capita income in Italy grew by just one-third. Between 1946 and 1963, the years of fastest growth, it doubled. Used to grinding poverty, Italians could only regard this sudden enrichment as miraculous, although, in truth, they had earned it by their own hard work.

Industrially, Italian economic growth was guided by the big private and public corporations. **FIAT** established itself as a mass manufacturer of automobiles, expanding production from a pre-war high of 78,000 vehicles in 1938 to over a million in 1963. The Italian state steel company, Finsider, under the guidance of Oscar

Singaglia, became one of the largest and most innovative manufacturers of finished steel products in the world. ENI, the oil and gas business of **Enrico Mattei**, gave Italian firms a cheap and plentiful source of fuel. Smaller producers of consumer goods, particularly domestic appliances and textiles, did their share: Italy became one of the world's largest producers of so-called "white goods" in these years. The chief market was Europe. The creation of the European Economic Community in 1958 opened the markets of northern Europe for the nimble and relatively cheap entrepreneurs of northern Italy, and they took full advantage of the opportunity. Exports grew even faster (approximately 10 percent per year on average) than the economy as a whole, and over 90 percent of sales abroad were in industrial merchandise rather than raw materials or services. In the late 1990s, over 70 percent of Italy's exports are made to other members of the **European Union.**

Italy, in short, had become a country that made and sold goods as well as thriving on service sector activities such as tourism. By 1961, nearly 40 percent of the working population was employed in manufacturing, and less than 30 percent in agriculture, a historic change from the over 60 percent who had hitherto worked the fields. Between 1958 and 1963, the peak years of the "miracle," nearly one million Southerners moved north, mostly to **Turin** and **Milan**, and many hundreds of thousands emigrated to Germany, Belgium, Switzerland, and the United States. But the phenomenon was not limited to the South: the region that lost the largest proportion of its inhabitants to migration was Venetia, whose rural population headed in their thousands to the fatter wage packets provided by the industrial cities of Lombardy. These demographic shifts led to an unprecedented construction boom, in which the outskirts of all of Italy's big cities became disfigured by housing projects hastily thrown up to provide the migrants with apartments. An unforeseen by-product was an upheaval in social mores. Freed from rural traditions, with money in their pockets for the first time, Italians of all classes began to experiment with more liberal sexual conduct, while church attendance plummeted. The diffusion of television contributed to altering the traditionally communal Italian way of life. Instead of sitting outside in the *piazze*, Italians—like the newly rich citizens of other European countries—became increasingly prone to entertain themselves in front of the flickering screen: more than half of all Italian families had a TV set by 1965.

Such economic and social changes left their mark on Italian culture. The disquiet felt by many intellectuals is captured in

Federico Fellini's 1957 film *La Dolce Vita*, while the disorientation of the southern migrants is the theme of **Luchino Visconti**'s moving *Rocco e i suoi fratelli* (*Rocco and His Brothers*, 1960). *See also* Tables 14 and 15 in Appendix.

EDUCATION. As in so much of Europe, Italy's entire public educational system is regarded as a responsibility of the collectivity and as being in the public interest from the *asilo* (kindergarten) through the university. Like the French system introduced under Napoleon, Italy's is meritocratic and elitist in that only those who meet the standards established by the Ministry of Education in **Rome** are advanced to the next grade. Others must repeat the entire year.

Municipalities—especially when administered by left-coalitions—often provide their own, free, preschool programs (the *Scuola Materna* is for toddlers; the *asilo* for the immediately pre-school ages) with preference given in admissions to mothers who work outside the home. Municipally regulated, the quality of care provided is widely recognized as high. The superintendent of schools in a city is an appointee of the ministry and is responsible for ensuring that there be properly operated pre-primary, primary, and secondary schools in his district.

High expectations begin in the elementary grades. The teacher in the pupils' first year stays with the class for the full five years, that is, until the pupils move on to the intermediate level (*Scuola Media*). At the end of three intermediate years, examinations are administered to determine fitness for moving on to the next level, either terminal or pre-university. The most prestigious secondary schools are the pre-university *licei* (like the French *Lycée* or German *Gymnasium*). The 14-year-old may choose either the Classical Liceo, the Scientific Liceo, Fine Arts, the Conservatory, or the *Liceo Linguistico* (Foreign Language Liceo). All are underwritten by the state. The curricular differences are chiefly in the balance between required courses and electives. Those individuals who do not aim at university studies may follow a separate track, concluding their education by studying Industrial Arts, Merchant Marine Academy, Bookkeeping, or Surveyors' Studies. The School-Leaving Examination for Liceo students has oral and written components. Judgments of candidates' readiness are made by a panel of eight: four from one's own high school, and four outside evaluators.

Whosoever completes liceo studies (as determined by the Maturity Examination most recently redefined in September of 1997) receives a School-Leaving Certificate that provides automatic entry to a university faculty (similar to a department in a United States institution) depending on the type of liceo chosen at age 14. For example, graduates of the Classical Liceo with its requirements of classical Greek, Latin, philosophy, and mathematics may choose any faculty, including medicine and law (jurisprudence). Those who "did" Fine Arts may choose architecture or art history; those from a Scientific Liceo may "major" in any of the laboratory sciences or medicine. In any university faculty, a prescribed program must be followed. Each student has a *libretto* (booklet) in which are recorded all examination results. Course exams are orally administered, normally by a panel of 3-5 professors. When the requisite courses have been successfully completed and the student selects, researches, writes, and defends a thesis, the student receives the laurel wreath (*la laurea*: the graduate is, therefore, *laureato/a*), entitling him/her to be styled *dottore / dottoressa*, or learned.

There are, and have been, private secondary schools as well that have traditionally served to offer a place to those (of means) who fail to meet the standards applied, fairly rigorously but uniformly, in the public institutions. Private parallel schools—many run by religious orders—exist at each level, from *asilo* to university. Some are treated as the equal of state schools (*parificati*: they conform to the curriculum, schedules, and examinations of the state schools), and others function experimentally, such as the *Libera Università Internazionale per gli Studi Sociali* (LUISS) / Free University for the Social Sciences, for business studies.

Heading each university is the "magnificent rector" who is elected by senior faculty of the university senate. This faculty member is expected to be an academic of some standing whose functions do not include fund-raising inasmuch as costs are met from the national budget. Faculty appointments are made after competitions in which candidates' publications are the chief criterion. (The perceived importance of senior sponsors is allegedly even more decisive.) There are normally hundreds of highly qualified candidates for each opening, wherever in the national system it might be located. The competition is fierce, even for places in the newest or least prestigious departments. Italian universities, however, are some of the oldest in the world. Bologna (which celebrated its 900th anniversary in 1988), Padua, Florence, the Sapienza University in Rome are all medieval institutions.

Limiting the number of students entering each year began only in the last few years and has met the unremitting hostility of the students. In February 1997, the Italian Council of State—the highest administrative court—questioned the legality of limiting the admission of qualified aspirants. Six thousand who had been excluded were readmitted. The total cost of Lit. 80 million ($50 thousand) for each degree weighs heavily on a government trying to reduce spending levels. When barely a third of those who begin university studies bring them to a successful conclusion, the government can be expected to view free access to university with misgiving. In ranking countries by the percentage of 20- to 24-year-olds pursuing higher (post-secondary) education, Italy ranks third in Europe. *See also* Women in Contemporary Italy; Table 17 in Appendix.

EINAUDI, LUIGI (1874-1961). A Piedmontese professor who became the first constitutionally elected president of the Italian Republic in 1948, Luigi Einaudi was the most prominent spokesman in Italy in this century for economic liberalism, and for a state whose role was strictly limited to what he called "the government of things." Born in Cuneo in 1874, the young Einaudi divided his time between his duties as a professor of finance at the University of Turin and as editorialist for *La Stampa* and *Corriere della Sera*. Like **Luigi Albertini**, his editor at the *Corriere della Sera*, Einaudi was an early opponent of **fascism**. He spoke out against the violence and authoritarianism of **Mussolini**'s movement even before the **March on Rome** and continued his criticisms after Mussolini had come to power. When Albertini was removed from the editorship of the *Corriere* in 1925, Einaudi's long collaboration with the paper also came to an end. There was no place in a fascist newspaper for a writer who praised free markets and European unification, and who signed the manifesto of anti-fascist intellectuals published by **Benedetto Croce** in 1925. In 1930, an academic review that Einaudi had edited since 1908, *Riforma sociale* (*Social Reform*), was also suppressed by the authorities. Einaudi was able to continue with his scholarly work, however. His key work on economics, *Principi della scienza delle finanze* (*Principles of the Science of Finances*), was published in 1932, and he also was able to write a series of studies on the classical economists.

After the fall of Mussolini in July 1943, Einaudi became rector of the University of **Turin**, but was swiftly forced to flee to Switzerland to avoid capture by the Germans. Upon his return to Italy, he was made governor of the Bank of Italy. He was elected to **Parliament** in June 1946 as a member of the **Partito Liberale Italiano** (PLI) / Italian Liberal Party and was soon given important economic responsibilities. In May 1947, Einaudi became budget minister and deputy prime minister in the first post-war government not to include the **Partito Comunista Italiano** (PCI) / Italian Communist Party, and introduced austerity policies that stabilized the plummeting **lira**. On May 10, 1948, he was elected president of the republic. Einaudi served as president until 1955. He was an active scholar and writer up to his death in October 1961. His *Prediche inutili* (*Useless Sermons)*—reflections on the classical themes of political economy—appeared between 1955 and 1959. These "useless" sermons did not find much of an audience in 1950s Italy, where both the **Democrazia Cristiana** (DC) / Christian Democracy Party and the PCI were in the grip of dirigiste economic philosophies, but Einaudi's insistence on limited but efficient government, and his lifelong attachment to the cause of a united Europe, have much more resonance in contemporary Italy. *See also* Banking.

ELECTORAL LAWS. When Italy was unified in 1861, it inherited the electoral laws of the Kingdom of Piedmont-Sardinia, which elected its **Parliament** through a dual ballot system of single-member constituencies. The Piedmontese system remained in force until 1882, when Italy moved to a plural-member constituency system in which, according to size, constituencies returned two to five deputies and the elector had as many votes as there were candidates to elect. This experiment failed, and a return to the former system took place in 1891 although the threshold for entering the second ballot was now reduced to one-sixth of the votes cast instead of the 30 percent required by the former law.

Universal male suffrage for men over 30 years of age was enacted in Italy in 1912. In 1919, **Francesco Saverio Nitti** introduced proportional representation, a move that allowed **Mussolini**'s nascent fascist party to gain a foothold in Parliament in 1921. Once in power, Mussolini introduced the "**Acerbo** Law" in 1923. Any party gaining a plurality in the popular vote was guaranteed two-thirds of the seats in Parliament. In 1928 a plebiscitary system was introduced whereby citizens were limited to voting yea or nay to an approved "big list" of approved fascist candidates.

Fully free elections with universal suffrage were introduced in Italy in 1946. Women were accorded the franchise not because of a great upsurge of demand but, quite possibly, because the leaders of the **Democrazia Cristiana** (DC) / Christian Democracy expected that women, thought to be traditionally churchgoing and suggestible by parish priests, would vote for the DC. In 1953, the DC tried to amend the system of proportional representation used in the elections of 1948 by introducing legislation (swiftly dubbed the "swindle law") that gave any coalition that obtained over 50 percent of the vote a "prize" in seats. In the 1953 elections, however, the DC and its allies failed to reach the 50 percent threshold and the law was never applied. Subsequently, Italy chose its representatives by proportional representation. For the Chamber of Deputies, election was by a convoluted form of the party-list system that guaranteed representation in Parliament to all but the very smallest formations, and that awarded seats in strict proportion to the number of votes cast with remainders put into a national pool for eventual assignment of seats. The result was the fragmentation of the party system and the prevalence of unstable coalition governments. For the Senate, a different system of proportional representation granted greater representation to the larger parties, but still meant that the upper chamber contained a plethora of mini-parties. An interesting peculiarity of elections for the Italian Senate was—and is—that only adults over 25 years of age may vote.

In the 1980s, dissatisfaction with the electoral system gave birth to a popular movement for electoral reform and to successful **referendums** on electoral reform in June 1991 and April 1993. Since August 1993, both the Chamber of Deputies and the Senate have been elected by an electoral law that reserves 75 percent of the seats in both chambers for direct election in single-member constituencies, and 25 percent of the seats for election by proportional representation. A German-style "threshold" excludes parties that obtain less than 4 percent of the vote from Parliament. This law has worked less well than many expected. Instead of leading to the development of a two-party system on the British or American model, Italy now has a "two-alliance" system of parties (more akin to France's Fifth Republic) in which two broad-based coalitions of mostly small parties confront each other. There is much talk in Italy of yet another new electoral law. *See also* Mario Segni.

ENCYCLICALS. Encyclicals are written by sitting Popes to instruct Catholic bishops concerning Papal views on specific matters. Those published since Italy's unification have been extremely important, none more so than *Rerum Novarum* prepared by Pope Leo XIII and published on May 15, 1891, in response to the growth of socialism as an apparent companion of early industrialism.

While undeniably conservative in tone (the document warned

that it was the duty of the state to intervene to preserve the "good workers" from the seductive doctrines of the revolutionaries and to prevent the expropriation of private property), *Rerum Novarum* nevertheless made concessions to the working-class movement. In particular, it argued that natural justice demanded that there be a minimum wage that guaranteed the frugal, clean-living worker an adequate standard of living, and it gave a Papal blessing to the formation of Catholic workers' associations. Fascist theorists subsequently cited this encyclical as a precursor of **corporatism**. The encyclical also urged the state to favor the growth of small-scale industrial enterprises, and to intervene to ensure that conditions and hours of work were not exploitative.

The thesis of *Rerum Novarum* was restated on its fortieth anniversary by Pius XI in *Quadragesimo Anno* (1931). Similarly, Pope Paul's *Popolorum Progressio* argued, in 1967, that the search for profits should not contravene Christian teaching. Both encyclicals took to task those whose only goal is profit, deplored the "inhumanity of bosses and the unfettered selfishness of competition," and advocated the organization of workers into categories able to negotiate with capital and thereby to prevent the abuses made possible by concentrated wealth.

Other encyclicals that address the balance to be struck between considerations of social justice and capital accumulation include John XXIII's *Mater et Magistra* (1961) and *Pacem in Terris* (1963); Paul VI's *Octogesima Adveniens* (1971); and John Paul's *Solecitudine Sociale* (1987).

ENVIRONMENTALISM. As in most other European countries, concern for the quality of the environment began to emerge in Italy in the 1970s and early 1980s. Overbuilding in Italian coastal resorts, increasing pollution in lakes and rivers, the growing problem of smog in the cities, the nascent nuclear program, a 1976 leak of dioxin at a chemical plant at Seveso near **Milan**, all contributed to an increased interest in environmental issues. Following the success of the German Green Party in the 1983 elections to the Bundestag, local Green associations successfully fielded lists of candidates in the two provinces closest to Germany, Trento and Bolzano, in 1983. In local elections held nationwide in 1985, local Green associations ran candidates in communal and provincial elections all over the country. To capitalize on this upsurge in interest, the "National Federation of Green Lists" was founded in November 1986, and in the 1987 general elections, the federation's symbol was on the ballot paper throughout the country. They won 2.5 percent of the vote and elected 13 deputies and two senators. In the fall of 1987, the Greens enjoyed a further triumph when Italians, alarmed by the Chernobyl disaster, voted in a national referendum to end Italy's nuclear power program. The formation of a rival force, the *Verdi arcobaleno* ("Rainbow Greens"), which appealed to Greens worried that the environmentalist movement was fossilizing into a traditional political party, did not slow the growth of Green sympathies among the electorate. In the European elections in June 1989, the two lists together obtained over 6 percent of the vote, the apex of Green support in Italy. Although the two rival movements merged in 1990, the *Verdi* have struggled to maintain electoral support in the changed economic climate of the 1990s. Only 2.8 percent of the electorate voted for Green candidates in the general elections of 1992, a figure that has been approximated in the two subsequent electoral tests. In April 1993, the former European commissioner for the environment, Carlo Ripa Di Meana, was appointed national spokesman for the Greens, and until December 1996, when he was deposed as party leader, he represented environmentalists within the **Olive Tree Coalition**.

Unless there is another nuclear or industrial calamity, the *Verdi* seem destined to remain marginal in Italian political life. Green sentiment, however, has become deeply rooted in Italy. Other single-issue organizations such as the *Lega ambiente* (Environmental League), Greenpeace, and the Anti-vivisection League all have substantial active memberships.

ETHIOPIA. *See* Abyssinia.

EUROCOMMUNISM. The peculiar brand of communism advanced by the leaders of the Italian, French, and Spanish communist parties advocated several positions regarded by the orthodox as anathema: that each country had to find its own path to socialism; that the Soviet party had no patrimonial rights or privileges in dealings with the western parties; and that the path to socialism might well entail accepting the constraints implicit in the parliamentary system. This phenomenon, so closely identified with **Enrico Berlinguer**, was already clearly enunciated at the 1969 Moscow conference of communist party leaders with such force that Brezhnev's aide stormed out of the hall. In October 1974, Berlinguer explicitly rejected, in another public forum, the "guiding function" of Soviet leadership. In a 1975 **Rome** meeting with Santiago Carrillo (of the Spanish Communist Party) and Georges Marchais (leader of the

French party), it was agreed that "true socialism is built on full confrontation among all political forces, socialist, social democratic, and Catholic." In Moscow at the Twenty-fifth Party Congress, the proponents of this "Eurocommunist" view tried to persuade others that they all had to accept "democratic conquests." That June, in Rome, Berlinguer added to an interviewer that "NATO is necessary to build socialism in liberty." By 1977, pluralism and democracy had become more important to those who followed Berlinguer than the dictatorship of the proletariat. "The propulsive force of Eastern Europe," Berlinguer added, "is exhausted." Indeed, in 1981, Berlinguer denounced the imposition of martial law in Poland by General Jaruzelski.

The implicit conclusion is that Eurocommunism contributed to the transformation both in name and direction of the **Partito Comunista Italiano** (PCI) / Italian Communist Party. The risks for the party included the possible disaffection of the militant base and the loss of appeal to younger members. The consequences for other Italian parties included losing that unifying menace on the revolutionary left: this loss widened the gaps among lay parties and between them and the Catholic center. Conservative voters began to look elsewhere than the **Democrazia Cristiana** (DC) / Christian Democracy Party for the defense of the status quo.

EUROPEAN UNION (EU). Italy has been one of the most vocal supporters of European unification since the 1940s. One of the earliest blueprints for a federal European state—the so-called Ventotene Manifesto—was drawn up in 1943 by the anti-fascist intellectuals Ernesto Rossi and **Altiero Spinelli**. In the 1950s, **Alcide De Gasperi** made European integration one of the core elements of his foreign policy and led Italy into the European Coal and Steel Community (ECSC) in 1952. The negotiations that led to the creation of the European Economic Community (EEC), or "Common Market," were carried out in Messina in **Sicily**, and became law in the Treaty of **Rome** (1958) with the signatures of the governments of France, Italy, West Germany, Belgium, the Netherlands, and Luxembourg. Participation in the EEC brought Italy substantial commercial benefits and was a major factor in the surge of economic growth in 1958-1963 known as the **economic miracle**.

Italy has since become a somewhat passive member of the European Community (EC) and then of the European Union (EU), although it has always subscribed to every attempt to expand the powers of "federal" institutions such as the European Parliament and

Commission at the expense of national sovereignty. Some critics argue that Italy's commitment to European unification is in reality somewhat flimsy. Italy was among the slowest of all member states to implement the single market in goods and services required by the 1986 Single European Act, and even today certain industries and services such as car manufacturing and **banking** enjoy a degree of informal protection from European rivals. Italy's state bureaucracy has also failed to exploit the opportunities for growth and industrial development offered by the various European funds for social and economic modernization. Finally, Italy's ability to enforce immigration controls required by the Schengen agreements (March 1995) has been called into question, especially by the German government. These agreements eliminate passport and other customs controls at EU borders for EU nationals. Italy's long coastlines, however, offer easy access for clandestine immigrants who can then move at will to other EU nations. For this reason, Italy only implemented the accords in October 1997.

It is fair to say that the process of European unification has compelled Italy's political parties to adopt deregulating, competition-inducing policies that they might otherwise not have followed. Particularly since signing the 1992 **Treaty of Maastricht,** the Italian government has had to introduce unprecedented economic austerity to meet its commitment to participating in European monetary union. Although Italian dairy farmers are very vocal in their disappointment with the milk production quotas assigned them, most of the Italian electorate remains enthusiastic toward European union. A Europe-wide poll taken by the European Commission in May 1997, showed that fully 73 percent of the Italians favored the introduction of the European single currency, the euro, regardless of the sacrifices entailed. This figure compares interestingly with 55 percent in France and only 39 percent in Germany.

-F-

FACTA, LUIGI (1861-1930). Italy's last liberal prime minister, Facta's two administrations in 1922 were the culmination of the lengthy and inexorable decline of liberal institutions in Italy. Facta, who had been minister for justice from January to June 1919 under **Vittorio Emanuele Orlando,** was a supporter of **Giovanni Giolitti.** When, following the resignation of **Ivanoe Bonomi** in February 1922, the **Partito Popolare Italiano** (PPI) / Italian People's Party vetoed Giolitti's nomination by the king, Facta emerged as a compromise candidate for the premiership. After the longest government crisis since 1848, Facta assembled a cabinet that gave three key ministries (finance, education, and agriculture) to the PPI. Six different parties or factions participated in the government, which was approved by Parliament on March 18, 1922, with the support of even the **Partito Nazionale Fascista** (PNF) / National Fascist Party.

Facta's first administration was characterized by huge fascist rallies in northern Italy and by unchecked fascist violence against socialists, trade unionists, and the PPI. On June 10, 1922, Facta feebly promised the Senate that he would overcome the crisis by applying the law "impartially." The absence of any threat to crack down on fascist *squadrismo* encouraged the worst violence yet in July 1922. Facta's government collapsed in mid-month after fascist squads devastated the headquarters of the **Partito Socialista Italiano** (PSI) / Italian Socialist Party and PPI in Cremona (Lombardy) and raided the homes of two PPI trade union leaders, Guido Miglioli and Giuseppe Garibotti. In his resignation speech, Facta denied that exceptional measures were needed and blamed local authorities for not enforcing the law. Facta formed a second, almost identical, government on August 1, 1922, promising to restore the "empire of the law." Within days, the fascists had occupied the city hall in **Milan**, destroyed the offices of *L 'Avanti!*, and started bloody riots in other northern Italian cities. No action was taken to punish these breaches of the law. Further acts of unpunished violence were recorded throughout the country in September and October. Facta again resigned on October 27, 1922, the day after the **March on Rome,** which the central government did not in any serious way oppose. He had asked the king for emergency powers to repress the fascist coup. The king refused and appointed **Mussolini** as premier.

How far was Facta culpable for the collapse of parliamentary democracy in Italy? In his defense, it should be said that Italian liberal opinion was demoralized; that nothing could have been done to stop the fascists without giving carte blanche to the PSI, which refused to undertake a permanent commitment to parliamentary democracy. Local police authorities under the command of prefects appointed in **Rome** could have done much more to ensure respect for the law. While all these points are true, an act of will on the part of Facta, and his political sponsor, **Giovanni Giolitti**, could have saved Italian democracy. As the fascist writer **Curzio Malaparte** pointed out, the crucial difference between the liberals and the fascists was that the fascists were prepared to use violence in pursuit of their ends and the liberals were not. Facta died in his native Pinerolo

(Piedmont) in 1930. *See also* Fascism.

FALCONE, GIOVANNI (1939-1992). The symbol of the Italian state's struggle against the **mafia**, Giovanni Falcone was brutally murdered in a bomb attack on May 23, 1992. He had risen rapidly to national prominence as an assistant district attorney in his native **Palermo**, where he was first the right-hand man of a heroic anti-mafia prosecutor, Rocco Chinnici (murdered by *Cosa nostra* in 1983), and then, between 1984 and 1987 the lead prosecutor in the huge trial of Michele "the Pope" Greco (the boss of the Sicilian mafia) and dozens of other gangsters. Falcone was the first prosecutor to breach the *omertà* (code of silence) that the mafia imposed upon its affiliates, by persuading a senior figure in the underworld, Tommaso Buscetta, to reveal all he knew of the organization's internal workings. Buscetta is now a key witness in the Italian state's investigation into former prime minister **Giulio Andreotti**'s alleged links to organized crime.

In the late 1980s, the efforts of Falcone and his anti-mafia "pool" of prosecutors in Palermo were hampered by the judicial and political hierarchies in Palermo. Falcone (who survived a bomb attack in June 1989) decided that he could continue the fight against the mafia better from **Rome**, and in 1991 with the encouragement of the justice minister, Claudio Martelli, he created the *Direzione nazionale antimafia* (DNA), a top-level, FBI-style task force that coordinates action against organized crime. Judicial politics prevented Falcone from becoming the first chief of this organization (the post went, instead, to another courageous prosecutor, Agostino Cordova), but the creation of the DNA was the decisive step in the struggle against organized crime. Literally hundreds of gangsters, including the boss of bosses, Toto Riina, have been arrested since 1991. This victory for legality is Falcone's legacy.

Falcone was murdered, while traveling between Palermo airport and the city center, by a buried bomb set off by remote control. It blew a huge crater in the highway, killing his wife, Franca, and three bodyguards, as well as Judge Falcone. The grief and rage that was felt throughout Italy at his death had profound political implications. It led directly to the election of **Oscar Luigi Scalfaro** as president of the republic, and stimulated growing public frustration with a political system that had for years tolerated and even collaborated with the bosses of *Cosa nostra*. *See also* Mafia.

FANFANI, AMINTORE (1908-). Born in Arezzo province (Tuscany), he was a boyhood member of the Catholic Boy Scouts and a founder of his hometown's **Azione Cattolica.** After serving in the army in **World War I**, he attended Milan's Catholic University of the Sacred Heart in the 1920s taking his research degree (*Libera Docenza*, 1932) in economics. He joined the **Partito Nazionale Fascista** (PNF) / National Fascist Party in 1933, then Catholic University's faculty where he served until 1955 when he was appointed at the University of **Rome**, a position he held until 1983. As an economist, he wrote the standard textbook for Italian secondary schools on fascist **corporatism.** His major biographer identifies him as an authoritarian as well as a confessional Catholic; he was to become a member of the inner circle of the **Democrazia Cristiana** (DC) / Christian Democracy Party after **World War II.** Chosen to serve on the steering committee (*Direzione Centrale*) in 1946, he was elected to the 1947 **Constituent Assembly.**

He served under **Alcide De Gasperi** and **Giuseppe Pella** between 1948 and 1953 as minister for agriculture and interior. In June 1949, he succeeded **Dossetti** as leader of the **integralist** faction of the DC. Finally, after an unsuccessful attempt at forming his own government, he was chosen party secretary in July 1954. In that post, he quickly showed himself able to match the organizational and technical skills of the **Partito Comunista Italiano** (PCI) / Italian Communist Party. Younger parliament members anxious to ride on his coattails were dubbed, in the press, *fanfaniani.* In July 1958, he became president of the Council of Ministers and foreign minister but resigned in February 1959. He also offered to resign as party secretary and was appalled when the offer was accepted by the National Council of the DC. An internal faction of centrists, the *Dorotei* (so called because they met in Rome's convent of Saint Dorothy), alarmed by his open preference for an **opening to the left** (i.e., to the **Partito Socialista Italiano** (PSI) / Italian Socialist Party), had decided to back **Aldo Moro.** After the **Tambroni** episode (1960), Fanfani and Moro became allies. Fanfani was again prime minister until June 1963, when unsatisfactory electoral results ended his attempt to govern with the parliamentary support of the PSI.

Between 1965 and 1968, Fanfani was foreign minister and, in 1965, became president of the United Nations General Assembly. In 1968, he was appointed to Italy's Senate. In 1972, he was made senator for life. He again served as party secretary between 1973 and 1976, the year in which he was elected to preside over the Senate. As party secretary, he led the DC's attempt to overturn the law on **divorce** warning the Italians—in lurid terms—that sexual morality would be undermined if the institution of marriage were threatened.

Following President **Giovanni Leone**'s resignation in June 1978, Fanfani served as president of the republic *pro tempore* for three weeks. In 1979, he was reelected president of the Senate.

In December 1982, he formed his fifth government, which lasted until the elections of June 1983. Again, in 1987, he formed a caretaker government that carried the country to the elections of that year. In the government of **Giovanni Goria** (August 1987 to February 1988), Fanfani was minister of the interior and, in its successor government led by **Ciriaco De Mita** (April 1988 to July 1989), he was budget minister. In sum, a man who began his political ascent in the 1930s continued to hold high office until the late 1980s. *See also* Democrazia Cristiana; Divorce; Aldo Moro; Opening to the Left; Table 6 in Appendix.

FARINACCI, ROBERTO (1892-1945). Before **World War I**, he had been a railway worker and prominent labor boss in Cremona. A street-fighter called by a British historian "one of the more illiterate and brutish of the hierarchy," he was rooted in the original revolutionary syndicalist left of the early fascist movement and was one of the first members of the **Partito Nazionale Fascista** (PNF) / National Fascist Party. While party secretary between 1925 and 1926, his desire to monopolize all veterans' organizations led him to order the dissolution of the Associazione dei combattenti (Combat Veterans' Association). He consistently preferred anti-bourgeois, anti-establishment violence so long as it was performed by PNF agencies.

Farinacci's reliance on violence is illustrated by two episodes: During the punitive expedition against **Milan**'s socialists on August 3-4, 1922, Farinacci not only broke up the presses of *L'Avanti!* but also evicted the socialist city government, having **Gabriele D'Annunzio** himself address the crowd from the city hall.

Similarly, when the acting Italian high commissioners —appointed by the government in **Rome** to win over the newly absorbed German-speaking population of *Süd Tirol* (Alto Adige)— pursued policies calculated to that end, Farinacci and allied nationalists rejected this "weak" approach. Under Farinacci's direction, fascist squads forcefully seized local government offices in Alto Adige.

By 1925, most of the opposition press had been silenced. Once uniformity had been imposed, it was a simple—and profitable—matter for local party leaders to begin publishing pro-party newspapers as was done by Farinacci in Cremona and **Italo Balbo** in

Ferrara. With a fraudulent university degree in law (he had attended few lectures and allegedly submitted another's dissertation), he actually began offering his "legal" services as an "insider" influence-peddler. As defense counsel for those accused after the **Matteotti** incident, he was seen by older, hard-line fascists as the savior of the party.

While he enriched himself in a number of ways, he was also consistent in his loyalty to the Duce. Farinacci was one of the few who were with **Mussolini** when he was captured by partisans on April 28, 1945, at Dongo, executed, and hung by his heels, together with Clara Petacci and **Achille Starace**. *See also* Fascism; Benito Mussolini; Squadrismo.

FASCISM. In December 1915, **Benito Mussolini** joined—and soon dominated—a small gathering of left-socialist interventionists who called their group a *fascio*, that is, a bundle, a *bund*, a league; he prepared their manifesto. This was eventually to become the Fasci Italiani di combattimento / Italian Combat League, thence the post-war **Partito Nazionale Fascista** (PNF) / National Fascist Party, born in Piazza di San Sepolcro, **Milan**, on March 23, 1919. (Those in attendance at this initial meeting were called, thereafter, Sansepolcristi.) Mussolini used the PNF to govern Italy for two decades (*il ventennio*) and—at least before **World War II**—was widely admired and imitated abroad, not least by Adolf Hitler. (Note that Mussolini had been in power for 11 years when Hitler became *Reichskanzler*.) Fascism's identifying characteristics include authoritarian conservatism, nationalism, and mobilization of the public to defeat, simultaneously, both Marxism and liberal democracy in favor of a "unanimous" society in which only one opinion on social or political questions has merit, and conflict would thus no longer arise. Contrary opinions were dealt with by a Special Tribunal (created in 1926) for offenses against the "revolution." Fascism was, therefore, anti-liberal, anti-pluralist and anti-parliamentary, anti-rational as well as hierarchical, hence its depiction as "romantic authoritarianism."

Many parliamentarians who endorsed the Mussolini government in 1922 were neither fascists nor nationalists but were convinced that Mussolini and the fascists would be made more tractable—and useful—once immersed in parliamentary ways. They included **Vittorio Emanuale Orlando, Giovanni Giolitti** himself, **Antonio Salandra, Alcide De Gasperi, Giovanni Gronchi**, and **Ivanoe Bonomi**, as well as King **Victor Emmanuel III**.

The movement's wide appeal, despite its internal contradictions, should not surprise the observer. The apparent inability of pre-war governments to deal with the social dislocations of industrialization and of waging war was hardly unique to Italy. But the costs of the war and the effect on savings, the rapid pace of industrial and social change and the loss of the stabilizing rigidities of the pre-war social order made it more likely that a mass movement offering new certainties would find adherents. The dimensions of the social devastation and the perceived humiliation of the peace settlement weakened the consensus—or at least the acquiescence—necessary to stability. If the invisible hand of market forces fails to ensure the attainment of goals such as full employment, steady growth, equitable distribution, and political stability, it seems clear that whole populations can be seduced by mercantilists and superpatriots.

After **World War I**, Mussolini used the nascent PNF to win parliamentary power. Once Mussolini had attained high office, it only took a few years for him to organize a plebiscite to endorse his assumption of dictatorial powers. In 1925, his status nearly equaled that of the king. He was to be styled head of government; by 1926, the power was his to legislate by personal decree without consulting a **Parliament**, which was—in any event—totally dominated by blackshirt-wearing fascists.

Even the most convinced anti-fascist would do well to recognize that Mussolini's power did not rely on brutality and repression alone. In the troughs of the depression, activities in fascist Italy were described admiringly by *Fortune* magazine in 1934 as including the launching of great ocean liners (the *Rex* and the *Conte di Savoia*). Trains ran on time and faster through the longest double-track tunnels in the world near the longest network of limited-access highways to be found anywhere. **Italo Balbo** and the Air Armada had flown seaplanes to Chicago and Brazil. The draining of the Italian marshlands had begun and the land prepared for agricultural production. Heavyweight prizefighter Primo Carnera had not yet been beaten by America's Joe Louis. Italy dominated European auto-racing circuits, air-speed records, and soccer fields. More important, fascism was widely perceived as having created, in **corporatism**, an imaginative structure for dealing with the industrial turmoil sweeping the world. Fascism struck many Italians and not a few foreigners as a salvation from what had gone before. Italy's attainments under fascism were attributed to its founder and leader, Benito Mussolini. *See also* Italo Balbo; Comitati di Liberazione Nazionale; Corporatism; Dopolavoro, Istituto Nazionale del; Roberto Farinacci;

Foreign Policy; Gran Consiglio del Fascismo; Quadrumvirate; Republic of Salò; Squadrismo; Achille Starace; World War I; World War II; Youth Movements; Table 4 in Appendix.

FASCIST IDEOLOGY. An articulated ideology was needed to justify the exercise of power by the new fascist elite in the name of what was claimed to be a permanent revolution. There are two proclamations of such an ideology but neither was adhered to in practice: one was the program enunciated by Mussolini at the 1919 birth of the **Partito Nazionale Fascista** (PNF) / National Fascist Party; the second was the program of the Repubblica Sociale Italiano at **Salò.** The former was anti-monarchical, anti-bolshevik, anti-socialist, anti-bourgeois, and anti-capitalist while claiming to embrace syndicalism. Specifically, the program called for an 80 percent levy on war profits, worker self-management, confiscation of church property, and the annexation of Dalmatia (the Croatian coast). Similarly, the 1943 program of the reborn party, now called the Partito Repubblicana Fascista / Republican Fascist Party, was—in Mussolini's eyes—a return to these origins. Hence, it was anti-monarchical, hostile to the Vatican, and opposed to the same enemies as were identified in 1919. The fascist spirit valued will over intellect, but intellectual trappings were thought useful all the same. Unlike Marxism, fascism had no "sacred text" to which the disputatious might refer. But in 1931, the *Enciclopedia Italiana* included an essay on fascist doctrine probably written by **Benito Mussolini** and edited by **Giovanni Gentile**, who was in charge of the encyclopedia. The slogans it contained and the quotable lines included in that essay were mined by party faithful for years afterwards.

Fascism was a nationalist, mobilizing, disciplining, ideological party able to rationalize rule by a self-styled elite aiming at "productivism." In this view, advanced by a number of comparativists, both fascism and Stalinism were developmental dictatorships, useful to effect rapid, forced modernization. The movement appealed to idealistic youths who had not been called to the colors, to returning veterans, to nationalists of all ages, to the urban middle class damaged by wartime inflation, and to assorted hangers-on. For many, the slogan *Più nemici, più gloria!* (The more enemies, the more glory!) was not empty tub-thumping but was an act of defiance by a nation tired of being on one of the bottom rungs of so many European rankings.

Much of **fascism**'s novelty, however, resided not only in its use of force or the commanding position of the maximum leader but in its rejection of all liberal democratic political assumptions. There was to be no pluralism but rather a single party. The state, the economy, and the society were to be bureaucratically, hierarchically, and *totally* organized (hence *Totalitarian*, Mussolini's coinage) integrating *all* activities—whether in religion, commerce, arts, leisure-hours, or the breeding of children—in consensual subordination to the party: *Tutto nello Stato; niente senza lo Stato; Tutto per lo Stato* (Everything within the State; nothing without the State; Everything for the State). It was from the totalitarian assumption that **corporatism** was born, perhaps the only original idea to be advanced by the fascist state.

That the emphasis was on action rather than doctrine helps explain its attraction to the unreflective. Such slogans as *Credere, Obbedire, Combattere* (Believe, Obey, Fight) did not necessarily invite obedience to a creed but rather to the person of Mussolini, whose beliefs were inconsistent and often contradictory. This absence of a doctrine was probably an advantage in courting diverse strata of society in acquiring power.

Mussolini had concluded from pre-war political activities and wartime experiences that liberal democracy and its parliamentary offshoot had shown themselves unable to reconcile their liberal assumptions with the needs of waging war effectively. All the belligerents had employed censorship, summary trials, compulsory economic planning, wartime economic and labor mobilization, and other statist measures. He also had drawn from Lenin the lesson that power would come to those able to transform the political party from an instrument born to garner votes in competitive elections to a device for enlisting mass support for the exclusive exercise of power by a single, hierarchical elite, justified by the mystique adhering to its members. Entry into leadership ranks was limited to those co-opted by the party. Indeed, *La Mistica Fascista* (Fascist Mystique) became a course in Italian universities and was eventually given ministerial status. Apologists describe fascism as dealing with new socio-economic realities by creating equally new political and economic institutions such as the fascist and corporatist state, providing the only *correct* way to accommodate order and diversity. *See also* Corporatism; Fascism; Gran Consiglio del Fascismo; Benito Mussolini; Partito Nazionale Fascista; Quadrumvirate; Youth Movements.

FEDERAZIONE UNIVERSITARIA CATTOLICI ITALIANA (FUCI) / Catholic University Graduates' Movement of Italy. Organized in 1896 as a part of **Azione Cattolica** (ACI) / Catholic

Action, FUCI provided a useful link between the nascent Christian democracy movement and university students, both male (fucini) and female (fucine). This necessarily drew them close to Don **Luigi Sturzo** and Don **Romolo Murri**. The autonomy of the fucini, most of whom were liberal Catholics, brought them into conflict with the more staid ACI, virtually an instrument of the Vatican. The close association with the **Partito Popolare Italiano** (PPI) / Italian Peoples' Party brought FUCI under close scrutiny by the fascist authorities after 1922 and led to its eventual dissolution in 1931. After reorganization (between 1935 and 1939) under the leadership of Giovanni Battista Montini (later Pope Paul VI) and such prominent laymen as **Aldo Moro** and **Giulio Andreotti**, FUCI became once again an assembly of liberal Catholics and a training ground for many of the political leaders of post-war Italy.

A special section of FUCI was organized in 1934, the university degree-holders' federation—FUCI-laureati (the *laurea* is the Italian university degree). They published a weekly magazine called *Azione Fucina* and, beginning in 1935, an intellectual review called *Studium*. To many in the regime, it was clear that fucini were engaged in little less than the preparation of a new elite to incorporate Catholic social doctrine into a new political order at the propitious moment, despite their outward conformity to regime requirements. *See also* Education; Florence; Guido Gonella.

FEDERZONI, LUIGI (1878-1967). Born in Bologna, Federzoni became the leader of the Italian nationalist association in 1910, which campaigned for Italian colonial expansion. Together with **Enrico Corradini**, Federzoni founded in 1911 the influential weekly *L'idea nazionale* in which Federzoni published (April 1913) a famous attack on freemasonry.

Federzoni became a parliamentary deputy in 1913, but nevertheless enrolled in the armed forces in 1915. In 1922 he became minister for the colonies in **Mussolini**'s first government. Following the disappearance of **Giacomo Matteotti** in June 1924, Federzoni was one of four ministers who resigned from Mussolini's government, publicly requesting that the fascist leader seek "national conciliation." A few days later, however, Mussolini made Federzoni minister for the interior, a post that he was forced to resign in 1926 after public criticism following two attempts on Mussolini's life, which made his position untenable. He was minister for the colonies once more until 1929.

Federzoni held several prestigious offices in the 1930s. He was president of the Senate from 1929 until 1939, editor of the fascist literary periodical *Nuova antologia* and, from 1938, the president of the **Accademia d'Italia**. A member of the Fascist Grand Council, he was one of 19 fascist leaders who signed the motion put by **Dino Grandi** asking King **Victor Emmanuel III** to resume his powers, thus isolating Mussolini who, by the same afternoon (July 25, 1943), was put into "protective custody" by order of the king and, after provisional imprisonments, was incarcerated atop the Gran Sasso in the Abruzzi mountains. After the ex-Duce was liberated (September 12) by German glider-borne commandos and established in the northern city of **Salò**, a half-dozen of the **Grandi** motion signers were tried for treason, Federzoni among them. He was condemned to death by the Republic of Salò but managed to flee to Portugal. For his role in **fascism**'s rise, he was sentenced to life imprisonment by the Republic of Italy after liberation in 1945 but was amnestied, and after a period of exile in Portugal and Brazil, he returned to Italy. He spent the last two decades of his life peacefully writing his memoirs. He died in **Rome** in 1967.

FELLINI, FEDERICO (1920-1993). Born after **World War I** in the provincial seaside town of Rimini, Federico Fellini began his career in the cinema as a writer for popular comedians in the 1940s. His first solo film was *Lo sceicco bianco* (*The White Sheik*, 1953), which was followed by *I vitelloni* (*The Spivs*, 1953). This latter film won the Silver Lion at Venice and affirmed Fellini's critical reputation. His next film, however, established Fellini as one of the best directors in the world. *La Strada* (*The Road*, 1954), which starred Fellini's wife, Giulietta Masina, is a film of almost unbearable pathos. It is the story of a simple peasant girl called Gelsomina (Masina) who is sold to a circus strongman called Zampanò (Anthony Quinn). Zampanò's brutish behavior drives Gelsomina to her death, at which point Zampanò realizes the extent of his attachment for her. He realizes, in short, what it is to be fully human. Too poetic for Italy's neo-realist critics, the film won more than 50 awards, including the Silver Lion and the Oscar for best foreign picture.

La Strada was the beginning of Fellini's creative peak. In the next eight years, he enjoyed an astonishing burst of sustained creativity. *La notti di Cabiria* (*The Nights of Cabiria*, 1956), a touching film about a prostitute, was followed by *La dolce vita* (*The Sweet Life,* 1959), which was both an ironic comment on high life during the Italian **economic miracle** and, more deeply, a meditation on how human beings should live. *Otto e mezzo* (*Eight and a Half,*

1962) is an equally complex film about a film director wrestling with his conscience. The latter two films provided Marcello Mastroianni with two of his greatest roles.

It is widely agreed that Fellini's work falls off after the early 1960s. His films became uneven, repetitive, and overly grotesque, although this does not mean that they are unrelieved failures. The surreal brilliance of the ecclesiastical fashion show, complete with roller-skating priests, saves the otherwise somewhat episodic *Fellini's Roma* (1972). The autobiographical and profoundly touching *Amarcord* (1973) won the Oscar for best foreign picture. Fellini's death in November 1993 was marked by national mourning: hundreds of thousands of people lined the streets of **Rome** to pay their last respects to the most poetic Italian artist of any genre in the post-war years.

FERMI, ENRICO (1901-1954). One of the finest theoretical physicists of this century, Enrico Fermi was one of the fathers of the atomic bomb and a pioneer in the field of nuclear fission. Fermi was born in **Rome** and was educated at the universities of Pisa and Göttingen. In 1926, when he was still in his mid-twenties, he returned to Italy to become professor of theoretical physics at the University of Rome. Initially Fermi cooperated with the fascist regime, accepting membership of the **Accademia d'Italia.** In 1938, Fermi was awarded the Nobel prize in recognition of the lasting importance of his work in atomic structure and the nature of radioactivity. **Mussolini**'s increasingly pro-Nazi policies had long been causing Fermi, whose wife was Jewish, great anguish and—after receiving the prize in Stockholm—he fled to the United States.

In 1942, he was one of the group of scientists at the University of Chicago who produced the first controlled nuclear chain reaction. In the closing years of the war, he worked on Project Manhattan and played a crucial role in ensuring that the Allies, rather than Nazi Germany, won the race to build the first nuclear weapons. After the war, Fermi returned to the University of Chicago to pursue his research on the behavior of neutrons. He died in Chicago in 1954. The chemical element Fermium (Fm), which is produced artificially in thermonuclear explosions, was named in his honor.

FIAT. The Fabbrica italiana automobili Torino is one of the world's largest producers of motor vehicles. Founded in 1899 by Giovanni Agnelli and an off-beat aristocratic inventor, Count Emmanuele Bricherasio di Cacherano, the nascent Italian auto industry rapidly achieved a reputation for making "horseless carriages" of high quality. Agnelli survived two trials in which he was accused of fraud and ramping FIAT's share price to emerge as the undisputed owner of the company by 1911, the year in which his close friend and political patron, **Giovanni Giolitti,** made him *cavaliere al merito di lavoro* (an award for businessmen similar to a British knighthood).

World War I was a bonanza for FIAT, which became the main supplier of vehicles and airplanes to the Italian army and also diversified into the manufacture of machine guns. By 1918, FIAT had become Italy's third-largest industrial concern. By the early 1920s, even visiting Americans recognized that FIAT's Turin car plant was among the most technologically advanced in the world.

Agnelli was one of the first people in Italy to recognize **Mussolini**'s rising star, and helped to finance Mussolini's newspaper *Popolo d'Italia* during the war. In 1923, Mussolini appointed Agnelli to the Senate. But FIAT's relations with the regime were never especially warm. Agnelli only joined the **Partito Nazionale Fascista** (PNF) / National Fascist Party in 1932. Nevertheless, FIAT's sales continued to grow in the 1930s and 1940s largely because of orders of military equipment from the Italian and German governments. When Agnelli died on December 16, 1945, he left a fortune estimated at one billion 1945 dollars.

Agnelli was succeeded as head of FIAT by Vittorio Valletta, a diminutive professor of banking who built the **Turin** carmaker into a global giant. Under Valletta's stewardship, FIAT mass produced the cheap minicars (especially the FIAT 600 and FIAT 500) that came to symbolize the **economic miracle.** Owning a car had been a novelty in pre-war Italy. By 1966, when Valletta stepped down, Italy had some of the most congested roads in the world, and FIAT was the world's fifth largest manufacturer of motor vehicles, deriving the maximum benefit possible from its protection of its domestic market.

Valletta's place was taken by Giovanni Agnelli's grandson, Gianni. Born in 1921, Gianni had served in the Italian army on the Russian front, and then, after his grandfather's death, became one of the world's most notorious playboys. Agnelli proved unable to cope with the oil shock and the degeneration of labor relations in Italy, and by the mid-1970s the company was in a potentially terminal crisis. The appointment in 1979 of a tough professional manager, Cesare Romiti, to run FIAT's day-to-day operations, while Agnelli concentrated upon lobbying and strategic policy, was arguably the event that put the company back on track. In October 1980, Romiti announced thousands of redundancies and then sat out the inevitable strike until the **trade unions** caved in.

Shortly afterward, the company produced the brilliant, award-winning FIAT *Uno*, which quickly became Europe's best-selling car, and car manufacturing once more became a cash cow for the group as a whole. In 1986, the company ruthlessly exploited its political connections to ensure that Ford did not buy the luxury Alfa Romeo from the Italian state's **Istituto per la Ricostruzione Industriale** (IRI) / Institute for Industrial Reconstruction. Instead, just as FIAT had acquired Lancia, it soon added Alfa Romeo to its product line, then Ferrari. Aircraft (including the Argentine FIAT fighter planes that attacked the Royal Navy during the Falklands War), busses, trucks of all sizes (marketed as *Iveco*), and robotics complete the offerings of this multinational giant. Today FIAT is Europe's third-largest automaker after Volkswagen and General Motors-Opel, and owns a stake or controlling interest in literally dozens of companies around the world. Joint enterprises in Eastern Europe, in South America, and in Asia add to its scope. In the summer of 1997, FIAT announced the intention to build, in three Indian cities, three separate factories to build cars, trucks, and tractors. One of Italy's leading newspapers, *La Stampa*, has been part of the FIAT empire since 1920, and the Juventus soccer team is also part of the group.

FINI, GIANFRANCO (1952-). Architect of the recent transformation of the neo-fascist **Movimento Sociale Italiano** (MSI) / Italian Social Movement into a new, conservative party, Gianfranco Fini is one of the smoothest performers in contemporary Italian politics. In the 1980s, the Bologna-born Fini was controversially chosen by **Giorgio Almirante** as his successor. Accordingly, in 1987, Fini became party secretary, and after Almirante's death assumed the leadership of the MSI's conservative wing. In 1990, at a party congress in **Rome** that was marred by fisticuffs between the factions, the MSI elected Pino **Rauti**, the ideologue of so-called "fascism of the left," to the secretaryship, although Fini's outstanding final speech consolidated his personal standing within the movement. Rauti's attempt to transform the MSI into a campaigning anti-capitalist force quickly proved itself a failure with the MSI's ultra-conservative electorate, and Fini returned to the party leadership in time for the collapse of the party system in 1992.

In December 1993, when he was narrowly defeated for the mayorship of Rome, Fini proved that there was a reservoir of former **Democrazia Cristiana** (DC) / Christian Democracy Party voters who were willing to vote for the MSI if the movement presented itself as a party of Catholic conservatives that was open to modern ideas of economic deregulation and the free market. In a masterstroke of political presentation, Fini seized upon an idea launched by Professor Domenico Fisichella—to assemble an electoral pact called the **Alleanza Nazionale** (AN) / National Alliance. Apart from a few former DC rightists, and a handful of conservative professors, the pact was the MSI by another name. In alliance with **Silvio Berlusconi** in the "Good Government Pole," the AN obtained twice as many votes as the former MSI in the general elections of March 1994 and entered Berlusconi's short-lived government.

Fini, who tainted his growing reputation by calling **Mussolini** the "greatest statesman of the twentieth century" shortly after the 1994 poll, completed the transformation of the MSI into the AN in January 1995. He has remained generally faithful to Berlusconi's leadership of Italy's right-wing "Liberty Pole," not least because the AN's electoral growth seems to have stalled at between 15 to 18 percent. In policy terms, Fini's most important commitment is to change Italy's **Constitution** to establish a strong elected president on the American, French, or even Russian model. Fini has altered the neo-fascist tradition in many ways, but a yearning for the "strong leader" is still discernible.

FLORENCE (*Firenze*). King **Victor Emmanuel II**, in 1865, moved Italy's capital from **Turin** to this Tuscan city while waiting to absorb **Rome.** The wealth accumulated by leading Florentine families during the Renaissance and displayed ever since then seemed to entitle Florence to this singular honor. Her museums—the Uffizi, the Bargello, the hidden gallery over the Ponte Vecchio—continue to draw tourists from the world over, all offering testimony to the Florentine treasures, among the finest in the Western world. During her prime, little trade between Europe and the East took place that was not financed by Florentine bankers and insured by Florentine entrepreneurs. Cultural primacy was evident in the adoption of the Tuscan dialect of Dante, Boccaccio, and Petrarch as the literary language for all Italians. **Curzio Malaparte**, Mario Tobino, Fidia Gambetti, Miriam Mafai, **Giovanni Papini**, and **Vasco Pratolini** are but a few of the literary figures of modern Tuscany, not to mention the British writers who have based much of their best work on their experiences, real or fancied, in the Tuscan hill-towns: E. M. Forster and the Brownings, Elizabeth and Robert. Americans closely associated with the city include Sargent, born there of expatriate parents, and the noted apologist and propagandist for fascism, Ezra Pound.

After the fall of **Mussolini** and the beginning of the civil war of 1943-1945, the Tuscan **Comitati di Liberazione Nazionale** (CLN) / National Liberation Committees harassed the German garrison so that the CLN might be in control of *their* city when Allied forces entered. In a preview of **consociationalism**, the city was divided among four commands to avoid conflicts among the **Partito Comunista Italiano** (PCI), the **Partito Socialista Italiano** (PSI), the **Partito d'Azione** (PdA), and Demochristians of the **Democrazia Cristiana** (DC) / Christian Democracy Party. Repressive measures ordered by German General Kesselring reflected his conviction that irregular, hence illegal, belligerence by those who should be non-combatants could be stopped by preventive hostage-taking, reprisals, public hangings and home burnings. These measures, however, served to draw Tuscans closer together despite class, political, and social differences.

Florence was the first, but not the last, Italian city to have been brought under CLN control prior to the arrival of Allied armies. When Allied political teams arrived on August 13, 1944, equipped with lists of Italian liberal notables, aristocrats, and Catholics to fill administrative jobs, they found that the CLN had effectively organized city government to perform municipal chores ranging from garbage collection to water supply. The Allies saw the wisdom of treating the CLN delegates as legitimate interlocutors rather than risking that the city's entire population turn against the liberators. The partisans had made clear that they would not accept being treated as mere auxiliaries.

Since the war's end, Florentine political life has been no less interesting than its wealth has been impressive. Between 1960 and 1962, Florence was one of those cities that "opened to the left," and its municipal government has, since then, more frequently been in the hands of left majorities than not. *See also* Dialects in Italy.

FO, DARIO (1926-). Dario Fo was born on March 24, 1926, near Lago Maggiore (Leggiuno Sangiano in Lombardy). Long a showman, playwright, designer, monologuist, director, actor, clown, and satirist, he—no less than the Italian intellectual community—was overwhelmed with surprise to learn that he was to receive the Nobel prize for literature in 1997, bringing to six the number of Italians to be so honored. Most of Fo's work (including 70 plays) consists of directing a carefully aimed thumb in the eye of those in authority, as well as of terrorists, Popes, and tycoons, all of whom are—in Fo's view—obtuse, at the very least. His plays have been likened to an absurdist type of British kitchen-sink drama. His most famous play, *La morte accidentale d'un anarchico* (The Accidental Death of an Anarchist, 1970) has been translated and staged all over the world. He has been allowed entry to the United States only once, in 1984. On two earlier occasions, he and his wife since 1953, the actress Franca Rame, had been denied U.S. visas because of his leftist associations and long membership in the **Partito Comunista Italiano** (PCI) / Italian Communist Party.

The **Vatican** seems to hold an equally negative view of Mr. Fo, having been the target of his humor on more than one occasion. *L'Osservatore Romano* deplored the action of the Swedish Academy, which selected this author "of questionable works." All the same, the Swedish Academy described this perfect jester as blending "laughter and gravity" in ways that reveal injustices and abuses by those in charge anywhere.

FOREIGN POLICY. Italy's foreign policy has generally had clear, but unassertive, objectives. Before unification, the lack of cohesion among mini-states and principalities under Austrian, Spanish, or Pontifical jurisdiction made unrealizable any territorial ambitions on the part of those few states that were autonomous. Moreover, a paucity of industrial raw materials and the vulnerability of two long coastlines warranted a certain modesty. After the peninsula's unification, however, the aim became to establish Italy's credentials as a power by pursuing a colonial policy in **Abyssinia** and in **Libya.** Successive governments also negotiated the so-called Triple Alliance, tying Italy to Germany and Austria-Hungary. In 1902, notes were exchanged between the Italian foreign minister and the French ambassador that allowed Italy great flexibility. Finally, reckoning that Italy's security required control over the mountain passes to her north and the absence of a rival power on the Adriatic, her government set about pursuing policy objectives meant to ensure that security. It was calculated that Austria would see no reason to share either mountain passes or seas with the Italians in the case of a joint victory in a European war. On the other hand, a victorious Anglo-French alliance would surely have no objection to parceling out formerly Austrian holdings to an Italian ally. Hence, Italy joined the British, French, and Russians in 1915.

Under **fascism**, similar objectives prevailed: to project Italy as a power convincingly enough to make her not only respected but actively feared. Boldness and initiative led **Mussolini**'s Italy to be the first state to recognize the Soviet government (1924), to shell the island of Corfù, to gradually absorb **Albania**, to face the 1934 Austrian crisis, the wars in **Abyssinia** and in the **Spanish Civil War**, and, finally, to join hostilities in 1940 lest an early German victory leave Italy with no gains whatsoever. Italy, one of the first states to endorse the post-war League of Nations, was also among the first to challenge it once Mussolini, self-proclaimed restorer of the grandeur of **Rome**, had come to power. All his actions were consistent with his view of the new fascist man. He would deal with problems not by programs and committees, but by action. For example, the 1923 assassination of Italian General Tellini and four members of his staff—allegedly by Greek patriots—while on duty working for the league in drawing boundaries between Greeks and Albanians, inspired Mussolini to issue an ultimatum to Greece and, simultaneously, to give units of the Italian fleet orders to shell and occupy Corfù. Although he was persuaded within a month to evacuate the island, and a Council of Ambassadors in Paris awarded Italy an indemnity from Greece and an apology, the impression made at home and abroad was clearly of a "strong leader" sensitive to perceived humiliations of the "new Italy."

In his other role as peacemaker and statesman, Mussolini signed the 1925 Locarno Treaties guaranteeing Belgian and French frontiers (while remaining silent about Germany's eastern frontiers to which the guarantees did not extend). In March 1933, Italy signed the Four Power Pact together with France, Germany, and Great Britain. The Duce hoped thereby to ensure Italy's place among the European Great Powers, which would reduce the influence of small powers in the League of Nations. At Stresa, in April 1934, Mussolini signed a Treaty with Britain and France in response to Germany's repudiation of the Locarno Treaties and of the disarmament clauses of the Treaty of Versailles.

In September 1936, Hitler invited Mussolini to Germany for a state visit and to watch German army maneuvers in order to convince the Duce that Germany would certainly triumph in any European war. The visit took place just three months after the opening of hostilities in Spain and just six months after Germany had reoccupied the Rhineland, contrary to both the Versailles and Locarno Treaties. Hitler succeeded so completely in flattering his guest's gargantuan vanity that, within a month, the Rome-Berlin Axis had been formed (October 25, 1936). By November, the anti-Comintern Pact had been created by the accession of Japan. By March 1938, Italy was so deeply committed to a fascist victory in Spain that Mussolini could not oppose the German absorption of Austria, a fact that at one stroke erased Italy's only concrete gain from her participation in **World War I**. For now, in place of the Austrian rump state and its weak successors beyond the mountains ringing Italy, there was a new Germanic empire far more powerful and more expansionist than the Hapsburgs had been. However, Mussolini's admiration of Germany's might led him to accept the Pact of Steel (May 1939), which bound Italy to Germany by military obligations that Italy was in no position to honor. Moreover, even a victorious Germany would be unlikely to satisfy what Mussolini defined as Italy's needs; and any German defeat must necessarily bring Italy down as well. The Pact of Steel was Mussolini's undoing.

Since the end of **World War II** and fascism's fall, Italy's policies have consistently aimed at identifying Italy as an Atlantic power, hence a loyal member of the **North Atlantic Treaty Organization** (NATO)—but not for use outside Europe and not as an assertive arm of U.S. policy. Indeed, when an Italian cruise ship—the *Achille Lauro*—plying the Mediterranean was hijacked by members of the Palestine Liberation Front (PLF), relations with the United States became, for a few months, quite seriously strained. Italy's "Mediterranean vocation" brought her close to collision with the United States.

Italy's aim is to make her one of the motors of the integration of Europe. She has regularly supported the deepening and broadening of the **European Union**. Noteworthy has been the relative consistency of the various governments' policies despite the presence, during the cold war, of the largest communist party in Western Europe. Such consistency could only have been possible with the tacit approval of the **Partito Comunista Italiano** (PCI) / Italian Communist Party whose leaders, especially in the years of the **compromesso storico** (historic compromise), were always ready to accept Italy's Atlanticist vocation. Contrary to many assumptions too easily made during the cold war, the size and political weight of the PCI served less to increase Soviet influence on Italy than to diminish that of the United States. *See also* London, Treaty of; Parallel War; Prinetti-Barrère Notes; World War I; World War II.

FORLANI, ARNALDO (1925-). A parliamentarian from 1958 to 1994, Arnaldo Forlani was most recently leader of the **Democrazia Cristiana** (DC) / Christian Democracy Party from 1989 to 1992. In this time, his own ambitions of becoming president of the republic were dashed, and the DC was crushed by bribery scandals. Forlani is a native of Pesaro, a middle-sized city in the Marches, his constant electoral base. He was elected to **Parliament** in 1958, and took office in the late 1960s first as minister for state participation in industry and then for relations with the United Nations. In 1969, he became party leader, a post he held until 1973.

In 1973, Forlani briefly became secretary general of the European Christian Democratic Union, but he was soon called back to high office in Italy, becoming minister of defense (1974-1976), foreign minister (1976-1979), and, finally, prime minister (1980-1982). During the first premiership of **Bettino Craxi**, Forlani was vice premier. Forlani became party leader once more in February 1989, when the DC's center faction, with the support of the faction of **Giulio Andreotti**, combined to vote out the then leader (and prime minister), **Ciriaco De Mita**. This move, which was strongly backed by Craxi, handed the reins of power in Italy over to the so-called "CAF" (Craxi-Andreotti-Forlani). The three men governed—or misgoverned—the country until the electoral and judicial disasters of 1992.

Forlani, perhaps because Craxi feared him less than Andreotti, was the triumvirate's choice to become president after the resignation of **Francesco Cossiga** in April 1992. Forlani obtained only 469 votes, 40 less than the required quota, and 80 less than the government parties theoretically controlled. Even after frantic arm-twisting by party whips, Forlani's vote only increased by ten in a subsequent ballot, and he was forced to drop out of the contest. His defeat symbolized the CAF's loss of control over the newly elected parliament.

Had Forlani won the presidency, he would have appointed Craxi prime minister, and the world would never have heard of the **Mani pulite** ("Clean Hands") investigation. Forlani himself was drawn into the bribery scandals and, in December 1993, was subjected to a ruthless cross-examination by **Antonio Di Pietro** when he was called (as a witness) to explain bribes paid to the DC by the chemical company Enimont. Forlani literally frothed at the mouth as he frantically tried to avoid the prosecutor's pointed questions. He left the witness box with his political career in ruins. *See also* Pentapartito.

FORTIS, ALESSANDRO (1842-1909). Born in Forlì in Emilia-Romagna, Alessandro Fortis took part as a young man in **Giuseppe Garibaldi**'s campaigns to liberate the Trentino in 1866 and **Rome** in 1867. One of the 28 purportedly anti-monarchist conspirators arrested in the coastal town of Rimini in August 1874, Fortis served three months imprisonment while awaiting trial, but the court eventually ruled that he had committed no crime. A moderate within the republican party, Fortis was elected to the Chamber of Deputies in 1880, and became increasingly connected with the figure of **Francesco Crispi**. He initially served in the government of General **Girolamo Pelloux** (June 1898-May 1899) as minister of agriculture, but joined his fellow republicans in opposing the restrictions upon political activity and free speech proposed by Pelloux. After the turn of the century, Fortis's ally of choice became **Giovanni Giolitti**, whose liberal reformism was closest to Fortis's own political views. When Giolitti's second administration resigned in March 1905, Fortis followed him as prime minister. His tenure of this office was characterized by a lengthy guerilla war in **Parliament** between Fortis and his conservative rival, **Sidney Sonnino**. Fortis's plans to introduce a partial nationalization of the railways, and to conclude a trade agreement between Italy and Spain that would have slashed Italian tariffs on Spanish wine, met with fierce parliamentary and public opposition. The tariff bill was defeated in Parliament, causing Fortis to reshuffle his government in December 1905. His government eventually fell in February 1906, despite Giolitti's support. Fortis visited Calabria and **Sicily** in September 1905 to examine firsthand the extent of **earthquake** damage. Shortly afterward, he put forward a special law to aid these regions. This was the first real recognition by the Italian state of the fundamental problems underlying southern underdevelopment. He died in Rome in 1909.

FORZA ITALIA. This wholly new party was born in the fall of 1993, when **Silvio Berlusconi**, alarmed by the collapse of the political system that had protected and nurtured his media interests, and worried by the growing strength of the **Partito Democratico della Sinistra** (PDS) / Democratic Party of the Left, ordered his marketing strategists to prepare his entry into politics. In December 1993, thousands of Forza Italia "clubs" were begun in cities and towns all over the country. Fifteen thousand such groups had been formed by the end of January 1994, when Berlusconi officially announced his intention to run for **Parliament**.

Berlusconi was well aware that the "clubs" did not constitute a genuine party organization. He accordingly allied his new movement, and his three national television networks, with the **Lega Nord** (LN) / Northern League in the so-called "Liberty Pole" alliance, and with the **Alleanza Nazionale** (AN) / National Alliance in the "Good Government Pole" in electoral districts in southern Italy. Two smaller parties, the Unione di Centro (UdC) / Center Union and the Centro Cristiano Democratico (CCD) / Christian Democratic Center, also struck electoral pacts with Forza Italia. Berlusconi's television networks propagated the idea that these electoral pacts stood for radical deregulation of the private sector, and promised that Berlusconi would use his business skills to create a million jobs within a year. The PDS and its allies, meanwhile, were portrayed as communists who would snuff out private enterprise and tax the savings of the middle class. Berlusconi warily warned that "Exile or the gallows" would follow a left victory.

These tactics paid off. Just three months after its foundation, Forza Italia became the biggest party in Italy, with 21 percent of the vote. In terms of parliamentarians, however, Forza Italia was underrepresented, with 99 seats in the Chamber of Deputies and 32 senators. The LN and the AN both had slightly more parliamentarians than Forza Italia as a result of the generosity of Berlusconi's pre-electoral deals. Forza Italia's deputies, moreover, were lacking in political experience (only 15 percent had had any political dealings prior to joining Berlusconi's movement) and did not provide Berlusconi with a pool of ready ministerial talent. It is a measure of Forza Italia's artificial nature that Berlusconi, to fill his party's quota of ministerial appointees in the government that he formed in May 1994, was forced to give top ministerial jobs to individuals from his own corporation, and to outside experts such as **Lamberto Dini** who had nothing to do with Forza Italia or with Berlusconi himself. Italians began to call Forza Italia *un partito azienda* (a company party).

Despite a smashing success in the June 1994 European elections (30 percent of the votes), and dignified performances in local elections in April 1995 and in the April 1996 general elections, Forza Italia has not shaken off its "company party" image. Its local organization remains thin to nonexistent, and Berlusconi's private fortune is its chief source of finance. Berlusconi's trusted associates continue to direct its operations. Forza Italia, in short, is arguably more like the electoral organization of an American senator than a traditional European mass party. *See also* Silvio Berlusconi.

FOSCOLO, UGO (1778-1827). A kind of Italian Shelley, Ugo Foscolo was a poet, classical translator, and patriot who was born to an Italian father and a Greek mother on the isle of Xante. He grew up in the then Venetian town of Spalato (modern-day Split, in Croatia), before moving to **Venice**. His first significant work, a pamphlet entitled *Bonaparte Libera tore* (*Bonaparte the Liberator*) was written in Venice in 1797 and celebrated the victory of the French revolutionary armies that occupied northern Italy and established the Cisalpine Republic in 1796. Foscolo moved to **Bologna** and **Milan** to take part in political activity in 1797 and fought bravely in defense of the Cisalpine Republic in 1799 when the Austro-Russian forces strove to restore absolutist rule in northern Italy. Foscolo subsequently served for some years in the French army in both Italy and France itself. Foscolo's literary masterpiece, his 1807 collection *Dei Sepolcri* (literally, *On Tombs*), was written after Napoleon had crowned himself king of Italy—a move that Foscolo, a former Jacobin, made no protest against. When Napoleon was defeated, Foscolo was treated kindly by the Austrians, despite the fact that he was by now one of the most well-known and most outspoken nationalists in all Italy. In March 1815, however, he fled to Switzerland, and from there to England, rather than accept the restoration of Austrian rule in Venetia and Lombardy. In England, he tried to live like a gentleman, but before long he had become a chronic debtor, with a string of mistresses and illegitimate children to maintain—or, more usually, to neglect. This last period of his life saw him produce some of his best work, however. His essay *Discorsi sulla servitù d'Italia* (*On the Servitude of Italy*, 1819) immensely influenced the young **Giuseppe Mazzini**, while his many essays on Italian literature, especially on Dante, are still regarded as important works of criticism even today. Foscolo died in disgrace and poverty in Burnham Green, near London, in September 1827. In 1871, after the liberation of **Rome**, the poet's remains were transferred to Italy, and Foscolo was interred in the vaults of Santa Croce Church in **Florence**, a building he had described as the last resting place of many "Italian glories" in *Dei Sepolcri*.

FOUR POWER PACT. *See* Foreign Policy.

FUTURISM. A literary, artistic, and cultural movement founded in the first decade of the twentieth century, *futurism* combined genuine artistic radicalism with a love of violence, power, and speed that led futurist thinkers and writers to extol the virtues of war, and to embrace fascism as their political creed.

The essence of futurism was its celebration of the beauty of modernity. A racing car could be as beautiful as a race horse; electric pylons as beautiful as trees or mountains. Literature and art should not, in short, be restful or contemplative, but should capture the noise, bustle, drama, and violence of industrial cities. In the words of the futurist manifesto published by **Filippo Tommaso Marinetti** in the French newspaper *Le Figaro* in 1909, the futurists wanted to "sing" of "the vast crowds energized by work, pleasure, or protest," to depict the "vibrant nightly fervor of the arsenals and workplaces lit by violent electric moons," the "bridges arched across rivers like gigantic gymnasts," and the "locomotives . . . like enormous steel horses in a harness of tubes." Despite the vigor and exuberance of Marinetti's prose in the manifesto, these tasks were fulfilled more memorably by the artists—**Umberto Boccioni**, Carlo Carrà, Giacomo Balla—than by the writers associated with the futurist cause.

Ideologically, the futurists subscribed to the anti-democratic philosophy of violence and power worship traceable to Nietzsche and popularized by Georges Sorel. Like the dadaists, they were hostile to traditional and classical forms in art, architecture, and esthetics. "The sound of a racing car engine is more beautiful than the greatest symphony" was a part of the futurist manifesto. **Giovanni Papini**, the editor of *Leonardo*, was the most prominent Italian thinker to fall under the sway of such ideas. Marinetti's manifesto, however, expressed the political thinking animating the futurists succinctly: "We want to glorify war—the world's only form of hygiene— militarism, patriotism, the destructive gestures of the anarchists, the fine ideas for which men die, and contempt for women." With a philosophy such as this, futurist intellectuals mostly became enthusiastic fascists, although their ardor cooled as **Mussolini**'s regime became increasingly institutionalized and conservative in the 1930s.

-G-

GARIBALDI, ANITA (1821-1849). The Brazilian-born first wife of **Giuseppe Garibaldi**, Anita Garibaldi (Anna Maria Ribeirao da Silva), was a heroine of the struggle for Italian unification. Already married when she met the Italian adventurer in 1839, she and Garibaldi had two sons and a daughter together. Both sons became prominent soldiers and statesman on the model of their father. Menotti (1840-1903) was born out of wedlock (Garibaldi and Anita were only able to marry after the death of her first husband in 1842). He fought with his father in the "Expedition of the Thousand" to **Sicily**, and won a gold medal for gallantry in the war against Austria of 1866. From 1876 to 1900, he was a parliamentary deputy. The second son, Raced (1847-1924), was also a war hero and adventurer who served in Parliament and took a leading role in the Italian-Turkish war when he was over 60 years old. Anita Garibaldi is remembered today, however, less for the exploits of her children than for her own extraordinary bravery and devotion. In 1849, against Garibaldi's will, she followed him to **Rome** and took part in the defense of the city from the French army. She accompanied him on the tragic retreat through the Papal states to Ravenna, where, overcome by exhaustion and hunger, she died when she was not yet 30 years old. Lodged between petrochemical plants and the Adriatic, the small hut in which she was ravaged by fever is still standing and is the object of sporadic pilgrimages.

GARIBALDI, GIUSEPPE (1807-1882). Born in Nice to a sea captain father, the young Garibaldi was a professional revolutionary. He took part in the Mazzinian uprising against the Piedmontese monarchy in 1834 and, following its suppression, was condemned to death for his role in the fighting. Garibaldi, however, had fled to Brazil. There, he met his first wife, **Anita**, and fought gallantly for six years (1836-1842) on behalf of the South Rio Grande republic, trying to achieve independence. Garibaldi ended the war as admiral of the would-be republic's small fleet. In 1846, he organized and commanded the Italian legion that fought for Uruguay in its war against Argentina. Garibaldi's reputation as the "hero of two worlds," and his familiar penchant for South American peasant garb, dates from this period.

News of the 1848 revolutions, however, prompted his return to Piedmont. Garibaldi fought bravely against the Austrians in Lombardy and in defense of the Roman republic in the spring of 1849. Together with a faithful band of volunteers and Anita, Garibaldi broke out of **Rome** and retreated toward **Venice**, which was still resisting Austrian rule. After suffering heavy casualties, he was forced to take refuge in the swamps surrounding Ravenna, where Anita died of exhaustion.

Garibaldi, at the lowest ebb of his fortunes, was expelled from Piedmont-Sardinia and was forced to lead the life of an exile once more. Briefly, he worked as a candle-maker in Camden, New Jersey, before returning to Europe in 1854. He established himself in a house on the Sardinian Island of Cabrera and gradually became more politically realistic. Under **Cavour**'s influence, Garibaldi accepted that the Piedmontese monarchy offered the best hope of unifying

Italy. This renunciation of his Mazzinian and revolutionary principles restored him to favor in **Turin**, and in 1859 Garibaldi was made a general in the Piedmontese army.

Garibaldi was violently critical of the Treaty of Villafranca. In January 1860, he endorsed the latest venture launched by **Giuseppe Mazzini**, the "Action party," which openly espoused a policy of liberating **southern Italy**, Rome, and Venice by military means. To this end, in the spring of 1860, Garibaldi led a corps of redshirted patriots from Genoa to the assistance of a Mazzinian uprising in **Palermo**. The "Expedition of the Thousand" is the most famous of all Garibaldi's military exploits. After landing near Palermo with the support of ships from the British fleet, Garibaldi swiftly took command of the island. On May 14, 1860, he became dictator of Sicily and head of a provisional government that was largely dominated by a native Sicilian who would play an important role in the political future of Italy, **Francesco Crispi**.

With the support of thousands of Sicilian peasants and workers, Garibaldi then invaded the Italian mainland, intent on marching on Rome. He entered **Naples** in September 1860. He was joined there by the principal republican theorists, Mazzini and **Carlo Cattaneo**, and for a brief moment it looked as if the process of Italian unification would take a radical turn. Cavour's shrewdness enabled him to outmaneuver Garibaldi. Piedmontese troops invaded the Papal states, blocking the road to Rome. Garibaldi decided not to compromise Italian unity by risking a conflict with the Piedmontese. On October 26, 1860, he consigned southern Italy to the monarchy.

Garibaldi, however, was unable to consider Italian unification complete while Rome remained under clerical domination, protected by French troops. He became a thorn in the side of the first Italian governments by carrying on his own independent foreign policy. In 1862, Garibaldi returned to Sicily to raise another army of volunteers willing to march under the melodramatic slogan "Rome or Death." The outraged reaction of Napoleon III compelled the Italian government to intervene, and Garibaldi's advance was halted by Italian troops at Aspromonte in Calabria. There was a skirmish, and Garibaldi was shot in the foot. Garibaldi was briefly imprisoned, but his international fame (especially in England to which he made a triumphal visit in 1864) soon led to his release.

In 1866, Garibaldi led Italian troops in the Trentino, liberating a great part of the Italian-speaking territory under Austrian rule before being ordered to relinquish his gains upon the end of the hostilities between Prussia and Austria. His short reply amply conveyed his disgust at the command: Garibaldi sent a one-word telegram saying "obbedisco" (I obey). His exploits in the Trentino were a prelude to further impolitic attempts to take Rome in the fall of 1867. Escaping from house arrest on Caprera, he joined 3,000 waiting volunteers in Tuscany. The courage of his amateur troops, however, was no match for the French army defending Rome, and at the small but bloody battle of Mentana on November 3, 1867, Garibaldi was decisively beaten. Once more, he was forced into exile in Caprera.

Garibaldi played no role in the liberation of Rome in 1870. His last campaign was on behalf of the French Republic. Garibaldi led a corps of Italian volunteers at the battle of Dijon in the fall of 1870, and his efforts were a decisive contribution to what was the only French victory of the Franco-Prussian war. In his last years, Garibaldi dedicated himself to writing his memoirs (and heroic poetry) and became a declared socialist. He died on Caprera in 1882, but his myth has been a powerful influence on Italian political life ever since, although northern popular views over a hundred years after his death sometimes blame him for including the south of Italy in the new Italy. *See also* Camillo Benso di Cavour; Risorgimento.

GENTILE, GIOVANNI (1875-1944). Born in Trapani (**Sicily**), Giovanni Gentile was both a philosopher of great distinction and a cultural propagandist on behalf of the fascist regime. His early studies were at Italy's most renowned institute of higher education, the *Scuola Normale* in Pisa, where he developed parallel interests in German idealism and the philosophy of Karl Marx. He disparaged all forms of positivism, materialism, or utilitarianism and was opposed to the political manifestations of these broad philosophical currents such as socialism, and laissez-faire liberalism, but he remained unusually aloof from political activity until **World War I**. During the war, which he enthusiastically supported, Gentile published what is arguably his most important philosophical treatise, *I fondamenti della filosofia di diritto* (*The Fundamentals of the Philosophy of Law,* 1916). It was in this book that he introduced the concept of the "moral state," which rested upon the belief that the individual only fully realizes himself when he obeys a state whose purposes are good. Service and sacrifice to the community, in this ethic, are higher virtues than independence and the pursuit of individual happiness. The implications of this position are obvious.

By the end of the war, Gentile was associated politically with the nationalists. In October 1922, **Mussolini** invited the philosopher to join his first cabinet. Gentile accepted and, in 1923, became both a member of the **Partito Nazionale Fascista** (PNF) / National Fascist Party and a senator. As minister, he was responsible in May 1923 for an important educational reform that laid the basis for the modern Italian school and university system. He was also responsible for the infamous "loyalty oath" that all Italian teachers, at whatever level, were asked to sign. Doing so pledged signatories to teach all their courses in such a way as to promote **fascism** and its values. Only 11 refused.

Gentile resigned from the government in June 1924 after the murder of **Giacomo Matteotti**, but remained the regime's most respected cultural and philosophical voice. In 1925, Gentile published a manifesto, signed by **Filippo Marinetti** and **Luigi Pirandello** among others, which urged on intellectuals a moral commitment to fascism's historical mission. In the same year, he wrote *Che cosa è il fascismo* (*The Nature of Fascism*), a highly readable short account of what he understood to be fascism's objectives and ideals. It is probable that **Mussolini** used parts of this essay in preparing his article on fascism for the Italian Encyclopedia, of which Gentile was the editor. Gentile was president of the Institute of Fascist Culture, and was a member of the **Gran Consiglio del Fascismo** (Fascist Grand Council) until 1929. In 1944, he became the last president of the **Accademia d'Italia** (Italian Academy). The encyclopedia was a huge undertaking and occupied most of Gentile's scholarly energies between 1929 and 1936. Most of Italy's leading intellectuals contributed, with the conspicuous exception of **Benedetto Croce.**

Gentile lost much direct political influence after the **Lateran pacts** in 1929, which he opposed on doctrinal grounds. He never renounced fascism, however, even after Mussolini's downfall. After some hesitation, Gentile backed the **Salò republic**, and this cost him his life. In 1944, he was assassinated in **Florence** by a squad of partisans.

GENTILONI PACT. Alarmed by the prospect of a victory of the **Partito Socialista Italiano** (PSI) / Italian Socialist Party in the elections of October 1913 (which were both the first elections held with universal male suffrage and the first in which the church allowed openly Catholic candidates to run), the president of the Unione Elettorale Cattolica (The Catholic Electoral Union), Count Vincenzo Ottorino Gentiloni, devised an electoral arrangement to maximize Catholic influence. Liberal candidates who promised to support Catholic schools and religious instruction in the public schools, who would oppose the introduction of **divorce**, and who agreed to several other key issues for "confessional" voters were offered the backing of the network of Catholic social organizations and parish clergy. The strategy was a striking success. Nearly 30 Catholic candidates were elected, and Gentiloni claimed that over 200 liberal candidates owed their victories to Catholic votes. Only 79 socialists of different denominations were elected, and the *Osservatore Romano* argued that "the party of subversion" would have won at least a hundred more deputies had the church not intervened. Many embarrassed liberal deputies later denied having reached an explicit accord with Gentiloni. Whatever the truth of their denials, the Gentiloni pact signaled that the church was the only institution with sufficient nationwide organization to contest the growing strength of the workers' movement. For better or worse, the church had reentered Italian politics.

GIANNINI, GUGLIELMO. *See* Qualunquismo.

GIOBERTI, VINCENZO (1801-1852). The radical political ideas of the Catholic philosopher Vincenzo Gioberti constrained him to live the life of an exile for much of his adult life. In the early 1830s, the young priest joined the clandestine organization *Giovine Italia* (Young Italy) and after a period of imprisonment was forced to move to Brussels in 1833, where he wrote and published several works of theology and philosophy. In 1843, he published his most famous work, *Del primato morale e civile degli italiani* (*The Moral and Civil Primacy of Italians*), a book that gave birth to so-called neo-guelphism. In retrospect, it might seem incredible that this somewhat obscure book, which argued that Catholicism, symbolized by the Papacy, was the heart of the primacy of Italian culture, should have aroused such passionate interest and debate. But Gioberti added a political dimension to his work by suggesting that it followed from his thesis that the most natural political form for Italy was a federation of sovereign principalities presided over by the Pope. This proposal was intellectually problematic since it in effect nationalized and politicized the supposedly universal and spiritual Church; at the same time, it presented political problems because its nationalist tone challenged Austrian rule. The huge success of his book launched Gioberti on a political career. Gioberti returned to **Turin** (his place of birth) after **Carlo Alberto** conceded a constitution to liberal opinion in March 1848. Gioberti rapidly became one of the principal political figures in the Piedmontese capital. He was elected to Parliament and after the Piedmontese defeat at Custoza in July 1848 became first a cabinet member and then prime minister. Consistent with his ideas, Gioberti strove to improve relations with the **Papacy**, but the plan was overtaken by the revolution in **Rome** in November 1848 and the defection of the Pope to **Naples**. After the defeat of the Piedmontese army at Novara, Gioberti took refuge once more in exile, fleeing to Paris where he remained until his death in 1852.

GIOLITTI, GIOVANNI (1842-1928). Giolitti's legacy is much contested, but no one doubts that this statesman from Mondovì in Piedmont made a critical contribution to Italian history. Giolitti entered politics in 1882 after a brilliant career in the Finance Ministry. In 1889 he was entrusted with the post of Treasury Minister by **Francesco Crispi**, and in 1892 he briefly held the office of prime minister. His appointment was controversial since he was the first politician to reach the highest office who had played no role in the **Risorgimento**. His premiership, however, was ended by the **Banca Romana** scandal, which was manipulated by his political rivals to make his position untenable. Giolitti returned to politics in 1897, but only in 1901 did he return to ministerial office. During his tenure as minister of the interior, Giolitti was severely criticized by industrialists and landowners for his lax attitude toward **trade unions**. Giolitti believed that the state should take no side in the class conflict and strongly defended the right to strike. He once told a landowner who complained in the Senate of having to plough his own fields that he should continue—for by so doing, he would realize how hard the peasants worked and would pay them more. Only a more equal distribution of income, Giolitti believed, would bring an end to the civil strife that had been plaguing Italy since the mid-1890s. Giolitti succeeded **Giuseppe Zanardelli** as prime minister in 1903, and for most of the next 20 years dominated Italian political life.

Giolitti added to the liberal reforms initiated by Zanardelli. His several pre-war administrations opened a dialogue with the labor movement, nationalized the railways in 1909, and introduced universal male suffrage with the electoral reform of 1912. Italy meanwhile joined the race of the European nations for "a place in the sun" by waging war with Turkey in 1911-1912 and seizing **Libya** as a colony.

Yet these achievements are overshadowed by what was not done. Giolitti did not campaign for the reform of the social injustices that were pushing the peasants and workers toward revolutionary doctrines, and honorably would not use the state to enforce the privileges of the wealthy. This position was an understandable one, but one that ultimately appeared as weakness. Giolitti was a master of the dark art of *trasformismo*. The Giolittian system of politics was a skillful balancing act that required him to incorporate radicals, republicans, moderate socialists, and finally Catholics into his governing coalition. His acceptance of the **Gentiloni pact** was a step too far for the radicals, however, and Giolitti was forced to resign on the eve of war. Giolitti opposed Italian entry into **World War I** and was widely suspected of working with the Austrians and Germans to prevent Italy's renunciation of the neutrality she adopted in August 1914. His opposition to the war derived from his sensitivity to Italy's military and economic weaknesses: he truly believed that the war might end with the Germans marching into **Milan**. So far as Giolitti was concerned, the Austrians and Germans had offered *parecchio* (a great amount) to ensure Italy's neutrality, and he could not see the point of spilling blood to obtain more. This calculating mentality was typical of Giolitti and flew in the face of the widely prevalent irrationalism and its consequent exaltation of action over reflection, an attitude soon elevated to dogma in the fascist regime.

Giolitti returned to power only in 1920-1921, just as disillusionment with the peace settlement and mounting industrial unrest were bringing the fundamental problems of liberal Italy to the crisis point. Giolitti initially tolerated **fascism**, believing that **Benito Mussolini** could be tamed and would both restore order and initiate social reforms. Events gradually robbed him of this illusion and convinced him to pass to the opposition. Until his death in **Turin** in 1928, Giolitti was an outspoken critic of the new regime.

GIUSTIZIA E LIBERTÀ (GL). An anti-fascist organization founded in Paris in 1929 by **Carlo Rosselli**, **Gaetano Salvemini**, and several other liberal socialist intellectuals, *Giustizia e Libertà* (Justice and Liberty) has a proud place in Italian history. Under the headline "we shan't win in a day, but win we shall," the movement's journal (also called *Giustizia e Libertà*) declared itself to be a revolutionary organization of republicans, liberals, and socialists committed to liberty, a republican form of government, and social justice. In July 1930, the movement publicized these ideals by launching a leaflet-raid over the cathedral square in **Milan** from an airplane purchased by Rosselli. This dramatic gesture caused the authorities to crack down and in October 1930 the leading organizers inside Italy,

Ferruccio Parri, Ernesto Rossi, and Riccardo Bauer, were arrested. Rossi and Bauer were sentenced to long prison terms in May 1931. In November, GL joined the so-called "anti-fascist concentration" uniting all the political forces in exile. The *giellisti*, as the movement's members became known, were made responsible for organizing resistance to the regime inside the country. This pact lasted until May 1934, when Rosselli broke with the major party in the "anti-fascist concentration," the **Partito Socialista Italiano** (PSI) / Italian Socialist Party, because of its increasing closeness to the **Partito Comunista Italiano** (PCI) / Italian Communist Party.

The movement was seriously harmed by the brutal murder of Carlo Rosselli and his brother, Nello, in 1937. Nevertheless, clandestine cells of Giustizia and Libertà were established in northern Italy in particular, and former *giellisti* later became influential figures in the PSI and the **Partito d'Azione** / Action Party after the fall of the regime.

GLADIO. Ostensibly a secret network of nearly 50 underground armed squads who would have organized resistance to an eventual Soviet invasion of Italy, Gladio (a *gladio* was the short, double-edged and pointed sword used by antique **Rome**'s infantry and in the arena) is one of the many murky chapters in Italian cold war history. The networks were discovered accidentally in 1990 during a judicial investigation in Venice into the murder of a policeman. Pressed by the leadership of the **Partito Comunista Italiana** (PCI) / Italian Communist Party, who suspected that the squads had existed to organize subversive activity in the event of a communist electoral victory, the then premier, **Giulio Andreotti**, first claimed that the networks had been disbanded in 1972. Subsequently, in October 1990, he was forced to admit that the squads were still in being. Furthermore, no fewer than 12 of the squads' 150 arms caches had been rifled by unknown hands. In January 1991, the gladiators' names were revealed, and it swiftly became clear that a substantial proportion had links to neo-fascist groups.

It is widely believed in Italy that Gladio was not a **North Atlantic Treaty Organization** (NATO) initiative, as the Andreotti government claimed, but was instead a CIA undercover operation in collaboration with the Italian secret service to subvert a communist government, even if legitimately elected. There are certainly grounds for believing this hypothesis. NATO headquarters initially denied its involvement and only retracted its denial after arm-twisting by the Italian government. The only first-rank Italian politicians to have been fully informed of the networks were Andreotti and President **Francesco Cossiga**, both of whom were notoriously close to the secret services, while other equally important, but less conspiratorial politicians, such as **Amintore Fanfani**, were seemingly not informed at all. Whatever the truth of Gladio's origins and purpose, the discovery of the network immediately led to a major institutional crisis as Cossiga used every power at his command to suppress an independent inquiry into his role in the affair. Most disturbingly of all, the revelation that the Italian state had been arming squads of right-wing extremists also provided an ominous explanation for the wave of neo-fascist terrorism in the 1970s that culminated in the bomb attack at the **Bologna** railway station on August 2, 1980, in which 80 people lost their lives.

GOBETTI, PIERO (1901-1926). In his tragically brief life, Piero Gobetti was the author of some of the most thought-provoking political philosophy written in Italy in this century. Born in **Turin** in 1901, he was a child prodigy—**Antonio Gramsci** made him the theater critic of *Ordine nuovo* when he was just 18 years old. While still a student, he founded and edited the anti-fascist periodical *Rivoluzione liberale (Liberal Revolution)*, which was banned by Mussolini in 1925. In 1923, he became a publisher: "Piero Gobetti editore" specialized in printing works by anti-fascist writers, including the poet and future nobel laureate **Eugenio Montale**. Gobetti's most famous essay, also called *La rivoluzione liberale*, was published in 1924; his other works include *Dal bolscevismo al fascismo (From Bolshevism to Fascism,* 1923) and *Risorgimento senza eroi (The Risorgimento without Heroes,* 1926). Gobetti's thought was characterized by an abiding faith in individualism and a profound suspicion of all bureaucratic and hierarchical forms of society. For this reason, he famously identified the Bolshevik revolution in Russia as "an experience in liberalism," since he regarded the Soviets established in St. Petersburg and Moscow as the embryo of a higher, more dynamic form of democracy than the parliamentarianism that had delivered Italy into the hands of Mussolini.

The violence of *squadrismo* forced Gobetti to emigrate to Paris in January 1926, where he died from the effects of a beating only a few weeks after his arrival. He was survived by his wife, Ada Prospero, who became a leading figure in the resistance to **fascism**.

GONELLA, GUIDO (1905-1982). Those Catholics who, during the fascist decades, were drawn to **De Gasperi** came largely from the **Federazione Universitaria Cattolici Italiana** FUCI-Laureati / Catholic University Graduates' Movement of Italy. It was responsible for publishing *Studium* so that it appeared to be independent of **Azione Cattolica Italiana**. Members included many post-war leaders of the **Democrazia Cristiana** (DC) / Christian Democracy Party, for example, **Aldo Moro, Giulio Andreotti** and Verona-born Guido Gonella. He was also editor of *Azione Fucina*.

As early as 1932, Gonella was the managing editor of the bimonthly *Illustrazione Vaticana*, an organ used to disseminate De Gasperi's views. He was also editor of *Rassegna Internazionale di documentazione*. Because of these journals' purported anti-fascist slant, he was arrested in 1939 on the eve of war in Poland. Catholic opinion favored (Catholic) Poland, but the regime was allied to Germany. When his sentence to *il confino* was changed to one of "political surveillance," Gonella became assistant editor of *L'Osservatore Romano*, the Vatican daily newspaper. In 1943, he founded the daily, *Il Popolo*, which was to become the organ of the DC. He remained at its helm until 1946. In the DC, his role included writing much of the program at the party's initial convention. From a Catholic background shared by his fellow DC militants, Gonella wanted to establish for his party a mass base among those who had been the backbone of **Mussolini**'s movement: small property-owners, and the lower middle class whose savings had been wiped out by **World War I** and who feared the left as a bolshevik menace. Artisans, shopkeepers, small businessmen, and white-collar workers sought assurances that Catholic morality and property rights would not suffer and that individual initiative would be protected from monopoly capitalism as well as from reformers' zeal.

He was elected to the **Constituent Assembly** and subsequently to the Chamber of Deputies in the first **Parliament** of the new republic. Consistently reelected to Parliament, he served as minister of education in De Gasperi's first five governments (1946-1951) and was also political secretary of the DC between 1950 and 1953. Minister of justice in De Gasperi's eighth government, he was eventually to serve with **Antonio Segni** (1955-1957), **Adone Zoli** (1957-1958), **Fernando Tambroni** (1960), **Amintore Fanfani** (1958-1959; 1960-1962), **Giovanni Leone** (1968), and **Giulio Andreotti** (1972-1973).

Gonella was elected to the Senate in 1972, reelected in 1976, and again in 1979. At the same time, he was elected to serve in the European Parliament.

GORIA, GIOVANNI (1943-1994). Republican Italy's youngest-ever prime minister, Goria was a native of the Piedmont town of Asti. His national political career began in 1976, when he was elected to the Chamber of Deputies; his ministerial career began just a few years later. In December 1982, Goria became minister for the treasury and he held this post until his accession to the premiership in July 1987. During his spell as treasury minister, a huge increase in public spending took place and the Italian state regularly ran annual budget deficits of 12-14 percent of GNP.

As prime minister, Goria soon discovered that he had little or no power to implement cuts in spending, or to follow any constructive policies at all. Closely allied to **Ciriaco De Mita**, the then secretary of the **Democrazia Cristiana** (DC) / Christian Democracy Party, Goria found that his government was hostage to the campaign being waged against De Mita by the **Partito Socialista Italiano** (PSI / Italian Socialist Party, and by the DC leader's own rivals within the party. His nine months as prime minister were a period of permanent political crisis in which Goria himself aged visibly. His treatment by the press was quite ruthless: to symbolize Goria's political nullity, one cartoonist began to represent the prime minister by drawing only his trademark wavy hair and full beard. Goria's government collapsed in March 1988. He returned to ministerial office only in 1991, as agriculture minister, and took the more prestigious post of finance minister in the administration formed by **Giuliano Amato** in June 1992. He resigned in January 1993 after he was briefly placed under investigation by the judiciary of his native Asti. He died there in May 1994 in his fifty-first year.

GRAMSCI, ANTONIO (1891-1937). Born in Cagliari, Sardinia, Gramsci overcame a serious childhood accident and his family's limited economic means to attend the university in **Turin**. It was here that he began his involvement in politics, joining the **Partito Socialista Italiano** (PSI) / Italian Socialist Party in 1913, and becoming a member of the editorial staff of the party paper *L'Avanti!* After the Bolshevik revolution in Russia, Gramsci founded *L'Ordine nuovo*, a periodical distributed mostly in Turin that published pro-Soviet views and took issue with what Gramsci saw as the timidity and futility of the PSI and organized labor in the face of the growing fascist menace. *L'Ordine nuovo* subsequently became the official paper of the **Partito Comunista Italiano** (PCI) / Italian Communist Party after its formation in January 1921, and Gramsci, as editor, became a member of the new party's central committee, as well as a parliamentary deputy in 1924.

Gramsci disapproved of the PCI's intransigent insistence upon an impractical policy of armed resistance to the fascists. Gramsci wanted to build a mass party that united the northern workers, the southern peasantry, and middle-class progressives against **fascism**. His more moderate line prevailed, and in 1926, the party's third congress, held in secret in Lyon, France, chose him as its new leader. Unlike his close friend from university, and successor as leader of the PCI, **Palmiro Togliatti**, Gramsci was unable to refrain from criticizing the degeneration of the Soviet regime. In October 1926, he condemned the dictatorial tendencies of the Soviet party in a famous letter to its central committee, which Togliatti, the Italian representative in Moscow, deliberately suppressed.

Shortly afterward, he bravely reentered Italy to oppose **Mussolini**'s repressive laws against the press and political freedom, but was arrested on November 8, 1926, before the parliamentary debate could begin. In 1928, he was sentenced to over 20 years of imprisonment. Between 1928 and 1933, he was held in jail in the southern city of Bari. While in prison, his health began to fail. International interest in his case caused the authorities to allow Gramsci to leave prison briefly in 1934, returning to jail in 1935. Finally released in April 1937, he died of a brain hemorrhage in the same month. He was survived by his wife and two children, who were living in the Soviet Union.

During his confinement, Gramsci wrote copiously on philosophical, political, historical, and social questions. When, after the war, his prison letters and notebooks were published by the progressive publisher Einaudi of Turin, it became clear that, despite the difficulties of his style, Gramsci was a thinker of the first order. In his view, it was mistaken to believe that there could be only one way to achieve the ultimate goal of socialism; each country would have to find its own individual road to achieving a socialist society. This idea assumed immense political importance after 1945, when Togliatti used it to justify the PCI's relative independence from Moscow. Eventually, the notion of "many roads to socialism" undergirded the *compromesso storico*. In Italy, Gramsci considered that socialism would only supersede capitalism after the PCI had attained cultural "hegemony" by controlling and shaping the means of intellectual production and hence the formation of ideas.

GRAN CONSIGLIO DEL FASCISMO (Grand Council of Fascism). The law of December 28, 1928, created the structure of this body, meant to be "the supreme organ entrusted with the prescription and coordination " of all regime activities.

The head of government (i.e., **Benito Mussolini**) was, by right, the president of the Grand Council, making this law the final step in the creation of his personal dictatorship. The normal prerogatives of a chairperson, that is to say, setting agenda and convening meetings, were spelled out in the law, a fact that makes clear the intention to leave all initiatives in the hands of the Duce. He could designate the secretary of the **Partito Nazionale Fascista** (PNF) / National Fascist Party, already the secretary of the Grand Council, as his surrogate, but the initiative lay with the head of government.

Automatic membership fell to the members of the **Quadrumvirate**, to former secretaries of the PNF, and to those cabinet members who had been members of the government for the entire three years since the fascist "revolution." Additional members pro tempore included the presidents of each house of Parliament, of the Chamber of Corporations (after the corporate system displaced the parliamentary houses), current cabinet officers, the general in command of the militia, the members of the PNF executive committee, the presidents of the **Accademia d'Italia**, of the Fascist Institute for Culture, of the Special Tribunal for crimes against the state, and of the **Confederazione Italiana Sindacati Nazionali Lavoratori** (CISNAL) / Italian Confederation of National Workers' Unions. The party apparently had absorbed the state.

Structural or constitutional changes were put within the purview of the Grand Council, but no such changes were introduced until the regime's end, brought about when Mussolini agreed to call a meeting on the afternoon of June 24, 1943 (the first meeting since December 1939: not even when Mussolini assumed the command [1940] of all the country's armed forces was a meeting held). There, **Dino Grandi** advanced a motion to restore power to the throne: it carried by a 19 to 7 majority with one abstention. Those in favor included **Giacomo Acerbo**, **Galeazzo Ciano**, **Giuseppe Bottai**, **Luigi Federzoni**, as well as **Emilio De Bono** and **Cesare De Vecchi**, both members of the **Quadrumvirate**. This action enabled King **Victor Emmanuel III** to have Mussolini arrested and put into "protective custody." *See also* Fascism.

GRANDI, DINO (1895-1988). A powerful provincial action-squad leader in Emilia-Romagna, he represented in **Bologna** what **Italo Balbo** and **Roberto Farinacci** did in the agrarian fascism of Ferrara and Cremona, respectively. One of the most popular of **Mussolini**'s early rivals for leadership, he was simultaneously intelligent, violent, and an eager social climber. He was a perfect choice to be an undersecretary at the Foreign Affairs Ministry in 1925 with the task of using bribery or intimidation—or both—to ensure that foreign journalists sent only government-approved stories to their newspapers. Cooperation meant easy access, free wire services, and even a stipend; failure to cooperate could mean anything from telegraph delays and "malfunctions" to a beating or even expulsion as a persona non grata.

At a time when Mussolini, as foreign minister in his own government, was busily supporting Croatian terrorists for eventual use in making Yugoslavia an Italian outpost in the Danube Basin, Grandi was given the assignment of supplying Macedonian dissidents with arms and money to be applied to the same end. In September 1929, Grandi was allowed to replace Mussolini at the Foreign Ministry. He remained at that post for three years at which time Mussolini resumed direction of foreign affairs, sweetening Grandi's dismissal by making him ambassador to the United Kingdom where he became known for his avid study of golfing, his belligerent posturing at the London Naval Conference (1930), and his reassurances to the British government in 1935 concerning Italian intentions in **Abyssinia**. In his eagerness to feed *Il Duce*'s vanity, Grandi exaggerated his reports of British admiration for Mussolini and consistently told the Italian dictator what he most wanted to hear. Mussolini repaid him by failing to keep him apprised either about initiatives in Ethiopia (Abyssinia) or, eventually, in Spain. Grandi, as a result, was often uninformed or ill-informed, forcing him to fabricate quite transparently. His standing in British circles declined steadily. He returned to Italy in 1939 and became minister of justice and president of the Chamber of Associations.

When Mussolini realized that, unless he went to war against France and Britain, he could not avoid becoming a mere *Gauleiter* of Italy, Grandi supported him. Subsequently, after the disasters in Greece, North Africa, and Russia were capped by the Anglo-American invasion of **Sicily**, the demoralization of the Italian army was complete. It was clear that changes were urgently needed.

On July 24-25, 1943, Mussolini opened the first wartime Grand Council meeting with a rambling speech in which it became clear that he had no policy objectives. Grandi and others renewed their vows of loyalty to Mussolini but cast about for ways to terminate a war that was going badly. Finally, Farinacci, the most outspoken and courageous critic, took Mussolini's direction of the war especially to task. Grandi, the most moderate of the critics, made the motion that inasmuch as dictatorship had undone Italy, the king should resume those powers of which he had been deprived. As chairman of the meeting, Mussolini could have arranged a substitute motion of confidence but, instead, allowed Grandi's motion to come to a vote and even offered no argument against it: the Grandi motion carried handily, 19 in favor, 7 opposed, and 1 abstention. Mussolini was arrested on the same day. Grandi sent a congratulatory letter to Marshal **Badoglio**, who had been designated by King **Victor Emmanuel III** as the new prime minister. Grandi subsequently escaped to Portugal, then Brazil, before returning to Italy under a presidential amnesty. While abroad, he had eked out a living by giving Latin lessons.

GRAZIANI, RODOLFO (1882-1955). Born in Frosinone just south of **Rome**, he finished **World War I** as a colonel but left army service for private life after that war. He returned to active duty in 1922 and was sent to **Libya** where he coordinated efforts at putting down Senussi irregulars, who had effectively slowed Italian colonization. By 1930, he had hanged the leaders in front of what remained of their clans after 60,000 of their number had been killed. When he returned to Italy in 1934, it was as a general commanding an army corps.

In the next year (1935), he was sent to Ethiopia (**Abyssinia**) to prepare the attack on that country. His success in subduing Abyssinian rebels by the methods employed in Libya led to his promotion to marshal. In 1936, he replaced **Pietro Badoglio**—his arch-rival—as viceroy of Ethiopia. When, in 1937, Graziani was repatriated, he was styled marquis of Neghelli. His place as viceroy was taken by the king's cousin, the duke of Aosta. In 1939, Graziani became chief of the General Staff, and in 1940 he was put in command of Italian forces in North Africa. They numbered over 300,000 but were still equipped with rifles of an 1891 design and had but 160 aircraft at their disposal. Accustomed to putting down nomadic tribesmen and inordinately proud of having been the first commander ever to use armored vehicles in the desert, he came too late to realize that the party placemen around him in command positions were singularly devoid of military experience. Far less numerous British and Commonwealth forces (two divisions faced Graziani's 10) were better led and far better organized: so much so that early in January 1941, they had forced him to retreat so rapidly that—after 100,000 of his troops were taken prisoner—he was relieved of his duties and summoned to Rome by a Commission of

Inquiry. After that, despite a spirited defense by the duke of Aosta, Italian East Africa fell.

Deprived of his commands, Graziani resumed private life until September of 1943 when he rejoined the Duce in the **Republic of Salò,** in which he served as defense minister. On being captured by the advancing Allies, he avoided execution but was tried by Italian courts in 1948 and sentenced to 19 years imprisonment for "collaboration with the German invader." Amnestied after five years, he became honorary president of the **Movimento Sociale Italiano** (MSI) / Italian Social Movement. He died in 1955 in Rome. *See also* Libya.

GRONCHI, GIOVANNI (1887-1978). Born in Pontedera (Pisa), by his early twenties, this Tuscan schoolteacher was among those liberal Catholics who eventually formed the **Partito Popolare Italiano** (PPI) / Italian People's Party in 1919. After **World War I,** he supported Don **Luigi Sturzo** in **Azione Cattolica** (ACI) / Italian Catholic Action, and by 1922, Gronchi was at the head of Catholic (white) labor unions. He publicly opposed Pius XI's involving Azione Cattolica in labor questions, fearful that it would inevitably lead to **trade unions'** subordination to the regime. When Gronchi realized the futility of his struggle for autonomy, he warned—in *Cronache Sociali d'Italia* beginning in 1926—that tying the church closely to the regime could only damage the church, the worker, and the nation, should fascist militarism and incompetence lead to disaster. Moreover, he argued that the new state, far from being consonant with Catholic doctrine as expressed in *Rerum Novarum*, was an instrument for the imposition of the state's will. When the policies of Pius XI transformed AC and isolated both the Catholic party and the white unions, Gronchi withdrew from political activities until 1943.

By September 1943, **Badoglio**'s new government made it possible for party life to resume. At that moment, Gronchi and colleagues from the PPI—figures like **Alcide De Gasperi, Mario Scelba, Guido Gonella** from the *Osservatore Romano*; **Aldo Moro** and **Giuglio Andreotti** from the **Federazione Universitaria Cattolici Italiana**-Laureati (FUCI-Laureati) / Catholic University Graduates' Movement of Italy—led the new Catholic party, which revived the name **Democrazia Cristiana** (DC) / Christian Democracy Party. Gronchi was conspicuous on the left of the DC after breaking with De Gasperi's center. He advocated an independent Italian foreign policy within Western Europe and an "opening" to the socialists. The Catholic and socialist masses could—in his view—by combining their strength, create a left Catholic regime in Italy. In 1955, his anticipation of what was to become the *compromesso storico* (historic compromise) drew the combined votes of the **Partito Comunista Italiano** (PCI) / Italian Communist Party, the **Partito Socialista Italiano** (PSI) / Italian Socialist Party, and left Demochristians to propel him into the presidency of the republic where he remained until 1962, when he became a life senator. While president, his official trip (February 1960) to the Soviet Union exposed him to criticism from the nationalist and conservative right both in and outside of Azione Cattolica Italiana. Active in the Senate as he had been in the party, he served on the Foreign Affairs Committee and—in the last parliament of his life (he died in **Rome** in 1978)—on the Defense Committee.

See also Encyclicals; Fernando Tambroni.

GUARENTIGIE, LEGGE DELLE. Following the occupation of **Rome** in 1870, relations with the **Papacy** became the major concern of the Italian government. Pope Pius IX was determined to maintain control of at least a symbolic portion of the city. This, no Italian government would allow for fear of foreign involvement (Pius asked Prussia to intervene on his behalf in the summer of 1870). A generous settlement was necessary. In May 1871, the Italian state unilaterally recognized the Pope as a head of state, conceded his right to free communication with foreign Catholics, gave diplomatic recognition to foreign ambassadors at the Vatican, and offered a substantial annual subsidy (later refused) for the Papal court's expenses. The government also renounced some of its powers over the nomination of bishops within Italian territorial boundaries, although it was prevented from abolishing all jurisdiction over church affairs by the strongly anti-clerical majority in Parliament.

These *guarentigie* (guarantees) were greeted with hostility by Pius IX. For the next 50 years, Pius IX and his successors treated themselves as prisoners of conscience, and refused to leave the walls of St. Peter's. Pius also unsuccessfully attempted to persuade the Catholic nations of Europe to maintain their embassies at **Florence**, the former capital, not Rome. A Papal ban forbidding Catholic heads of state to visit Rome was enacted and remained in force until 1920. Pius's reaction was not mere pique. The Pope could not afford to bow to the law for fear that foreign countries would use his subordination to the Italian state as an excuse to interfere with his spiritual powers over their Catholic citizens. Even without the Pope's participation, however, the guarantees provided a modus vivendi between church and state until they were superseded by the signature of the **Lateran pacts** in 1929.

-H-

HISTORIC COMPROMISE. *See* Compromesso Storico.

HOARE-LAVAL PACT. Sir Samuel Hoare was Great Britain's foreign minister in the government of Samuel Baldwin at a time when Pierre Laval headed the government of France. Together, they had agreed to resolve the Italo-Abyssinian border dispute by offering to cede to **Abyssinia** a port in British Somaliland if Haile Selassie would cede to Italy the Ogaden territory. Furthermore, Britain and France would recognize Italian economic paramountcy in the rest of Abyssinia (Ethiopia). That is, Haile Selassie, king of Abyssinia, was to give up two-thirds of his national territory and give to Italy a de facto protectorate over what remained.

This offer was rejected by **Mussolini**, who really wanted a formal Italian protectorate. Before negotiations could resume, the Hoare-Laval proposals were leaked to the French press by several enterprising French correspondents assigned to London. The result was a furor, especially in Britain. Baldwin dismissed Sir Samuel (who was to resume a political role a few years later as British ambassador to Spain), blaming the initiative on Laval; British distrust of the French increased. Thus, not only was Mussolini in a position to conquer the territory but the onus for the breakdown of negotiations could be put on the democracies.

In fact, Italy had already begun to move troops into Ethiopia when this dismemberment was proposed. By May of 1936, the Italian army entered Addis Ababa, the Abyssinian capital. In July, the League of Nations lifted sanctions that had not proven effective in the absence of the United States from the league. Mussolini had been able to claim that Italy had stood up to 60 nations arrayed against her. Together with Anglo-French "non-involvement" in the Spanish Civil War, the conflict in Ethiopia made clear the incapacity of the league to act without the concurrence of Britain and France; and that their incompatible foreign policies were governed by disparate notions of political realism, not by commitments to collective security.

-I-

IMMIGRATION. Among densely populated European states with relatively high unemployment, Italy is one of the chief destinations of migrants from Africa, East Europe, and Turkey. Her lengthy coastline seems to invite a commercial traffic of clandestine immigration. Over one-third of new arrivals "regularize" their position under the provisions of legislation that offer them legal status in exchange for registering, a move that gives them access to education, housing, and health care. By a decree of January 2, 1990, any immigrant may apply for a residency permit (permesso di soggiorno) within four months of arrival even without an entry visa so long as either two Italian nationals with no prior penal convictions or two "regularized" fellow nationals can testify to the applicant's identity. Many immigrants find employment in seasonal labor, fishing, and construction work where they are often exploited because of their vulnerability to deportation if their status has not been "regularized."

Most immigrants into Italy in the 1980s came from Morocco, the Philippines, Tunisia, Senegal, Egypt, Ghana, and Nigeria. More recently, Eastern Europe has been the chief source. As Turkey's war on the Kurdish population increased in intensity, many Kurds entered Europe by way of Italy, giving rise to fears among **European Union** (EU) partners that their own immigrant populations would swell as a result. Under current regulations, once arrived in Italy, immigrants have 15-day temporary visas. They can, and many do, risk remaining without documents; or they "regularize" themselves; or they leave for elsewhere in the EU.

In many cities, especially those with a left tradition, language-training and job-training programs are available as are municipal centers to offer assistance in finding housing and in adjusting to Italian life. The major **trade unions** make the hiring of immigrant labor a condition in new contracts. Italy has one of the lowest demographic growth rates in the world. Consequently, predictions are freely made that her economy needs immigrants to fill those jobs that may otherwise go begging.

In 1990, the Italian statistical agency (ISTAT) estimated at 700,000 the number of non-Caucasians or "people of color" living in Italy. Of those, a full 230,000 legalized their status, which entitles them to Italian social benefits such as health care and access to schools. Unlike earlier immigrants, most come from urban areas in their own countries to Italian cities. A full 16 percent are university graduates, which does not protect them from a good deal of hostility. Many of those who find no work in the building trades eke out a living by becoming itinerant salesmen of (often bogus) designer-label jewelry and clothing, of cigarette lighters and trinkets, or of artifacts evoking images of exotic crafts. *See also* Albania.

INGRAO, PIETRO (1915-). Born in Latina province near **Rome**, Ingrao began a lifetime of anti-fascist activity in adolescence. After joining the **Partito Comunista Italiano** (PCI) / Italian Communist Party in 1940, he earned the distinction of being sought by the fascist police because he had become one of the leaders of the clandestine communist group operating in Rome. From a temporary safe-house in Calabria, he managed to reach **Milan** where he became one of the editors of the clandestine newspaper, *L'Unità*, a post in which he was confirmed for 10 years beginning in 1947.

Since his first election in 1948, Ingrao has served steadily as a member of the Chamber of Deputies. In 1963, he was chosen vice president of the Communist Parliamentary Group. Five years later, he was elected president of the Parliamentary Group and retained that post until 1972 when he was put in charge of interregional coordination. In 1975, he became director of the party's Study Center for State Reform. He was elected to serve as president of the Chamber of Deputies between 1976 and 1979, and when he was redesignated for that post he refused in order to serve on the Committee for Constitutional Affairs.

Ingrao, long identified as one of the most influential members of the Central Committee, left the party in 1993 over the issues involved in its transformation. At the **Bologna** convention of the PCI, Ingrao had struggled to retain much of the traditional symbolism of the West's leading Communist party. While he did not carry the day, it was clear that he spoke for much of the working-class base of the party. Some analysts, in their search for an explanation of the left's losses in the 1994 elections, have pointed to tensions between the old Resistance militants like Ingrao and the younger party-members. It is noteworthy that Ingrao's daughter, Chiara, is a deputy of the **Partito Democratico della Sinistra** (PDS) / Democratic Party of the Left.

INTEGRALISM. The devout of any faith who advocate the application of its sociology and teachings to political and social life are "integralists" since they seek to integrate faith and policy. Islam is not alone in producing this view: it exists as well in Roman Catholic states, Italy being a case in point. Beginning in 1948, Luigi Gedda organized civic committees that were meant to check the perceived threat of bolshevism by ensuring the coherence of the Catholic vote as part of **Azione Cattolica** / Catholic Action, which also organized newly enfranchised women. By 1949, Italian Catholics voting for Marxist parties risked excommunication. These initiatives linked the Roman Catholic Church with the right-most wing of the **Democrazia Cristiana** (DC) / Christian Democracy Party.

The most aggressive Catholics were often active in the cities deep in the "Red Belt" of Emilia-Romagna and northward. Cardinal Lercaro of **Bologna**, for example, with the support of local industrialists, had small trucks and school busses converted into mobile chapels (the famous *cappelle volanti* or flying chapels) that, together with a priest, would drive on Sunday mornings into working-class neighborhoods, there to play over loud-speakers recordings of church bells and hymns while serving mass to passersby. Others sought expression through a faction of the early DC ably led by Professor Giorgio La Pira and **Giuseppe Dossetti** (1913-1996), an ex-partisan member of the **Constituent Assembly**. *See also* Guido Gonella.

IOTTI, LEONILDE (1920-). The first woman ever to become speaker of the Italian Chamber of Deputies, "Nilde" Iotti was born in Reggio Emilia (Emilia-Romagna). She became a communist activist while in her teens, and in 1946 she was one of the very few **women** elected to the **Constituent Assembly**. After the war she was elected to the Central Committee of the **Partito Comunista Italiano** (PCI) / Italian Communist Party and to its *direzione*, or inner cabinet, and played an important role in making party policy, especially over women's issues. Iotti was in fact even closer to the heart of the PCI's leadership than these institutional posts suggest: she was the companion of **Palmiro Togliatti**, the party leader, until his death in 1964. In Parliament, she was especially active in the struggle to obtain a **divorce** law during the late 1960s, and then to defend the law from a **referendum** challenge in 1974.

Iotti became deputy speaker of the Chamber in 1972, and in 1979 replaced another communist, **Pietro Ingrao**, as speaker. She held the post until 1992. In 1987, during a lengthy and confused government crisis, Iotti was briefly given an exploratory mandate by President **Francesco Cossiga** to form a new government. Although her attempts failed, it was the first time that a member of the PCI had been entrusted with this task. *See also* Referendums.

IRREDENTISMO. The occupation of **Rome** in 1870 still left a number of "unredeemed" Italian territories such as the Trentino and **Trieste.** In 1877, the radical politician Matteo Renato Imbriani formed, with the patronage of **Giuseppe Garibaldi,** an association called *L'Italia irredenta* whose goal was the liberation of these "unredeemed" territories from Austrian rule. The Italian government's refusal to push Italy's claims at the Congress of Berlin (1878), and the pro-German foreign policy followed by the administrations of **Agostino Depretis** and **Francesco Crispi** after the signature of the **Triple Alliance** in 1882, led the association to become one of the main opposition forces in liberal Italy. An offshoot of the association, the "Committee for Trento and Trieste" was banned by Crispi in 1889 as—the following year—were clubs of citizens named in honor of an Italian nationalist from Trieste, Guglielmo Oberdan, who had been hanged by the Austrians.

After 1900, the movement became more prone to violence and illegality, and many irredentists transmuted their beliefs into nationalism and even imperialism. *Irredentismo* was at the bottom of the decision of many socialists, radicals, and republicans to support the war in 1914, although unlike the nationalists, the irredentists were usually in favor of entering the war on the side of the Entente. By 1919, when **Gabriele D'Annunzio** seized Fiume to general popular approval, the movement had lost its authenticity. **Mussolini** also used the rhetoric of *irredentismo* to justify Italian adventures in Dalmatia, **Albania,** and the eastern Mediterranean—a perversion of the original ideal.

ISTITUTO PER LA RICOSTRUZIONE INDUSTRIALE (IRI). For most of the latter half of this century, the state holding company, IRI, has held a central position in the Italian economy. The company was set up in 1933, as the fascist administration struggled to rescue the country's financial system from the huge losses the principal investment banks had incurred lending to depression-hit manufacturing firms. In essence, the state bailed the banks out and was left with a ragbag of industrial companies whose activities included steel, shipbuilding, electricity generation, and telephones. The initial goal was to restore IRI's component parts back into private ownership as soon as their profitability warranted it, but in 1937, the regime's increasingly belligerent foreign policy goals led it to desire greater planning over economic production and IRI, with the cooperation of the industrial elite, was thus used to coordinate the Italian state's (somewhat inefficient) transition to a war economy. After the war,

IRI's member firms employed almost 100,000 people and faced immense problems with readjusting to a peacetime economy. After a decade of drift, the Italian government acted, establishing, in December 1956, the Ministry for State Participation in Industry, which established a three-tier system of control for state-owned businesses. The bottom, operating tier was occupied by individual joint-stock companies, who were grouped into *enti di gestione* (management structures) answerable to the ministry and wholly owned by it. The *enti di gestione*, of which IRI was the biggest, were supposed to be run as ongoing economic concerns, with the government providing strategic direction. In particular, from 1957 onward, IRI was directed to spend at least 40 percent of its capital investment budget in southern Italy.

IRI itself was divided into six main *società finanziarie* (financial holding companies). These controlled the company's telephone, shipping, engineering, shipbuilding, steel, and electricity generation activities. In addition, the company controlled a number of banks, the Italian television service, **RAI**, and the national airline, Alitalia. By the early 1960s, IRI controlled nearly 7 percent of total manufacturing output, and its largest subsidiary, *Finsider* the steel company, had become one of the highest producing steel corporations in the world.

The early 1960s were the high point of IRI's success. Gradually, the shortcomings of state-controlled enterprises everywhere began to take a toll on the institution's efficiency. Investment decisions were too often taken for political reasons; lay-offs were shirked; over-generous pension, job security, and fringe benefit rights were awarded to the workforce; bureaucratic empire building took place; strategic decision-making, which required broad ministerial, union, and managerial consensus, was slow and unresponsive to changes in market demand. By 1982, when **Romano Prodi** took over as chairman of the company, IRI was losing Lit 3 trillion every year and had Lit 35 trillion of accumulated debt. Prodi brought a measure of financial discipline and attempted to solve the debt problem by asset sales, but his plans swiftly ran into political opposition. In 1986, Prodi wanted to sell off the Alfa Romeo car firm to the American carmaker Ford, but the government intervened and forced him to sell the company to FIAT instead. When Prodi's political backer, **Ciriaco De Mita**, was forced from power in 1989, the privatization program was halted completely and Prodi lost his job. The European Union has succeeded, however, where Prodi failed. The need to meet EU guidelines has led to significant privatizations since 1992, notably in the telecom sector, although skeptical Italian economists claim that not enough has been done to liberate the newly privatized firms from political control.

-L-

LABRIOLA, ANTONIO (1843-1904). One of the most prominent Marxist philosophers of the late nineteenth century, Antonio Labriola was the son of a schoolteacher from Cassino (Campania). A brilliant student who won prizes for essays on Spinoza and Greek interpretations of Socrates' thought before he was 30 years of age, Labriola became *ordinario* (full professor) of history in 1877. Labriola's conversion to socialism was a slow process. The seemingly scientific approach of Marxism to social questions, his disgust at the increasingly corrupt form of parliamentary democracy practiced in liberal Italy, contacts with workers' study groups, and the intolerance of right-wing students toward his ideas (Labriola was forced to abandon a course on the French Revolution in February 1889 by riotous students) were the chief factors that led him to embrace the socialist cause, which can be dated to a speech he gave to a study group of Roman workers in June 1889.

In the 1890s, Labriola established an international reputation as a Marxist theorist. Between April 1895 and 1897, he published three long essays on historical materialism in the journal *Devenir Social*, edited by the French theorist Georges Sorel. In these essays, Labriola introduced the notion of Marxism as a practical doctrine—a guide to understanding historical development rather than a dogma—that would later be taken up by **Antonio Gramsci**. In Italy, the same essays were edited for publication by **Benedetto Croce**, and they had an enormous influence on Croce's early thought.

Despite his doctrinal flexibility, Labriola was hostile to the reformism of **Filippo Turati**. He opposed the **Partito Socialista Italiano** (PSI) / Italian Socialist Party's collaboration with the forces of Italian liberalism, and evinced at times an intemperate hostility toward the Italian bourgeoisie. Paradoxically, however, he supported the imperialist adventures of the Italian state in Libya and East Africa, arguing somewhat coldly that imperialism was a necessary stage in the development of European capitalism, from which Italy could not refrain without condemning itself to social backwardness. Labriola died of throat cancer in 1904.

LABRIOLA, ARTURO (1873-1959). The most noted Italian follower of the French syndicalist, Georges Sorel, Labriola was viewed as a heretic by the socialist movement in Italy, which he had joined in 1895, the year of receiving his *laurea* in jurisprudence from the University of **Naples**. Syndicalist thinking was one of the mainsprings of the general strike of September 1904, in which Labriola played an important organizational role. His contempt for parliamentary democracy and the pacific resolution of political disputes that pervaded the thinking of the Italian right in the early twentieth century runs through his pre-war writings. Unsurprisingly, in his periodical, *L'Avanguardia socialista* (*The Socialist Vanguard* published between December 1902 and October 1906) and in his many books and pamphlets, he espoused an interpretation of Marxism that differed from both the moderate social democracy of **Leonida Bissolati** and the mainstream of the **Partito Socialista Italiano** (PSI) / Italian Socialist Party, which believed that socialism would occur through revolutionary action only when historical conditions were ripe.

Labriola, like Sorel and the young **Benito Mussolini**, believed that the working class should accelerate the historical process and smash the institutions of the state through violent action by the **trade unions.** He was "intransigently revolutionary," having bolted the PSI in 1907. Elected to Parliament in 1913 as an independent socialist, he found convoluted reasons for defending Italy's war against Turkey and against Germany and Austria. He accepted the post of minister for labor in the last government of **Giovanni Giolitti** in 1921 and opposed **fascism** both in **Parliament** and in a much-discussed book, *La dittatura dei borghesi* (*The Dictatorship of the Middle Class*, 1924). Labriola was dismissed from his appointment as a professor at Messina for having criticized the regime. Thereupon, he emigrated to France and Belgium and lived in exile until the 1935 invasion of **Abyssinia**, which he openly supported, induced him to return.

After the fall of fascism, Labriola resumed an active political role. He was elected to the **Constituent Assembly** in 1946 and became a life senator in 1948. In 1956, he was elected to the **Naples** city council as an independent on the list of the **Partito Comunista Italiano** (PCI) / Italian Communist Party. He died in his native Naples in 1959.

LA MALFA, UGO (1903-1979). One of Italy's most honest and talented post-war leaders, the **Palermo**-born Ugo La Malfa was an exponent of a socially humane brand of liberal capitalism that found few converts in post-war Italy. As a student, he distinguished himself for both scholarly brilliance and anti-fascist activism (he was arrested briefly in 1934 and took part in the clandestine movement *Giustizia e Libertà*). A founder of the **Partito d'Azione** (PdA) / Action Party in 1942, he was its representative in the **Comitati di Liberazione Nazionale** (CLN) / National Liberation Committees after the Italian surrender in September 1943.

La Malfa's ministerial career began immediately after the war: he was minister for transport under **Ferruccio Parri** and for foreign trade in the first of **Alcide De Gasperi**'s eight governments (November 1945-June 1946).

Discontented with the policies being followed by Emilio Lussu, leader of the PdA, La Malfa—together with Parri—left the party in February 1946 to form the "Movement for Republican Democracy," which later merged with the **Partito Repubblicana Italiano** (PRI) / Italian Republican Party. Over the next 30 years, La Malfa came to symbolize the tiny PRI, whose reputation for being the "conscience" of the Italian center-left owed much to La Malfa's intellectual rigor and personal integrity. He became party leader in 1965 after a period as budget minister under **Amintore Fanfani** (1960-1963). La Malfa was the minister responsible for the policy of austerity that followed the 1973 oil shock. He served as vice premier under **Aldo Moro** between 1974 and 1976, and continued to preach a message of fiscal prudence. The need for financial stability led La Malfa to become Italy's most vocal exponent of entry into the European Monetary System in 1979.

President **Sandro Pertini** offered La Malfa the chance to form a government in March 1979. Blocked by the **Democrazia Cristiana** (DC) / Christian Democracy Party, whose members distrusted his reforming zeal, La Malfa was forced to accept second best and become vice premier and budget minister under **Giulio Andreotti**. La Malfa immediately proposed large spending cuts, but did not live long enough to put them into effect. Tired out by overwork, he died suddenly in **Rome** in the spring of 1979. His son, Giorgio, has followed in his father's footsteps, becoming budget minister under **Cossiga** in 1981, and leader of the PRI in 1987.

LA MARMORA FERRERO, ALFONSO (1804-1878). One of four brothers, all of whom rose to the rank of general in the Piedmontese army, Alfonso La Marmora was the first military officer to become prime minister of Italy, in September 1864. He had earlier served as prime minister of the Kingdom of Sardinia for six months in 1859, after the peace of Villafranca and the subsequent resignation of

Camillo Benso di Cavour. During his first spell in office, a law unifying local administration throughout the country was promulgated. Building upon earlier laws presented by **Urbano Rattazzi** in 1863, the new local government arrangements established tight central control over the peninsula. In addition, Italian law was harmonized with Sardinian law in matters of public health, the classification of roads, railways, canals, and other public works. During La Marmora's period as premier (he continued to govern until June 1866, interrupted only by a brief government crisis in December 1865), the new civil code was introduced. The code, which has been in force since January 1866, permitted civil marriage for the first time, but backed away from introducing **divorce**. The judicial inferiority of **women** and children born outside marriage was established.

La Marmora gave up politics in June 1866 to lead the Italian forces in the war against Austria. Despite his creation of the **Bersaglieri**, his military leadership was less than inspiring: Italian troops under his command were defeated at Custoza in June 1866, largely as a result of his errors as a commander. After the war, La Marmora was the target of bitter public criticism both for his conduct in the field and the wider failure of his governments to prepare the new kingdom's armed forces. He retired into reclusion, emerging only in 1870 when King **Victor Emmanuel II** made him Lieutenant of **Rome**. He died in Florence in 1878.

LAMPEDUSA. *See* Di Lampedusa, Prince Giuseppe Tomasi.

LAND REFORM. One of the most contentious measures introduced in the immediate post-war period, the 1950 land reform was a major step in the modernization of Italian agriculture and reduced the political power of the landowning class in southern and central Italy. Pressure for land reform arose after the death of **Mussolini** when peasants in **Sicily** and other parts of Italy occupied and began to cultivate land left fallow by absentee landlords. Fausto Gullo of the **Partito Comunista Italiano** (PCI) / Italian Communist Party, as minister for agriculture in Allied-occupied Italy, introduced a series of decrees in 1944 that, among other important considerations, allowed peasant **cooperatives** to take over arable land left uncultivated by its owners. Over the next two years, tens of thousands of peasants formed such cooperatives and a considerable quantity of land was put to productive use. Gullo's decrees met with uncompromising opposition from the **Democrazia Cristiana** (DC)

/ Christian Democracy Party, worried that the PCI would reap a harvest of votes among the rural poor, and from the **Partito Liberale Italiano** (PLI) / Italian Liberal Party.

Under **Antonio Segni**, minister for agriculture in the cabinet formed by **Alcide De Gasperi** in July 1946, the legal balance was restored to favor the landowners. In 1949, grievances boiled over and all of southern Italy, save Calabria and Basilicata, saw mass occupations of private land. The police intervened to defend private property, and a number of people were killed. Such repressive tactics only exacerbated tensions in the Mezzogiorno and won the DC no friends in Washington. Starting in May 1950, therefore, De Gasperi and Segni promoted three laws (one for Sicily, one for Calabria, and one for the marshland areas near **Rome** and the Po River valley) that aimed to break up the great estates and redistribute the land among the peasants who worked them. State land development agencies were created to improve uncultivated terrain and to sell it, at discounted prices, to landless peasants. Generous land improvement grants were provided, and the Italian government made an expensive effort to provide infrastructure for normally neglected rural regions.

Over the next two decades, agricultural productivity rose dramatically in Italy, and the net harvest of the main crops (grain, grapes, vegetables) increased despite a sharp fall in farmworkers as peasants migrated to the booming factories of the industrial cities and to northern Europe. Such gains in production, however, were less due to the land reform, which affected only a few hundred thousand people directly, than to the huge allotments poured into agriculture by the DC in the 1950s and 1960s. More than one-third of the average farmer's income came from state subsidies by the 1970s: unsurprisingly, the agricultural producers' associations (*consorzie*) became a bastion of support for the DC. *See also* Cassa per il Mezzogiorno; Latifondi; Southern Italy.

LANZA, GIOVANNI (1810-1882). By training, a doctor of medicine, Giovanni Lanza's historical legacy was the stiff and painful cure that he gave to the Italian economy during his premiership from 1869 to 1873. Elected to the Piedmontese Parliament for the first time in 1849, he served as minister of education and minister of finance under **Cavour** in the 1850s. After reunification he became one of the leading figures of the parliamentary right. He was minister of the interior in 1864 in the **La Marmora** government, but resigned in opposition to the grist tax (*dazio sul macinato*) imposed by **Quintino Sella.**

Lanza became premier in 1869. In economic policy, he and his treasury minister, **Marco Minghetti**, struggled to put the nation's accounts in order; in foreign policy Lanza successfully persuaded King **Victor Emmanuel II** not to side with the French in the Franco-Prussian war. Instead, Lanza took the opportunity to complete the unification of Italy by occupying **Rome** and proclaiming it capital on March 27, 1871. Lanza unsuccessfully tried to put relations with the church on a firm footing after the occupation of Rome. The *legge delle guarentigie,* though not recognized by the church, served as a *modus vivendi* between the spiritual and temporal powers within the Italian state until the signature of the **Lateran pacts** in 1929. Lanza was forced to resign in 1873. He continued to serve as deputy for his native Casale Monferatto (Piedmont) until his death in 1882.

LATERAN PACTS. The Lateran pacts were an agreement reached between **Mussolini** and Pope Pius XI which substituted the *legge delle guarentigie* of 1871 as the basis for church-state relations in Italy. They were the fruit of a lengthy period of secret negotiations between Pius, the Vatican's foreign minister, Cardinal Pietro Gasparri, **Mussolini**, and the fascist justice minister, **Alfredo Rocco**. Negotiations began in August 1926, but ran into severe difficulties over education, which the church was not prepared to wholly cede to the fascist state. Eventually, in February 1929, in the Lateran palace near the Vatican, Mussolini and the Pope came to a deal that granted unique privileges within the fascist state to the Catholic Church.

The agreement consisted of three separate pacts. The first was a treaty of mutual recognition between the Vatican and the Italian state, whereby Italy acknowledged the territorial rights of the Pope over the Vatican palaces and a number of other churches in **Rome**, and accepted that the Vatican was an independent state that could maintain diplomatic relations with other states even during times of war. The Pope, in return, recognized the kingdom of Italy. A financial convention appended to the treaty constrained Italy to pay substantial reparations for church property expropriated after the **Risorgimento**.

An additional concordat established the role that the church would play in the civil life of the nation. Here, too, the church won substantial concessions. Mussolini recognized that Catholicism should be the official state religion; that the state's existing veto power over episcopal appointments should be reduced to a consultative power only; that religious instruction would be provided at all levels of primary and secondary education (though not in the universities); that the Catholic Church would be permitted to organize youth associations, including **Azione Cattolica** and the Boy Scouts; and that church weddings would have civil recognition. The concordat effectively gave the church legal autonomy from the totalitarian state. As such, it was greeted with consternation by many fascists, notably **Gentile** and **Farinacci**. Catholic democrats like Don **Luigi Sturzo, Giovanni Gronchi**, and **Alcide De Gasperi,** by contrast, worried that the church would become too closely identified with the fascist state. Pius XI, however, was satisfied. The pacts were a legal bulwark of genuine strength against fascist encroachment on the church's traditional activities.

The Lateran pacts were subsequently affirmed—with **Partito Comunista Italiano** (PCI) / Italian Communist Party support—in Article 7 of the 1948 **Constitution**, which reiterates the independence and sovereignty of the Catholic Church and, in paragraph 2, states that "Relations between [state and the church] are governed by the Lateran pacts. Alterations of these pacts, if accepted by both parties, shall require no constitutional amendments."

In 1984, the pacts were, in fact, renegotiated to give full status to church weddings so long as they conformed with civil law. Vatican annulments of marriages were made reviewable by Italian courts, religious teaching in Italian public schools was left to the discretion of parents, limited tax exemptions were granted to church properties of a strictly religious function, state stipends to the clergy were ended, and it was agreed that all disputes between the Vatican and Italy were to be settled in Italian courts, a concession that established the primacy of Italian law. This tilting of the balance toward the state reflects Italy's increasing secularization. *See also* Papacy.

LATIFONDI. As late as the 1940s, land tenure in **southern Italy** was based on the tradition of the *latifondo*, or large estate. Such estates practiced an essentially feudal system in which the landowner was entitled to most (as much as 75 percent even after 1945) of the crops raised on his land. Tenants had no permanent right to the terrain they cultivated, but usually rented, for a fixed period of time, several thin strips of land, often far apart from each other, to which they had to walk every working day. Richer peasants sublet such strips to poorer ones, whose entire income thus depended upon tilling a patch of (often poor) land on behalf of two classes, both of which were profiting from his labor. The peasants were in constant competition with each other for the best strips of land and for the favor of the landowner's *campieri* (overseers) and *gabellotti,* responsible for tax collection on behalf of the landlord. The *campieri* enforced compliance and kept wages low among agricultural laborers, the most oppressed of all Italian social categories. Incomes among the landlords, meanwhile, were huge, but only rarely were they ploughed back into farm modernization.

The social costs of this system were enormous. Southern Italy had a rural standard of living that was hardly higher than Africa's by the end of the fascist period; hundreds of thousands of peasants lived in one-room homes, without running water or electricity; few Southerners had been able to accumulate capital and hence there was a minuscule entrepreneurial middle class able to lead an economic resurgence; and a cultural pattern of dependency on the powers-that-be had been established. Perhaps most seriously of all, the **mafia** was a product of the *latifondi.* The landowners and the *gabellotti,* anxious to preserve their positions, paid "men of honor" to intimidate upstart laborers. Convinced that "there is neither law nor justice except by one's own initiative," to quote an old Calabrian saying, many Sicilians and Calabrians became mafiosi, a grim and risky form of social mobility.

The social injustice engendered by the *latifondo* system periodically caused political turmoil in southern Italy. In the mid-1890s, when Piedmont's trade policies deprived **Sicily** of its traditional French market for sulphur exports with a resultant shift of labor from mining to already overcrowded agriculture, the result was a series of peasant uprisings that were savagely repressed by an invading army of over 80,000 Piedmontese troops. During **fascism**, the landowners' privileges were preserved by the full weight of the state. After the fall of **Mussolini**, however, the peasantry of the *Mezzogiorno* was politicized by the **Partito Comunista Italiano** (PCI) / Italian Communist Party. In a series of decree laws, the PCI agriculture minister in the **Bonomi** government, Fausto Gullo, authorized peasant **cooperatives** to take over vast swaths of uncultivated land used by the landowners for hunting; limited the landowners' tithe to 50 percent; banned the *gabellotti*; and established state-owned grain stores to which the peasants could take their produce. These policies were wildly popular with the peasants (and account for a good deal of residual leftism in the rural South even today), but were met by unrelenting opposition and widespread violence from the landlords, and political obstruction from the **Democrazia Cristiana** (DC) / Christian Democracy Party and the **Partito Liberale Italiano** (PLI) / Italian Liberal Party. The decrees were soon ruled illegal by the high courts, and the peasants had to wait until the agricultural reform of July 1950 for serious improvement in their conditions of life. *See also* Cassa per il Mezzogiorno; Land Reform; Southern Italy.

LAW. Most Italians, legally trained or not, take pride in the fact that the basis of the most widely adopted legal system in the non-Anglo-Saxon world is, in fact, Roman law and the medieval glosses prepared by those who systematized it, the glossators. Its crowning modern achievement is the French *Code Civil*, of which the Italian *Codice Civile* is a virtual translation.

Some differences between the civil (or Roman) law and the English Common Law used in former English colonies are worth explicating. Prosecutors are part of the career magistracy as are prefects, magistrates, notaries, and praetors. Competitive examinations provide the entrance route. Plea bargaining is out of the question since courts seek the truth, rather than an accommodation between contending interests. In response to the **Brigate Rosse** and to the difficulty of finding evidence against members of the **mafia**, Italy has recently begun offering lower penalties for *pentiti*, repentant wrong-doers who turn state's evidence. Procedure follows the premise of an accusatorial trial (or inquisitorial—perceived as an improvement over vengeance taken with one's own hands for a wrong).

Courts use only written evidence, allowing no surprise witnesses. The right to appeal a judgment is guaranteed: the first on both law and facts, the last, on law only. The result is slow trials, and long waits to appear on a court's calendar. Thus, by the 1980s, great demand for the modernization of penal procedure led to adopting some elements of Anglo-American procedure, drawn from an entirely different tradition, culture, and set of assumptions.

Canon law of the Roman Catholic Church is still studied in all faculties of jurisprudence. A third element of contemporary Italian law (in addition to Roman law and Canon law) is the commercial law of the Italian city-states that dominated medieval trade between Europe and the Eastern Mediterranean. This is the element in Roman law that is not scholars' law but is pragmatic, drawn by businessmen who had formed guilds and had devised appropriate rules. Commercial law, applied by merchants rather than ecclesiastics or royally appointed temporal judges, spread to all of Europe.

Civil law studies address a civil code, commercial code, code of civil procedure, penal code, and code of penal procedure. All were meant to be complete and coherent, accessible to all literate persons without regard to specialized legal training. The modern nation-state gave rise to the view that the highest source of law was statutory, followed by administrative regulations, then customary usage and such general principles of natural law as good faith, public order, and morality.

Aside from conciliators (for small claims) and praetors (who also hear labor cases), the tribunal of the first instance is followed by an appeals court, then by the Court of Cassation, which can quash a decision and remand to a lower court for a new hearing on points of law. Since **World War II**, an added Constitutional Court reflects the need to ensure the constitutionality of new legislation. Most trials are heard by a panel of judges rather than by a jury. The entire system is supervised by the Consiglio Superiore della Magistratura (CSM) / High Council of the Magistracy.

In penal procedure, an accused who has been arrested by the police faces an investigating magistrate who may call witnesses, effect confrontations and reenactments, warrant phone taps and mail-opening, to compile a dossier that is then examined by both sides.

Administrative courts are seated in each regional capital as the Tribunale Administrativo Regionale (TAR) / Regional Administrative Court. Appeal may be made to the Consiglio di Stato (Council of State), the highest administrative tribunal. *See also* Constitution of 1948.

COURT	No. COURTS	No. JUDGES
Cassation	1	7
Appeal	23	5
Assize	91	2 (+ 6 lay people)
Tribunals of First Instance	156	3
Praetors	893	1
Conciliatori	8000	1

LEGA NORD (LN) / Northern League. The Lega is the name taken in

February 1991 by a confederation of regional leagues campaigning for a federalist reform of the Italian **Constitution**, fiscal reform, privatization, and strong anti-immigrant measures. By far the most important of the leagues was the Lega Lombarda (Lombard League), which redefined localist feeling in much of northern Italy in the 1980s. Formed in 1982, the Lega Lombarda was initially regarded as a political oddity. However, the skillful leadership of **Umberto Bossi**, the worsening corruption of the Italian political system, the growing influx of non-European migrants, and unscrupulous "anti-Southerner" rhetoric added to the league's appeal. In the 1987 general elections, Bossi was elected to the Senate.

The real electoral breakthrough, however, came in local elections in May 1990. Exploiting dissatisfaction with the party system, the Lega Lombarda won 19 percent of the vote in Lombardy; autonomy candidates did unprecedentedly well in other parts of the North. In August 1991, Bossi proposed the division of Italy into three self-governing and fiscally independent "macro-regions": the North, the South, and the Center. In the 1992 general elections, the LN took 8 percent of the national vote (17 percent in the North) and became Italy's fourth largest party with more than 50 representatives in the Chamber of Deputies. Bossi himself was the most popular candidate in the country, receiving more than 250,000 preference votes. In local elections in June 1993, the Lega Nord won the mayoral race in **Milan** with over 40 percent of the poll.

However, three factors prevented the LN from replacing the **Democrazia Cristiana** (DC) / Christian Democrats as the natural home for Italy's middle-class electorate. First, its appeal stopped at the river Po: only northern voters showed any interest in the league's ideas. Second, in December 1993, Bossi was charged with (and eventually found guilty of) accepting an illegal donation to the party funds. The charge was trivial by comparison with the financial abuses committed by Italy's political old guard, but the episode tarnished his claim of opposing the "money politics" of the traditional parties. Third, and most important, the rise of **Silvio Berlusconi's** party, **Forza Italia**, denied the Lega Nord a firm hold on conservative, middle-class voters.

The Lega Nord fought the March 1994 general elections as part of the "Liberty Pole"—the right-wing electoral alliance formed by Berlusconi in the North of Italy. In numerical terms, the league secured slightly fewer votes than in 1992. Its parliamentary representation, however, thanks to the introduction of first-past-the-post voting, increased enormously, to more than 100 deputies and 50 senators. The league was awarded a deputy prime ministership, several key ministerial positions, and the speakership of the Chamber of Deputies, but it was soon at odds with Berlusconi and with the former fascists of the **Alleanza Nazionale** (AN) / National Alliance. The LN, despite its strident right-wing rhetoric on social questions, is strongly opposed to the centralized, corporatist state traditionally supported by Italian **fascism**. Accordingly, in December 1994, Bossi brought down the government in a vote of confidence. This move split his own party and led to a challenge to his leadership in February 1995. To everybody's surprise, however, the LN was able to fight the April 1996 elections without allies and remain the largest party in Italy's alpine regions. Overall, the party took 10 percent of the national vote, and even won some electoral districts directly. Bossi celebrated this by threatening to create a new state, to be called "Padania," from the regions of northern Italy, and in September, after a symbolic journey down the river Po, he "founded" the new republic. Since September 1996, the LN has antagonized the rest of Italy by establishing an unofficial "government" of Padania, and holding "elections" in the fall of 1997. *See also* Umberto Bossi, Electoral Laws.

LEONE, GIOVANNI (1908-1998). In 1929, Leone was a student of **Enrico De Nicola**, who was to be the first president of Italy. The young Leone took degrees in law as well as in political and social sciences and began his own academic career at the University of **Naples** in 1933 as a *libero docente* in criminal law and procedure. Attaining the rank of professor in only two years, he was given tenure in 1936 with an appointment at Sicily's University of Messina. His academic career subsequently took him to Bari, Naples, and **Rome**.

In 1944, Leone enrolled in the **Democrazia Cristiana** (DC) / Christian Democracy Party and served for a year as political secretary of the Naples section. In 1946, he was elected to the **Constituent Assembly** and, in 1948, to the first republican **Parliament**. In 1950, he was chosen vice president of the Chamber of Deputies. He replaced **Giovanni Gronchi** as president of the lower house when the latter was elected head of state.

In 1963, Leone formed a government to steer the budget through Parliament. His first candidacy (1964) for the presidency of the republic was unsuccessful although he was his party's official nominee. The victor, **Giuseppe Saragat** of the **Partito Socialista Democratico Italiano** (PSDI) / Italian Social Democratic Party, made Leone a life senator. In June 1968, he followed **Moro**'s third government, forming a *monocolore* cabinet (i.e., one made up entirely of deputies from a single party—in this case, DC). It held until November of that year. In December 1971, he was elected president of the republic. In September 1974, he was the first head of state to be invited to the White House by President Gerald Ford.

Inquiries in the U.S. Senate led to newspaper assertions that, like industrial leaders elsewhere in the world, several Italian ministers and President Leone had accepted bribes from the Lockheed Corporation to facilitate aircraft sales to the Italian Air Force. Leone resigned his office in June 1978 under this cloud of scandal, thus making way for **Alessandro Pertini** to become president. As a life senator, however, he retained his seat in Parliament. *See also* Mariano Rumor.

LEONE, SERGIO (1929-1989). The inventor of the "spaghetti western," Sergio Leone was uniquely able to make films that were both a critical and a box office success. Born in **Rome**, Leone was what Italians call a *figlio d'arte* insofar as both his father and mother were prominent figures in the Italian silent cinema. After a lengthy apprenticeship in Hollywood (he made more than 50 films as an assistant director), Leone directed, in 1964, the seminal western *A Fistful of Dollars* under the pseudonym of "Bob Robertson." This film, which starred Clint Eastwood as "the man with no name" cost less than $200,000 to make, but revived the western genre in a new, more brutally realistic, form. The film's sequel, *For a Few Dollars More* (1965), was equally successful.

Leone, by now internationally famous, was able to make the two big-budget westerns that permanently established his reputation as one of the great contemporary film directors: *The Good, the Bad, and the Ugly* (1966) and *Once Upon A Time in the West* (1968). Complex, violent, and philosophical, these movies combined art and entertainment with outstanding skill. The same is true of Leone's last film, the epic gangster movie *Once Upon a Time in America* (1984). This saga of a band of Jewish gangsters was a lengthy and complicated study in themes of friendship and betrayal. Drastically cut by its American distributors, the film, when seen in its entirety, can only be described as an intellectual and visual triumph. Leone died in Rome in 1989.

LEOPARDI, GIACOMO (1798-1837). The precocious son of a noble southern Italian family, Giacomo Leopardi was the greatest Italian poet of the nineteenth century, and one of the finest romantic poets in any language.

Born near Macerata (Marches), Leopardi was an introspective, studious, sickly boy who practically lived in his erudite father's capacious library from the age of 11 until his late teens, teaching himself Greek, astronomy, classical history, and poetry. By 1815—still only 17 years of age—he translated Homer and Virgil, and wrote an essay on the "popular errors of the ancients" worthy of a first-rate classical scholar. The first poems that Leopardi would later include in his *Canti* (*Lyrics*, 1831) were written around 1819: *L'infinito* (*Infinity*) is best known, with its haunting final stanza *Così tra questa immensità s'annega il pensier mio / e il naufragar m'è dolce in questo mare* (Thus, in this immensity, my thought drowns and to drown seems sweet to me, in this sea).

By this time, Leopardi was desperate to lead a less cloistered life away from home. His father eventually allowed his son to move to an uncle's house in **Rome**, where the young poet hoped to find a job. The experience was a delusion, however, and Leopardi soon returned home. In 1825 he moved to **Milan**, where Lo Stello, a publisher, had invited him to edit a volume of Cicero's collected works. Lo Stello published Leopardi's main collection of philosophical reflections, *Operette morali (Moral Essays)* in 1827 and two anthologies of Italian renaissance prose and poetry. The next three years were the peak of his mature poetic gift: in 1828 he wrote *Il Risorgimento*, and the following year the collection of poems known as *Grandi Idilli* (*Great Idylls*). The most famous of these is perhaps *La quiete dopo la tempesta* (*The Quiet After the Storm*). Between 1830 and his death in 1837, his failing health and a succession of unhappy love affairs inspired a final creative burst; his last poems were written on the slopes of Vesuvius, overlooking cholera-ridden **Naples**.

LEVI, CARLO (1902-1975). A gifted painter as well as an outstanding neo-realist writer, Carlo Levi's principal legacy is the famous novel *Cristo si è fermato a Eboli* (*Christ Stopped at Eboli*, 1945). This novel, which is autobiographical, tells the story of a northern Italian intellectual who is confined to a small, remote village in rural Calabria by the fascist government. The book's moving portrayal of the peasants' economic and cultural backwardness yet great personal dignity swiftly won it a worldwide audience. It remains one of the most translated post-war Italian novels even today.

Levi had already established his reputation as an artist by the time he wrote his classic novel. Before his arrest and exile for anti-fascist activity in 1935-1936, he had been one of the founders of the so-called "group of six," a school of painting in **Turin** that, in open contrast to the preferences of the regime, attempted to bring French influences such as impressionism and fauvism to bear on their work.

Levi was elected to the Senate as a member of the **Partito Comunista Italiano** (PCI) / Italian Communist Party in 1963. He died in **Rome** in 1975.

LEVI, PRIMO (1919-1987). A Jewish Italian who initially specialized in chemistry, Levi's documentary novel, *Se questo è un uomo* (translated as *If This Is a Man*, 1947), is regarded as one of the classics of holocaust literature, and has been one of the most widely debated books of the century. The book is based on Levi's own experiences after he was deported to Auschwitz in 1944. In 1963, he wrote a sequel to the book, *La Tregua (The Truce)*, which described his homecoming through war-torn Eastern Europe after the end of hostilities. The highlights of Levi's later work were *Il sistema periodico (The Periodic System*, 1975) and *La chiave a stella (The Wrench*, 1978). The former of these consists of 21 short stories that narrate the difficulties of Levi's generation during **fascism**; the second novel, which is thematically experimental, is a series of involved accounts by a skilled manual worker of how he overcame various complex technical problems. *La chiave a stelle* won the Strega prize, Italy's most prestigious literary award. His last novel, *Se non ora, quando? (If not now, when?* 1982) won the scarcely less prestigious Viareggio and Campiello prizes. Levi committed suicide in 1987 by throwing himself down the stairwell of his **Turin** home.

LIBERAL PARTY / *See* **Partito Liberale Italiano** (PLI) / Italian Liberal Party.

LIBYA. In the sixteenth century, Ottoman Turks had combined Tripolitania, Cyrenaica, and Fezzan to proclaim Libya. Two hundred years later, a Libyan dynasty established independence from Turkey. Turkish control was reestablished in 1835.

By 1887, Italy had secured the acquiescence of Europe's Great Powers for eventual Italian initiatives in Libya. Once France and Germany resolved their differences over the Moroccan question, the Italian government insisted on a counter for French gains. In 1911, Italy landed troops and quickly proclaimed the annexation of Libya. Within months, 150,000 Italian settlers came to Libya. Determined resistance, initially by Turkey's Enver Bey, continued until 1931, when Italian forces under **Rodolfo Graziani** captured and executed the Senussi leader, 'Umar al-Mukhtār.

In April and May 1912, Italian warships had entered the Dardanelles and shelled, then occupied, the island of Rhodes and some of the Dodecanese Islands. By the fall, several Balkan states had declared war on Turkey, leading her to sign the Treaty of Lausanne with Italy on October 18, 1912. Under its terms, Italy was to end her occupation of the islands (which she failed to do) in exchange for the Turks leaving Tripoli (although they were to retain religious primacy by appointing a *caliph*).

Libya's role in **World War II** was to be a springboard for Italian moves against Egypt—and subsequently, as a theater of Italian military debacles. As a consequence, the United Nations established Libyan independence from Italy (1951) under a Senussi monarch, Idris I. By 1969, oil revenues inspired a group of ambitious army officers, led by Mu'ammar al-Gadhafi, to overthrow the monarchy in favor of "modernization." Between January and July 1970, Colonel Gadhafi announced the nationalization of the Libyan holdings of Royal Dutch Shell, Standard Oil of New Jersey, and AGIP, the major Italian petroleum firm. Moreover, he also seized all property belonging to Jews and to 35,000 Italians. While the Jewish community was compensated in 15-year bonds, the Italian community was denied any compensation, allegedly because the Italian colonization before **World War I** and under **fascism** had been depredations for which Libya should be compensated. **Mariano Rumor** was prime minister at the time and **Aldo Moro** was his foreign minister. Relations were extremely strained, especially because international law, while it accepts nationalization as a legitimate exercise of territorial sovereignty, insists that foreign property holders be compensated. The dispute seemed to be resolved in February 1974 when Italy and Libya signed an accord in **Rome** that committed Libya to sending to Italy 30 million tons of oil (up from 23 million) in exchange for technical assistance in building petrochemical facilities and shipyards, and improving agriculture. *See also* Pietro Badoglio; Italo Balbo; Balkan Wars; Foreign Policy; Rodolfo Graziani.

LIRA. The Italian unit of currency is the lira (lire in the plural form: hence written as Lit. or Lire Italiane). Its origins lie in the monetary reforms of Charlemagne, undertaken between 793 and 794. Twenty *soldi* or 240 *denari* constituted a lira. By the thirteenth century, there were Lombard lire, Venetian lire, Genoese lire, Florentine lire, and others, the value of each determined by the precious-metal content of the coins. Prior to Italy's unification, currencies were issued by local banks within the regions that eventually became parts of the Italian state of Piedmont-enlarged.

The first Italian lire (valued at 5 grams of silver) were in the Regno Italico of 1806, established by Napoleon. The bimetallic lira of united Italy was introduced on August 24, 1862, at 4.5 grams of silver or 0.293 grams of gold. At the same time, six banks were authorized to print paper currency. The states of the church (Lazio, Emilia-Romagna, Marche, Umbria) did not begin to use the lira until 1866. In 1926, the Banca d'Italia was given a monopoly on the printing of paper currency.

World War I, in Italy as elsewhere, created such changes in public attitudes toward public debt and inflationary monetary policies that wild inflation ruined many bourgeois families, small landowners, and those living on rents. By 1920, the lira was valued at one-fifth of its 1914 level. The ruination of the old bourgeoisie was accompanied by the creation of "new rich," black-marketeers, and arms manufacturers particularly. Exchange controls that had been established in 1918 by agreement with Britain, France, and the United States had run their one-year course and duly expired: the result was the further collapse of the lira's value on international markets. Whereas in 1914, $100 would purchase Lit. 518, the same $100 bought Lit. 2,857 in 1920. Since Italy depended on imports of many foodstuffs, especially wheat, and industrial energy sources such as coal and oil, the effect on the cost of living was devastating.

Mussolini, ever sensitive to matters of prestige, saw the falling lira as an affront to national honor. Ignoring the advice of those economic counselors who foresaw that an overvalued lira would have a deflationary effect, he apparently thought that what mattered was public enthusiasm and he coined the slogan *quota novanta* suggesting, thereby, that no rate of exchange below Lit. 90 to the British pound would be tolerated (in 1925, it had been near 145), and in December 1927, the Duce decreed the exchange rate of 92.46, which had the predicted effect of making Italian goods prohibitively expensive to foreign buyers.

Further devaluations characterized the worldwide depression of the 1930s, all meant to lower the costs of a nation's exports. Britain and the United States devalued in 1934, making it even more difficult for Italian exporters to find foreign buyers. Only after the **Abyssinian** War in 1935-1936 did Mussolini devalue the lira 40.94 percent.

As an occupied country after **World War II**, Italy found its currency pegged to the United States dollar at Lit. 630. Italy became a member of the International Monetary Fund in 1960 and the exchange rate stabilized at Lit. 625 to the dollar until 1973, when the floating exchange rate was begun worldwide. Since market forces now determine the lira's worth, it has oscillated between a high of the aforementioned Lit. 630 to a low of Lit. 2,007 in 1997.

LOCARNO TREATIES. *See* Foreign Policy.

LOMBARDI, RICCARDO (1901-1984). One of the founding members of the **Partito d'Azione** (PdA) / Action Party in 1942, Riccardo Lombardi was born in Enna (Sicily). He was the PdA's representative in the **Comitato di Liberazione Nazionale**-Alta Italia (CLNAI) / National Liberation Committee-Northern Italy and was one of the resistance leaders who negotiated the unconditional surrender of the **Salò** republic with **Mussolini** in April 1945. Following these negotiations, Lombardi was appointed prefect of **Milan** by the CLNAI. One of his first tasks was to save the bodies of Mussolini and his mistress, Clara Petacci, from further vilification by the crowd that had strung them up in Piazza Loreto.

Lombardi served as transport minister in **De Gasperi's** first post-war government (December 1945-July 1946) and was elected to the **Constituent Assembly** as a member of the PdA. He was the secretary of the PdA until its dissolution in 1947. Lombardi was reelected to the Chamber of Deputies in 1948 as a member of the **Partito Socialista Italiano** (PSI) / Italian Socialist Party. He edited the Socialist daily, *L'Avanti!*, in 1949-1950, and rapidly became the theoretical voice of the PSI's left wing and the main rival within the party to **Pietro Nenni**. Lombardi reluctantly agreed to the PSI's decision to form a coalition government with the **Democrazia Cristiana** (DC) / Christian Democracy Party in 1963; he theorized that the PSI would be able to undermine the capitalist system in Italy from within the state by promoting radical social reforms. He did not take ministerial office, however, and thus was unable to press his case. His position further weakened by the loss of **Lelio Basso** and others of the party's far left who left the PSI to form the Partito Socialista Italiano d'Unità Proletaria (PSIUP) / Italian Socialist Party of Proletarian Unity in 1964. He remained the focal point of the PSI's left throughout the 1960s and 1970s, but his supporters were only a minority faction within the party. Lombardi was briefly president of the PSI in 1980. He died in **Rome** in 1984.

LONDON, TREATY OF. The agreements signed in London on April 26, 1915, induced Italy to join the war as an Anglo-French ally with the objective of neutralizing Austria. At war's end, she was to gain control over Süd Tirol, Trentino, Gorizia, Gradisca, **Trieste**, Istria, and portions of the Dalmatian Coast. She was also to get a protectorate over Durazzo (**Albania**), sovereignty over the Dodecanese Islands, and—in Asia Minor— Adalia, if Turkey should be partitioned in Asia. Moreover, if Britain and France divided Germany's colonies, Italy would receive compensation enlarging **Libya**, Eritrea, and Somalia.

After the war, Italy's allies used the creation of Yugoslavia as a pretext to deny to Italy some of these commitments, giving rise to Italian nationalists' deploring the "mutilated peace." On Italy's part, she was to go to war within a month of signing, that is, before May 26, 1915. Not only was the text of this treaty not discussed in Parliament but it was not made public until Russian archives had been opened by the Soviets in the last year of the war and many documents published in the neutral Swedish press.

In 1916, an agreement between Britain and France regarding oil-rich lands (Sykes-Picot, May 16) excluded Italy, thus necessitating a special treaty to placate her. This was the Treaty of St. Jean de Maurienne (April 17, 1917), which promised Italy Smyrna as well as Adalia—thus, for the first time, showing a readiness to put Ottoman Turks under foreign rule. Although never ratified, this treaty served as a grievance for post-war Italian governments.

Each belligerent seems to have calculated that a short, victorious war—such as those fought in the nineteenth century by France and **Sardinia** against Austria, Austria and Prussia against Denmark, Prussia against Austria, and Prussia against France—would produce highly desirable results. Italy was no exception. How else might she control the mountain passes through which invaders had traveled for centuries? How else could she make the Adriatic an Italian lake? A war beside Austria, her natural antagonist, would yield less than a victory over Austria.

Once the United States entered the war and Russia had withdrawn (after the 1917 Revolution and the Treaty of Brest-Litovsk), the Treaty of London was a dead letter. The Soviets opposed concessions made at Serbia's expense and the United States had not been a signatory so was not bound to overlook the contradictions between the treaty and President Wilson's Fourteen Points, one of which promised Serbia access to the sea. Moreover, national self-determination was sure to run afoul of the absorption of many German-speaking Tyroleans into Italy.

LONGO, LUIGI (1900-1980). After serving as a soldier in **World War I** and studying engineering, Luigi Longo joined the **Partito Socialista Italiano** (PSI) / Italian Socialist Party where he worked on the party newspaper and took part in the **Turin** factory occupations of 1920. At the Livorno (Leghorn) Congress of the PSI in 1921, he supported the minority who wished the PSI to enter the Communist International on Lenin's terms and who split away to form the **Partito Comunista Italiano** (PCI) / Italian Communist Party. In 1922, Longo was one of the PCI's delegates to the International's Fourth Congress. Between 1923 and 1924, he was arrested twice, but served less than a year in prison. In 1927, he escaped fascist persecution by fleeing to France where he lived until 1932, with the task of providing falsified documents to those who would enter Italy to conduct anti-fascist activity. Between 1933 and 1935, he was sent to the USSR as a representative of the PCI. There, he became a member of the political committee of the Comintern.

During the **Spanish Civil War**, Longo served in the Garibaldi Battalion and was the political commissar of the Second International Brigade, which had the distinction of inflicting a serious defeat on the Italian expeditionary force at Guadalajara. At the end of 1936, he became inspector general of the 50,000-man International Brigades and took part in the final defense of Madrid.

In 1938, Longo was arrested in France and turned over to the Italian authorities who imprisoned him for five years. Freed in September 1943, he directed the PCI's partisan activity in **Rome**. For his efforts, he was awarded a Bronze Star by the U.S. government. Elected to the **Constituent Assembly** in 1946, he served in the first parliament and was continually reelected thereafter. For ten years, beginning in 1956, he was joint editor (with **Alessandro Natta**) of the PCI's main theoretical journal, *Critica Marxista*. A lifetime of party service led to his succeeding **Palmiro Togliatti** as party secretary in August 1964. During Longo's tenure as leader, the PCI made its first tentative steps away from pro-Soviet orthodoxy by strongly criticizing the Russian suppression of the Prague Spring in 1968. Longo died in Rome in 1980.

LOTTA CONTINUA. The extra-parliamentary left parties or "ultras" of the 1960s and 1970s included the Movimento Studentesco (Student Movement), Servire il popolo (Serve the People), Avanguardia Operaia (Workers' Vanguard), Potere Operaio (Worker Power), Il

Manifesto (The Manifesto), Autonomia Operaia (Worker Autonomy), Lotta Operaia (Workers' Struggle), and Lotta Continua (Constant Struggle), which was the largest.

Heightened class tensions in the 1960s were caused, in part, by the accumulated anger of southern immigrant workers, the inflexibility of the labor market, the gap between skilled and unskilled both in pay and in union representation, and dramatically increased worker literacy. The French students' movement of 1968 was duplicated in Italy; each hierarchy insisted on an ideological coherence that made united action unlikely. All of these groups were quick to criticize both the **Partito Comunista Italiano** (PCI) / Italian Communist Party and national **trade unions** as being too ready to compromise for the sake of stability and industrial peace.

By the autumn of 1969—the "hot autumn"—a genuine working alliance seemed to be emerging—especially in **Turin**—between university students and factory workers. The better to adapt to these changed conditions, the trade unions insisted on autonomy from the parties. Shop-floor agitation was to become a reformist tool in the hands of an evolving trade union leadership rather than an instrument of party hierarchs.

The most fervently revolutionary elements became increasingly authoritarian. Just as in other revolutions, moderates were displaced by radicals. In some cases, Lotta Continua had become a stepping stone between adolescent religious idealism and the **Brigate Rosse**, an impatient resort to violence to hasten the attainment of a utopian future. Some from Lotta Continua went, instead, to Nuclei Armati Proletari, but they were less well led than the Red Brigades, were more easily infiltrated by the **police**, and, therefore, were soon neutralized.

By 1976, **women** who were dissatisfied with their roles in Lotta Continua occupied meeting halls, held counter-meetings and assemblies, and at the Rimini Congress in October, women and workers broke off, obliging the leadership to agree that the basic assumptions of the organization had to be reexamined. Although its newspaper continued to appear, Lotta Continua dissolved. A residual group, joined by the remnants of others in similar straits, drifted into Democrazia Proletaria, a party that has held seats in **Parliament** since the elections of June 1976.

In those years, the courts were hearing appeals of the conviction of three Lotta Continua members accused of having killed Luigi Calabresi, a police commissioner present in the fourth-floor headquarters room from which Giuseppe Pinelli, an anarchist employed as a trolley-car driver, had allegedly jumped to his death after having been questioned in relation to the 1969 terrorist bombing of a bank in Piazza Fontana in **Milan** (purportedly timed to coincide with the bombing of another bank in Italy's capital). Having decided that anarchists were to blame, those whose names were on file were rounded up and questioned. Pinelli's death was attributed by the police to suicide. In 1975, the court asserted that Pinelli had been innocent of charges of complicity in the bombing. In 1988, three men were arrested and imprisoned for the murder of Calabresi, a sentence confirmed by the court of cassation in 1997. *See also* Law.

LOTTIZZAZIONE. *See* Patronage.

LUZZATTI, LUIGI (1841-1927). Born in **Venice**, Luigi Luzzatti was one of Italy's longest-serving politicians. After an early career in academic law, he entered **Parliament** in 1871, where he remained until 1921, generally identified with the moderate right of the **Partito Liberale Italiano** (PLI) / Italian Liberal Party. During this half-century of parliamentary experience, he was minister for the treasury under **Antonio Starabba Di Rudinì** (1891; 1896-1898), **Giovanni Giolitti** (1903-1905), and **Sidney Sonnino** (1906).

Luzzatti was briefly a caretaker prime minister between 1910 and 1911. He took office after an arcane dispute over the Italian merchant marine brought down the Sonnino government. His spell as prime minister was dominated by the question of extending the suffrage. Luzzatti proposed to reduce the severity of the norms for ascertaining electors' educational standards, to introduce nationwide state elementary **education**, and to introduce election for a part of the Senate. Additionally, he proposed making the vote a compulsory duty. These proposals initially won him widespread parliamentary support (his government was backed by 386 deputies, including the **Partito Socialista Italiano** (PSI) / Italian Socialist Party), but by December 1910, the PSI and the radicals had decided that these proposals did not go far enough. His government fell over the electoral reform issue in March 1912, and he was replaced by Giovanni Giolitti who introduced universal male suffrage. Nominated to the Senate in 1921, Luzzatti died in **Rome** in 1927. His memoirs are a source of great importance for historians.

-M-

MAASTRICHT, TREATY OF. Signed by the then 12 member states of the European Community at the Dutch city of Maastricht on February 7, 1992, the treaty on **European Union** (EU) has had immense effects on the Italian economy and government. The treaty's rigid timetable for European Monetary Union (EMU), and the equally rigid economic conditions laid down as a prerequisite for membership in the group of countries that will use the "Euro," obliged Italy and other aspirants to endure five years of unprecedented fiscal austerity. Since Maastricht, Italy has managed to reduce its annual public spending deficit from 10 percent of GDP in 1993 to less than 3 percent in 1998, and thus met the most stringent of the treaty's tests for membership. Accumulated national debt has stabilized at approximately 120 percent of GDP, far above the figure established at Maastricht, and Italy, together with Belgium and Ireland, was forced to ask for a special dispensation in this respect. Inflation, however, has fallen to less than 2 percent —the lowest figure since the 1960s—and interest rates have fallen to German levels. In 1996, the **lira** reentered the European Monetary System (EMS) and over the next two years proved that it could maintain a stable exchange rate with the German mark. In recognition of these improved economic fundamentals, in 1998 Italy was invited to become one of the 11 founding members of the single currency. The lira will be replaced by the Euro in electronic transactions from January 1999 and Euro notes and coins will be used from January 2002.

Entry into the Euro has been a personal success for **Carlo Azeglio Ciampi**, the treasury minister in the **Olive Tree Coalition** government since April 1996. Without Ciampi's international reputation and negotiating ability, it is likely that countries such as Germany would have blocked Italy's path. The Italian people also deserve much of the credit. Entry into the single currency has meant falling living standards, especially in 1997 when Ciampi was forced to introduce a heavy "Eurotax" as a one-off measure to keep Italy on track to meet the EU's conditions. The Italians' willingness to make sacrifices for Europe reflects both Italy's economic dependence on the EU (70 percent of exports go to other EU countries), and the symbolic importance of EU membership for the Italians. Culturally, Italians are very sensitive to any suggestion that their Mediterranean location implies less than "European" levels of efficiency and development. Qualifying for Maastricht thus became a matter of national pride. *See also* Olive Tree Coalition; Romano Prodi; Table 18 in Appendix.

MAFIA. The Sicilian mafia originated during the rule of the Bourbons. In a society where the state existed merely to collect taxes and preserve the privileges of the nobility and the large landowners, justice was a matter for individuals, and the *mafioso* ("man of honor") who would defend his family's property, and avenge insults to the family name or its women, became the most respected man in his community. According to the Italian scholar Pino Arlacchi, *mafiosi* passed through two stages in their social development. In the first "anomic" stage, they established themselves as men to be feared by virtue of their ferocity in conducting *vendette*. Thereafter, they performed the role of government in the small village, or the neighborhood in which they lived. The *mafioso* and his "family" or "clan" of friends provided protection from thieves and bandits, punished social deviants, and acted as mediator, patching up quarrels over seduced daughters and marriage dowries before they led to bloodshed. They brooked no interference and dealt brutally with informers, giving rise to the phenomenon known as *omertà*, which prohibits collaborating with "outsiders," that is, the Italian state or its judiciary or police. Men of honor were courted by the political class, especially after the introduction of universal male suffrage in 1912. Becoming a "man of honor," indeed, could arguably be seen as a dangerous form of social mobility: a way for the most ruthless peasants to emerge as social leaders.

Mussolini waged war on the mafia clans after his accession to power in 1922. Thousands of Sicilians, whether or not proven to be *mafiosi*, were arrested and sent into internal exile. The arrival of the Allies in 1943, however, gave the leading mafia bosses a new lease on life. Assuming that imprisoned *mafiosi* were anti-fascists, the British and American armies released and even gave political responsibilities to well-known men of honor.

Italy's post-war **economic miracle** reduced the power of the traditional mafia. Fewer young Sicilians were tempted into becoming men of honor, and the (relative) modernization of social and sexual mores and customs meant that the clans lost their mediating function. The word "mafia" increasingly became associated with criminal gangs trafficking in contraband cigarettes and, from the 1970s onward, drugs. The Italian state fought these gangs with zeal. By the end of the 1960s, **Sicily** was a more law-abiding place than at any previous time in its modern history.

Three factors saved the mafia from extinction. First, the economic miracle came to an end in the 1970s. Second, the gangs became entrepreneurs and used the proceeds from their illicit activities to buy up large sections of the economy of **southern Italy**, especially in low-technology construction, agriculture, tourism, and transport. Aside from providing services that are illegal such as prostitution, intimidation of competitors, and contract-rigging, its activities include legitimate businesses and investments, particularly in construction industries. Third, the degeneration of the Italian political class allowed the mafia to regain its influence over the political process: in exchange for votes, the politicians funneled public works contracts to companies beholden to—if not owned by—by the mafia. In exchange for campaign funds and the delivery of votes, political figures can offer protection against investigation and a share of public contracts.

By the 1980s, it is no exaggeration to say that three southern Italian regions—Campania, Calabria, and Sicily—had largely become fiefs of local crime bosses. Politicians who crossed the leading clans, such as Piersanti Mattarella (DC), the president of the Sicilian regional government, were brutally murdered, as was a grisly list of judges and policemen. The early 1980s also saw the emergence of the *Corleonesi*. Led by Totò Riina, they exterminated the older clans and became the occult de facto government of the island. In Naples and Calabria (where the criminal gangs are known as the *Camorra* and the 'ndrangheta, respectively), the domination of the political-criminal elite was arguably even more complete. **Earthquake** relief funds, together with the profits to be made in narcotics dealing, added further to the sums at stake and have contributed to the viciousness of the struggle among rival clans for dominance. Occasionally—as in July of 1997—the government has sent troops into **Naples** to enhance citizen security in periods of warfare between rival *Camorra* clans for territorial control.

Perhaps the worst effect of the mafia's presence is its stifling of local entrepreneurial spirit. Those who succeed are threatened with violence, either to their persons, their families, or their enterprise, if they fail to pay the *pizzo* or "cut" as protection money: extortion, pure and simple. Those seeking a bank loan to undertake an enterprise will find that bank discomfort with the conditions in mafia-controlled territory adds 4 percent to the interest rates charged elsewhere in Italy. Estimates put at 15 to 20 percent the share of total gross income in western Sicily produced by profits from criminal enterprises. The sale of illegal drugs alone brought in Lit. 11,600 billion ($7 billion).

The Italian state's fight was led by a determined prosecutor, **Giovanni Falcone**, who persuaded several mafia associates to break the ancient code of *omertà* and turn state's evidence. A huge trial of literally hundreds of gangsters between 1984 and 1987 concluded in a personal triumph for Falcone, and the imposition of 19 life sentences. Despite this triumph, the anti-mafia judges and policemen of southern Italy were denied the political backing that they needed to prosecute the battle efficiently, and by the early 1990s lawlessness had reached unprecedented levels.

The turning point in the battle against the mafia was the murders in 1992 of Falcone and of his colleague Paolo Borsellino. The heads of the *Corleonesi*, including Totò Riina, were hunted down in 1993, and the political collapse of the **Democrazia Cristiana** (DC) / Christian Democracy Party robbed the gangs of their protection in southern Italy. Former prime minister **Giulio Andreotti**, like several other prominent DC politicians, is currently standing trial on charges of association with the mafia. Riina, meanwhile, has been sentenced to eleven life sentences, and many of his henchmen have also been condemned to heavy prison sentences.

MALAGODI, GIOVANNI (1904-1991). The scion of a well-established liberal family (Malagodi's father, Olindo, was a prominent journalist and Anglophile who was appointed to the Senate), Malagodi's initial career was in international banking. After the war, he was one of the technical experts who contributed to the drawing up of the Marshall Plan and, in the late 1940s, represented the Italian government, as minister plenipotentiary, in international trade negotiations. In 1950, Malagodi became the president of the fledgling Organization for Economic Cooperation and Development (OECD).

Malagodi's political career began in 1953 when he was elected to Parliament for the **Partito Liberale Italiano** (PLI) / Italian Liberal Party. He became leader of the PLI in 1954 and held the post until he became treasury minister under **Giulio Andreotti** in 1972. This was his only ministerial experience: his staunch opposition to statist and interventionist economic policies prevented the PLI from cooperating with the governments of the center-left preferred by such **Democrazia Cristiana** (DC) / Christian Democracy Party leaders as **Amintore Fanfani** and **Aldo Moro** in the 1950s and 1960s. Despite his economic conservatism, Malagodi was strongly in favor of liberal social reforms such as **divorce**.

Malagodi became honorary president of the PLI in 1976. He was elected to the Senate in 1979, and was briefly president of the upper chamber in 1987. He died in **Rome** in 1991.

MALAPARTE, CURZIO (pseud. Kurt Erich Suckert, 1898-1957). An intriguing figure, Malaparte (who Italianized his name during his service as a volunteer in the Italian army in 1915) was an active fascist in his native Tuscany. In 1924, he founded a review, *La Conquista dello stato* (*The Conquest of the State*), which became the theoretical journal of the revolutionary wing of the **Partito Nazionale Fascista** (PNF) / National Fascist Party headed by **Roberto Farinacci**. Malaparte subsequently curried favor with **Benito Mussolini** by attacking Farinacci in *La Conquista*. High in the esteem of the Duce, he was sent to the Soviet Union as a correspondent, which led him to write *L'Intelligenza di Lenin* (*The Intelligence of Lenin*, 1930) full of scarcely disguised admiration for Soviet totalitarianism. He became editor of the **Turin** newspaper *La Stampa* in 1929, but was hounded from his job by Mussolini for publishing too many articles critical of fascist industrial policy. This, at any rate, was Malaparte's explanation.

Exiled in Paris, Malaparte wrote the Europe-wide best-seller *Technique du Coup d'état* (*Technique of the Coup d'Etat*, 1931), which described recent seizures of power in various European countries and argued that the essential element of political power was the willingness to use violence in pursuit of one's ends. Malaparte argued, for instance, that Mussolini had been successful less for his own merits than the spinelessness of Italy's liberals, who had been unwilling to defend their own values and state. Such a position did nothing to enhance his standing with the fascist dictator. Malaparte also disparaged Hitler and the Nazi movement, and extracts from his book were used as propaganda material by the anti-fascist parties in the German elections of 1932. *Technique du Coup d'État* was banned in Italy and burned in Germany. Malaparte was arrested upon his return to Italy in October 1933 and served several years of confinement in the mid-1930s. He was a correspondent in Russia and Finland during the war. After the war, he embraced the Chinese brand of communism and had just returned from a visit to Red China—one of the first foreigners permitted to see the Maoist state—when he died from cancer in 1957.

Malaparte's literary output was vast, but three books in particular have withstood the test of time: *Kaputt* (1944), *La Pelle* (*The Skin,* 1949), and *Maledetti toscani* (*Damned Tuscans*, 1956). In addition to his prodigious literary output, Malaparte also designed his own house on the Isle of Capri. It is still regarded as a classic example of modernist architecture.

MANI PULITE. The "Clean Hands" investigation into corruption began in **Milan** in February 1992 with the arrest by prosecutor **Antonio Di Pietro** of Mario Chiesa, a **Partito Socialista Italiano** (PSI) / Italian Socialist Party politician with close links to the party leader, **Bettino Craxi**. Chiesa's arrest triggered corruption inquiries all over the country, but the Milan "pool" of prosecutors would remain the spearhead of the investigations into illicit activities by politicians over the next three years.

In retrospect, the "Clean Hands" investigation developed in five main phases. The first phase was the easiest: the discovery of the corruption surrounding public works contracts in Milan and dozens of other cities all over Italy. By the fall of 1992, literally thousands of businessmen had confessed to paying politicians. Soon, dozens of politicians at local and regional level, as well as parliamentary deputies from all the main parties, had been indicted on charges of corruption, extortion, and illegal financing of the political parties. Politicians were shown to be taking 5 to 10 percent on almost every project involving public spending. The second phase of the investigation, by the Milanese prosecutors in particular, of the leadership of the PSI, was the one that brought down the political system. By the end of April 1993, the Milan "pool" had asked **Parliament** for authorization to indict Bettino Craxi on diverse counts of corruption and extortion. When Parliament refused to lift immunity, there were street demonstrations all over Italy and the one-day-old government of **Carlo Azeglio Ciampi** collapsed ignominiously. During the summer of 1993, the investigation spread into health care contracts. When a government official responsible for authorizing new pharmaceuticals for the Italian market was arrested in his home, the police discovered thousands of Kruggerrands and other gold coins, gold ingots, and Swiss bank accounts stuffed worth tens of millions of francs. The health minister, Francesco De Lorenzo of the **Partito Liberale Italiano** (PLI) / Italian Liberal Party, was also arrested and charged with organizing rake-offs from the public money being spent to combat AIDS.

By the spring of 1993, it was clear that none of the former parties of government was clean (and the opposition **Partito Democratico della Sinistra** (PDS) / Democratic Party of the Left had not escaped unscathed either). In December 1993, **Antonio Di Pietro** used the trial of Sergio Cusani to put the entire Italian political class on trial. Cusani was a Milanese financier who had disbursed "the mother of all bribes" (Lit. 150 billion or $100 million) from the chemical company Enimont. One by one, the heads of the **Democrazia**

Cristiana (DC) / Christian Democracy Party, the PSI, the **Partito Socialista Democratico Italiano** (PSDI) / Italian Social Democratic Party, and the **Partito Repubblicano Italiano** (PRI) / Italian Republican Party were called as witnesses and subjected to merciless cross-examination. In front of some of the largest television audiences in Italian history, they collectively admitted to taking immense sums. The treasurer of the DC, Senator Severino Citaristi, admitted in court that the DC had raised Lit. 85 billion ($57 million) a year in illicit contributions like the one from Enimont. Even **Umberto Bossi** admitted that he had received an undeclared "donation" from Enimont to help the activities of the **Lega Nord.**

The Cusani trial was the apex of the third phase of the Mani pulite investigation. In 1994, the fourth phase began when attention shifted to the media empire of **Silvio Berlusconi**. In November, it was officially announced that Berlusconi, who was by now prime minister, was under investigation. Shortly afterward, Antonio Di Pietro announced that he was resigning from the legal profession, complaining of the climate of suspicion and hostility that surrounded his person, in particular, and the Milan "pool" in general. Di Pietro would be compelled to spend the whole of 1995 disproving allegations that he was guilty of abusing his official position, and that he had received unlawful gifts from a businessman.

The rest of the Milan "pool"—Piercamillo Davigo, Gherardo Colombo, Francesco Saverio Borrelli, and Gerardo Ambrosio (who survived an attempt on his life in 1994)—have found themselves increasingly on the defensive since Di Pietro's resignation. In this fifth act of the investigation, politicians across the political spectrum have accused the Milan prosecutors of usurping political power in order to establish "a republic of judges." The "pool" has already beaten off two attempts by the politicians (in February 1993 and June 1994) to pass an amnesty for the hundreds of politicians still awaiting judgment by Italy's notoriously slow system of appeal courts. So far, only a handful of people (including Craxi) have been definitively condemned to prison sentences, and the remainder are plainly hoping that a solution will be found that will allow them to wriggle out of their predicament.

MANIFESTO, IL / *The Manifesto.* Initially a weekly from its beginnings in June 1969, it became a daily newspaper in 1971 and continues to maintain a substantial readership among students and politically active workers even today. The main goal of its renegade founders, Luigi Pintor, Aldo Natoli, and Rossella Rossanda—all deputies of the **Partito Comunista Italian** (PCI) / Italian Communist Party—was to press for a definitive break between Italian communism and the Soviet Union. After the fifth edition of the paper argued that the PCI's response to the Soviet invasion of Czechoslovakia had been insufficiently critical, the group was accused of factionalism by the central committee of the PCI and expelled. In the 1970s, *Il Manifesto* was the newspaper of choice for the many individuals and groups who felt that the PCI had lost its revolutionary ideals and had become integrated into the political system.

MANIN, DANIELE (1804-1857). A lawyer born into one of **Venice**'s noblest families, Daniele Manin became one of the symbolic figures of Italian nationalism. Briefly arrested by the Austrians in January 1848, he became the focus of the nationalist uprising in the city. At the end of March, after a tumultuous fortnight of street conflict, a republic was declared, with Manin being chosen as the first president of the new state. When, however, in July 1848, the Venetian national assembly voted for unification with the Kingdom of Sardinia, the anti-monarchist Manin resigned from the presidency. In 1849, when Austrian victories over the Kingdom of Sardinia left Venice without allies, Manin heroically guided the city's resistance. The city was blockaded by the Austrians at the end of May 1849, and resisted—until the end of August—land, sea, and aerial bombardment (by lighter-than-air balloons) and a serious outbreak of cholera. Under the terms of the armistice, Manin and some 40 other citizens were compelled to leave the city. He emigrated to France where he lived in poverty. In 1856, he was persuaded by **Cavour** to end his distrust of the Sardinian royal family and accept the presidency of the Italian National Society, a body uniting all strands of the nationalist movement except the Mazzinians, and which pledged itself to unite Italy under the direction of the Kingdom of Sardinia. He died the following year. His son, Giorgio, took part in **Giuseppe Garibaldi**'s expedition to **Sicily** in 1861 and became aide de camp to King **Victor Emmanuel II**.

MANZONI, ALESSANDRO (1785-1873). Born in **Milan**, Manzoni was the grandson of **Cesare Beccaria**, the enlightenment philosopher and jurist. As a writer, his most creative period was between 1812 and 1827. In these years, he wrote his most influential poetry and plays and, after 1821, began working on the huge manuscript of *I promessi sposi* (*The Betrothed*), which was originally called *Fermo e Lucia*.

The novel was published in 1827.

I promessi sposi tells the story of two weavers, Renzo and Lucia, who wish to marry but whose love is endangered by Don Rodrigo, a libertine who has other plans for Lucia. The couple flee, are separated, undergo seemingly endless vicissitudes, but are eventually reunited in happy married life. Summarized so briefly, the novel might seem to be a mere melodrama. In fact, it was a momentous step for Italian literature. For the first time since Boccaccio, ordinary people took the stage in Italian literature, speaking in their native dialects and being described faithfully as dignified individuals rather than as caricatures. There was nothing artificial or rhetorical about Manzoni's style, while the powerful Christian humanism suffusing the novel was an equally radical innovation for the time. *I promessi sposi* remains a subject of close study in Italian schools.

After the publication—and immediate public and critical success—of *I promessi sposi*, Manzoni fell silent. He was made a life senator in 1861. He dedicated his later years to writing a historical essay comparing the French Revolution with the **Risorgimento**. This work was published after his death in Milan in 1873.

MARCH ON ROME. In fascist myth-building, few events were as exalted as the March on Rome, with its implication of near-insurrectionary public demands that King **Victor Emmanuel III** form a government headed by **Benito Mussolini**, leader of the **Partito Nazionale Fascista** (PNF) / National Fascist Party. The reality, however, was quite another.

In pursuit of domestic tranquility, Prime Minister **Ivanoe Bonomi** (July 1921 to February 1922) attempted a "Conciliation Pact" between the **Partito Socialista Italiano** (PSI) / Italian Socialist Party and the fascists, but faced with Mussolini's intransigence, Bonomi began to consider suppression of the *squadristi*. Mussolini reacted by enrolling *all* fascists in the action squads, an action that, by raising the specter of civil war, divided Bonomi's coalition partners so completely that governmental inaction was inevitable. Finally, in February 1922, his government lost a vote of confidence and Bonomi was replaced by **Luigi Facta**, the man soon to be displaced by Mussolini.

The failure of successive Nitti, Bonomi, and Facta governments to combat the reign of terror imposed by *squadrismo* led the PSI to proclaim a general strike in August 1922. This move played directly into Mussolini's hands. For he was now able to announce that the fascist squads stood ready to break the strike if the government did nothing; the squads could thus be presented as forces of law and order. On August 3, 1922, action squad *camicie nere* (blackshirts) took over many cities in the north, most conspicuously **Milan**, where they burned the buildings of *l'Avanti!* and smashed its presses.

By then, local fascist leaders and *squadristi* had come to believe that by marching on Rome they could end the general strike called by the socialists. Facta had failed to persuade the king to use the army to stop the preannounced march. For his part, the king saw **fascism** as a tool to be used in forestalling the rise of bolshevism. The Royal Army could have put an end to fascism's punitive expeditions and the March on Rome, but the king was apparently convinced that he could "tame" this obstreperous Romagnole journalist by appointing him to join—and then head—the government.

While Mussolini moved to a position near the Swiss border, the **Quadrumvirate** mobilized squads from provincial cities to proceed to Rome. Premier Facta claimed that the king had promised to sign an enabling order should circumstances warrant military action against the fascists. The king's refusal to make good on that undertaking reflected the repugnance he felt for civil war as well as his conviction that he would be able to control Mussolini. He was also concerned lest his dashing cousin, the duke of Aosta, who was on good terms with the fascists, might plot to depose him.

When the king finally summoned Mussolini to Rome from Milan, the man who headed fascism insisted on a telegraphed invitation to form a government (as opposed to merely *joining* a government headed by another) and reached Rome by train, only after the cable had arrived. The subsequent demonstrations by blackshirted columns of *squadristi* were made to appear to have been headed by Mussolini, ever sensitive to the importance of showing himself a leader. *See also* Fascism; Benito Mussolini; Table 4 in Appendix.

MARCONI, GUGLIELMO (1874-1937). The inventor of the wireless, Guglielmo Marconi was not only one of the most important scientists of the twentieth century, but an adept businessman and diplomat. Born into a well-off family from **Bologna** (Emilia-Romagna), Marconi was attracted by the physical sciences from his earliest youth. Unable to find financial support for his ideas in Italy, in 1896 he patented the first prototype of the wireless in England. In 1901, he successfully sent a trans-Atlantic message between Britain and the United States. This feat, which at the time seemed little short of miraculous, won Marconi the Nobel prize for physics in 1909.

Marconi was far from being an ivory tower academic. He had founded a company to exploit his discoveries commercially as early as 1897, and as the military and commercial implications of wireless technology were realized, he became an important political figure. Between 1912 (the year in which he was nominated as senator) and 1915, he played an important role in Anglo-Italian relations and in the negotiations that eventually led to Italy joining the war on the side of the Entente. In 1919, he was one of the Italian delegation to the Paris peace conference.

Marconi joined the **Partito Nazionale Fascista** (PNF) / National Fascist Party in 1923. The regime showered honors upon him, including the presidency of the **Accademia d'Italia.** He died in Rome in July 1937.

MARINETTI, FILIPPO TOMMASO (1876-1944). Born in Alexandria, Egypt, and educated in French-language schools, Marinetti was caught up in the "free style" poetry that was coming into vogue at the turn of the century. Indeed, between 1902 and 1908, he had written three collections of poetry in free verse. Faced with the social tension between dreams and reality, Marinetti chose the urban, technological, industrial reality, and the mystique of the superman. His *Mafarka le futuriste* (*Mafarka the Futurist,* 1910) pointed the way toward what was to become the **futurist** movement. He defined it in his Manifesto of 1909. "We sing the love of danger, courage, rashness, and rebellion . . . [not] thoughtful immobility and ecstasy [but] the new beauty of speed . . . we glorify war, militarism and patriotism." The breaking of constraining rules, being agitated and nervously aware—these were the elements of futurism, identifying order and tradition with the dead past. Museums, libraries, and elite schools should be closed (or, indeed, burned) and the Pope expelled from **Rome.** Futurist libertarians, anti-clerical and anti-monarchist, by making common cause with the nationalists, were able to satisfy the apparent longing among many of the young generation for a party of the right that would free Italy from the status of "also-ran," and from alternating between being imitation-French and imitation-German.

Early fascists—similarly nationalist, anti-monarchical, and anti-clerical (at least until the 1919 elections moved **Mussolini** to re-shape the movement to court those who held real power)—talked of being "not conservatives or reactionaries but rather radicals or revolutionaries who repudiate bourgeois culture and institutions of the nineteenth century." The similarities explain the presence in the original *Fasci Italiani di Combattimento* (Combat Veterans' League) of Marinetti himself whose home in **Milan** was used by an organization of *arditi.*

Marinetti was not only a *Sansepolcristo* (fascists of the first hour, present at the initial meeting in Milan's Piazza di San Sepolcro) but was elected to the central committee of the fascist movement in the founding session of March 23, 1919. **Mussolini** welcomed Marinetti's support in the early years, but when faced with choosing between Catholic support and the support of the futurists, he found no difficulty in turning his back on Marinetti who—in June 1920—resigned from the central committee of the PNF because of what he saw as the transformation of fascism by its appeasement of the Church. Marinetti had also defended modern art and Jewish painters.

Despite the implicit defection from all futurist dogma, Marinetti accepted being among the first appointees (all chosen by Mussolini himself) to the newly created **Accademia d'Italia**. Despite the studied antiquarianism of the academy's eighteenth- century uniforms, replete with feathers and braid, Marinetti was ever eager to be identified with the latest technology; for example, the radio and the official public broadcasts. In the martial tones to which Americans had grown accustomed in the "March of Time" documentaries and newsreels of the 1930s, Marinetti's voice announced the dramatic return to Italy of **Italo Balbo** and the Air Armada from its New World visits in August 1933.

So total was his nationalist commitment that when Italy went to war in **Abyssinia**, Marinetti volunteered. When Italy subsequently went to war with the Soviet Union, he rejoined his regiment on the Don River. Subsequently, he joined Mussolini at **Salò**, where he was made president of the Accademia. His death in Bellagio (Como) in 1944 occasioned a major state funeral. *See also* Italo Balbo; Futurism.

MARTINAZZOLI, MINO (1931-). The last secretary of the **Democrazia Cristiana** (DC) / Christian Democracy Party before its demise in January 1994, Mino Martinazzoli had long been the party's conscience. Born in the province of Brescia (Lombardy), Martinazzoli made his way to national politics via local politics. He was elected to the Senate in 1972 and was reconfirmed in the subsequent elections of 1976 and 1979. In 1983, he switched houses and was elected to the Chamber of Deputies.

Martinazzoli served as minister of justice in the first **Craxi** government, and as minister for defense under **Giulio Andreotti** between 1989 and 1991. In October 1992, the DC turned to him in desperation as the corruption investigations grew in intensity and the full extent of the DC's misgovernment became clear. As party secretary, Martinazzoli did his best to revive the DC, but its electoral fate was signed by the allegations of links between leading DC politicians and the **mafia** in the spring of 1993. After an electoral calamity in local elections in June 1993, and further, even graver, defeats in November-December 1993, Martinazzoli decided that the DC was beyond saving. While the party's right split away to form the Centro Cristiano Democratico (CCD) / Christian Democratic Center, he—and the majority of the former DC—transformed its remnants into the **Partito Popolare Italiano** (PPI) / Italian People's Party, apparently hoping that the revival of that name would provide the party with new vigor and renewed credibility.

That was not to be. The 1994 elections were something of a disaster for the PPI, which overestimated its electoral support and was not able to hold the balance of power in the new Parliament, as Martinazzoli had hoped. Martinazzoli was replaced as party leader by **Rocco Buttiglione** after the elections. He returned to local politics and since April 1995 has been mayor of Brescia.

MATTEI, ENRICO (1906-1962). Enrico Mattei was founder and head of the great oil and natural gas trust, Ente Nazionale Idrocarburi (ENI). He was born in the Marches, the son of a police officer. He had left school at 15 and, after working in a tannery, went to **Milan** as a salesman of German industrial equipment. He established, before 1940, his own chemical company. In 1943, he was prominent in the **Democrazia Cristiana** (DC) / Christian Democracy Party.

He was put in charge of the moribund agency that had been established under the fascists, Azienda Generale Italiana Petroli (AGIP) / Italian General Petroleum Agency. Mattei transformed AGIP by the intensive exploitation of the methane gas discovered in the Po Valley a few years after the war. The appetite of private firms was whetted by the prospect of abundant cheap energy, but Mattei, aided considerably by Prime Minister **De Gasperi** and Finance Minister Vanoni, succeeded in ensuring that all Po Valley natural gas exploitation would be under the control of ENI, created for this purpose in February 1953.

A financial buccaneer, he managed to build an empire in the next decade that created such spin-offs as petrochemicals, motels, restaurants, steel oil-ducts, construction contracting, textiles, nuclear power, and research. His acumen and accomplishments required cutting through the bureaucratic "red tape" of Italy's patrimonial tradition. He bribed, ignored regulations, and made clientelistic appointments on a regular basis—with spectacular results that were faithfully reported in *Il Giorno*, a newspaper controlled by ENI.

His aggressive bidding in offering Arab oil producers terms far more favorable than those of the Anglo-American "Seven Sisters" made many foreign enemies. Because he supported the Algerian independence movement, his execution was ordained by the Organisation Armée Secrète (OAS), the private army of French settlers who took up arms against France to induce the government to keep Algeria French.

In October 1962, his private airplane crashed on a flight from Sicily to Milan. In a setting where charges of conspiracy are quickly made and readily attended, the accidental nature of a successful populist's death was not easily accepted by popular opinion. The **mafia**, the Central Intelligence Agency (CIA), the international oil cartel, the OAS were all accused of having caused his death in the press, in novels, and in films (such as *Il Caso Mattei* by Francesco Rosi, 1972).

MATTEOTTI, GIACOMO (1885-1924). A Socialist martyr, Giacomo Matteotti's murder by the fascists signaled the definitive end of liberal Italy and the advent of **Mussolini**'s dictatorship. Matteotti was born in Rovigo, near Venice, the son of a lower-middle-class family. He studied law and seemed embarked on a career as a jurist, but his socialist sympathies led him toward political activism and journalism. He opposed **World War I**, but was nevertheless called up and served in the army for three years. In 1919, he was elected to Parliament as a deputy for the **Partito Socialista Italiano** (PSI) / Italian Socialist Party. Matteotti belonged to the reformist wing of the PSI, however, and in 1922 he joined **Filippo Turati** in forming the Partito Socialista Unitaria (PSU) / United Socialist Party, becoming its secretary and chief organizer.

In 1923, Matteotti published a searing condemnation of **fascism**'s intellectual and economic pretensions, *Un anno di dominazione fascista* (*A Year of Fascist Domination*) and, in May 1924, made a historic speech in the Chamber of Deputies denouncing the electoral frauds and acts of intimidation that had falsified the 1924 elections throughout Italy. On June 10, five fascist *squadristi* kidnapped him as he walked along the banks of the Tiber in **Rome**. His body was found two months later.

Matteotti's murder provoked the liberal and democratic

opposition to walk out of **Parliament** on June 13, and the widespread disgust with the violence and illegality of the fascist militias might have brought Mussolini down but for the zeal of **Roberto Farinacci**, long the putative leader of the revolutionary wing of the **Partito Nazionale Fascista** (PNF) / National Fascist Party. In the end, therefore, the *delitto Matteotti* (the Matteotti crime) served to consolidate Mussolini's power. After Mussolini was directly accused (December 1924) of having ordered Matteotti's murder, he accepted political responsibility for the killing in a brilliant speech in January 1925. This was a prelude to the widespread closings of "subversive" publications and organizations, indiscriminate arrests of critics, the substitution of proportional representation with single-member constituency districts. Together, these measures—given the proven illegalities of the action squads—ended all remnants of liberal democracy in Italy.

MAZZINI, GIUSEPPE (1805-1872). One of the most influential political theorists of the nineteenth century, Giuseppe Mazzini was born in Genoa, where he studied law and philosophy and developed the advanced republican and democratic ideas that he propounded for the rest of his life. He became a member of the *carboneria* in 1827. In November 1830, he was betrayed by an informer and served four months in jail. Prison was followed by exile to Marseilles where, in 1831, he founded a new clandestine movement, Giovine Italia. In a sense, Giovine Italia can be seen as a prototype for the revolutionary parties of the twentieth century. Mazzini demanded great commitment and personal virtue from the movement's members; insisted that the point of political theorizing was to provide not sterile discussions but a guide for action; and underlined the need for a dictatorship of the revolutionary elite in the immediate aftermath of a revolution. In concrete terms, Giovine Italia (which gave birth to similar movements in Poland, Germany, and Switzerland) achieved little. An abortive uprising in Piedmont-Sardinia in 1834 was its only serious attempt to upset the absolutist order, and the movement disintegrated by 1837.

Mazzini was the first Italian revolutionary to pay attention to the needs of the urban working class. Strongly influenced by English Chartism (he lived at length in England), Mazzini argued in strikingly similar terms to Marx that the industrial revolution was producing a two-class system in which the worker "denied land, capital and credit" was a slave at the mercy of the property-owning class. Unlike Marx, however, Mazzini thought that this divide could be filled by a democratic government instituting concrete social reforms to improve wages and conditions, and reduce the working day. He was, in short, an early social democratic reformist.

No democratic revolution was possible in Italy while the Austrians continued to hold much of the country. Accordingly, in 1848, Mazzini argued in favor of national unity against the common enemy and temporarily made his peace with the monarchy of Piedmont-Sardinia. In March 1849, Mazzini rushed to **Rome**, anticipating a revolutionary upheaval directed against the **Papacy**. He was immediately made a parliamentary deputy, and became one of the triumvirate of leaders in charge of the city's defense against the advancing French forces. Mazzini drew up the republican constitution that was symbolically promulgated on the day that Rome was forced to surrender. Expelled from Rome, he was forced, once more, into exile in Switzerland and England.

In the 1850s, Mazzini lost influence over the nationalist movement. In 1853, he started a new revolutionary movement called the **Partito d'Azione** (PdA) / Action Party, but its one attempt to promote simultaneous insurrections in Genoa and **Naples** in 1857 ended in disaster. An expeditionary force led by the anarcho-socialist Carlo Pisacane was slaughtered by angry peasants near Salerno; Mazzini had to flee from Genoa with the police on his trail. As a consequence, frustrated former Mazzinians such as **Giuseppe Garibaldi** joined the Italian Nationalist Society with its motto "For Italy and **Victor Emmanuel**." Mazzinians were responsible for the uprising in **Palermo** in 1860 that led to the expedition of Garibaldi's "Thousand." The policies enacted by Garibaldi's dictatorship in **Sicily** were also Mazzinian in inspiration and were enforced by one of his most loyal followers, **Francesco Crispi**. Mazzini himself, however, played only a relatively minor role in the **Risorgimento**. In September 1860, he went to Naples, intent on launching the idea of a national Constituent Assembly that would freely decide whether or not to accept annexation by Piedmont-Sardinia, but nothing came of this plan.

In the last decade of his life, Mazzini was deserted by Francesco Crispi and others among his few remaining supporters, who became royalists and leaders of the constitutional left. He was sharply criticized by Italy's nascent workers' movements. In 1870, he was arrested while attempting to promote an uprising in Rome. Released after the liberation of the capital, he lived the last few months of his life in Pisa under the pseudonym of Dr. Brown. *See also* Revolutions of 1848; Risorgimento.

MENABREA, LUIGI FEDERICO (1809-1896). Born in Chambéry, in the Savoy region of modern-day France, Luigi Federico Menabrea was a distinguished theoretical engineer who served in the engineering corps of the Sardinian army. Elected to the Sardinian Parliament in 1848, he swiftly became one of the leaders of the *destra storica* (the historic right). He served as minister for the navy and for public works in the early 1860s, and as ambassador to Vienna in 1866. At the end of October 1867, Menabrea formed his first government, which lasted little more than a month. During this month, **Giuseppe Garibaldi** was defeated at the battle of Mentana, outside **Rome**, by French forces. Menabrea's administration subsequently came under fire from Italian patriots for doing too little to make Rome the capital of Italy. The huge debts incurred by Italy during the war with Austria in 1866, and fear of a further war with France if the Roman question were pushed too hard, led Menabrea to a course of prudence.

His second and third cabinets (January 1868 to May 1869; May 1869 to December 1869) concentrated on restoring the public finances. During Menabrea's tenure of office, the notorious grist tax on milled grain was introduced in January 1869. Menabrea's government also "privatized" the state tobacco industry, selling it to a consortium of Italian and foreign bankers for 15 years in exchange for a 40 percent tax on its profits and Lit. 180 million in cash (about $36 million). Both decisions were unpopular. The former led to widespread rioting in rural areas, which the government suppressed at the cost of over 200 lives; the latter, to predictable accusations of corruption. Nevertheless, they were the beginning of a period of austerity that enabled the Italian state to put its finances on a sound footing by the mid-1870s. Menabrea served as ambassador to France and Great Britain for the remainder of his career. He died in his native Savoy in 1896.

MEZZOGIORNO. *See* Cassa per il Mezzogiorno; Latifondi; Southern Italy.

MICHELINI, ARTURO (1909-1969). Michelini, who was born in **Florence** in February of 1909, had volunteered to fight in the **Spanish Civil War** as well as on the Russian front in **World War II**. He became the leader of the **Movimento Sociale Italiano** (MSI) / Italian Social Movement in 1954, having offered an alternative to longing for the **Republic of Salò** and for the street-brawling of the faction around Pino Rauti. The only avenues open to the MSI seemed to be either placating these nostalgics by becoming the public manifestation of semi-clandestine and violent grouplets; or competing for the conservative backers of the **Partito Liberale Ialiano** (PLI) / Italian Liberal Party by completely integrating with the democratic system. A respected businessman, Michelini wanted an MSI that was a respectable right-wing party allied with the monarchists and able to gain access to the clientelism used by those who share in power to crystallize the loyalty of beneficiaries, especially among the petit bourgeoisie of **southern Italy**'s cities and towns, still ready to trade political support for political favors. At his funeral in June 1969, the highest authorities of the state were present in testimony to his accomplishment, rendering innocuous a party of former fascists. His successor was **Giorgio Almirante.**

MILAN (*Milano*). Even by European standards, Milan is an ancient city. It has been an important municipal center since Roman times and, in A.D. 285, Mediolanum, as the Romans called it, became the capital city of the western half of the Roman Empire. The city's modern history begins in 1737, after the War of the Spanish Succession, when the peace of Utrecht assigned Milan to Austria. In the next century, under Napoleon, Milan was to enjoy relative freedom becoming the capital of the Republic of Italy in 1802, then of the Kingdom of Italy in 1805. The Milanese, therefore, were disgruntled by the decision of the Congress of Vienna in 1815 to restore Austrian rule. Milan was the center of the **revolutions of 1848** in northern Italy. It was liberated by the Piedmontese army in 1859. In the late nineteenth century, Milan was the stronghold of Italian socialism and trade unionism. Prior to the advent to power of **fascism** in 1922, the city was the setting for fierce street battles between the **Partito Socialista Italiano** (PSI) / Italian Socialist Party and **Mussolini**'s squads. In 1945, the city's working class liberated the city without waiting for Allied forces.

Since 1945, Milan has become Italy's premier commercial, financial, and manufacturing center. Over four million people live in the city of Milan and its hinterland, and measured by the proportion of its citizens who work in manufacturing industry, Milan has become one of the most highly industrialized areas in the world. The high levels of industry have brought both an enviably high standard of living—the per capita value of the city's product is approximately $30,000—and a less enviable reputation for pollution, chaotic traffic, and urban sprawl. Political corruption has also marred the city's image. In 1992-1993, the city was the center of the **Mani pulite** investigations into political wrongdoing that eventually led to the disgrace of the PSI leader (and Milanese political boss) **Bettino Craxi**. *See also* Lega Nord; Mani Pulite; Risorgimento.

MINGHETTI, MARCO (1818-1886). Born in **Bologna**, Marco Minghetti was a close collaborator and friend of **Cavour**. He served as minister of the interior under Cavour in 1860-1861 and rose to be prime minister in March 1863. In this role, he signed, in 1864, the treaty with Napoleon III that led to the withdrawal of all French forces from Italy in exchange for a guarantee of the Pope's authority over **Rome**. The treaty also established **Florence** as capital of Italy. The diplomatic caution was wildly unpopular with Italian nationalists and radicals, notably **Giuseppe Garibaldi**, and with the deputies of the parliamentary left. Popular feeling against the treaty brought Minghetti's administration to an end in September 1864.

Minghetti occupied no further cabinet posts until July 1873 when he succeeded **Giovanni Lanza** as premier and also held the key post of finance minister. In office, Minghetti followed a policy of unremitting rigor that balanced the nation's books within three years. This financial rectitude naturally had political costs: Minghetti's unpopular policies were one of the principal causes of the so-called "parliamentary revolution" that brought **Agostino Depretis** and the left to power in 1876.

Minghetti led the parliamentary opposition from 1876 to 1882. In that year, however, he and his faction in Parliament shifted their support to Depretis, allowing the premier to "transform" the political situation by forming a centrist majority. Minghetti died in Rome in 1886.

MINORITIES. Linguistic minorities in Italy abound. Many Italians speak so-called "standard," school-taught Italian (*la lingua letteraria*) as a second language; second, that is, to their *spoken* language, which is their local dialect. In 1945, 50 percent of Italians spoke *only* a dialect. Widespread exposure to films and television and longer school attendance have greatly reduced the influence of dialects on young Italians. Three million Italians belong to non-Italian linguistic groups scattered throughout the peninsula as the following data suggest. *See also* Dialects in Italy.

LINGUISTIC MINORITIES		
Language	**Number of Speakers**	**Areas where spoken**
Albanian	100,000	7 southern regions
Catalan	15,000	Alghero (Sardinia)
German	200,000	South Tyrol, Trento, Verona, Vicenza, Belluno, Udine, Novara, Vercelli
French	100,000	Aosta, the city of Turin, and two towns in Puglia
Greek	20,000	Lecce and Calabria
Ladino-Dolomitico	30,000	Bolzano, Trento, and Belluno
Ladino-Friulano	700,000	Pordenone, Venezia, Udine
Occitanian	100,000	Provinces of Turin and Cuneo
Sardinian	1,500,000	Sardinia
Serbo-Croatian	4,000	Region of Molise
Slovenian	100,000	Trieste, Gorizia, Udine

Drawn from Salvi, Sergio. 1975. Le lingue tagliate. Milano: Rizzoli.

MODIGLIANI, AMEDEO (1884-1920). One of the most distinctive of all twentieth-century artists, Amedeo Modigliani was born into a wealthy Jewish family from Livorno (Leghorn) on the Tuscan coast but spent most of his adult life in Paris, where he began working as a sculptor and was greatly influenced, like many artists of the time, by African art. His life in Paris was the classic tale of the neglected genius: he had only one one-man show in his lifetime, and that was swiftly shut down by the police on the grounds of obscenity. He was interested in the work of Cézanne, but otherwise was little influenced by either the principal movements in the art world (fauvism, **futurism,** and cubism) or the left-wing politics of the Parisian art scene. The last five years of his brief life were the most memorable ones of his artistic production. In these years, Modigliani painted the portraits and the strikingly erotic (some would say pornographic) nudes that established his artistic reputation. His *Portrait of Leopold Zborowski* (1916), epitomizes his uniquely stylized form of portraiture. Zborowski, Modigliani's closest male friend, sits in the center of the canvas, a bulky figure in a brown suit, whose shoulders taper like a wine bottle to a perfectly oval-shaped head. Detail is reduced to a minimum: the eyes are no more than a dab of unexpressive green, the sitter's hair and beard are merely precisely defined areas of brown paint, the face is absolutely flat, the skin of the face is unwrinkled and almost monochromatic, the brown suit has a virtually unseeable lapel but no other adornment, the background is an unfeatured grey-green cloth or curtain. Yet the picture conveys both an undeniable sense of character—one perceives Zborowski's poise and intellect—and a powerful sense that the sitter has been accurately represented. From about 1912 onward, Modigliani was chronically addicted to alcohol and hashish. Several glasses of whisky were required to set his creative gifts in motion: he made a conscious philosophy out of living a life of excess. He died of tubercular meningitis in 1920. His last companion, Jeanne Héburtane, killed herself the following day.

MONARCHY (*House of Savoy: SAVOIA*). One of Europe's oldest ruling families, the lineage of the dukes of Savoy stretches back to the Middle Ages. Though theoretically subjects of the Holy Roman Empire, the Savoy family enjoyed great autonomy and, from **Turin,** governed a substantial tract of territory straddling the Alps. Chambéry and Annecy in modern-day France, and territories within the modern Italian regions of Piedmont, Aosta, and Liguria constituted the dukedom's boundaries. The dukes achieved regal status as a result of the enterprising Duke Amadeus II (Amadeo II, 1675-1730), who deserted King Louis XIV of France at a crucial moment in the War of Spanish Succession and was rewarded for his behavior by elevation to kingship and the addition of the island of Sicily to Savoyan territory in 1718. In 1720, under Austrian pressure, he was obliged to exchange Sicily for Sardinia. His heirs were henceforth known as the Kings of Sardinia, although many historians refer to the state as Piedmont-Sardinia to reflect the fact that Turin continued to be the administrative and social capital of the new state. The new state added to its domain during the War of the Polish Succession, when the son of Amadeus II, Charles Emmanuel III, defeated the Austrians and conquered Lombardy, although at the peace of Vienna in 1738, he was obliged to give Lombardy back in exchange for the province of Novara and other minor territorial gains.

Austria, as the primary power in Lombardy and Venetia, was thus the long-standing enemy of the Savoy family. Nevertheless, the family was an absolutist dynasty, and the Savoys therefore rallied to the side of imperial Austria against the challenge of revolutionary France after 1789. Napoleon defeated the Austro-Piedmontese forces at the battle of Mondovì in 1796; two years later, Charles Emmanuel IV of Savoy was forced to flee to Sardinia when French forces occupied Turin. The Savoys, in the person of King Victor Emmanuel I, were only restored to their throne in 1815 at the **Congress of Vienna**.

The importance of the Savoy family, of course, is that they became the ruling family of all Italy. Victor Emmanuel I was succeeded to the throne of Sardinia by his pro-Austrian brother, Charles Felice (reigned 1821-1831), and only then by his son, **Carlo Alberto** (1831-1849). Italian unification was achieved during the reign of **Victor Emmanuel II** (1849-1878). His son, Humbert I (1878-1900), was a reactionary who backed the conservative governments of the 1890s and was killed by an emigré anarchist who returned from the United States with the express intention of revenging the innocent peasants and workers slaughtered by Italian troops during the Sicilian uprisings of 1894 and the Milanese bread riots in 1898. Humbert's son, **Victor Emmanuel III** (1900-1946), initially backed relative progressives in the Italian political establishment, but ultimately acquiesced in the accession to power of **Benito Mussolini**. His son, Humbert II was king for two months in 1946 prior to the referendum on the future of the monarchy. By a very close margin (12.7 million votes to 10.7 million, with 1.5 million invalid votes), Italy elected to become a republic.

The Savoy family were subsequently debarred from ever stepping foot in Italy again, though this ban was ended in 1997. Even today, many Italians, particularly in the North, regard the Savoy family as traitors and unpunished war criminals and would require serious evidence of contrition by the current head of the family, Victor Emmanuel IV, before they would allow the royal family to return as residents. There is no monarchist political party in Italy today, although there is a surprising amount of public interest in the Savoy family's jet-set lifestyle. *See also* Constitution of 1948; Girolamo Pelloux; Rome.

MONTALE, EUGENIO (1896-1981). One of the greatest twentieth-century poets, Eugenio Montale became the fifth Italian in this century to win the Nobel prize for literature.

Montale established his reputation in 1925 when the anti-fascist publisher and philosopher **Piero Gobetti** printed his remarkable collection *Ossi di seppia* (*Cuttlefish Bones*). Along with Eliot's *Wasteland* (which Montale translated into Italian), the poems in *Ossi di seppia* are perhaps the most poignant expression of the malaise experienced by the generation who had survived **World War I**. Spare in style, self-consciously rejecting the pompous, rhetorical form of **Gabriele d'Annunzio**, they also refused to make any concessions to the ardent, committed poetry prized by the new fascist regime.

Montale "discovered" **Italo Svevo** in a famous essay in 1925, and as one of the principal figures connected with the literary magazine *Solaria*, he played an important role in preserving independent Italian literature during the dictatorship. His relations with the regime were never easy, and in 1939 his refusal to swear allegiance to **Mussolini** led to his losing his job at a Florentine literary foundation. In the same year, he published his second great collection of poems, *Le occasioni* (*Occasions*).

After **World War II**, Montale worked as a cultural and music critic (his collected short essays and criticism were published in Italy in 1996) for *Il Corriere della sera*, and produced a masterful collection of poems, *Il Bufera e altri* (*The Storm and Others*) in 1956. The death of his wife, in 1963, inspired him to write a series of lyric poems that were later collected in *Saturna* (1971).

Honors were showered upon Montale in his last years. He became a life member of the Italian Senate in 1967 and, in 1975, was awarded the aforementioned Nobel prize. He died in **Milan** in September 1981.

MONTANELLI, INDRO (1909-). Perhaps the most famous living

Italian journalist, Indro Montanelli fought a long intellectual battle against Italian communism, but in the mid-1990s became one of the sternest critics of the right-wing politicians who had emerged in Italy since the collapse of the **Democrazia Cristiana** (DC) / Christian Democracy Party in 1992-1993.

Born near **Florence**, Montanelli made his name as a war correspondent for the *Corriere della sera* in Finland during the winter of 1939-1940. For most of the post-war years, Montanelli was the chief columnist for the *Corriere*, but, in 1974, dismayed by the paper's increasing willingness to compromise with the **Partito Comunista Italiano** (PCI) / Italian Communist Party, he left the Milanese daily to found a new newspaper, *Il Giornale nuovo*, which he edited until January 1994. At *Il Giornale*, Montanelli was vehemently critical of both the PCI and the DC, whose corruption and political malpractice he denounced in brilliant, incisive prose. He nevertheless continued to urge his readers to "hold their noses" and vote for the DC so long as there was any risk of the PCI's taking power. Montanelli's defense of the DC made him unpopular with the radical left in the turbulent 1970s; in June 1977, he was shot in the legs by zealots of the **Brigate Rosse** (BR) / Red Brigades.

Montanelli's career as editor of *Il Giornale* was brought to an end by his refusal to condone and support the political career of **Silvio Berlusconi**, the paper's owner. Berlusconi brusquely sacked Montanelli, and the veteran journalist was forced to start a new broadsheet, *La Voce*, which soon failed.

Almost 90, Montanelli continues to play an active role in Italian public life and to publish regular articles on the political scene. In addition to his journalism, he is the author of numerous works of popular history including a multivolume history of Italy, as well as several plays and stories.

MONTESSORI, MARIA (1870-1952). One of this century's most famous and innovative educational theorists, Maria Montessori was born in Ancona (The Marches). The so-called "Montessori method," which has been used in experimental schools all over the world, and which has had a huge impact upon curricular and school reform in all advanced industrial countries, prizes the use of didactic materials that spontaneously awaken the curiosity of young children and incite them to learn. It was thus in opposition to the highly disciplined and teacher-centered methods common in the early part of this century. Children taught by the Montessori method are encouraged to read, write, and develop spatial skills at a very early age. This aspect of the method has led to criticism from educational progressives who believe that early education should allow children to adjust to their environment and experience rather than fostering precocious academic achievement.

As one would expect from someone who put so much emphasis upon free inquiry and curiosity, Montessori was no friend of the fascist regime. Rather than endure the dictatorship, she left Italy and eventually established herself permanently in the Netherlands. She died near The Hague in 1952.

MORANTE, ELSA (1918-1985). An important figure in post-war Italian fiction, Elsa Morante was the author of four major novels, *Menzogna e Sortilegio* (*The House of Liars*, 1948), *L'Isola di Arturo* (*Arturo's Island*, 1957), *La Storia* (*History: A Novel*, 1974), and *Aracoeli* (*Aracoeli: Altar of Heaven*, 1982). In all her works, childhood recurs as an obsessive theme and child-characters are often employed as a foil to the corruption and alienation of the adult world. Morante became famous almost overnight with the publication of *La Storia*, which became a best seller and which stirred a huge debate between those critics who condemned its profound pessimism and those who praised Morante's warmth toward the ordinary people who are history's principal victims. Initially more successful in France than in Italy, few would now doubt that Morante is one of the most important contemporary Italian novelists, and one of the most talented women writers to emerge in any language since 1945. She died in her native **Rome** in 1985.

MORAVIA, ALBERTO (pseud. Alberto Pincherle, 1907-1990). One of Italy's most prolific and controversial contemporary writers, Alberto Moravia was an exceptionally precocious novelist. *Gli indifferenti* (*The Indifferent*, 1929), his first novel, was published when he was hardly more than 20 years old. Many still regard this study of bored, corrupt, worthless, and indecisive upper-class Romans as his best work. Its sexual frankness won it a large audience, but its merciless depiction of the feebleness and rottenness of the Italian ruling class aroused the censure of the regime, and Moravia was obliged to leave Italy for exile in Mexico and the United States.

Several of Moravia's later novels were turned into films, the most successful being *Il Conformista* (*The Conformist*, 1952) with an adaption of which **Bernardo Bertolucci** won his first Oscar; while the influence of Moravia's novel *La Noia* (literally "Boredom" but translated as *The Empty Canvas*) is very evident in the films of **Michelangelo Antonioni**. Both of these novels were of the same existentialist genre as *Gli indifferenti,* but Moravia also wrote several realist novels, the best of which is probably *La Romana* (1947). Moravia was close politically and personally to the leaders of the **Partito Comunista Italiano** (PCI) / Italian Communist Party. In 1986, he married the young Spanish novelist Carmen Llera: he had previously been married to the Italian novelists **Elsa Morante** and Dacia Moraini. Moravia died in **Rome** in 1990.

MORO, ALDO (1916-1978). Born in Apulia, the heel of the Italian boot, Moro became a professor of law and criminal procedure at the University of Bari. During the war years, he was simultaneously president of the **Federazione Universitaria Cattolici Italiana** (FUCI) / Catholic University Graduates' Movement of Italy, a member of the Catholic Movimento Laureati (Graduates' Movement) and editor of *Studium*, its major publication, and a member of the Gioventù Universitaria Fascista (GUF) / Fascist University Youth. Elected to the **Constituent Assembly** and subsequently to the first republican Parliament, he was identified with **Alcide De Gasperi**, in whose fifth government Moro was undersecretary for foreign affairs. Consistently reelected to the Chamber, by 1953, he was floor leader of the **Democrazia Cristiana** (DC) / Christian Democracy Party. In **Antonio Segni**'s government, he served as minister of justice. He was minister of education in the 1958 **Amintore Fanfani** government. In 1959, he became secretary of the DC. By 1963, he had formed his own government, which lasted until 1968. By 1976, he had been prime minister five times.

Moro had also served as minister for foreign affairs in governments headed by **Mariano Rumor** (1969-1970;1973-1974), **Emilio Colombo** (1970-1972), and **Giulio Andreotti** (1972). It was in this capacity that he met Henry Kissinger, then Secretary of State of the United States, who described Moro as wily, imperceptibly maneuvering, the most formidable among the DC leaders. Moro was, indeed, as the **Tambroni** episode reveals, the supreme party strategist and a man of extraordinary intellectual subtlety. His detractors describe him as obfuscating. Some of his more memorable formulations are still quoted, for example, "parallel convergencies."

Chief architect of the *apertura a sinistra* (**opening to the left**), he had been engaged in enlarging that opening to include the **Partito**

Comunista Italiano (PCI) / Italian Communist Party. In their boldest
move, the **Brigate Rosse** (BR) / Red Brigades kidnapped Aldo Moro
in broad daylight on March 16, 1978. After he had been held for 55
days in captivity, and after bitter quarrels as to his fate, BR leaders
offered to negotiate with the government the exchange of Moro for
13 jailed companions but were spurned. The rejection was as divisive
of DC opinion as making the offer had been to the Red Brigades.
Moro was executed and his body left in the trunk of a small
automobile in central **Rome**, midway between PCI national offices
and the national headquarters of the DC in Piazza del Gesù.

His murder produced vitriolic exchanges among political leaders
of all parties but most especially within the DC. His policy is seen by
his admirers as aiming at widening the consensus in Italy to embrace
the working class as well as the bourgeoisie, thus resolving a
perennial Italian conundrum. His detractors, on the other hand, see
him as a cunning dissimulator who sought to declaw the left by
seducing first the socialists, and then the communists, into supporting
an unjust status quo. *See also* Federazione Universitaria Cattolici
Italiana; Fernando Tambroni.

MOSCA, GAETANO (1858-1941). One of the democratic age's most
uncomfortable thinkers, Gaetano Mosca is chiefly remembered today
for his conviction that democratic regimes—like all other types of
regime—are controlled by elites, who manipulate public opinion and
the levers of power for their own ends.

Born in **Palermo** in 1858, Mosca's critique of democracy first
surfaced in his 1884 work *Teorica dei governi* (*Theory of
Governments*). But it was his 1896 work, *Elementi di scienza politica*
(*Elements of Political Science*), that established his reputation. For
Mosca, who by now was a close advisor of the conservative
statesman **Antonio Starabba Di Rudinì**, the rhetoric of popular
sovereignty was simply a device used by Machiavellian politicians
to facilitate their own pursuit of power. Moreover, paucity of political
sophistication, shaky institutions, and a high tolerance for political
corruption meant that democratic reforms were a gift horse that
should be carefully examined for unscrupulous agitators willing and
able to exploit popular prejudices and ignorance. For this reason,
Mosca, who was elected to Parliament in 1909, opposed the
introduction of universal male suffrage in 1912.

Mosca, however, must be regarded as a liberal-conservative, not
as a proto-fascist or a reactionary (his most famous pupil, **Piero**

Gobetti, described him as a "conservative gentleman"). His objection to democracy was precisely that it increased the likelihood that an anti-liberal elite would come to power—and post-1918 politics in Italy hardly persuaded him to question this analysis. Like **Benedetto Croce**, Mosca was initially inclined to give **Mussolini** the benefit of the liberal doubt, but by 1925 he had passed to the opposition. Mosca signed the manifesto of anti-fascist intellectuals published by Croce in the newspaper *Il Mondo* on May 1, 1925. Mosca's final years were spent finishing off an enormous history of political thought, which was published in 1933. He died in **Rome** in 1941.

MOVIMENTO SOCIALE ITALIANO (MSI) / Italian Social Movement. Survivors of the **Republic of Salò** joined returning veterans, former war prisoners, and nostalgics for **fascism**'s certainties to found the MSI in December of 1946. **Giorgio Almirante**, the party's first secretary, had been a member of the *Decima mas* (former naval personnel of the *Motoscafi Antisommergibile* / Antisubmarine Patrol Boats, who were used in the republic to find, arrest, and terminate Italian partisans) and preferred violent confrontations to political compromise. At Salò, the original hundred party members (including Almirante) grew to 4,000, led by Roman Prince Junio Valerio Borghese who refused to be subordinate either to the Germans or to fascist party functionaries. The presence of additional right-wing groups, such as the Monarchists and factions within the newly formed MSI, made cohesion difficult.

Despite his undeniable abilities and skill as an orator, Almirante was replaced in 1950 by Augusto De Marsanich, who was determined to make the party an accepted player in the Italian Republic. The MSI continued on this path under the leadership of **Arturo Michelini**, chosen in 1954, whose network of contacts in his native **Rome** provided entry to both Vatican and bourgeois Roman circles. Events surrounding the **Tambroni** government, however, made it difficult to put the MSI at the core of a parliamentary right.

When Michelini died unexpectedly in 1969, the party chose Almirante to replace him. He began to combine the strategies of anti-regime agitation with the pursuit of legitimation as the party of "law and order." Almirante managed to tie to himself **Pino Rauti**, the hot-headed street-fighter and founder of Ordine Nuovo. A few senior military officers (Admiral Birindelli, General Giovanni De Lorenzo, and General Vito Miceli) were drawn to the party after the 1972 merger with the monarchists of the Destra Nazionale (DN) / National

Right, thus creating the MSI-DN.

By 1980, the MSI had put aside the cudgel in favor of the double-breasted suit, becoming the party of opposition to (leftist) terrorism, the drug culture, abortion, and **divorce**, and—with similar energy—becoming the advocate of a U.S.-style presidency for Italy. The renewal of public interest in the culture of **fascism**'s two decades manifested itself in the appearance at MSI Congresses of party leaders from the **Democrazia Cristiana** (DC) / Christian Democracy and other parties, including **Panella** of the **Partito Radicale** (PR) / Radical Party and **Bettino Craxi** of the **Partito Socialista Italiano** (PSI) / Italian Socialist Party, who argued against the continued "ghettoization" of the MSI. Almirante visited the United States and even paid homage at the funeral of **Berlinguer** in the Rome headquarters of the **Partito Comunista Italiano** (PCI) / Italian Communist Party. The reborn MSI-DN offered **corporatism** as an alternative to unbridled capitalism. A strong state, hierarchy, discipline, authority and obedience, acceptance of the fascist years as an integral part of Italy's recent past and not an anomaly; these core beliefs purported to defend the "dignity and interests of the Italian people" in the Mediterranean, in Europe, and the world.

Before Almirante died in the spring of 1988, he led the MSI to elect as secretary **Gianfranco Fini**, born seven years after **World War II**. Fini held that position since 1988, exception made for the period January 1990 to July 1991 when Pino Rauti was secretary. Fini's program included the death penalty, lower taxes, harsh anti-immigrant legislation, and revision of the 1975 Treaty of Osimo settling the borders with Yugoslavia. Fini was the last leader of the MSI. Under his guidance, the party transformed itself into the **Alleanza nazionale** (AN) / National Alliance in 1994-1995 in an attempt to make the neo-fascist movement a pole of attraction for the many conservative voters disillusioned by the moral decline of the DC and alarmed by the growing strength of the Italian left. *See also* Alleanza Nazionale; Giorgio Almirante.

MURRI, ROMOLO (1870-1944). Born in the Marches, this leader of radical **Catholicism** in pre-1914 Italy had become a priest in 1893. Like many young priests born after the **Risorgimento**, he chafed under the church's ban on political activity and found the Vatican-approved social movements (the most important of which was the so-called Opera dei congressi) intolerably conservative. Beginning in 1898, Murri edited a magazine, *Cultura sociale*, a

Catholic rival to the Socialist Party's intellectual journal *Critica sociale*. Spurred by the state's repression of workers' movements throughout Italy in 1898-1899, Murri's critique of Italian society assumed nearly Marxist tones—so far as he was concerned, the state was merely the expression of the desires and ideas of the property-owning classes; an essentially repressive organization that had to be transformed into *una democrazia cristiana* (a Christian democracy).

Disenchanted with the conservatism of the Vatican-controlled "popular unions" that replaced the Opera dei congressi in 1905, Murri founded the Lega Democratica Nazionale (National Democratic League) in 1905. The new movement openly proclaimed its intention to recruit young working-class activists who would spread democratic and socialist ideas within Catholic organizations in Italy. Displeased, the church banned priests from participating in the new movement, and eventually suspended Murri from the priesthood in 1907 after he openly called for state supervision of religious schools and the ending of religious instruction in elementary schools. Undaunted, Murri was elected to Parliament as a radical for his native Ascoli Piceno (Marches) in 1909. The church responded by excommunicating him.

Murri's hostility to Giolittian liberalism, and the influence of the philosophy of **Giovanni Gentile** later caused his political views to turn rightward, however. He won the plaudits of the fascist hierarchy by publishing a paean to the strong state entitled *La conquista ideale dello stato* (*The Ideal Conquest of the State*, 1923). After the publication of this book, **Piero Gobetti** dismissed him as "the perfect example of a failed prophet." In 1943, he was reconciled to the church, and died in the following year.

MUSSOLINI, BENITO (1883-1945). Born in the foothills of the Apennines in Predappio (Romagna), Benito Mussolini's father and grandfather were both peasants who were jailed for their commitment to the nascent socialist movement, while his mother was a schoolmistress and a devout Catholic. Mussolini, though a voracious reader, seems to have been an ill-tempered child who was twice suspended from school for knifing fellow students. After leaving school, he had a number of teaching appointments, but everywhere he went he managed to antagonize the authorities. After fleeing to Switzerland and France to avoid military service in 1903-1904, his political activities and riotous conduct led to his being arrested and expelled. Fascist historians subsequently misrepresented this ignominious period in Mussolini's life by asserting that he had studied at the University of Geneva. A general amnesty for deserters, however, allowed him to repatriate and clear his record by 18 months of military service. While Mussolini was serving in the military, his mother died: Mussolini returned to Predappio as soon as his period of conscription was over and became both a (rather incompetent) schoolteacher and a socialist activist of growing notoriety.

In 1909, Mussolini emigrated once more, this time to the Trentino (then under Austrian rule) where he honed his growing skills as a propagandist as editor of *Il Popolo* (The People), an irredentist newspaper published by the leader of the Italian community, **Cesare Battisti**. Repeatedly arrested by the Austrian authorities, Mussolini's inevitable expulsion only enhanced his standing among Italian nationalists.

Mussolini opposed the war in **Libya**, which the reformist majority of the **Partito Socialista Italiano** (PSI) / Italian Socialist Party had backed, and served a five-month prison sentence in 1911 for anti-war activities. One of his cell mates was **Pietro Nenni**. On his release Mussolini was determined to wrest control of the PSI from the reformists. Taking advantage of the membership's hostile reaction to a visit to the royal palace made by party leader **Leonida Bissolati** to congratulate the king on escaping from an assassination attempt, Mussolini made a violent speech against Bissolati's policy of obtaining social reforms through cooperation with the Italian state. Mussolini's motion to expel Bissolati and the other leaders of the PSI's moderates achieved an unexpectedly large majority, and Mussolini became the party's dominant personality.

Mussolini became editor of the party newspaper, *L'Avanti!* In 1914, he was torn between the party line of neutralism and the will to intervene. His hope appears to have been that a military bloodbath would stimulate revolutionary conditions. Unilaterally, he changed the editorial policy of the paper to one backing interventionism, but was unable to carry the party leadership with him, and he was expelled. Undaunted, Mussolini launched a paper of his own, *Il Popolo d'Italia* (The People of Italy) in November 1914, with substantial financial aid from businesses in the war industries. By 1915, he had become an expansionist, advocating the creation of an Italian empire in the eastern Mediterranean and Middle East. Mussolini was called up in September 1915 and seems to have performed his duties as a soldier competently, being promoted to corporal, but without particular distinction. In February 1917, he was wounded by an accidental explosion during grenade training: fascist hagiographers would later make much of this injury and claim that the war began to go badly for Italy when Mussolini was constrained to leave the front! Mussolini returned to *Il Popolo d'Italia*, where he took an increasingly nationalist and populist line, and abandoned socialism, as he himself put it, with a "sigh of relief."

In March 1919, Mussolini founded the *Fasci Italiani di Combattimento*. The new movement had no clear ideology: Mussolini's speeches and articles drew upon a mishmash of anarchist, socialist, nationalist, and syndicalist themes. But the movement's appeal for *action*, which it backed up by a campaign of terror against the PSI in the streets and fields of Italy, appealed to Italy's numerous disaffected ex-soldiers, and Mussolini showed great skill in trimming his tactical sails to suit the needs of the moment. He became prime minister in October 1922 quite legally, but legality was not the hallmark of his premiership. In his first speech to Parliament, he made clear his contempt for the institution, saying that he could have bivouacked his blackshirts in "quest'aula sorda e grigia" ("this deaf, gray hall"). Fascist bullyboys terrorized the rival parties, the opposition leader **Giacomo Matteotti** was murdered, and in 1925-1926 all opposition parties, newspapers, and independent political activity was banned. He had become Duce: the leader, and his word was law.

Like the rulers of Soviet Russia, Mussolini set out to create a new man for a new century, but his methods seem somewhat infantile in retrospect. An assertive and arrogant *costume fascista* (fascist behavior) was imposed on ordinary life. Italians had to say "voi" (the second person plural) to each other instead of "lei" (the first person polite form) since the latter was regarded as less virile. Shaking hands was abolished to encourage use of the Roman salute, and Saturday afternoons were given over to compulsory communal sports or meetings. Great emphasis was put on flag waving rallies, grandiose architecture, and educational propaganda. Mussolini himself struck heroic poses, spoke to what the fascist press called "oceanic crowds" of carefully choreographed enthusiasts, and launched symbolic battles for grain, land reclamation, and fertility. Quite a number of foreign visitors were taken in by the facade: Winston Churchill and a stream of other eminent upper-class British visitors regarded Mussolini as one of the great men of the age. In retrospect, however, we can see that he was merely a fraud with a certain gift for propaganda and political intrigue: Mussolini was extremely skilled

244 • Muti, Ettore

at making sure that rivals for influence within the fascist movement such as **Italo Balbo** were promoted to jobs distant from the power centers in Rome. Above all, although he invented the word, he was not a totalitarian dictator on the model of Stalin and Hitler, though he may have liked to have been. He was much lazier, less ruthless, less obsessed, more human, and Fascist Italy was consequently a much more liveable place than the great dictatorships of Nazi Germany and Communist Russia.

Mussolini was also prone to vainglory. His downfall can ultimately be traced to the fact that he began to believe his own propaganda. Contemptuous of democratic Britain and France, puffed up by Italy's military victory in **Abyssina**, his ego flattered by Hitler's skillful diplomacy (notably during a five-day official visit to Germany in September 1937 and Hitler's return visit in April 1938), Mussolini threw in Italy's lot with Nazi Germany. Mussolini soon became the junior partner in Hitler's plans, though the German dictator continued to the end to regard the Duce with esteem and friendship. As the war progressed, Mussolini, who was also suffering from a serious stomach illness, proved to be an inadequate war leader: out of touch with reality and unable to direct the war effort with the energy and rationality that the fascist system, where power was entirely concentrated in the Duce's own hands, demanded. When, after the Allied invasion of Sicily in July 1943, the Fascist Grand Council deposed Mussolini from power, there was no popular protest even among active fascists. *Il Popolo d'Italia*, announcing the news, simply substituted Mussolini's photograph on the front page with one of Marshal **Badoglio**.

Mussolini was rescued by the Germans from his hotel-prison on top of the Gran Sass mountain in September 1943. For the last two years of his life he ruled the puppet **Republic of Salò**, and must bear great responsibility for the savagery of the civil war fought in northern Italy in those years. Mussolini died on April 28, 1945, as he, his mistress Clara Petacci, and a handful of diehards were trying to escape into Switzerland. He was captured by the partisans, summarily executed and hung by his heels in Milan's Piazza Loreto, where his corpse was vilely treated by the crowds. *See also* Luigi Facta; Fascism; Fascist Ideology; Gran Consiglio del Facismo; Foreign Policy.

MUTI, ETTORE (1902-1943). Ettore Muti was secretary of the **Partito Nazionale Fascista** (PNF) / National Fascist Party between 1939 and

1941 when he was succeeded by Vidussoni, having himself succeeded Starace at a moment when the latter's standing with the Duce had declined precipitously because he questioned the wisdom of the alliance with Germany. Muti, on the other hand, was a congenial friend of **Galeazzo Ciano**, son-in-law of **Mussolini.** Ciano regarded Muti as "like a child" in his company. Muti's service in the **Arditi** in **World War I** had led to frequent decoration. After becoming party secretary, his penchant for wearing all his medals on any occasion resulted in his description as having "the most magnificent chest in Italy." He had also participated in **D'Annunzio**'s filibuster in Fiume. Both in the war in **Abyssinia** and in the **Spanish Civil War,** he was Ciano's co-pilot in bombing raids.

Memorialist Fidia Gambetta described Muti's penchant for driving his Bugatti two-seater at break-neck speeds into the main square of small Italian towns. The scene was reproduced by **Federico Fellini** in his film-memoir, *Amacord* (*I Remember*) (in Romagnole dialect). Muti's limited administrative abilities led to his dismissal in May and his replacement by Adelchi Serena, who was, in turn, replaced by a young, unknown, and administratively inexperienced law student, Aldo Vidussoni. He had lost a hand and an eye in the Spanish Civil War, for which he had been awarded a gold medal. His detractors suggested that the post of PNF secretary was another form of compensation. However, he proved no more capable than his predecessors of stemming the hemorrhage of party morale.

When **Pietro Badoglio** came to power, he had Muti arrested. Muti was killed in an attempt to escape. Born in Ravenna on the Adriatic, he died at Fregene, a popular seaside city outside **Rome.** *See also* Fascism; Table 4 in Appendix.

-N-

NAPLES (*Napoli*). Italy's third-largest city, with nearly 1.5 million inhabitants, Naples is the center of a conurbation that stretches along the coast and includes such important towns as Erculano (site of the ancient town of Pompeii), Torre Del Greco, and the famous village of Sorrento. Population density, at nearly 3,000 inhabitants per square kilometer, is one of the highest in the world: only Hong Kong and a handful of other cities in Asia are more crowded. The islands of Capri and Ischia, famous for their natural beauty, are also part of the province of Naples. Mount Vesuvius, a huge active volcano, looms above all.

The city's history has been turbulent. It was founded in the fifth century B.C. In 327 B.C. it became a self-governing province of the Roman Empire. After the empire's fall, Naples was successively occupied by the Goths (A.D. 493) and the Byzantine empire (A.D. 536). Gradually, the city achieved greater independence and became an important trading center. Both Lombards and Saracens tried to conquer Naples for this reason, but it was not until A.D. 1138, when the Normans captured the city, that Naples succumbed. In the later Middle Ages, the Kingdoms of Aragon, France, and Spain successively ruled Naples.

The city's modern history begins with the Spanish, whose corrupt rule, many argue, left a trace in the political culture of the city that endures today. In 1647, the city rose in revolt against Spanish misgovernment. In 1734, after a brief period of Austrian rule, Charles of Bourbon became monarch of an independent Kingdom of Naples that lasted until French troops occupied the city in 1798. In 1799, the people of Naples established a republic, but Bourbon troops supported by the British fleet crushed the nascent democracy. Napoleon reoccupied Naples in 1806. For two years, Joseph Bonaparte, Napoleon's brother, ruled over the city; after Joseph became king of Spain, his place was taken by one of Napoleon's most successful generals, Joachim Murat. After the fall of Napoleon in 1814-1815, the Austrians restored the Bourbons to power in what became known as the Kingdom of the Two Sicilies. In both 1820 and 1848, the city was the center of uprisings against absolute rule that were suppressed by the Austrian army. The city was finally liberated by **Garibaldi** in 1860. During **World War II,** the city's insurrectionary traditions came to the fore once more: in four days of bloody street fighting (September 28 to October 1, 1943), the people of Naples managed to liberate the city from its Nazi occupiers in advance of the Allies' arrival.

Despite its glorious history, Naples has a reputation for being one of Europe's problem cities. The ubiquitous *Camorra* (the Neapolitan mafia) and exceptionally high rates of poverty are the most troublesome issues. Illegal construction, insane traffic, widespread political corruption, and decaying infrastructure are additional concerns. In 1993, the city elected a prominent former communist, Antonio Bassolino, to the mayoralty, ahead of **Mussolini's** granddaughter Alessandra. Bassolino has been widely praised for reviving the city, but much work remains to be done.

NAPOLEONIC ITALY. The idea of a united Italy first took concrete political form under the rule of Napoleon Buonaparte. In 1793, the Papal states, the Kingdom of **Naples**, and the absolutist rulers of northern Italy, declared war on revolutionary France. Commanded by Napoleon, the French invaded what is today Piedmont and defeated the Austro-Piedmontese army at the battles of Millesimo and Mondovì. The peace of Paris between France and Piedmont-Sardinia (May 1796) assigned Nice and Savoy to France, and after further defeating the Austrians at Lodi, northern Italy was reorganized on republican lines. In July 1797, the Cisalpine Republic was founded, with the tricolor as its flag, uniting all of northern Italy from the French border to Emilia-Romagna. In October 1797, the Treaty of Campo Formio ceded Venetia to Austria in exchange for Austrian recognition of the revolutionaries' gains.

In 1798, Napoleon continued his conquests into southern Italy. The Papal states and Naples were occupied and briefly transformed into a republic; Piedmont itself was occupied by French troops; Pope Pius VI was forced to move to France. Internal developments in France, however, allowed the Austrians, aided by the English navy and the Russian army, to launch a counter-attack in 1799 and reconquer most of the peninsula after bloody fighting, especially in Naples. In 1800, Napoleon launched his second Italian campaign and destroyed the Austrian army at Marengo. The subsequent peace of Lunéville in 1801 assigned the duchies of Parma and Piacenza to Piedmont, and the isle of Elba to France; the Pope was restored to his throne in **Rome**, but **Bologna**, Ferrara, and Ravenna were retained by the Cisalpine Republic. The following year, the Cisalpine Republic became the republic of Italy, with **Milan** as its capital. The Napoleonic legal codes were introduced throughout the republic in 1805, just two years after their introduction in France.

Also in 1805, Napoleon turned the republic of Italy into a kingdom and took the crown. The new kingdom's territories were extended at the peace of Pressburg between France and Austria to include Venetia and Istria (Istria is now part of Croatia). The following year, Napoleon invaded Naples and appointed his brother Joseph to the throne. In 1808, French troops occupied the Papal states and took the Pope prisoner once more. In 1809, the Trentino was occupied. All of modern-day Italy except **Sicily** had been united into one kingdom, and although Buonaparte by now had become as much a crowned prince as any of the continent's hereditary monarchs, a culture of assertive nationalism as well as of liberal and constitutionalist thinking had been injected into Italy's politically influential classes. The subsequent attempt to restore absolute monarchy at the **Congress of Vienna** in 1814-1815 flew in the face of these decisive developments.

NAPOLITANO, GIORGIO (1925-). A native of **Naples,** Giorgio Napolitano joined the **Partito Comunista Italiano** (PCI) / Italian Communist Party in 1945 after a period of youthful anti-fascist activity. He was elected to the Chamber of Deputies for the first time in 1953 and has represented first the PCI, then the **Partito Democratico della Sinistra** (PDS) / Democratic Party of the Left in **Parliament** for most of the next 40 years. Napolitano was closely identified with the PCI's social-democratic wing, the so-called *miglioristi* (reformers), and their leader, **Giorgio Amendola.** In the 1970s and early 1980s he was the chief theoretician of the PCI's move away from the Soviet bloc and its adoption of a foreign policy that defended international institutions and sharply condemned Soviet expansionism. Napolitano believed, as he argued in a famous 1979 book, that the PCI was wallowing "in the middle of the ford" between communism and social democracy. In domestic policy, he was a strong proponent of an electoral alliance with the **Partito Socialista Italiano** (PSI) / Italian Socialist Party. The PSI's integration into the structure of political power in the 1980s, however, rendered this project impossible. Neither **Craxi** nor the majority of the PCI's membership would have been willing to turn it into a political reality.

Napolitano has held several of the highest positions in the Italian state. Between 1981 and 1986, he was the PCI's floor leader in the Chamber of Deputies; between 1992 and 1994, he was speaker of the Chamber of Deputies. In May 1996, he became minister for the interior in the center-left government formed by **Romano Prodi.**

NATIONAL ALLIANCE. *See* Alleanza Nazionale (AN) / National Alliance.

NATTA, ALESSANDRO (1918-). Born in Imperia (Liguria) in the last year of **World War I**, he studied literature at the University of Genoa before he began teaching in an Imperia secondary school (*liceo*) prior to becoming an artillery lieutenant in **World War II**. He was wounded in action against the Germans after Italy's surrender to the Allies on September 8, 1943, was taken prisoner on Rhodes, and sent to a series of prison camps. While a prisoner, he organized fellow officers to render their captors' lives as difficult as possible. After the war, he joined the **Partito Comunista Italiano** (PCI) / Italian Communist Party, returned to his teaching duties, served on his local city council, and in 1948, was elected to the Chamber of Deputies. He has edited *Rinascita*, was co-editor with **Luigi Longo** of *Critica Marxista* between 1956 and 1966, and served on the Central Committee as well as on the Steering Committee of the PCI.

Because he was a reliable party functionary, Natta was made general secretary upon **Berlinguer**'s untimely death in 1984. He was confirmed in that post at the Florence Congress of the PCI in April 1986. Like others who try to lead by consensus, he seemed torn between the forces that were wrenching the party apart: one pulling in the direction of renewed Stalinist-Leninist orthodoxy and the other, toward northern European social democracy, anathema to the party's left. However, PCI losses in the 1987 elections led to pressures for easing him out when a heart attack brought on his resignation. His place was taken by **Achille Occhetto**. At the all-important Bologna Congress where the PCI was transformed into the **Partito Democratico della Sinistra** (PDS) / Democratic Party of the Left, Natta—like **Ingrao**—was among those reluctant to give up the symbolism of the largest Western Communist party.

Unsympathetic observers have remarked on the "grayness" of one who was essentially a party worker and who lacked the charisma that had characterized **Berlinguer**. Tempted by the possibilities opened, on the one hand, by unity on the left with **Craxi** and, on the other, by collaboration with **De Mita**'s left-Demochristians, Natta proved unable to make a clear choice or to articulate a clear party position.

NENNI, PIETRO (1891-1979). The dominant figure in the **Partito Socialista Italiano** (PSI) / Italian Socialist Party for much of this century, Pietro Nenni began his political career in his native province of Forlì (Emilia-Romagna) as a militant of the **Partito Repubblicana Italiano** (PRI) / Italian Republican Party. One of the organizers (**Benito Mussolini** was another) of a series of strikes and public protests against Italy's 1911 colonial war in **Libya**, Nenni was arrested and sentenced to several months' imprisonment. His opposition to war was not repeated in 1915, however. In line with his party, Nenni supported intervention and served at the front as an infantryman. This experience made him strongly critical of the PSI's hostility to the war. In 1919, Nenni was even one of the founding members of **Bologna**'s *fascio di combattimento* (Combat Veterans' League).

Instead of evolving into a fascist, however, his experience during the turbulent "red biennial" (1919-1921) caused him to reexamine his most fundamental ideological views and to edge toward reconciliation with the PSI. Nenni became a journalist for the PSI daily *L'Avanti!* in 1921 and, in December 1922, as editor of the paper, opposed the party leadership's attempts to woo Moscow by merging with the breakaway **Partito Comunista Italiano** (PCI) / Italian Communist Party. Believing, pragmatically, that the PSI should rather concentrate on rallying all of Italy's democratic forces against the common fascist enemy, Nenni became an isolated figure and, in 1925, was forced to resign from the paper's editorial board. The following year, he took refuge in France.

While in exile in Paris, Nenni was the architect of the reunification of the reformist and "maximalist" wings of the Italian socialist movement in 1930. He became party leader in 1933, and also editor of *L'Avanti!* Despite his past hostility to the PCI, Nenni supported the "Popular Front," fighting personally in the International Brigade in Spain. His anti-fascist activities were interrupted in 1941 when he was taken prisoner by the Germans and handed over to the Italian government, which imprisoned him on the island of Ponza (Campania). His daughter, Vittoria, was less fortunate: she died in Auschwitz in 1944.

Released from prison, Nenni took a leadership role in the **Comitato di Liberazione Nazionale**–Alta Italia (CLNAI) / National Liberation Committee-Northern Italy. Under his direction, the PSI—unlike the PCI—refused to join the cabinet of **Ivanoe Bonomi**. In April-May 1945, Nenni was the primary contender to head the new all-Italian government. The British viewed this prospect with frank horror, and **Ferruccio Parri** was eventually chosen as prime minister. Nenni did become vice premier and minister in charge of organizing the elections to the **Constituent Assembly** in the first administration formed by **Alcide De Gasperi** in December 1945.

The PSI fought the elections of June 1946 in the company of the PCI, emerging as the second-largest party in Italy after the **Democrazia Cristiana** (DC) / Christian Democracy Party, with 20 percent of the vote. Nenni had the sensitive post of foreign minister in De Gasperi's second administration, but was unable to follow a pro-Soviet foreign policy. Within a few months, the wily De Gasperi had reshuffled his government to exclude the left.

Nenni became increasingly convinced in the 1950s that the PSI had to assert its independence from the PCI. After regaining the party leadership in 1953, he seized the opportunity provided by the Soviet crushing of the Hungarian revolution in 1956 to inch away from the PCI and eventually, between 1960 and 1963, to join the DC in government. Nenni believed that the PSI's participation would lead to major changes in the structure of Italian society, but he overestimated the extent to which the PSI could make its voice count. Nenni was the principal architect of the failed attempt to merge the **Partito Socialista Democratico Italiano** (PSDI) / Italian Social Democratic Party with the PSI between 1966 and 1968. He died in **Rome** in 1979. *See also* Fernando Tambroni.

NEO-REALISM. The goal of neo-realist writers and artists was to represent ordinary working-class life faithfully, and find poetry in the lives of the poor and oppressed. This emphasis on working-class experience was influenced by the theories of the communist philosopher **Antonio Gramsci** who believed that culture in Italy had always been hegemonized by the elite, and that the communist movement needed to produce a "national-popular" literature of its own. The neo-realists were also influenced by the sometimes grim realism of American writers such as Steinbeck, Hemingway, and Dos Passos.

Among the film directors who worked in the neo-realist idiom were **Vittorio De Sica, Roberto Rossellini,** and **Luchino Visconti.** These directors used ordinary citizens in preference to established actors, allowed the use of dialect instead of literary Italian, and set the films in working-class settings.

The main subject matter of neo-realist novels and reportage was working-class and peasant life during the war, and novels about the resistance to the Nazis. **Carlo Levi, Primo Levi, Italo Calvino,** and **Cesare Pavese** are four remarkable writers on these themes.

Many of the leading intellectuals associated with neo-realism were socialists or communists, but almost without exception they found the **Partito Comunista Italiano** (PCI) / Italian Communist Party too insistent in its demands that their realism be transformed into socialist realism, that is, propaganda. The short-lived neo-realist literary periodical, *Il Politecnico*, was soon the target for ideologically motivated attacks by the leader of the PCI, **Palmiro Togliatti,** and by the PCI's stable of politically orthodox critics and

252 • Nicòtera, Giovanni

scholars. *Il Politecnico* was all but boycotted by the PCI and its
sympathizers and had to close in 1947.

By the early 1950s, the best neo-realist artists were chafing at the
genre's limits. Rossellini and Visconti increasingly made visually
beautiful films with psychological themes set (often) in upper-class
settings; Pavese's last novel before his suicide, *La Luna e i falò* (*The
Moon and the Bonfire*s, 1950), was introspective and nostalgic in
tone; Calvino increasingly became a *favolista*, or writer of fables.
Few of the Italian writers and directors of the first rank who emerged
in the 1950s were neo-realist in approach. For all neo-realism's
limits, however, in the hands of its finest artists, the suffering,
poverty, and endurance of the Italian working class was transmuted
into artistic form.

NICÒTERA, GIOVANNI (1828-1894). Born in Catanzaro (Calabria),
Giovanni Nicòtera was a hero of the struggle against absolutism in
the Kingdom of the Two Sicilies. In 1857 he was sentenced to death
for his part in the abortive attempt of a group of revolutionaries, led
by Carlo Pisacane, to raise an insurrection in southern Italy; this
sentence was commuted to life imprisonment on the isle of
Favignana, off Sicily. Nicòtera was rescued by **Garibaldi**'s forces in
June 1860.

Nicòtera was elected to **Parliament** in 1861, but he continued to
support Garibaldi's efforts to complete the reunification of Italy.
Nicòtera was at Garibaldi's side during the clash with the Italian
army in Aspromonte in 1862; in Garibaldi's successful campaign
against the Austrians in the Trentino in 1866; and at the disastrous
battle of Mentana in 1867.

Nicòtera gradually abandoned the radicalism of Garibaldi and
compromised with the Italian state. When the parliamentary left took
power in 1876, Nicòtera became minister of the interior under
Agostino Depretis. His support for Depretis did not extend to
accepting the policy of *trasformismo* and, during the 1880s, Nicòtera
was one of the leaders of the parliamentary opposition to Depretis's
center-right government. Nicòtera served as interior minister under
Di Rudinì in 1891-1892, and in his final years, the authoritarian and
nationalistic policies propounded by **Francesco Crispi** increasingly
attracted him.

NITTI, FRANCESCO SAVERIO (1868-1953). One of the few
politicians of national standing to emerge from the rural southern

region of Basilicata (another is **Emilio Colombo**), Francesco Saverio Nitti entered politics in 1904 after a career as a university teacher of jurisprudence. He served as a minister in the **Giolitti** governments from 1911 to 1914 and, in 1917, became minister of the treasury in the government of **Vittorio Emanuele Orlando**.

Nitti succeeded Orlando as prime minister in June 1919 and was forced to deal with a country that was on the point of institutional and social collapse. He vainly tried to hold together a territory ravaged by the economic costs of the war, the violence and nationalism of the disillusioned former soldiers enrolled in the *Fasci italiani di combattimento* (Italian Combattants' League, precursor of the **Partito Nazionale Fascista** (PNF) / National Fascist party), and the rising tide of working-class revolutionary syndicalism, but the effort was too much for him. His failure to deal with the challenge posed to his authority by **Gabriele D'Annunzio**'s seizure of Fiume in the summer of 1919 was symptomatic of his entire experience as prime minister. Nitti's professorial, abstract, rational approach to government was simply inadequate for the demands of the time. In June 1920, he was forced to hand over the reins of government to Giolitti.

Nitti was willing to give **fascism** a chance to prove itself, but his tolerance was not reciprocated. Forced to flee abroad on the eve of the 1924 elections, he spent the years of **Mussolini's** dictatorship in exile—and was even briefly held prisoner by the Nazis in 1943. He returned to Italy in 1945, and together with **Benedetto Croce**, **Vittorio Emanuele Orlando**, and **Ivanoe Bonomi** fought the elections of June 1946 under the colors of the so-called Unione Nazionale / National Union Party. Nitti was elected to the **Constituent Assembly,** but he was only able to play a marginal role in a Parliament dominated by the **Democrazia Cristiana** (DC) / Christian Democracy Party, the **Partito Repubblicana Italiano** (PSI) / Italian Socialist Party, and the **Partito Comunista Italiano** (PCI) / Italian Communist Party.

Nitti was made a life senator in 1948. He died in **Rome** in 1953. In addition to his long political career, Nitti was the author of several interesting, if not particularly profound or original, works of political philosophy during his years in exile.

NOBEL PRIZE. Thirteen Italian citizens have won prizes in the various disciplines (chemistry, economics, literature, medicine, peace, physics) recognized by the Swedish foundation. The Nobel prize for literature was awarded to the Tuscan writer, **Giosuè Carducci**, in 1906; to the Sardinian, **Grazia Deledda**, in 1926; to **Luigi Pirandello**, in 1934; to the poet, **Salvatore Quasimodo**, in 1959; to **Eugenio Montale**, in 1975; and to **Dario Fo**, in 1997.

Three Italians have won the Nobel prize for physics. **Guglielmo Marconi** took the prize in 1909, **Enrico Fermi** in 1938, and, most recently, Carlo Rubbia, whose research has mostly been carried out in the United States and Switzerland, won in 1984.

The Nobel prize for chemistry was won by Giulio Natta of Milan's Politecnico University in 1963; in 1986, Rita Levi-Montalcini won the prize for medicine. She was the second Italian to win this prize. In 1906, Camillo Golgi, a pioneer in the field of neurology, shared the prize for medicine with the Spanish researcher Ramon y Cajal.

The Nobel peace prize was awarded to the radical journalist Enrico Teodoro Moneta in December 1907 for his work as editor of the pacifist journal *Vita Internazionale*. In addition to these Italian citizens, two Italian emigres to the United States, Emilio Segrè and Franco Modigliani, won the prizes for physics and economics in 1959 and 1985, respectively.

NORTH ATLANTIC TREATY ORGANIZATION (NATO). Italy's role in the North Atlantic Treaty Organization, to which she was admitted in 1949, has been to provide unquestioning support for its initiatives. Equipped by the United States, Italian forces have been a reliably subordinate NATO partner. The Mediterranean Command of the organization is in **Naples,** and NATO bases began in the 1950s to appear in the north, center, and south, welcomed by the NATO chain of command as advance bases to meet any challenge in the Middle East or the Balkans, welcomed by local communities as a source of income. The cadre at *Italian* bases, on the other hand, was to train Italian conscripts during their 18-month *naja* or compulsory-service "training period."

Much Catholic opinion in the immediately post-war years was ready to support a neutralist Italy. But as the cold war unfolded and the dramatic choice came to be between a Marxist and a Western-oriented future, all the parties fell into line. The **Tambroni** experiment left the **Democrazia Cristiana** (DC) / Christian Democracy Party, under **Moro**'s skillful leadership, with no choice beyond "**opening to the left**." Whether to accept that proposition was **Pietro Nenni**'s decision to make. At the **Partito Socialista Italiano**

(PSI) / Italian Socialist Party Congress in 1961, the determination to form a government with the DC necessarily involved embracing the NATO alliance as well. Equidistance between East and West was no longer the Socialist position.

In December 1979, Italy was one of the first NATO members to accept cruise missiles on her soil despite the risk that this initiative presented in the event of hostilities. Italy has also participated both in NATO and non-NATO overseas enterprises (Beirut, Somalia) and cooperated in Bosnia, where she sent 2,100 **Bersaglieri** to Gorazde. These initiatives have been taken despite Italy's standing—with Luxembourg—at the bottom of any ranking of NATO members by proportion of gross domestic product dedicated to military expenditures.

-O-

OCCHETTO, ACHILLE (1936-). Although born in **Turin**, Achille Occhetto has represented **Palermo** (**Sicily**) in the Chamber of Deputies since 1976. Elected to the central committee of the **Partito Comunista Italiano** (PCI) / Italian Communist Party in 1979, it was to Occhetto that the PCI turned when it entered in crisis in the late 1980s. In July 1988, he was chosen to replace a sick **Alessandro Natta** as party secretary by the central committee, a post in which he was confirmed by the Eighteenth Congress of the PCI in March 1989. At this congress, the party, at Occhetto's behest, did away with all references in the party statute to Marx, Lenin, and former leader **Palmiro Togliatti,** and greatly expanded its leadership cohort to allow the influx of new, more reform-minded individuals. In November 1989, after the collapse of the Berlin wall, Occhetto realized that these changes were insufficient and led the process of renewal by which the PCI was transformed between 1989 and 1991 into the **Partito Democratico della Sinistra** (PDS) / Democratic Party of the Left.

In the general elections of March 1994, Occhetto was the architect of the so-called "Progressive Alliance," a motley collection of left-wing parties that did not possess enough general appeal to win centrist votes. Although the PDS improved its individual share of the vote, the alliance as a whole fared poorly. In elections to the European Parliament three months later, the PDS was defeated even more clearly. After this second rebuff, Achille Occhetto resigned as secretary of the PDS and was replaced by **Massimo D'Alema.**

Occhetto's fundamental vision was to turn the PCI into a radical, campaigning movement that would expand and improve the conditions of women, immigrants, and the lowest paid. In the highly regulated, high taxation Italy of the 1990s, this hope was destined to failure. The magnitude of his achievement, however, has been understated by many commentators. Had Occhetto not had the drive to make the necessary break with communism in 1989, the PCI would have seemed an unbearable anachronism in the Italian political crisis of 1992-1993. *See also* Partito Comunista Italiano.

OLIVE TREE COALITION (Ulivo). This name was chosen by the broad coalition of a dozen center-left parties assembled, under the leadership of **Romano Prodi**, in the spring of 1995. The Olive Tree Coalition governed Italy between the general elections of April 1996, when it obtained 284 seats in the Chamber of Deputies, and the government crisis of autumn 1998 when Prodi's cabinet was brought down by the contrary vote of the **Partito di Rifondazione Comunista** (PRC) / Communist Refoundation Party, which had previously provided the Coalition with a slender parliamentary majority.

Despite the difficulties caused by the Olive Tree Coalition's heterogeneous character—conservatives, ex-communists, socialists, environmentalists, neo-liberals, and Catholic centrists were all represented within the government—it should be said that Prodi's cabinet scored some useful policy triumphs. Laws proposing the devolution of power to local tiers of government were enacted in 1997, an overdue reform of the education system was begun, public aid was directed toward economic blackspots in southern Italy. Most importantly of all, public finances were brought under control by a prolonged period of austerity and Italy, as a consequence, was allowed to participate in the single European currency, the Euro, from 1999 onward. The Olive Tree Coalition significantly fell apart once membership of the Euro had been attained. As a movement, it had never achieved the cohesion necessary to replace the political parties which composed it. *See also* Maastricht, Treaty of; Partito di Rifondazione Comunista; Romano Prodi.

OPENING TO THE LEFT (*l'apertura a sinistra*). This term describes attempts made in the early 1960s by several leaders of the **Democrazia Cristiana** (DC) / Christian Democracy Party to lure the **Partito Socialista Italiano** (PSI) / Italian Socialist Party out of its alliance with the **Partito Comunista Italiano** (PCI) / Italian Communist Party and to broaden the consensus in the Italian polity to include the socialists as representatives of the workers. The ultras on the left assert that its "real" purpose was to divide the working class' loyalties, setting their most credible representatives against one another to the political advantage of the ruling center. Italian political inventiveness is illustrated by such post-war devices as the opening to the left, **Eurocommunism**, the *compromesso storico*, and "concertation" or collaborative planning among industry, government, and labor.

Dealings between **Aldo Moro**, then secretary of the DC, and the PCI were abruptly altered when he was kidnapped and murdered. His courtship of the communists themselves aimed either at enlarging the opening to the left or, alternatively, at furthering the emasculation of the working-class parties in order to retain the status quo. Which explanation one accepts is dependent on one's basic political persuasion and level of optimism.

Those who accept the conventional view that Moro really intended to maneuver the working class, through their representatives, into accepting the status quo are divided. On the one hand are those who see this as a progressive move and, on the other, are those so cynical as to see it as a device for retaining a system in which the Demochristian party remained dominant and in which change would continually be postponed and delayed. *See also* Giovanni Gronchi; Aldo Moro; Fernando Tambroni.

ORLANDO, LEOLUCA (1948-). One of the most flamboyant personalities of recent Italian politics, Leoluca Orlando made his reputation as a reformist **Democrazia Cristiana** (DC) / Christian Democracy Party mayor of **Palermo**. An academic lawyer, Orlando entered Sicilian politics in the 1970s and swiftly became one of the most outspoken critics of the DC's established leadership on the island. In 1985, he became mayor of Palermo for the first time, at the head of a conventional five-party alliance that included all the DC's national allies. In 1987, he broke with the **Partito Socialista Italiano** (PSI) / Italian Socialist Party and formed a new administration that included the Greens and representatives from the numerous civic renewal groups and anti-**mafia** initiatives that had sprung up in the city during the 1980s. In 1989, he added the **Partito Comunista Italiano** (PCI) / Italian Communist Party to his majority. This so-called "Palermo spring" won Orlando national attention; his increasingly unambiguous accusations that leading DC politicians such as **Giulio Andreotti** were collaborating with the mafia made him notorious. Orlando became a hero for Italy's liberal press, but some skeptics, notably the Sicilian writer **Leonardo Sciascia**, regarded him as an opportunist who was making his career as a "professional opponent of the mafia."

Orlando broke with the DC in 1990 and launched a new political party, **La Rete**, in October of that year. Orlando was elected to the Chamber of Deputies in April 1992 with an enormous number of personal preference votes and, in November 1993, won the mayoralty of Palermo for La Rete by a plebiscite-like 75 percent majority, but his party has failed to take root outside of Palermo. Orlando, who once seemed destined to become a national political figure, and who was the beneficiary of much international media attention, now increasingly seems destined to remain an essentially regional politician.

ORLANDO, VITTORIO EMANUELE (1860-1952). A Sicilian professor of law, he was a member of the pre-fascist cabinets of **Giolitti**, **Salandra**, and **Boselli** ranging from the Ministry of Public Education to Justice to Interior. In 1917, he became prime minister himself when the **Caporetto** disaster brought about Boselli's resignation. A better risk-calculator than his predecessor, he ordered General Diaz (**General Cadorna's** replacement) to counter-attack in late October. By the end of the month, Italian forces with British reinforcements inflicted a major defeat on the Austrian army at Vittorio Veneto and, on November 5 (nearly a week before the armistice in France), the guns were silenced on the Austrian front. Orlando was called the "President of Victory."

Italy's role in formulating the settlement was limited to the northeastern Italian borders with Austria and with the new state of Yugoslavia. President Wilson, showing more hubris than tact, sought the support of the Italian public for the settlement by a visit to Italy. The warmth of the reception given the American president by the Italian public so angered Orlando, resentful of this direct appeal to public opinion over his head, that he led the Italian delegation in storming out of the French capital and retiring to **Rome**, assuming that the Allies would offer terms to persuade him to return. Instead, Orlando and **Sonnino** eventually returned to Paris barely in time for the German signatures.

Orlando's resentments were nourished by the question of Fiume

(Rijeka), which had not been mentioned in the 1915 **Treaty of London** (which neither the Serbs nor the United States had signed). In the end, Italy got **Trieste** but not Dalmatia; and Fiume became a free state (later to be occupied in **D'Annunzio**'s famous private invasion). The Treaty of Lausanne with Turkey (July 1923) confirmed Italian sovereignty over the Dodecanese Islands, exercised de facto since 1912.

The perception that the settlement had been mishandled and Italy denied her just deserts led to Orlando being turned out by **Parliament** in a humiliatingly lopsided vote, 262-78. His successor, **Francesco Nitti,** had the sense to abort a naval expedition to annex Soviet Georgia that Orlando had devised.

In 1924, hoping to be able to effect the embourgeoisement of **Mussolini,** Orlando consented to being included on a joint electoral list. Within a year, he realized the futility of his hopes, broke with Mussolini, and resigned from the Chamber of Deputies and from all political activity. Like many liberal leaders, he found the fascists repugnant; but less so than the two mass parties, Socialist and Catholic, which threatened Liberal Party primacy.

When, in 1931, the regime obliged university professors to pledge allegiance to fascism, only 11 in the entire system refused and resigned their posts. One of them was Professor Orlando. In 1944, the **Bonomi** government named Orlando president of the Chamber of Deputies. In 1948, he became a life senator by right, a position he held until his death. *See also* Giovanni Gentile; Partito Popolare Italiano; Partito Socialista; World War I.

-P-

PADANA, PIANURA. The area drained by Italy's longest river, the Po, the *Pianura padana* (the Po Plains) is Italy's industrial and commercial heartland. Its biggest manufacturing centers (**Turin, Milan, Bologna**, Brescia, Varese) are among the busiest in Europe. Income per head is extremely high—over $24,000 on average—and unemployment, which has rarely exceeded 4 percent in recent years, is far below the Italian national average. Per person productivity in manufacturing has been estimated to be higher than anywhere in the world except the United States. Apart from the giant **FIAT** car company, most of the industrial production of the region is concentrated in small- and medium-sized companies specializing in a vast range of niche products for export as well as domestic consumption. Ceramics, textiles, optical equipment, and food processing are just some of the major providers of employment in the region, which is the size of Denmark.

Politically, the region has been traditionally divided between the "red zones," where the **Partito Comunista Italiano** (PCI) / Italian Communist Party held sway (Bologna, Parma, Turin), and the "white zones," dominated by the **Democrazia Cristiana** (DC) / Christian Democracy Party (Milan, Brescia, Verona, Vicenza, Padua). To a certain extent, this right-left division still holds. Lombardy and the western parts of Venetia have voted for the **Lega Nord** (LN) / Northern League and **Forza Italia** since 1993; Emilia-Romagna and, to a lesser extent, Turin and its surroundings remain bastions of the **Partito Democratico della Sinistra** (PDS) / Democratic Party of the left. Despite being only the third party in the region, the Northern League has announced its intention to bring into being an independent republic called "Padania." This project is very unlikely to be realized, but it does show that some political figures think to gain from appeals to self-conscious local pride in being both a political and an economic model for the rest of Italy.

The countryside is flat and uninteresting, and is covered by thick fogs from November to April. Cities such as Verona (with its remarkable Roman amphitheater), Cremona (with its covered arcades and small workshops where craftsmen continue to construct violins using techniques not significantly different from those employed by Stradivarius), Vicenza (with its superb Palladian architecture), Ravenna (with its Roman mosaics), Padua, and Bologna (with their ancient universities) are of great artistic and historical interest. The region's cooking, with Parma and Bologna as the undisputed gastronomic capitals, is internationally famous. *See also* Lega Nord.

PALERMO. The largest city in **Sicily** with over 700,000 inhabitants, Palermo is the island's political center and principal port. Founded around 700 B.C. by the Phoenicians, Palermo is one of the oldest cities in the world. Part of Carthage from 480 B.C. to when it became part of the Roman Empire in 254 B.C., Palermo has endured wave after wave of foreign conquest. The Vandals, Goths, Byzantines, Arabs, and Normans all conquered the city after the fall of the Roman Empire. The last two invasions, in particular, left an indelible architectural impression on the city. The "Palace of the Normans," one of the finest buildings in Italy, is a ninth-century Arab building that was restructured by the Normans in the twelfth century.

The city's modern history can be said to start in 1738, when the city became a possession of the Bourbons. In 1820, Palermo revolted against rule from **Naples** (the capital of the Bourbon Kingdom of the Two Sicilies), but the populist uprising was put down by troops sent by the constitutional liberal government of Naples, which itself was crushed by the Austrians shortly afterward. In 1831, there were further riots in Palermo against Bourbon rule, and then, in 1848, an insurrection in Palermo was the trigger that set off the famous "year of revolutions" throughout Europe. In 1860, the city's people rebelled again, ensuring victory for the redshirts of **Giuseppe Garibaldi**.

The contemporary city has been scarred by persistent misgovernment and by the pervasive presence of the **mafia**. Probably nowhere in Italy was the link between the political class and organized crime so strong. Since the early 1970s, in particular, Palermo has been the scene of a dozen so-called "excellent crimes"—the murders of leading figures whether judges, politicians or police commanders opposed to the mafia. The death by bombing of **Giovanni Falcone** in April 1992 is the most notorious killing of this kind.

PANNELLA, MARCO (1930-). The historic leader of the **Partito Radicale** (PR) / Radical Party, Marco Pannella is a political showman who has nevertheless changed Italian history. He cut his political teeth as a student activist in the 1950s, and was one of the PR's founding members in 1956. He became leader in 1962 and for the last 35 years has been a constant presence in Italian political life, campaigning for changes to the **divorce** laws, for a more liberal abortion law, for electoral reform, and for action against a vast range of domestic and international abuses and injustices. The important constitutional role occupied by **referendums** in Italy is largely due to Pannella's single-minded use of the referendum as an instrument for achieving social reforms.

Pannella was first elected to Parliament in 1976, and led the PR's minuscule delegation in the Chamber of Deputies until the 1992 elections, which the PR fought under the name of the *Lista Pannella*. During his leadership—though reign may well be a more fitting description—the PR was regarded as a libertarian fringe group, and as such it became popular with the urban, university-educated young. In 1994, however, after the collapse of the **Democrazia Cristiana** (DC) / Christian Democracy Party and its system of dominance,

Pannella allied his movement with **Silvio Berlusconi**'s right-wing coalition, and engaged in a spirited defense of the indicted leaders of the old regime. This perverse move has robbed the veteran radical of credibility with his electoral constituency, and Pannella's fortunes have ebbed visibly.

Pannella nevertheless adds his own particular spice to the already highly flavored dish of Italian politics. His volcanic television monologues, his penchant for chaining himself to railings, his frequent hunger strikes, the radical party candidacy of Cicciolina, the porno star, have made him one of Italy's most recognized public figures. His most recent escapade was to hold a cannabis "smoke-in" outside the Chamber of Deputies in a bid to draw attention to what he regards as Italy's absurdly restrictive drug laws. *See also* Partito Radicale; Women in Contemporary Italy; Referendums.

PAPACY. Since Italy became a unified nation in 1861, there have been ten Popes. All but one (the current incumbent, John Paul II) have been Italian. The moral teachings and political opinions of these men have exercised an enormous influence upon Italian politics and society.

Pius IX (Pope 1846-1878). Giovanni Maria Mastai Ferretti was born in Senigallia (the Marches) in 1792. Initially regarded as a liberal, he was forced to flee from **Rome** during the 1848 revolution. Restored to his throne by French troops in 1849, he became a rigid conservative. Chiefly remembered for pronouncing the doctrine of Papal infallibility in 1869, he rejected all attempts by the Italian state to reach a compromise on the role of the church within Italy after the occupation of Rome.

Leo XIII (Pope 1878-1903). Vincenzo Gioacchino dei conti Pecci was born near Rome in 1810. More genuinely liberal than his predecessor, he nevertheless refused to acknowledge the authority of the Italian state over Rome and defined himself as the "prisoner in the **Vatican**." He barred Catholics from participating in Italian political life. His main doctrinal innovation was the **encyclical** *Rerum Novarum*, which criticized free market economics as well as socialism.

Pius X (Pope 1903-1914). Giuseppe Melchiorre Sarto was born in the province of Treviso (Venetia) in 1835. In terms of his influence on Italian life, he is chiefly important for giving his tacit consent to the so-called "**Gentiloni pact**," by which the church indicated a list of conditions that liberal candidates should respect in order to be assured of Catholics' votes. He was sanctified in 1954.

Benedict XV (Pope 1914-1922). Giacomo Della Chiesa was born in Genoa (Liguria) in 1854. He is most famous for his condemnation of **World War I** as a "useless slaughter" in 1917. Within Italy, he promoted the formation of the **Partito Popolare Italiana** (PPI) / Italian People's Party in 1919.

Pius XI (Pope 1922-1939). Ambrogio Damiano Achilli Ratti was born near **Milan** in 1857. As Pope, his primary duty was that of maintaining the church's independence from the fascist regime. The **Lateran pacts**, signed in February 1929, succeeded in this objective though liberal Catholics believed that they made the church an accomplice of **Mussolini's** repressive rule. Violently anti-communist, Pius XI backed the fascist side during the **Spanish Civil War** (1936-1939).

Pius XII (Pope 1939-1958). Eugenio Pacelli was born in Rome in 1876. He strove to keep Italy out of **World War II** and preached a negotiated end to the conflict at every opportunity. Widely criticized for not having condemned Hitler's persecution of the Jews with sufficient vigor, Pius undertook an anti-communist crusade after 1945, interfering directly in Italian domestic politics by threatening to excommunicate communist voters and by mobilizing the clergy in support of the **Democrazia Cristiana** (DC) / Christian Democracy Party.

John XXIII (Pope 1958-1963). Angelo Giuseppe Roncalli was born in Bergamo (Lombardy) in 1881. As Pope, he initiated a period of liberalization for the church. He prompted the liturgical and doctrinal renewal of the Second Vatican Council between 1961 and 1965, giving it the specific task of "enabling the Church to contribute more usefully to solving the problems of modern life." Domestically, he sought to disengage the Vatican from Italian politics. His popularity soared after he visited Italian prisons and showed a humility at one with his humble origins. Politically, he followed a policy of détente toward the communist bloc.

Paul VI (Pope 1963-1978). Giovanni Battista Montini was born in Brescia (Lombardy) in 1897. Paul was the first Pope to make pastoral visits overseas, visiting Israel in 1964, and several other countries in the following years. Within Italy, he refrained from turning issues such as **divorce** and abortion into a crusade, while affirming the church's objections to liberalization in these matters.

John Paul I (Pope 1978). Albino Luciani was born in the province of Belluno in 1912. A much-loved figure who spurned traditional pomp and ceremony during his investiture, John Paul was expected to renew the policies of Pope John. His sudden death in September 1978, after just 34 days as Pope, put an end to these hopes.

John Paul II (Pope 1978-). Karol Wojtyla was born in Wadowice (Poland) in 1920. He is the first non-Italian Pope since the Dutchman Hadrian VI (1521-1523). He played a significant role in supporting Poland's Solidarnosč, which accelerated the disintegration of the Warsaw Pact system and of even Soviet communism. Despite his theological conservatism, John Paul has won rueful respect from progressives in Italy for his opposition to the Gulf War and for his strictures against the materialism of modern life. He was the target of an unsuccessful assassination attempt in May 1981. *See also* Encyclicals; Vatican.

PAPINI, GIOVANNI (1881-1956). A self-taught intellectual of formidable energy and power, but little precision, Giovanni Papini was a tireless editor and literary entrepreneur. Nevertheless, he is chiefly remembered today for his paean of praise for **fascism**, *Italia mia* (*My Italy*, 1941).

Born in **Florence**, Papini came to public attention as a literary figure between 1903 and 1907 as the editor of the little magazine, *Leonardo*, and as a contributor to *Il Regno*, a review edited by **Enrico Corradini**. A violent nationalist, Papini was also attracted by pragmatism, which, unlike American philosophers such as John Dewey and William James, he interpreted as an ideology of power that would lead to the "twilight of the philosophers" rather than as a practical tool for the achievement of social reform.

After experimenting with nationalism, **futurism**, and pragmatism, Papini turned to the church, becoming a devout Catholic in the 1920s. He also started his final literary venture, *Frontespizio*, and warmed somewhat to **Mussolini**. After he was invited to join the **Accademia d'Italia** (1937), he became an ardent admirer. *Italia mia* was one of the low points of intellectual fellow-traveling with Mussolini's regime. A tirade of invective against plutocratic Britain, the sinister forces of freemasonry and Jewry, and a plea for Italy to achieve her historical role and reemerge as the guiding hand in European civilization, the book was a study in the power of nationalist ideology to detach its followers from the moorings of common sense. By the end of the war, however, the Florentine intellectual had come to realize that the irrationalist philosophy he had propagated throughout his life had been one of the causes of the immense destruction that was all around him. He did not support the **Salò republic.** Papini died in Florence in 1956.

PARALLEL WAR. At the time of the formation of the "Pact of Steel" (May 6-7, 1939) Italian General Ugo Cavallero gave German Foreign Minister von Ribbentrop a memorandum for Hitler from **Mussolini**—the Duce—informing him that Germany's chief ally would not be able to enter a European war at any time before 1942 unless Germany agreed to replace the military supplies that Italy had used in **Abyssinia** (Ethiopia) and in the **Spanish Civil War.** Mussolini wanted to conduct, at a moment of his own choosing, a war parallel to Hitler's but independent of Hitler's attempt to consolidate Germany's position in northern Europe. Italy's ambitions focused on the Mediterranean and the Balkans.

German moves into Slovakia (March 1939) induced Mussolini to anticipate his planned invasion of **Albania**, the better to demonstrate to Hitler his capacity for autonomous action. When Hitler made war on Poland and within weeks had forced her to submit, Mussolini saw the prospect loom of a reordering of Europe's power relations without Italy's participation. Hence, he declared war on Britain and France on June 10, 1940, so that "a few thousand [Italian] dead" would entitle him to a seat at the peace settlement that he believed to be imminent.

Subsequently, in response to Germany's swift move into Rumania in early October 1940, Italy undertook an invasion of Greece (October 28, 1940) that went so badly that Germany had to intervene to prevent a total debacle. (In December, the Greeks had broken the Italian line, occupied southern Albania, and taken thousands of prisoners.) Not only did the German reinforcements reverse the Axis' fortunes in Greece, but they put an end to Mussolini's ambitions in the Eastern Mediterranean and the Balkans. The war was no longer to be fought separately: henceforth, Italy was to be more a German vassal than an ally. *See also* Foreign Policy; World War II.

PARETO, VILFREDO (1848-1923). One of the most important economists of the nineteenth century, Vilfredo Pareto was also a challenging sociologist and political scientist. For economic theorists, Pareto is chiefly remembered as the inventor of the so-called "Pareto optimalization" in 1906, which describes efficient and inefficient states in a market economy. Pareto was one of the leading proponents of laissez-faire theories in late-nineteenth-century Italy, especially after the Italian state's adoption of protectionism in 1887. He did not shirk political polemic: in June 1896, in a devastating article, he ironically attacked numerous leading politicians, and in particular **Antonio Starabba di Rudinì**, as heading a "ministry of gentlemen," for not having investigated the role played by political corruption in the **Banca Romana** scandal.

As a sociologist, Pareto's reputation rests upon his colossal (2,000-page) *Trattato di sociologia generale* (*Treatise of General Sociology*, 1916). The central theme of his work in social theory was that human history is nothing other than a perpetual struggle between elites to obtain power or to conserve it. Political ideologies (such as liberalism or conservatism or socialism) are merely elaborate justifications with which the elites mask their intentions from others and even from themselves. Contemporary Europe, moreover, Pareto believed, was guided by a uniquely inept ruling class that did not even defend its own values with energy and was destined to yield to the rising power of the working class.

Pareto's academic career was largely spent in Switzerland. He took the chair in political economy at the University of Lausanne in 1893. In his final years, he lived at Celigny on the shores of Lake Geneva. He died there in 1923.

PARLIAMENT. The Italian Parliament consists of a Camera dei Deputati (Chamber of Deputies) of 630 members elected by universal suffrage and the Senato (Senate) of 315 elected members plus life senators (ex-presidents of the republic and up to five presidential nominees named for "social, scientific, artistic, or literary" merit). Only citizens over 25 can vote in Senate elections; those who have reached their majority (at 18) may vote for deputies.

The Italian Parliament sits for a maximum of five years although the president can dissolve the legislature if he sees an election as the only way to resolve a crisis—understood in a parliamentary system as meaning that the government of the day is no longer able to command a parliamentary majority. Both chambers of Parliament must give an initial vote of confidence to a government before it can take office. Meeting in joint session, the Parliament also chooses the president of the republic for a seven-year term, and five of the 15 members of the Constitutional Court.

To calm the fears inspired by a strong executive, and the better to ensure that level of representation that **fascism** had denied, the writers of the **Constitution of 1948** revived the pre-fascist parliamentary system with only a few changes. Parliament was given strong powers to curb the executive (including secret voting, which meant that the power of party whips to coerce their deputies into obedience of the party line was greatly reduced), and an extremely representative system of proportional representation was adopted. In a society as divided as Italy is by region, economic function, and class, this decision ensured that politics would be conducted by multi-party coalitions.

As in all coalition systems, the Italian government's capacity to undertake bold initiatives has thus been limited by what a parliamentary majority is willing to support. The emblematic feature of post-war Italian democracy has been the *crisi di governo*, intra-government rows over policy or **patronage**, which have usually ended with the reshuffling of cabinet seats and a familiar face at the head of the executive. Since 1945, the average Italian government has lasted less than one year. Critics call this state of affairs "assemblyism" and—pointing to the failure of the third and fourth republics in France—argue that allowing Parliament to hold the executive hostage in this way is anachronistic in a modern state. Moreover, such a weakened executive has emboldened the bureaucracy to create virtual fiefdoms independent of all supervision or coordination.

Between 1946 and 1994, the parties of Italy's Parliament can be grouped into four main categories: the Catholic, the lay non-socialist, the Marxist, and the regionalist. The **Democrazia Cristiana** (DC) / Christian Democracy Party, before the corruption scandals in the 1990s, regularly received almost 40 percent of the vote. The lay parties polled less than 15 percent, and the Marxist subculture usually polled somewhat over 40 percent of the electorate. Since both the neo-fascists and the communists were regarded as "anti-system" parties, coalitions had to be built around the dominant DC.

The current Parliament, despite the partial renunciation of proportional representation since the 1994 elections, is more thronged than ever with mini-parties. The **Olive Tree Coalition** depends upon the parliamentary support of the neo-communist **Partito di Rifondazione Comunista** (PRC) / Communist Refoundation Party. It is faced by an opposition determined to use every one of Parliament's many permissible powers of obstruction to block the government's legislative program, especially in budgetary allotments for pensions and health care. Not surprisingly, voices demanding reform are once again heard. *See also* Electoral Laws.

PARRI, FERRUCCIO (1890-1981). Born near **Turin**, Parri fought bravely in **World War I**, and was wounded on three occasions. He proved equally brave as an uncompromising anti-fascist. In December 1926, together with **Carlo Rosselli** and **Alessandro Pertini**, he helped **Filippo Turati** to escape from Italy, and he was one of the organizers of the clandestine movement **Giustizia e libertà**. In October 1930, he was arrested in **Milan** and was sentenced to a period of *confino*. At the end of 1941, Parri acted as the coordinator of the negotiations that led to the formation of the **Partito d'Azione** (PdA) / Action Party in June 1942.

Parri was active both as a diplomat and as a commander during the German occupation. In December 1944, on behalf of the **Comitato di Liberazione Nazionale-Alta Italia** (CLNAI) / National Liberation Committee-Northern Italy, he signed the agreement by which the British agreed to furnish the partisans operating in northern Italy with arms and money in exchange for a commitment to post-war disarmament and recognition of the government approved by the Allies. As "Partisan Maurizio," he was one of the heroes of the popular military struggle against the Germans. In January 1945, he was arrested by the Nazis in Milan but was saved from certain death when the Allies required his restitution as a sign of German good faith in secret surrender talks that began in March 1945.

After liberation, the British and Americans realized that they had to respect the "wind from the North" and incorporate the main partisan parties into the provisional government. In June 1945, Parri, whose politics alarmed the British, but who was personally greatly esteemed by the Allies, became post-war Italy's first prime minister. His government, however, lasted only until November, when the **Partito Liberale Italiano** (PLI) / Italian Liberal Party and the **Democrazia Cristiana** (DC) / Christian Democracy Party —alarmed by the influence of the left in Parri's administration—withdrew their ministers.

In February 1946, Parri's dislike of the increasingly pro-communist position of the PdA led him to join with **Ugo La Malfa** to form the so-called Concentramento Democratico Repubblicano / Democratic Republican Concentration. After receiving just 97,000 votes in the 1946 elections to the **Constituent Assembly**, Parri and La Malfa became members of the **Partito Repubblicano Italiano**

(PRI) / Italian Republican Party. In 1953, however, Parri broke with the PRI over its support for an electoral reform known as the "swindle law." In the subsequent election, Parri's Unità Popolare / Popular Unity party obtained 170,000 votes, which tipped the balance and ensured that the swindle law's provisions never came into effect. In 1955, Parri received over 300 votes in the first ballot for the presidency, though eventually **Giovanni Gronchi** was elected. In March 1963, he was made senator for life. He died on December 8, 1981, in **Rome**. *See also* Electoral Laws.

PARTITO COMUNISTA ITALIANO (PCI) / Italian Communist Party. Founded in 1921 by a breakaway faction of the **Partito Socialista Italiano** (PSI) / Italian Socialist Party. The new party's first leader was **Amadeo Bordiga**, but his doctrinaire approach led to his substitution in 1926 by **Antonio Gramsci**. Gramsci's successor as party leader was **Palmiro Togliatti**.

Togliatti returned to Italy from his Comintern exile in the Soviet Union in 1944. Under his guidance, the PCI cooperated fully with the conservative governments of **Pietro Badoglio** and **Ivanoe Bonomi** established in Allied-occupied Italy, and after the war participated in the first two governments of **Alcide De Gasperi**. The international situation dictated this moderate line: Stalin and Churchill had agreed that Italy would fall within the British sphere of interest, and British troops would have crushed any overtly revolutionary activity, but Togliatti seems to have taken conciliation beyond what was necessary. The Italian state was not cleansed of former fascist functionaries; progressive taxation reforms were not introduced; the peasants of southern Italy were denied immediate relief. In March 1947, De Gasperi reshuffled his government to exclude the PCI and the PSI without having made any concession of substance to the working class. On the other hand, under Togliatti the PCI became Italy's largest mass party, with nearly two million members, establishing its claim to being the authentic voice of Italian workers.

In international policy, the PCI was closely linked to the USSR. The party defended the Soviet takeover of Eastern Europe, organized immense demonstrations against Italian membership in the **North Atlantic Treaty Organization** (NATO) and the American intervention in Korea, and greeted the news of the death of Stalin with an outpouring of public grief. Only after Khrushchev's secret speech to the Twentieth Congress of the Soviet Communist Party in 1956, admitting the scale of Stalin's repressions for the first time, did a serious debate begin about the totalitarian character of the USSR. This debate heated up after the Soviet repression of the Hungarian uprising in the same year. Togliatti backed the Soviet Union, but tens of thousands of party members, especially intellectuals, resigned their membership in the wake of these events.

The PCI shifted perceptibly toward a more moderate position in international affairs after Togliatti's death in 1964. The new leader, **Luigi Longo,** was outspoken in his condemnation of the Soviet Union's 1968 repression in Czechoslovakia. In domestic policy, the decade was dominated by a major theoretical debate between the party's left and right wings. **Pietro Ingrao** on the left argued that the PCI should democratize its internal politics while the right-wing's leader, **Giorgio Amendola**, wanted the PCI to merge with the PSI around a platform of social democratic reforms. The party seemed to be becoming incurably conservative.

Under the leadership of **Enrico Berlinguer**, there was hope that the PCI would achieve a historic *sorpasso* (overtaking) and obtain more votes than the **Democrazia Cristiana** (DC) / Christian Democracy Party. In the event, neither party could form a government, thus the compromise reached allowed the DC to head the government with the PCI's parliamentary support. In the next elections (1979), the party was relegated to its familiar opposition role. By now, the PCI had become a "Eurocommunist" party, which no longer accepted Moscow's primacy and was openly critical of human rights' abuses in the Soviet bloc.

After Berlinguer's death in 1984, he was succeeded by the intelligent but bureaucratic **Alessandro Natta**, who let the party drift until a disaster in the 1987 general election compelled change. The party chose a dynamic young leader, **Achille Occhetto,** and at the Eighteenth Party Congress in March 1989 abandoned all references to Marx, Lenin, and Togliatti in its party statutes.

The collapse of the Soviet client states in Eastern Europe prompted Occhetto to announce (November 14, 1989) that he intended to turn the PCI into a leftist party "new even in name." By February 3, 1991, Occhetto had a large majority for replacing the PCI with the **Partito Democratico della Sinistra** (PDS) / Democratic Party of the Left. A minority group, unable to renounce the link with communism, formed the **Partito di Rifondazione Comunista** (PRC) / Communist Refoundation Party on the same day. *See also* Enrico Berlinguer; Armando Cossutta; Compromesso Storico; Eurocommunism; Palmiro Togliatti.

PARTITO D'AZIONE (PdA) / Action Party. The PdA was founded in May 1942 by a diverse group of radicals, liberals, libertarians, and socialists. Many former members of **Giustizia e Libertà** joined the ranks of the new formation, as did some liberal communists. From the beginning, the party was gravely divided internally over points of political principle. It did have three main areas of common ground, however: it was anti-fascist, opposed to the bureaucratic and totalitarian form of communism practiced in the Soviet Union, and violently anti-monarchical. Unlike the **Partito Comunista Italiano** (PCI) / Italian Communist Party, the PdA refused to join the wartime governments set up in Allied-occupied territory by **Pietro Badoglio** and **Ivanoe Bonomi** in the latter stages of the war. Instead the PdA, via its military arm, the "Justice and Liberty Brigade," threw itself into the partisan struggle and bore a disproportionate share of the fighting against the Germans and their fascist allies. In all, the PdA contributed over 30,000 partisans, perhaps a fifth or a quarter of those active in the partisan struggle, and they suffered heavy casualties: more than 4,000 were killed in action. Only the PCI made a greater contribution to the domestic Italian war against nazism.

When the war was over, the PdA's commander in northern Italy, **Ferruccio Parri**, was made prime minister. It was said that this would bring a "wind from the North" for radical social change, but the PdA was the smallest and least well-organized party in the post-war coalition, and the PdA, which was disliked by both the PCI and the Democrazia Cristiana (DC) / Christian Democracy, was soon shunted out of office. The PdA did not even manage to arrive at the elections for the 1946 **Constituent Assembly** as a united force: in February 1946, at the movement's first real congress, Parri and **Ugo La Malfa**, the party's right-wing left to form the "Movement for Republican Democracy." In the elections of 1946, the party made a miserable showing and gradually fizzled out.

Why, therefore, regard the PdA as an important political movement? The answer to this question is that it acted as a bridge that enabled the liberal-socialist ideas of the early anti-fascist resistance to be transmitted into the main post-war political parties. Every major party except the DC, including the PCI, was in some ways influenced by the PdA, and it is widely agreed that former *azionisti* have possessed an importance in Italy's intellectual and political development out of all proportion to their numbers.

PARTITO DEMOCRATICO DELLA SINISTRA (PDS) / Democratic

Party of the Left. Since its birth in February 1991, the PDS—the heir to the Partito Comunista Italiano / Italian Communist Party—has been the principal leftist force in Italian politics. The PDS's short history can be divided into two short periods. In the first period, the party was led by **Achille Occhetto**. Under Occhetto, the party survived the 1992 general elections, the first after the collapse of communism in the Soviet bloc, obtaining a creditable 16 percent of the vote, and emerged from the **Mani pulite** corruption scandals in better shape than any other party. Proposing itself at the head of a "Progressive Alliance" of radical parties, the PDS did well in local and regional elections held in the late fall 1993. The March 1994 general elections were a different story, however. Occhetto was outperformed on the campaign trail by the new leader of the Italian right, the media entrepreneur **Silvio Berlusconi**, and the Italian left was soundly defeated at the polls by the conservative and populist right. The PDS's own share of the vote nevertheless increased to 20 percent.

After further losses in the June 1994 elections to the European Parliament, Occhetto was replaced as leader by his deputy, **Massimo D'Alema**. Under D'Alema, the PDS worked in conjunction with **Romano Prodi** and the more progressive elements of the former **Democrazia cristiana / Christian Democracy** party in the **Olive Tree Coalition**. The PDS provided nine senior ministers, including deputy prime minister, minister of the interior, and finance minister, in the cabinet formed by Prodi after the general elections of April 1996. The PDS was, by a narrow margin, the party which attracted most votes in this poll. Under D'Alema, the party's political platform has been radically changed. The PDS has committed itself to the market economy, privatization and welfare reform: policies that are far away from its ex-communist heritage. D'Alema has also tried to broaden the party to encompass small parties from the non-communist left. In February 1998, the PDS absorbed several of these parties, but in the process changed its own name to the Democratici di Sinistra / Democrats of the Left. The new formation retains the PDS's oak tree symbol, but at the roots of the tree, the red rose of European social democracy has replaced the old hammer and sickle emblem of the PCI. *See also* Partito Comunista Italiano.

PARTITO LIBERALE ITALIANO (PLI) / Italian Liberal Party. Formed in 1943, the PLI occupied a minority position on the right of the Italian political spectrum until the political scandals of the 1990s brought about the party's dissolution. Its early leaders included **Luigi Einaudi** and **Benedetto Croce,** who was elected president of the party in 1946, and was made its president for life in 1947. In November 1945, the PLI conspired with **Alcide De Gasperi** to bring down the government of **Ferruccio Parri,** which the Liberals regarded as ineffectual. The PLI in this period was split between a relatively progressive wing, which was willing to countenance some measure of social and agricultural reform, state regulation of industry, and a republican form of government, and a conservative faction that was prepared to back none of these things. The conservatives were numerically stronger, and the party consequently saw many of its most gifted leaders, notably **Manlio Brosio,** leave to join the **Partito Repubblicana Italiano** (PRI) / Italian Republican Party.

In June 1946, the PLI fought the elections in the company of a cluster of survivors from pre-fascist Italy: together they took just under 7 percent of the vote. In 1948, the party was allied with the *Uomo qualunque* movement, but obtained less than 4 percent of the ballots cast. The PLI's showing in 1948, in fact, set a precedent that would be repeated until the 1980s: whenever the threat from the **Partito Comunista Italiano** (PCI) / Italian Communist Party seemed strong, the PLI would lose votes to the **Democrazia Cristiana** (DC) / Christian Democracy Party; when the DC was riding high, the prosperous upper-middle-class professionals who constituted the PLI's main base of support resumed their backing for the PLI.

Apart from a brief spell in government in 1954-1955, and again in 1972-1973, the PLI's hostility to state ownership and to the creation of the welfare state kept it out of government until 1981. For most of this period, the PLI was led by a highly respected economist, **Giovanni Malagodi.** The PLI's peak electoral performance came in 1963 when it obtained 7 percent of the votes and 39 deputies in the Chamber.

Despite its conservative economic credentials, the PLI was progressive on social issues. It strongly backed **divorce** and campaigned vigorously to protect the 1970 law instituting divorce rights from a DC-led referendum in 1974. At the end of the 1970s, the PLI began to tilt toward cooperation with the DC, but the PLI's access was blocked by the **Partito Socialista Italiano** (PSI) / Italian Socialist Party. The necessity of forming a solid majority eventually led to the formation of the five-party coalition called the *pentapartito.* The PLI—which by the 1980s could count upon little more than 2 percent of the vote—played a subordinate role in the governments it entered. Nevertheless, several of its chief figures became enmeshed in the bribery scandals of 1992-1993. In the 1994 elections, the party split, with some leading members siding with the center-left, and others forming a new party called the Unione di Centro (UdC) / Center Union, which allied itself with media entrepreneur **Silvio Berlusconi**. *See also* Qualunquismo.

PARTITO NAZIONALE FASCISTA (PNF) / National Fascist Party. Derived from the Italian Combat Veterans' Association, the PNF was one of the concrete results of the March 1919 rally held by **Benito Mussolini** in **Milan**'s Piazza San Sepolcro. Little more than 50 people were in attendance, despite claims made after the PNF held national power. Those 50 were called Sansepolcristi. In each province, a party secretary headed the fascist *Federazione* and was called the *Federale*. Each was chosen by the PNF in **Rome**, which is to say, by Mussolini.

The Duce's use of parallel structures suggests that he placed little trust in the institutions that antedated his rise to power: the army, the Parliament, the cabinet, the police, each was to have a party counterpart. The militia (the MVSN or *Milizia Volontario di Sicurezza Nazionale*), made up initially of the street-toughs who were the original components of *squadrismo*—with its own hierarchy, discipline, and expectations of obedience—was strongly resented by the Royal Army. The **Gran Consiglio del Fascismo** / Grand Council of Fascism, by 1926, functioned as a cabinet although it rarely met and took no initiatives until July 1943 when a majority voted down Mussolini. Finally, the OVRA was effectively the fascist police, secret and unaccountable to anyone other than Mussolini himself, who allegedly took pleasure in having devised these initials with no publicized meaning, hoping thereby to inspire fear.

Fascism's claim to be revolutionary rests, in part, on the contributions to increased social mobility made by these parallel arrangements—that is, in rigidly class-structured traditional Italian life, membership, and rank earned by a member of the *milizia* gave parity with "better-born" subordinates and a rank similar to officers of the Piedmontese military tradition. A source of strength (the army) was thus balanced by the creation of the militia. Those able to influence youth (Ministry of Education) found themselves sharing quarters with the Opera Nazionale Balilla (ONB) responsible for fascism's **youth movements**. The National **police** found that the

OVRA or party police was subject to no legal restraints. Even the judiciary had to accept the creation of the Special Tribunal for Crimes against the State: a Star Chamber. These parallel structures put the party on the same level as the state, which was apparently Mussolini's design. So successful was he in realizing his design that the chief concern of the Allies in the surrender of Italy on September 29, 1943, was the disbanding of all the institutions and instruments of the PNF. *See also* Benito Mussolini; Fascism; Fascist Ideology; Peace Treaty of 1947; Youth Movements, Fascism; Table 4 in Appendix.

PARTITO POPOLARE ITALIANO (PPI) / Italian People's Party. The PPI was founded by Don **Luigi Sturzo** in January 1919 with the blessing of Pope Benedict XV. The decision to found a mass party open to non-Catholics and, theoretically, independent of the Church hierarchy was the product of the Vatican's growing alarm at the strength of the **Partito Socialista Italiano** (PSI) / Italian Socialist Party after 1918. At the PPI's First Congress in June 1919, Don Sturzo outlined a progressive program that emphasized the need to defend the family, to extend **education**, welfare, and pensions to create a social safety net, to increase the nation's productive powers and divide the nation's wealth more equitably, and to work for peace in the world. The PPI also asked for proportional representation, an elected Senate, and **women**'s suffrage. Proportional representation was in fact introduced in August 1919. The PPI obtained 1.2 million votes in the November 1919 elections, securing 20.5 percent of the total, making it the second-largest group in Parliament, after the PSI.

By the next spring, the party had 250,000 members and took part in **Giovanni Giolitti's** last government (June 1920-July 1921). It did not join the anti-socialist *blocco nazionale* that was liberal Italy's last-ditch effort to retain its hold on power. In the general elections of May 1921, the PPI repeated its 1919 result and subsequently had three ministers in the cabinet formed by **Ivanoe Bonomi.**

At its Third Congress (October 1921), an attempt by the leader of the party's left to commit the PPI to non-cooperation with the fascists was rejected. The leadership underestimated the threat posed by **Mussolini**. The PPI in fact entered the government formed after Mussolini's coup in October 1922. At the PPI's Fourth Congress in April 1923, the leadership's position toward **fascism**, as sustained by the head of its parliamentary group, **Alcide De Gasperi**, was clarified as one of "conditional collaboration"—support for the government so long as it kept within constitutional boundaries. This was not enthusiastic enough for one delegate who declared that Italy should "thank divine providence for sending her a man like Mussolini."

The PPI split over the 1923 **Acerbo Law**, with most of the party abstaining, but a small minority voting in favor. Before the vote, Don Sturzo had been pressured into resigning as leader by the Vatican, which was worried that his continuance in office would wreck relations with Mussolini. In the elections of March 1924, the PPI, fighting on an openly anti-fascist platform, obtained 650,000 votes (9 percent) and 39 deputies. These results made it the largest opposition party. After the poll, the PPI chose De Gasperi as its new leader. Under his direction, the PPI took a prominent role in the boycott of Parliament that followed the murder of **Giacomo Matteotti**. The PPI's deputies attempted to retake their seats in the Chamber in January 1926, but were physically ejected by the fascist members. The party was suppressed in November 1926. Its leaders were mostly allowed to live an unmolested life, and made no attempt to set up a clandestine organization.

In January 1994, the rump of the **Democrazia Cristiana** (DC) / Christian Democracy renamed the party the PPI in a bid to recall the original Christian democratic movement. The party nevertheless did poorly in the March 1994 elections. After the elections it chose **Rocco Buttiglione** to be its leader, but his divisive strategy caused the party to split in March 1995. The revived PPI is a member of the **Olive Tree Coalition**. *See also* Papacy.

PARTITO RADICALE (PR) / Radical Party. The PR was founded in 1955 by a group of intellectuals drawn from among the disaffected within the **Partito Liberale Italiano** (PLI) / Italian Liberal Party who had grown impatient with the economic conservatism of **Giovanni Malagodi**. Originally hardly more than a club of intellectuals associated with the weekly newspaper *Il Mondo*, the PR nevertheless articulated a penetrating critique of the economic and political tendencies of Italian society. The PR's principal figures, Mario Pannunzio and Ernesto Rossi, waged war against the dogmatism of both the Catholic Church and the **Partito Comunista Italiano** (PCI) / Italian Communist Party and against the growing corruption and clientelism of the chief political parties, and argued that the Italian state was interfering too much in the workings of the free market.

In 1962, a generational change in the leadership brought the PR under the control of **Marco Pannella**, who has been the dominant figure in the party ever since. Until the late 1970s, Pannella's small band of activists was merely a **Rome**-based pressure group that agitated for social reforms, but the PR's sponsorship of a **referendum** to liberalize the 1978 abortion law brought genuine electoral popularity, especially among the urban young. In the 1979 general elections, the PR could boast the votes of 3.5 percent of the electorate, up from just 1 percent in 1976, and as much as 7 percent in big cities such as Rome, **Milan**, and **Turin**. The PR also persuaded nearly four million Italians to vote for its amendment to the abortion law in May 1981—nearly 12 percent of the electorate. Since 1981, the PR has made the referendum its chief political weapon, sponsoring or co-sponsoring plebiscites on nuclear power, the judiciary, hunting, and electoral reform. Cicciolina, a performer in pornographic films and night-club acts, was elected to the Chamber of Deputies as a Radical. In June 1995, PR-promoted referendums were held on (among others) shopping hours, compulsory union dues, and the privatization of the state TV networks. The leadership has also made good use of the adherence of the Movimento della Liberazione delle Donne Italiane (MLD) / Freedom for Italian Women Movement, a major actor on the scene of women's rights to equality and autonomy.

In the 1980s, the PR developed into a campaigning movement that resembled Greenpeace or Amnesty International more than a traditional political party. The PR's primary concerns became world hunger, environmental questions, the fight against the death penalty, and the decriminalization of drugs. PR members were allowed to join other parties, and the party essentially became a forum for Pannella. In 1992, the PR actually fought the election as the *Lista Pannella*, which symbolized the unhealthy extent of the PR's enthrallment to its charismatic leader. Also in 1992, the PR staved off extinction by a recruitment drive that attracted 37,000 new subscriptions. This testified to the affection that the increasingly eccentric PR inspired, but this affection was put to the test by Pannella's perverse decision to defend the politicians involved in the corruption investigations, and, in 1994, to side with **Silvio Berlusconi**'s right-wing coalition. Pannella aside, few PR activists have achieved nationwide recognition. One exception is Emma Bonino, who is currently the **European Union**'s commissioner for fishing, human rights, and third world issues. *See also* Women in Contemporary Italy.

PARTITO REPUBBLICANO ITALIANO (PRI) / Italian Republican

Party. Officially founded in April 1895 (though the party's roots can be traced back to **Mazzini** and the various political movements that he inspired), the PRI was little more than a parliamentary fringe group when **Mussolini** took power. Banned during the fascist dictatorship, the PRI was active in the resistance to **fascism**, although its anti-monarchist principles prevented it from taking part in the **Comitati di Liberazione Nazionale** (CLN) / National Liberation Committees after Italy's surrender to the Allies on September 8, 1943.

The PRI was reborn as an organized party in 1946. It obtained 4 percent of the vote in the elections to the **Constituent Assembly** and was subsequently strengthened when **Ferruccio Parri** and **Ugo La Malfa**, and former **Partito Liberale Italiano** (PLI) / Italian Liberal Party leader **Manlio Brosio** joined the party.

The PRI's policy stance in this period was founded upon a progressive attitude toward social and economic reform and hostility to the **Partito Comunista Italiano** (PCI) / Italian Communist Party. This stance made the PRI a natural ally for **Alcide De Gasperi**, who—despite the **Democrazia Cristiana's** (DC) / Christian Democracy Party's narrow overall majority in the Chamber of Deputies in the May 1948 elections—included the PRI in all his governments. PRI ministers held such portfolios as foreign affairs, defense, and foreign trade at various times and thus enjoyed an influence on national policy out of all proportion to their electoral support. In 1953, the PRI split after the party majority backed the DC's attempt to introduce the so-called *Legge truffa* (swindle law). **Ferruccio Parri** and the party's left wing deserted the PRI in protest and formed a new group, Unità popolare (Popular Unity), which campaigned against the new law and was decisive in denying the DC the majority it needed to put the law's provisions into effect. The PRI's vote sank to just 1.6 percent in 1953.

Chastened by this experience, and by the DC's rightward move after the death of De Gasperi, the PRI played no further governmental role until 1962. Under the leadership (from 1965) of **Ugo La Malfa**, the PRI acted as the "critical conscience of the center-left" during the 1960s and 1970s, speaking out against the political parties' increasing power over the institutions of the Italian state and arguing vehemently for social reforms such as **divorce** and abortion. La Malfa, after a contentious spell as treasury minister during the 1973 "oil shock," became vice premier during the 1974-1976 administration of **Aldo Moro**. La Malfa died in 1979. His place was taken by **Giovanni Spadolini**. Spadolini argued that the PRI was capable of providing political leadership, not just moral tone, to Italian government. In the 1983 elections, the PRI's electoral support was its best ever—5.1 percent.

Yet despite the generally high quality of the PRI's ministerial appointees in the 1980s, the party became a powerless spectator as the DC and the PSI struggled for power and patronage. Eventually, in April 1991, the newly elected party secretary, Ugo La Malfa's son, Giorgio, pulled the PRI out of the governing coalition. The PRI was the cleanest party of government in the first Italian Republic, although it did not emerge unscathed from the bribery scandals in 1992-1993. Still led by Giorgio La Malfa, the PRI supports the **Olive Tree Coalition**, although it is but a shadow. *See also* Tables 7, 8 in Appendix.

PARTITO DI RIFONDAZIONE COMUNISTA (PRC) / Communist Refoundation Party. This splinter group bolted the Twentieth Party Congress of the **Partito Comunista Italiano** (PCI) / Italian Communist Party in February 1991 manifesting its rejection of the party's transformation into the **Partito Democratico della Sinistra** (PDS) / Democratic Party of the Left. Led initially by **Armando Cossutta,** and from 1994 by Fausto Bertinotti, it has displayed unexpected electoral and organizational resilience. In the 1994 general elections, it obtained 6 percent of the poll, a figure that rose in 1996 to 8 percent. The party boasts 100,000 dues-paying members and more than 30 deputies.

Since April 1996, Rifondazione has been a necessary but sometimes difficult parliamentary ally for the **Olive Tree Coalition.** Holding the balance of power in Parliament, the party has blocked the government's attempts to reform Italy's system of so-called "baby pensions" (pensions available to workers in certain occupations after as little as 15 or 18 years of employment) and to initiate privatizations of the state's industrial holdings, especially in the telecommunications sector. The party has also conditioned Italy's strenuous efforts to restore order to its public finances by insisting that the burden of new taxation fall on the upper middle and middle classes, not the manual workers. Right-wing opposition parties claim that Bertinotti and Rifondazione have undue influence on policymaking.

Despite its attachment to the red flag, and to the wooden jargon of communist ideology, Rifondazione Comunista is in a sense a conservative party in its steadfast defense of the institutions and practices of the all-encompassing welfare state. Insofar as Italy, like every other major Western democracy, is rethinking the role of the state as a provider of goods and services, Rifondazione has a ready-made electorate among people anxious about job security, pensions, and social benefits. In October 1997, PRC withheld its support for the **Prodi** budgetary cuts in pensions and health care, but the public reaction was so hostile that Bertinotti and Cossutta backed down, accepting a pledge that Prodi would seek a 35-hour work week by 2001 and would reduce by 10 percent the pension and health care cuts proposed in the 1998 budget. In 1998, the PRC brought down the Prodi government when further changes to the welfare system were proposed. The party split, with Bertinotti leading the majority faction into opposition. The PRC returned to its external support of the government. *See also* Romano Prodi.

PARTITO SOCIALISTA DEMOCRATICO ITALIANO (PSDI) / Italian Social Democratic Party. The first step toward the creation of a social democratic party in Italy was taken in January 1947 when **Giuseppe Saragat** led 52 of the 115 Partito Socialista Italiano d'Unità Proletaria (PSIUP) / Italian Socialist Party of Proletarian Unity deputies in the **Constituent Assembly** to form the Partito Socialista dei Lavoratori Italiani (PSLI) / Italian Socialist Workers Party. In December 1947, this new formation entered the government, with Saragat becoming vice premier. In May 1948, the PSLI fought the elections in the company of the Unione Democratico Socialista (UDS) / Democratic Socialist Union, a movement headed by the writer **Ignazio Silone.** The results were promising: in all, the new ticket received over two million votes (7 percent of the electorate).

The PSLI's internal politics were turbulent after the 1948 elections. A further schism in the **Partito Socialista Italiano** (PSI) / Italian Socialist Party led to the formation of a mini-party headed by the former interior minister, Giuseppe Romita, which quickly merged with the UDS and numerous defectors from the PSLI to form the Partito Socialista Unitario (PSU) / Unitary Socialist Party. The political line of the new party was more neutralist in foreign affairs, and more critical of Saragat's policy of cooperating with the **Democrazia Cristiana** (DC) / Christian Democracy Party. This fragmentation of Italian social democracy was unsustainable, however, and in January 1952, a unifying congress took place in

Bologna, and the PSDI was born. Romita was the first party secretary; the following year he was replaced by Saragat. The PSDI's electoral baptism came in 1953, when its vote fell to just 4.5 percent.

The PSI's shift away from the **Partito Comunista Italiano** (PCI) / Italian Communist Party and toward the political center after 1962 raised the question of the reunification of Italian socialism. The PSI's votes contributed to Giuseppe Saragat's election as president of Italy in 1964, and in 1966, the PSI and the PSDI merged into a new party known as the Partito Socialista Unificato (PSU) / Unified Socialist Party. The experiment was not a success. The PSU obtained just 14.5 percent of the votes in the elections of 1968, 5 percent less than its two component parties had obtained in the previous electoral test in 1963. The PSU fell apart in July 1969, and in 1970, it re-formed under the leadership of Mario Tanassi.

Lacking a mass electoral base (over the next 20 years the PSDI's support would never be higher than 5 percent of the electorate), the PSDI became a satellite of the DC and adopted the corrupt and clientelistic policies that were the DC trademark. In 1976, party leader Tanassi was accused of having accepted bribes from the American aerospace company Lockheed while minister of defense under **Mariano Rumor** from 1971 to 1974. He would eventually be found guilty and sentenced to two years' imprisonment. Most of Tanassi's successors were little better. One of them, Pietro Longo, was found to be a member of the subversive masonic lodge Propaganda Due (P2) and was later arrested on corruption charges. The last two secretaries of the PSDI, Antonio Cariglia and Carlo Vizzini, were swept away by the corruption investigations of 1992-1993. The PSDI took part in every administration between August 1979 and July 1992, but it made no apparent contribution to improving Italy's political and economic life. *See also* Opening to the Left.

PARTITO SOCIALISTA ITALIANO (PSI) / Italian Socialist Party. The PSI was founded, under the name of the "Italian Workers' Party" in Genoa in 1892. In its early years, the party was dominated by **Filippo Turati** and his companion, Anna Kuliscioff. Turati's "reformist" socialism came into increasing disrepute with the party's revolutionary "maximalist" wing. At the party's Eighth Congress in 1912, the revolutionaries, led by **Benito Mussolini,** expelled the party's moderates, and Turati was left to fight an increasingly lonely battle until his own expulsion in 1922. For the most part, the PSI remained faithful to the Marxist view that **World War I** was a product of imperialism that the working class of all nations had the duty to oppose. Earlier—in November 1914—Mussolini was himself expelled for violating the party's neutralist line on intervention in the war.

The PSI's Marxism did it no harm with a working-class electorate inspired by the Bolshevik revolution in Russia. In the 1919 general elections, the second held under universal male suffrage, the PSI became the largest party with almost 33 percent of the vote and 156 deputies. This electoral triumph was a prelude to the so-called *biennio rosso* (1920-1922), two years of heated industrial action and street battles between fascists and socialists.

Resistance to **fascism** was hampered by the doctrinaire manner of the "maximalists." Even after the fascists broke a "pact of pacification" signed with the PSI in August 1921, the PSI's leadership refused to join a government that would use force to restore law and order; at the same time, the PSI polemicized futilely with the **Partito Comunista Italiano** (PCI) / Italian Communist Party over whether conditions were ripe for outright revolution. The consequence was that Mussolini seized power, and the PSI, though still theoretically a legal party, was soon subjected to police harassment and the arbitrary arrest of many of its local and national leaders. The party was outlawed, along with the rest of the opposition, in November 1926.

The party's "reformist" and "maximalist" wings composed their differences at a congress of exiles in Paris in July 1930. The architect of this deal was **Pietro Nenni,** who became from this moment onward the chief figure in Italian socialism. Within Italy, however, the Partito Socialista Italiano became almost moribund during the dictatorship. In August 1943, it was forced to merge with **Lelio Basso**'s Movimento di Unità Proletaria (MUP) / Movement of Proletarian Unity, to form the Partito Socialista Italiano d'Unità Proletaria (PSIUP) / Italian Socialist Party of Proletarian Unity. Lacking organization, the new party soon became subordinate to the PCI within the resistance. It did not, however, endorse the PCI's decision to join the government formed by **Ivanoe Bonomi** in August 1944.

The PSIUP participated in the **Parri** and **De Gasperi** administrations that governed the country prior to the election of the **Constituent Assembly** in June 1946. In the elections, which it fought in alliance with the PCI, the PSIUP obtained 20 percent of the vote and emerged as the second party after the **Democrazia Cristiana** (DC) / Christian Democracy Party. The Partito Socialista Italiano (as it was again called after 1947) continued its Unity of Action pact with the PCI until 1953, even presenting joint lists of candidates in 1948, but this close identification with communism did not serve the party's interests. In January 1947, the party's moderates, led by **Giuseppe Saragat**, left the party, weakening its electoral support, and the PCI soon overtook the PSI as the point of reference for the working class.

The Partito Socialista Italiano definitively broke with the PCI in 1956 after Khrushchev's secret speech on Stalin's crimes, and Soviet suppression of the Hungarian revolution. Nenni, who had been a convinced "frontist," had received a Stalin prize, which he now returned. He then began a flirtation with the DC. In 1963, Nenni took the plunge and entered the cabinet formed by **Aldo Moro** in December of that year. The party remained in office more or less constantly until 1974, but the move was not an electoral success. In the 1968 elections, the PSI and the **Partito Socialista Democratico Italiano** (PSDI) / Italian Social Democratic Party, running joint lists, obtained only 14.5 percent, over 5 percent less than the sum of their independent scores in 1963. In terms of social reforms, the PSI's experience of government was also a delusion. The PSI played a major role in introducing a **divorce** law in 1970, but the Italian economy remained in mostly private hands. Worst of all, the PSI, hitherto incorruptible, began to taste the pleasures of **patronage**.

In 1972, the PSI obtained its worst electoral result ever: just 9.6 percent. This poor performance was repeated in 1976. The consequence of these electoral disasters was a generational change in the party's leadership. In July 1976, **Bettino Craxi** was elected leader. After an opportunistic and electorally unrewarding spell in opposition during the **Andreotti-Berlinguer** compromise of that year, Craxi made the PSI the fulcrum of Italian politics in the 1980s. Even by Italian standards, the PSI's top politicians were notoriously venal. When the bribery investigations began, the PSI was hit harder than any other party, and its electoral support withered. In March 1994, the PSI, now led by a trade unionist, Ottaviano Del Turco, obtained just 2.2 percent of the votes. Later in 1994, the party split into four fragments (the "Italian Socialists," the "Laborists," the "Reformists," and a minuscule group of die-hard *"Craxiani"*). *See also* Bettino Craxi; Pietro Nenni; Opening to the Left; Filippo Turati; Tables 7, 8 in Appendix.

PASOLINI, PIERPAOLO (1922-1975). Director, novelist, poet, and critic, Pierpaolo Pasolini was born and educated in **Bologna** studying first art history, and then (after an interlude in which he was drafted into the Italian army) modern literature. After graduating, Pasolini went to **Rome** and drifted into the underworld of prostitutes—both male and female—their procurers, and petty criminals that populate his films and stories. His first novel was banned for obscenity, a punishment that did not stop his book of poems, *Le ceneri di Gramsci* (*The Ashes of Gramsci*, 1957) from winning the prestigious Viareggio prize. In 1959, he published a second, better, novel about slum life, *Una vita violente* (*A Violent Life*).

Pasolini's first feature film, *Accatone*, was issued in 1961. The film's naturalism—like his novels set in the Rome underworld—aroused an uproar in Italy, but was rewarded with international critical acclaim. The following year, Pasolini was given a suspended prison sentence for blasphemy after the release of *RoGoPaG*, a collection of four shorts directed by **Roberto Rossellini**, Jean-Luc Godard, Pasolini, and Ugo Gregoretti. Paradoxically, his next major film, *Il Vangelo secondo Matteo* (*The Gospel According to St. Matthew*, 1964) is widely recognized as one of the finest biblical movies ever made: even the Vatican awarded it a prize. Pasolini, a Marxist and non-believer, strove to make a sober presentation of the story of Christ (who was played by a Spanish architecture student) and to portray the spirituality of the Christian religion—a dimension he believed that Marxists neglected. He followed *Matteo* with the fable-like *Uccellacci e uccellini* (*The Hawks and Sparrows*, 1966).

Pasolini's subsequent films were for the most part concerned with explicit sexual themes. *Teorema* (*Theorem*, 1968) was prosecuted unsuccessfully for obscenity; he also made a brilliantly bawdy film version of Boccaccio's *Decamerone* (*The Decameron*, 1971). His last film, *Salò, o le centoventi giornate di Sodoma* (*Salò, or the 120 days of Sodom*, 1975), was an adaption of De Sade set in the dying days of **Mussolini's** regime. The film displays his fascination with cruelty and sexual violence, to which he fell victim. In 1975, he was murdered near Rome by a homosexual prostitute.

PATRONAGE (*Lottizzazione*). It is a commonplace to say that political stability is aided by one of two factors: ideology or patronage. Doing favors, providing sinecures and other jobs, assuring contracts in exchange for electoral support, is the essence of patronage, called in Italian, *lottizzazione* or parcelling-out. It is within the expectations of many people that whoever has access to power will utilize it to the benefit of relations and friends in such a way as to increase the number of those caught in what one scholar has called the "network of obligations."

If one is to avoid politics as "denatured civil war," in Walter Lippman's happy phrase, it is best to share power with adversaries in order to give them a stake in preserving the present order of things—the status quo. One way to share power is by sharing legislative appointments to committee assignments; another is to share the power to appoint the administrators of state-controlled enterprises. That is the pattern evolved in Italy inasmuch as an exceptionally high portion of Italy's industry and services long operated as instruments of the state. The list would include insurance companies, banks, telephones, telegraph, television and radio, public sector producers and holding companies, state agencies, and the state's bureaucracy: all are headed by persons answerable to politicians responsible to the public. Not only is such a system democratic, it also helps ensure stability and continuity in a generally volatile political environment.

In Italy, the traditions of *trasformismo* and **consociationalism** have long since laid the groundwork for the readiness to ensure the acquiescence of adversaries by sharing both power and influence. However, one of the effects is that the three publicly financed television channels were for years headed by, respectively, a Demochristian, a Socialist, and a Communist. Which faction of each party is rewarded by the appointment in question is, of course, an internal party matter closely watched by the press as a measure of the various factions power.

In sum, the net effect is to reward party solidarity rather than managerial competence; and the possibilities of corruption are self-evident.

The **opening to the left** was intended to modify the behavior of the **Democrazia Cristiana** (DC) / Christian Democracy Party by introducing the socialists and, through them, the working class into the halls of power. Far from transforming the DC, however, the new equilibrium changed the socialists.

The stabilizing effect of patronage seems to have waned since judicial inquiries begun in 1990 have revealed the extent of the corruption to which patronage makes such a mighty contribution. *See also* Istituto per la Ricostruzione Industriale; Mani Pulite.

PAVESE, CESARE (1908-1950). One of the leading novelists associated with **neo-realism**, Cesare Pavese was born in Cuneo (Piedmont). He took his degree in literature in 1930 and worked as a teacher of English while publishing critical essays on modern American writers such as Walt Whitman, Mark Twain, Sinclair Lewis, and, above all, Herman Melville, whose *Moby Dick* Pavese translated into Italian.

In 1936 (the year in which his first volume of poems appeared) Pavese was sentenced to a period of *confino* in a remote Calabrian village for passing on politically compromising letters to a communist militant with whom he was having an affair. As a known anti-fascist, Pavese was forced to live in hiding in the countryside during the last months of the war, and this experience—together with the political fervor engendered in him by his decision to join the **Partito Comunista Italiano** (PCI) / Italian Communist Party—led him to produce by 1950 a string of novels and stories that have become classics of contemporary Italian literature. *La Casa in collina* (*The House on the Hill*), *Il Compagno* (*The Comrade*), and *La Luna e i falò* (*The Moon and the Bonfires*) all appeared between 1947 and 1950, and they permanently established Pavese's reputation as one of the most acute writers in modern fiction. Certainly of all the Italian neo-realist writers, he is the one whose work seems most likely to stand the test of time, though some of his later work, notably *La Bella Estate* (*The Fine Summer*), a 1949 collection of three stories, showed that he was chafing under the restrictions of the neo-realist genre.

Pavese committed suicide in 1950. The publication of his diaries in 1952 illustrated that he had long been struggling with a profound sense of personal anguish.

PEACE TREATY OF 1947. On September 29, 1943, an "instrument of surrender" was signed in Malta by General **Badoglio**, then prime minister of the Kingdom of Italy, and General Eisenhower for the Allies. It provided for the unconditional surrender of Italian air, sea, and land forces. Italy was to be occupied by Allied armies. All organizations of the **Partito Nazionale Fascista** (PNF) / National Fascist Party (e.g., OVRA [fascist secret police with deliberately mystifying nonsense initials], Milizia Volontaria di Sicurezza Nazionale [MVSN], and the Organizzazione Nazionale Balilla [ONB]) were to be immediately disbanded. All Italian laws that provided for discrimination on grounds of race, creed, or opinion were to be rescinded under the supervision of an Allied Control

Commission.

King **Victor Emmanuel III** declared war on Germany in October 1943 and thus Italy became a "co-belligerent." Opinion on the left, certainly, expected this new status to entitle Italy to favored treatment in the final peace treaty. But the February 10, 1947, treaty signed in Paris obliged Italy to cede the Italian border cities of Tenda and Briga to France after a plebiscite. Under pressure from the USSR, always protective of Slavs, Italy had to cede Fiume, Zara, Pola, and most of Venezia Giulia to Yugoslavia. Even **Trieste** and its hinterland, fruit of the sacrifices made as allies of the Entente powers between 1915 and 1918, were to be turned over to the Allies as a free territory. Italy's colonial losses included some areas acquired not only before **World War II** and **fascism**, but even before **World War I**. For example, the Dodecanese Islands were assigned to Greece, and Italy's African colonies—not only **Ethiopia** but Eritrea and Italian Somaliland—were turned over to the United Nations. Finally, Italy was effectively disarmed (until she joined the North Atlantic Treaty Organization [NATO]) and was to pay reparations to **Albania**, **Abyssinia**, Greece, the United Kingdom, the United States, the U.S.S.R., and Yugoslavia. The United States and the United Kingdom renounced their share. The Soviet Union received $100 million; the others divided a total of $260 million.

The signing and ratification of the treaty added to the troubles of **De Gasperi** and **Democrazia Cristiana** (DC) / Christian Democracy Party. Runaway inflation, high unemployment, and rural unrest (including land occupations) were worrisome enough, but the DC's 1947 election losses, and U.S. pressure to "dump" the Marxist parties, pushed De Gasperi to do what seemed to have been contrary to his preferences. In May, he formed a new government of Demochristians with centrist and right-wing parties, excluding both the **Partito Socialista Italiano** (PSI) / Italian Socialist Party and the **Partito Comunista Italiano** (PCI) / Italian Communist Party, thus substituting for the anti-fascist coalition an anti-communist one. The U.S.-U.K. proposal that Italy be admitted to the UN was vetoed by the Soviets until December of 1955. *See also* Fascism; Land Reform.

PELLA, GIUSEPPE (1902-1981). Once a *podestà* (a fascist equivalent of an appointed mayor), he came to the **Democrazia Cristiana** (DC) / Christian Democracy Party by way of **Azione Cattolica Italiana** (ACI) / Catholic Action. As a cautious economist first elected to **Parliament** in 1946, he acquired policy experience by serving as chair of the Finance Committee, became deputy minister of finance and, within a year, was minister of finance serving also as minister of the treasury and budget. In August 1953, he became president of the Council of Ministers covering foreign affairs and budget simultaneously. Even after leaving these responsibilities, he served again in **Zoli**'s cabinet (1957-1958) as vice premier in charge of foreign affairs. Subsequently, he served in governments headed by **Antonio Segni** (1959-1960) and by **Amintore Fanfani** (1960-1962) at budget and finance. He died in **Rome** in 1981.

PELLOUX, LUIGI GIROLAMO (1839-1924). General Pelloux fought in all three of the wars that established Italian independence and reunification. In 1870, he commanded the artillery that breached the walls of **Rome**. His political career began in 1880, when he was elected to the Chamber of Deputies. A troublesome and ambitious minister of war under both **Di Rudinì** and **Giolitti**, Pelloux was identified by King Umberto in June 1898 as a strong leader who could restore calm after the bloody rioting of the previous months. In his initial statements to **Parliament**, Pelloux claimed that he would have no need of the restrictive laws against political organization and free speech proposed by his predecessor, Rudinì. In February 1899, however, Pelloux reneged on his word. His second government, formed in May 1899 with the center-right deputies led by **Sidney Sonnino**, struggled for several weeks to pass a harsh packet of repressive measures. The left, especially the **Partito Socialista Italiano** (PSI) / Italian Socialist Party, responded with a filibuster—the first time this tactic had been used in the Italian Parliament. At the end of June 1899, Pelloux lost patience and had the law passed by royal decree. King Humbert I (Umberto) closed Parliament until November. The next year, following a sentence by the High Court declaring the royal decree of June 1899 constitutionally invalid, Pelloux tried again to get parliamentary approval for the measures. He was not successful; parliamentary filibustering caused the government to withdraw the proposals.

Pelloux therefore decided that there was no option but to go to the polls and have the electorate confirm or reject his policies. Elections were held at the beginning of June 1900. The PSI, Radicals, and Republicans together obtained almost 100 deputies, and the traditional left of **Zanardelli** did well, too. Pelloux's majority had been considerably reduced and on June 18, 1900, he resigned and returned to the armed forces, in command of the garrison in **Turin**.

He played no further role in politics. He died in Bordighera (Liguria) in 1924.

PENTAPARTITO. This term was used to describe the five-party coalition of the **Democrazia Cristiana** (DC) / Christian Democracy Party, the **Partito Socialista Italiano** (PSI) / Italian Socialist Party, the **Partito Repubblicana Italiano** (PRI) / Italian Republican Party, the **Partito Socialista Democratico Italiano** (PSDI) / Italian Social Democratic Party, and the **Partito Liberale Italiano** (PLI) / Italian Liberal Party that governed Italy between June 1981 and April 1991, with two brief interludes. Between December 1982 and September 1983, the veteran DC statesman, **Amintore Fanfani**, presided over a government that did not contain the PRI; between April and July 1987, Fanfani also headed a short-lived DC-only minority government (a *monocolore*).

In all, there were nine separate governments that fitted the *pentapartito* model. The first two were formed by the PRI's **Giovanni Spadolini** (July 1981-December 1982). After the first Fanfani interlude, direction of the government passed to the leader of the PSI, **Bettino Craxi**, who was prime minister from August 1983 to April 1987, the longest duration of any government. Between 1987 and 1991, the premiership passed back into the hands of the DC. Three senior DC politicians headed administrations in the last four years of the *pentapartito*: the late **Giovanni Goria** who was in office from July 1987 to April 1988, **Ciriaco De Mita**, then secretary of the DC, who was in power from April 1988 to August 1989, and **Giulio Andreotti** who became premier for the sixth time after the June 1989 elections. His variation on the *pentapartito* formula lasted until April 1991, when he attempted to reshuffle the cabinet to remove the PRI's hold on the ministry of post and telecommunications. The PRI left the government in a huff, and Andreotti reconstituted his government with representatives from the four remaining parties and with a heavy presence of ministers from the PSI.

This account of the numerous ministerial changes underlines the most important feature of party politics during the *pentapartito* decade: their extreme tendentiousness. The Craxi governments were sabotaged by the DC, which feared the PSI leader's emergence as a national figure; between July 1987 and June 1989, the PSI repaid the compliment with interest. The political instability of the *pentapartito* coincided with extraordinary misgovernment. The national debt expanded from approximately 60 percent of GNP in 1981 to over 100 percent in 1991; there were several years in which annual government spending exceeded tax revenues by as much as 12-14 percent of GNP. In **southern Italy**, the mafia's influence grew sharply. **Law** and order all but broke down in regions such as Calabria and **Sicily**. Worst of all, these years saw the cancer of endemic corruption metastasize within the Italian body politic. Apart from **Spadolini** and **Fanfani** (who in any case belonged to an earlier, cleaner generation of politicians), most of the principal figures of the *pentapartito* era were tarnished by the anti-corruption and anti-mafia investigations of 1992-1994.

PERTINI, ALESSANDRO (1896-1990). "Sandro" Pertini was an icon of the Italian left, and probably the most popular president of the first republic. Born in Savona (Liguria), he served during **World War I** as an officer in a machine-gun battalion. After 1918, Pertini joined the **Partito Socialista Italiano** (PSI) / Italian Socialist Party, but in 1922 passed to **Turati** and **Matteotti**'s socialist reformists. He was an active anti-fascist. In May 1925, he was arrested while printing a pamphlet entitled *Sotto la dittatura barbara fascista (Under the Barbaric Fascist Dictatorship)*, which earned him eight months' imprisonment. Amnestied, he was one of a group of youthful socialists who spirited **Filippo Turati** out of Italy (crossing from Savona to Corsica in a motorboat) and then accompanied the veteran socialist leader to Paris. Pertini was sentenced in his absence to ten years' imprisonment for this feat. Unable to return to Italy, he settled in Nice and operated a clandestine radio station. In 1928, he was arrested by the French police. His trial, in January 1929, became a cause célèbre. Pertini used the trial as an opportunity to denounce the fascist regime publicly and escaped with a suspended one-month prison sentence.

In 1929, Pertini, calling himself Luigi Roncaglia, returned to Italy intent on assassinating **Mussolini**. Unluckily seen and recognized by a lawyer from Savona, he was arrested once more and sentenced to ten years' imprisonment in November 1929. Subjected to solitary confinement, Pertini's health collapsed, and only an international campaign by anti-fascist exiles abroad succeeded in getting him transferred to an easier jail in Foggia (Apulia), where he was a fellow prisoner of **Antonio Gramsci**. Despite his precarious health, Pertini staunchly resisted attempts by his family to obtain a pardon for him. Indeed, in November 1933 he was given a further nine-year prison sentence for insulting a notoriously sadistic prison officer.

Pertini spent the period 1940-1943 in the prison camp for anti-fascist intellectuals on the Isle of Ventotene. Liberated in August 1943, he rushed to **Rome**, where he became a member of the central committee of the newly reconstituted PSI. He was given responsibility for organizing the party's military resistance to the Nazis. He took a leading role in the street battles that followed Italy's surrender on September 8, 1943, but in October he was captured and condemned to death by the Nazis. A daring rescue by partisans in January 1944 saved his life. Pertini spent the rest of the war in permanent danger of death and torture as one of the principal leaders of the **Comitato di Liberazione Nazionale**-Alta Italia (CLNAI) / Committee of National Liberation-Northern Italy, and in March 1945 was one of the organizers of the popular insurrection in **Milan**. He was awarded the gold medal for valor for his services to the resistance.

After the war, Pertini naturally became a leading figure in the PSI, even though his political line was only rarely in accord with the party leadership's. Pertini was elected to **Parliament** in 1953 and retained his seat in the Chamber of Deputies until 1978. From 1968 to 1976, he was speaker of the Chamber.

In 1978, Pertini was elected president of the republic with 832 votes out of a possible 995. As the British historian Paul Ginsborg has remarked, Pertini's selection was an "extraordinarily felicitous choice." Pertini brought the presidency closer to the people by inviting thousands of schoolchildren to visit him in the presidential palace; he took the bold political step of going outside the **Democrazia Cristiana** (DC) / Christian Democracy Party for the premiership; he invoked the values of the resistance as a basis for a rebirth of Italy's stagnant democracy. Perhaps the most enduring image of Pertini's presidency occurred during the 1982 World Cup final between Italy and West Germany. Throwing protocol to the winds, Italy's first citizen celebrated Italy's winning goal with a patriotic joy that was published on the front pages of newspapers throughout the world. Pertini died in Rome in February 1990 at nearly 94. His death was marked by widespread public mourning.

PIANO SOLO. *See* Solo Plan.

PIRANDELLO, LUIGI (1867-1936). Italy's greatest twentieth-century playwright, Luigi Pirandello was also a novelist of distinction. His political legacy, however, is less inspiring: like **Gentile** and **D'Annunzio**, he yielded to the flattery of the fascist state. Pirandello was born in Girgenti (modern-day Agrigento), **Sicily**, in 1867. He was educated in Germany, at Bonn, where he was briefly the Italian language instructor at the university. He returned to Italy in 1897 to work as a teacher of Italian literature and language in **Rome**, a post he retained until 1922. His life in this period was vexed by the irrational behavior of his wife, who believed, apparently without grounds, that Pirandello was a persistent adulterer. This domestic anguish insinuated itself into his work: the protagonist of Pirandello's first novel, *L'esclusa* (*The Outcast*, 1901), is a woman who is unjustly accused of being an adulteress.

Pirandello's second novel, *Il fù Mattia Pascal* (*The Late Mattia Pascal*, 1904), was a study in alienation and irony. The protagonist, Mattia Pascal, a timid, perfectly ordinary middle-class man, argues furiously with his wife one day, and leaves her. Then, two events occur that make it possible for him to begin life afresh. First, he wins the lottery and becomes financially independent. Second, he is wrongly identified as the victim of a road accident. Liberated from all his past ties, he takes a new name, Adriano Meis. However, he soon finds that it is impossible to live in modern society without the "form" that is given to us by bureaucratic recognition. Adriano Meis cannot fully exist because nobody has an official document proving it. Mattia Pascal thus fakes Adriano Meis's suicide and attempts to return to his former life, but his wife has remarried. Nothing remains of his former life except his tomb. He has truly become "The late Mattia Pascal." The novel conveys a sense of human absurdity and estrangement with great poignancy.

Pirandello began writing for the theater in 1916, creating a cycle of somewhat traditional plays set in Sicily and spoken in dialect. The two plays that made his reputation, however, *Così è . . . se vi pare* (*That's how it is . . . if you like*, 1917) and *Sei personaggi in cerca di un autore* (*Six Characters in Search of an Author*, 1921) were astonishingly original. As well as being formidably intellectual, they broke with the tradition of theatrical realism (of the play as the presentation of a finished drama portraying "reality") and established a new dramatic custom: the play as an artifice for interpretation. There is no "truth" in Pirandello's plays, just contrasting and conflicting meanings explained at length by characters on a bare stage that compels the audience to concentrate upon the dialogue and think about, not just accept, what is being said. Modern drama—Ionescu, Beckett, Pinter, Stoppard—owes a great debt to Pirandello and his near contemporary, Berthold Brecht.

Pirandello was lauded by the fascist state, greatly flattering his vanity. He signed Gentile's 1925 manifesto of fascist intellectuals and, in 1929, agreed to become a member of the **Accademia D'Italia**. His identification with **Mussolini**'s regime did not affect his growing international reputation, however. In 1934, he was awarded the Nobel prize for literature. He died in 1936 in Rome. By his express wish, there were no speeches or ceremonies at his funeral, and even his children were forbidden to accompany him to his grave.

PIVETTI, IRENE (1963-). Born in **Milan**, she earned her degree in modern literature at the Catholic University of Milan. Despite her relative youth and lack of parliamentary experience (her political past is limited to the Associazione Cristiana Lavoratori Italiani [ACLI] / Italian Association of Christian Workers and militance in the **Federazione Universitaria Cattolici Italiana** [FUCI] / Catholic University Graduates' Movement of Italy, both Catholic lay organizations), Irene Pivetti became Speaker of the Chamber of Deputies in April 1994. Not only was she the youngest person ever to hold this high institutional office, she was only the second woman: and this in the face of having been a member of **Parliament** for a bare two years. The strongly Catholic Pivetti first entered Parliament in 1992 as a deputy for the **Lega Nord** (LN) / Northern League, which she entered in 1990, moving from the Lombard League to which she had been a Catholic consultant. As speaker, she proved able to control a sometimes boisterous assembly, although she was occasionally criticized for lacking impartiality by taking too active a role in the inner politics of the LN. Her relations with the League's leader, **Umberto Bossi**, have soured since he began to evoke the specter of northern secessionism in the spring of 1996.

After an initial flirtation with this scheme, Pivetti has since argued that the LN is abandoning its original goal of achieving the reorganization of Italy as a federal state and is taking an extremist position that is bound to damage the movement electorally. This conflict of opinion led to her expulsion from the increasingly intolerant league at the end of July 1996, although there is no question that she commands widespread, if muted, support among the party's membership. It is unlikely that Pivetti's career is over. *See also* Leonilde Iotti; Women in Contemporary Italy.

POLICE. Italy has an abundance of police forces administered by various public authorities. The *Vigili Urbani* (municipal traffic police) are appointed and paid locally. The interior ministry in **Rome** is in charge of the 82,000 *Pubblica sicurezza* (public security) police whose subdivisions include the highway patrol (*Polizia stradale*) and railway police. Organized in 1946, their numbers included many former fascist militia members among its recruits and thus came to be seen as a holdover from the former regime. In the immediate post-war period, Interior Minister **Mario Scelba** relied upon the public security police when he formed the so-called *Celere* (riot squad) to break up leftist demonstrations and picket lines. Equipped with shields, face-guards, and riot sticks (euphemistically called "crowd dispersers" or "*sfollagente*"), these police adapted an earlier, horse-mounted century's tactics of crowd control to the possibilities offered by small, maneuverable, engine-powered jeep-like vehicles. After the prefect had ordered three times the sounding of the ritual trumpet call to disperse, any group of demonstrators (but conspicuously, those on the left) would find the *piazza* ringed with jeeps, each with wire mesh covering the windshield. Three police armed with riot sticks were able to reach outside the sides as each vehicle described a circle beginning at the outer edges of the crowd. While three swung their clubs indiscriminately, the driver propelled his vehicle, engine shrieking in some low gear and shrill siren wailing, in tighter and tighter circles. Finally, when the several jeeps had isolated a manageable group of demonstrators, they were carted off for eventual trial.

The Ministry of Agriculture administers the *Corpo forestale* or forestry corps. Under the control of the Treasury Ministry are the *Guardie di finanza* (GdF), the gray-uniformed finance guards (more than 40,000 in number) whose responsibilities include border controls, customs collection, anti-smuggling activity, and the collection of taxes. Discussions were underway in 1997 to demilitarize the Guardie di Finanza. Like other Italian police (save the municipal police), the GdF are para-military and equipped with automatic rapid-fire weapons, light armored vehicles, and helicopters.

The senior and most respected force remains the *Carabinieri*, part of the armed forces who serve as military police at army installations and as battle police in wartime. Accordingly, they are administered by the Ministry of Defense and are variously called *La Benemerita* (The Most Deserving) and *L'Arma Fedelissima* (The

Arm Most Faithful or Loyal—to the monarch and now, to the republic). The 20 *Carabinieri* legions (one in each region) are subdivided into provincial groups, and dispersed in 4,700 local stations, each of which is headed by a *Maresciallo* (a non-commissioned officer). Each public prosecutor's office has a detachment of *Carabinieri* to execute arrests, carry out searches, and conduct investigations. There are also specialist armored brigades, helicopter-borne forces, parachutists, "frogmen," and the *Gruppo d'intervento speciale* (GIS), which has trained with Britain's and Germany's anti-terrorist commandos. Not all are volunteers. Conscripts can choose to do their military service in either Police, *Carabinieri* or Firefighters. Aside from giving a shorter period of service, it provides an early career start for some.

Many *Carabinieri* have been killed in the last two decades by the terrorists of the **Brigate Rosse** (BR) / Red Brigades or by the **mafia**. This may help explain why they are seen as a disciplined force at the service of the public rather than enforcers of particular political persuasions. In fact, commemorative plaques at sites of German or fascist executions of partisans (e.g., Fiesole near Florence; Ardeatine caves outside Rome) reproduce accounts of individual *Carabinieri* who volunteered to take the place of terrified civilians pleading for their lives. Even more recently, when *Carabinieri* are ambushed and killed by criminal elements, it is not unusual for spontaneous offerings of flowers to mark the spot. *See also* Brigate Rosse; Gladio; Antonio Segni; Solo Plan; Fernando Tambroni.

PRATOLINI, VASCO (1913-1991). Born in a working-class district on the "wrong" bank of the Arno River (Florence's *Oltrarno*), he did not have the classical training of most Italian literary luminaries. He was self-taught by following his insatiable literary curiosity. By the time he was 19, he was part of the fascist literary left, collaborating with the editors of a well-known fascist weekly, *Il Bargello*. By 1938, his enthusiasm for the party's polemics against the traditionally privileged bourgeoisie seemed to be waning. In fact, he had begun another periodical, *Campo di marte*, which lasted for just one year (August 1938 to August 1939) before being closed by the minister of culture because its **neo-realism** and concern for social issues convinced some fascists that the editors were leftists.

After World War II, Pratolini began a period of feverish writing: he published *Il Quartiere* (*The Neighborhood*, 1943), *Cronaca familiare* (*Family Chronicle,* 1947), and *Diario sentimentale*

(*Sentimental Diary*, 1957), all perceptions from the *Oltrarno.*
Probably his most important books followed: *Cronache di poveri
amanti* (*Chronicle of Poor Lovers,* 1947) was followed by *Le ragazze
di San Frediano* (*The Girls of San Frediano,* 1949) and *L'eroe del
nostro tempo* (*The Hero of our Times*, 1949). His major undertaking
was a three-part *Una storia italiana* made up of *Metello (1955), Lo
sciallo* (*The Shawl,* 1960), and *Allegoria e derisione* (*Allegory and
Derision,* 1966). Several of his books have been made into highly
successful films.

PRESIDENTE DEL CONSIGLIO DEI MINISTRI / President of the
Council of Ministers. The Italian **Constitution of 1948**, prepared
after the 1946 referendum created the First Republic, reflected
deliberate choices by its authors. The provisional government had
been built around the anti-fascist forces of the **Democrazia Cristiana**
(DC) / Christian Democracy Party, the **Partito d'Azione** (PdA) /
Action Party, the **Partito Comunista Italiano** (PCI) / Italian
Communist Party, and their allies of the **Partito Socialista Italiano**
(PSI) / Italian Socialist Party. One choice was to impede the
reappearance of a "Man on Horseback." If executive powers had
been concentrated in the hands of either **Palmiro Togliatti** (PCI) or
Alcide De Gasperi (DC), the other would have perceived a threat.
The system was to return to being parliamentary in which elections
would choose members of **Parliament** from among competing
parties whose leaders then decide on a de facto steering—or
executive—committee (the cabinet, Council of Ministers, or
"government of the day"), the head of which is the prime minister or,
in Italy, the president of the Council of Ministers. The post-war
Italian republic was created on this parliamentary model, which is to
say that the executive is chosen by and depends for its life on the
support of the legislature. In parliamentary systems, the prime
minister is chosen by the parliamentary majority, be it a single party
with an absolute majority or a coalition of parties. In Italy's
multi-party democracy, the choice of chief executive has almost
invariably emerged after prolonged consultations among the party
leaders of the majority coalition. This fact has given rise to the
observation that Italy's system is less a democracy than a
"partitocracy" in which the electorate determines the negotiating
strength of the various parties but ultimately has no direct voice in
selecting the country's leader.
  The president of the Council of Ministers has had much less

control than, say, an English prime minister over the composition of his cabinet. Cabinets have normally been chosen from among the coalition partners' leaders, with account being taken of the intense rivalry among intra-party factions. The number of government members of cabinet rank has depended on the negotiations. However, always included are such central ministries as Foreign Affairs, Budget and Finance, the Treasury (which controls the revenue police and customs service), Defense (which includes command of the armed forces including the *Carabinieri*), Interior (which includes control over the public security **police**), and Agriculture.

One consequence of the dominance of the political parties has been the ease with which parties excluded from a share of power and its perquisites can join forces to bring down a government without necessarily being able to agree on the composition of an alternative. In all, Italy had 55 prime ministers in the first 50 years of the republic, almost all of whom, however, were drawn from the centrist factions of the DC. The exceptions were **Giovanni Spadolini** (whose government lasted 17 months beginning in June of 1981), **Bettino Craxi** (1983-1987), **Carlo Azeglio Ciampi** (1993-1994), **Silvio Berlusconi** (May-December 1994), **Lamberto Dini** (1995-1996), and **Romano Prodi**, made president of the Council in May 1996. Ciampi and Dini were apolitical technocrats pressed into service by President **Oscar Luigi Scalfaro** because Parliament was unable to agree upon a nominee from the political parties. Dini's government, in particular, was unique in that it did not contain a single member of either branch of the legislature, only jurists, professors, economists, and military men brought in to head the main departments of state.

Enhancing the powers of the chief executive is a central theme in Italian politics today even though it clearly reverses one of the fundamental institutional choices made in the **Constituent Assembly.** *See also* Parliament; Presidente della Repubblica.

PRESIDENTE DELLA REPUBBLICA / President of the Republic. In parliamentary republics, the president is a surrogate monarch with the right "to encourage, to advise, and to be warned" in Bagehot's famous dictum. Normally, however, the office disposes of little or no executive power. Article 83 of the Italian **Constitution** assigns the task of electing the president to an electoral college composed of the two chambers of **Parliament** and representatives from Italy's regional governments. A two-thirds majority is necessary until the fourth round of balloting; thereafter, a simple majority is sufficient.

The party leaders have the task of finding a nominee who will be supported by a broad coalition of electors—a task that is rendered all the more difficult by the fact that the ballot is secret and the influence of the party whips cannot be brought to bear. The negotiations often go on for weeks as the number of ballots grows without conclusion.

The Italian president, chosen for a seven-year term, is more institutionally powerful than a German president but much less powerful than the president of France or the United States. He is the titular head of the High Council of the Judiciary (the executive committee of the legal profession) and has the right to nominate five members of the Constitutional Court. He can nominate senators for life. Most important of all, he formally nominates the prime minister (who must be approved by Parliament) and decides whether or not to resolve a government crisis by dissolving Parliament and calling an election.

For most of the post-war period these powers meant little beyond interviewing prospective prime ministers in order to encourage the parties to find a nominee acceptable to a majority of Parliament, but in recent years the president's role as a crisis-manager has propelled him to center stage. President **Oscar Luigi Scalfaro** played a decisive role in the establishment of the governments of **Carlo Azeglio Ciampi** and, above all, of **Lamberto Dini**. The three last presidents—**Sandro Pertini**, **Francesco Cossiga**, and Scalfaro —have all been accused by their detractors of seeking to expand the powers of the office, especially in the area of foreign affairs. There is growing support for a presidentialist reform, especially from the ex-fascist **Alleanza Nazionale** (AN) / National Alliance.

PRINETTI-BARRÈRE NOTES. On the heels of the June 1902 renewal of the Triple Alliance pledging Austrian, German, and Italian cooperation in the event of a general European war, Italy sought to ensure her own freedom of maneuver. Essentially, she did what the German Foreign Office had accomplished with "Reinsurance Treaties": leaving in one's own hands the final decision of whether or not to commit military forces to the side of an ally in the event of war.

In **Rome**, the French Ambassador was Camille Barrère, to whom the Italian Foreign Minister, Giulio Prinetti (1851-1908), presented in 1902 a note assuring Barrère that should France be attacked, Italy would remain neutral. The same would occur even if, as a consequence of a direct attack, France felt herself "compelled, in defense of her honor or her security," to declare war. This meant that Italy might join in hostilities if, in *Italy's* view, France was attacking Germany without provocation. Reciprocal recognition of Italian claims in **Libya** and French claims in Morocco were also included.

Italy's agreements with Germany specified that in the event of a French attack on Germany, Italy should come to Germany's assistance. On the other hand, if Germany attacked France, Italy would remain "benevolently neutral." Only neutrality was pledged, just as Germany's secret "Reinsurance Treaties" had left in Germany's hands the question of which to choose in the event of an Austro-Russian conflict: assistance to Austria or "benevolent neutrality"—that is, only if France attacked Germany was Italy pledged to provide assistance.

Historians use a different measure in looking at Germany's diplomacy in this period from the one used when examining Italy's initiatives, however. Germany's protection of Germany's freedom of maneuver is defined as a stunning exercise of realpolitik while Italy's efforts bent in the same direction allegedly reveal a basically duplicitous nature. These commitments were not made known beyond their principals until the 1920 publication in France of collections of Foreign Ministry documents (in Yellow Books).

PRODI, ROMANO (1939-). Romano Prodi was born in the province of Reggio Emilia (Emilia-Romagna) in August 1939. Like all but two of his eight brothers and sisters, he initially followed an academic career, becoming a professor of economics at the University of Bologna and a visiting professor at Harvard. In 1978, he became minister for industry in **Andreotti**'s short-lived fourth government.

In 1982, Prodi was asked to take over the chairmanship of the **Istituto per la Ricostruzione Industriale** (IRI), the huge holding company that manages the Italian state's widespread industrial interests. When Prodi took over IRI, the company was sinking under the burden of its debts. By rationalizing the company's steel production in particular, Prodi was able to transform IRI into a profit-making concern by 1989, although his attempts to privatize substantial segments of IRI's activities were blocked by his political opponents. Prodi's career at IRI was linked to the continuance of **Ciriaco De Mita** as secretary of the **Democrazia Cristiana** (DC) / Christian Democracy Party. When De Mita was ousted in 1989, Prodi soon lost his post.

Prodi—whom the Italian left has long regarded as the acceptable face of the DC—was spoken of as a potential premier during the government crises of April 1993 and January 1995. In February 1995, Prodi launched himself into politics, nominating himself as the candidate for the premiership of a broad coalition of center-left parties, including the **Partito Democratico della Sinistra** (PDS) / Democratic Party of the Left, and **Partito Poplare Italiana** (PPI) / Italian People's Party. This coalition, whose symbol is the *ulivo* (olive tree) spent most of 1995 in internal disputation, but rallied to form a common front with the Rinnovamento Italiano / Italian Renewal Party of outgoing Prime Minister Lamberto Dini in the 1996 elections. Led by Prodi, the **Olive Tree Coalition** scored a historic victory in the general elections held on April 21, 1996. In the middle of May, Prodi became prime minister at the head of a government that contained ten PDS ministers.

Prodi has grown in the job as prime minister. He has handled the government's shaky majority, which depends on the votes of Rifondazione Comunista / Communist Refoundation, with skill and has followed a strongly pro-European policy. Under his leadership, the government deficit was brought down from 6.8 percent to just over 3 percent in 1997, and in November 1997, Prodi and the trade unions agreed to reforms of the pension system that will bring the deficit even lower. Thanks to Prodi, and his finance minister, **Carlo Azeglio Ciampi**, Italy seems sure to qualify for European Monetary 1999. *See also* European Union; Maastricht, Treaty of; Partito di Rifondazione Comunista; Olive Tree Coalition.

PROPAGANDA DUE (P2). A secretive masonic lodge, the P2 was described as "an association for criminal purposes" by President **Alessandro Pertini** in October 1981. The existence of the lodge—which boasted over 900 members of Italy's political, business, military, and journalistic elite—was discovered in March 1981 by prosecutors investigating the illegal activities of two of its members, the financier Michele Sindona (poisoned in prison in 1987) and "God's banker," Roberto Calvi, who had made huge illegal payments to **Bettino Craxi**, leader of the **Partito Socialista Italiano** (PSI) / Italian Socialist Party, shortly before being found hanging under Blackfriars Bridge in London in June 1982. The lodge's political objectives, as revealed by its grand master, the ex-Nazi collaborator, Licio Gelli, were to infiltrate members into the highest ranks of the state and media (the TV entrepreneur **Silvio Berlusconi** was a member of the lodge) and to press for a presidential republic as a better bulwark against the danger thought to be posed by the **Partito Comunista Italiano** (PCI) / Italian Communist Party.

The Italian Parliament outlawed the organization in December 1981 and established a Commission of Inquiry whose May 1984 report confirmed that the P2 had indeed intended to manipulate Italy's democratic institutions. Only then did Pietro Longo, as leader of the **Partito Socialista Democratico Italiano** (PSDI) / Italian Social Democratic Party, as senior politician directly involved in the scandal, resign from the government. During the inquiry, it also became clear that Gelli had been closely connected with the Italian secret services and with right-wing terrorist groups, and with **Giulio Andreotti**, who was accused of being the godfather of the secretive association. No proof of this charge—which Andreotti indignantly denied—has ever been found. It does seem certain, however, that the P2 had friends in high places. Gelli was subsequently treated with extraordinary leniency by the authorities, and Italy's high court has since denied—in the face of all the evidence—that the P2 was a subversive organization.

PUCCINI, GIACOMO (1858-1924). Second only to **Giuseppe Verdi** in the annals of Italian opera, Giacomo Puccini was born in Lucca (Tuscany) to a family of musicians. He studied at the conservatory in **Milan** between 1880 and 1883, but his first publicly performed works did not achieve any great critical or popular success. His third and fourth scores, *Manon Lescaut* (1893) and *La Bohème* (1896), by contrast, won international acclaim and remain today two of the most frequently performed classical operas. His two subsequent works, *Tosca* (1900) and *Madame Butterfly* (1904), were initially greeted with skepticism by musical critics, but met with overwhelming enthusiasm from audiences.

After 1904, Puccini collaborated with some of the finest orchestras in the world, producing a series of comparatively minor works. At the time of his death, in 1924 in Brussels, he was working on what is arguably his masterpiece, *Turandot*, which was finished by the composer Franco Alfano and presented at the Scala Theater in Milan in 1926. During the performance, the conductor, **Arturo Toscanini**, famously halted the music in the middle of the third act to tell an emotional audience "At this point, the *maestro* died." Less musically innovative than Verdi, Puccini's operas are nevertheless characterized by rich orchestration, a wonderful gift of melody, great dramatic intensity, and pervasive eroticism.

-Q-

QUADRUMVIRATE. The four men who led the **March on Rome** were designated after the fact by **Mussolini** Field Marshals of the Fascist Revolution: **Italo Balbo, Emilio De Bono, Cesare Maria De Vecchi,** and **Michele Bianchi,** secretary general of the **Partito Nazionale Fascista** (PNF) / National Fascist Party until 1923. These four constituted the quadrumvirate. All were "fascists of the first hour." Of the four, Italo Balbo was the only one toward whom Mussolini showed a certain wariness.

The only institutional function filled by the quadrumvirate was membership in the **Gran Consiglio del Fascismo,** as set down in Article 4 of the 1928 legislation, which, by creating the Grand Council, completed the construction of a personal Mussolinian dictatorship. The only meeting after 1939 of the Grand Council was the essential one of July 24-25, 1943 in which Grandi's motion to restore the king's prerogatives was passed, thus ending Mussolini's rule. *See also* Fascism; Squadrismo; Victor Emmanuel III.

QUALUNQUISMO. In Italian, *l'uomo qualunque* is "the man in the street" or "every man." *Qualunquismo* in the vocabulary of Italian politics means promoting populist, intellectually discreditable policies by demagogic means. The term has its origin in the 1944 political party called the *Fronte dell'Uomo Qualunque* (UQ) / The Ordinary Joe's Front. Its founder was a playwright and journalist called Guglielmo Giannini. Well financed by wealthy businessmen who had enjoyed close ties with the fascist regime, Giannini's party fought the June 1946 election to the **Constituent Assembly** under the slogan (the translation sanitizes the mildly obscene original) "we've had it with people bossing us about" and polled 1.2 million votes. In local elections in November 1946, the party actually obtained more votes in **Rome** than the **Democrazia Cristiana** (DC) / Christian Democracy Party. This was the high point of its success. In 1947, when the DC ended its joint government with the **Partito Socialista Italiano** (PSI) / Italian Socialist Party and with the **Partito Comunista Italiano** (PCI) / Italian Communist Party, the UQ lost its main reason for being. The party fought the 1948 elections in the company of the **Partito Liberale Italiano** (PLI) / Italian Liberal Party, but then declined in significance, with many of its members joining the neo-fascist **Movimento Sociale Italiano** (MSI) / Italian Social Movement or the Monarchists. Giannini died in Rome in

1960. In recent times, the politician most regularly accused of *qualunquismo* has been **Umberto Bossi**.

QUASIMODO, SALVATORE (1901-1968). Born in one of Italy's southernmost cities, Ragusa (**Sicily**), Quasimodo was brought up in a railwayman's family and was given a technical education. He attended the University of **Rome** (La Sapienza) in 1921, initially to study engineering, but soon gave up his studies, and eventually found work as a clerk. In 1930, his first collection of poems, *Acque e terre* (*Water and Earth*), appeared after he was introduced into literary circles by his brother-in-law, **Elio Vittorini**. Two further collections were published in the 1930s, and during the war he published two great collections of lyrics translated from ancient Greek. In 1941, he was appointed professor of Italian literature in **Milan**.

Quasimodo's pre-war poetry had taken no particular social position, but the tragic experience of **World War II** convinced him that the poet needed to take a stand on social issues. His overall body of work (which included translations of modern classics such as e.e. cummings [sic.], Ezra Pound, and Pablo Neruda) was recognized in 1959 by the award of the **Nobel prize**. Upon his death in 1968 in **Naples**, Quasimodo was widely regarded as one of the greatest poets in any language in this century.

-R-

RACIAL LAWS. Not until September-October 1938—after joining the anti-Comintern Pact with Germany and Japan—did fascist Italy approximate German racial legislation, making it illegal for Jews to be teachers at any level, work as journalists, join the **Partito Nazionale Fascista** (PNF) / National Fascist Party, study in state schools, or hold any government positions. Italians of "Aryan race" were forbidden to marry Jews. Limited exemptions were granted for Jews who had served Italy with distinction (for instance by being wounded in battle, or having joined the PNF before 1922). These restrictions were the culmination of a series of previous initiatives in the field of racial policy: in April 1937, all sexual relations between Italians and Africans had been forbidden by law, and in July 1938 a "Manifesto of Racial Scientists" was published in the *Giornale d'Italia* with the approval of the government. The fascist authorities also sponsored an anti-semitic magazine entitled *La Difesa della Razza* (*Defense of the Race*) from August 1938 onward. A moving picture of the plight of Italy's Jews after the publication of the racial laws is to be found in a famous novel by **Giorgio Bassani**, *Il giardino dei Finzi-Contini* (*The Garden of the Finzi-Continis*, 1956), made into a film directed by **Vittorio De Sica**.

While these new restrictions severely wounded many Italian Jews, and caused many prominent Italian Jews to leave the country, the legislation was not as ruthlessly enforced as in Germany. Moreover, compared with France and many other countries in Nazi-occupied Europe, non-Jewish Italians showed an unusual degree of solidarity with their Jewish fellow citizens. During the German occupation of **Rome**, the contributions of Christian Italians enabled the Jewish community to pay—indeed exceed—the huge ransom in gold demanded by the Nazis as a price for not herding Rome's Jews off to forced labor camps. Italian commanders and diplomats in Croatia, Greece, and southern France used bureaucratic cavils of every kind to block shipments of Jews. In November 1942, when **Mussolini** learned that Jews sent to Germany from Croatia were being gassed, he ordered that the delaying tactics should be continued. Even after Nazi minister Von Ribbentrop visited Mussolini in February 1943 to deplore the failure of Italian officers to comply with an ally's requests on racial policy, obstruction continued. Mussolini appointed a chief of racial **police** whose deputy, Angelo Donati, was Jewish, and the police, in fact, often conspired to protect Jews from the Nazis.

RADICAL PARTY (PR). *See* Partito Radicale.

RADIO AUTODIFFUSIONE ITALIANA (RAI and RAI-TV). Italian television first went on the air in January 1954. The new state-owned service transmitted fewer than 1,500 hours of programs in the first year of service, and viewers were numbered in the tens of thousands only. This number increased rapidly as the **economic miracle** brought the cost of a television set within the reach of ordinary middle-class Italians. In the early years of Italian broadcasting, the most popular programs were reproductions of American game shows such as "Double or Nothing" and the "Sixty-Four Thousand Dollar Question." The star of these shows, a young Italian American named Mike Buongiorno, remains one of Italy's most popular television personalities today.

For the first seven years, only the first channel, RAI-1, was broadcasting; but in 1961, a sister channel, RAI-2, appeared. RAI-3 came on the air in 1979 (there are also three parallel radio channels). In the 1980s, RAI's monopoly over nationwide broadcasting was broken by an upstart entrepreneur, **Silvio Berlusconi**, who— beginning with a local TV station in **Milan** —rapidly expanded to build three national networks called Rete 4, Canale 5, and Italia 6. A politically sanctioned duopoly emerged, which has made Italy one of the least advanced countries in the industrialized world in the increasingly crucial field of entertainment technology and services. High union costs and Berlusconi's reliance on cheap American imports (which are dubbed into Italian with astonishing realism) have also ensured that none of the television companies has achieved a particularly good record in producing quality programs of their own. Italy is one of Hollywood's biggest export markets.

RAI is one of the most politicized television companies in the democratic world. During the 1980s, the three RAI channels, especially their news programs, were fiefs of the main political parties. One of the first acts of the recently elected **Olive Tree Coalition** government in the summer of 1996 was to pack the five-person board of directors in charge of the RAI with its own nominees. In a June 1995 **referendum**, Italians voted by 55-45 percent to privatize the RAI. Despite cross-party support for the referendum, **Parliament** has so far failed to act consistently with that vote. *See also* Patronage.

RATTAZZI, URBANO (1808-1873). A native of Alessandria (Piedmont), Rattazzi became a parliamentary deputy in 1848. In 1852, Rattazzi, leader of the relatively radical wing of the Parliament, made the political agreement known as the *connubio* (union) with **Cavour**, and established himself as the second most important political figure in pre-Risorgimento Piedmont. The alliance between the two men dissolved on the eve of the war with Austria in 1859. Rattazzi, who was a favorite of King **Victor Emmanuel II**, became minister of the interior in the short-lived government formed by **General La Marmora** after the Treaty of Villafranca in July 1859, which had provoked **Cavour**'s resignation. As minister of the interior, Rattazzi initiated an important reform of local government that extended the Piedmontese form of provincial and communal administration to Lombardy. The same law, in slightly modified form, was extended throughout the peninsula after unification and established Italy as a centralized state whose lower levels of administration were conceded little autonomy.

In March 1862, Rattazzi formed his first cabinet, taking the offices of foreign and interior minister as well as the premiership. His government took the important decision to introduce a single Italian currency, which increased Italy's ability to borrow in the international markets, but fell afoul of public opinion in September 1862 when the government used troops to prevent **Giuseppe Garibaldi** from marching on **Rome**. Rattazzi's administration resigned in November 1862, but he returned to the premiership in April 1867. The most important act of his short-lived administration was a law in August 1867 that nationalized and auctioned off the land and property held by thousands of religious institutions all over Italy. Garibaldi's attempts to seize Rome in 1867, which ended in the disaster of Mentana, once more brought down Rattazzi's government. Caught between public opinion, which regarded him as too cautious on the Roman question, and France, which suspected him of aiding and abetting Garibaldi, Rattazzi dithered and lost the favor of the king. He died in Rome in 1873. Contemporary writers judged his political record harshly, but in retrospect, it seems that circumstances, rather than ineptitude, were the chief cause of Rattazzi's ministerial failures.

RAUTI, GIUSEPPE UMBERTO (1926-). "Pino" Rauti has been the most vocal and uncompromising fascist leader in post-war Italy. As a youth, he served in the armed forces of the **Republic of Salò**. Rauti has always remained faithful to the anti-capitalist rhetoric of the Salò Republic: for him **fascism** is a revolutionary ideology whose main goal should be the overthrow of the institutions of the bourgeois state. These radical sentiments were frowned upon by the leadership of the **Movimento Sociale Italiano** (MSI) / Italian Social Movement for much of the post-war period, and Rauti's relationship with Italy's neo-fascist party has thus always been a troubled one. Between 1956 and 1969, in fact, Rauti was not a member of the MSI, preferring to act as the theoretician of a neo-nazi group with the ominous name of *Ordine Nuovo* (New Order). Inspired by the political thought of the philosopher Jules Evola, the "New Order" group propagated a sub-Nietzscheian ideology deriding safe bourgeois weaklings and utilitarian values of democratic civilization; while exalting the superman, the hero, the aristocrat, and the warrior. The "New Order" would prove to be the breeding ground for many of the neo-fascist terrorists who plagued Italy in the 1970s, but by then Rauti, finding some of his disciples too extreme, had returned to the MSI.

Rauti became a parliamentary deputy for the MSI in 1972. He swiftly became an influence among the party's most youthful members, and diffused his belief in the necessity of a "fascism of the left." His conviction that the fascist movement should take aim at the egoism, materialism, and superficiality of modern life, and abandon all thought of cooperating with the political parties of Italy's corrupt democracy, gradually won over a majority of the MSI's members. Rauti became secretary of the MSI at a heated party conference in Rimini in January 1990. "Fascism of the left," however, was not popular with the MSI's intensely conservative petty bourgeois electorate and the party suffered the worst defeat of its history in the 1990 local elections, obtaining just 4 percent of the vote. After a further disaster in regional elections in **Sicily** in June 1991, Rauti was obliged to resign.

Despite the electoral success brought to the neo-fascist movement in Italy by his successor, **Gianfranco Fini,** Rauti has been unable to digest the transformation of the MSI into the **Alleanza Nazionale** (AN) / National Alliance. At the Seventeenth and last Party Conference of the MSI at Fiuggì in January-February 1995, Rauti left the party rather than accept Fini's apparent abandonment of fascist ideology and objectives. *See also* Giorgio Almirante; Movimento Sociale Italiano.

RED BRIGADES. *See* Brigate Rosse.

REFERENDUMS. Article 75 of the **1948 Constitution** permits the electorate to repeal all or part of a law (or decree that has the force of law) by popular referendum, though not to write new legislation, which is the explicit function of **Parliament**. Only international treaties, amnesties, or pardons, and all fiscal and budget legislation cannot be abrogated in this way. A referendum can only be called if five regional governments or 500,000 legal adults petition for it. It must also be approved by the Constitutional Court, and may not coincide with a general election. On three occasions (in 1972, 1976, and 1987) Italian governments engineered elections to postpone referendums on **divorce**, abortion, and nuclear power, though all three were eventually held. To pass, a majority of all eligible voters must vote, and a simple majority of them must back the wording of the referendum's sponsors.

The first referendums were on the divisive social issues of divorce (May 12-13, 1974) and abortion (May 17-18, 1981). On both issues, there was a huge turnout (80 percent) and clear decisions in favor of the existing laws.

Since 1981, referendums have become a characteristic feature of the Italian political system: apart from Switzerland, no other country relies upon popular plebiscites as much. Among other issues, referendums have been held on reinstating wage-indexing (1985), abolishing the nuclear power program (1987), and banning hunting and the use of pesticides (1990). Only the last of these failed to meet the 50 percent participation requirement. Deciding whether or not hunting should be banned was, of course, really a question that should have been decided by Parliament. The culmination of this growing use of the referendum was the campaign for electoral reform led by **Mario Segni** between 1988 and 1993. The referendums of June 1991 (on preference voting) and April 1993 (on the repeal of proportional representation in elections to the Senate) were decisive affirmations of the people's will for radical change to the political system.

The triumph of the April 1993 referendum on electoral reform disguised some of the serious defects inherent in overuse of the referendum strategy. In both April 1993 and June 1995, voters were asked to make absurdly technical changes to the law on a vast range of subjects, as well as deciding major issues such as electoral reform and the privatization of the state broadcasting system. Other referendums have been promised. These initiatives are the surest sign of Italy's urgent need for constitutional and political reform. *See also* Divorce; Partito Radicale; Mario Segni.

REGIONALISM. The 1948 **Constitution**, in Articles 114-133 (Title V), sets out the powers and limitations on Italy's regions, of which there are the following 20, subdivided in 95 provinces: Piedmont, Lombardy, Veneto, Liguria, Emilia-Romagna, Tuscany, Umbria, The Marches, Latium, Abruzzi, Molise, Campania, Puglia, Basilicata, and Calabria. Five regions—**Sicily**, **Sardinia**, Trentino-Alto Adige, Friuli-Venezia Giulia, and the Valle d'Aosta are accorded semi-autonomous status. Note that Sicily and Sardinia are islands; the other "special status" regions are border regions with large non-Italian-speaking minorities.

At the close of **World War II**, General de Gaulle's government in France sought to make good its territorial claims against Italy by occupying the Val d'Aosta and parts of Piedmont. Anglo-American counter-pressure, including President Truman's threat to halt aid to

France, obliged de Gaulle to withdraw, whereupon the Italian government announced that the Valdostani would have some administrative autonomy and that public schools would be instituted in which French would be the language of instruction. Val d'Aosta, therefore, had the status in 1945 that was given the other "special status" regions in 1948.

The **World War I** settlements had included Austria's cession of Trento (predominantly Italian-speaking) and Bolzano (Süd Tirol or Alto Adige), predominantly German-speaking. **Mussolini**'s government had sought to Italianize both Val d'Aosta and Trentino-Alto Adige by the selective assignment of teachers and other civil servants, investment policy, and labor transfers. In 1939, Hitler and Mussolini had agreed to allow the local German-speaking population in Trentino-Alto Adige, which was to be recognized as "forever Italian," to choose, in a plebiscite, between being Italian or being German. Those choosing the latter option were to be transferred to the Third Reich. Others would accept Italianization. Of the nearly 267,000 voting, over 185,000 (nearly 70 percent) voted to go to Germany. The onset of World War II interrupted the transfer of such a large number of persons. When Italy surrendered to the Allies in 1943, many German-speakers were still in Alto Adige, which Germany quickly annexed. When the region was returned to Italy, two-thirds of the region's population was—and remains—ethnically German. On September 5, Prime Minister **De Gasperi** signed agreements with the Austrian government (the De Gasperi-Gruber Accord) guaranteeing the administrative, cultural, and economic autonomy of Alto Adige. Thus, two years before the Constitution created "special status," both Val d'Aosta and Trentino-Alto Adige had acquired that status.

The settlement with Yugoslavia concerned the Istrian Peninsula, flanked by Fiume (Rijeka) and **Trieste**. The number of allies (Britain, France, the United States, and the Union of Soviet Socialist Republics) ensured that the conference would degenerate into tests of strength among these victors rather than between them and the vanquished. The Yugoslav monarchy-in-exile and the Tito-led communist partisans vied for the right to represent Slav interests. When Tito occupied Trieste in May 1945, Britain and the United States—backed by the USSR—persuaded him to withdraw in favor of the establishment of the Free Territory of Trieste, divided into Zone A (under Anglo-American occupation) and Zone B (the rest of the peninsula, under Yugoslav occupation). The reabsorption of

Trieste by Italy was finally accepted by Yugoslavia in the 1975 Treaty of Osimo.

Each of the 20 aforementioned regions, according to the enabling legislation passed by the **Parliament**, is to be governed by a legislative body (the Regional Council), which elects from among its members both the executive Giunta (cabinet) and the region's president, who "represents the Region; promulgates regional laws and regulations; directs the administrative functions delegated by the State to the Region, in conformity with the instructions issued by the central government." The better to ensure that conformity, the Constitution also calls for a resident commissioner to reside in the regional capital, whose duty it will be to "supervise the administrative functions of the State and ensure their coordination with those exercised by the Region." That commissioner must counter-sign all regional legislative acts "within 30 days." These regional entities were brought into existence only in 1970, 22 years after the Constitution called for them. Earlier attempts to implement the devolution to the regions of the powers exercised by the central government ran afoul of what, for the dominant **Democrazia Cristiana** (DC) / Christian Democracy Party, was an unacceptable reality: that such a reform would add to the power of the **Partito Comunista Italiano** (PCI) / Italian Communist Party in the "Red Belt" of central Italy.

It was not until 1977 that the strength of the left could be applied to the question of regional devolution. The regions were given a measure of financial autonomy, especially in health care and city planning. The great divergences to be found in the success with which the gains in regional autonomy are utilized to the advantage of the citizenry have been the subject of a major study that has concluded that those regions with a strong tradition of civic order are quicker to organize, to utilize the funds provided by the state, and to monitor expenditures.

Whether the decentralization sought by the **Lega Nord** is a transient phenomenon remains to be seen. *See also* Bologna; Dialects in Italy; Minorities; Movimento Sociale Italiano; Trieste.

REPUBBLICA SOCIALE ITALIANA (RSI) / Italian Social Republic. *See* Salò, Republic of.

REPUBLICAN PARTY. *See* Partito Repubblicano Italiano.

RERUM NOVARUM. *See* Encyclicals.

RESISTANCE. *See* Bologna; Comitati di Liberazione Nazionale; Florence; Rome.

RETE, LA (The Network). A political movement of pronounced progressive sympathies, La Rete provided a political vehicle for the social and civic activism of many thousands of mostly young people who were already involved in voluntary, church, and local associations against scourges such as the **mafia**, unemployment, urban degradation, and political corruption.

La Rete was officially founded in January 1991. Its first leader—or, more accurately, "national coordinator"—was the former mayor of **Palermo, Leoluca Orlando**, who had left the **Democrazia Cristiana** (DC) / Christian Democracy Party the previous year after the party hierarchy insisted that he should govern in conjunction with the party's national allies, and should abandon the heterogeneous local coalition of progressives supporting his administration. Palermo has ever since been the heart of La Rete's support, but the new movement took root in other cities where there were strong traditions of urban activism and Christian socialism, notably **Milan, Turin**, and Trento. From the very beginning, La Rete attempted to renounce all the traditional forms of party organization, allowing the maximum possible local autonomy for the small self-financed cells of citizens who constitute its membership.

In the 1992 general elections, La Rete obtained over 700,000 votes—2 percent of the electorate—despite the fact that it did not run candidates throughout the country, but only in areas where it had some semblance of local organization.

La Rete failed to fulfill its promise, however. Anxious not to be wiped out by a change in the electoral laws, it reneged on its earlier commitment to abolish the proportional system of parliamentary representation during the **referendum** on the question in April 1993. In the June 1993 local elections, the party headed broad leftist coalitions in Turin, Milan, and Catania (Sicily). Despite the favorable circumstances (the elections were held shortly after **Giulio Andreotti** and other DC leaders were accused of links to the mafia), all three of its candidates lost, a defeat that was only partially remedied by Orlando's triumphant reelection—by a 75 percent plurality—as mayor of Palermo in a second round of local elections in November 1993.

La Rete fought the 1994 election as part of the progressive coalition headed by the **Partito Democratico della Sinistra** (PDS) / Democratic Party of the Left. It was unexpectedly overtaken in **Sicily** by **Forza Italia** and did not advance beyond the 2 percent of the vote it had obtained in 1992. Under the new electoral law, this meant that it was not awarded any of the seats allocated by proportional representation, and the movement was reduced to a handful of directly elected members, all of whom were from Sicily. While officially still in being, La Rete has virtually ceased to exist as a political force outside Sicily. *See also* Electoral Laws.

REVOLUTIONS OF 1848. Even by the turbulent standards of the "year of revolutions," Italy endured a period of exceptional upheaval in 1848-1849. Tension had been building throughout 1847. Poor harvests, the liberal reformism of Pius IX, resentment at the heavy taxes levied by the Austrians (which gave rise to the so-called "smokers' strike" in Lombardy in January 1848) all contributed to a favorable climate of opinion for a revolt against absolutism. The catalyst for revolution was the successful revolt of the people of **Palermo** and **Naples** in January 1848, which compelled Ferdinand II to concede a constitutional monarchy, and then the French Revolution of February, which ignited public opinion in Berlin and Vienna, where Metternich himself was deposed by a popular insurrection on March 13.

The first stage of revolutionary activity in Italy was liberal and constitutionalist. As soon as news of the downfall of Metternich reached **Milan**, Lombardy and **Venice** rose in revolt against the Austrians in March 1848. During the "five glorious days" (March 18-23, 1848), the Milanese drove the Austrians from the city. In Venice, the people seized power and hoisted the tricolor, declaring a republic. Insurrections broke out in **Bologna**, Parma, Piacenza, and other northern Italian cities. Against the wishes of some of their most influential leaders, the cities and republics of northern Italy voted to unify themselves with Piedmont-Sardinia, which declared war on Austria in March after already having adopted a liberal constitution. Defeat at Custoza was followed by an armistice with the Austrians and the reoccupation of Milan by General Joseph Radetzky's forces.

The reoccupation of Milan only inflamed the peninsula further. The peoples of the Papal states, angered by Pius IX's tacit support for Austria, rose in revolt in **Rome** in November and imposed on the Pope a government of pronounced liberal sympathies. On November

24, Pius IX fled to Naples (where Ferdinand and the forces of reaction had bloodily regained control). The revolt in Rome, and similar uprisings in **Florence**, Livorno (Leghorn), and Genoa, were explicitly republican and democratic—even socialist—in tone. In Rome, the liberal government appointed by the Pope lasted but a few days. On January 21-22, 1849, free elections by universal male suffrage were held, and on February 9, Rome became a republic. Church property was confiscated, public workshops and housing were provided, certain taxes were abolished. **Mazzini** arrived in Rome in March 1849, and was swiftly given executive power.

Papal authority was restored in Rome by the French army. Louis Napoleon, anxious to curry favor with French Catholics, sent an expeditionary force of 10,000 men to Italy in April 1849. Led by **Giuseppe Garibaldi**, the Romans mounted a spirited resistance, and it was only after reinforcements arrived from Naples and Spain, and a month of destructive bombardment, that the city surrendered to the French at the beginning of July 1849. Venice was the last bastion of revolution to fall: it eventually surrendered to General Radetzky after a bloody siege, on August 23, 1849. *See also* Papacy.

RICASOLI, BETTINO (1809-1880). A wealthy Tuscan landowner who delighted in experimenting with modern techniques in agriculture, Ricasoli took an equally earnest interest in promoting Italian unification. His first venture in this direction was the publication of a newspaper, *La Patria* (*The Motherland*), in 1847. He was an active organizer of the Italian National Society in Tuscany and in 1859-1860 emerged as one of the leaders of the Florentine nationalists. **Florence** rose in support of the Kingdom of **Sardinia** in April 1859 and Ricasoli was appointed minister of the interior for Tuscany by the representative of the Sardinian throne, Count Carlo Boncompagni, who was voted dictatorial powers for the duration of the war.

After the peace of Villafranca in July 1859, Ricasoli took the lead in ensuring that ducal rule was not restored in Tuscany, and guided the plebiscite in March 1860 by which Tuscany voted to join the Kingdom of Sardinia. His success in this endeavor made him a political figure of national standing, and when **Camillo Benso di Cavour** died unexpectedly in June 1861, King **Victor Emmanuel II** turned to the energetic and dignified Ricasoli as a replacement.

Ricasoli thus became prime minister on June 12, and reserved for himself the portfolios of foreign and interior minister. He soon won the nickname of "the Iron Baron." His government initiated a policy of fierce repression in southern Italy, where disgruntled peasants were in revolt, and established a highly centralized form of local government in October 1861. In February 1862, Ricasoli lost the confidence of the king and was replaced by **Urbano Rattazzi**. He was out of power until June 1866, when he became prime minister on the day of the outbreak of war with Austria. Ricasoli's second premiership was dominated by the dismal performance of the Italian army and fleet, which were defeated at the battles of Custoza and Lissa, respectively, and by the decision to block **Giuseppe Garibaldi**'s advance in the Trentino for political reasons. Ricasoli also ordered the savage repression of a popular uprising against the monarchy in **Palermo** in September 1866—hundreds of rebels were shot, thousands arrested, and much of **Sicily** was put under martial law until December. In February 1867, Ricasoli's government was defeated in Parliament over the question of relations with the church. The king asked Ricasoli to form a new government, but after elections in March 1867, he resigned once more and never again held high office. *See also* Camillo Benso di Cavour; Giuseppe Garibaldi.

RIFONDAZIONE COMUNISTA. *See* Partito di Rifondazione Comunista.

RISORGIMENTO. The creation of Italian political unity took place in a remarkably brief time span, 1859-1861. This brevity was due to a felicitous combination of international and domestic factors. First, the international context was favorable for the reduction of Austrian power in Italy. Austria had isolated herself during the Crimean War by staying neutral and was facing France's challenge to her role as the power broker in Europe. Liberal England, moreover, wished to see the end of the anachronistic absolutist regime of the Bourbons in southern Italy. Within Italy, Piedmont-Sardinia, thanks to the modernizing efforts of **Cavour**, had emerged as a power of some weight capable of attracting the middle classes of Lombardy, Tuscany, and the rest of northern Italy to its cause. Liberal and nationalist ideas, moreover, were widespread by the end of the 1850s. The views of **Vincenzo Gioberti**, **Cesare Balbo**, and **Massimo D'Azeglio** had been read by every educated Italian; republicans and democrats such as **Carlo Cattaneo** and **Giuseppe Mazzini** also had a substantial following, particularly in central Italy.

Cavour's unique diplomatic skills turned these favorable

conditions into political action. First, he persuaded Napoleon III to ally France to Piedmont in July 1858 at Plombières by promising France Nice and the duchies of central Italy (the eventual status of Savoy was left open) in exchange for French assistance to liberate Lombardy and Venetia from Austrian rule. The four northern Italian regions so liberated were then to form a federation under the presidency of the Pope. Cavour then goaded Austria into declaring war in April 1859, allowing Piedmont-Sardinia to appear as the innocent victim of an act of aggression by a larger power. As the bloody battles of Magenta and Solferino demonstrated, without French support the Piedmontese army would never have been able to defeat the Austrians. Simultaneous insurrections in Tuscany, Modena, and Parma in favor of unification with **Turin** were in large part organized by Cavour's agents, thus nullifying the Plombières agreement by thwarting Napoleon III's ambitions. The peace in July 1859—which granted Lombardy to Piedmont, but which insisted on the return of absolute rule in central Italy—was a tardy attempt by Napoleon and the Austrians to close the Pandora's box opened by their own ambition. The treaty provoked Cavour's resignation, but by now the movement for unification with Piedmont in central Italy was too strong to be blocked by anything short of a bloody war of repression. Cavour returned triumphantly to office in January 1860 and, in exchange for the cession of Savoy as well as Nice to France, was allowed to incorporate all of north-central Italy into Piedmont-Sardinia.

Mazzini and **Giuseppe Garibaldi** regarded Cavour's patient diplomacy as too cautious, however. At the beginning of 1860, the so-called "Action Party" was founded with the specific goal of liberating **Rome**, **Venice,** and **southern Italy** from absolutist and Papal rule. In April 1860, Garibaldi and his "Thousand" redshirts sailed to **Palermo** to assist the Mazzinian uprising that had broken out against Bourbon rule. With the assistance of the British fleet, Garibaldi disembarked and swiftly established his personal dictatorship over the island. In August 1860, he crossed the Strait of Messina at the head of an army of Sicilians and marched on **Naples**, which he entered without encountering resistance in September. He was joined by Mazzini and **Cattaneo** who openly argued that the redshirts' conquests should herald a democratic and republican solution to the unification of Italy.

Cavour, alarmed by this project, used the threat of a democratic revolution in Italy to persuade France to give him a free hand in southern Italy. Piedmontese troops invaded the Papal states and blocked Garibaldi's road to Rome, and at Teano on October 26, 1860, Garibaldi ceded his conquests to Piedmont's king. This decision was confirmed by regional plebiscites in February 1861. Only the wealthiest citizens were allowed to vote, and, particularly in the south, ballot fraud was widespread. Italy had completed its liberal revolution, but had installed a regime that was ignorant of the needs of the southern peasantry and strongly identified with the interests of northern upper classes. It is not fanciful to claim that many of Italy's subsequent problems stemmed from the political settlement of the process of unification. *See also* Camillo Benso di Cavour; Giuseppe Garibaldi; Giuseppe Mazzini; Southern Italy; Monarchy.

ROCCO, ALFREDO (1875-1935). Rocco, a legal scholar from **Naples** who had been one of the leading lights of the Italian nationalist movement, became one of the foremost ideologues of **fascism**. In 1918, he had begun publishing *La Politica*, a review in which he articulated the classic precept of the supremacy of the state over the individual. Elected president of the Chamber of Deputies after the 1924 elections, he held that position throughout the **Matteotti** crisis before, in January 1925, becoming minister of justice. In this post, his first duty was to introduce a law banning secretive associations such as the Freemasons. **Antonio Gramsci** made his only parliamentary speech in opposition illustrating that the law gave the government the power to ban opposition associations of any kind. This measure was a prelude to Rocco's drastic measures dissolving all opposition parties, reintroducing the death penalty, and instituting special tribunals for political activity in October 1926.

In 1928, he was responsible both for the new electoral law, with its plebiscitary character, and the law that precisely defined the role and functions of the Fascist Grand Council and transformed it from a party body to an organ of the state. Rocco capped his spell at the Justice Ministry by introducing new penal codes in 1930-1931. These included the *Testo unico di pubblica sicurezza* or "Consolidated Public Security Laws" still in force in post-fascist Italy: more generally, they were intended to enshrine Rocco's fundamental principle of jurisprudence—the priority of collective institutions over individual rights and the primacy of the monolithic state above all other institutions of any kind. Rocco opposed the **Lateran pacts** in 1929 because he believed that they would weaken the power of the state.

Rocco also played a key role in the creation of **corporatism**. In 1926, he wrote the Labor Charter, which prohibited strikes and effectively closed down all **trade unions** except the fascist Confederazione Italiana Sindacati Nazionali Lavoratori (CISNAL) / Italian Confederation of National Workers' Unions. When the Ministry of Corporations was created in 1926, he was called on to head it since corporatism was the institutional core of the entire fascist system. He also headed the subsequent (1930) Consiglio Nazionale delle Corporazioni (National Council of Corporations) to which all workers' syndicates were automatically attached. At the time of his death in 1935, he was rector of the University of Rome. *See also* Fascism.

ROME (*Roma*). Before Italy's unification, Rome was often regarded by Anglo-American tourists as a backwater of Europe, notable chiefly for being the seat of the Holy See and the Roman Catholic Church. The wealth of architecture and art produced there over earlier centuries reflected the wealth, most often, of Papal sponsors. The population was often likened to those of southern Italy. Commerce, rather than manufacture (in the 1980s, manufacturing employed barely one-fifth of Rome's work force), seemed its chief producer of wealth. After the Napoleonic turmoil and its attendant nationalism, pan-Italian militants identified the church as the temporal power whose grip had, somehow, to be loosened. As in much of the Italian peninsula, such struggles were rarely left only to Italians: foreign governments regularly intervened in Italian affairs. Whether it was French forces in the 1849 Roman Republic; or a Piedmontese army (seen by Romans as foreign) in 1870; or the German *Wehrmacht* after September 8, 1943; or the American Fifth Army in June 1944; foreign armies have made their weight felt in modern Italy.

Unique among Western cities, Rome is two capitals: that of the Holy See, and that of the secular Italian state. Like most Italian cities, contemporary Rome is ringed by the remnants of medieval defensive walls interrupted by the former portals. At one, *Porta Pia* (the Pious Portal), a monument has been erected to the Piedmontese **Bersaglieri** who breached the wall there when Rome became Italian. The city was under Papal jurisdiction, and its defense was in the hands of the Papal Zouaves, remnants of a French garrison left behind when the rest were withdrawn to assist in the defense of Paris in the Franco-Prussian war. Their commander was ordered by the Pope to fire a single cannonade in order to establish that violence had been done to the Papal state, to be followed by surrender to the Piedmontese forces. When the Bersaglieri entered the city, therefore, they met no resistance.

Instead, memorialists recall that from the windowsills along the entry route, Piedmontese flags with the heraldic symbol of the House of Savoy suddenly appeared in place of the theretofore ubiquitous white and gold of the Papal banner. Cries of "Long Live the King!" and "Long Live Italy!" accompanied the fanfares of Bersaglieri bands. A provincial plebiscite held two weeks later showed 133,681 votes in favor of annexation and only 1,507 opposed. The probability of becoming the national capital had an immeasurable influence on that electoral outcome.

The **March on Rome**, which established **Benito Mussolini** as Italy's chief executive for two decades, is chronicled elsewhere among the entries in this volume. However, it should be noted that whether under a liberal monarchy, a fascist dictatorship, or a democratic state dominated by the **Democrazia Cristiana (DC)** / Christian Democracy Party, the Italian state—legally, an extension of the Piedmontese state—has been unitary and centralized, thereby putting enormous power in the hands of the bureaucracy, which, by virtue of the relative weakness of the post-war executive, is in a position to frustrate all initiatives able to threaten bureaucratic discretionary power.

After September 8, 1943, Rome's population waited for the Allies to arrive as liberators. Meanwhile, the Germans had to deal with non-compliance rather than insurrection by armed bands. Those few groups who were armed were either ex-military who saw themselves as "reserve units" to assist the Allies—whensoever they should reach Rome; adolescents of the periphery of Rome whose raids on bakeries produced flour for distribution to the neighborhood and something left over to trade on the black market; and, finally, the active left-partisan groups made up of intellectuals, craftsmen, and organized workers.

On March 23, 1944, Roman partisans bombed a truckload of German guards, killing 32. For each dead German, the outraged commander had ten prisoners (starting with Jews) killed in the Ardeatine caves. Although the entrance to the caves was blown up and sealed after the massacre, witnesses were aware of what had been done and the site was uncovered within a month. It is today the site of an annual commemoration ceremony. The German officer in charge, Erich Priebke, was extradited and placed on trial for war crimes in 1996.

At the time, the heavy-handed assassination of 335 unarmed civilians (the warden, in fact, sent 15 too many), who could have had nothing to do with the guerrilla action, seemed to augment popular support of the partisan *Gruppi d'Azione Patriottica* (GAP). Yet the fact remains that Rome is the only Italian city not to have experienced an insurrection, even at the moment when the Germans were withdrawing northward to establish new defensive lines against the Allied advance.

Since then, Rome—the Eternal City—continues to be the center of Italian political life. National headquarters for all the parties are located there as are the ministries and the thousands of civil servants employed by them, either directly or in public works projects. People from far poorer cities, especially from the South and the islands of **Sicily** and **Sardinia**, have long flocked there in the hope of finding a job or a sinecure. In 1871, the population was 200,000. By 1909, it had more than doubled (542,000). A million had been reached by 1926. Between 1951 and 1961, a half-million newcomers per year added to the city's population so that by 1961, there were 2.2 million inhabitants. By 1971, it had grown to 2.8 million. Of these, 40 percent were from regions south of Rome or from the islands. In the next decade, immigration from the South and from insular Italy eased, and by 1975, the number of emigrants surpassed the number of immigrants. *See also* Umberto Bossi; Fascism; Lega Nord; Benito Mussolini; Papacy; Squadrismo.

ROSSELLI, CARLO (1899-1937) and **NELLO** (1900-1937). Anti-fascist martyrs, the Rosselli brothers were two of the bravest and most intellectually sophisticated leaders of the struggle against **Mussolini**. Born in **Rome** to a wealthy Jewish family from Tuscany, the brothers were brought up in **Florence**, which in the early 1920s was the scene of some of the worst acts of *squadrismo* in Italy. Greatly influenced by **Gaetano Salvemini** and **Piero Gobetti**, Carlo, when a professor of political economy at the University of Genoa, was among the organizers of a "cultural circle" for the propagation of democratic ideas and free thought, which was shut down in Florence by fascist bullies in December 1924. Beaten—literally, but not bowed—the brothers, together with Salvemini, printed and distributed a subversive leaflet, *Non Mollare!* (*Don't Give Up*) in 1925 and participated in the escape from Italy of **Filippo Turati** and

Salvemini.

Carlo was arrested and sentenced to five years' imprisonment on the island of Lipari in 1927, but he managed to escape in 1929. In 1930, he published, in Paris, his most important work, *Socialismo liberale* (*Liberal Socialism*), a book that was not only anti-fascist, but critical of the authoritarian tendencies of Soviet communism, and a plea for a form of socialism founded upon liberal principles of human rights. *Socialismo liberale* was secretly distributed within Italy and made Carlo the undisputed leader of the clandestine organization known as *Giustizia e libertà*. Carlo Rosselli, in fact, can be regarded as the principal influence on the young intellectuals who would later form the **Partito d'Azione** (PdA) / Action Party and occupy an important role within the **Partito Repubblicano Italiano** (PRI) / Italian Republican Party, **Partito Socialista Democratico Italiano** (PSDI) / Italian Social Democratic Party, and **Partito Socialista Italiano** (PSI) / Italian Socialist Party after 1945.

Carlo did not restrict his anti-fascist activity to theorizing. In 1936, he organized a column of Italian anti-fascist volunteers and served in the **Spanish Civil War**. Struck down by illness, he returned to Paris, where he was joined by Nello, who in the meantime had become a historian of the **Risorgimento**, and had seen the inside of several fascist jails. In June 1937, the two brothers were stabbed to death by a group of French hoodlums hired by the fascists: it has since been established that Mussolini gave the order for the brothers' murder.

ROSSELLINI, ROBERTO (1906-1977). Regarded by many as Italy's greatest film director, Rossellini made his international reputation with a depiction of the resistance to the Nazi occupation: *Roma, città aperta* (*Open City*, 1945). Shot on location in war-torn **Rome**, using a jumble of film types and with a cast of largely unprofessional actors, the film tells the story of the unsuccessful attempt of an underground leader, Manfredi, to elude the Gestapo. Manfredi is helped by a defiant group of Roman workers, and by a Catholic priest, Don Pietro. Both Manfredi and Don Pietro are captured and tortured. In the moving final scene, Don Pietro is shot by a firing squad. Yet the message of the film is one of hope. From a distance, the children from Don Pietro's church in the slums witness his brave death and walk down the hill from the place of execution to a city that will be theirs. The film is notable also for the performance of a brilliant actress, Anna Magnani, who plays the resourceful Pina, a pregnant slum woman who works, feeds a family, and aids the resistance with courage and good humor. The scene in which Pina is shot by German soldiers after having arrested her lover is one of the most evocative images in the history of cinema.

Rossellini continued to work in the neo-realist idiom, producing the classic films *Paisà* (*Paisan*, 1947) and *Germania, anno zero* (*Germany, Year Zero*, 1947). But his film *Stromboli, terra di Dio* (*Stromboli*, 1949) was criticized both by neo-realist critics for its unsympathetic portrayal of the Stromboli peasants and for its unabashed religious content; and by the Catholic Church, which regarded the film as the product of sin (the film starred Ingrid Bergman, with whom Rossellini had an affair and whom he married after she divorced her Swedish husband).

Rossellini's break with **neo-realism** came in 1953 when he directed *Viaggio in Italia* (*Journey to Italy*), a film about a prudish English couple whose relationship is threatened by the emotions that they experience upon visiting **Naples**. The film's overt religious content and taxing *longeurs* were excoriated in Italy. In France, however, Rossellini's film, and all his subsequent work in the 1950s and 1960s, was greatly admired by both critics and filmmakers, especially Godard and Truffaut.

Rossellini returned to popular and critical favor in Italy only in 1959 with *Il generale Della Rovere* (*General Della Rovere*, 1959). Starring **Vittorio De Sica**, this story about a confidence trickster hired by the German occupiers to discover the identity of a resistance leader, but who ultimately rejects his paymasters and dies a hero's death, won the Golden Lion at the Venice Film Festival and was a huge commercial success. In the 1960s, Rossellini was one of the first directors to experiment with the new medium of television. Between 1966 and 1973, he made a series of masterful historical dramas as well as a number of documentaries. When he died in 1977, he was regarded as one of the most original figures in the history of film.

RUMOR, MARIANO (1915-1990). Benjamin Disraeli's observation that becoming prime minister is much like climbing a greasy pole is well illustrated by Mariano Rumor. One of many Christian Democrats to serve as premier, he reached the pinnacle by devoted service to the party. A high school teacher who was active on the provincial **Comitato di Liberazione Nazionale** (CLN) / National Liberation Committee in his native Vicenza after September 8, 1943, he served his party at both national and local levels. Elected to the **Constituent Assembly** in 1946 and subsequently to the Chamber of Deputies in every election until his death, Rumor was also president of the Associazione Cristiana Lavoratori Italiani (ACLI) / Christian Association of Italian Workers and vice secretary of the **Democrazia Cristiana** (DC) / Christian Democracy Party in 1950-1951 and again between 1954 and 1958.

His first ministerial appointment was as deputy secretary in the agriculture ministry under **De Gasperi** (1951) and **Giuseppe Pella** in 1954. One of the leading lights of the centrist *doroteo* faction, he became a fixture in subsequent DC administrations until in December 1968 he became president of the Council of Ministers in his own right, a post he retained until August 1970 heading three different coalitions. His period as prime minister was characterized by both intricate political maneuvering within the DC and growing social tensions and political violence in Italy. His government did, however, pass the enabling legislation that authorized the holding of **referendums** and instituting a regional layer of government.

Rumor returned to the premiership in July 1973, and his administration lasted, in two incarnations, until November 1974. In these years, public dissatisfaction with the DC's corruption and misrule came to a head. Rumor was subsequently implicated personally in the Lockheed bribery scandal (which forced **President Giovanni Leone** to resign before his term had expired) but was exonerated by **Parliament** in 1978. The following year, he was elected to the Italian Senate and was reelected in 1983 and 1987. He died in **Rome** in 1990. *See also* Regionalism; Fernando Tambroni.

-S-

SAINT GERMAIN, TREATY OF. The Treaty of Saint Germain between the victorious Allies and Austria was signed on September 10, 1919. The former Austro-Hungarian empire was broken up and new nations—Czechoslovakia, Hungary, Yugoslavia—were created. Italy's territorial claims against Austria were one of the thorniest issues in the peace settlement and the treaty left the Italian public feeling that Italy had been betrayed by her fellow powers. The secret **Treaty of London** (April 1915), which had secured Italian accession to the war on the side of the Entente, and a subsequent deal between the wartime premiers of France, Britain, and Italy in April 1917, had promised Italy large gains at the expense of Austria, control over much of the Dalmatian coastline (modern-day Croatia), the Dodecanese Islands, Smyrna in Asia Minor, and colonial compensation.

These exorbitant promises, made at a moment when the Entente powers were desperate to get Italy into the conflict, seemed excessively generous compensation for Italy's contribution once the war was over. Moreover, the United States had entered the war in 1917, and President Woodrow Wilson was determined to shape the post-war peace in accordance with the principle of self-determination of racial minorities. In particular, he was adamant that Italy would not acquire sovereignty over several hundred thousand Slavs in Dalmatia. Despite Italy's representative at Paris, Prime Minister **Vittorio Emanuele Orlando**, walking out of the peace conference in protest, Italy's expectations were cut back sharply. Wilson conceded Italy the Brenner frontier (ensuring that hundreds of thousands of German nationals were incorporated into Italy) and allowed Trieste and Istria, but not Dalmatia, to become Italian territory. Italy also maintained de facto control over the Dodecanese Islands but had to renounce her territorial ambitions in Asia Minor. Cunningly, Britain and France took advantage of Italy's self-imposed exclusion from the conference table to ensure both that Italy was not given any of the former German or Turkish colonies as a "mandate" from the League of Nations and that she was not compensated with territorial gains in Africa.

In objective terms, Italy was not badly treated by the peace settlement. Italy's statesmen, however, had been convinced that the settlement would transform the Mediterranean into an "Italian lake" and that Italy would emerge as one of the indisputably great powers. The disillusionment was therefore enormous, with even moderates denouncing Italy's betrayal at the hands of the other powers. Resentment at the peace settlement enabled **Gabriele D'Annunzio** to seize the town of Fiume (which had been given to Yugoslavia) on the Dalmatian coast, and fanned the already smouldering flames of nationalism and fascism.

SALANDRA, ANTONIO (1853-1931). When **General Pelloux** was prime minister (1898-1890), he turned to those who were also conservative nationalists, like Professor Salandra, who was subsequently to serve in **Sidney Sonnino**'s 1906 and 1909 governments. Later, when Salandra was prime minister (1914-1916), he negotiated the **London Treaty of 1915** under the terms of which Italy, if she were to join the Anglo-French Entente against the Central Powers, would receive Trento and **Trieste**, South Tyrol (Alto Adige), the Dalmatian Coast, the Aegean Islands, and a share in the Ottoman Empire in the event of its partitioning. These arrangements were not revealed to the Italian **Parliament**, whose members might well have opposed them.

No friend of reform, he was a political gambler quite prepared to plot with King **Victor Emmanuel III** to undo the Giolittian system even if at the risk of war. Austria's July ultimatum to Serbia, given without consulting her Italian ally, put Austria in violation of the **Triple Alliance,** which bound Italy to retain benevolent neutrality should Austria go to war. But Salandra saw neutrality consistent with the Triple Alliance as offering a special advantage: Austria was under obligation to compensate Italy for any change in the Balkan status quo. Indeed, while Italy was secretly negotiating in London, she was also dealing with one-time German Chancellor von Bülow who was gingerly offering to satisfy some Italian claims on "unredeemed" territories in the northeast in exchange for benevolent neutrality. Salandra, in fact, seems to have hoped that the new state of **Albania** might become Italian as compensation: in December 1914, Italian forces had already occupied Valona. As it was, just three weeks before Italian entry into hostilities as required by the secret Treaty of London, Salandra informed the Austrian and German governments of his renunciation of the Triple Alliance.

Anxious to keep Italy from joining the war against them, Austria offered to satisfy most Italian territorial demands. Salandra delayed the reopening of Parliament so that the decision was really in the hands of the king who was by now so deeply committed by his signature of the London Treaty that he had no honorable alternative to waging war against Austria. With a logic not unlike **Mussolini**'s in 1940, Salandra reckoned that the time had come for Italy to choose (what seemed at the time) the winning side. His subsequent reference to *sacro egoismo* was as ill-timed as it was candid. Austria made early advances against an Italian army whose general staff learned of the switch in alliances only three weeks before war was declared. Salandra was forced to resign.

It was well after the war that Salandra again became a candidate for premier. Fascist street violence had forced **Luigi Facta** to recognize his impotence and resign in 1922. Salandra hoped to head a government including the fascists. Nationalist leaders recommended that **Mussolini** accept such an arrangement, but the fascist leader held out for nothing less than forming his own government.

Only after the publication of documents connecting Mussolini directly with the murder of **Matteotti** did Salandra join the opposition which was, by then, totally ineffective. *See also* March on Rome.

SALÒ, REPUBLIC OF. Two weeks after Anglo-American forces landed in **Sicily** (July 10, 1943), the **Gran Consiglio del Fascismo** (Grand Council of Fascism) supported a document submitted by **Dino Grandi** urging the king to resume command of Italian forces and resume "that supreme initiative in making decisions which our institutions attribute to him." The vote was 19 in favor, 7 opposed, and 1 abstention. King **Victor Emanuel III** thereupon ordered **Mussolini**'s arrest and transfer to a prison on the Gran Sasso Mountain in Abruzzo where he was kept under close guard until being freed by German glider-borne paratroopers in a daring raid on September 12.

The king initially chose Marshal **Badoglio** to head what became a royal-military dictatorship still intent on continuing the war, at least while negotiations with the Allies could proceed. When Italy surrendered on September 8, 1943, the king, Badoglio, and the government fled south to Brindisi by way of Pescara leaving the Royal Army without orders; this proved the final blow to the **monarchy**. Italian forces stationed abroad were crushed between the hatred of local populations and the contempt of the betrayed German army. Among other actions, the German army massacred nearly 10,000 Italian soldiers on the Isle of Cefalonia (Greece) after a ten-day battle. In Italy, few units offered organized resistance to the Germans although many individuals, both officers and enlisted men, subsequently joined the Resistance.

Even before Mussolini's rescue from Gran Sasso, several hierarchs (**Roberto Farinacci**, Vittorio Mussolini, and Alessandro Pavolini) had announced from East Prussia the creation of a new fascist government. By September 23, an ailing Mussolini was installed by the Nazis at the head of a puppet regime at the town of Salò on Lake Garda. He immediately renamed the **Partito Nazionale Fascista** (PNF) / National Fascist Party. It was now to be the Partito Repubblicano Fascista / Fascist Republican Party, infuriated with the monarchy and with those fascists who had voted against Mussolini. Adherents of the **Republic of Salò** were *repubblichini*. A party congress held in nearby Verona between November 14-16, 1943, established the new regime's fundamental principles in an 18-point program that announced the end of the monarchy and articulated an ideology that paid lip service at least to the necessity of limiting the power of private capitalism. In January 1944, several members of the Grand Council who had voted against Mussolini were convicted of treason and executed, including Mussolini's son-in-law, **Galeazzo Ciano**.

The true believers (*repubblichini*) who stayed with Mussolini or were conscripted in the North were teamed with German units to function as "order maintainers" and as an anti-partisan militia. Anxious to prove their mettle to their diffident German comrades-in-arms, they were responsible for especially brutal acts of repression in Emilia-Romagna and other northern regions. The *Decima mas*—a private army headed by Prince Valerio Borghese—was drawn from a group of Italian naval personnel who had used small motor-powered craft to attack submarines. Together with the so-called Black Brigades, it constituted the chief anti-partisan arm of the **Repubblica Sociale Italiana** (RSI) / Italian Social Republic and included in its ranks **Giorgio Almirante**, who after the war became the charismatic leader of the neo-fascist **Movimento Sociale Italiano** (MSI) / Italian Social Movement.

The Italian Social Republic at Salò came to a brutal end in the spring of 1945. As Allied forces advanced on both the Tyrrhenian and Adriatic fronts and German General Karl Wolff, in Switzerland, began negotiations with the Allies for the surrender of the German forces in Italy, Mussolini sought to escape to Switzerland, then Austria. Together with his mistress, Clara Petacci, he was apprehended—despite the German uniforms they wore to assist in their escape—and summarily executed by partisans on April 28, 1945.

Most of the Salò survivors returned to their homes and drifted, politically, into the MSI. The savagery of the fascist militias left a scar on Italy's conscience and it is only recently, with the emergence of **Gianfranco Fini**'s "fascism in a double-breasted suit," that the passions aroused by the memory of Salò have begun to subside.

SALVEMINI, GAETANO (1873-1957). A historian best known for his work on the French Revolution, a journalist, and a liberal-socialist, he preferred exile to pledging loyalty to **fascism**. He held a chair of modern history at the University of **Florence** and was editor of a weekly magazine called *L'Unità* (no relation to the Communist Party daily newspaper of the same name), which lasted until 1920, a year after his election to Parliament. In 1925 (he was 52) Salvemini resigned his chair rather than sign the "loyalty oath" required of all state employees (including professors). He was one of a bare handful of academics daring to make public their disdain for fascist conformity and the "servile adulation of the party in power" that it exacted. His exile lasted for 20 years.

Electoral manipulation was the aspect of the **Giolitti** system of *trasformismo* (bringing the opposition to support the governing majority by generous **patronage** and programmatic concessions) that Salvemini attacked in *L'Unità,* calling Giolitti *il ministro della malavita* (the minister of the criminal underworld), a view he disavowed only in 1945 in the introductory essay to a study of the Giolittian era.

He bitterly opposed the war in **Libya** and the whole idea that poverty-stricken Italy, unable even to face its own southern question, should benefit from the absorption of even poorer territories in North Africa. Both an Anglophile and a Francophile, he favored entry into **World War I** on the side of these democratic states, especially after the attack on Belgium. When the question of a Yugoslavian state was raised, Salvemini was among the renouncers, that is, those who thought that friendly relations with a new state replacing Austria would be useful, and therefore justified renouncing any claims to (Slav) Dalmatia.

At the time of the **Matteotti** kidnapping, Salvemini wrote to **Filippo Turati** that—based on **Mussolini**'s relative isolation immediately after the fact—it was fair to assume that fascism would be destroyed by a combination of passive resistance like the **Aventine Secession** and propaganda abroad recounting fascism's wrongdoing. He had split with the **Partito Socialista Italiàno** (PSI) / Italian Socialist Party over the southern question. In 1925, he went into exile in Paris where he worked with the **Rosselli** brothers, Ernesto Rossi, and others on the anti-fascist publication *Non Mollare! (Don't Give Up!)*. Finally, in 1934, he accepted an appointment to Harvard's history department. While dissident opinion often sought to blame socialist intransigence for the rise of fascism, Salvemini put the blame on the political class of liberal Italy in several books written during his exile. Most conspicuous among them were *The Fascist Dictatorship in Italy* and *Under the Axe of Fascism.*

On his return to the University of Florence in 1948, he is said to have opened his first lecture by saying, "*Stavo dicendo* . . . ." (As I was saying . . .). *See also* Giovanni Gentile.

SARAGAT, GIUSEPPE (1898-1988). Born and educated in **Turin**, he served in **World War I** as an enlisted man (although a university graduate), becoming an officer (artillery) by battlefield promotion. In 1922, he joined the **Paritito Socialista Italiano** (PSI) / Italian Socialist Party. Together with **Pietro Nenni** and **Alessandro Pertini**, Saragat entered the executive committee in 1925 but soon left Italy to protest **fascism**, fleeing first to Austria, then to France. He reentered Italy in 1943, was arrested, and escaped, then resumed secret activity in the Partito Socialista Italiano d'Unità Proletaria (PSIUP) / Italian Socialist Party of Proletarian Unity, eventually being elected to its executive committee.

In January 1947, a group of dissident socialists around Saragat met in **Rome**'s Palazzo Barberini to give birth to the Partito Socialista Lavoratori Italiano. The name was later changed to **Partito Socialista Democratico Italiano** (PSDI) / Italian Social Democratic Party after the **Constituent Assembly**, of which Saragat had been chairman, had completed its work. He found that the socialists' unity on the left had come to mean subordination to the larger Communist Party. While expressing admiration for the organizational skills of the **Partito Comunista Italiano** (PCI) / Italian Communist Party militants, he deplored the "democratic centralism" that distanced the militants from policy choices made at the top. Where Communists win, "capitalism dies but Socialism is not born." Saragat wanted what **De Gasperi** apparently sought: a reformist coalition with legal limits established by a constitutional framework.

He served as vice premier in the **Mario Scelba** and **Antonio Segni** governments between 1954 and 1957. He also served as foreign minister in several **Moro** governments (1964-1968). In fact, the PSDI took part in **Democrazia Cristiana** (DC) / Christian Democracy Party coalitions so regularly that they were derisively called the "secular arm of the DC." The PSI, on the other hand, continued their Unity of Action Pact with the PCI until 1956 when the Soviet crushing of the Hungarian uprising caused a break between Nenni and **Palmiro Togliatti** that was never healed. In fact, Nenni met secretly with Saragat to discuss reunification, but nothing came of the meeting until a decade had passed. In October 1966, the PSI-PSDI Unificato (the United PSI-PSDI) came into existence but lasted only until the elections of 1968 in which the Partito Socialista Unificato (PSU) lost 27 percent of the voters (14.5 percent cf. 19.9 percent) of its former component elements. The PSI and PSDI quickly returned to their former autonomy.

At the end of **Giovanni Gronchi**'s term as president of the republic, **Antonio Segni** and Saragat were the leading contenders to replace him. Saragat was supported by Communists, Socialists, Social Democrats, **Partito Repubblicano Italiano** (PRI) / Italian Republican Party, and, initially, by the supporters of **Amintore Fanfani** (*fanfaniani*) in the DC. However, calls for party unity brought the *fanfaniani* back to the DC fold with the result that Segni, supported by the entire DC, the monarchists, and the neo-fascists, was elected **presidente della repubblica.**

In January 1964, another Socialist schism was to affect Saragat's future. Nenni's entry (after the **opening to the left**) into a Moro-led government so alienated the left wing of the PSI that the party splintered, the left faction forming the Partito Socialista Italiano d'Unità Proletaria (PSIUP) / Italian Socialist Party of Proletarian Unity. When Antonio Segni resigned from the presidency because of failing health in December 1964, the ensuing stalemate between the DC candidates to replace him, **Giovanni Leone** and Fanfani, enabled the PCI to support Saragat as a (relatively) left candidate. On the fourteenth day of balloting, he became the fifth president of the Italian republic.

His presidency was marred by a tacit tolerance of right-wing terrorism and judicial obfuscation. Thus, when Saragat sought a second term in 1971, only the **Partito Liberale Italiano** (PLI) / Italian Liberal Party, the PRI, and his own PSDI supported his candidacy. After 20 ballots, the DC produced Giovanni Leone as a compromise candidate and Saragat lost. As a matter of right, ex-President Saragat became a life senator; as a matter of courtesy, his party made him president of the Social Democrats for life.

SARDINIA (*Sardegna*). Like **Sicily**, Sardinia possesses a rich history that has bred a strong independent cultural tradition. Unlike Sicily, whose capital city of **Palermo** was once among the leading cultural centers of Europe, no Sardinian tradition of grandeur exists. To be sure, the island has been inhabited since neolithic times, and the Phoenician, Carthaginian, and Roman civilizations all left their traces on its history. With the decline of the Roman Empire, the islands of the Mediterranean were threatened by the rising power of the Arabs.

To defend itself, Sardinia was divided (at about A.D. 900) into four states called *giudicati*, forming the basis for the territorial boundaries of the modern-day provinces of Cagliari, Sassari, Oristano, and Nuora. The *giudicati* became, in effect, independent, small kingdoms, although they were also early examples of constitutional regimes insofar as an assembly of the people known as the *corona de logu* decided major questions of national interest. The rule of the *giudicati* came to an end in the late Middle Ages, after which political power was exercised by Spanish dynasties. Sardinia remained Spanish until the early eighteenth century, and Sardinian culture and its distinctive language has been greatly influenced by Spain's long domination. In 1718, at the end of the War of the Spanish Succession, Sardinia was awarded to the House of Savoy, although it continued to maintain its formal independence from the Savoy's other domains until 1847, when Sardinia and Piedmont fused into a single state with a single parliament, legal system, and government. The subsequent transformation of the Kingdom of Sardinia into the Kingdom of Italy did not lead to special favors. Like the rest of **southern Italy** it remained a semi-feudal backwater. As late as 1911, more than half of adult Sardinians could not read or write. Few were conversant in Italian; most spoke only *Sardu,* a language similar to Catalan.

In 1948, the island became one of five special regions that enjoy a certain legal autonomy from **Rome**, particularly in questions of urban planning. This autonomy has permitted the development of one of the Mediterranean's most skillfully marketed tourist industries: environmental activists claim that it has also led to the "cementification" of one of the most beautiful coastlines in the world. The Emerald Coast was effectively colonized by the Aga Khan, drawing in his wake jet-setters and yachtsmen tying up indescribably luxurious seaworthy vessels. Such an influx of well-off individuals in the 1950s and 1960s (even today, Sardinia has managed to maintain an "elite" tourism) revived one of the island's most insidious traditions: banditry. As late as the 1980s and 1990s, there have been frequent cases of kidnapping for ransom, which have occasionally led to tragic murders. In the mid-1960s, a special unit of the Italian police was sent to Sardinia to hunt down the most notorious bandits, in hiding in some of the wildest terrain in Europe. Tourism remains, however, the mainstay of an economy that has suffered greatly since the late 1970s when traditional industries such as sulphur and coal mining became obsolete. Sardinia's current gross regional product is approximately Lit. 15 million ($8,600) per head, less than half the figure achieved by the richer regions of the country, and unemployment has reached 30 percent in the poorest parts of the island.

A few leading Sardinian families have provided many of republican Italy's leading politicians. President **Antonio Segni**, his son **Mario Segni**, **Francesco Cossiga**, and the PCI leader **Enrico Berlinguer** all hailed from these influential and interrelated families in the province of Sassari. This is not to mention **Antonio Gramsci**, certainly one of the leading theoreticians on the historical left. The DC dominated post-war politics in the island, although the nationalist Partito Sardo d'Azione / Sardinian Action Party could count upon an important minority vote. *See also* Cassa per il Mezzogiorno; Dialects in Italy; Land Reform; Regionalism; Southern Italy; Table 18 in Appendix.

SCALFARO, OSCAR LUIGI (1918-). Born in Novara (Piedmont), Scalfaro, who is a fervent Catholic, entered politics by way of his activism in **Azione Cattolica Italiana** (ACI) / Catholic Action. In 1946, as a young public attorney, he was elected to the **Constituent Assembly** for the **Democrazia Cristiana** (DC) / Christian Democracy Party. Never identified with any of the DC's factions, or associated with the party's power brokers, Scalfaro took nearly 20 years to reach cabinet rank, although he was entrusted with several junior ministerial posts in the 1950s and early 1960s. Minister of transport between 1964 and 1968, and again in 1972, Scalfaro was also briefly education minister in the second **Andreotti** government from 1972 to 1973.

An astute and knowledgeable parliamentarian, Scalfaro became vice speaker of the Chamber of Deputies in 1976. He was again called to ministerial office once more in 1983, when he became minister for the interior under **Bettino Craxi**. Scalfaro lasted all four years of Craxi's premiership, but by the late 1980s he had begun to speak out against the rising corruption and moral degeneracy of the Italian political system.

Scalfaro by 1992 was regarded as one of the "grand old men" (he was 74) of Italian politics. Elected to the speakership of the Chamber of Deputies following the elections of April 1992, his personal probity and uncompromising honesty became immense assets during the presidential election of May 1992. Initially Scalfaro was not the candidate of any party, but in the mood of national revulsion at petty party politics caused by the **mafia**'s murder of the prosecutor **Giovanni Falcone**, Scalfaro emerged as a figure who might restore public opinion's shaken faith in the country's institutions.

It is generally agreed that Scalfaro has performed exceptionally well as president. Making shrewd use of his constitutional power to nominate the premier for **Parliament**'s approval, he has played an active political role since 1992 and has filled the institutional vacuum caused by the collapse of the former party system. In particular, he was the architect of the non-political 1995-1996 administration of **Lamberto Dini** whose technocratic competence arguably saved Italy from an international crisis of confidence. Scalfaro has also sturdily defended the public attorneys investigating political corruption and, in early 1997, strongly criticized the **Lega Nord**'s plans for secession. Despite his somewhat priestly manner, and a fondness for high-flown rhetoric, his standing with public opinion is probably the highest of any post-war Italian head of state except **Alessandro Pertini.**

SCELBA, MARIO (1901-1991). Born in the Sicilian province of Catania, he was a militant in Catholic youth federations, including the **Federazione Universitaria Cattolici Italiani** (FUCI-*Laureati*) / Catholic University Graduates' Movement of Italy. For a time, he was secretary to Don **Luigi Sturzo** and an early member of the **Partito Popolare Italiano** (PPI) / Italian People's Party, forerunner of the **Democrazia Cristiana** (DC) / Christian Democracy Party. During the fascist years, together with other like-minded Catholic activists (**Guido Gonella, Alcide De Gasperi, Giovanni Gronchi**), he sought to keep a Catholic party alive. Indeed, at war's end, he was one of five or six leaders of the new DC. After early ministerial service (with **Parri** in 1945 and, subsequently, with De Gasperi, 1945-1947) at post and telegraph, he became minister of the interior in De Gasperi's second government in 1947 and stayed at that post through successive governments until 1953. In 1954, he formed his own government in which he also was both prime minister and minister of the interior: it lasted for 17 months.

Scelba is perhaps best remembered for this period as minister of the interior. In that capacity, he reorganized the *Polizia* (public security **police**) purging from the ranks all ex-partisans who had joined the force. He also inspired the creation of the *Celere*, or rapid-response anti-riot police, used with telling effect on labor, left, or other demonstrators against government policies.

After the fall of the **Tambroni** government, Scelba joined **Fanfani**'s third government as minister of the interior (1960-1962). In 1968, he was elected to the Senate and was president of the European Parliament between 1969 and 1971. He died in 1991 at the age of 90. *See also* Police.

SCIASCIA, LEONARDO (1921-1989). Born near Agrigento in **Sicily,** Sciascia's literary career began in the 1950s, but it was in the early 1960s that he published the two works that have since received most attention outside Italy, *Zii siciliani* (*Sicilian Uncles,* 1960) and *Il giorno della civetta* (*The Day of the Owl,* 1961). The latter book, with its portrayal of the vain efforts of a northern Italian policeman to get to the bottom of a murder committed in a provincial Sicilian town, was made into a successful film by Damiano Damiani.

Sciascia was a prolific writer, but two further books must be mentioned. *Il mare di colore vino* (*The Wine Dark Sea,* 1973) is an extraordinary collection of short stories that mix humor, black irony, and pathos as few contemporary writers have succeeded in doing; *Candido ovvero un sogno fatto in Sicilia* (*Candido Or a Dream that took place in Sicily,* 1977), which portrays a guileless Sicilian whose personal idealism leads him into disillusioning experiences with the equally dishonest philosophies of Catholicism and communism. It is a brilliant contemporary reworking of Voltaire's *Candide.*

Sciascia was essentially a moralist. Since the Italian political class is not distinguished by its integrity, Sciascia inevitably became involved in political polemic. He famously argued in the 1970s that he was neither for the terrorists of the **Brigate Rosse** (BR) / Red Brigades nor the Italian state, a moral equation that struck many as repulsive. He was a parliamentary deputy for the **Partito Radicale** (PR) / Radical Party. In an interview-book toward the end of his life, he summarized the purpose of his own work as being that of using "Sicily as a metaphor" for the human condition. He died in Palermo in June 1989.

SECCHIA, PIETRO (1903-1973). Born in Vercelli near **Turin,** Pietro Secchia was a powerful figure in the **Partito Comunista Italiano** (PCI) / Italian Communist Party from the early 1930s until the mid-1950s and the leader of the party's Stalinist wing. A founding member of the PCI in 1921, Secchia became the leader of the Federazione Giovanile Comunista Italiana (FGCI) / Italian

Communist Youth Federation and in 1928 a member of the party's central committee with a place on the party's politburo. In this role, he cast the decisive vote, in January 1930, that led the PCI to approve underground activities against the fascist regime and to construct a network of clandestine cells within Italy. In July 1930, the first head of the party's "internal center," Camilla Rovera, was arrested by the police. Secchia was named as her substitute. In April 1931, he himself was arrested in Turin and condemned to 18 years in prison.

Secchia was only liberated in August 1943, when he immediately resumed his role as one of the party's most influential figures and took an active role in the resistance against the Nazis as the chief commissar of the PCI's partisan forces. At the Fifth Congress of the PCI in January 1946, Secchia was placed in charge of the vital task of forming the political consciousness of the PCI's rapidly growing membership. **Palmiro Togliatti** apart, Secchia was by now the most important figure in the PCI, a fact that was recognized by his appointment as vice secretary at the Sixth Congress of the PCI in 1948. Working with fanatical dedication, Secchia built a party that boasted over two million members by the early 1950s, but that was also dominated by an unblushing personality-cult of Stalin, and an uncritical belief in the superiority of the Soviet model. Secchia's influence decreased after Stalin's death in 1953, and a scandal involving one of his most trusted assistants, who had absconded with secret party documents and a considerable sum of money in July 1954. In January 1955 Secchia was compelled to undergo "self-criticism" and was removed from his post as the PCI's chief organizer. From 1955 to his death in 1973, Secchia opposed the PCI's gradual move away from Moscow under Togliatti and his successor, **Luigi Longo**. In 1965, he published a two-volume history of the "war of liberation" fought by the partisans in Italy between 1943 and 1945.

SEGNI, ANTONIO (1891-1972). Sardinian born, he studied law at Sassari University. He then was appointed to the law faculty at the University of Perugia, where he taught until 1925. While a student, he had organized a section of **Azione Cattolica Italiana** (ACI) / Catholic Action, the first in Sassari. A member of the National Council of the **Partito Popolare Italiano** (PPI) / Italian People's Party, he was its candidate in the elections of 1924. With the advent of **fascism**, he withdrew from political life altogether.

Segni's academic career next took him to Cagliari, then to Pavia, then back to Sassari before becoming rector of its university between 1946 and 1951, when he accepted a teaching assignment in **Rome**. He had resumed political life in 1942 by collaborating in the founding of the **Democrazia Cristiana** (DC) / Christian Democracy Party, being made its head for **Sardinia**. He was chosen as a deputy to the **Constituent Assembly**, then to the first **Parliament** and to all subsequent Parliaments.

In the second **Bonomi** government (January-June 1945), Segni was made deputy minister for agriculture and forests, a post he retained in the **Parri** government and under **De Gasperi** until July 1946, when he became minister of that department, a post he retained until 1951. For the next three years he was minister of education. In 1955, he was invited to form a government that lasted until 1957. After an interval of serving under **Fanfani** (1958-1959), he was once again asked to form a government in 1959 in which he was also minister of interior. This government was succeeded by that of **Fernando Tambroni** (April-July 1960). In the subsequent government, he was foreign minister until his election to the presidency of the republic in May 1962. He resigned for reasons of health 30 months later, becoming automatically a life senator.

His resignation ended a stormy presidency. The **opening to the left**, for which he had no sympathy whatsoever, had, indeed, induced **Pietro Nenni**'s **Partito Socialista Italiano** (PSI) / Italian Socialist Party to break with the **Partito Comunista Italiano** (PCI) / Italian Communist Party. The price exacted included reforms such as the nationalization of the electrical industry. That measure alarmed investors while antagonizing the left socialists, who split from the party to form the Partito Socialista Italiano d'Unità Proletaria (PSIUP) / Italian Socialist Party of Proletarian Unity. Meanwhile, widespread and successful industrial action had added to labor costs, thus fueling both inflation and the sense of losing control. President Segni conferred with military leaders and with the president of the Senate, known to favor an emergency government to put a stop to socialist-inspired reforms. Subsequent parliamentary and journalistic investigation discovered that a coup d'état had been a real possibility. Segni was exonerated, but the episode left a sour taste for Italian democrats. Soon after this crisis, Segni was struck with a partial paralysis and resigned from the presidency. *See also* Solo Plan.

SEGNI, MARIO (1939-). Mario Segni, the son of President **Antonio Segni,** was born in the Sardinian city of Sassari in June 1939. Like his father, Segni followed a career as a law professor before entering the Chamber of Deputies in 1976 as a standard bearer for the **Democrazia Cristiana** (DC) / Christian Democracy Party.

By 1986, he had become convinced of the need for a reform of Italy's narrowly proportional system of electing its **Parliament**. In that year, Segni formed a pressure group dedicated to advocating the introduction of majoritarian principles of election to the Italian political system. This initiative was backed by nearly 200 members of Parliament from all the parties except the **Partito Comunista Italiano** (PCI) / Italian Communist Party and the neo-fascist **Movimento Sociale Italiano** (MSI) / Italian Social Movement. In 1988, Segni also founded the Comitato per la Riforma Elettorale (COREL) / Committee for Electoral Reform, which pressed, as a starting point, for the direct election of mayors in all urban centers.

The rigid opposition of the leadership of the DC and the **Partito Socialista Italiano** (PSI) / Italian Socialist Party to this proposal convinced Segni that it was necessary to resort to a **referendum**. In 1990, the COREL introduced three referendum proposals: the first eliminated the practice of multiple preference voting in elections to the Chamber of Deputies; the second sought to introduce the direct election of mayors in towns with more than 5,000 inhabitants; the third to introduce majoritarian principles in elections for three-quarters of the seats in the Senate, with one quarter being assigned by proportional representation. In January 1991, the Constitutional Court allowed a referendum on the first of these proposals. On June 9, 1991, the referendum became the only one in post-war Italian history to be backed by a majority of all adults (not just of those voting)—a historic slap in the face for the party leaderships, which had opposed the referendum strenuously.

Once the June poll was over, Segni began campaigning for the two referendums denied by the Constitutional Court. In March 1993, the Italian Parliament enacted the scheme for the direct election of mayors into law: this law was first used in local elections in June 1993. In April 1993, Italians voted in a fresh referendum by a four-to-one margin to introduce a primarily majoritarian system of election for the Italian Senate. Immediately prior to the April poll, Segni left the DC. Many believed that he would be able to parlay his success as the leader of the referendum campaigns into a position of national political leadership.

Since the April 1993 election, however, Segni has lost most of his luster. His "Segni Pact" did very badly in the March 1994 elections, winning no seats directly. Despite this fall from grace, Segni remains one of the most well-known figures in Italian politics. In February 1995, he supported the entrance of **Romano Prodi** into politics, becoming a founding member of the **Olive Tree Coalition**. *See also* Referendums.

SELLA, QUINTINO (1827-1884). Born in Biella (Piedmont) to a wealthy family of cloth manufacturers, Sella was a mathematician and geologist by training. Encouraged to take up politics by **Cavour**, he became finance minister in 1862 during **Rattazzi**'s premiership and conserved the position for most of the next ten years. Personally austere, and a skilled administrator, he imposed a policy of rigid economy on Italy. Sella was the architect, in 1868, of the deeply unpopular grist tax which, from January 1869, imposed a tax of two lire for every hundred kilograms of milled grain. This tax was deeply regressive (it removed ten days' income from the pocket of the average agricultural laborer), and it provoked widespread riots that cost more than 200 lives. Sella won for himself the reputation as the "starver of the people." Nevertheless, if by the time of the "parliamentary revolution" in 1876, Italy's national accounts were in the black, much of the credit must be given to Sella, and to his bitter rival, but fellow fiscal conservative, **Marco Minghetti**.

Sella was a strong anti-cleric. As finance minister, he sold off the Catholic Church's assets in Italy at discount prices, and joined the constitutional left in restricting the amount of independence allowed to the church by the **legge delle guarentigie** in 1871. Sella was a great lover of the mountains, and one of his most lasting achievements was to found the Italian Alpine Association in 1863. Despite his national standing as a politician, he did not disdain local office, and between 1870 and his death in 1884, he was president of the provincial council of Novara.

SFORZA, CARLO (1872-1952). A career diplomat, Sforza played a crucial role in restoring Italy to the society of nations in the immediate post-1945 period. He began his career in 1896 and swiftly rose in the ministerial hierarchy to become ambassador to China between 1911 and 1915. **Francesco Saverio Nitti** gave him his first ministerial post as undersecretary for foreign affairs in 1919, and in the same year he was appointed to the Senate. In 1920, in the last cabinet formed by **Giovanni Giolitti**, Sforza became foreign minister, and in this role negotiated the treaty of Rapallo with

Yugoslavia that ended the diplomatically sensitive crisis over Fiume. In 1922, Sforza became ambassador to France. He was in Paris when **Benito Mussolini** took power in October 1922. Unlike many Italian liberals, Sforza denounced the fascist coup immediately. Returning to Italy, he collaborated with the democratic forces who tried to organize opposition to the dictatorship after the murder of **Giacomo Matteotti**, and wrote articles critical of the regime for the *Corriere della Sera*. In October 1926, his home was sacked by a fascist squad in the wake of a failed attempt on Mussolini's life, and he was constrained to emigrate first to Belgium and then to the United States. For the next 15 years, he was one of the dictatorship's most uncompromising public critics.

In July 1942, at a conference of anti-fascist exiles in Uruguay, Sforza unveiled an eight-point plan for a Constituent Assembly that would draw up a democratic republic in Italy after the fall of **fascism**.

This move presaged his return to Italy after the fall of **Mussolini**, when he became foreign minister in the government formed in Allied-held territory in October 1943 by **Pietro Badoglio**. Sforza held office in Badoglio's second, short-lived administration in April 1944, and then joined the Salerno-based government of **Ivanoe Bonomi**. When, in November 1944, Bonomi resigned, Sforza was nominated as his successor, but his republicanism caused the British to veto his election. He held no place of significance in the second Bonomi cabinet (December 1944 to June 1945), but was given the sensitive post of high commissioner for the punishment of the fascists' crimes. He resigned from this post in January 1945.

In February 1947, Sforza returned to the ministry of foreign affairs, a post he continued to hold until 1951. Almost his first action as foreign minister was to request amendments to the harsh treaty of peace signed by Italy on February 10, 1947. Sforza followed a strongly pro-American policy during his tenure as foreign minister. The culmination of his political and diplomatic career was Italy's accession to **North Atlantic Treaty Organization** (NATO) in 1949, and the active role he took in promoting European economic integration. Sforza died in **Rome** in 1952.

SICILY *(Sicilia)*. The largest island in the Mediterranean, and Italy's largest region, Sicily is inhabited by slightly more than five million people. Its largest cities are **Palermo**, the regional capital, Catania, Messina, Siracusa, Enna, Agrigento, and Caltanisetta. Throughout its history, Sicily has been the victim of wave after wave of foreign invaders—the ancient Greeks, Carthaginians, Romans, Moors, Normans, French, and Spaniards (Sicilian wags add that the Italians are the last in the list) all occupied the island over the centuries and left their genetic and cultural imprint. Sicily has the most remarkable remnants of Greek civilization in the whole Mediterranean (the Greco-Roman Theater in Taormina, the Greek Theater in Siracusa, and the majestic Valley of the Temples near Agrigento prove this assertion).

In economic terms, Sicily is one of the poorest regions of Italy. The outskirts of the major towns are dominated by half-built projects, often without roofs, that were quickly flung up to house migrants from the countryside in the 1960s. Unemployment and drug abuse are rife, and foreign and mainland Italian investment is scared off by the ubiquitous intrusion of the **mafia**. Nevertheless, there are some success stories, particularly in the eastern part of the island. Messina and Siracusa, for instance, are bustling, commercial cities.

Politically, the island is one of Italy's five special autonomous regions. Its own elected assembly (whose members pay themselves generous salaries) and the regional government exercise considerable authority. For most of the post-war period, local government has been in the hands of the **Democrazia Cristiana** (DC) / Christian Democracy Party, but the anti-corruption and anti-mafia investigations of the 1990s have ended this hegemony. In the elections of March 1994, **Forza Italia** emerged as the largest political force, but this victory has since been marred by allegations about the mafia links of some of the party's local organizers.

Sicily has made a remarkable contribution to contemporary Italian and world culture. The writers **Luigi Pirandello, Giuseppe Verga, Leonardo Sciascia**, Vittorio Brancati, **Salvatore Quasimodo, Elio Vittorini**, and **Giuseppe Tomasi Di Lampedusa** were all Sicilians, as was the painter Renato Guttuso. The island is craggy, in places arid, but of spectacular natural beauty. The eastern part of the island is dominated by Mount Etna, a 3,510 meter (11,000 feet) active volcano whose frequent eruptions are a regular source of disturbance. *See also* Regionalism.

SILONE, IGNAZIO (pseud. Ignazio Tranquillini, 1900-1978). Ignazio Silone was a native of the province of Aquila (the Abruzzi) who was orphaned by an earthquake in his early teens. After the death of his parents, Silone was obliged to break off his studies. He became involved in the workers' movement and in the anti-war struggle. An ardent socialist, he was implacably opposed to the fascists from the very beginning, and in the early 1920s worked for a **Trieste** newspaper, *Il Lavoratore*, a frequent target for fascist squads.

After **Mussolini** had introduced the series of repressive measures outlawing all political dissent and organization in 1925-1926, Silone, who by now was a member of the **Partito Comunista Italiano** (PCI) / Italian Communist Party, joined **Antonio Gramsci** in clandestine activities against the regime. He narrowly escaped arrest and incarceration, escaping to Switzerland with the police on his trail in 1928. As one of the most important exiled Italian communists, he took an active role in the Communist International, but this first-hand experience of the communists' doctrinaire subordination to Stalinism led him to break with the PCI in 1930.

Silone's most important books were first published in Switzerland. *Fontamara* was published in 1933, first in German, then in over 20 other languages. *Vino e pane* (*Bread and Wine*, 1936), his greatest novel, followed three years later. It tells the story of a communist intellectual, Pietro Spina, who disguises himself from the fascists by pretending to be Don Paolo Spada, a priest. Living among the peasants in an out-of-the-way mountain village in the Abruzzi, Pietro comes to doubt that political solutions—particularly the narrow dogmatism of the Communist Party—can bring about an improvement in the lot of the ordinary people. By the end of the novel, he is in despair, but in fact his own humanity and decency have already been an example for the villagers. Like Orwell, Silone's contemporary and friend, Silone believed that common decency was the key to creating a better society. While in exile, Silone also wrote two important treatises on politics, *Fascismo, le sue origini e il suo sviluppo* (*Fascism: Its Origins and Development*, 1935), and *La scuola dei dittatori* (*The School for Dictators*, 1938).

After World War II, Silone played a major role in the formation of the anti-communist **Partito Socialista Democratico Italiano** (PSDI) / Italian Social Democratic Party. His implacable and active opposition to Stalinism may have cost him the place in Italian letters that he deserved. One of the most widely read and translated Italian authors in this century, his works are scantily represented in Italian school textbooks and university courses even today. Silone died in Geneva in 1978. *See also* Confino; Fascism; Squadrismo.

SOCIAL DEMOCRAT PARTY. *See* Partito Socialista Democratico

Italiano.

SOCIALIST PARTY. *See* Partito Socialista Italiano.

SOLO PLAN. In July 1964, during lengthy negotiations over the formation of a new government, the then president **Antonio Segni** invited the head of the *Carabinieri*, General Giovanni De Lorenzo, to the presidential palace for formal talks. In 1965, De Lorenzo was made Army Chief of Staff, and seemed to be en route to becoming the head of the armed forces. In 1967, however, the news magazine *L'Europeo* published extracts from secret files that De Lorenzo had accumulated, in his former role as head of army intelligence, on the private lives of prominent politicians, including Segni's successor as president, **Giuseppe Saragat.** On May 10, 1967, another magazine, *L'Espresso*, broke the news of the so-called *Piano Solo* (Solo Plan) drawn up by De Lorenzo at the beginning of 1964. The Solo Plan foresaw the arrest and imprisonment of lists of persons who were regarded as subversive; the occupation of prefectures, television studios, telephone exchanges, and party headquarters; unilateral action by the *Carabinieri* rather than joint action with other, less trustworthy branches of the armed forces. On June 26, 1964, the day that the center-left coalition led by **Aldo Moro** collapsed, De Lorenzo apparently gave orders for detailed local contingency plans to be drawn up, although his orders were greeted with some perplexity, and little enthusiasm, by the *Carabinieri* officers who would have had to carry them out. The press outcry led to a parliamentary investigation that found that De Lorenzo was merely engaging in defensive emergency planning for the eventuality of an institutional breakdown. This conclusion, unsurprisingly, was not shared by the putative targets of the Solo Plan. How much Segni knew of De Lorenzo's schemes has never been clarified, and **Francesco Cossiga**, who acted as liaison between De Lorenzo and Segni, has never been trusted by Italian progressive opinion since. The military coups in Greece in 1967 and Chile in 1973 suggested that the left's fears were not entirely misplaced. De Lorenzo was elected to Parliament as a monarchist in 1968, and he later joined the neo-fascist **Movimento Sociale Italiano** (MSI) / Italian Social Movement. He died in **Rome** in 1973. *See also* Gladio; Police; Antonio Segni.

SONNINO, BARON GIORGIO SIDNEY (1847-1922). The Tuscan-born Sonnino (his mother was Welsh) entered politics only in 1880 after beginning a successful diplomatic career. Shortly after becoming a parliamentary deputy, he was one of the leaders of the movement to introduce universal suffrage into the electoral reform act of 1882. Sonnino's first ministerial job was as minister of finance in the second **Crispi** government from 1893 to 1896. He skillfully steered bank reforms through **Parliament** and all but balanced the budget despite the outlays caused by Italy's adventures in **Abyssinia**.

In 1897, he published an article entitled *Torniamo allo statuto* (*Back to the Constitution*), which urged the Crown to reclaim its right under the **Statuto Albertino** to name the executive independently of Parliament. Sonnino argued that Parliament was inept and corrupt and that its role should be merely consultative. These views were immensely influential, and they underlay the authoritarian attempts of the conservative governments of **Antonio Di Rudinì** and **Luigi Pelloux** from 1898 to 1900 to combat social unrest and the nascent workers' movement by authorizing emergency measures with a royal decree rather than with a vote of Parliament.

Sonnino, in short, was the conservative counterpart of **Giovanni Giolitti.** Since the first decade of this century was dominated by Giolitti, Sonnino was only briefly prime minister in 1906 and again from December 1909 to March 1910. In October 1914, he became foreign minister and kept that role throughout **World War I**. He negotiated Italy's entrance into the war on the side of the Entente in 1915, winning the promise of substantial territorial gains in Dalmatia and the eastern Mediterranean from Britain and France. After the war, however, Britain and France did not support Italy's claims at the Paris peace conference, and the Italian government briefly walked out of the talks. The report on the **Caporetto** disaster by the Commission of Inquiry, published in 1919, roundly criticized him for not having sought a separate peace with Austria. Nominated to the Senate in 1920, Sonnino died in **Rome** in 1922. His diaries are one of the outstanding historical sources for the politics of this period. *See also* Vittorio Emanuele Orlando.

SOUTHERN DEVELOPMENT FUND. *See* Cassa per il Mezzogiorno.

SOUTHERN ITALY (*Il Mezzogiorno*). The *mezzogiorno* comprises Abruzzi, Apulia, Basilicata, Calabria, Campania, Lazio (south of **Rome**), and Molise, as well as **Sardinia** and **Sicily**. With unification, two economies, one industrializing and the other pre-industrial, were hammered together in the 1860s, then left on their own for 85 years. It is therefore not surprising that they move at different paces: Calabria, in 1980, had the same rate of illiteracy as 1880 Piedmont. Land tenure in the South was based on the *latifondi*, that is, the *feudo* of a central manor surrounded by retainers' dwellings. The *gabella* was the rent paid by the *gabellotto* or tenant. He, in turn, could sublet his land and pocket the difference. The *campieri* (overseers) enforced compliance and kept wages low. The landowners, most trusted *campieri* and "enforcers" were not unlike a private army, their loyalty ensured by the fact that many had a criminal past known to their employer. Together, in the view of many modern students of the **mafia**, these elements became a surrogate for an ineffective state, rendering a crude justice in exchange for loyalty in a local version of the Roman patron-client relationship.

Unification meant the enforced conformity of all Italian regions to Piedmontese practices and laws. In the South, this was brought home by a military occupation by as many as 80,000 Piedmontese troops to suppress local resistance by "brigands." Resentment was wed to long-standing hostility directed at absentee landlords.

Piedmont's trade policies led to bloody peasant uprisings for which the socialists were blamed by the **Crispi** government. Landowners exploited the fear inspired by the *fasci siciliani* (Sicilian peasants' leagues leading the peasants' uprisings). Indeed, in some towns, local councils under landowners' control outlawed public education for peasants' children since it left the poor dissatisfied with their lot. Sicilian intellectuals often describe Italy as the last in a long list of foreign invaders of Sicily.

Southern problems also have their origins in a lack of rainfall, alternating in extremely mountainous settings with periods of flood and mudslides, inadequate transportation, minuscule holdings not amenable to large-scale or specialized cultivation, and cultural isolation. Conscription into national military service, as early as **World War I**, and emigration brought home to many Southerners the enormity of the gap separating them from compatriots in Italy's North or elsewhere in Europe.

The *Cassa per il Mezzogiorno* (Southern Development Fund) was created in 1950 to overcome these disparities. Yet in the first decade of its program, three million Southerners left for either northern Italy or northern Europe in search of work. All efforts notwithstanding, the gulf separating South from North not only persists but widens as gains made in the South are more than equaled in the North. The latest studies by the Tagliacarne Institute show that the 1994 per capita disposable income in Bologna, the richest city in Italy, was Lit. 30 million while in Crotone (Calabria), it was less than Lit. 12.5 million (i.e., $18,500 cf. $7,737 at the 1994 rate of exchange).

Neo-fascism continues to draw much of its strength from the southern regions and the cities of **Naples**, Bari, Catanzaro, Reggio Calabria, Messina, Catania, and **Palermo**. Rome has the additional problem of marginalized minor civil servants, nostalgic for a **patronage**-dispensing state. *See also* Latifondi; Mafia.

SOUTH TYROL PEOPLE'S PARTY. *See* Süd Tirol Volkspartei.

SPADOLINI, GIOVANNI (1923-1994). The first prime minister of the Italian republic not to be a member of the **Democrazia Cristiana** (DC) / Christian Democracy Party, Giovanni Spadolini was one of the few first-rank figures in recent Italian history whose reputation was enhanced by his years at the head of the principal institutions of the state. Spadolini was a latecomer to political life. Before 1972, when he was elected to the Senate on the **Partito Repubblicana Italiano** (PRI) / Italian Republican Party ticket, Spadolini had been a successful newspaperman for more than 20 years. Since 1968, in fact, he had been editor of Italy's most prestigious newspaper, *Il Corriere della Sera*.

Spadolini served as a minister twice in the 1970s. Between 1974 and 1976, he was minister for the arts and national monuments. In 1979 he became minister for education. In the same year, he replaced **Ugo La Malfa** as leader of the PRI, a position he retained until 1987. In June 1981, Spadolini headed the first government containing all five main non-communist parties, the so-called *pentapartito*. His premiership was dominated by financial-political scandals and by the **mafia**'s increasingly assertive and brutal role in **Sicily**, but Spadolini and the PRI emerged from this period in Italian history with its reputation enhanced. In the June 1983 elections, the PRI obtained more than 5 percent, its best showing since the war.

During the **Craxi** governments, Spadolini was minister for defense (July 1983 to March 1987), although he briefly resigned in objection to Craxi's position during the Achille Lauro dispute in October 1985. Spadolini fervently supported Italy's membership in the **North Atlantic Treaty Organization** (NATO) and saw no utility in antagonizing Italy's most powerful ally. Spadolini was president of the Senate from 1987 to 1994, and in 1991 was made a life senator. In April 1994, he was the center-left's candidate for the presidency of the Senate but he lost by a single vote to Carlo Scognamiglio, formerly a member of the **Partito Liberale Italiano** (PLI) / Italian Liberal Party.

Spadolini was a hugely successful writer of popular history books, and a leading scholar of the Giolittian period in Italian history. A noted bibliophile, his private library contained thousands of rare books. He died in August 1994.

SPANISH CIVIL WAR. Well before the outbreak of hostilities in Spain in 1936, Italian air force planes had made emergency landings in Morocco. Their papers revealed plans for Italy's military contribution to the forthcoming insurgency in the Spanish Republic.

With the absorption of **Abyssinia**, Italy had reason to be a "satisfied" power that could be expected to sustain a newly pleasing status quo. But at the same time, fascist doctrine insisted that it was "unfascist" to be a "satisfied" power. This division largely reflected the differences between fascists of the first hour and the younger members of the party hierarchy. When Count **Galeazzo Ciano**, **Mussolini**'s son-in-law, was suddenly elevated to be minister for foreign affairs, an opportunity was presented to him to make his own mark. War in Spain would be *his* generation's war balancing the Abyssinian War of older fascists. Thus, when Franco initiated his invasion of Iberia from Spanish Morocco, he was sure of Italian assistance.

The first troops sent were the blackshirted militia, called—for the occasion—Legionnaires under the command of General Carlo Roatta. Mostly ex-*squadristi*, they found little to their liking in combat against even the relatively shabbily armed and poorly disciplined Republican forces against whose determination the Legionnaires fared poorly. After a stinging defeat at Guadalajara (at the hands chiefly of the Italian Garibaldi Battalion of the International Brigades), the blackshirts were stiffened by an infusion of regular Italian army troops. By 1937, their number exceeded 70,000.

Low morale oppressed Italian troops who, while they had been persuaded that the Ethiopian highlands might provide economic opportunities to Italy's poverty-ridden southern rural populations, found little reason to be in Spain, poorer than the poorest parts of

Italy. Moreover, young Italian peasants in uniform found no reason to be killing young Spanish peasants (or to be killed by them) whether in uniform or not.

Both Nazi Germany and Fascist Italy claimed to be "stemming the tide of Bolshevism." The help so gingerly offered to the Republicans by the USSR reflected Stalin's aversion to helping establish a communist government in a country so far from Soviet borders. Foreign anti-fascists and republic sympathizers of whatever stripe began to find their way to Spain with the help of Spanish Republican recruiters in Paris who enrolled foreigners into the International Brigades that were sent to Spain, untrained and ill-equipped, to fight for the republic and, in many cases, to fight on Spanish soil the anti-fascist wars that they could not or would not undertake at home.

Once engaged, Mussolini's preoccupation with prestige would not allow him to accept defeat. Thus, Italy's involvement increased with time while Polish, German, Italian, and Greek anti-fascists joined forces with North Americans, British, and others, whether drawn by romantic idealism or simply by the will to "*do* something" more useful than continued rhetorical pyrotechnics. Many Italian partisans received their battlefield training on the rugged soil of Spain: **Luigi Longo, Pietro Nenni, Carlo Rosselli**, and at least 5,000 others among them.

By March 1939, when Madrid fell to Franco, Italy had expended untold millions of lire. Indeed, at the beginning of her intervention in Spain, the costs of sending the militia came so close on the campaign in Ethiopia (Abyssinia) that Mussolini had to devalue the lira (October 1936) and declare to Hitler that Italy would not be able to honor the obligations undertaken in the treaty with Germany for four years at the earliest. *See also* Foreign Policy.

SPINELLI, ALTIERO (1907-1986). While a law student in **Rome**, he was arrested as a member of the Federazione Giovanile Comunista Italiana (FGCI) / Italian Communist Youth Federation and sentenced by the special tribunal to ten years' imprisonment and to *confino* for six more. On his release, he left the **Partito Comunista Italiano** (PCI) / Italian Communist Party because of the Stalinist purges and founded the European Federalist Movement. Together with Ernesto Rossi, he wrote the *Manifesto for a Free United Europe* and led the Federalist movement first from Paris, then from Switzerland during the years before the Resistance, which he joined in **Milan** where he also joined the **Partito d'Azione** (PdA) /Action Party. Spinelli left its secretariat in 1946 to become secretary of the Federalist Movement. In that capacity, he worked closely with **Alcide De Gasperi**, Paul-Henri Spaak (of Belgium), Konrad Adenauer of West Germany, and Jean Monnet of France toward the building of a more united Europe. Spinelli directed the Italian Institute of International Affairs between 1967 and 1970 when he became a member of the European Commission where he stayed until 1976. In that year, he won a seat in the Chamber of Deputies as an independent on the PCI ticket and repeated that victory in 1979. Simultaneously, he served in the European Parliament, having been elected there as well in both 1976 and 1979.

Spinelli had argued in 1966 that three routes to power lay open to the communists: the Marxist tradition of seizing cities and assuming that the rest would follow; the Titoist tradition that taught that if one can seize control of the countryside the cities will follow; and the Stalinist "salami" tactic of playing the parliamentary game until, by getting control of the ministry of the interior, a coup can be staged (1945-48). In each attempt, the PCI failed, but each contributed to producing Italy's democracy. In the first period, sacrifices and discipline were acquired by the PCI that put it in a position to lead the partisan stage, in which, by contributing to the downfall of **fascism**, it made possible the new republic. In the third stage, it compromised on such basic items as the **Lateran pacts** because it was convinced that, in the long run, power would come to it by the voters' choice.

In this way, the PCI acquired a stake in the republic's establishment. In Spinelli's view, increasing its share of governmental power would further its identification with the establishment and its stake in a stable order.

SQUADRISMO. Formerly subservient farmhands and factory workers who had served in the mountain campaigns of **World War I** no longer deferred to property owners who controlled political power on the local scene and enjoyed easy access, through prefects and parliamentarians alike, to national power as well. Action squads (*squadre d'azione*) served to put the unruly workers in their place. Punitive expeditions by *squadristi* (members of action squads) were especially used in the Po Valley where landowners sought to crush **trade unions**, both Catholic and socialist, which were challenging their traditional political primacy. The socialist victory in the 1919 elections (fascists failed to elect a single deputy) frightened conservatives who began to see fascist expeditions as effective instruments against the rise of unions trying to organize farmworkers and factory workers alike. Financial support for the fascist movement swelled.

Black-shirted, black-fez-wearing action squads were equipped with small arms and blackjacks (*il santo manganello* or "holy club"), using vehicles often provided by sympathizers in army motor pools to reach neighboring villages and towns not their own. There, they would beat union organizers, administer massive doses of castor oil with humiliating effect, pillage union headquarters, and create as much confusion on the left as possible. Police rarely appeared on the scene until the squads had been able to leave. Even less frequently did they make arrests. Local fascists who led the action squads took the title, *Ras,* derived from Abyssinian tribal chiefs. A brief list of outrages committed by the squads gives a clear idea of the lawlessness that prevailed in the last years of liberal Italy. In November 1920, nine socialists were killed, and more than 50 wounded, when 500 armed fascists burst into a meeting of **Bologna** city council. In July 1921, 18 people died in a pitched battle between a fascist squad and the townsfolk and *Carabinieri* of Sarzana (Liguria). On May 1, 1922, clashes between the squads and socialists left dozens dead and wrecked rallies of the **Partito Socialista Italiano** (PSI) / Italian Socialist Party all over Italy.

The failure of the **Nitti, Bonomi,** and **Facta** governments to combat the reign of terror imposed by the *Ras* led the PSI to proclaim a general strike in August 1922. This move played inexpertly into **Mussolini**'s hands. For he was now able to announce that the fascists stood ready to break the strike if the government did not respond and to present the squads as forces of law and order. On August 3, 1922, blackshirts took over many cities in the north, most conspicuously **Milan**, where they burned the offices of *l'Avanti!* and smashed its presses.

Mussolini owed his accession to power to *squadrismo* and to the timidity of the politicians of liberal Italy who were unwilling to meet illegal violence with the force of law. One of Mussolini's first acts as premier was to transform the squads into the Milizia Volontario di Sicurezza Nazionale (MVSN) / Voluntary Militia of National Security. Flushed by this institutional legitimization, the squads continued their reign of terror throughout the first years of

Mussolini's premiership, and were only brought to heel after Mussolini had consolidated his regime. By 1932, the original *squadristi* who had participated in the **March on Rome** were styled La Vecchia Guardia (The Old Guard), thus emphasizing that their role was in the past and not in the future of **fascism**. *See also* World War II; Comitati di Liberazione Nazionale; Roberto Farinacci; Republic of Salò; Achille Starace.

STARACE, ACHILLE (1889-1945). This Pugliese "fascist of the first hour," decorated for bravery in **World War I**, was a "Fascist of the first hour." He was to become secretary of the **Partito Nazionale Fascista** (PNF) / National Fascist Party between 1931 and 1939, the longest tenure of any individual in this office. The position was a powerful one. The secretary nominated (and **Mussolini**—as the Duce—appointed) all secretaries of the PNF's provincial federations and had a seat on the party's National Directorate.

Starace remained faithful to the militantly anti-bourgeois program of San Sepolcro (the Milan Fascist Congress of 1919). In ever-stylish Italy, for example, he undertook to discourage all forms of dress that underscored class distinctions as well as the frequenting of night clubs. He considered abolishing the class system in railway compartments and even talked of closing the stock exchange. Starace also invented much of the mock-Roman symbolism of the regime. At Starace's prompting Mussolini even introduced the slogan, *Usate l'italianissimo voi!*—a campaign to make Italians use the second person plural (*voi*) as the formal form of address, rather than the deferential and formal third person singular (*Lei*). Ever ready to ritualize **fascism**, he became known as its choreographer, assuring that each public appearance of the Duce or of the party hierarchs was greeted with shouted slogans: *Saluto al Duce! Eja, eja, alalà!* and other forms of pageantry.

Starace was eased out only when Mussolini hesitated about going to war before the completion of military preparations. A leading member of the war party, Starace had given the Duce estimates of public morale that were flatly contradicted by all other advisors. After 1941, Starace lost favor with Mussolini and was even imprisoned in a forced labor camp during the **Republic of Salò**. This fall from grace did not save him from the partisans, however. Starace was tried and shot in **Milan** on the same day as his former leader, and his body was exposed to the crowd in Piazza Loreto along with the other members of the PNF hierarchy. *See also* Fascism; Benito

Mussolini.

STATUTO ALBERTINO (1848). The basis of constitutional government in Italy until the foundation of the First Republic in 1948, the Statuto Albertino (named after King **Carlo Alberto**) ended the absolute power of the House of Savoy. The statute was drawn up by a committee of liberal noblemen, including **Cesare Balbo** and **Camillo Benso di Cavour**, in order to head off popular discontent in Piedmont. In this respect, it was very successful: the Piedmont-Sardinian throne escaped relatively unscathed in the so-called "year of revolutions."

Most of the statute's 88 articles were concerned with delineating the relative powers of the sovereign and the Parliament. The king was made chief executive, nominal head of the judiciary and was given a legislative veto. He could appoint ministers, but the ministers themselves were subject to a vote of confidence from Parliament. The legislature itself was divided into two branches. The Senate was composed of life members appointed by the king; the Chamber of Deputies was elected by an electoral law that was not specified in the statute itself, but featured an extremely restrictive property qualification. Voters had to be at least 25 years of age, be literate, and pay at least 40 lire in taxes every year. Approximately 80,000 people—barely 2 percent of the population—met these conditions.

The statute guaranteed important civil rights. Equality before the law was established "for all subjects, whatever be their rank"; the freedoms of property, press, and person were sanctioned. Catholicism was stated to be the "sole religion of the State," but the principle of toleration for other faiths was established. At the end of March 1848, Carlo Alberto put legal flesh to these constitutional bones by signing a new press law that authorized any writing except those that offended against public decency or obstructed the "regular functioning of government." This formulation was ambiguous, but it was regarded as a step forward from the previous system of ecclesiastic and temporal censorship. Between March and June 1848, Jews were admitted to the same civil status as Catholics throughout the kingdom.

STRESA FRONT. *See* Foreign Policy.

STURZO, LUIGI (1871-1959). Born in Caltagirone (**Sicily**), Luigi Sturzo was ordained in 1904. Convinced of the need for the church to involve itself in the lives of the working class, and to provide a Catholic alternative to socialism, "Don" Sturzo (the Sicilian honorific is nearly always applied by Italians—even non-Sicilians—to refer to a priest) interpreted his calling to include social and political action. He held elected office in Caltagirone, wrote for the Catholic press, and was secretary of **Azione Cattolica Italiana** (ACI) / Catholic Action between 1915 and 1917. With the tacit support of the Vatican, which had previously blocked any attempt to found a political movement that was not under the church's direct control, Don Sturzo launched the **Partito Popolare Italiana** (PPI) / Italian People's Party in January 1919. The new movement sought to offer the working class a moderate alternative to the corruption and ineptness offered by Italian liberalism and the revolutionary politics of the **Partito Socialista Italiano** (PSI) / Italian Socialist Party. The message found plenty of listeners: in the elections of November 1919, the PPI obtained nearly 21 percent of the votes and 100 seats in the Chamber of Deputies.

Don Sturzo early recognized the dangers for democracy presented by **fascism**, but despite the frequent acts of intimidation toward the PPI's local organizations and activists, the party as a whole was more afraid of the PSI. In October 1922, the party was passive in the face of **Mussolini**'s coup and decided, against Don Sturzo's will, to participate in the government formed by the fascist leader.

Don Sturzo's critical attitude toward Mussolini was too controversial for the Vatican that, since the election of Pope Pius XI in February 1922, had cultivated good relations with the fascists. Prior to the parliamentary debate over the "**Acerbo** Law" on electoral reform in 1923, the fascists threatened to wage war against the church if the Vatican did not disown the "priest from Caltagirone." The church replied to this open threat by inviting Don Sturzo to step down, which he did in July. He continued to remain a member of the PPI's national council. In 1924, the PPI, with Don Sturzo to the fore, endorsed the boycott of Parliament by the democratic parties after the murder of **Giacomo Matteotti**. In October 1925, the Vatican bowed to fascist pressure and instructed Don Sturzo to leave for London.

He spent the next 20 years in foreign exile. During his time abroad, he wrote numerous books under the watchful eye of the church authorities, and finally returned to Italy in 1946. He took only a consultative role in the political development of the **Democrazia**

Cristiana (DC) / Christian Democracy Party. In 1953, he was appointed senator for life of the Italian republic. He died in **Rome** in 1959. *See also* Papacy; Partito Popolare Italiano.

SÜD TIROL VOLKSPARTEI (SVP) / South Tyrol People's Party. The official voice of the German-speaking majority in the province of Bolzano, the SVP was founded in May 1945 by Erich Ammon, the recognized leader of those Italian citizens of German mother tongue who had chosen not to take German citizenship or to emigrate to Germany during the war. The new party's representatives, after the collapse of Hitler Germany and the reconstitution of Austria, played an important background role in the talks between Italy and Austria that led, in September 1946, to the signature of a crucial accord between **Alcide De Gasperi** and the Austrian chancellor, Karl Gruber. Under its terms, Italy, in exchange for a guarantee of her borders, made a commitment to allow citizens who had opted for citizenship of the Third Reich to regain their Italian nationality, and promised to introduce measures that would permit the German-speaking minority to exercise considerable local autonomy.

The SVP's political activity since 1946 has mostly been concerned with securing and amplifying the guarantees of autonomy provided by the De Gasperi-Gruber accord. The 1948 decision to make Trentino-Alto-Adige one of five special autonomous regions recognized by Italy's constitution gave the two provinces of Trento and Bolzano substantial political autonomy while continuing subsidies from **Rome**. In 1964, after a period of prolonged international pressure from the Austrian government, the SVP persuaded Italy to grant a "packet" of measures ensuring greater attention for the rights of the German- and Romansch-speaking minorities in Bolzano, and in the early 1970s the party succeeded in making knowledge of German compulsory for anybody employed in the public services. This measure enormously embittered the tens of thousands of Italians living in Bolzano and allowed the neo-fascist **Movimento Sociale Italiano** (MSI) / Italian Social Movement to establish itself as the main opposition party. Despite the concessions to the German-speaking minority, Alto Adige was the theater for sporadic outbursts of terrorist activity in the 1970s by nationalists organized as *Ein Tirol* ("One Tyrol"). The SVP did not always condemn the activities of this organization.

The SVP has dominated general and local elections in the province of Bolzano throughout the post-war years. It survived the crash of its main ally in Rome—the DC—with aplomb. Bolzano's tranquility is only skin-deep, however. Only the Italian taxpayers' largesse has prevented the growth of a movement in favor of rewriting the De Gasperi-Gruber accords to allow either outright independence or unification with Austria. *See also* Alps; Regionalism.

SVEVO, ITALO (pseud. Ettore Schmitz, 1861-1928). Born in **Trieste**, Italo Svevo was a neglected genius who, by bitter irony, was killed in a road accident just as he was winning European-wide fame for his dense, intellectually challenging novels. Svevo worked in obscurity for most of his career. Financial problems forced him to skip a university education and to work as a bank clerk from 1880 until 1899 (when he became a partner in his father-in-law's business). He was accordingly self-educated, reading widely in German idealist philosophy and the French realists.

Svevo's first novel, *Una Vita* (*A Life*), was published in 1892 to general critical indifference. His second novel, *Senilità* (*Senility*, 1898), met the same fate. Yet both novels were remarkable and meticulously observed portrayals of ordinary middle-class individuals unable to escape their own deficiencies and the circumstances of their lives. After the critical disappointment of *Senilità*, Svevo was silent for over 20 years. In 1905, he met James Joyce, who was living in Trieste at that time. He became a close friend of the great Irish writer, and in 1925, after Joyce had achieved international renown, he was able to bring Svevo's masterpiece, *La coscienza di Zeno* (*The Conscience of Zeno*, 1923), to the attention of the leading literary critics of the day. Svevo, after years of anonymity, was suddenly recognized as one of the most insightful contemporary novelists.

La coscienza di Zeno merited this extraordinary acclaim. The novel is the diary of Zeno Cosini, a middle-aged man who has been encouraged by his analyst to write down his memoirs as a way of curing himself of nicotine addiction. As the tale unfolds, it becomes obvious that Zeno's compulsive smoking is only a symptom of a deeper malaise, a manifestation of his profound alienation from the structures of modern life. Like Joyce and Proust, Svevo concentrates upon the depiction of his central character's inner life, not, as in nineteenth-century fiction, upon the external events that constitute the story. Svevo's novel is today recognized as one of the classics of literary modernism and as one of the most successful literary representations of Freudian theories of the unconscious.

-T-

TAMBRONI, FERNANDO (1901-1963). Born in Ascoli Piceno, he was—by the mid-1920s—an ambitious young lawyer, a prominent activist in the **Federazione Universitaria Cattolici Italiana** (FUCI) / Catholic University Graduates' Movement of Italy and a functionary of the **Partito Popolare Italiana** (PPI) / Italian People's Party. His detractors argue that the aftermath of his 1926 arrest for alleged anti-regime activity—which was cited in his 1963 obituary notice—revealed a certain opportunism. His arrest was presented as showing him to be anti-fascist, but no mention was made of his immediate joining of the **Partito Nazionale Fascista** (PNF) / National Fascist Party. Such expediency, while not unusual in itself, makes more comprehensible his brief, but turbulent, spell in 1960 as the head of a government with dramatic implications for the future.

Tambroni returned to the PPI in time to be elected to the Chamber of Deputies in 1946 and to take up a place in the **Democrazia Cristiana** (DC) / Christian Democracy Party. Service in several of **Alcide De Gasperi**'s governments (January 1950 to June 1953) and in governments headed by **Giuseppe Pella** (August 1953 to January 1954) and **Amintore Fanfani,** to whom he grew very close (July 1958 to January 1959), led to service as minister of the interior under **Antonio Segni** (February 1959 to February 1960). When the **Partito Liberale Italiano** (PLI) / Italian Liberal Party withdrew its support from that government, it became dependent on the neo-fascist **Movimento Sociale Italiano** (MSI) / Italian Social Movement for a parliamentary majority. Segni, consequently, resigned. After several unsuccessful attempts at forming another government, President **Gronchi** turned, in March, to Tambroni, asking him to form a government pledged to resign after completing the budgetary process. When Tambroni's government won a vote of confidence in the Chamber of Deputies (April 8, 1960) through the support of four monarchists and the MSI, three cabinet members and an undersecretary immediately resigned. President Gronchi thereupon, with the backing of the executive committee of the DC, persuaded **Parliament** to give Tambroni a limited mandate to steer the budget through both houses, then resign. Tambroni, however, had other ambitions. He announced sweeping schemes for new investment as well as higher wages and subsidies for entire categories of the workforce.

Emboldened by its entry into Italian political life, the heretofore ostracized MSI declared its intention to hold its annual convention in Genoa in July 1960 and to appoint as convention chairman Carlo Emanuele Basile. Genoa was the city in which partisans had accepted the surrender of General Meinhold's 11,000 German troops in 1945 and had the port operating when Allied armies arrived. Basile, prefect of Genoa from 1943 until this Liberation, had carried out the deportation policies of the **Republic of Salò** and its German sponsors and was especially hated. A neo-fascist convention was seen as a calculated affront.

From Sicily to Milan spontaneous protests erupted. Police repression was of a ferocity not seen in a decade. By mid-July, ten demonstrators had been killed. The political right extolled Tambroni for restoring order while moderate and left opinion deplored the rebirth of the conditions that had preceded the advent of **fascism.** Italy seemed on the verge of civil war. On July 19, Tambroni resigned. His party had no alternative but to become what **Aldo Moro** cited Alcide De Gasperi as having called a "center party moving to the left." From 1960 until 1994, the MSI was excluded from any part in national governments, Moro used the incident to persuade major DC constituencies that there is no alternative to **opening to the left**, while Tambroni sank into an obscurity from which he never recovered. He died in **Rome** three years after his dramatic fall from grace. *See also* Aldo Moro.

TITTONI, TOMMASO (1855-1931). Elected to Parliament when he was just over 30 years old, Tittoni was one of the leading conservatives in liberal Italy. He was nominated to the Senate in 1902, and the following year became foreign minister in the second government of **Giovanni Giolitti**. Prime minister for two weeks during a government crisis in 1905, Tittoni maintained the post of foreign minister, with one brief interlude as ambassador to Britain, until 1910. As foreign minister at a complex and difficult moment in European history, Tittoni skillfully managed to keep Italy from definitively joining either of the two armed camps forming in Europe and to keep tensions with Austria from boiling over into war. Between 1910 and 1916, he was ambassador to Paris; in 1919, he became foreign minister under **Francesco Saverio Nitti**. Tittoni supported the advent of **fascism**, and served as president of the Senate until 1929, whereupon he became president of the

Accademia d'Italia / Italian Academy, and a member of the **Gran Consiglio del Fascismo.** He died in his native **Rome** in 1931.

TOGLIATTI, PALMIRO (1893-1964). Togliatti was born in Genoa of Piedmontese parents. In 1911, while entered in an academic scholarship competition, Togliatti met **Antonio Gramsci**, another of the competitors. (Gramsci finished sixth; Togliatti second). While both studied at the University of Turin, they joined the **Partito Socialista Italiano** (PSI) / Italian Socialist Party. After his degree in **law**, Togliatti interrupted his studies for a second degree (in Philosophy) for service in **World War I**. On discharge, he collaborated with Gramsci in the Torinese weekly newspaper, *Il grido del popolo* (*The People's Cry*). At the Livorno (Leghorn) PSI Congress (January 21, 1921), he helped lead the creation of the **Partito Comunista Italiano** (PCI) / Italian Communist Party with 58,000 members at birth. In the next two PCI congresses, he was elected to the central committee and to its executive committee. After several short-term arrests (1923 and 1925), he was a major organizer of the clandestine congresses of the PCI held in Lyons, France (1926), and in Cologne, Germany (1931), as well as the Anti-War Congress held in Brussels, Belgium, in the year of the beginning of the Italian invasion of **Abyssinia**. Between 1936 and 1939, during the **Spanish Civil War**, he served in the International Brigade. Subsequently, Togliatti left Europe to serve as a member of the Comintern, eventually rising to be its vice secretary. He spent the war years in Moscow broadcasting as Mario Correnti.

He returned in 1944 to preside at the party's Salerno Congress as the party's general secretary, a post to which he was re-elected in 1947. The party proclaimed that it had but one goal: the defeat of the Nazi occupiers and their fascist underlings. He should join the government although it was Catholic, conservative, and headed by a royally appointed army officer whose career had been advanced by his service to **fascism.** Liberation had a higher priority than revolution. This was the so-called *svolta di Salerno* (the Salerno turnabout).

The central role of the PCI in the resistance, other parties' compromises with the regime, and the prowess shown by the Red Army led Togliatti to think that a socialist revolution by electoral means was not only possible but likely. Once parliamentary democracy was restored, a coalition might unite all those workers, peasants, youths, and intellectuals who shared the vision of a progressive democracy. The presence of Allied armies on Italian soil was an additional argument against any premature insurrection to install a "dictatorship of the proletariat." Togliatti himself served in the governments headed by **Pietro Badoglio** (April-June 1944), **Ivanoe Bonomi** (June 1944 to June 1945), **Ferruccio Parri** (June-December 1945), and **Alcide De Gasperi** (December 1945 to July 1946). In July 1948, he was the target of an unsuccessful assassination attempt in **Rome**. When an interlocutor suggested mobilizing ex-partisans and arming communist cells, Togliatti's astounded reaction, allegedly, was, "What do you want to do: start a revolution?"

Togliatti's greatest achievement was transforming a small group of militants into the largest non-revolutionary communist party in the non-Soviet world. He was constantly alert to the risk of actions that might provide the political elite with a pretext for anti-communist measures. Nothing was to be allowed to threaten the grand coalition that he saw as the only road to socialism. At the party's head until his death, his main contributions were two: the stabilization of political life in the early post-fascist years; and the conversion of the PCI from a vanguard party to a mass organization that added communist political culture to much of Italian society. Its demonstrated ability to create an alternative civic sense with recreation centers for both members and non-members, its libraries open to all (even during the midday break when most libraries close), even its annual fund-raising, *Feste dell'Unità*, made for a strong sense of solidarity.

However, these attributes were counterbalanced by several negative features. For one, the party was—at least until' the 1990s—totally lacking in internal democracy. This may have been a necessary price to pay for the avoidance of the sorts of factionalism that tormented other Italian parties. Second, not only was it hierarchical but—especially after Stalin's death in 1953—given to virtual beatification of its saints, Gramsci and Togliatti.

He had used the Twentieth Congress of the Communist Party of the USSR to proclaim his doctrine of polycentrism, that is, each communist party taking its own road to socialism. He had already opposed the excommunication of parties from the Comintern for not accepting Soviet instruction. Togliatti's death at Yalta in the summer of 1964 ended the career of a supremely adaptable leader.

TOSCANINI, ARTURO (1867-1957). One of the greatest orchestral conductors of modern times, Toscanini was born in Parma, where he studied at the conservatory. After a distinguished early career as a musician and conductor, he became the first director of **Milan**'s La Scala Theater in 1898. Much of his subsequent career was spent in the United States as the director of New York's finest orchestras. Between 1937 and 1954, he was the director of the NBC symphony orchestra, which was dissolved upon his retirement in 1954. Famously choleric with wayward musicians, Toscanini preached and practiced a policy of strict fidelity to the original musical scores. His repertoire included Verdi, Puccini, Wagner, Beethoven, and Brahms, but few post-1918 works. Toscanini's relationship with the fascist regime was a mixed one. He actually ran as a candidate for the **Partito Nazionale Fascista** (PNF) / National Fascist Party in the 1919 elections, but gradually lost sympathy with the regime. In May 1931, he refused to play the fascist hymn *Giovinezza* as the prelude to a concert in **Bologna**, and was brutally beaten by the blackshirts. Toscanini emigrated to the United States following this episode and only returned in 1956. He died within a year.

TRADE UNIONS. The pre-fascist trade unions, whether of Catholic or Marxist inspiration, were equally the targets of systematic violence at the hands of fascist action squads, then of outright prohibition. During the resistance, however, the **Comitati di Liberazione Nazionale** (CLN) / National Liberation Committees drew many of their leaders together. The collaborative spirit that informed the resistance also moved its component parties to work together in reconstituting the Confederazione Generale Italiana del Lavoro (CGIL) / Italian General Confederation of Labor in 1944. Giuseppe di Vittorio of the **Partito Comunista Italiano** (PCI) / Italian Communist Party was its first post-war president. In the early reconstruction years, the union made continual concessions, eager to avoid antagonizing the dominant **Democrazia Cristiana** (DC) / Christian Democracy Party. By late 1946, factory committees had been effectively emasculated, thus silencing for a time the workers' voice on the shop floor.

    After the 1948 elections and the onset of the cold war, nothing could prevent Catholic members from leaving the CGIL and forming their own Confederazione Italiana Sindacati Lavoratori (CISL) / Italian Confederation of Workers' Unions. They were soon followed by the Social Democrats and Republicans who had formed the Unione Italiana del Lavoro (UIL) / Italian Union of Labor. The CGIL, from being a three-party union, became "transmission belt" for the **Partito Comunista Italiano** (PCI) / Italian Communist Party. This led to a persistent employers' offensive, generously backed by the U.S. embassy and the American Federation of Labor (AFL), so that by 1955, the influence of the CGIL had noticeably slipped. It was not until July 1972 that a CGIL-CISL-UIL federation was formed. The components cooperated but retained their independence.

In the late 1960s, many young Italian workers, especially "immigrants" from the South, inspired by what they saw happening in France, concluded that the moment had come for a New Left. Disruptive and often violent, it led to immediate results. Union leaders demanded total autonomy from political parties, the better to respond to this uncompromising spirit. Thereafter, the unions began to recover some of their lost standing among workers.

At the end of the "hot autumn" of 1969, concessions included the right to convene shop-floor assemblies for up to ten hours annually at employer expense, the 40-hour week, and the beginnings of wage-leveling. In 1970 and 1971, the unions began to reintroduce elected factory councils. Union training schools offered courses on trade-union history and political theory. In 1973, the metalworkers' contract entitled them to up to 150 hours paid time off every three years for instruction in public institutions in pursuit of higher qualifications. Feminist collectives became widespread by the use of this provision.

In 1980, **FIAT** pointed to a declining market share to explain a chain of dismissals. The reaction was a union call for a total shutdown. After 34 days, in a spontaneous counter-strike, up to 40,000 foremen, white-collar workers, and line workers who wanted to return to work paraded through the streets of **Turin**. A turning point was reached when the union capitulated.

Hard times strained solidarity even in a setting where collective bargaining covered more than wages and benefits. Like their counterparts in much of Europe, Italian unions were rooted in the Marxist view of labor organizations as instruments in the class struggle. It was to the trade unions that successive governments turned to reach a consensual position with industry and labor in the period of **consociationalism**. That consociational role apparently worked to management's advantage in the private sector. A labor movement defined by a Confindustria vice-president as "reformist rather than revolutionary" was—in management eyes—a legitimate interlocutor. Union readiness to sustain the system was best revealed on November 1, 1997, when leaders agreed to change the pension system by raising the retirement age. This single measure is expected to lower the public spending deficit to 2.8 percent of the GDP, a figure below the required 3 percent set by the European Commission. *See also* Fascism; Corporatism; Lotta Continua; Maastricht, Treaty of; Romano Prodi.

TRASFORMISMO. A key term in Italian politics, *trasformismo* was born in 1882, when **Agostino Depretis**, anxious to widen his parliamentary majority and to lessen his dependence on the parliamentary left, invited members of the parliamentary right to "transform themselves" into centrists and join with him in carrying out a specific program of common policies while sharing in the good things of government. Led by **Marco Minghetti**, a substantial group of former rightists did in fact reinforce Depretis's cabinet in 1883. **Giovanni Giolitti** was a flawed master of the same technique. His decision to open the doors of parliamentary respectability to **Mussolini**'s fascists in the 1921 election campaign illustrates the dangers of this brand of accommodating, inclusive politics. A more modern example is the **opening to the left** in the 1960s, when the **Democrazia Cristiana** (DC) / Christian Democracy Party successfully persuaded the **Partito Socialista Italiano** (PSI) / Italian Socialist Party to join its majority. The word *trasformismo* is thus commonly used to describe the practice of ruling politicians to seek a stable majority by **patronage** rather than by ideological solidarity.

TREVES, CLAUDIO (1869-1933). Born in **Turin** of an affluent family, he studied jurisprudence at the University of Turin and became a leading deputy of the **Partito Socialista Italiano** (PSI) / Italian Socialist Party. Together with **Leonida Bissolati** he bent his efforts to persuading his constituents to accept reform as preferable to revolution. For Bissolati, this could even mean agreeing to join bourgeois governments. **Filippo Turati** and Giuseppe Modigliani shared Treves's view that this was taking reform too far. Yet when the PSI supported a more intransigent position than his, Treves began publishing *Critica Sociale* (*Social Criticism*), which came very close to justifying the war in **Libya**, contrary to the party's position. He seemed unable to choose between violent revolution (which he rejected) and sharing power with the bourgeoisie (which he also rejected).

Even in the Socialist Party's internal affairs, the importance attached to doctrinal purity was often self-defeating. Turati and

Treves, for example, who were on the left wing of the reformists, were the right wing of the official party once it was in the hands of intransigents. Convinced that the maximalists' policies were bound to fail, the reformists refused to accept places offered them on the party's executive committee. These maneuvers, not surprisingly, left the party divided as between equally unyielding reformists and revolutionaries and quite unable to respond effectively to changing circumstances.

They refused to cooperate with the **Partito Popolare Italiano** (PPI) / Italian People's Party to impede the seizure of power by the fascists. Events were to prove that time was not on their side: no compromises, no alliances, no results.

At the 1919 Socialist Congress, Treves and the other moderates were outvoted by four to one. Even after the most radical wing of the PSI split from the party at Livorno (Leghorn) in January 1921 to form the Partito Comunista d'Italiano, Treves and Turati remained in a minority, and were eventually expelled in October 1922. They formed the Partito Socialista Unitario (PSU) / Unitary Socialist Party and decided—too late—to cooperate with the Catholic Party to oppose **fascism**. In November 1926, Treves, together with **Giuseppe Saragat** and **Ferruccio Parri,** fled to Paris where Treves edited *La Libertà* (Liberty). By the mid-1920s, most reform-socialists were to be found in Paris. Treves died there in 1933.

TRIESTE. The largest city in Italy's northeast, with some 300,000 inhabitants, Trieste marks the border with the republic of Slovenia and is one of the most important ports on the Adriatic. While its history goes back to pre-Roman times, it was under the dominion of the Hapsburgs from 1382 to 1918. The foundation of the city's commercial wealth goes back to 1719, when it became a free port. Briefly occupied by the French during the Napoleonic wars, it was restored to Austria in 1813, and became an autonomous province within the Austrian empire in 1850. The population was nevertheless mostly Italian-speaking, and after the **Risorgimento**, nationalist sympathies began to spread. The 1882 hanging by the Austrians of Guglielmo Oberdan, an irredentist, only inflamed pro-Italian feeling. During **World War I,** Trieste was the prize for which Italian troops fought 11 battles on the Isonzo River, which empties into the Adriatic near the city. Italian troops entered the city in November 1918. Trieste, along with the Istrian Peninsula, became Italian with the Treaty of **Saint Germain** in June 1919. Half a million Slovenes were thereby placed under Italian rule.

In 1945, after two years of Nazi occupation, Istria and Trieste were captured by Yugoslav partisans who carried out a ruthless policy of "ethnic cleansing" at the expense of the Italian-speaking community. Thousands were murdered, and tens of thousands more fled to Italy. In June 1945, the former province of Trieste was divided into a small "zone A," which was administered by the British and Americans and included the city, and a much larger "zone B" left in the hands of the Yugoslav government. The peace treaty of February 1947 defined the city itself as a free territory. Italy reoccupied "zone A" in 1953, and in 1954 the Yugoslav government recognized Italian sovereignty over the city. The present border was fixed by the Treaty of Osimo in November 1975. The treaty's terms are frequently challenged by nationalists of the **Alleanza Nazionale** (AN) / National Alliance, heirs of the fascist tradition.

The loss of its hinterland in Istria after 1945 explains why, at 220 square kilometers (85 square miles), Trieste is by far the smallest Italian province. Trieste is anomalous in other ways. Its long domination by Austria has ensured that the city's architecture has little in common with the rest of Italy, and much in common with mid-European cities such as Prague or Vienna. Trieste is also the windiest city in Italy. The so-called *bora* can blow for weeks on end; special railings are in place along the most exposed streets to protect citizens from being blown off their feet.

TRIPLE ALLIANCE. A secret treaty signed between Germany, Austria-Hungary, and Italy on May 20, 1882, the Triple Alliance bound the signatories to offer mutual assistance in the event that any one of them should be attacked by two or more powers—Russia and France being perceived as the main dangers. It was to be renewed at five-year intervals and was in effect until 1915. The alliance was motivated by Bismarck's desire to isolate France and by Austria-Hungary's desire to obtain backing against Russia for its adventures in the Balkans. For Italy, allying with her historic enemy, Austria, represented a sea change in foreign policy and signaled that the cabinet of **Agostino Depretis** did not intend to listen to the nationalists who, since the mid-1870s, had been pressing the Italian government to put the liberation of Trento and **Trieste**—the two largest cities still under Austrian domination—at the core of its foreign policy. Foreign Minister Felice Nicolis di Robilant, the architect of the new policy, was motivated by Italy's need for diplomatic support against France, which was blocking her attempts to expand into Tunisia and to build a North African empire. French support for the Pope was feared as well. While the alliance offered none of the guarantees of Italy's position in **Rome** sought by Italy, it did provide assurances against an attack by France.

The threat of the alliance prompted France to ally herself with Russia in 1894 and to enter an entente cordiale with Great Britain in 1904, thus dividing Europe into two counterposed blocs of powers. Many historians believe that the origins of **World War I** are to be found in the frictions between the powers that this situation inevitably provoked. In 1915, however, Italy entered the war on the side of Britain and France, rather than Austria-Hungary and Germany. *See also* Foreign Policy; London, Treaty of; World War I.

TRIVENETO. The name given to the northeastern corner of Italy, the Triveneto consists of the regions of Venetia, Friuli-Venezia-Giulia, and the Trentino. The northern part of all three regions is extremely mountainous; the southern part is a continuation of the Paduan Plain. The region is nevertheless a distinct cultural and industrial entity. In recent years cities such as Treviso (Venetia), Belluno (Venetia), Udine (Friuli), Padova (Venetia) have formed one of the most competitive economic zones in the world with rates of growth in income per head matched only by the Asian "tigers." Several local companies—the most famous of which is Benetton—have become world leaders in their sector of the market: Venetia alone, with a population of just over four million (about 7 percent of the nation's total) provides over 13 percent of Italian exports, more than all of southern Italy, and as much as Piedmont, whose figure is boosted by the presence of **FIAT**. Production is concentrated in small and medium-sized enterprises with notable capacity for innovation. In some towns in the area, so many new jobs are being created that an influx of new residents is required every year to satisfy demand, thus creating negative unemployment.

This remarkable economic success has brought with it a decline in traditional moral values. Secularization has proceeded apace, and some argue that the search for *schei* (the local dialect word for money) has replaced religious belief (traditionally very strong) in the value structure of young people in particular. The crime rate is one of the highest in Italy, second only to relatively very poor areas like Calabria. Drug abuse is rife among adolescents and young adults.

Politically, the area traditionally voted for the **Democrazia**

Cristiana (DC) / Christian Democracy Party by large pluralities, but since the late 1980s, the area has looked toward the **Lega Nord** (Northern League), which finds a ready audience for its secessionist and anti-government rhetoric among the local population.

TURATI, FILIPPO (1857-1932). Turati was the most prominent reformist voice in the early days of the Italian Socialist movement. From 1891, he was editor of the review *Critica sociale*, and in 1892 was the author, together with his beloved companion, the former Russian revolutionary Anna Kuliscioff, of the newly formed **Partito Socialista Italiano** (PSI) / Italian Socialist Party's political program. He became a parliamentary deputy in 1896, a role that did not save him from arrest and imprisonment in 1898 during the indiscriminate repression of the Socialist movement ordered by the Rudinì government in that year.

Despite the Italian state's heavy-handed treatment of the workers' movement, Turati was no revolutionary. In November 1900—at his behest—the PSI committed itself to a gradual transformation of Italian society via parliamentary institutions and gave parliamentary backing to the liberal **Zanardelli-Giolitti** government in 1901. Although this approach was criticized by many in the PSI, it remained the primary strand of thinking within the PSI until the 1912 party conference. In that year, the so-called "maximalists," led by **Mussolini**, became the majority voice in the party, while the reformists of the right, who wished to turn the PSI into a labor party on the British model, were expelled. Turati, who subscribed to neither group, was left in the middle.

Turati bitterly opposed Italy's entry into **World War I**. He foresaw that the war would heighten Italy's class divisions and block the economic modernization that was a precondition for a peaceful transition toward socialism. After the disaster of **Caporetto** in 1917, however—to the disgust of many in the PSI—he did support the defense of Italian territory.

The PSI entered the Third International created by the Bolsheviks in 1919, and one of Lenin's explicit conditions for the party's continued membership was the expulsion of Turati and his fellow moderates. Many even of the "maximalists" balked at this demand, but by 1922 Turati's studied moderation, and defense of parliamentary institutions, was in any case anathema to the PSI's militants. On October 1, 1922, Turati was expelled by the narrow margin of 32,000 votes to 29,000. Undeterred, he organized a new leftist party, the Partito Socialista Unitario (PSU) / Unitary Socialist party, which attracted many of the bravest young socialists in Italy. Following the murder of his friend and comrade **Giacomo Matteotti** by the fascists, Turati joined with **Alcide De Gasperi** and **Giovanni Amendola** in boycotting **Parliament**. The failure of the boycott left Turati in personal danger, and he escaped to Paris where he continued the resistance to **fascism** and sought to reunify the PSI into a single anti-fascist force. He died in exile.

TURIN (*Torino*). Located in the northwest corner of Italy, near the French border, Turin rivals **Naples** for the honor of being the third-largest city in Italy, with a population of approximately 1.2 million. Like **Milan**, Turin can trace its history to Roman times, but its modern history begins in 1718, when it became the capital of the kingdom of Sardinia. During the Napoleonic wars, the city was a constant battleground. In 1798, it fell to the French. Austro-Russian forces fighting in Italy reconquered it in 1799, and the French retook the city in 1800. It remained in French hands until 1815, when the Congress of Vienna restored the Sardinian throne. In 1821, the city rose in revolt and demanded the granting of a constitutional monarchy: only the intervention of Austria restored absolute rule. After the **Risorgimento** in 1859-1861, Turin was the seat of the kingdom of Italy until 1865 when the capital was transferred first to **Florence** and then, in 1870, to **Rome**. The decision to move the capital provoked massive popular demonstrations in Turin in September 1864 that left 50 dead.

At the end of the nineteenth century, Turin was Milan's only rival for the title of Italy's industrial capital. **FIAT**—still the city's largest employer—began operations in 1899 and was soon giving work to tens of thousands of workers at its Mirafiori plant. The city's workers gallantly resisted the Nazis during the German occupation in the latter stages of the war. During the 1950s and 1960s, the city became the home to hundreds of thousands of southern Italian migrants, who were housed in hastily built projects on the city's outskirts. Turin naturally became one of Italy's most highly unionized cities and the city has frequently been the scene of street clashes between the authorities and striking workers, most particularly during the "hot autumn" of 1969. Apart from FIAT, Turin is chiefly famous outside of Italy for being the home of the Juventus soccer club, the current world club champions.

The city's fifteenth-century cathedral houses the "shroud of

Turin," a cloth that appears to have an imprinted image of Christ, and that is popularly believed to be the sheet in which Jesus was wrapped when he was taken down from the Cross. Carbon dating has confirmed that the shroud dates back to well before the Middle Ages. In 1997, the shroud miraculously escaped destruction in a major fire that has left lasting damage to the cathedral. *See also* Napoleonic Italy.

-U-

UNGARETTI, GIUSEPPE (1888-1970). A personal, autobiographical poet, Giuseppe Ungaretti was born in Egypt and schooled in France, where he attended the Sorbonne and imbibed the philosophy of Bergson at its source. He arrived in Italy in 1914, where he began to publish poetry in the Florentine review *Lacerba*. Loudly pro-war, Ungaretti fought in **World War I** as a common soldier, and his war poetry, gathered in the collection *L'Allegria* (*Happiness*, 1917) is the greatest poetic testimony of the war on the Italian front. The experience of combat transformed his jingoism into a more reflective understanding of the horrors that war inevitably brings. In the poem *San Martino del Carso*, he superbly conveyed the anguish he felt on seeing a village that had been battered by artillery: Of these houses / Nothing remains / But a few / Broken Walls / Of the many / Who wrote me / None now are here / But in my heart / No cross is missing / My heart / Is the most shattered village of all.

Ungaretti's second major collection, *Sentimento del tempo* (*The Sentiment of the Time,* 1933), saw the poet experimenting with religious themes, and with more traditional metrical structures, as he attempted to recapture the "song" of classical Italian poetry. Between 1936 and 1942, Ungaretti lived in Brazil, where he taught Italian literature in Sao Paolo. His stay was marked by the tragic death of his son, Antonietto, whom he later remembered in the lyrics that constituted half of his 1947 collection, *Il dolore* (*Grief*). The remainder of the poems were dedicated to "occupied **Rome**," and many critics regard them as his finest work. Ungaretti's collected works were published in Italian in 1970, shortly before his death.

UNIONE DELLE DONNE ITALIANE (UDI) / Union of Italian Women. The relatively advantageous position of the **Democrazia Cristiana** (DC) / Christian Democracy Party on all matters touching the family led the **Partito Comunista Italiano** (PCI) / Italian

Communist Party to make this addition to its formidable capillary organizations (others include sporting clubs and cultural and recreational societies). The Unione delle Donne Italiane (UDI) / Union of Italian Women publishes its own magazine, *Noi Donne* (*We Women*), and by 1954 had over a million members in 3,500 local circles, each one typically holding fortnightly meetings, which —while largely political—circulated, among members, petitions regarding issues of apparent concern to traditional, working-class Italian **women**: housing, care of the elderly, unemployment among women, and summer camps for children. The UDI also organizes trips to museums to "raise the cultural level" of members. *See also* Dopolavoro; Youth Movements, Fascist.

UOMO QUALUNQUE. *See* Qualunquismo.

-V-

VATICAN. An independent city-state of 0.44 square kilometers (0.17 square miles), the Vatican consists of Saint Peter's cathedral (so named because it was built by Emperor Constantine in the fourth century A.D. on what legend reputed to be the tomb of the apostle Peter), its surrounding palaces (which include the Pope's private quarters and the Vatican library), and a substantial walled park behind Saint Peter's. The city has fewer than 1,000 residents, of whom approximately 400 carry the Vatican passport. The Pope's territorial authority also extends over a handful of important buildings elsewhere in **Rome**, including the cathedral.

The Pope rules as absolute monarch over the tiny city-state, which has its own railway station, its own newspaper (*L'Osservatore Romano*, the official organ of the Vatican), and its own currency, the Vatican lira, which is worth exactly the same as the Italian lira. A regiment of (volunteer) Swiss guards, in colorful costumes designed by Raphael, maintain a symbolic defense of the tiny state. The Vatican maintains an observer at the United Nations, but is not a member. Nevertheless, since the signing of the **Lateran pacts** in 1929, it has been recognized as a sovereign state. The Vatican is full of priceless works of art by the great Renaissance masters. The frescoes painted by Michelangelo on the ceilings of the Sistine chapel continue to draw awed art lovers from around the world. *See also* Catholicism; Guarentigie, Legge delle; Lateran Pacts; Papacy.

VELTRONI, WALTER (1955-). While still in a Roman secondary school, Veltroni joined the Federazione Giovanile Comunista Italiana (FGCI) / Italian Communist Youth Federation and was soon elected secretary of his cell. In 1975, he was elected provincial secretary and a member of the national executive of the FGCI. The next year (he was just 21), he was elected to the city council of **Rome** and, within another year, was put in charge of propaganda for the Roman federation of the **Partito Comunista Italiano** (PCI) / Italian Communist Party. By 1980, he was second in charge of propaganda and relations with the press of the national party.

By 1987, he headed the Committee on Propaganda and Information. Later that year, he was elected to the Chamber of Deputies and was reelected in 1992 and in 1996 as a member of the **Partito Democratico della Sinistra** (PDS) / Democratic Party of the Left. He currently serves in the government of **Romano Prodi** both as deputy prime minister and as minister for culture. In the latter capacity, he is largely credited with overseeing—even with monthly personal visits—the final stages of restoration of the Borghese Art Museum, a seventeenth-century villa that has been the property of the Italian state since 1902. It includes paintings by Caravaggio, Titian, and Raphael as well as sculptures by Canova and Bernini. Its reopening to the public in summer 1997 has been regarded as a coup by Minister Veltroni.

VENICE (*Venezia*). One of the most famous and visited cities in the world, Venice was long one of Europe's most powerful independent states: she was *La Serenissima Repubblica* (The Most Serene Republic). The Doges of Venice (chosen by a popular assembly until A.D. 1172 and by a Grand Council of noblemen thereafter) dominated the eastern Mediterranean and trade between Europe and the East until the eighteenth century, when Venice's centuries-long struggle against the power of the Ottoman Turks was brought to an end by the Peace of Passerowitz in which the Venetians lost all their colonies except for settlements along the Dalmatian coastline.

The city's modern history began in 1797, when a century of economic decline ended in a popular revolt against the aristocracy and the institution of a short-lived democracy. Briefly under Austrian rule, Venice became part of Bonaparte's Kingdom of Italy, but at the **Congress of Vienna** was restored to Austria. In 1848, under the leadership of **Daniele Manin**, the city established a republic that held out against the Austrians until August 1849. It subsequently remained under Austrian rule until 1866 when, after a plebiscite, it passed into Italian hands.

With the possible exception of **Florence**, it is probably fair to say that no city in the world has so large a share of the world's artistic and cultural heritage as Venice. Its long politically dominant position and its commercial wealth made the city a mecca for artists during the Renaissance and after. Bellini, Giorgione, Tiziano, Tintoretto, Veronese, Tiepolo, and Canaletto are all "Venetian" artists.

The modern city has 70,000 inhabitants, down from 150,000 just a few decades ago. On the other side of the lagoon is the large industrial satellite-city of Mestre, with its nearly 400,000 citizens. Tens of millions of tourists every year take a gondola down the Grand Canal or visit Saint Mark's Square. Tourism, while an immense source of income for the local economy, has inflicted substantial environmental costs, and on some days during the high season the city has to block the road link from Mestre to prevent overcrowding. Venice is currently sinking into its lagoon at a dangerous rate, and the city council, the Italian government, and UNESCO are studying various projects to stop the slide.

VERDI (Greens). *See* Environmentalism.

VERDI, GIUSEPPE (1813-1901). Born near Parma, Verdi's early musical and private life was characterized by setbacks. His attempt to enter the conservatory at **Milan** in 1832 was rebuffed on the grounds of his excessive age and insufficient piano technique. Between 1838 and 1840, he had to endure the tragedy of losing his wife and children to illness. Only in 1842, when he composed *Nabucco*, did his luck begin to turn. In the next 15 years he wrote nearly 20 operas, including *Rigoletto* (1851) and *La Traviata* (1853). By now internationally famous, he began writing and presenting operas all over the world: *Aïda* (1871), perhaps his most famous work, was first produced in Cairo with the pyramids as a backdrop. Verdi was a patriot and a supporter of the unification of Italy, and was elected to the first Italian Parliament in 1861. During the 1850s, audiences who wanted to show their support for Italian nationalism would hang banners in the theater reading "*Viva* V.E.R.D.I." As well as showing their affection for a great composer, the letters stood for "Vittorio Emanuele Re d'Italia."

After *Aïda*, his production became less intense. In 1874, he composed the requiem mass for the novelist **Alessandro Manzoni**. His last two great works were both based on Shakespeare's plays: *Otello* (1877) and *Falstaff* (1893). Musically less challenging than his great German contemporary, Wagner, Verdi's operas have nevertheless lost none of their appeal for audiences all over the world. In Italy, he remains a popular composer in the widest sense of the word, and new productions of *Rigoletto* or *La Traviata* are whistled off stage if they do not meet the public's demanding standards for singing and orchestration.

VERGA, GIOVANNI (1840-1922). The greatest exponent of *verismo* (naturalism) in Italian literature, Giovanni Verga's exceptional powers of realistic description have led to comparisons with such writers as Emile Zola and D. H. Lawrence. Verga was born in Catania, **Sicily**, but spent much of his life in **Florence** and **Milan**. Between 1866 and 1881, Verga produced several novels and plays, but with *I Malavoglia* (*The House of the Medlar Tree,* 1881) he established himself as a writer of international repute. *I Malavoglia* is the story of a family of Sicilian fishermen who tempt fate by foolishly speculating on a cargo of lupins. This act of vainglory is the harbinger of a series of disasters that lead the family into misery and dishonor. Verga's theme, in short, is the pessimistic one of determinism: the inability of human beings to escape the circumstances of their birth. The book inspired **Luchino Visconti**'s classic neo-realist film, *La terra trema* (*The Earth Trembles,* 1948).

In 1886, Verga published a second novel with a similar fatalistic theme, *Mastro Don Gesualdo*, which is the story of a man who is determined to acquire possessions, *roba*, at all costs. He succeeds, but at the end of the novel, despite his daughter's brilliant marriage, he dies without the family love and affection which, Verga seems to imply, alone give meaning to life. In the mid-1890s, Verga returned to Catania and worked half-heartedly at a third book, this time set in high society, portraying "the defeated," but never finished it. Nominated to the Senate in 1920, he died in his ancestral home in Catania in 1922.

VICTOR EMMANUEL II / Vittorio Emanuele II (1820-1878). Born in Turin on March 19, 1820, this last king of Sardinia and first king of united Italy grew up in Tuscany and Piedmont. He was the son of Carlo Alberto and Maria Teresa of Tuscany. As a young man (22), he married Maria Adelaide, daughter of the Austrian Viceroy in

Lombardy-Venetia. Despite his lack of command experience, he led a division in the War of Independence of 1848-1849. Defeat at Novara led his father to abdicate the throne and brought young Victor Emmanuel to be king. In that position, he negotiated an armistice with General Radetzky.

He revealed his absolutist inclinations by twice dissolving Parliament when its majority objected to the resultant treaty. The king twice called for new elections until the majority that he preferred was realized. Parliament approved the treaty with Austria in 1850. He further circumvented Parliament by making a secret arrangement with France for the dispatch of Piedmontese troops to the Crimea in 1854, just as he was later to make a secret alliance with France in the event of war with Prussia.

After **Giuseppe Garibaldi** had ceded southern Italy to Piedmont (March 18, 1861), his influence with the new king of Italy grew, to the intense chagrin of **Cavour**. In fact, Victor Emmanuel retained secret contacts with both **Mazzini** and Garibaldi throughout his reign. When **Rome** was absorbed, the Piedmontese king of united Italy began to be called "Father of his Country." His dynastic policy often put him at odds with his government, his claims to uphold the **Statuto Albertino** notwithstanding. His maneuvering brought down the governments of both **Ricasoli** and **Minghetti**. One of his sons, Amadeo, was king of Spain, 1870-1873.

His wife, having produced eight children (three of whom died in childhood), passed away in 1855. Within 14 years, he had remarried morganatically. His new wife was Rosa Vercellana Guerrieri whom he created Countess of Mirafiore e Fontanafredda.

Victor Emmanuel laid the groundwork for the Triple Alliance by visiting both Berlin and Vienna in 1873. He died in **Rome** in 1878 at 58 and was succeeded by his son, Humbert I (Umberto I). *See also* Camillo Benso di Cavour; Giuseppe Garibaldi; Rome; Victor Emmanuel III.

VICTOR EMMANUEL III / Vittorio Emanuele III (1869-1947). Born in **Naples** in November 1869, he was the son of Humbert I and Margherita di Savoia (Margaret of Savoy). His education, despite his minimal stature (he was barely five feet tall), was military. By 1897, not yet 30 but already a general, he commanded an army corps. Additional studies included law, history, and political subjects. In 1896, he married Elena of Montenegro. When an anarchist assassinated his father (July 1900 in Monza), Victor Emmanuel succeeded to the throne. The centrality of the governments of the right ended with **Zanardelli** and his successor, **Giolitti**, with whom the king fell out over the intervention issue. Neutralist Giolitti was not in tune with Victor Emmanuel's interventionist spirit: the king would have preferred **Antonio Salandra** as prime minister but accepted the constitutional limitations on his powers of initiative.

When Italy emerged impoverished and torn by **World War I**, Victor Emmanuel III came to see fascism as a tool to be used in forestalling the rise of bolshevism. Apparently convinced that he could avoid civil war and could tame **Benito Mussolini**, the king failed to act or to use the Royal Army to put an end to **fascism's** political terrorism and the **March on Rome.** By 1925, legal opposition having been ended, only the **Partito Nazionale Fascista** (PNF) / National Fascist Party was legitimate. Ceremonial powers were all that was left to the monarch, especially after the title president of the Council of Ministers was changed by law (December 24, 1925) making Mussolini head of the government. This pill was eventually sweetened by the conferring on the king of the titles of emperor of Italian East Africa (1936) and king of **Albania** (1939). The king's acceptance of a subservient role vis-à-vis Mussolini prevented the officers' corps of the army, always loyal to the throne, from opposing what was, after all, the legitimate Italian government. Resentment ran deep among officers raised in Piedmontese traditions, especially when Mussolini gave status equal to the Royal Army to the blackshirts of the *Milizia*, made up largely of former squadristi and street-fighters.

It was a full three years after Italy's invasion of France in 1940 that humiliating defeats in North Africa and the USSR, together with the imminence of Allied landings in Italy itself, combined to convince the king to save what he could. On July 25,1943, he sought to preserve the monarchical institution by having Mussolini arrested and putting **Marshal Badoglio** in charge of the government. After 40 days, on September 8, the marshal announced an armistice with the Allies and Victor Emmanuel, together with his court and Badoglio, fled Rome to travel south to areas already under Allied occupation, leaving the Italian army without orders in the face of the inevitable German drive to occupy immediately all of Italy as far south as **Naples** and to suppress Italian forces everywhere. Those who resisted were quickly overrun. Many simply shed their uniforms and headed home. Others joined the resistance, playing a leading role in establishing short-lived autonomous republics in the north administered by the **Comitato di Liberazione Nazionale**-Alta Italia (CLNAI) / Committee for National Liberation-Northern Italy. The king declared war on Germany in October 1943 thus making Italy a "co-belligerent." Given the post-war climate of hostility to all identifiable supporters of fascism, his flight from Rome and his failure to act against fascism in any way before 1943 ensured defeat for the monarchy in the referendum held to choose between its perpetuation and its termination. The Savoy dynasty's role in Italy was ended by popular will. Victor Emmanuel III abdicated on May 9, 1946, and went into exile in Alexandria, Egypt, where he died on December 28, 1947. *See also* Fascism; Monarchy; Mussolini; Peace Treaty of 1947.

VIENNA, CONGRESS OF. So far as Italy was concerned, the Congress of Vienna (November 1814 to June 1815) represented an attempt by the great powers, especially Austria, to restore absolutism in the Italian peninsula. The Trentino, South Tyrol, and Venezia Giulia were all reabsorbed into the Austrian empire; Lombardy-Venetia became an Austrian colony ruled over, from January 1816, by an Austrian viceroy applying Austrian law. The Duchies of Modena, Parma, and Lucca, and the Grand Duchy of Tuscany were allowed nominal independence, but were ruled by individuals related by ties of marriage to the Austrian court. Elsewhere in Italy, absolutism was reinforced by the restoration of the pre-Napoleonic order. The Papal states, comprising the modern regions of Emilia-Romagna, the Marche, Umbria, and Lazio, were re-created, and, in southern Italy, Metternich insisted upon the return of the Bourbon Ferdinand IV of **Naples**, whose authority was also extended over **Sicily**, thereby creating—in December 1816—the Kingdom of the Two Sicilies. The only part of Italy where Austria's writ did not run was the Kingdom of Piedmont-Sardinia, but this, too, was an absolute monarchy ruled over by King Victor Emmanuel I.

The return of absolutism did not go unchallenged. In July 1820, the people of **Naples**, led by a large part of the armed forces, rebelled and imposed on Ferdinand a constitutional monarchy modeled on the Spanish Constitution of 1812. Seizing the opportunity to declare independence, the city of **Palermo** also rose in revolt, and a bloody civil war began in Sicily between supporters and opponents of unification with Naples. At the conference of Troppau in October 1820, the Holy Alliance powers (Austria, Russia, and Prussia) warned that they would intervene to protect the principle of absolute monarchy, and in March 1821 Austrian troops restored Ferdinand to power. Violent repression of the Carboneria, intricately organized sects of liberal revolutionaries, followed. The revolts in southern Italy were a prelude to similar unrest in Piedmont-Sardinia. On March 10, 1821, the Carboneri seized **Turin**, proclaimed a constitutional monarchy, and declared Victor Emmanuel I to be the king of all Italy—thereby effectively declaring war on Austria. Rather than concede a constitutional monarchy, Victor Emmanuel handed power to Prince **Carlo Alberto** who, as regent, first agreed to the constitutional monarchy, but refused to make war on Austria. On March 23, reneging on his word, Carlo Alberto fled to join the loyalist forces of Victor Emmanuel's brother, Carlo Felice, who with massive Austrian support crushed the constitutionalists at the battle of Novara at the beginning of April. On April 19, 1821, Victor Emmanuel abdicated, allowing Carlo Felice to ascend to the throne.

The restoration of absolutism in Italy was confirmed by the Congress of Verona (October-December 1822). *See also* Carlo Alberto; Statuto Albertino; Carboneria.

VISCONTI, LUCHINO (1906-1976). The scion of one of Italy's oldest and most aristocratic families, Visconti entered the cinema relatively late, and was nearly 30 when a chance social contact enabled him to work with the great French director Jean Renoir. Visconti's first film, *Ossessione* (*Obsession*, 1942), was based on the American novel *The Postman Always Rings Twice* and aroused an uproar in Italy for its frank sexuality. Visconti had to make a personal appeal to **Mussolini** to get the film past the censors. Fortunately, the dictator allowed this first masterpiece of **neo-realism** to appear with only limited cuts. Visconti was later arrested by the authorities and charged with aiding the resistance. For some time, he was at grave risk of execution. In 1947, Visconti made his second great film, *La terra trema* (*The Earth Trembles*), which was based upon **Giovanni Verga**'s novel *I malavoglia*. Set in the Sicilian fishing village of Aci Trezza, the film manages both to show the hardship and agony of the villagers' lives, and include scenes of ravishing poetic beauty. Visconti used no professional actors in the film, and the film had to be subtitled into Italian for non-Sicilian viewers.

Visconti produced two masterpieces in the 1950s. *Senso* (*Feeling*, 1954) was his first foray into the use of color, but its visual opulence and subject matter (the film is a love story set during the

Risorgimento) were regarded with suspicion by the neo-realists. *Rocco e i suoi fratelli* (*Rocco and his Brothers*, 1960), by contrast, marked a return to the naturalism of his earlier films, and was a major critical and box office success. From 1960 onward, however, Visconti turned more toward the big-budget, visually enchanting style of *Senso*. Turning his back on neo-realism and Italy's Marxist critical establishment, Visconti chose to adapt **Di Lampedusa**'s novel *Il Gattopardo* (*The Leopard*, 1963), even though the book had been derided as reactionary when it first appeared in the late 1950s. The film won the *Palme d'Or* at Cannes. Visconti's last major film was *Morte a Venezia* (*Death in Venice*, 1971). The depiction of the decadent beauty of Venice is the most successful aspect of the film; the psychological trauma undergone by Aschenbach, the protagonist, is portrayed somewhat ponderously. In addition to his film career, Visconti was Italy's preeminent opera and theater director. He died in **Rome** in 1976.

VISCONTI-VENOSTA, EMILIO (1829-1914). One of liberal Italy's most adept diplomats and statesmen, Emilio Visconti-Venosta was the scion of a prominent Milanese family. In his youth he was a follower of **Mazzini**, but by 1861, when he entered Parliament, he had become fully reconciled to constitutional liberalism. Visconti-Venosta was foreign minister almost continuously from 1863 to 1876; in this time he promoted the policy of close relations with Bismarck's Germany that enabled Italy to complete the process of unification begun in 1860-1861, and played a major role in resolving the crisis of relations with the **Vatican** after the occupation of **Rome** in 1870 by promoting the so-called **legge delle guarentigie**. The rise of **Depretis** and **Crispi** signaled the end of his career for 20 years.

Finally, in 1896, after the Italian defeat at the battle of Adowa brought a rude awakening from Crispi's imperialistic dreams, **Di Rudinì** called Visconti-Venosta back to office. The veteran diplomat subtly steered Italy away from its alliance with Austria and Germany, improving relations with France and maintaining good relations with Britain even as Germany began to challenge British dominance. Unlike Crispi, Visconti-Venosta was a realist who was aware that diplomacy, not force of arms, was the key to a successful foreign policy for Italy. He relinquished his office in 1901, but played an important role as mediator between France and Germany at the Algeçiras conference in 1906. He died in **Rome** in 1914.

VITTORINI, ELIO (1908-1966). Born in 1908 in Syracuse (**Sicily**), Vittorini was one of the most influential editors and writers of post-war Italy. His first steps into the literary world came during the late 1920s when he began to collaborate with *Solaria*, the Florentine literary periodical edited by **Eugenio Montale**. In 1933, *Solaria* began publishing his first novel, *Il garofano rosso* (*The Red Carnation*), in installments, but the censor, disliking this study of a youth whose adolescent rebelliousness finds an outlet in the violence and camaraderie of the fascist movement, suspended publication. In the late 1930s, Vittorini translated American realists such as Steinbeck and Hemingway. Their influence can be seen on his two most important novels, *Conversazione in Sicilia* (*Conversations in Sicily*, 1942) and *Uomini e no* (*Men and Others*, 1945), which were based upon his experiences as a wartime partisan in **Milan**.

In 1945, Vittorini became a member of the **Partito Comunista Italiano** (PCI) / Italian Communist Party and founded *Il Politecnico*, the theoretical journal of the neo-realist movement in the arts. The review closed in 1947 after Vittorini clashed with **Palmiro Togliatti**, the secretary of the PCI, who accused Vittorini of privileging literary culture over political commitment. Vittorini replied that the PCI should not expect writers to merely "blow the revolution's flute." To preserve his independence, Vittorini left the PCI in 1951.

In 1950, he became an editor for Einaudi, responsible for discovering and nurturing new writers of talent. Vittorini's political and literary preferences were not always helpful in this role. In 1957, he rejected **Di Lampedusa**'s remarkable novel, *Il Gattopardo* (*The Leopard*), on the grounds that it was reactionary in sentiment and over-literary in language and style. After the mid-1950s, Vittorini published no more novels. He was joint editor, however, with **Italo Calvino**, of the avant-garde journal *Menabò* from 1960 onward. He died in Milan in 1966.

-W-

WOMEN IN CONTEMPORARY ITALY. Since the fall of **fascism,** women's roles have changed not only for ideological reasons but because of the reduced centrality of the home. In its turn, this has resulted from changing aspirations among the young, eager to strike out on their own (if they can find affordable housing); the increase in two-income families; changing sexual behavior; and general emulation of what are considered American (modern) ways. The role of women in making family purchases and increased consumerism are additional factors contributing to the change in the position of women. Still, progress has not always been easy, especially in strongly conservative regions where it was impeded by traditions, by Catholicism, or both.

In north-central regions, as many as 70 percent of Italian women work outside the home, and in the South as well as the North, many who stay in the home work in *lavori sommersi* (hidden cottage industries). In the eleventh legislature chosen in 1992, 30 women made up 9.2 percent of the **Parliament**. In the lower house, of 631 members, 51 (8.08 percent) are women. While still low, these figures mark a considerable progress considering that women only got the franchise in 1949. More than half of the 30 women in the Italian Senate represent the **Partito Democratico della Sinistra** (PDS) / Democratic Party of the Left; one of their number (**Leonilde Iotti**) has been a highly respected president of the Chamber of Deputies.

In December 1975, 20,000 women marched in a Roman demonstration that was disrupted by the forceful intervention of male militants from **Lotta Continua,** unwilling to accept the principle of a "women only" march. On the issue of abortion, the women's movement collected 800,000 signatures—300,000 over the legal requirement—for a **referendum.**

Aside from political careers, many women are active participants in Italian professions. Nearly 80 percent of elementary teachers are women; two-thirds of intermediate (*medie*) school teachers and nearly half of *liceo* teachers. A full 21 percent of university faculty are also women (although the proportion who are tenured [*di ruolo*] is smaller). Half the metropolitan police in many larger cities are women, and they draw street duty (including mounted patrol) as well as desk work. All of these tasks have built on their role in the resistance and the activities of the **Unione delle Donne Italiane** (UDI) / Union of Italian Women. *See also* Black Economy.

WORLD WAR I (1914-1918). In hindsight, World War I can be seen as another contest for primacy on the continent of Europe. For the French, that primacy was theirs almost as a right traceable to Louis XIV. For the Germans, victory in the Franco-Prussian war entitled the new Germany to that primacy; yet France was still regarded as Europe's cultural and creative center. Even in German popular speech, one who experienced great joy was described as being *Glücklich wie ein Gott in Frankreich!* (As happy as a God in

France!) as though that were a *non plus ultra.*

Britain entered the war after Belgium had been successfully invaded and German subjugation of the continent seemed plausible. Whether against Frederick the Great, Napoleon, or the Kaiser, Britain fought to see that no state would dominate the resources—human and material—of the continent across the Channel.

For Italy, on the other hand, interest in the war focused on Austria, the traditional Italian nemesis, to whom she was joined in the **Triple Alliance.** Seen by the Italian government as purely defensive, the treaty promised Italy's assistance to Germany and Austria should either be the victim of an attack. As Austria's displeasure mounted concerning Serbian aggrandizement at Turkey's expense in the **Balkan Wars,** Italy made clear that the Triple Alliance would never be a license for Austria to engage in aggressive war against the Serbs.

Thus, when the assassination of Archduke Francis Ferdinand led to Austria's ultimatum to Serbia, Italy—claiming that the Triple Alliance's conditions had not been met—declared her neutrality while Serbia's and Austria's allies mobilized for what each thought would be a swift war resolving outstanding problems of national aspirations, imperial ambition, and the settling of scores.

It soon became clear that the most an Austrian victory might yield to Italy would be concessions in Africa (perhaps Tunisia, French since 1830). But a French victory over Austria and Germany could mean that territories such as the Trentino might become Italian—if Italy were France's ally, continued neutrality might favor either Austria or Serbia at war's end but certainly not Italy.

The decisive factor was the desire to establish Italian credentials as a power and to take part in establishing the post-war equilibrium. Thus, the **Treaty of London** of 1915 formalized Italian entry into the war as an ally of France and Britain. It was accepted by the Italian **Parliament** only after **Gabriele D'Annunzio** and other nationalists had manipulated crowds in the public squares of Italy to rout opposition opinion that, in fact, held the majority in Parliament. War fever, however, was followed by shock.

Hostilities in Europe's highest mountains could not have begun at a worse time. Russian forces had suffered defeats that obliged them to withdraw from (Austrian) Galicia, thus freeing Vienna to reinforce its positions in the Alps. In 1916, a determined Austrian offensive devised to drive Italy out of the war failed and the fighting, which was rarely carried to the Austrians, settled into trenches and shelling between mountaintops. Eleven bloody but indecisive battles at the Isonzo River had been fought on a 96 kilometer (60 mile) front and had advanced Italian forces barely 10 miles toward **Trieste**. When the Austrians learned of a massive Italian offensive being planned by General **Cadorna** for the spring of 1918, they sought, and received, assistance from their German ally in the form of experienced troops and officers. The twelfth battle of the Isonzo, begun in October 1917, ended at Caporetto where the Italian line broke.

Rumors of a rout became self-fulfilling. It was only at the Piave River that the line finally held. British and French reinforcements soon arrived and enabled the Italian army to counter-attack with a vengeance, driving Austria to ask for an armistice after a stunning defeat at Vittorio Veneto. The armistice came on November 3, 1918, eight days before the armistice on the western front.

Meanwhile in Italy, the war had reduced respect for Parliament and for the liberals who controlled it. The growing gap between the wealthy and the poor had heightened social tension. Moreover, many returning veterans found that even the newer engineering and metallurgical industries, made rich by the conflict, now faced shrinking markets and needed no new workers. Thus, not only were social divisions sharper than they remembered but the consequent bitter tensions did not stand comparison with the comradeship of the military life. All of these factors contributed to the rise of **fascism**. *See also* Treaty of Saint Germain.

WORLD WAR II (1939-1945). Hitler's conviction that Germany had been unfairly treated after her defeat in **World War I** was shared by some of Germany's one-time enemies. For British leaders, especially, substituting French hegemony in Europe for German was no great improvement. Moreover, the absence of a stabilizing force among the so-called successor states of the defunct Austrian empire made Hitler's initial appearance on the scene less problematic than it afterward appeared. National self-determination, after all, suggested the logic of Austro-German merger; that France should stand in the way of German militarization of German territory—the Rhineland—was offensive to much Anglo-American opinion. Finally, on each occasion when Hitler challenged the victors of World War I, he immediately offered a friendship pact or some agreement at which British officials grasped as at a straw.

Mussolini sought to dominate the Mediterranean and the

Balkans by creating a network of obligations. He assisted Franco in his seizure of power, thus compromising the Spanish *caudillo*; he sought Hitler's gratitude by not resisting the Anschluss with Austria in 1938; and the good will of both Britain and France by playing a mediatory role in the first Czechoslovakian crisis. Finally, he thought to please Hitler further by an alliance that was given effect only when it seemed clear that the *Blitzkrieg* might reorder European borders without any consideration given to Italian pretensions.

Once having entered the war on June 10, 1940, the Italian government—which is to say, Mussolini—decided on an invasion of France. Within a month, Italian forces attacked France's British ally in the Sudan and Kenya from garrisons in Abyssinia. By mid-August, British Somaliland had been occupied and Egypt was being threatened by the Italian army in Libya.

The tide of battle soon turned, however, and, in January 1941, South African and Indian forces had strengthened British positions adequately to carry the war to the Italians in **Libya**, **Abyssinia**, and the occupied British territories. By April, Haile Selassie had been returned to Addis Ababa by British-led forces. Fighting in North Africa continued throughout 1941 as thousands of Italians, severely demoralized by incompetent leadership and inadequacies of supply, were taken prisoner at a cost of hundreds of British casualties.

Even more humiliating was the fate of the Italian army in its Greek campaign begun in October 1940. By the end of November, Italian frontal attacks had worn down the troops, to such a point that—despite reinforcements—Greek counter-offensives had pushed Italian troops back into **Albania**. In order to preclude British occupation of Greek bases that could then be used against German sources of Rumanian oil and Balkan foodstuffs, and to prevent the total humiliation of his Italian ally, Hitler ordered the invasion of Greece (where they accomplished in two weeks what had eluded the Italians for six months).

Mussolini found it ever harder to refrain from accepting the assistance that he obviously needed from Germany. Once General Erwin Rommel had been sent into North Africa to assist **Graziani** and German troops had been sent to Greece, Mussolini lost control over the only area of the world in which Italy had a genuine interest. From that moment, Italy was clearly an underling and old traumas were revived of *Untermenschlichkeit* (sentiment of being inferior). The final testimony came when the Greeks agreed to surrender to Germany but not to Italy. Only Mussolini's personal appeal persuaded Hitler to include Italy in the April 1941 armistice proceedings. Hitler's respect for the Greek soldiers led him to order the release of all Greek prisoners.

Italian humiliations—the battle at El Alamein and the surrender of Italy's units in North Africa, losses of half of the country's forces in Russia, German reverses after Stalingrad—combined with the Allied invasion of **Sicily** to persuade the king to do what was needed to save what he could. The war, quite clearly, could not be won. On September 8, 1943, **Victor Emmanuel III** had the Duce of Italy arrested after a meeting of the Grand Council of Fascism had voted to terminate Mussolini's powers. A new government, while promising Germany to continue the war, entered into negotiations with the Allies, seeking and receiving status as a "co-belligerent," meaning that Italian forces (wearing British uniforms) would serve with the advancing British Eighth Army moving up the Adriatic coast toward the Po River valley.

Italian losses between 1940 and 1945 amounted to 165,000 military and naval personnel (and as many civilians), fewer than the losses of World War I but far from trivial. Moreover, the destruction of railway rolling-stock, productive facilities, and civilian housing was astronomical, surpassed only by Germany, Poland, and the USSR. Partisan activity often liberated northern cities even before Allied armies arrived, thus preserving major factories from war damage. *See also* Comitati di Liberazione Nazionale; Fascism; Benito Mussolini; Spanish Civil War.

-Y-

YOUTH MOVEMENTS, FASCIST. The organization of youth by age groups began with the paramilitary *Balilla* (Organizzazione Nazionale Balilla)—organized in January 1926—for 8- to 14-year-olds. At 14, one enrolled in the *Avanguardisti* for those between 14 and 19 and, finally, in Fascist University Youth (Gioventù Universitaria Fascista) that aimed at continuing the inculcation of military values in young Italians (18- to 29-year-old male and female university students). This system was proclaimed by nationalists as ensuring that in any future war, a race of warriors would meet the enemy with "eight million bayonets." (A favorite comment on this Mussolinian boast was that the enemy, unfortunately, was equipped with tanks.)

Similarly, young females were brought into *Piccole Italiane*

(Little Italians—female) to acquire and perfect the skills needed to be the mothers of tomorrow's warriors, the true heirs of Roman military prowess. It also served as a sporting, athletic, and disciplinary body. *Giovani Italiane* / Italian [Female] Youth drew Italian adolescent females (ages 14-18). Once adulthood approached, it was expected that all these young people, male and female alike, would move into membership in the **Partito Nazionale Fascista** (PNF) / National Fascist Party.

One of the functions of senior members of these organizations was to take a supervisory part in the summer camps, which were widely admired abroad. These camps exposed urban children to fresh air, exercise, and sunshine at seaside and mountain resorts established for them. Special trains were laid on for the participants and camping kits were distributed while they were taught patriotic and party songs. Healthy bodies and high spirits, it was assumed, make better soldiers. *See also* Fascism.

-Z-

ZANARDELLI, GIUSEPPE (1826-1903). Born in Brescia, Giuseppe Zanardelli was an active participant as a young man in the nationalist struggle. In 1848, and again in 1859, he led the citizens of Brescia in insurrections against Austrian rule. He entered Parliament in 1860 as a member of the **Partito Liberale Italiano** (PLI) / Italian Liberal Party constitutional left. After **Agostino Depretis**'s accession to power in 1876, he became minister for public works, then minister of the interior. In this role, he was responsible for the first liberalization of the **electoral law** in 1880. Between 1881-1883 and 1887-1891, he was minister of justice under both Depretis and **Francesco Crispi.** During the second of these spells in office, he successfully introduced a new penal code that among other provisions abolished the death penalty.

Zanardelli's progressive sympathies caused him to look upon the *trasformismo* of Depretis with a less than charitable eye. His opposition to Crispi's autocratic methods also prevented him from taking part in Crispi's second government. From December 1897, Zanardelli did, however, participate in the second **Rudinì** government, and was one of the architects of the panicky repression of the socialist and Catholic movements in May 1898. Following the accession to power of **Pelloux,** however, Zanardelli performed an enviable feat of political acrobatics and allied himself with **Giolitti** and the socialists against the right. In addition to his occasional ministerial duties, Zanardelli held the post of president of the Chamber of Deputies for much of the decade.

Zanardelli became prime minister in 1901, in the aftermath of the assassination of King Humbert I. His government, which was dominated by his political heir, Giovanni Giolitti, was the most liberal administration Italy had experienced since 1861. While prime minister, Zanardelli unsuccessfully tried to introduce a **divorce** law. He held the post until his death in 1903.

ZOLI, ADONE (1887-1960). Born in Cesena in the province of Forlì (Emilia-Romagna), Adone Zoli was a close collaborator of Don **Luigi Sturzo** after the foundation of the **Partito Popolare Italiana** (PPI) / Italian People's Party in 1919. He took an active role in the Tuscan **Comitati di Liberazione Nazionale** (CLN) / National Liberation Committees during the resistance from which position he moved to being vice mayor of **Florence** and a member of the national council of the **Democrazia Cristiana** (DC) / Christian Democracy Party. He was elected to the Senate in 1948 and reconfirmed in the elections of 1953 and in 1958. He was briefly vice president of the Senate before becoming minister of justice in 1951. Zoli also served as finance minister and as minister for the budget between 1955 and 1957. Zoli briefly headed a DC-only cabinet between May 1957 and June 1958. Close, politically, to **Amintore Fanfani**, Zoli's government nevertheless represented all strains of opinion within the DC, with important ministerial positions being held by **Fernando Tambroni** (interior), **Giulio Andreotti** (finance), and **Aldo Moro** (education).

Appendix

This appendix has been compiled from several useful works of reference. For Tables 2, 6, 12, 13, and 14 we are particularly indebted to the appendix to *Diario d'Italia: Due secoli di storia italiana giorno per giorno*, a chronology of modern Italian history published by the daily newspaper *Il Giornale* in 1994. For Tables 3, 7, 8, 9, and 11 our main source was Maria Serena Piretti, *Le elezioni politiche in Italia dal 1848 a oggi* (1995), Bari: Laterza, although we have taken the liberty of rounding out some figures and have limited ourselves to presenting only the principal political parties. Table 10 is based upon figures produced by the Italian Parliament after the 1996 election. For Tables 15 and 16, we are indebted to ISTAT, the Italian national statistical agency, whose annual reviews of Italian society are published by Il Mulino of Bologna, and whose web site (http://www.istat.it) is a feast of useful information about Italy. For more detailed information on politics, the economy, the regions, and the Italians' private lives, we recommend Paul Ginsborg, ed. *Stato dell'Italia* (1994), Milan: Mondadori, and the statistical appendixes to the series of annuals on Italian politics and society, which has been published since 1986 by the Istituto Cattaneo in Bologna in both English and Italian.

Table 1

Royal Heads of State

The Kingdom of the Two Sicilies

Ferdinand I of Bourbon	1815-1825
Francis I of Bourbon	1825-1830
Ferdinand II of Bourbon	1830-1859
Francis II of Bourbon	1859-1860

Kingdom of Sardinia

Victor Emmanuel I	1814-1821
Charles Felice	1821-1831
Charles Albert	1831-1849
Victor Emmanuel II	1849-1861

Kingdom of Italy

Victor Emmanuel II	1861-1878
Humbert I	1878-1900
Victor Emmanuel III	1900-1946
Humbert II	May-June 1946

Table 2

Heads of Government, 1861-1945

Cavour	March-June 1861
Ricasoli I	June 1861-March 1862
Rattazzi I	March-December 1862
Farini	December 1862-March 1863
Minghetti I	March 1863-September 1864
Lamarmora I	September 1864-December 1865
Lamarmora II	December 1865-June 1866
Ricasoli II	June 1866-April 1867
Rattazzi II	April-October 1867
Menabrea I	October 1867-January 1868
Menabrea II	January 1868-May 1869
Menabrea III	May-December 1869
Lanza	December 1869-July 1873
Minghetti II	July 1873-March 1876
Depretis I	March 1876-December 1877
Depretis II	December 1877-March 1878
Cairoli I	March-December 1878
Depretis III	December 1878-July 1879
Cairoli II	July-November 1879
Cairoli III	November 1879-May 1881
Depretis IV	May 1881-May 1883
Depretis V	May 1883-March 1884
Depretis VI	March 1884-June 1885
Depretis VII	June 1885-April 1887
Depretis VIII	April-July 1887
Crispi I	July 1887-March 1889
Crispi II	March 1889-February 1891
Di Rudinì I	February 1891-May 1892
Giolitti I	May 1892-December 1893
Crispi III	December 1893-March 1896
Di Rudinì II	March-July 1896
Di Rudinì III	July 1896-December 1897
Di Rudinì IV	December 1897-June 1898
Di Rudinì V	June 1898
Pelloux I	June 1898-May 1899
Pelloux II	May 1899-June 1900
Saracco	June 1900-February 1901
Zanardelli	February 1901-November 1903

Giolitti II	November 1903-March 1905
Fortis I	March-December 1905
Fortis II	December 1905-February 1906
Sonnino I	February-May 1906
Giolitti III	May 1906-December 1909
Sonnino II	December 1909-March 1910
Luzzatti	March 1910-March 1911
Giolitti IV	March 1911-March 1914
Salandra I	March-November 1914
Salandra II	November 1914-June 1916
Boselli	June 1916-October 1917
Orlando	October 1917-June 1919
Nitti I	June 1919-May 1920
Nitti II	May-June 1920
Giolitti V	June 1920-July 1921
Bonomi I	July 1921-February 1922
Facta I	February-August 1922
Facta II	August-October 1922
Mussolini	October 1922-July 1943
Badoglio I	July 1943-April 1944
Badoglio II	April-June 1944
Bonomi II	June-December 1944
Bonomi III	December 1944-June 1945

Source: "Diario d'Italia." 1994. *Il Giornale.*

Table 3

Elections to the Chamber of Deputies, 1861-1924

Year	Number votes cast	% voting	Largest party	(%)
1861	239,746	57.1	Moderate Rt.	(47.6)
1865	271,522	54.4	Moderate Rt.	(42.0)
1867	258,119	52.0	Moderate Rt.	(44.2)
1870	240,731	45.4	Moderate Rt.	(47.2)
1874	319,493	55.8	Moderate Rt.	(44.7)
1876	358,899	59.2	Constl. Left	(62.6)
1880	369,953	59.2	Constl. Left	(55.1)
1882	1,222,555	60.6	Constl. Left	(58.3)
1886	1,406,658	58.2	Constl. Left	(52.2)
1890	1,479,475	53.7	Constl. Left	(51.8)
1892	1,643,417	56.1	Constl. Left	(53.6)
1895	1,257,888	59.3	Constl. Left	(48.2)
1897	1,242,657	58.6	Constl. Left	(40.6)
1900	1,310,480	58.3	Constl. Left	(43.7)
1904	1,593,886	62.7	Constl. Left	(45.7)
1909	1,903,687	65.0	Constl. Left	(43.1)
1913	5,100,615	59.0	Constl. Left	(33.3)
1919	5,793,507	56.6	Socialist Party	(32.3)
1921	6,701,496	58.4	Socialist Party	(24.7)
1924	7,614,451	63.1	Fascist Party	(65.0)

Notes
Percentage figures have been rounded to the nearest tenth.
1913 first year with universal male suffrage.
1924 election conditioned by fascist violence.

Source: Piretti. 1995. *Le elezioni politiche in Italia dal 1848 a oggi.*
    Bari: Laterza.

Table 4

National Secretaries of the PNF

Name	Tenure
Michele Bianchi	Nov. 20, 1921 - Jan. 13, 1923
Nicola Sansanelli	Jan. 13, 1923 - Oct. 15, 1923
Francesco Giunta	Oct. 15, 1923 - Apr. 23, 1924
Provisional Directorate	Apr. 23, 1924 - Aug. 7, 1924
National Directorate	Aug. 7, 1924 - Feb. 12, 1925
Roberto Farinacci	Feb. 12, 1925 - Mar. 30, 1926
Augusto Turati	Mar. 30, 1926 - Oct. 8, 1930
Giovanni Giuriati	Oct. 7, 1930 - Dec. 7, 1931
Achille Starace	Dec. 7, 1931 - Oct. 31, 1939
Ettore Muti	Oct. 31, 1939 - Oct. 30, 1940
Adelchi Serena	Oct. 30, 1940 - Dec. 26, 1941
Aldo Vidussoni	Dec. 26, 1941 - Apr. 19, 1943
Carlo Scorza	Apr. 19, 1943 - July 25, 1943

Source: Cannistraro, Philip V. 1982. *Historical Dictionary of Fascist Italy*. Westport, CT: Greenwood Press. Appendix E.

Table 5

Presidents of the Republic, 1946-1997

Enrico Di Nicola	1946-1948
Luigi Einaudi	1948-1955
Giovanni Gronchi	1955-1962
Antonio Segni	1962-1964
Giuseppe Saragat	1964-1971
Giovanni Leone	1971-1978
Alessandro Pertini	1978-1985
Francesco Cossiga	1985-1992
Oscar Luigi Scalfaro	1992-

Table 6

Italian Cabinets and Prime Ministers since 1945

Premier	Composition	Tenure
Parri	DC-PCI-PSIUP-PLI-**PdA**	June-Nov.1945
De Gasperi I	**DC**-PCI-PSIUP-PLI-PdA	Dec.1945-July 1946
De Gasperi II	**DC**-PCI-PSI-PRI	July1946-Jan.1947
De Gasperi III	**DC**-PCI-PSI	February-May 1947
De Gasperi IV	**DC**-PSLI-PRI-PLI	May1947-May 1948
De Gasperi V	**DC**-PSLI-PRI-PLI	May 1948-Jan.1950
De Gasperi VI	**DC**-PSLI-PRI	Jan. 1950-July 1951
De Gasperi VII	**DC**-PRI	July 1951-June 1953
De Gasperi VIII	**DC**	July 1953
Pella	**DC**	Aug. 1953-Jan. 1954
Fanfani I	**DC**	January 1954
Scelba	**DC**-PSDI-PLI	Feb. 1954-June 1955
Segni I	**DC**-PSDI-PLI	July 1955-May 1957
Zoli	**DC**	May-June 1957
Fanfani II	**DC**-PSDI	July 1958-Jan.1959
Segni II	**DC**	Feb. 1959-Feb.1960
Tambroni	**DC**	March-July 1960
Fanfani III	**DC**	July 1960-Feb. 1962
Fanfani IV	**DC**-PSDI-PRI	Feb.1962-May 1963
Leone I	**DC**	June-November 1963
Moro I	**DC**-PSI-PSDI-PRI	Dec.1963-June 1964
Moro II	**DC**-PSI-PSDI-PRI	July 1964-Jan.1966
Moro III	**DC**-PSI-PSDI-PRI	Feb. 1966-June 1968
Leone II	**DC**	June-November 1968
Rumor I	**DC**-PSU-PRI	Dec.1968-July 1969
Rumor II	**DC**	Aug.1969-Feb. 1970
Rumor III	**DC**-PSI-PSDI-PRI	March-July 1970
Colombo	**DC**-PSI-PSDI-PRI	Aug. 1970-Jan.1972
Andreotti I	**DC**	February 1972
Andreotti II	**DC**-PSDI-PLI	June 1972-June 1973
Rumor IV	**DC**-PSI-PSDI-PRI	July 1973-Mar. 1974
Rumor V	**DC**-PSI-PSDI	March-Oct.1974
Moro IV	**DC**-PRI	Nov. 1974-Jan. 1976
Moro V	**DC**	February-April 1976
Andreotti III	**DC**	July 1976-Jan. 1978
Andreotti IV	**DC**	Mar.1978-Jan. 1979

Andreotti V	DC-PRI-PSDI	March-Aug.1979
Cossiga I	DC-PSDI-PLI	Aug.1979-Mar.1980
Cossiga II	DC-PSI-PRI	April-Sept. 1980
Forlani	DC-PSI-PSDI-PRI	Oct.1980-May 1981
Spadolini I	DC-**PRI**-PSI-PSDI-PLI	June 1981-Aug. 1982
Spadolini II	DC-**PRI**-PSI-PSDI-PLI	Aug.-Nov. 1982
Fanfani V	DC-PSI-PSDI-PLI	Dec.1982-April 1983
Craxi I	DC-**PSI**-PSDI-PRI-PLI	Aug. 1983-June 1986
Craxi II	DC-**PSI**-PSDI-PRI-PLI	Aug.1986-Mar. 1987
Fanfani VI	**DC**	April -July 1987
Goria	DC-PSI-PSDI-PRI-PLI	July 1987-Mar. 1988
De Mita	DC-PSI-PSDI-PRI-PLI	Apr. 1988-May 1989
Andreotti VI	DC-PSI-PSDI-PRI-PLI	July 1989-Mar. 1991
Andreotti VII	DC-PSI-PSDI-PLI	Apr. 1991-April 1992
Amato	DC-**PSI**-PSDI-PLI	July 1992-April 1993
Ciampi	Government formed without negotiations with the parties	Apr.1993-Jan. 1994
Berlusconi	**FI**-LN-AN-CCD-UC	May-December 1994
Dini	Government of non-party experts	Jan. 1995-Feb. 1996
Prodi	ULIVO (PDS+PPI+ minor parties)	May 1996-Oct. 1997
Prodi	ULIVO (same as above)	Oct. 1997-

Note: prime minister's party in boldface type.

Source: "Diario d'Italia" 1994. *Il Giornale.*

Table 7

Elections to the Chamber of Deputies, 1946-1992
Share of Vote Obtained by Main Political Parties

Election Year				Party			
	DC	PCI	PSI	MSI	PSDI	PRI	PLI
1946	35.2	18.9	20.7	—	—	4.4	6.8*
1948	48.5	31.0*		2.0	7.1*	2.5	3.8
1953	40.1	22.6	12.7	5.8	4.5	3.0	1.6
1958	42.3	22.7	14.2	4.8	4.6	1.4	3.5
1963	38.3	25.3	13.8	5.1	6.1	1.4	7.0
1968	39.1	26.9	14.5	4.5	*	2.0	5.8
1972	38.7	27.1	9.6	8.7	5.1	2.9	3.9
1976	38.7	34.4	9.6	6.1	3.4	3.1	1.3
1979	38.3	30.4	9.8	5.3	3.8	3.0	1.9
1983	32.4	30.8	11.4	8.8	4.1	5.1	2.9
1987	34.3	26.6	14.3	5.9	2.9	3.7	2.1
1992	29.7	21.7*	13.6	6.5	2.6	4.7	2.8

Notes
* (1946). "Liberal" opinion represented by the Unione Democratico Nazionale (UDN).
* (1948). PCI and PSI presented a joint list. PSDI figure obtained by Unitê Socialista (US).
* (1968). PSI and PSDI presented joint list under the name Partito Socialista Unitario (PSU).
* (1992). PCI vote obtained by adding the share of the vote obtained by the PDS (16.1%) to the share obtained by Rifondazione Comunista (5.6%).

Source: Piretti. 1995. *Le elezioni politiche in Italia dal 1848 a oggi.* Bari: Laterza.

Table 8

Elections to the Senate, 1948-1992
Share of Vote Obtained by Main Political Parties

Election Year				Party			
	DC	PCI	PSI	MSI	PSDI	PRI	PLI
1948	48.1	30.8	0.7	4.2	2.6	5.4	
1953	39.9	20.2	11.9	62.1	4.3	1.1	2.8
1958	41.2	21.8	14.1	4.4	4.4	1.4	3.9
1963	38.3	25.3	13.8	5.3	6.3	0.8	7.4
1968	38.3	30.0	15.2	4.8	—	2.2	6.8
1972	38.1	28.1	10.7	9.1	5.4	3.0	4.4
1976	38.9	33.8	10.2	6.6	3.1	2.7	1.4
1979	38.3	31.5	10.4	5.7	4.2	3.4	2.2
1983	32.4	30.8	11.4	7.3	3.8	4.7	2.7
1987	33.6	28.3	10.9	6.5	2.4	3.9	2.2
1992	27.3	23.6	13.6	6.5	2.6	4.7	2.8

Source: Piretti. 1995. *Le elezioni politiche in Italia dal 1848 a oggi.*
Bari: Laterza.

Table 9

The General Election of March 27, 1994
Composition of the Chamber of Deputies and the Senate

Coalition	Chamber	Senate
Polo della libertê (FI, LN, Panella, UC)	191	82
Polo del buon governo (FI-AN-CCD)	164	64
Other AN	10	8
Total Right-Wing	355	54
Patto Italia (PPI, Patto Segni)	46	31
Progressisti (PDS, Rifondazione, Rete, +minor parties)	213	122
Others	5	8

Source: Piretti. 1995. *Le elezioni politiche in Italia dal 1848 a oggi.*
Bari: Laterza.

Table 10

The General Election of April 21, 1996

Party or Coalition	Deputies	Senate
Ulivo (PDS-PPI-Prodi+minor parties)	284	157
Rif. Com/Progressisti	35	10
Lega Nord	59	27
Polo per la Libertê (FI-AN-CCD-CDU)	246	116
Others	6	5

Table 11

**General Elections of March 27, 1994, and April 21, 1996
Share of Vote Obtained by the Main Political Parties**

	FI	PDS	AN	LN	R.COM	PPI	CCD-CDU
1994	21.0	20.4	13.5	8.4	6.0	15.7*	—
1996	20.6	21.1	15.7	10.1	8.6	6.8	5.8

* *Includes Segni Pact*

Source: Piretti. 1995. *Le elezioni politiche in Italia dal 1848 a oggi.*
Bari: Laterza.

Table 12

Italian Resident Population by Census Return, 1861-1991
(in thousands)

Year	Male	Female	Total	Average Ann. Increment (%)
1861	13,399	12,939	26,328	—
1871	14,316	13,835	28,151	6.7
1881	15,134	14,657	29,791	5.7
1901	16,990	16,788	33,778	6.6
1911	18,608	18,313	36,921	8.6
1921	18,814	19,042	37,856	2.4
1931	20,181	20,862	41,043	8.6
1936	20,826	21,573	42,339	6.5
1951	23,259	24,257	47,516	7.4
1961	24,784	25,840	50,624	6.4
1971	26,476	27,661	54,137	6.7
1981	27,506	29,051	56,557	4.4
1991	27,406	29,006	56,411	-0.3

Source: "Diario d'Italia." 1994. *Il Giornale.*

Table 13

Distribution of Working Population by Sector, 1861-1991

Year	Agriculture	Industry	Services	Percentage Working
1861	69.7	18.1	12.2	59.0
1871	67.5	19.2	13.3	56.6
1881	65.4	20.2	14.4	54.0
1901	61.7	22.3	16.0	49.4
1911	58.4	23.7	17.9	47.4
1921	55.7	24.8	19.5	46.1
1931	51.7	26.3	22.0	44.4
1936	49.4	27.3	23.3	43.8
1951	42.2	32.1	25.7	41.2
1961	29.1	40.6	30.3	38.7
1971	17.2	44.4	38.4	34.8
1981	12.8	36.3	50.9	36.6
1991	8.5	32.0	59.5	42.0

Source: "Diario d'Italia." 1994. *Il Giornale.*

Table 14

Italian GNP at Constant 1938 Figures, 1861-1951

Year	GNP (billion lire)	Income per Capita* (lire)
1861	49.7	1,845
1871	54.6	1,897
1881	55.5	1,877
1891	63.0	1,906
1901	74.9	2,259
1911	95.0	2,455
1921	100.0	2,884
1931	125.0	3,029
1941	161.0	3,022§
1951	186.0	3,479

*Per head income calculated as a ten-year average, except for 1941
   and 1951.
§ 1941-1951 average per head income 2,655 lire.
Value of 1938 lira: one pound sterling = approximately 90 lire; one
   U.S. dollar = approximately 20 lire.

Source: "Diario d'Italia." 1994. *Il Giornale.*

Table 15

Annual Economic Growth, 1952-1974: The Economic Miracle

Year	Real GNP growth (%)
1952	4.4
1953	7.5
1954	3.6
1955	6.7
1956	4.7
1957	5.3
1958	4.8
1959	6.5
1960	6.3
1961	8.2
1962	6.2
1963	5.6
1964	2.6
1965	3.2
1966	5.8
1967	7.0
1968	6.3
1969	5.7
1970	5.0
1971	1.6
1972	3.1
1973	6.9
1974	3.9

Source: ISTAT.

Table 16

The Steady Growth of a Mature Economy:
The Italian Economy in the 1990s
All figures in trillion lire.

Year	In 1990 prices	GNP in current prices
1989	1,282,905	1,191,960
1990	1,310,659	1,310,659
1991	1,325,582	1,360,480
1992	1,333,072	1,437,524
1993	1,317,668	1,474,526
1994	1,346,267	1,546,819
1995	1,385,830	1,663,421
1996	1,395,408	1,759,449

Source: ISTAT.

Table 17

Total School Enrollment, 1993-1994

National Population = 57,268,578.

Pre-primary	1,578,420
Primary	2,863,279
Secondary:	
Intermediate	1,996,037
Higher Secondary	
Technical	1,210,166
Vocational	524,886
Teachers' Training	190,225
Fine Arts Liceo	97,084
Liceo	756,992
Universities	1,628,715

Source: "Statistical Survey, Education." *The Europa World Year Book, 1996*. vol.1, London: Europa Publications, Ltd. 1,707.

Table 18

**The European Union:
1996 Populations (in millions),
Gross Domestic Product (in billions of U.S. dollars)
and Approximate GDP Per Capita
(in thousands of U.S. dollars).**

Country	Population	GDP	GDP/capita
Austria	8.1	$ 218	27
Belgium	10.1	261	26
Britain	58.7	1131	19
Denmark	5.3	173	35
Finland	5.1	123	25
France	58.3	1526	26
Germany	81.8	2325	28
Greece	10.5	122	12
Ireland	3.6	69	17
Italy	**57.3**	**1199**	**21**
Luxembourg	0.4	18	45
Netherland	15.5	387	25
Portugal	9.9	103	10
Spain	39.2	581	15
Sweden	8.8	247	27

Source: *The New York Times* (Sept. 18, 1997) A10.

Bibliography

The bibliography of Italian studies in English is a patchy one. Some subjects—the mafia being a predictable example—have been treated in great detail, and have inspired a very large number of outstanding monographs. More generally, the social history of Italy's rural, peasant communities and studies of the folkways of southern Italy have provided a rich source of material for scholars and writers. Italy's economic history is more sketchily treated, but there are several outstanding general histories, the most recent of which is Vera Zamagni's *Economic History of Italy* (1993). Political and intellectual history, by contrast, is—the fascist interlude apart—full of gaps. Only a handful of Italian statesmen have been the subject of full-length biographies in any period (including fascism, where Mussolini has hogged the attention), and Italy's most representative writers, philosophers, and political thinkers simply have not been accorded as much attention as—for instance—their French and German peers. This relative neglect of Italian political and intellectual life has three major contributory causes. First, Italian is not as widely read as French or German in Britain and the United States; second, Italian politics and culture is (wrongly) considered to be less important, or less influential; third, Italy's fascinating social culture, and the modern preference for sociological history over narrative history on political subjects, seems to have taken precedence. It cannot be denied, however, that the fact that there exists no English-language biography of (and this is an abbreviated list) Agostino Depretis, Francesco Crispi, Giovanni Giolitti, Alcide De Gasperi, Palmiro Togliatti, Aldo Moro, Enrico Berlinguer, and Giulio Andreotti represents a serious shortcoming for anybody anxious to expand his or her knowledge of the country's history.

Intellectuals and writers have been similarly neglected: Vilfredo Pareto, Gaetano Mosca, Antonio Labriola, Benedetto Croce, Giovanni Gentile, and Gaetano Salvemini are social thinkers of the first rank, and although there has been a revived interest in Croce recently, it cannot be said that any of these remarkably influential figures have received their due. Only Antonio Gramsci has been canonized by English-language writers, and in his case the problem is almost the abundance of studies on the former Communist leader's life and thought. In other aspects of cultural life—the cinema, art, architecture, and even literature—Italy emerges very satisfactorily. Anybody wishing to read about Roberto

Rossellini, Federico Fellini, Vittorio De Sica, or Pier Paolo Pasolini is faced with an embarrassing range of choice. The body of literature describing Italy's towns, regions, and cuisine, of course, can only be described as monumental, and this bibliography has merely hinted at its size.

The bibliography follows the standard procedure for general texts on Italy by arranging the material by historical period, after a brief section listing books that give Italian political, economic, and social history the broad-brush treatment. These periods are the Risorgimento (i.e., from 1815 to 1861 approximately); Liberal Italy (1861-1922); Fascist and wartime Italy (1922-1946); Republican Italy (1946-). Each section is divided into subsections separating general works on each period from specific texts in politics, society, and economics. The final section, on Republican Italy, has been enriched with two further sub-sections dealing with the literature on the mafia phenomenon and on the crisis of the Italian state between 1992 and 1995, which has generated a substantial literature in English, and a vast one in Italian. To round off the bibliography, there are sections on intellectual and cultural history, on Italy's regions and cities, and on guidebooks. With few exceptions, the bibliography concentrates on relatively recent texts (1970 or later with exceptions in outstanding cases). There are two recent bibliographies in English that deal with Italian subjects, Martin J. Bull's, *Contemporary Italy: A Research Guide* (1996) and F. J. Coppa and M. Roberts, *Modern Italian History: An Annotated Bibliography* (1990).

An important point about the bibliography is the number of texts in Italian. For the reasons given above, it is almost impossible to comprehend the country's political history in particular unless one reads the original language. Parallel lists of books in Italian therefore accompany every section of the bibliography, and political subjects are given special prominence. It should be noted in passing that political historians and contemporary writers on politics in Italy are of an extremely high standard and naturally deal with many issues in a detail that English language writers cannot match. Italian history is partisan history, with liberals, communists, and Catholics still struggling to capture the country's past, but it is hard to see why this should be regarded as a defect when it imparts such vitality to the scholarly debate.

Despite the fact that so much of the best writing on modern Italian history has never been translated, and despite the gaps that exist in the English-language bibliography, it remains true that Italy's political, economic, and social history has inspired some very fine and readable scholarship by English-language authors. A reader wishing to become acquainted with Italy's modern history should certainly start with

Christopher Duggan's *A Concise History of Italy* (1994), or Denis Mack Smith's *Italy: A Modern History* (1969), both of which are splendid introductory texts. Martin Clark's *Modern Italy 1871-1995* (1995) is an undoubted achievement, though he downplays the role of politics excessively. Mack Smith's *The Making of Italy 1796-1866* (1986), and his biographies of Cavour, Mazzini, and Garibaldi, are very readable introductions to the Risorgimento. Harry Hearder's *Italy in the Age of the Risorgimento* (1983) is also a fine book. Liberal Italy's politics are treated in magisterial fashion by Christopher Seton-Watson's *Italy from Liberalism to Fascism 1870-1925* (1967). Benedetto Croce's *A History of Italy 1870-1915* (1929) is both a classic of historical writing and a revealing insight into Italian liberalism.

Fascism has inspired several important books in English. To name just two, Mack Smith's *Mussolini* (1982) is a highly critical and well-researched account of the dictator's life. Adrian Lyttleton's *The Seizure of Power: Fascism in Italy 1919-1929* (1973) is the definitive text in either language of the regime's birth and early years in power. The doyen of historians of fascism, however, is Renzo De Felice, whose five-volume study of Mussolini's life and times is regrettably only available in Italian. His 1977 *Interpretations of Fascism,* however, in an excellent translation by Brenda Huff Everett, provides a more than adequate introduction to his work. De Felice is just one of several indisputably great Italian historians (others are Giorgio Candeloro, Federico Chabod, Arturo Jemolo, and Rosario Romeo) whose skill in the neglected art of writing narrative is a delight for anyone with a basic knowledge or better of the Italian language.

The annual reports published by ISTAT, the Italian government statistical agency, can be very useful. Perhaps the best snapshot of contemporary Italian life, however, is a book edited by an English academic who lives in Italy, Paul Ginsborg, whose *Stato d'talia (The State of Italy*, 1994) is a compendium of articles written by experts on every aspect of Italian society. The same scholar's *A History of Contemporary Italy: Society and Politics, 1943-1988* (1990) is probably the best available introduction to post-war Italy. Other accessible introductions in English to contemporary Italian life might include Luigi Barzini (1971), Giuseppe Di Palma (1977), Spencer Di Scala (1995), Joseph La Palombara (1987), Giuliano Procacci (1973), Frederic Spotts, and T. Wieser (1986). Each is cited in the bibliography below.

A remarkable piece of social anthropology that deserves mention is David I. Kertzer's *Comrades and Christians* (1980), which describes the competing strategies used by the church and the Communist Party to win the attention of the working class in Bologna and leaves an indelible picture of what life in the popular quarters of 1970s Bologna was like. The phenomenon of the mafia is skillfully dissected in Pino Arlacchi's *Mafia Business: The Mafia Ethic and the Spirit of Capitalism* (1988). More recently, Robert Putnam's book, *Making Democracy Work: Civic Traditions in Modern Italy* (1993), uses detailed historical research into the communes of northern and southern Italy to make a broad case for the importance of civic associations for the well-being of democratic government: both the method and the conclusions of the book have aroused spirited controversy.

Relatively few journal articles have been mentioned in the bibliography, which makes this an appropriate place to list some of the journals that most closely occupy themselves with Italy. Of the major scholarly reviews, the *Journal of Modern History* and the *Journal of Contemporary History* have both given considerable space in recent times to Italian subjects, especially fascism. A new *Journal of Modern Italian Studies*, which is published by Routledge three times a year, has also been started: it contains reviews that are essential sources for would-be Italianists. *Passato e presente, Storia contemporanea, Rivista storica italiana, Italia contemporanea, Nord e Sud, Quaderni storici, Clio*, and *Società e storia* are all excellent historical and cultural journals. Contemporary political issues are discussed in the lively bimonthly *Il Mulino*, and such publications as *Democrazia e diritto, Il Ponte, MicroMega,* and *Reset* testify to the vitality of Italian intellectual debate. The news magazines *Panorama* and *L'Espresso* offer dozens of pages every week giving "insider" accounts of Italian politics, publishing leaked documents and analyzing the economy. They also carry articles on all aspects of political, social, and economic history from 1700 to the present day. The Association for the Study of Modern Italy, a British academic body, produces an annual called *Modern Italy*. A vital source for contemporary events is the annual *Italian Politics* series published in Italy by Il Mulino of Bologna since 1986, and in English by Pinter publishers until 1993 and by Westview Press since then. Each edition consists of nine to twelve essays by well-known experts on significant developments in the political, economic, and institutional life of Italy in the previous year. Literary and cultural subjects can be found in the *Italian Quarterly* and *Italica*.

Bibliography Contents

General Histories

In English:

Absolom, Roger. 1995. *Italy Since 1880. A Nation in the Balance?* London: Longman.

Barbagli, M. 1982. *Educating for Unemployment: Politics, Labor Markets and the School System 1859-1973*. New York: Columbia University Press.

Bell, Rudolph M. 1981. *Fate and Honor, Family and Village: Demographic and Cultural Change in Rural Italy Since 1800*. Chicago: University of Chicago Press.

Bull, Martin J. 1996. *Contemporary Italy: A Research Guide*. Westport, CT: Greenwood Press.

Cappelletti, Mauro, J. Merryman, and J. M. Perillo. 1967. *The Italian Legal System; An Introduction*. Stanford, CA: Stanford University Press.

Clark, Martin. 1995. *Modern Italy 1871-1995*. London: Longman.

Clough, Shepard, and Salvatore Saladino. 1968. *A History of Modern Italy*. New York: Columbia University Press.

Coppa, F. J., and M. Roberts. 1990. *Modern Italian History: An Annotated Bibliography*. Westport, CT: Greenwood Press.

Cotta, Maurizio. 1994. "Italy." In *Parliaments in the Modern World*, ed. Gary W. Copeland and Samuel C. Patterson. Ann Arbor, MI: University of Michigan Press.

Di Scala, Spencer M. 1995. *Italy from Revolution to Republic: 1700 to the Present*. Boulder, CO: Westview.

Duggan, Christopher. 1994. *A Concise History of Italy*. Cambridge: Cambridge University Press.

Federico, Giovanni. 1996. "Italy, 1860-1940: A Little Known Success Story." *Economic History Review.* 59, 4: 764-786.

Jemolo, Arturo. 1960. *Church and State in Italy 1850-1950.* Oxford: Blackwell.

Kertzer, David I., and Richard P. Saller, eds. 1991. *The Family in Italy from Antiquity to the Present.* New Haven, CT: Yale University Press.

Leo XIII. 1891. *Rerum Novarum.* No. 1, Collana Magistero. Alba: Figlie di San Paolo.

Livi-Bacci, M. 1977. *A History of Italian Fertility during the Last Two Centuries.* Princeton, NJ: Princeton University Press.

Mack Smith, Denis. 1969. *Italy: A Modern History.* Ann Arbor, MI: University of Michigan Press.

Pius XI. [1931] 1979. 7th ed. *Quadragesimo Anno.* Alba: Figlie di San Paolo.

Procacci, Giuliano. [1968] 1973. *History of the Italian People.* Trans. Anthony Paul. Hammondsworth, UK: Penguin Books.

Redford, Bruce. 1996. *Venice and the Grand Tour.* New Haven, CT: Yale University Press.

Sereni, Emilio. 1997. *History of the Italian Agricultural Landscape.* Princeton, NJ: Princeton University Press.

Spotts, Frederic, and Theodor Wieser. 1986. *Italy: A Difficult Democracy.* New York: Cambridge.

"Statistical Survey, Education." 1996. *The Europa World Year Book*, vol. 1. London: Europa Publications.

Tannenbaum, E. R., and E. P. Noether, eds. 1974. *Modern Italy: A Topical History since 1861.* New York: New York University Press.

Woolf, Stuart J. 1979. *A History of Italy, 1700-1860: The Social Constraints of Political Change.* New York: Methuen.

412 • Bibliography

Zamagni, Vera. 1993. *The Economic History of Italy 1860-1990*. Oxford: Clarendon Press.

In French:

David, René. 1982. *Les grands systèmes de droit contemporains*. 8th ed. Paris: Librairie Dalloz.

In Italian:

Bosworth R. J. B., and Sergio Romano, eds. 1991. *La politica estera italiana 1860-1985*. Bologna: Il Mulino.

Barbagli, A. 1988. *Sotto lo stesso tetto: mutamenti di famiglia in Italia dal XV al XX secolo*. Bologna: Il Mulino.

Barbaro, I. 1973. *Storia del sindacalismo italiano*. 3 vols. Firenze: La nuova Italia.

Bevilacqua, P. 1989-1991. *Storia dell'agricoltura italiana in età contemporanea*. 3 vols. Venice: Marsilio.

_____. 1993. *Breve storia dell'Italia meridionale dall'Ottocento a oggi*. Roma: Donizelli.

Candeloro, Giorgio. 1970-1986. *Storia dell'Italia moderna*. 12 vols. Milano: Feltrinelli.

Cappelletti, Mauro. 1972. *Giustizia e società*. Milano: Comunità.

Carocci, Giampiero. 1963-1984. *Storia del parlamento italiano dal 1848 al 1968*. 20 vols. Palermo: Flaccovio.

Castronovo, Valerio. 1995. *Storia economica d'Italia. Dall'Ottocento ai nostri giorni*. Torino: Einaudi.

Castronovo, Valerio, and Nicola Tranfaglia. 1970. *Storia della stampa italiana. La stampa italiana dall'unità al fascismo*. Bari: Laterza.

Daneo, C. 1980. *Breve storia dell'agricoltura italiana 1860-1970.* Milano: Mondadori.

D'Antone, Leandra, ed. 1997. *Collezione di Studi Meridionali,* vol. 37. Roma: Ed. Bibliopolis.

De Bernardi, Alberto, and Luigi Canapini. 1996. *Storia d'Italia, 1860-1995.* Milano: Mondadori.

De Felice, Renzo, ed. 1976-1983. *Storia d'Italia dall'unità alla repubblica.* 7 vols. Naples: Edizioni scientifiche italiane.

Di Giorgio, M. 1992. *Le italiane dall'unità a oggi.* Bari: Laterza.

Di Rosa, G. 1966. *Storia del movimento cattolico in Italia.* 2 vols. Bari: Laterza.

Galasso, Giuseppe. 1979. *Storia d'Italia.* vols. 20-23. Torino: UTET.

Ghisberti, Alberto. 1967. *Storia costituzionale d'Italia 1849-1948.* Bari: Laterza.

Melograni, Piero, ed. 1988. *La famiglia italiana dal Ottocento a oggi.* Bari: Laterza.

Nicolò, Rosario, ed. 1975. *Codice civilecon la costituzione e le principali leggi speciali.* Milano: A. Giuffrè Editore.

Piretti, Maria Serena. 1995. *Le elezioni politiche in Italia dal 1848 a oggi.* Bari: Laterza.

Romano, R., ed. 1990-1991. *Storia dell'economia italiana.* Torino: Einaudi.

Romeo, Rosario. 1991. *Breve storia della grande industria in Italia.* Milano: Il Saggiatore.

Rossi, Ernesto. 1957. *I padroni del vapore.* Bari: Laterza.

Salvi, Sergio. 1975. *Le lingue tagliate.* Milano: Rizzoli.

Sorcinelli, P. 1993. *Eros. Storie e fantasie degli italiani dal 800 a oggi.* Bari: Laterza.

Italy 1815-1861: The Risorgimento

General Histories

In English:

Beales, D. 1981. *The Risorgimento and the Unification of Italy.* London: Longman.

Berkeley, G. F. H. 1968. *Italy in the Making.* 3 vols. Cambridge: Cambridge University Press (Reprint).

Davis, John A., and Paul Ginsborg, eds. 1979. *Society and Politics in the Age of the Risorgimento: Essays in Honour of Denis Mack Smith.* Cambridge: Cambridge University Press.

Grew, Raymond. 1963. *A Sterner Plan for Italian Unity.* Princeton, NJ: Princeton University Press.

Hearder, Harry. 1983. *Italy in the Age of the Risorgimento 1790-1870.* London: Longman.

Mack Smith, Denis. 1986. *The Making of Italy 1796-1866.* London: Macmillan.

Riall, Lucy. 1994. *The Italian Risorgimento: State, Society and National Unification.* New York: Routledge.

Whyte, Arthus J. 1959. *The Evolution of Modern Italy.* New York: Norton.

In Italian:

Balbo, Cesare. 1855. *Delle speranze d'Italia.* Firenze: Felice le Monnier.

Gobetti, Piero. 1976. *Risorgimento senza eroi.* Torino: Einaudi.

Gramsci, Antonio. 1955. *Il Risorgimento*. Torino: Einaudi.

Omodeo, Adolfo. 1960. *L'età del risorgimento italiano*. Naples: Edizioni scientifiche italiane.

Romeo, Rosario. 1961. *Dal Piemonte sabauda all'Italia liberale*. Torino: Einaudi.

_____. 1963. *Risorgimento e capitalismo*. Bari: Laterza.

Rosselli, Nello. 1980. *Saggi sul Risorgimento*. Torino: Einaudi.

Sabbatucci, Giovanni, and V. Vidotto, eds. 1994. *Storia d'Italia*, vol. 1. *Le premesse dell'unità. Dalla fine del Settecento al 1861*. Bari: Laterza.

Salvatorelli, Luigi. 1974. *Pensiero e azione del Risorgimento*. Torino: Einaudi.

Salvemini, Gaetano.1961. *Scritti sul Risorgimento*. Milano: Feltrinelli.

Scirocco, Alfonso. 1990. *L'Italia del Risorgimento*. Bologna: Il Mulino.

Studies in Biography, Politics, and Society

In English:

Acton, Harold. 1961. *The Last Bourbons of Naples (1825-1861)*. London: Methuen.

Broers, Michael. 1996. "The Police and the Padroni: Italian Notabili, French Gendarmes and the Origins of the Centralized State in Napoleonic Italy." *European History Quarterly.* 26:331-354 (July).

Budden, Julian. 1987. *Verdi*. New York: Random House.

Coppa, Frank J. 1973. *Camillo Di Cavour*. New York: Twayne.

_____. 1992. *The Origins of the Italian Wars of Independence*. White Plains, NY: Longman.

Davis, John A. 1988. *Conflict and Control: Law and Order in Nineteenth Century Italy*. Basingstoke: Macmillan.

Eisenstein, Elizabeth. 1959. *The First Professional Revolutionary: Filippo Michele Buonarotti*. Cambridge: Cambridge University Press.

Finley, Milton. 1994. *The Most Monstrous of Wars: The Napoleonic Guerilla War in Southern Italy*. Columbia, SC: University of South Carolina Press.

Ginsborg, Paul. 1979. *Daniele Manin and the Venetian Revolution of 1848-1849*. Cambridge: Cambridge University Press.

Hearder, Harry. 1994. *Cavour*. New York: Longman.

Hibbert, Christopher. [1965] 1987. *Garibaldi and His Enemies: The Clash of Arms and Personalities in the Making of Italy*. London: Penguin Books.

Hughes, Steven C. 1994. *Crime, Disorder and the Risorgimento: The Politics of Policing in Bologna*. Cambridge: Cambridge University Press.

Kertzer, David I. 1989. *Family, Political Economy and Demographic Change: The Transformation of Life in Casalecchio, Italy, 1861-1921*. Madison, WI: University of Wisconsin Press.

King, Bolton. 1911. *The Life of Mazzini*. New York: Dutton.

Lovett, C. M. 1972. *Carlo Cattaneo and the Politics of the Risorgimento 1820-1860*. The Hague: Martin Nijhoff.

_____. 1982. *The Democratic Movement in Italy, 1830-1876*. Cambridge, MA: Harvard University Press.

Mack Smith, Denis. 1982. *Garibaldi*. London: Hutchinson.

_____. 1985. *Cavour*. London: Weidenfeld and Nicholson.

_____. 1985. *Cavour and Garibaldi: A Study in Political Conflict*. Cambridge: Cambridge University Press.

_____. 1994. *Mazzini.* New Haven, CT: Yale University Press.

Rath, R. J. 1964. "The Carbonari: Their Origins, Initiation Rites, and Aims." *American Historical Review.* 69.

Reinerman, Alan J. 1974. "Metternich, Alexander I and the Russian Challenge in Italy." *Journal of Modern History.* 46, no. 2:20-38 (June).

Ridley, Jasper. 1974. *Garibaldi.* London: Constable.

Roberts, William. 1989. *Prophet in Exile. Joseph Mazzini in England 1837-1868.* New York: Peter Lang.

Robertson, Priscilla. 1971. *Revolutions of 1848: A Social History.* Princeton, NJ: Princeton University Press.

Romani, G. T. 1950. *The Neapolitan Revolution of 1820-1821.* Evanston, IL: University of Illinois Press.

Sarti, Roland. 1997. *Mazzini: A Life for the Religion of Politics.* Westport, CT: Greenwood Press.

Taylor, A. J. P. 1934. *The Italian Problem in European Diplomacy.* Manchester: University of Manchester Press.

In Italian:

Lepre, A. 1967. *La rivoluzione napoletana del 1820-1821.* Roma: Riuniti.

Moretti, Emilia. 1984. *Giuseppe Mazzini: Quasi una biografia.* Roma: Edizioni dell'Ateneo.

Romeo, Rosario. 1984. *Cavour.* 3 vols. Bari: Laterza.

Spadolini, Giovanni. 1986. *Cattolicismo e risorgimento.* Firenze: Le Monnier.

Ugolini, Romano. 1982. *Garibaldi: genesi di un mito*. Roma: Edizioni dell'Ateneo.

Villani, P. 1978. *L'Italia napoleonica*. Naples: Guida.

Liberal Italy

General Histories

In English:

Bosworth, R. J. B. 1979. *Italy, The Least of the Great Powers: Italian Foreign Policy before the First World War*. New York: Cambridge University Press.

Cafagna, Luciano. 1973. "Italy 1830-1914." In *The Fontana Economic History of Europe*, ed. Carlo Cipolla. London: Fontana.

Coppa, Frank J., ed. 1986. *Studies in Modern Italian History: From the Risorgimento to the Republic*. New York: Lang.

Croce, Benedetto. 1929. *A History of Italy 1871-1915*. Oxford: Oxford University Press.

Lowe, C. J., and F. Marzari. 1975. *Italian Foreign Policy 1870-1940*. London: Routledge and Kegan Paul.

Mack Smith, Denis. 1990. *Italy and Its Monarchy*. New Haven, CT: Yale University Press.

Salomone, A. William. 1960. *Italy in the Giolittian Era: Italian Democracy in the Making 1900-1914*. Philadelphia: University of Pennsylvania Press.

Seton-Watson, Christopher. 1967. *Italy from Liberalism to Fascism 1870-1925*. London: Methuen.

Toniolo, Gianni. 1990. *An Economic History of Liberal Italy, 1850-1918*. London: Routledge.

In Italian:

Amendola, Giorgio. 1976. *Una scelta di vita*. Milano: Rizzoli.

Aquarone, Alberto. 1981-1988. *L'Italia Giolittiana*. 2 vols. Bologna: Il Mulino.

Chabod, Federico. 1971. *Storia della politica estera italiana dal 1870 al 1896*. Bari: Laterza.

Croce, Benedetto. 1928. *Storia d'Italia, 1871-1915*. Bari: Laterza.

Gambetti, Fidia. 1978. *Gli anni che scottano*. Milano: Mursia.

Gentile, Emilio. 1990. *L'Italia giolittiana*. Bologna: Il Mulino.

Mafai, Miriam. 1987. *Pane Nero*. Milano: Arnaldo Mondadori.

Romanelli, Raffaele. 1990. *L'Italia Liberale*. Bologna: Il Mulino.

Sabbatucci, Giovanni, and V. Vidotto, eds. 1995. *Storia d'Italia*, vol. 2. *Il nuovo stato e la società civile (1861-1887)*. Bari: Laterza.

Volpe, Gioacchino. 1958. *L'Italia moderna, 1815-1915*. Firenze: Sansoni.

Studies in Biography, Politics, and Society

In English:

Agocs, Sandor. 1988. *The Troubled Origins of the Italian Catholic Movement*. Detroit: Wayne State University Press.

Bagnoli, Paolo. 1997. "Piero Gobetti and the Liberal Revolution in Italy." *Journal of Modern Italian Studies*. 4, 2:34-44 (Spring).

Bell, Donald Howard. n.d. *Sesto San Giovanni: Workers, Culture and Politics in an Italian Town 1880-1922*. New Brunswick, NJ: Rutgers University Press.

Bernardini, Paolo. 1996. "The Jews in Nineteenth Century Italy: Towards a Reappraisal." *Journal of Modern Italian Studies*. 1, 2:292-310.

Bosworth, R. J .B. 1983. *Italy and the Approach of the First World War*. New York: St. Martin's Press.

Caroli, Betty Boyd. 1973. *Italian Repatriation from the United States, 1890-1914*. New York: Center for Migration Studies.

Coppa, Frank J. 1971. *Economics and Politics in the Giolittian Age: Planning, Protection and Politics in Liberal Italy*. Washington, DC: Catholic University Press.

_____. 1979. *Pope Pius IX: Crusader in a Secular Age*. Boston: Twayne Publishers.

_____, ed. 1985. *Dictionary of Modern Italian History*. Westport, CT: Greenwood Press.

Craver, Earlene. 1996. "The Third Generation: The Young Socialists in Italy, 1907-1915." *Canadian Journal of History / Annales canadiennes d'histoire*. 31: 199-226 (August).

Di Iorio, Anthony. 1980. *Italy, Austria-Hungary and the Balkans 1904-1914*. Urbana, IL: University of Illinois Press.

Di Scala, Spencer. 1980. *Dilemmas of Italian Socialism: The Politics of Filippo Turati*. Amherst, MA: University of Massachusetts Press.

Forsyth, D. J. 1993. *The Crisis of Liberal Italy 1914-1922*. Cambridge: Cambridge University Press.

Gerschenkron, A. 1962. *Economic Backwardness in Historical Perspective*. Cambridge, MA: Harvard University Press.

Gibson, Mary. 1986. *Prostitution and the State in Italy 1860-1915*. New Brunswick, NJ: Rutgers University Press.

Gonzales, Manuel G. 1980. *Andrea Costa and the Rise of Socialism in the Romagna*. Washington, DC: University Press of America.

Gooch, J. 1989. *Army, State and Society in Italy, 1870-1915.* Basingstoke: Macmillan.

Hess, Robert L. 1966. *Italian Colonialism in Somalia.* Chicago, IL: Chicago University Press.

Kertzer, David I. 1984. *Family Life in Central Italy 1880-1910: Sharecropping, Wage Labor and Co-residence.* New Brunswick, NJ: Rutgers University Press.

_____. 1993. *Sacrificed for Honor: Italian Infant Abandonment and the Politics of Reproduction.* Boston: Beacon Press.

Ledeen, Michael A. 1977. *The First Duce: D'Annunzio at Fiume.* Baltimore, MD: Johns Hopkins University Press.

Lyttleton, Adrian. 1988. *The Language of Political Conflict in Pre-Fascist Italy: Occasional Paper No. 54.* Bologna: Johns Hopkins University Research Institute.

Maloney, John M. 1977. *The Emergence of Political Catholicism in Italy: Partito Popolare 1919-1926.* Totowa, NJ: Rowman and Littlefield.

Morris, Jonathon. 1993. *The Political Economy of Shopkeeping in Milan, 1885-1922.* Cambridge: Cambridge University Press.

Pernicone, Nunzio. 1993. *Italian Anarchism, 1864-1892.* Princeton, NJ: Princeton University Press.

Puzzo, Dante A. 1959. "Gaetano Salvemini: Historiographical Essay," *Journal of the History of Ideas.* 20:235 (April).

Randeraand, Nico. 1993. *Authority in Search of Liberty: The Prefects of Central Italy.* Amsterdam: Thesis Press.

Renzi, William A. 1987. *In the Shadow of the Sword: Italy's Neutrality and Entrance into the Great War 1914-1915.* New York: Peter Lang.

Snowden, Frank M. 1986. *Violence and the Great Estates in the South of Italy: Apulia 1900-1922.* Cambridge: Cambridge University Press.

_____. 1996. *Naples in the Time of the Cholera 1884-1911.* Cambridge: Cambridge University Press.

Webster, Richard A. 1975. *Industrial Imperialism in Italy 1908-1915.* Berkeley, CA: California University Press.

Whittam, John. 1977. *The Politics of the Italian Army 1861-1918.* Hamden, CT: Archon Books.

In Italian:

Arfè, G. 1965. *Storia del socialismo italiano 1892-1926.* Torino: Einaudi.

Ballini, Pierluigi. 1988. *Le elezioni nella storia d'Italia dall'unità al fascismo.* Bologna: Il Mulino.

Battaglia, R. 1958. *La prima guerra d'Africa.* Torino: Einaudi.

Candeloro, Giorgio. 1972. *Il movimento cattolico in Italia.* Roma: Riuniti.

Capone, A. 1981. *Destra e sinistra da Cavour a Crispi.* Torino: UTET.

Cardini, Antonio. 1981. *Stato liberale e protezionismo in Italia, 1890-1900.* Bologna: Il Mulino.

Carocci, Giampiero. 1992. *Il trasformismo dall'unità ad oggi.* Milano: Unicopli.

_____. 1956. *Agostino Depretis e la politica interna italiana dal 1876 al 1887.* Torino: Einaudi.

Corner, Paul R. 1993. *Contadini e industrializzazione: Società rurale e impresa in Italia dal 1840 al 1940.* Bari: Laterza.

Galante Garrone, Alessandro. 1973. *I radicali in Italia 1849-1925.* Milano: Garzanti.

Isnenghi, Mario, ed. 1972. *La prima guerra mondiale*. Bologna: Zanichelli.

Luzzatto, G. 1968. *L'economia italiana dal 1861 al 1894*. Torino: Einaudi.

Mola, A. A. 1980. *L'imperialismo italiano: la politica estera dall'unità al fascismo*. Roma: Riuniti.

Pacifici, Vincenzo G. 1979. *Le elezioni nell'Italia unita: assenteismo e astensionismo*. Roma: Edizioni dell'Ateneo.

Perfeti, F. 1984. *Il movimento nazionalista in Italia 1903-1914*. Roma: Bonacci.

Petricioli, Marta. 1983. *L'Italia in Asia minore: equilibrio mediterraneo e ambizioni imperialiste alla vigilia della prima guerra mondiale*. Firenze: Sansoni.

Polsi, Alessandro. 1993. *Alle origini del capitalismo italiano. Stato, banche e banchieri dopo l'unità*. Torino: Einaudi.

Ricolfi, M. 1992. *Il Psi e la nascita del partito di massa 1892-1922*. Bari: Laterza.

Spadolini, Giovanni. 1954. *L'opposizione cattolica da Porta Pia al 1898*. Firenze: Vallechi.

_____. 1991. *Giolitti e i cattolici 1901-1914*. Firenze: Le Monnier.

Valeri, Nino. 1972. *Giovanni Giolitti*. Torino: Einaudi.

Fascism

General and Theoretical Works

In English:

Adamson, Walter L. 1995. "The Culture of Italian Fascism and the

Fascist Crisis of Modernity: The Case of 'Il Selvaggio.'" *Journal of Contemporary History.* 30:555-575 (October).

Borgese, G. A. 1937. *Goliath: The March of Fascism.* New York: Viking Press.

Cannistraro, Philip V. 1982. *Historical Dictionary of Fascist Italy.* Westport, CT: Greenwood Press.

Cassels, Alan. 1975. *Fascism.* New York: Thomas Crowell.

Chabod, Federico. 1963. *A History of Italian Fascism.* London: Weidenfeld and Nicholson.

Collier, R. B., and D. Collier. 1979. "Inducements v. Constraints: Disaggregating Fascism." *American Political Science Review.* 73:967-986.

De Felice, Renzo. 1977. Interpretations of Fascism, trans. Brenda Huff Everett. Cambridge, MA: Harvard University Press.

——————. 1976. *Fascism: An Informal Introduction to Its Theory and Practice.* New Brunswick, NJ: Transaction Books.

De Grand, Alexander. 1982. *Italian Fascism: Its Origin and Development.* Lincoln, NE: University of Nebraska Press.

Diggins, John P. 1972. *Mussolini and Fascism.* Princeton, NJ: Princeton University Press.

Fermi, Laura. 1961. *Mussolini.* Chicago: University of Chicago Press.

Finer, Herman. 1935. *Mussolini's Italy.* New York: Grosset and Dunlap.

Florinsky, Michael T. 1936. *Fascism and National Socialism.* New York: Macmillan.

Forgacs, David, ed. 1986. *Rethinking Italian Fascism: Capitalism, Populism and Culture.* London: Lawrence and Wishart.

Fortune Magazine. 1934. "Fascist Italy. " July.

Halperin, S. William. 1974. *Mussolini and Italian Fascism*. New York: Van Nostrand.

Mack Smith, Denis. 1982. *Mussolini*. New York: Knopf.

Morgan, Philip. 1995. *Italian Fascism 1919-1945*. New York: St. Martin's Press.

Payne, Stanley G. 1996. *A History of Fascism, 1914-1945*. Madison, WI: University of Wisconsin Press.

Salvemini, Gaetano. [1942] 1973. *The Origins of Fascism in Italy*. New York: Harper and Row.

_____. 1936. *Under the Axe of Fascism*. New York: Viking Press.

_____. 1927. *The Fascist Dictatorship in Italy*. New York: Henry Holt.

Schmitter, P. C. 1974. "Still the Century of Corporatism." In *The New Corporatism*, ed. F. B. Pike and T. Stggritch. Notre Dame, IN: Notre Dame University Press.

Tannenbaum, Edward R. 1972. *The Fascist Experience: Italian Society and Culture, 1922-1945*. New York: Basic Books.

Von Plehwe, Friedrich-Karl. 1971. *The End of an Alliance*. London: Oxford University Press.

Webster, Richard A. 1960. *The Cross and the Fasces*. Stanford, CA: Stanford University Press.

Whittam, John. 1995. *Fascist Italy*. Manchester: Manchester University Press.

Wiskemann, Elizabeth. 1969. *Fascism in Italy: Its Development and Influence*. London: Macmillan.

In French:

Manoilesco, Mihail. 1934. *Le Siècle du Corporatisme*. Paris: Felix Alcan.

In Italian:

Aquarone, Alberto. 1965. *L'organizzazione dello stato totalitario*. Torino: Einaudi.

Bordoni, Carlo. 1981. *Fascismo e politica culturale*. Bologna: Brechtiana Ed.

Chabod, Federico. 1961. *L'Italia contemporanea 1918-1948*. Torino: Einaudi.

_____. 1962. *Fascismo e antifascismo, 1918-1948*. 2 vols. Milano: Feltrinelli.

Ciano, Galeazzo. [1946] 1950. *Diario, 1937-1943*. 3 vols. Milano: Rizzoli

Galli, Giorgio. 1995. *Il Fascismo: Dallo squadrismo a Dongo*. Verona: Teti Editore.

Hertner, Peter, and Giorgio Mori, eds. 1983. *La transizione dell'economia di guerra all'economia di pace in Italia e Germania dopo la prima guerra mondiale*. Bologna: Il Mulino/Istituto Italo-Germanico (Trento).

Salvatorelli, Luigi, and Giovanni Mira. 1964. *Storia d'Italia nel periodo fascista*. Torino: Einaudi.

Salvemini, Gaetano. 1961. *Trent'anni di storia italiana 1915-1945*. Torino: Einaudi.

Santarelli, E. 1973. *Storia del fascismo*. Roma: Riuniti.

Tasca, Angelo. 1950. *Nascita e avvento di fascismo*. Firenze: La Nuova Italia.

Toniolo, G. 1980. *L'economia dell'Italia fascista*. Bari: Laterza.

Veneruso, Danilo. 1990. *L'Italia fascista*. Bologna: Il Mulino.

Studies in Biography, Politics, and Society

In English:

Adamson, Walter L. 1993. *Avante-garde Florence: From Modernism to Fascism*. Cambridge, MA: Harvard University Press.

Adler, Franklin Hugh. 1995. *Italian Industrialists from Liberalism to Fascism: The Political Development of the Industrial Bourgeoisie, 1906-1934*. New York: Cambridge University Press.

Baer, George W. 1976. *Test Case: Italy, Ethiopia and the League of Nations*. Stanford, CA: Hoover Institution.

Bessel, Richard, ed. 1996. *Fascist Italy and Nazi Germany*. Cambridge: Cambridge University Press.

Cordoza, Anthony L. 1983. *Agrarian Elites and Italian Fascism: The Province of Bologna 1901-1926*. Princeton, NJ: Princeton University Press.

Corner, Paul. 1975. *Fascism in Ferrara*. New York: Oxford University Press.

Coverdale, J. F. 1975. *Italian Intervention in the Spanish Civil War*. Princeton, NJ: Princeton University Press.

Deakin, F. W. 1962. *The Brutal Friendship: Mussolini, Hitler and the Fall of Italian Fascism*. London: Weidenfeld and Nicholson.

_____. 1966. The Last Days of Mussolini. London: Harmondsworth.

De Grand, Alexander. 1978. *The Italian Nationalist Association and the Rise of Fascism in Italy*. Lincoln, NE: University of Nebraska Press.

_____. 1972. "Curzio Malaparte: The Illusion of a Fascist Revolution." *Journal of Contemporary History*. 7:73-89.

De Grazia, Victoria. 1981. *The Culture of Consent: The Mass Organization of Leisure in Fascist Italy*. New York: Cambridge University Press.

_____. 1992. *How Fascism Ruled Women: Italy 1922-1945*. Berkeley, CA: University of California Press.

Delzell, Charles. 1961. *Mussolini's Enemies: The Italian Anti-Fascist Resistance*. Princeton, NJ: Princeton University Press.

Duggan, Christopher. 1989. *Fascism and the Mafia*. New Haven, CT: Yale University Press.

Ecksteins, Modris. 1989. *Rites of Spring: The Great War and the Birth of the Modern Age*. New York: Anchor Books.

Fraddosio, Maria. 1966. "The Fallen Hero: The Myth of Mussolini and Fascist Women in the Italian Social Republic (1943-1945)." *Journal of Contemporary History*. 31:99-124 (January).

Gentile, Emilio. 1990. "Fascism as a Political Religion." *Journal of Contemporary History*. 25:229-251.

_____. 1986. "From the Cultural Revolt of the Giolittian Era to the Ideology of Fascism." In *Studies in Modern Italian History*, ed., Frank J. Coppa. New York: Peter Lang. 103-119.

Gregor, A. James. [1974] 1997. *Interpretations of Fascism*. New Brunswick, NJ: Transaction Publishers.

_____. 1979. *Young Mussolini and the Intellectual Origins of Fascism*. Berkeley, CA: California University Press.

_____. 1979. *Italian Fascism and Developmental Dictatorship*. Princeton, NJ: Princeton University Press.

_____. 1974. *The Fascist Persuasion in Radical Politics*. Princeton, NJ: Princeton University Press.

Griffin, Roger. 1993. *The Nature of Fascism*. London: Routledge Press.

Hamilton, Alexander. 1971. *The Appeal of Fascism*. London: Blond.

Hardie, Frank. 1974. *The Abyssinian Crisis*. Hamden, CT: Archon.

Hibbert, Christopher. 1962. *Il Duce*. Boston, MA: Little, Brown and Co.

Hood, Stuart. 1985. *Carlino*. Manchester, UK: Carcanet Press.

Joes, Anthony J. 1977. "On the Modernity of Fascism." *Comparative Political Studies*. 10:259-268.

Keegan, John. 1989. *The Second World War*. New York: Penguin Books.

Kelikian, Alice A. 1986. *Town and Country under Fascism: The Transformation of Brescia 1915-1926*. New York: Oxford University Press.

Kent, Peter. 1981. *The Pope and the Duce: The International Impact of the Lateran Accords*. New York: St. Martin's Press.

Knox, McGregor. 1982. *Mussolini Unleashed, 1939-1941: Politics and Strategy in Fascist Italy's Last War*. Cambridge: Cambridge University Press.

Koon, Tracey H. 1985. *Believe, Obey, Fight: Political Socialization of Youth in Fascist Italy*. Chapel Hill, NC: University of North Carolina Press.

Lussu, Emilio. 1992. *The March on Rome and Thereabouts*. Lewiston, NY: Edwin Mellen.

Lyttleton, Adrian. 1973. *The Seizure of Power: Fascism in Italy 1919-1929*. London: Weidenfeld and Nicholson.

MacGregor-Hastie, Roy. 1963. *The Day of the Lion: The Life and Death of Fascist Italy*. New York: Coward-McCann.

Mack Smith, Denis. 1982. *Mussolini*. New York: Alfred A. Knopf.

_____. 1976. *Mussolini's Roman Empire*. New York: Viking.

Michaelis, Meir. 1978. *Mussolini and the Jews: German-Italian Relations and the Jewish Question in Italy 1922-1943*. Oxford: Clarendon Press.

Mockler, Anthony. 1985. *Haile Selassie's War: The Italian-Ethiopian Campaign 1935-1941*. New York: Random House.

Modernism/Modernity. 1994. (A special issue devoted to Marinetti and the Italian Futurists.) Vol. 1, no. 3 (September).

Passerini, Luisa. 1987. *Fascism in Popular Memory: The Cultural Experience of the Torino Working Class*. New York: Cambridge University Press.

Pollard, John F. 1985. *The Vatican and Italian Fascism 1929-1932: A Study in Conflict*. New York: Cambridge University Press.

Rhodes, Anthony. 1973. *The Vatican in the Age of the Dictators*. London: Hodder and Stoughton.

Roberts, David D. 1979. *The Syndicalist Tradition and Italian Fascism*. Chapel Hill, NC: University of North Carolina Press.

Robertson, E. M. 1977. *Mussolini as Empire-builder: Europe and Africa 1932-1936*. London: Macmillan.

Sarti, Roland. 1971. *Fascism and the Industrial Leadership in Italy 1919-1940: A Study in the Expansion of Private Power under Fascism*. Berkeley, CA: California University Press.

_____. 1974. *The Ax Within: Italian Fascism in Action*. New York: New Viewpoints.

Schmitz, David F. 1988. *The United States and Fascist Italy 1922-1940*. Chapel Hill, NC: University of North Carolina Press.

Segrè, Claudio. 1974. *Fourth Shore: The Italian Colonization of Libya*. Chicago, IL: University of Chicago Press.

_____. 1987. *Italo Balbo: A Fascist Life*. Berkeley, CA: California University Press.

Snowden, F. M. 1989. *The Fascist Revolution in Tuscany 1919-1922*. Cambridge: Cambridge University Press.

Spackman, Barbara.1996. *Fascist Virilities, Rhetoric, Ideology and Social Fantasy*. Minneapolis, MN: University of Minnesota Press.

Sternhall, Zeev. 1994. *The Birth of Fascist Ideology*. Princeton, NJ: Princeton University Press.

Stille, Alexander. 1991. *Benevolence and Betrayal: Five Italian Jewish Families under Fascism*. New York: Summit Books.

Thompson, Doug. 1991. *State Control in Fascist Italy: Culture and Conformity, 1925-1943*. Manchester: Manchester University Press.

Toscano, Mario. 1968. *The Origins of the Pact of Steel*. Baltimore: Johns Hopkins University Press.

Wanroji, Bruno. 1987. "The Rise and Fall of Italian Fascism as a Generational Revolt." *Journal of Contemporary History*. 22:401-418.

Wilhelm, Maria De Blasio. 1988. *The Other Italy: Italian Resistance in World War Two*. New York: Norton.

Wilson, Perry R. 1993. *The Clockwork Factory: Women and Work in Fascist Italy*. Oxford: Clarendon Press.

Wiskemann, Elizabeth. 1966. *The Rome-Berlin Axis*. London: Fontana.

In Italian:

Aga Rossi, Elena. 1985. *L'Italia nella sconfitta. Politica interna e situazione internazionale durante la seconda guerra mondiale*. Naples: Edizioni scientifiche italiane.

Biagi, Enzo. 1995. *Lunga è la notte*. Milano: Nuova Eri.

432 ● Bibliography

_____. 1977. *La repubblica di Mussolini*. Bari: Laterza.

Bocca, Giorgio. 1966. *Storia dell'Italia partigiana*. Bari: Laterza.

Colarizi, Simona. 1976. *L'Italia antifascista dal 1922 al 1940*. Bari: Laterza.

Consulta di Napoli. 1978. *Anni della Resistenza: lezioni e testimonianze su fascismo e società italiana dello stato liberale alla resistenza*. Napoli: Cooperative l'Informazione.

De Felice, Renzo. 1965-1981. *Mussolini*. 5 vols. Torino: Einaudi. (i) 1965. *Mussolini il rivoluzionario*. (ii) 1966. *Mussolini il fascista: la conquista del potere 1921-1925*. (iii) 1968. *Mussolini il fascista: l'organizzazione dello stato fascista 1925-1929*. (iv) 1974. *Il Duce: gli anni di consenso*. (v) 1981. *Il Duce: lo stato totalitario*.

De Grand, Alexander. 1978. *Bottai e la cultura fascista*. Bari: Laterza.

Del Boca, A. 1976-1984. *Gli italiani in Africa orientale*. 4 vols. Bari: Laterza.

_____. 1986-1988. *Gli italiani in Libia*. 2 vols. Bari: Laterza.

Di Donato, Riccardo. 1970. *Da Vittorio Veneto alla marcia su Roma*. Firenze: La Nuova Italia.

Gentile, Emilio. 1989. *Storia del partito fascista 1919-1922: movimento e milizia*. Bari: Laterza.

_____. 1995. *Il culto del littorio: la sacralizzazione della politica nell'italia fascista*. Bari: Laterza.

_____. 1995. *La via italiana al totalitarismo*. Roma: Nuova italia scientifiche.

Giovagnoli, A. 1991. *La cultura democristiana tra chiesa cattolica e identità italiana 1919-1941*. Bari: Laterza.

Melograni, Piero. 1972. *Gli industriali e Mussolini*. Milano: Longanesi.

Mussolini, Arnaldo. 1937. *Fascismo e Civiltà*. Milano: Hoepli Ed.

Nello, P. 1987. *Dino Grandi: la formazione di un leader fascista*. Bologna: Il Mulino.

Nolte, Ernst. [1968] 1970. *La crisi dei regimi liberali e i movimenti fascisti*. Bologna: Il Mulino.

Pavone, Claudio. 1995. *Alle origine della repubblica: scritti su fascismo, antifascismo e continuità della Stato*. Torino: Bollat Berlinghieri.

Sarfati, Michele. 1994. *Mussolini contro gli ebrei: cronaca dell'elaborazione delle leggi razziali del 1938*. Torino: Zamorani.

Scoppola, Pietro. 1971. *La Chiesa e il fascismo*. Bari: Laterza.

Stille, Alessandro. 1994. *Uno su mille: cinque famiglie ebraiche durante il fascismo*. Milano: Mondadori.

Vaudagna, Maurizio. 1981. *Corporativismo e New Deal*. Torino: Rosenberg and Sellier.

Vivarelli, Roberto. 1981. *Il fallimento del liberalismo: studi sulle origini del fascismo*. Bologna: Il Mulino.

The First Italian Republic

General Works and Collections

In English:

Barzini, Luigi. 1971. *From Caesar to the Mafia*. London: Hamish Hamilton, Ltd.

Bellavita, Gino. 1962. *Il paese delle cinque polizie*. Milano: Ed. Comunità.

Belloni, Frank P., and Dennis B. Beller, eds. 1978. *Faction Politics: Political Parties and Factionalism in Comparative Perspective.* Santa Barbara, CA: Clio Press.

Colombo, Furio, ed. 1981. *In Italy: Postwar Political Life.* New York: Karz Publishers.

Di Palma, Giuseppe, and P. Siegelman, eds. 1983. *Italy in the 1980s: Paradoxes of a Dual Society.* San Francisco, CA: Frank V. de Bellis Collection.

Duggan, Christopher, and Christopher Wagstaff. 1995. *Italy in the Cold War.* Washington, DC: Berg Publishers.

Ellwood, David. 1985. *Italy 1943-1945.* Leicester: Leicester University Press.

Ginsborg, Paul. 1990. *A History of Contemporary Italy: Society and Politics 1943-1988.* London: Penguin.

Hughes, H. Stuart. [1953] 1965. *The United States and Italy.* Cambridge, MA: Harvard University Press.

Kogan, Norman. 1983. *A Political History of Post-War Italy.* New York: Praeger.

Leonardi, Robert, and Raffaella Y. Nanetti, eds. 1986. *Italian Politics: A Review*, vol. 1. London: Congrips/Pinter.

_____, and Piergiorgio Corbetta, eds. 1989. *Italian Politics: A Review*, vol. 3. London: Pinter.

Nanetti, Raffaella Y., Robert Leonardi, and Piergiorgio Corbetta. 1988. *Italian Politics: A Review,* vol. 2. London: Pinter.

_____, and Raimondo Catanzaro. 1990. *Italian Politics: A Review,* vol. 4 [1988]. London: Pinter.

Quartermaine, L., and J. Pollard. 1985. *Italy Today: Patterns of Life and Politics.* Exeter: Exeter University Press.

Riscossa, S. 1973. "Italy 1920-1970." In *The Fontana Economic History of Europe*, ed. Carlo Cipolla, vol. 6. London: Fontana.

Sassoon, Donald. 1986. *Contemporary Italy*. London: Longman.

Woolf, Stuart J. 1972. *The Rebirth of Italy 1943-1950*. London: Longman.

In French:

Chassériaud, Jean-Paul. 1965. *Le Parti Démocrate Chrétien en Italie* Paris: Librairie Armand Colin.

In Italian:

Anderlini, F., and R. Leonardi, eds. 1991. *Politica in Italia: i fatti dell'anno e le interpretazioni: Edizione 1991*. Bologna: Il Mulino/Istituto Cattaneo.

Caciagli, Mario, and David I. Kertzer, eds. 1996. *Politica in Italia: i fatti dell'anno e le interpretazioni: Edizione 1996*. Bologna: Il Mulino/Istituto Cattaneo.

Castronovo, Valerio. 1976. *L'Italia contemporanea, 1945-1975*. Torino: Einaudi.

Catanzaro, Raimondo, and Raffaella Y. Nanetti, eds. 1989. *Politica in Italia: i fatti dell'anno e le interpretazioni: Edizione 1989*. Bologna: Il Mulino/Istituto Cattaneo.

_____, and Filippo Sabetti, eds. 1990. *Politica in Italia: i fatti dell'anno e le interpretazioni: Edizione 1990*. Bologna: Il Mulino/Istituto Cattaneo.

Colarizi, Simona. 1994. *Storia dei partiti nell'Italia repubblicana*. Bari: Laterza.

Corbetta, Piergirogio, and Robert Leonardi, eds. 1986. *Politica in Italia: i fatti dell'anno e le interpretazioni: Edizione 1986.* Bologna: Istituto Cattaneo.

_____. 1987. *Politica in Italia: i fatti dell'anno e le interpretazioni: Edizione 1987.* Bologna: Il Mulino/Istituto Cattaneo.

_____. 1988. *Politica in Italia: i fatti dell'anno e le interpretazioni: Edizione 1987.* Bologna: Il Mulino/Istituto Cattaneo.

Della Porta, Donatella, and Maurizio Rossi. 1984. *Cifre crudeli: bilancio dei terrorismi italiani.* Bologna: Istituto Carlo Cattaneo.

Galleni, Mauro, ed. 1981. *Rapporto sul terrorismo.* Milano: Rizzoli.

Gambino, Antonio. 1978. *Storia del dopoguerra: dalla liberazione al potere DC.* Bari: Laterza.

Graziano, Luigi. 1980. *Clientelismo e sistema politico: il caso d'Italia.* Milano: Franco Angeli.

Hellman, Stephen, and Gianfranco Pasquino, eds. 1992. *Politica in Italia: i fatti dell'anno e le interpretazioni: Edizione 1992.* Bologna: Il Mulino/Istituto Cattaeneo.

_____. 1993. *Politica in Italia: i fatti dell'anno e le interpretazioni: Edizione 1992.* [1991] Bologna: Il Mulino/Istituto Cattaneo.

Ignazi, Piero, and Richard S. Katz. 1995. *Politica in Italia: i fatti dell'anno e le interpretazioni: Edizione 1995.* Bologna: Il Mulino/Istituto Cattaneo.

Ingrao, Pietro. 1977. *Masse e potere.* Roma: Ed. Riuniti.

Lanaro, Silvio. 1992. *Storia dell'Italia repubblicana: dalla fine della guerra agli anni novanta.* Venice: Marsilio.

Mamarella, Giuseppe. 1993. *L'Italia contemporanea.* Bologna: Il Mulino.

Mershon, Carol, and Gianfranco Pasquino, eds. 1994. *Politica in Italia: i fatti dell'anno e le interpretazioni: Edizione 1994.* Bologna: Il Mulino/Istituto Cattaneo.

Navicella, La. 1949. *I deputati e senatori del primo parlamento repubblicano.* Roma: La Navicella.

_____. 1954. *I deputati e senatori del secondo parlamento repubblicano.* Roma: La Navicella.

_____. 1958. *I deputati e senatori del terzo parlamento repubblicano.* Roma: La Navicella.

_____. 1963. *I deputati e senatori del quarto parlamento repubblicano.* Roma: La Navicella.

_____. 1965. *I deputati e senatori del quarto parlamento repubblicano,* rev. ed. Roma: La Navicella

_____. 1969. *I deputati e senatori del quinto parlamento repubblicano.* Roma: La Navicella.

_____. 1972. *I deputati e senatori del sesto parlamento repubblicano.* Roma: La Navicella.

_____. 1976. *I deputati e senatori del settimo parlamento repubblicano.* Roma: La Navicella.

_____. 1979. *I deputati e senatori dell'ottavo parlamento repubblicano.* Roma: La Navicella.

_____. 1983. *I deputati e senatori del nono parlamento repubblicano.* Roma: La Navicella.

_____. 1987. *I deputati e senatori del decimo parlamento repubblicano.* Roma: La Navicella.

_____. 1992. *I deputati e senatori dell'undicesimo parlamento repubblicano.* Roma: Editoriale Italiana.

Pasquino, Gianfranco, ed. 1995. *La politica italiana. Dizionario critico 1945-95*. Bari: Laterza.

Romano, Sergio. 1993. *Guida alla politica estera italiana dal crollo del fascismo al crollo del comunismo*. Milano: Rizzoli

Salvati, Michele. 1986. *L'economia italiana dal dopoguerra a oggi*. Milano: Garzanti.

Scoppola, Pietro. 1991. *La repubblica dei partiti. Profilo storico della democrazia in Italia 1945-1990*. Bologna: Il Mulino.

Vassallo, Salvatore. 1994. *Il governo di partito in Italia 1943-1993*. Bologna: Il Mulino.

Politics and Institutions

In English:

Aliboni, Roberto, and Ettore Greco. 1996. "Foreign Policy Renationalization and Internationalism in the Italian Debate." *International Affairs*. 72: 43-51 (January).

Allum, Percy. 1973. *Italy: Republic without Government?* London: Weidenfeld and Nicholson.

Carandini, Nicolò. 1958. *The Alto Adige: an Experiment in the Devaluation of Frontiers*. Rome: Il Mondo.

Diani, M. 1995. *Green Networks. A Structural Analysis of the Italian Environmental Movement*. Edinburgh: Edinburgh University Press.

Di Palma, Giuseppe. 1978. *Political Syncretism in Italy: Historical Coalition Strategies and the Present Crisis*. Berkeley, CA: University of California Press.

_____. 1977. *Surviving without Governing: The Italian Parties in Parliament*. Berkeley, CA: University of California Press.

Di Scala, Spencer. 1988. *Renewing Italian Socialism: Nenni to Craxi.* New York: Oxford University Press.

Drake, Richard. 1989. *The Revolutionary Mystique and Terrorism in Contemporary Italy.* Bloomington, IN: Indiana University Press.

Evans, Robert H. 1976. *Life and Politics in a Venetian Village.* Notre Dame, IN: Notre Dame University Press.

Farneti, Piero. 1985. *The Italian Political System, 1945-1980.* London: Pinter.

Feiler, Michael. 1996. "South Tyrol: Model for the Resolution of Minority Conflicts?" *Aussenpolitik.* 47, 3:287-299.

Ferrajoli, Luigi. 1996. "Democracy and the Constitution in Italy." *Political Studies.* 44: 457-472.

Ferraresi, Franco. 1996. *Threats to Democracy: The Radical Right in Italy after the War.* Princeton, NJ: Princeton University Press.

Galli, Giorgio, and Alfonso Prandi. 1970. *Patterns of Political Participation in Italy.* New Haven, CT: Yale University Press.

Hales, E. E. Y. 1965. *Pope John and His Revolution.* London: Eyre and Spottiswoode.

Hine, David. 1988 "Italy: Condemned by Its Constitution?" In *Constitutions in Democratic Politics*, ed. Vernon Bogdanor. London: Aldershot.

_____. 1993. *Governing Italy: The Politics of Balanced Pluralism.* Oxford: Clarendon Press.

Ignazi, Piero. 1993. "The Changing Profile of the MSI." In *Encounters with the Contemporary Radical Right*, ed. P. H. Merkl and Leonard Weinburg. Boulder, CO: Westview Press.

_____. 1996. "The Intellectual Basis of Right-Wing Anti-partyism." *European Journal of Political Research.* 29, 3:279-296 (April).

Lange, Peter, and Sidney Tarrow. 1980. *Italy in Transition: Conflict and Consensus*. London: Cass.

_____, and M. Vannicelli. 1982. *Unions, Change and Crisis: French and Italian Union Strategy and the Political Economy, 1945-1980*. London: George Allen and Unwin.

Leonardi, Robert, and Douglas A. Wertman. 1989. *Italian Christian Democracy: The Politics of Dominance*. Basingstoke: Macmillan.

La Palombara, Joseph. 1987. *Democracy, Italian Style*. New Haven, CT: Yale University Press.

_____. 1988. "Partitocrazia." *Wilson Quarterly*. 99-117 (Spring).

Lumley, Robert. 1990. *States of Emergency: Cultures of Revolt in Italy 1968-1978*. London: Verso.

Mershon, Carol. 1996. "The Costs of Coalition: Coalition Theories and Italian Governments." *American Political Science Review*. 90:534-554 (September).

Miller, J. E. 1986. *The United States and Italy: The Politics of Diplomacy and Stabilization*. Chapel Hill, NC: University of North Carolina Press.

Morlino, Leonardo, and M. Tarchi. "The Dissatisfied Society: The Roots of Political Change in Italy." *European Journal of Political Research*. 30, 1:41-63 (July).

Nappi, Chiara. 1996. "A Tale of Two School Systems: Funding in the United States and Italy." *Dissent*. 60-66 (Spring).

Nilsson, K. Robert. 1989. "Mini-industries and Cooperatives: The Italian Model." *Proceedings of the Fourteenth European Studies Conference*. Omaha, NE: University of Nebraska Press.

_____. 1987. "The Italian Socialist Party." In *Italy at the Polls: 1983*, ed. Howard Penniman. Durham, NC: Duke University (for the American Enterprise Institute).

_____. 1981. "The EUR Accords and the Historic Compromise: Italian Labor and Eurocommunism," *Polity.* 14:29-50 (Fall).

Panebianco, Angelo. 1988. "The Italian Radicals: New Wine in an Old Bottle." In *When Parties Fail*, ed. Kenneth Lawson and Peter Merkl. Princeton, NJ: Princeton University Press.

Pasquino, Gianfranco. 1987. "Party Government in Italy: Achievements and Prospects." In *Party Governments: European and American Experiences*, ed. Richard Katz. Berlin: De Gruyter. 202-242.

Pridham, G. 1988. *Political Parties and Coalition Behavior in Italy.* London: Routledge.

Putnam, Robert D. 1973. *The Beliefs of Politicians: Ideology, Conflict and Democracy in Britain and Italy.* New Haven, CT: Yale University Press.

Seton-Watson, Christopher. 1980. "Italy's Imperial Hangover." *Journal of Contemporary History.* 15, no. 1:169-179.

Spini, Valdo. 1972. "The New Left in Italy." *Journal of Contemporary History.* 7, no. 1-2:51-72.

Tarrow, Sidney. 1977. *Between Center and Periphery: Grassroots Politicians in Italy and France.* New Haven, CT: Yale University Press.

_____. 1989. *Democracy and Disorder: Protest and Politics in Italy, 1965-1975.* Oxford: Clarendon Press.

In French:

Bartolini, Stefano, and Roberto d'Alimonte. 1995. "Les élections parlementaires de 1994 en Italie: compétition majoritaire et réalignement partisan." *Revue Française de Science Politique.* 45: 915-954 (Décembre).

Bibes, Geneviève, and Jean Ranger. "Les élections municipales de 1993 en Italie." *Revue Française de Science Politique.* 45:955-979 (Décembre).

In Italian:

Abbate, Michele. 1968. *L'Alternativa meridionale.* Matera: Basilicata Ed.

Agosti, A., L. Passerini, and N. Tranfaglia, eds. 1991. *La Cultura e i luoghi del 68.* Milano: Franco Angeli.

Alberoni, Francesco. 1976. *Italia in trasformazione.* Bologna: Il Mulino.

Amato, Giuliano. 1980. *Una repubblica da riformare.* Bologna: Il Mulino.

_____, and Luciano Cafagna. 1982. *Duello a sinistra. Socialisti e comunisti negli lunghi anni 70.* Bologna: Il Mulino.

Amendola, Giorgio. 1978. *Il rinnovamento del PCI.* Roma: Ed. Riuniti.

Angioni, Franco. 1984. *Un soldato italiano in Libano.* Milano: Rizzoli.

Baget-Bozzo, G. 1974. *Il partito cristiano al potere. La DC di De Gasperi e di Dossetti 1945-1954.* Firenze: Vallecchi.

_____. 1977. *Il partito cristiano e l'apertura a sinistra. La DC di Fanfani e di Moro 1954-1962.* Firenze: Vallecchi.

Baldassare, A., and C. Mezzanotte. 1985. *Gli uomini del Quirinale. da Di Nicola a Pertini.* Bari: Laterza.

Bandiera, Orana. 1996. "Presidenzialismo e semi-presidenzialismo: due sistemi a confronto nel caso italiano." *Italian Politics and Society.* No. 46:44-48 (Autumn).

Barbagli, Marzio, and Alessandro Maccelli. 1985. *La partecipazione politica a Bologna.* Bologna: Il Mulino.

Barbera, Augusto. 1978. *Governo locale e riforma della Stato*. Roma: Ed. Riuniti.

Belligni, Silvano, and Fausto Bertinotti, et al., eds. 1978. *Cogestione o controllo? Partiti e sindacato al bivio*. Torino: Istituto Gramsci.

Bevacque, Stefano, and Giuseppe Turani. 1978. *La svolta del '78*. Milano: Feltrinelli.

Bigi, Giulio. 1960. *I fatti del 7 luglio*. Reggio Emilia: Tecnostampa.

Brancoli, Rodolfo. 1980. *Spettatori interessati: gli Stati Uniti e la crisi italiana, 1975-1980*. Milano: Garzanti.

Caciagli, Mario, and A. Spreafico, eds. 1990. *Vent'anni di elezioni in Italia 1968-1987*. Padova: Liviana.

Chimenti, Anna. 1993. *Storia dei referendum*. Bari: Laterza.

Del Bocca, Angelo. 1994. *La trappola somala: dall'operazione 'Restore Hope' al fallimento delle Nazione Unite*. Bari: Laterza.

_____. 1993. *Una sconfitta dell'intelligenza: Italia e Somalia*. Bari: Laterza.

De Luna, Giovanni. 1982. *Storia del partito d'Azione*. Milano: Feltrinelli.

De Lutiis, G. 1991. *Storia dei servizi segreti in Italia*. Roma: Riuniti.

De Mita, Ciriaco. 1984. *Ragionando di Politica*. Milano: Rusconi.

Diamanti, Ilvo, and Renato Mannheimer, eds. 1994. *Milano a Roma. Guida all' Italia elettorale del 1994*. Roma: Donizelli.

Di Loreto, P. 1993. *La difficile transizione. Dalla fine del centrismo al centro-sinistra 1953-1960*. Bologna: Il Mulino.

Ferraresi, Franco, ed. 1984. *La Destra radicale*. Milano: Garzanti.

Galli, Giorgio. 1966. *Il bipartitismo imperfetto. Comunisti e democristiani in Italia*. Bologna: Il Mulino.

_____. 1978. *Storia della Democrazia cristiana*. Bari: Laterza.

_____. 1983. *L'Italia sotterranea: Storia, politica e scandali*. Bari: Laterza.

_____. 1975. *Fanfani*. Milano: Feltrinelli.

_____. 1986. *Storia del partito armato, 1968-1982*. Milano: Rizzoli.

Gandolfi, Francesco. 1960. *A Genova, non si passa*. Milano: Ed. Avanti!

Ghirotti, Gigi. 1970. *Rumor*. Milano: Longanesi.

Girardi, Giulio. 1973. *Marxismo e Cristianesimo*. Assisi: Citadella Ed.

Graziano, Luigi, and Sidney Tarrow. 1979. *La crisi italiana*. 2 vols. Torino: Einaudi.

Guarnieri, C. 1993. *Magistratura e politica in Italia*. Bologna: Il Mulino.

Ignazi, Piero. 1989. *Il Polo escluso. Profilo del Movimento sociale italiano*. Bologna. Il Mulino.

Ilari, Virgilio. 1994. *Storia militare della prima repubblica 1943-1993*. Ancona: Nuova Ricerca.

Malgeri, F., ed. 1987-1990. *Storia della Democrazia cristiana*. 5 vols. Roma: Edizioni cinque lune.

Mannheimer, Renato, and Giacomo Sani. 1987. *Il mercato elettorale: identikit dell'elettore italiano*. Bologna: Il Mulino.

Manzella, A. 1991. *Il Parlamento*. Bologna: Il Mulino.

Messina, Sebastiano. 1992. *La Grande Riforma*. Bari: Laterza.

Palandri, Enrico, Claudio Piersanti, Carlo Rovelli, and Maurizio Torrealta, eds. 1977. *Bologna marzo 1977 . . . fatti nostri. . . .* Verona: Bertani Ed.

Pasquino, Gianfranco. 1980. *Crisi di partiti e governabilità*. Bologna: Il Mulino.

_____, ed. 1985. *Il sistema politico italiano*. Bari: Laterza.

_____. 1991. *La repubblica dei cittadini ombra*. Milano: Garzanti.

Piró, Aldo. 1982. "Sandro Pertini: il primo socialista in Quirinale," *In 1892-1982: PSI Novanta anni di storia*. Roma: Almanacco Socialista.

Pizzinelli, Corrado. 1969. *Moro*. Milano: Longanesi and Co.

Sabbatucci, Giovanni. 1991. *Il riformismo impossible: storia del socialismo italiano*. Bari: Laterza.

Sartori, Giovanni. 1982. *Teoria dei partiti e caso italiano*. Milano: SugarCo.

Setta, Sandro. 1995. *L'Uomo Qualunque, 1944-1948*. Bari: Laterza.

Valiani, Leo. 1982. *L'Italia di De Gasperi 1945-1954*. Firenze: Le Monnier.

Studies in Society, Economics, and Culture

In English:

Acquaviva, S. S., and M. Santuccio. 1976. *Social Structure in Italy*. London: Martin Robertson.

Adler Hellman, Judy. 1987. *Journeys among Women: Feminism in Five Italian Cities*. Oxford: Oxford University Press.

Allum, Percy. 1973. *Politics and Society in Post-War Naples*. London: Cambridge University Press.

Amyot, Grant. 1996. "The Relatively Autonomous State: The Italian Case." *Studies in Political Economy*. 46:153-174 (Spring).

Angotti, T. 1977. *Housing in Italy: Urban Development and Political Change*. New York: Praeger.

Banfield, Edward C. 1958. *The Moral Basis of a Backward Society*. Glencoe, Il: The Free Press.

Baranski, Z. G., and R. Lumley, eds. 1990. *Culture and Conflict in Post-War Italy: Essays on Mass and Popular Culture*. Basingstoke: Macmillan.

Barkan, Joanne. 1984. *Visions of Emancipation: The Italian Workers' Movement since 1945*. New York: Praeger.

Birnbaum, Lucia Chiavola. 1986. *Liberazione della donna: Feminism in Italy*. Middletown, CT: Wesleyan University Press.

Carnevali, Francesca. 1996. "Between Markets and Networks: Regional Banks in Italy." *Business History*. 38:84-100 (July).

Chandler, B. J. 1988. *King of the Mountains: The Life and Death of Giuliano the Bandit*. Dekalb, IL: Northern Illinois University Press.

Chubb, Judith. 1982. *Patronage, Power and Poverty in Southern Italy: A Tale of Two Cities*. Cambridge: Cambridge University Press.

Cowell, Alan. 1994c. "Affluent Europe's Plight: Graying." *New York Times*. September 8, A 8.

De Cecco, Marcello. 1996. "Italy and the International Economy." *International Spectator*. 31:37-50 (June).

Dolci, Danilo. [1956] 1966. *Poverty in Sicily*. Trans. P. D. Cummins. Hammondsworth, UK: Penguin Books.

Esposito, Nicholas J. 1989. *Italian Family Structure*. New York: Peter Lang.

Golden, M. 1988. *Labor Divided. Austerity and Working Class Politics in Contemporary Italy*. Ithaca, NY: Cornell University Press.

Harper, John L. 1986. *America and the Reconstruction of Italy, 1945-1948.* Cambridge: Cambridge University Press.

King, R. L. 1973. *Land Reform: The Italian Experience.* London: Butterworth.

_____. 1985. *The Industrial Geography of Italy.* Beckenham (GB): Croom Helm.

Laviosa, Flavia. 1997. "1970s: a Decade of Legislative Reforms for Italian Women's Protection and Equality." *Italian Politics and Society.* No. 47:57-63 (Spring).

Luporini, Annalisa, and Bruno Parigi. 1996. "Multi-task Sharecropping Contracts: The Italian Mezzadria." *Economica.* 63:445-457 (August).

Podbielski, G. 1978. *Twenty-Five Years of Special Action for the Development of Southern Italy.* Rome: SVIMEZ.

Putnam, Robert, and Robert Leonardi. 1993. *Making Democracy Work: Civic Traditions in Modern Italy.* Princeton, NJ: Princeton University Press.

Sabetti, Filippo. 1984. *Political Authority in a Sicilian Village.* New Brunswick, NJ: Rutgers University Press.

Sarti, Roland. 1985. *Long Live the Strong: A History of Rural Society in the Apennine Mountains.* Amherst, MA: University of Massachusetts Press.

Schneider, J., and P. 1976. *Culture and Political Economy in Western Sicily.* New York: Academic Press.

Woods, Dwayne. 1995. "The Crisis of Center-Periphery Integration in Italy and the Rise of Regional Populism: The Lombard League." *Comparative Politics.* 27: 187-203 (January).

In French:

Palomba, Rossella, and Lucana Quattrociocchi. 1996. "Images de la famille italienne en mutation." *Population.* 51:353-367 (Mars-Avril).

In Italian:

Barbagli, M. 1991. *Provando e riprovando. Matrimonio, famiglia e divorzio in Italia e in altri paesi occidentali.* Bologna: Il Mulino.

_____. 1980. *I signori dello sciopero.* Milano: Longanesi.

Bocca, Giorgio. 1980. *I signori dello sciopero.* Milano: Longanesi.

Brunetta, G., and A. Longo., eds. 1991. *Italia cattolica: fede e pratica religiosa negli anni 90.* Firenze: Vallechi.

Caciagli, Mario, ed. 1986. *Governo locale, associazionismo e politico culturale.* Padua: Liviana.

Castronovo, Valerio. 1971. *Giovanni Agnelli.* Torino: U.T.E.T.

Cavazza, Fabio Luca, and Stephen R. Graubard. 1974. *Il caso italiano.* 2 vols. Milano: Garzanti.

Cigno, Alessandro, and Furio Rosati. 1996. "Nuove prospettive teoriche ed empiriche su risparmio delle famiglie e sicurezza in Italia," *Economic Politica.* 13:83-111 (Aprile).

De Brunhoff, Suzanne. 1979. *Stato e capitale: ricerche sulla politica economica.* Milano: Feltrinelli.

Dore, Lorenzo. 1974. *Fabbrica e scuola: le 150 ore.* Roma: Ed. Sindacale Italiana.

Fornasiero, Franco. 1992. "Comportamenti degli extracomunitari nel mercato del lavoro: un'analisi su microdati," *Economia e Lavoro.* 26:37-47 (October-December).

Galli, Georgio, and Alessandra Nannei. 1975. *Il capitalismo assistenziale*: *Ascesa e declino del sistema economico italiano 1960-1975*. Milano: SugarCo.

Garelli, F. 1991. *Religione e Chiesa in Italia*. Bologna: Il Mulino.

Gennaro, Giovanni. 1977. *L'operaio immaginario: la figura del operaio in una società non industrializzata*. Bologna: Il Mulino.

Graziosi, Andrea. 1979. *La ristrutturazione nelle grandi fabbriche, 1973-1976*. Milano: Feltrinelli.

Lerner, Gad. 1988. *Operai. Viaggio all'interno di una classe che non c'è più*. Milano: Feltrinelli.

Manzini, Giorgio. 1994. *Indagine su una brigatista rosso: la storia di Walter Alasia*. Torino: l'Unità/Einaudi.

Selvatici, Antonio. 1994. *Più uguali degli altri. indagine su un'amministrazione al di sopra di ogni sospetto*. Bologna: Il Fenicottero.

Soldani, S., and G. Turi. 1994. Fare gli italiani. Scuola e cultura nell'Italia contemporanea. 2 vols. Bologna: Il Mulino.

Sylos Labini, P. 1982. *Le classi sociali negli anni 80*. Bari: Laterza.

Tanda, Paola. 1994. "Partecipazione femminile in Italia: evidenza empirica su dati individuali." *Economia e Lavoro*. 28:123-134 (January-March).

Zanchetta, P. L. 1991. *Essere stranieri in Italia*. Milano: Franco Angeli.

Communism and Intellectual Politics

In English:

Amyot, Grant. 1981. *The Italian Communist Party: The Crisis of the Popular Front Strategy*. London: Croom Helm.

Blackmer, Donald, and Sidney Tarrow, eds. [1975] 1977. *Communism in Italy and France.* Princeton, NJ: Princeton University Press.

Bobbio, Norberto. 1995. *Ideological Profile of Twentieth-Century Italy.* Trans. L. Cochrane. Princeton, NJ: Princeton University Press.

Bull, Martin J. 1997. "From PDS to Cosa 2: The Second Congress of the Democratic Party of the Left." *Italian Politics and Society.* No. 47:9-20 (Spring).

Clark, Martin. 1977. *Antonio Gramsci and the Revolution That Failed.* New Haven, CT: Yale University Press.

Claudín, Fernando. 1978. *Eurocommunism and Socialism.* London: NLB.

De Grand, Alexander. 1989. *The Italian Left in the Twentieth Century: A History of the Socialist and Communist Parties.* Bloomington, IN: Indiana University Press.

Evans, Robert H. 1967. *Coexistence: Communism and Its Practice in Bologna 1945-1965.* Notre Dame, IN: Notre Dame University Press.

Gramsci, Antonio. 1957. *The Modern Prince and Other Writings.* Trans. Louis Marks. New York: International Publishers.

Hellman, Stephen. 1988. *Italian Communism in Transition: The Rise and Fall of the Historic Compromise in Torino 1975-1980.* New York: Oxford University Press.

Joll, James. 1977. *Antonio Gramsci.* New York: Viking.

Kertzer, David I. 1996. *Politics and Symbols: The Italian Communist Party and the Fall of Communism.* New Haven, CT: Yale University Press.

_____. 1980. *Comrades and Christians: Religion and Political Struggle in Communist Italy.* Cambridge: Cambridge University Press.

Moss, D. 1989. *The Politics of Left-Wing Violence in Italy, 1969-1985.* Basingstoke: Macmillan.

Ranney, Austin, and Giovanni Sartori, eds. 1977. *Eurocommunism: The Italian Case*. Washington, DC: American Enterprise Institute.

Ruscoe, James. 1982. *On the Threshold of Government: The Italian Communist Party, 1976-1981*. New York: St. Martin's Press.

Sassoon, Donald. 1981. *The Strategy of the Italian Communist Party: From the Resistance to the Historic Compromise*. London: Pinter.

Serfaty, Simon, and Lawrence Gray, eds. 1980. *The Italian Communist Party: Yesterday, Today, Tomorrow*. Westport, CT: Greenwood.

Tarrow, Sidney. 1967. *Peasant Communism in Southern Italy*. New Haven, CT: Yale University Press.

Urban, Joan Barth. 1986. *Moscow and the Italian Communist Party: From Togliatti to Berlinguer*. London: Tauris.

In Italian:

Ajello, Nello. 1979. *Intellettuali e il PCI 1944-1958*. Bari: Laterza.

Amendola, Giorgio. 1978. *Il rinnovamento del PCI*. Roma: Ed. Riuniti.

Berlinguer, Enrico. 1973. "Imperialismo e coexistenza alla luce dei fatti cileni," 28 September; "Via democratica e violenza reazionarie," 5 October; "Riflessioni sull'Italia dopo i fatti di Cile," 12 October. *Rinascita*.

_____. 1994. *Il principe disarmato: con una scelta di testi del leader del Pci su questione morale, riforma della politica e ruolo dei partiti*. Roma: Sisifo.

Braga, Giorgio. 1956. *Il comunismo fra gli italiani*. Milano: Ed. Comunità.

Cafagna, Luciano. 1993. *La Grande Slavina*. Venice: Marsilio.

Croce, Benedetto. 1900. *Materialismo storico ed economia marxista.* Milano: Sandron.

D'Alema, Massimo. 1994. *Dialogo su Berlinguer.* Firenze: Giunti.

Davidson, Alastair. 1995. "Dilemma of Liberal Socialism. The Case of Norberto Bobbio." *Australian Journal of Politics and History.* 41: 47-54.

De Felice, Franco, and Valentino Parlato, eds. 1966. *Antonio Gramsci: la Questione Meridionale.* Roma: Ed. Riunti.

De Giovanni, Biagio, V. Gerrattana, and L. Paggi. 1977. *Egemonia, Stato, partito in Gramsci.* Roma: Ed. Riuniti.

Fiori, Giuseppe. 1989 *Vita di Enrico Berlinguer.* 2 vols. Bari: Laterza.

Fubini, Elsa, ed. 1967. *Antonio Gramsci: Il Vaticano e l'Italia.* Roma: Ed. Riuniti.

Galli, Giorgio. 1983. *Storia del PCI.* Milano: Kaos edizioni.

_____. 1958. *La Sinistra italiana nel dopoguerra.* Bologna: Il Mulino.

Gorresio, Vittorio. 1976. *Berlinguer.* Milano: Feltrinelli.

Gramsci, Antonio. 1955. *L'Ordine nuovo, 1919-1920.* 2nd ed.,Torino: Giulio Einaudi.

Ignazi, Piero. 1992. *Dal PCI al PDS.* Bologna: Il Mulino.

Napolitano, Giorgio. 1979. *In mezzo al guado.* Roma: Riuniti.

Ricchini, Carlo, et al., eds. 1987. *Gramsci: le sue idee nel nostro tempo.* Roma: Ed. L'Unità.

Salinari, Carlo, and Mario Spinella. 1963. *Antonio Gramsci: Antologia degli scritti.* 2 vols. Roma: Ed. Riuniti.

Santucci, Antonio A., ed. 1988. *Gramsci: lettere dal carcere*, vol. 2. Roma: Ed. L'Unità.

Sassoon, Donald. 1980. *Togliatti e la via italiana al socialismo*. Torino: Einaudi.

Spriano, Paolo. 1975. *Storia del partito comunista.* 6 vols. Torino: Einaudi.

_____. 1988. *Gramsci in carcere e il partito*. Roma: Ed. L'Unità.

Tatò, Antonio, ed. 1977. *Comunisti e mondo cattolico oggi*. Roma: Ed. Riuniti.

Vacca, Giuseppe. 1987. *Tra compromesso e solidarità. La politica del PCI negli anni 70*. Roma: Riuniti.

The Mafia and Corruption

In English:

Arlacchi, Pino. 1988. *Mafia Business: The Mafia Ethic and the Spirit of Capitalism*. Oxford: Oxford University Press.

Blok, Anton. 1974. *The Mafia of a Sicilian Village, 1860-1960*. Oxford: Blackwell.

Gambetta, Diego. 1993. *The Sicilian Mafia*. Cambridge, MA: Harvard University Press.

Pantaleone, Michele. 1966. *The Mafia and Politics.* London: Chatto and Windus.

Stille, Alexander. 1995. *Excellent Cadavers*. New York: Pantheon.

Walston, James. 1988. *The Mafia and Clientelism: Roads to Rome in Post-War Calabria*. London: Routledge.

In French:

Namer, Gérard. 1996. "Clientélismes et mafia." *L'Homme et la Societé.* 119: 33-41.

In Italian:

Canosa, Romano. 1995. *Storia della criminalità in Italia dal 1946 a oggi.* Milano: Feltrinelli.

Catanzaro, Raimondo. 1991. *Il delitto come impresa: storia sociale della mafia.* Milano: Rizzoli.

Cazzola, F. 1992. *L'Italia del pizzo.* Torino: Einaudi.

Ciconte, Enzo. 1992. *'Ndrangheta dall'unità a oggi.* Bari: Laterza.

Dalla Chiesa, Nando. 1990. *Storia di boss, ministri, tribunali, giornali, intellettuali, cittadini.* Torino: Einaudi.

Della Porta, Donatella. 1992. *Lo scambio occulto.* Bologna: Il Mulino.

Falcone, Giovanni, and M. Padovano. 1991. *Cose di Cosa Nostra.* Milano: Rizzoli.

Lupo, Salvatore. 1993. *Storia della mafia dalle origini ai giorni nostri.* Roma: Donizelli.

Mosca, Gaetano. 1993. *Che cosa è la mafia. e altri scritti su Palermo, la Sicilia e il Mezzogiorno.* Mandurla: P. Lacalta.

Pezzino, Paolo. 1995. *Mafia: Industria della violenza.* Firenze: La Nuova Italia.

Sales, Isaia. 1988. *La Camorra, le camorre.* Roma: Riuniti.

Tranfaglia, Nicola. 1992. *Mafia, politica e affari 1943-1991.* Bari: Laterza.

_____, ed. 1994. *Cirillo, Ligato e Lima: tre storie di mafia e politica*. Bari: Laterza.

Turone, S. 1984. *Corrotti e corruttori dall'unità d'Italia alla P2*. Bari: Laterza.

The Italian Political Crisis of the 1990s

In English:

Abse, Tobias. 1996. "The Left Advances in Italy." *New Left Review*. 217:123-130 (May-June).

Attina, Fulvio. 1996. "Italy's EU Presidency." *Ecsa Review*. 9, 3: 9-14 (Fall).

Bardi, Luciano. 1996. "Anti-party Sentiment and Party System Change in Italy." *European Journal of Political Research*. 29, 3:345-363 (April).

_____. 1996. "Change in the Italian Party System." *Italian Politics and Society*. No. 46:9-22 (Autumn).

Bordignon, Massimo. 1993. "Taxing Lessons from Italy." *International Economic Insights,* 4:10-13 (November-December).

Bufacchi, Vittorio. 1996. "The Coming of Age of Italian Democracy, Part I: Literature on Italian Elections 1992-1994." *Government and Opposition*. 31:322-346 (Summer).

Caciagli, Mario, and David I. Kertzer, eds. 1996. *Italian Politics: The Stalled Transition*. Boulder, CO: Westview Press.

Campi, Alessandro. 1995. "What Is Italy's National Alliance?" *Telos*. 105:122-132 (Fall).

Cowell, Alan. 1994e. "Italian Government in Turmoil . . ." *New York Times*. October 6, A 13.

D'Alimonte, Roberto, and David Nelken, eds. 1997. *Italian Politics: The Center-Left in Power.* Boulder, CO: Westview Press.

Della Cananea, Giacinto. 1996. "Reforming the State: The Policy of Administrative Reform in Italy under the Ciampi Government." *West European Politics.* 19:321-339 (April).

Gilbert, Mark. 1995. *The Italian Revolution: The End of Politics, Italian Style.* Boulder, CO: Westview.

Gobetti, Daniela. 1996. "La Lega: Regularities and Innovation in Italian Politics." *Politics and Society.* 24:57-82 (March).

Gundle, Stephen, and Simon Parker, eds. 1995. *The New Italian Republic: From the Fall of the Berlin Wall to Berlusconi.* London: Routledge.

Guzzini, Stefano. 1995. "The Long Night of the First Republic: Years of Clientelistic Implosion in Italy." *Review of International Political Economy.* 2:27-61 (Winter).

Harper, John L. 1996. "The Transformation of the MSI to AN." *West European Politics.* 19, 4:693-714 (October).

Katz, Richard, and Piero Ignazi, eds. 1995. *Italian Politics: The Year of the Tycoon.* Boulder, CO: Westview.

Katz, Robert S. 1996. "Electoral Reform and the Transformation of Party Politics in Italy." *Party Politics.* 2:31-53 (January).

Levy, Carl. 1996. *Italian Regionalism: History, Identity and Politics.* Washington, DC: Berg.

Magri, Lucio. 1995. "The Resistible Rise of the Italian Right." *New Left Review.* 214:125-133 (December).

McCarthy, Patrick. 1997. "Italy at a Turning Point." *Current History.* 96, 608: 111-115 (March).

_____. 1995. *The Crisis of the Italian State: From the Origins of the Cold War to the Fall of Berlusconi.* New York: St. Martin's Press.

_____. 1993. "Italy: The Absent State." *International Economic Insights*. 4:6-9 (November-December).

_____, and Gianfranco Pasquino, eds. 1993. *The End of Post-war Politics in Italy: The Landmark Elections of 1992*. Boulder, CO: Westview Press.

Morlino, Leonardo. "Crisis of Parties and Change of Party System in Italy." *Party Politics*. 2:5-30 (January).

Newell, James L., and Martin J. Bull. "The Italian Election of 1996: The Italian Left on Top or on Tap." *Parliamentary Affairs*. 49, 4:616-647 (October).

Pasquino, Gianfranco, and Carol Mershon, eds. 1994. *Italian Politics: Ending the First Republic*. Boulder, CO: Westview Press.

Recchi, Ettore. 1996. "Fishing from the Same Schools: Parliamentary Recruitment and Consociationalism in the First and Second Italian Republics." *West European Politics*. 2:340-359 (April).

Rosenthal, Lawrence. 1996. "Dateline Rome: The New Face of Western Democracy." *Foreign Policy*. 154-168 (Fall).

Salvati, Michele. "The Crisis of Government in Italy." *New Left Review*. 213:76-96 (September-October).

Seisselberg, Jorg. 1996. "Forza Italia: A Media-Mediated Personality-Party." *West European Politics*. 19, 4:715-743 (October).

In French:

Lazar, Marc. 1996. "L'Italie au-delà du Rubicon?" *Politique Internationale*. 337-351 (Summer).

Manzella, Andrea. 1996. "La logique proportionelle." *Pouvoirs. Revue française d'études constitutionnelles et politiques*. 76:151-158.

_____. 1996. "Le referendum italien." *Pouvoirs. Revue française d'études constitutionnelles et politiques*. 77:137-148.

In Italian:

Bocca, Giorgio.1990. *La Disunità d'Italia*. Milano: Garzanti.

_____. 1988. *Gli italiani sono razzisti?* Milano: Garzanti.

Bossi, Umberto. 1992. *Vento dal Nord*. Milano: Sperling and Kupfer.

Caciagli, Mario, and David Kertzer, eds. 1996. *Politica in Italia: Edizione 1996*. Bologna: Il Mulino/Istituto Cattaneo.

Carioti, Antonio. 1995. "Dal ghetto al palazzo," *Politica in Italia, Edizione 1995*, ed. Piero Ignazi and Richard Katz. Bologna: Il Mulino.

Diamanti, Ilvo. 1993. *La Lega. Geografia, storia e sociologia di un nuovo soggetto politico*. Roma: Donizelli.

Di Nicola, Primo. 1993. *Mario Segni*. Milano: Sperling and Kupfer.

Fabbrini, Sergio. 1994. *Quale democrazia: L'Italia e gli altri*. Bari: Laterza.

_____. 1997. *Le regole della democrazia*. Bari: Laterza.

Follini, Marco. 1994. *C'era una volta la DC*. Bologna: Il Mulino.

Giuliani, Marco. 1997. "L'Italia fra political intera e politica europea." *Italian Politics and Society*. No. 47:21-33 (Spring).

Ignazi, Piero. 1995. *Postfascisti?* Bologna: Il Mulino.

_____. 1996. The Transformation of the MSI to AN." *West European Politics*. 19, 4:693-714 (October).

Mannheimer, Renato, ed. 1991. *La Lega Lombarda*. Milano: Feltrinelli.

Maraffi, Marco, and Paolo Segatti. 1997. "Partiti ed elettori dal 94 al 96." *Italian Politics and Society*. No. 47:34-41 (Spring).

Pamparana, Andrea. 1994. *Il processo Cusani*. Milano: Mondadori.

Pasquino, Gianfranco, ed. 1995. *L'alternanza inattesa: le elezioni del 27 marzo e le loro consequenze.* Catanzaro: Rubbettin.

Ruggeri, Giovanni, and Paolo Guarini. 1994. *Berlusconi: inchiesta sul Signor TV.* Milano: Kaos edizioni.

Salvadori, Massimo L. 1996. *Storia d'Italia e crisi di régime.* Bologna: Il Mulino.

Art, Cinema, Literature, Theater

Amoia, Alba. 1996. *Twentieth Century Italian Women Writers.* Illinois University Press.

Baranski, Zymunt G., and Pertile, Lino, eds. 1994. *The New Italian Novel.* New York: Columbia University Press.

Bondanella, Peter. 1989. *Italian Cinema: From Neorealism to the Present.* Woodland Hills, CA: Continuum.

_____. 1992. *The Cinema of Federico Fellini.* Princeton, NJ: Princeton University Press.

_____. 1993. *The Films of Roberto Rossellini.* New York: Cambridge University Press.

Braun, Emily, et al., eds. 1995. *Italian Art in the Twentieth Century: Painting and Sculpture, 1900-1988.* New York: Te Neues.

Bruno, Giuliana. 1993. *Streetwalking on a Ruined Map: Cultural Theory and the City Films of Elvina Notari.* Princeton, NJ: Princeton University Press.

_____, and Nadotti, Maria, eds. 1988. *Off-screen: Women and Film in Italy.* New York: Routledge.

Buss, Robin. 1989. *Italian Films.* New York: Holmes and Meier.

Cannon, JoAnn. 1989. *Postmodern Italian Fiction: The Crisis of Reason in Calvino, Eco, Sciascia, Malerba.* Cranbury, NJ: Fairleigh Dickinson University Press.

Cardullo, Bert. 1991. *What is Neorealism? A Critical English-Language Bibliography of Italian Cinematic Neorealism.* Lanham, MD: University Press of America.

Ciolli, Marco. 1993. *The Theater of Eduardo de Filippo.* New York: Vantage.

Cottino-Jones, Marga. 1995. *A Student's Guide to Italian Film.* Dubuque, IA: Kendall-Hunt.

Goldthwaite, Richard A. 1981. *The Building of Renaissance Florence: A Social and Economic History.* Baltimore, MD: The Johns Hopkins University Press.

Goy, Richard. 1994. *The Buildings of Venice.* San Francisco: Chronicle Books.

Gunzberg, Lynn M. 1992. *Strangers at Home: Jews in the Italian Literary Imagination.* Berkeley, CA: University of California Press.

Haller, Hermann W. 1986. *The Hidden Italy: A Bilingual Edition of Italian Dialect Poetry.* Detroit: Wayne State University Press.

Hay, James. 1987. *Popular Film Culture in Fascist Italy.* Bloomington, IN: Indiana University Press.

House, Jane, and Artisani, Antonio, eds. 1995. *Twentieth Century Italian Drama, an Anthology: The First Fifty Years.* New York: Columbia University Press.

Jaffe, Michael. 1994. *Bolognese and Emilian Schools.* San Francisco: Chronicle Books.

_____. 1994. *Roman and Neopolitan Schools.* San Francisco: Chronicle Books.

_____. 1994. *Tuscan and Umbrian Schools.* San Francisco: Chronicle Books.

_____. 1994. *Venetian and North Italian Schools.* San Francisco: Chronicle Books.

Japanese architect. n.d. *Italian Architecture, 1945-1985.* New York: Gingko Press.

Landy, Marcia. 1985. *Fascism in Film: The Italian Commercial Cinema, 1931-1943.* Ann Arbor, MI: Books on Demand.

Lazzaro-Weiss, Carol M. 1993. *From Margins to Mainstream: Feminism and Fictional Modes in Italian Women's Writing, 1968-1990.* Philadelphia: University of Pennsylvania Press.

Patruno, Nichalas. 1995. *Understanding Primo Levi.* Columbia, SC: University of South Carolina Press.

Riccio, Peter. 1977. *Italian Authors of Today.* N. Stratford, NH: Ayer.

Rumble, Patrick, and Bart Testa, eds. 1993. *Pier Paolo Pasolini: Contemporary Perspectives.* Toronto: University of Toronto Press.

Soby, James T., and Alfred H. Barr, Jr. 1972. *Twentieth Century Italian Art.* No. Stratford, NH: Ayer.

Traldi, Alberto. 1987. *Fascism and Fiction: A Survey of Italian Fiction in Fascism.* Lanham, MD: Scarecrow.

Vermilye, Jerry. 1994. *The Great Italian Films: From the Thirties to the Present.* New London, CT: Citadel Press.

Wickin, Karen. 1996. *Giorgio Morandi.* New York: Rizzoli International.

Guidebooks

Baedeker staff. 1996. *Baedeker's Italy.* New York: Macmillan.

Blanchard, Paul. (forthcoming). *Southern Italy*, 7th ed. New York: Norton [Blue Guides].

Catling, Christopher. 1994. *Umbria, the Marches and San Marino*. NTC Publishing Group.

Facaros, Dana, and M. Pauls. 1996. *The Bay of Naples, Amalfi Coast and Southern Italy*. 2nd ed. Globe Pequot.

Hoffman, Paul. 1995. *The Sunny Side of the Alps and Year-round delights in South Tyrol and the Dolomites.* New York: Henry Holt and Co.

Mecadam, Alta. 1991. *Northern Italy.* Norton [Blue Guides].

Touring Club Italiano. Separate volumes on Italy, Florence, Rome, Venice (new volumes forthcoming).

About the Authors

Mark F. Gilbert was born in Chesterfield (Great Britain) in 1961. He was educated at University College, Durham, and the University of Wales, College of Swansea, where he took his Ph.D. in December 1990. After teaching for Dickinson College's European Studies program in Bologna, Italy, he was assistant professor of political science at Dickinson College's home campus in Carlisle, Pennsylvania, between 1993 and 1996. Since September 1997, he has been lecturer in Italian Studies in the Department of European Studies and Modern Languages at the University of Bath, England. Mark Gilbert is the author of *The Italian Revolution: The End of Politics, Italian Style?* Boulder, CO: Westview, 1995, and has published numerous articles and reviews on contemporary Italian political history.

K. Robert Nilsson was born in Kearny, New Jersey, in 1927. After service in the U.S. Army Air Corps (1945-1947), he received his B.A. from Temple University and the M.A. in International Relations from The Johns Hopkins University School of Advanced International Studies (including a year at the Bologna [Italy] Center of SAIS that made for an abiding interest in that country). While studying for his Ph.D. at Columbia University, he was enabled to return to Bologna for dissertation research by a Fulbright grant. In 1962, he began teaching European political systems, international relations, and the politics of modernization at Dickinson College in Carlisle, Pennsylvania. In 1965, he was the first director of the Dickinson College Center for International Studies in Bologna, a post to which he returned for a total of nine years by the time of his 1990 retirement. He also spent sabbatical years in Rome and in Florence.

For a time, he was chairman of the Italy Seminar at the Foreign Service Institute of the Department of State and was editor of the newsletter of the Conference Group on Italian Politics and Society. He has written on international questions in general and Italian issues in particular in publications in the United States and Italy, and is a member of the monthly University Seminar on Modern Italy at Columbia University. He is retired in Carlisle, Pennsylvania, and returns to Europe at least once a year.